ENGLISH LITERATURE

精编英国文学教程

◎ 陈庆生 陈 许 主编

ZHEJIANG UNIVERSITY PRESS
浙江大学出版社

序

今年夏初，杭州电子科技大学英美文学研究所所长陈许教授、外国语学院副院长高丙梁教授和英美文学教研室陈庆生副教授一行三人来河南高校学习考察，顺访我院，送来他们刚刚编写完成的《精编英国文学教程》和《精编美国文学教程》两书的书稿，恳请我在付梓之前协助审读。我早先知道该院开设的《英美文学导论》是一门广受同行赞誉、深受学生欢迎的课程，2007 年被浙江省教育厅评为浙江省普通高校精品课程。因此，我想这是他们给我的一个学习的好机会，让我享受"先睹为快"的幸事，欣然同意。

于是，我利用暑假较仔细地翻阅了这套教材。这次阅读不仅使我重温了英美文学，同时也勾起了我对英美文学教学的种种回忆与遐想。

英美文学教学，特别是英国文学教学在我国有着悠久的历史。根据史料记载，鸦片战争之后，"洋务运动"的兴起和清廷外交事务的加重，迫切需要培养外语人才，从而大大推动了我国外语教育事业的发展。外语开始作为一门独立的学科列入各级学校的教学计划。专门培训外语人才的学校相继成立。1862 年创立的京师同文馆首先设立英文馆，尔后又开设法文馆、俄文馆、日文馆等。上海、广州也分别于 1883 年和 1884 年成立了类似的外语学校。1898 年我国第一所国立的综合性大学——京师大学堂成立，也就是北京大学的前身。1901 年同文馆并入该校，改名为京师大学堂译学馆，相当于今日综合性大学中的外语院系，揭开了我国高校外语教育新的一页。英语是该馆的主要语种。

1911 年孙中山先生领导的辛亥革命推翻了封建帝制，宣告了中华民国的诞生，至 1949 年国民党政府退出中国大陆，民国时期也就此结束。在这个时期我国高等教育和外语教学都有一定的发展，据不完全统计，新中国成立前夕，我国共有 205 所高等学校，其中 41 所设有英语系或英语专业，专业教学都偏重文学，开设的课程多为英美小说、诗歌、散文、戏剧等，没有开设听、说、读、写、译等训练语言技能的课程，主要通过大量阅读文学作品和写作来提高外语水平和文化修养，深受当时英美高等学校英语系教学思想和方法的影响。

中华人民共和国成立初期,由于受当时国内外形势与国家政策的影响,俄语教学大发展,而英语和其他语种的教学任务大为压缩,教学力量严重削弱。1953 年经过院系调整,我国高校仅剩下 9 个英语教学点,学生人数锐减,大批英语教师改行教授俄文或其他专业,甚至转业做其他工作。就以我当时在读的北京大学西语系为例,英语专业本科四个年级学生人数仅一百多人,而师资力量十分雄厚,可谓群英荟萃,拥有像李赋宁、俞大絪、杨周翰、赵萝蕤、吴兴华、朱光潜等等一大批高水平的知名教授和学者,却苦于没有多少学生可教,没有多少课可开设,造成宝贵的人才资源的极大浪费。

1956 年开始中央发觉了这种情况,出台了一系列政策纠正原先政策上的偏颇,英语及其他一些语种得到了较大的发展。到 1957 年年底全国高校设有英语专业的学校增至 23 所,招生数量也倍增,教学也逐步走入正规。可惜好景不长。全国范围内开展的"反右运动"、"大跃进运动"、"反右倾运动"、"四清运动"等连绵不绝的政治运动,"左"倾思潮泛滥,严重地阻碍了教学工作的健康发展。所谓批判资产阶级教育路线,批判"西方资本主义腐朽文化",批判"文学路线"等使英语教学,特别是英美文学教学再次受到严重打击。1966 年开始的"文化大革命",极"左"路线发展到了登峰造极的地步,教育战线和其他战线一样,受到重创。外语教育首当其冲,灾难深重,教学工作基本处于瘫痪状态。这种状况持续了整整十年之久,直至"四人帮"被打倒,"文化大革命"宣告结束,外语教育重获新生。

党的十一届三中全会给高校外语教育带来了复苏的春风。1978 年教育部根据当年邓小平同志主持召开的全国科学大会和全国教育工作会议的精神,举行了全国外语教育座谈会。会议对如何恢复和发展外语教育提出了明确的方针和具体的措施。从此开创了我国外语教育的新局面,正如原国务院副总理李岚清在为上海外语教育出版社 2008 年出版的《改革开放 30 年中国外语教育发展丛书》写的"序"中说的那样,"……可以说,改革开放 30 年,是中国外语教育事业大发展的 30 年。"外语教育的面貌同全国其他战线一样"发生了历史性的变化"。高校英语专业发展的势头更是迅猛。据不完全统计,目前我国英语教学点已经超过 1000 个,与 1953 年时硕果仅剩的 9 个相比,增长了百倍以上,其发展速度真可谓"史无前例","世界第一"。英语专业在校学生近 60 万。2004 年英语专业招收新生 102388人,排在所有专业的第一位。

在这里我想特别要提出的是,在各类高校英语专业的发展中,理工科院校的英语专业是发展最为迅速的。据我了解在目前 1000 多个英语专业本科教学点中,有三分之一设在理工类院校。他们利用本校学科的优势,在教学改革和提高教学质量方面都创造了许多佳绩。杭州电子科技大学的外国语学院就是这样的一个范例。他们的办学历史和教学经验虽然不如一些"老牌"的学校悠久和丰富，但是通过他们的辛勤工作，创造出了令人钦佩的业绩。摆在我面前的这套英美文学教材就是一个明证。

由陈许和陈庆生两位教授主持编写的《精编英国文学教程》和《精编美国文学教程》是该院精品课程的有机组成部分，也是颇有特色的大学本科英语专业的文学教材。诚如他们在书的"前言"中总结归纳的那样，这套教材具有内容全面，脉络清晰；结构合理，重点突出；浅显易懂，易于自学；图文并茂，增添兴趣等鲜明特点。

这里我想强调指出的是，众所周知，英国文学具有较悠久的历史，产生了很多著名的作家，他们的作品浩如烟海，要从中选出最重要的、最具有代表性的作家和作品，又要适合我国高校，特别是理工类院校英语专业学生的实际水平和需要实是一件很不容易做好的工作。但是，这本教材的编写者们做了大量的准备工作，精心设计，精挑细拣，选择了50多位作家，90多篇作品，个个有特色，篇篇是珠玑。他们为这些作家和作品写的介绍、评析和注释也是精心安排，精益求精，正如本书的书名《精编英国文学教程》表明的那样，"精"字当头，名副其实。

我相信这套教材的出版和使用，不仅会给浙江省高校的英美文学的教学有很大的帮助，而且对其他地区的各类院校的英美文学教学也会有所裨益。在此我也向广大爱好英美文学的读者推荐本书。

我在上面用了较多篇幅简要地回忆我国外语教育发展的历史，为的是要告诉人们我们当前外语教学的大好形势来之不易，应十分珍惜。杭州电子科技大学外国语学院的同仁们做的工作正是为保持和发展这种局面作出的很好努力，也是对建国60周年的最好献礼，可喜可贺！可敬可佩！

是为序。

解放军外国语学院英语教授、博导　姚乃强

2009 年 8 月于洛阳

前 言

21 世纪的特点是政治多极化、经济全球化、文化多元化和信息社会化。在这个瞬息万变、飞速发展的新世纪里，我国的高等教育事业在前十年里加速腾飞，由此带来了英语专业的迅猛发展，使得英语语言文学专业的本科生和硕士生人数每年递增。作为英语专业教学的重要组成部分，英美文学教学所受到的关注程度还不尽如人意。我们编写这本《精编英国文学教程》，希望能够在提高学生的英国文学学习兴趣和鉴赏能力方面尽绵薄之力，给予一定的帮助。

英国文学是世界文学的重要组成部分。在 16 世纪上半叶，英国文学便异军突起；到 16 世纪下半叶，以莎士比亚为代表的一批作家将英国文学的旗帜插上了欧洲文艺复兴运动的顶峰。从此，英国文学一直屹立于世界文学之林。

《精编英国文学教程》是杭州电子科技大学"英美文学导论"校级与省级精品课程建设的重要组成部分。在多年的课程建设中，课程组所有成员认真备课，精心制作出内容丰富、生动形象的教学课件，搜集了大量的教学资料，如英国文学经典影片、文化背景等视频图像，并不断总结、积累和交流教学经验，这些都为本教材的编写打下了良好的基础。它的编写原则充分体现了本学科先进的教学思想，编写过程中紧紧围绕英语人才培训的目标和思路，力求层次分明，条理清晰，章节安排合理，既突出重点、难点，又强调对本课程基础知识的全面理解和掌握。与当前市场上已有的各种版本的教材相比，本教材具有以下主要特色：

1. 内容全面，脉络清晰。全书按照英国文学发展的七个阶段分为七个部分，即：早期和中古文学、16 世纪文学、17 世纪文学、18 世纪文学、浪漫主义文学、维多利亚文学、20 世纪文学。本书涉及了 40 位作家及其代表作品 60 余篇。学生通过课堂学习和课外自学对英国文学有一个比较清晰的认识和理解。

2. 结构合理，重点突出。本书每章由三个部分组成：第一部分内容介绍不同时期的历史、重大事件等相关背景知识；第二部分内容主要包括文学综述、文学史实、文学流派、重要作家简介等知识；第三部分内容为主要作家（附照片)的生平和主要作品介绍、作品简介和赏析、作品选读、作品注释和思考题。各部分侧重点不同，但相互关联、相互补充，从不同角度帮助学生，使他们对英国文学有一个全面而深刻地了解和把握。

3. 浅显易懂，易于自学。我们针对中国学生英语水平的状况，以及他们的需求和学习特点，在编写本书时力求文字简洁易懂、语言浅显流畅、论述深入浅出。并在每篇作品后附有较为详细的注释，以便降低学生的学习难度，提高他们的阅读速度和学习效率。

4. 图文并茂，增添兴趣。我国以前出版的英国文学教材，大多数没有提供图片资料，实为欠缺。针对青年学生的兴趣特点，我们为每一位作家配备了相关的图片，并附以文字说明，使得教材生动鲜活，有吸引力，也有助于学生更好的了解作家，理解作品的内涵。

5. 资料详实，观点新颖。本书在编写过程中力求观点客观全面，同时注意吸收多年来国内外有关英国文学的研究成果，努力做到资料详实、评价客观、分析深刻、观点新颖，使之更好地服务于我国高等院校英语专业的教师和学生，以及勤奋好学的英语爱好者。

参加本教材编写工作的有陈庆生、陈许、方璞、黄巍、蓝云春、秦宏、田野、田颖、王银瓶、杨鲁萍、郑玮、周小娉等老师，他们在选材、录入、注释、校对、搜集图片等方面做了大量的工作。全书的构思设计和选材安排都由主编负责。

在《精编英国文学教程》即将付梓之际，我们要衷心感谢解放军外国语学院资深望重的姚乃强教授，他对我们编辑本教材给予了充分肯定，并在百忙之中为本教材作序；我们还要衷心感谢浙江省教育厅、杭州电子科技大学及其教务处和外国语学院领导对本教材编写的大力支持和资助；我们也要衷心感谢浙江大学出版社的编辑，他们为本教材的出版做了大量辛勤的工作。

最后，由于水平所限和成书仓促，疏漏和谬误之处在所难免，敬请专家、学者和读者匡正，以便今后改进。

陈庆生　陈　许

2009 年 8 月于杭州电子科技大学

Contents

Part One   Early and Medieval English

Literature (449—1485)

I. Historical Background

Early and medieval period covers more than 800 years, beginning with the invasion in large numbers of the three Germanic tribes into Britain during the 5th and 6th centuries. Prior to the invasion, Britain had been a province under the control of the Roman Empire between AD 43 and 410. Towards the end of the 4th century, with the withdrawal of the Roman troops, Britain came under an increasing pressure from continental barbarian attacks on all sides. The invasion of the three tribes of Angles, Saxons and Jutes marked a new era in the history of Britain.

1. The Anglo—Saxon Period (449—1066)

The Anglo-Saxon period begins with the immigration of three Germanic tribes Angles, Saxons and Jutes, who came from the northern part of the European continent. Seemingly independent of each other, they were closely connected in terms of their Germanic cultural heritage. Before their invasion, Britain had been inhabited by the Celts—the native Britons. In their confrontation with the invasion, the native Celts fought bravely for their independence, but they failed to keep away their powerful enemies. Towards the end of the 5th century, the Angles, Saxons and Jutes succeeded in their conquest of Britain. In consequence of their final conquest, the English nation came into being. Their language, the English, also called Old English, became the dominant one in Britain.

When they settled down in the new home, the Anglo, Saxons and Jutes were heathens, believing in the old mythology of northern Europe. Later in AD 597, a group of missionaries, headed by Saint Augustine, came to Britain from Rome, and within 100 years, the Anglo-Saxons were Christianized. Among them, the first person to be converted into a pious Christian was the King of Kent. The introduction of Christianity into England is a very important event because the religion exerts a very strong influence on the life of the British people and on English literature as well, especially during its early periods.

Soon after their invasion, the Anglo-Saxons set up seven kingdoms gradually in Britain. Wars were constantly fought among themselves. The second half of the 9th century witnessed the new Germanic invasion of the Viking Danes who began their fierce attacks on the Anglo-Saxons. Headed by King Alfred the Great of Wessex (849—899), the English people fought against the Viking invaders and succeeded in repulsing them. In the early 11th century, the Danish invaders again stepped on the British soil. This time they succeeded in their subjugation of the English nation and kept the land under their control for more than two decades.

2. The Medieval Period (1066—1485)

The year of 1066 ushered in a new era in British history. William the Duke of Normandy assembled a fleet of approximately 600 ships and an army of 7,000 men to invade. Under his leadership, the Romans fought hard and won a decisive battle near Hastings. Thus, William declared himself William I, King of England, crowned on December 25, 1066, in Westminster Abbey.

After the Norman Conquest, the Anglo Norman, or Old French, retained a prestigious status for nearly 400 years as the official language and it was used by the royal, the noble and the rich. The native English became the daily speech of the common people. The third language Latin was used in churches and other religious institutions. So it was a funny thing to see that three languages were seen existing in Britain at the same time, each with a different, special function. The native English, though in a humble status, kept its strong vitality. It borrowed from the other two languages a good many of words and terms, which greatly enriched the English language itself. As time elapsed, the English assumed its dominance and replaced French in many functions. In the middle of the 14th century, English became the literary as well as the spoken language in England. By the end of this period, English took its officially dominant role in the educational institutions and at courts of law.

The Norman Conquest was a crucial turning-point in English history for several reasons. First, it linked Britain more closely with continental European nations by introducing a Norman aristocracy. Secondly, it created one of the most powerful monarchies in Europe and brought about a sophisticated governmental system. Next, it changed the English language and culture. Finally, it had an iconic role in English national identity as the last successful military conquest of Britain.

II. Literary Review

1. The Anglo–Saxon Literature

The literature of this period is, comparatively speaking, rather primitive. With their arrival in Britain, the Anglo-Saxons brought with them their own custom, tradition and culture. So the Anglo-Saxon literature, in its early stage, mainly dealt with the events that were happening far away in their European homeland. The earliest form of their literary works was not written but oral. Interesting events were circulated or passed downed from mouth to mouth, and fancy stories were narrated orally or sung to the public. Later, some monks, well-informed and well-educated, took the task of writing down some of the stories.

1.1 Old English Poetry

The Old English poetry in the Anglo-Saxon period can be classified into two types: the pagan and the Christian. The pagan poetry is mostly heroic in the form of oral sagas, dealing with pre-Christian Germanic myth and history. The most important and beautiful works of this group are *The Wanderer*, *Deor*, *The Seafarer*, and *The Wife's Complaint*. An elegiac and melancholy tone is prevailing in all these poems, most likely with a happy past contrasted with a precarious and desolate present.

Much of the Old English Christian poetry is distinct in its simple belief in an unsophisticated Christianity, mainly dealing with the themes from Bible and the lives of the saints. The names of two Christian authors are well known. The first is Caedmon, the earliest known English poet, who is universally hailed as the "Father of English Song". His greatest work, *Paraphrase*, tells the story of Genesis. The second person is Cynewulf, famous for his religious compositions. He is said to have signed four poems *The Christ*, *Elene*, *Juliana*, and *The Fates of the Apostles*.

1.2 Beowulf

Beowulf is a national epic of the Anglo-Saxons with its anonymous authorship and uncertain date, probably composed in the oral form by some English bards in the early 8th century. The story has nothing closely associated with England because the materials for the poem are derived mainly from Scandinavian history, folklore, and mythology.

The whole poem comprises two parts. The first narrates two battles. In the first battle, Hrothgar, the King of the Danes, has built a great hall called Heorot, where Hrothgar and his warriors spend their time singing, eating and drinking. But Grendel, a monster who lives in the swamplands, attacks the hall and kills many of Hrothgar's warriors. Beowulf, a young warrior of the Geats, learns of Hrothgar's trouble, and sails to Denmark, determined to defeat Grendel. Beowulf and his men spend the night in Heorot. After they fall asleep, Grendel enters the hall to resume his attack. Beowulf leaps up and fights heroically with Grendel. Finally, Beowulf tears Grendel's arm from his body and the monster runs back home in the marshes to die.

The second battle relates Beowulf's fight with Grendel's revengeful mother. The next night, Grendel's Mother, a more powerful monster, appears and attacks the hall in revenge for Grendel's death. Beowulf pursues Grendel's Mother to her lair under a lake, where Beowulf and the mother monster engage in a fierce combat. In the end, Beowulf cuts her head off.

In the second part of the epic, Beowulf returns home and eventually becomes a King, loved and respected by his own people. One day, late in Beowulf's old age, one of his slaves steals a golden cup from an unnamed dragon's cave. When the dragon learns that his golden cup has been stolen, it flies in a fury and destroys everything in sight. Beowulf succeeds in killing the dragon. But unfortunately, Beowulf is mortally wounded in the final battle and falls back dead.

The world and the theme that *Beowulf* portrays are a relic of pre-Anglo-Saxon culture. The setting of the story is in Scandinavia, prior to the Anglo-Saxon migration. The work was composed in England, but it presented an interesting though incomplete picture of the life of the upper class and the warriors among the northern Germanic tribes on the Continent and in England.

1.3 Old English Prose

Old English prose dates from the latter part of the Anglo-Saxon period and it is made up of two groups of literary works: religion and history.

The first important and famous English prose writer is Bede (673—735), also called the Venerable Bede, generally considered "the Father of the English learning". His most important work, and also the first English history book—the *Ecclesiastical History of the English People*, is fascinating to read even now with its combination of accurate information and immense credulity.

King Alfred the Great of Wessex, (871—899) displayed his heroic deeds in fighting against the Viking invaders. He was also a learned scholar and great educator, working hard to revitalize the indigenous English culture after the Danish invasions. Alfred's great contributions to the English literature are threefold. First, under his guidance, a lot of Latin books of great educational value were translated into the English vernacular. He himself took the initiative in translating half a dozen of the best informational manuals of history, philosophy, and religion of his time. Secondly, Alfred took charge of the launching of *the Anglo-Saxon Chronicle*. It is extremely valuable, not only as a record of events from Caesar's conquest up to 1154, but also as a literary monument showing the development of the English language. Alfred's third contribution is that he created the first English prose that is clear and familiar.

Another important figure of the Old English prose is Aelfric (955—1025), an English abbot of Eynsham. He wrote voluminous works of homilies, saints' lives, biblical commentaries, and other genres. The main theme of his literary creation is God's mercy. He wrote, for example: "The love that loves God is not idle. Instead, it is strong and works great things always. And if love isn't willing to work, then it isn't love. God's love must be seen in the actions of our mouths and minds and bodies. A person must fulfill God's word with goodness." (*For Pentecost Sunday*)

2. The Medieval English Literature

In the first part of the Medieval period from 1066 up to the mid-14th century, probably the most important writer was Geoffrey Monmouth (1100—1154), a Welsh monk, whose *Historia Regum Britanniae* (*The History of the Kings of Britain*) is of great value as abundant sources from which many later writers would draw their literary materials. The next writer worth our consideration was Roger Bacon, (1214—1294), an English scholastic philosopher and scientist, who placed considerable emphasis on empiricism, one of the earliest European advocates of the modern scientific method. His important book *Opus Maius* was a sort of encyclopedia of facts about the sciences of his time. Another important figure was Layamon (born in 1200), the first prominent Middle English poet, whose *Brut* (1215) is a long poem written in a form of Middle English. *Brut* is a chronicle in 32,341 short lines on the history of Britain, from the fall of Troy to the arrival of Brutus in Britain and continuing through the death of Cadwaladr (a Welsh king).

From the mid-14th century on, Britain began to see the appearance of writers like Geoffrey Chaucer, John Wycliffe, William Langland, John Gower, and John Mandeville. Compared with the Anglo-Saxon literature, Medieval English literature covered a wider range of subjects. Literary writings of various kinds in different styles, tones and genres were produced. English literature came into its first flourishing period in history.

2.1 Religious literature

The literature of the Medieval period can be roughly divided into two groups: the religious and the secular. Many songs were written to be addressed to the Virgin, showing the people's sincere and tender devotion and speaking for the finer spirits in an age of crudeness and violence, but by today's standards, only a few can be considered fine and beautiful as poetry. Perhaps what is worth our special mention among so many works is the *Cursor Mundi* (*Surveyor of the World*), an early 14th century poem of 24,000 lines, dealing with the universal history from the beginning, on the basis of the Biblical narrative. There were some didactic poems, of which the most well-known was *The Pearl*, an allegorical and elegiac poem, relating the vision of one who had lost his pearl. The "Pearl" was, in fact, the poet's young daughter. In an allegorical vision of singular beauty, he saw her as a maiden in paradise, and as a result of his final decision to give up of all the joys and sorrows of earthly existence, he became reconciled to her death.

2.2 Secular literature

In secular literature the variety was greater than in religious writings. The best known of all is the exuberant *Summer Is Icumen In* of the 13th century, intended to be sung in harmony by four voices. It is a traditional English round (A round is a musical composition in which two or more voices sing exactly the same melody over and over again, but with each voice beginning at different times).

There were political and satirical songs and miscellaneous poems of various kinds, of which some significant ones were *On the Evil Times of Edward II*, *When Holy Church Is Under Foot*, *Satire on the Monks and People of Kildare*, and *Sir*

Penny. The majority of the prose works were the *Chronicles*, generally written by the monks of the monasteries in the 12th and 13th centuries, with most of them in Latin, some in French, and a few in English. Many of the *Chronicles* were mere annals just like the *Anglo-Saxon Chronicle*, but some were the lifelong works of men, full of some enlightenment of genuine historical vision. Some dealt merely with the history of England, others with that of the entire world.

2.3 Medieval Romances

The most important form of medieval literature during the period, beginning in the middle of the 12th century, is the romance, especially the metrical romance—the romance written in metrical verses. The typical romance was the literary expression of chivalry (the quality and ideal of knightly conduct), a spirit of great value prevailing in Europe at that time.

The romances were composed by the professional minstrels or bards, who recited their works from memory, in the great halls or in the ladies' bowers, to the accompaniment of their harps. The themes of the romances were mainly love and chivalry. The heroes are knights, and the characters are fair ladies in distress, warriors in armor, giants, dragons, enchanters, and various enemies of Church and State. Love in the romances was displayed through the honest, serious, and unyielding admiration and worship of a fair and noble woman by men or knights, who voluntarily and patiently went through various dangers and adventures to win her favor. Apart from love and chivalry, religion was also a major concern in the romances.

In subject matters, romances can be classified into three categories:

(1) The matter of France: Some of the romances deal with the military exploits of Charlemagne, King of the Franks and French national hero in the 8th century. The most well known piece is *Chanson de Roland*.

(2) The matter of Rome: Some romances deal with materials from ancient Roman and Greek civilizations.

(3) The matter of Britain: The Arthurian legend originated out of stories of Celtic mythology, and was brought to France, and the English people later took the material from the French tales. There exist many cycles of Arthurian romances, among which are tales about Sir Gawain, Launcelot, Merlin, the quest for the Holy Grail, and the death of King Arthur.

2.4 The Arthurian Legend

To the English reader, of all the romances, the Arthurian are by far the most important and interesting, because of their peculiarly close connection with English literature and history. Rich in varied characters and incidents, the Arthurian legend deals with the exploits of King Arthur of Britain and his Knights of the Round Table.

Arthur was the illegitimate son of Uther, king of Britain, and Igraine, the wife of Gorlois, the Duke of Tintagel. After the death of his father, Arthur, who had been brought up secretly, obtained the throne of Britain by successfully pulling a sword from a stone. Merlin, the court magician and guide to Arthur, then revealed the real parentage of the new king.

Though King Arthur is a fabled, prominent figure in Britain's legendary history, he has been exalted, since then, as the ideal of kingship both in war and in peace. Even now in modern times he has been ranked as one of the 100 Greatest Britons of all times. The stories of King Arthur have caught such widespread interest that he is no longer identified as the legendary hero of a single nation. Numerous new legends, stories, revisions, books, and films have been produced, in which the depictions of King Arthur are enlarged and expanded.

Geoffrey Chaucer (ca. 1343—1400)

Life and Major Works

Geoffrey Chaucer was born in London in the early 1340s. His father was John Chaucer, a wealthy wine merchant. Instead of training his son in the family business, the father sent the young Geoffrey to serve as a page in the household of the countess of Ulster. After learning the manners and skills required for a career in the service of the ruling class, Chaucer eventually began to serve the countess's husband, Prince Lionel, the second son of King Edward III. In 1359, Chaucer was captured by the French in the

Chaucer

Hundred Years War and was taken prisoner at a place called "Retters". Chaucer was liberated on ransom by March 1360, and the king (Edward III) subscribed £16 towards the sum paid. In the late 1360s, Chaucer married Philippa Roet, one of the damsels serving in the queen's chamber. Philippa was the daughter of Sir

Paon Roet of Hainaul and the sister to the third wife of John of Gaunt, the duke of Lancaster.

In his lifetime, Chaucer held various positions at court and traveled abroad on numerous diplomatic missions. In 1372, Chaucer was sent to Genoa to fulfill a diplomatic mission. This visit and a subsequent one to Florence brought him into direct contact with the Italian Renaissance. In 1374, Chaucer was appointed Controller of Customs of hides, skins, and wools in the port of London. In 1386, Chaucer was sitting in parliament as knight of the shire for Kent, where Canterbury was located. In 1394, Chaucer received from Richard the king a pension of £20 a year.

Chaucer died on Oct 25, 1400, and was buried in Westminster Abbey, in the chapel of St. Benedict, a place that has since become known as the Poet's Corner.

The works of Chaucer can be divided into three periods, in relation to the three stages of his life: from 1360 to 1372; from 1372 to 1386; and from 1386 to his death. During the first period, Chaucer was influenced by the leading French poets of his day such as Guillaume de Machaut (1300?—1377) and Jean Froissart (1333?—1400). Most of their poems were lyrics and narratives about courtly love, usually told in the form of a dream. In the second period, Chaucer was under the influence of Italian literature. His trip to Italy in 1372 for diplomatic mission is regarded as a milestone in his literary development. The most outstanding work in this period is *Troilus and Criseide* (ca. 1385), a story of the tragic love between the Trojan prince Troilus and Criseide, the daughter of a soothsayer. This second period also saw other important poems: *The House of Fame*; *The Parliament of Fowls*; and *The Legend of Good Women*. *The House of Fame* describes a journey of the poet in the dream vision to the celestial palace of the goddess Fame. *The Parliament of Fowls* tells the meeting of all the birds on St. Valentine's Day to choose their mates. Concerning the topic of love, different thoughts and talks of different classes in the society are humorously depicted in this poem. *The Legend of Good Women* was an unfinished long poem, recounting 10 stories of virtuous women in nine sections. The third period covers the last 15 years of Chaucer's life. *The Canterbury Tales*, his most famous and critically acclaimed work was written in this period. The long poem begins with a general prologue, telling us how, one spring day, the poet meets a group of pilgrims in an inn in the southern suburb of London and how they decide to kill the time by telling tales on their journey to and from Canterbury. Although the poet originally planned to write about 120 stories (two for each pilgrim to tell on the way to Canterbury and two more on the way back), he never finished, leaving us the general prologue, 22 complete tales, and two more in fragments. Besides the above prominent works, Chaucer also wrote moral and religious works, chiefly translations. For example, he translated the Latin *Consolation of Philosophy*, a work written by the sixth-century Roman statesman Boethius and enjoyed popularity in the Middle Ages.

Chaucer is usually regarded as the father of English poetry and his contribution to English language and literature is tremendous. First, he introduced from France the rhymed stanzas of various types to English poetry (Originally, old English poems are mainly alliterative verses with few variations). For example, in *The Romance of the Rose*, he first introduced the octosyllabic couplet to English; while in *The Legend of Good Women*, he used for the first time in English the heroic couplet. Second, he wrote his masterpiece *The Canterbury Tales* in his native language at a time when French and Latin were prevailing. Thus, he greatly contributed to the founding of the English language, the basis of which was formed by the London dialect.

Brief Introduction and Appreciation

The Canterbury Tales, as Chaucer's masterpiece, includes a general prologue which is acclaimed to be the best part of the book, and 24 tales. In the general prologue, the poet begins his story: one day in spring, the narrator joins a group of pilgrims at the Tabard Inn, a tavern in Southwark, near London. These pilgrims are people from all walks of life: Knight, Squire, Yeoman, Prioress, Monk, Friar, Merchant, Clerk, Man of Law, Franklin, Haberdasher, Carpenter, Weaver, Dyer, Tapestry-Weaver, Cook, Shipman, Physician, Wife, Parson, Plowman, Miller, Manciple, Reeve, Summoner, and Pardoner. The same destination to the shrine of the martyr Saint Thomas Becket in Canterbury gets all these people together at the inn owned by a man called Harry Bailey. Being a hearty man, Harry the host joins the pilgrims and proposes a way to entertain one another on their journey: each pilgrim tells two tales on the way to Canterbury and another two on the way back. The person who has provided the best tales—the host being the judge—will receive a meal (paid by the other pilgrims) at the host's tavern. This proposal is accepted and the pilgrims begin to draw lots to determine the order of story-telling. The Knight is the first story-teller. And the rest of the book turns out to be an assembly of various types of tales, with a retraction of the author at the end of it. There are romances, vulgar stories, legends of saints, fables, and sermons, etc.

The stories told by the Miller, the Wife of Bath, the Pardoner, and the Nun's Priest are especially interesting and innovative. The Miller tells the story of a foolish carpenter who is cheated by his wife and her lover. John, the carpenter, has a sexy and young wife called Alisoun. Nicholas, a poor student boarding in his house, persuades Alisoun to spend the night with him. Nicholas makes John believe the coming of the second flood and tricks John into spending the night in a tub hanging from the ceiling of his barn. Absolon, another adorer of Alisoun, passes the window of the room where Nicholas and Alisoun lie together and asks the latter for a kiss. The mischievous Alisoun tricks Absolon into kissing her rear end. Infuriated by the insult, Absolon returns with a red-hot poker and asks for another kiss. This time Nicholas sticks his bottom out the window and receives the hot poker. When Nicholas cries for water, the carpenter cuts the rope connecting his tub to the ceiling, falls down and breaks his arm.

The Wife of Bath tells an Arthurian story. A young knight of King Arthur's court is sent by the queen to discover what women want most to make amends for his misdoing. On his way, he meets an ugly old woman who promises to tell him the answer on condition that he promises to do anything she asks for. The knight consents, and is told that women want control of their husbands and their own lives. When this answer is accepted by the queen, the old woman tells the knight that he must marry her. Knowing that the knight is sick of her appearance, the old woman asks him to choose between an ugly and faithful wife, and a beautiful and unfaithful wife. The knight leaves the choice to the old woman herself and is rewarded with a wife both beautiful and faithful.

The Pardoner's story is about greed and death. Three young men go out to look for Death, thinking that they can kill him. An old man informs them that they will find Death under a tree. However, they find eight bushels of gold under a tree and decide to bring the gold to town under cover of darkness. When the youngest one who is sent to fetch food and drink comes back, he is killed by the other two, who die just a moment later when they drink the poisoned drink the youngest one has fetched.

The Nun's Priest tells an interesting fable. The protagonist of the story is Chanticleer, a Rooster. Chanticleer is carried off by a cunning fox who tricks him into closing his eyes and showing off his crow abilities. However, the Chanticleer lures his foe into bragging about his victory. As soon as the fox opens his mouth, Chanticleer falls down and escapes.

Chaucer ends his book with a retraction in which he asks the readers to thank Jesus Christ for anything pleasing in the book, and to ascribe the fault to the author for anything displeasing in it.

The Canterbury Tales bears historical significance in the development of English language and literature. First, the native language Chaucer adopted in *Canterbury* established the prestige of English. Second, the heroic couplet Chaucer used with ease in *Canterbury* set a good example for the later poets such as Alexander Pope. Third, the structure of Boccaccio's *Decameron* (hooking together the collection of stories by gathering the story-tellers in one place) inspired Chaucer, but he improved the structure in an ingenious way (there are interplays between the tales and the tale-tellers in *Canterbury*). Fourth, Chaucer's *Canterbury* gives us a realistic and comprehensive picture of the England in his time. If Dante's journey in *The Divine Comedy* ended in spiritual purification, Chaucer's pilgrims learned about the weakness of human nature. Chaucer's grand plan to create a literature and poetic language for all classes of society was successful. By the time of English Renaissance, Chaucer had been identified as the father of the English literary canon by poetry critic George Puttenham. Even today, Chaucer is still regarded as one of the great shapers of literary narrative and character.

The following selections are from "the General Prologue", and "the Wife of Bath's Prologue Tale".

Selected Reading

The Canterbury Tales
(The General Prologue)

When the sweet showers of April have pierced

The drought of March, and pierced it to the root,

And every vein is bathed in that moisture

Whose quickening force will engender the flower;

And when the west wind too with its sweet breath

Has given life in every wood and field

To tender shoots, and when the stripling sun

Has run his half-course in Aries, the Ram,[1]
And when small birds are making melodies,
That sleep all the night long with open eyes,
(Nature so prompts them, and encourages);
Then people long to go on pilgrimages,
And palmers[2] to take ship for foreign shores,
And distant shrines, famous in different lands;
And most especially, from all the shires
Of England, to Canterbury they come,
The holy blessed martyr[3] there to seek,
Who gave his help to them when they were sick.
It happened at this season, that one day
In Southwark at the Tabard where I stayed
Ready to set out on my pilgrimage
To Canterbury, and pay devout homage,
There came at nightfall to the hostelry
Some nine-and-twenty in a company,
Folk of all kinds, met in accidental
Companionship, for they were pilgrims all;
It was to Canterbury that they rode.
The bedrooms and the stables were good-sized,
The comforts offered us were of the best.
And by the time the sun had gone to rest
I'd talked with everyone, and soon became
One of their company, and promised them
To rise at dawn next day to take the road
For the journey I am telling you about.
...
There was a business woman, from near Bath[4],
But, more's the pity, she was a bit deaf;
So skilled a clothmaker, that she outdistanced
Even the weavers of Ypres and Ghent[5].
In the whole parish there was not a woman
Who dared precede her at the almsgiving,
And if there did, so furious was she,

That she was put out of all charity.

Her headkerchiefs were of the finest weave,

Ten pounds and more they weighed, I do believe,

Those that she wore on Sundays on her head.

Her stockings were of finest scarlet red,

Very tightly laced; shoes pliable and new.

Bold was her face, and handsome; florid too.

She had been respectable all her life,

And five times married, that's to say in church,

Not counting other loves she'd had in youth,

Of whom, just now, there is no need to speak.

And she had thrice been to Jerusalem;

Had wandered over many a foreign stream;

And she had been at Rome, and at Boulogne,

St James of Compostella, and Cologne;[6]

She knew all about wandering—and straying:

For she was gap-toothed, if you take my meaning.[7]

Comfortably on an ambling horse she sat,

Well-wimpled, wearing on her head a hat

That might have been a shield in size and shape;

A riding-skirt round her enormous hips,

Also a pair of sharp spurs on her feet.

In company, how she could laugh and joke!

No doubt she knew of all the cures for love,

For at that game she was a past mistress.

…

(The Wife of Bath's Prologue)

Experience—and no matter what they say

In books—is good enough authority

For me to speak of trouble in marriage.

For ever since I was twelve years of age,

Thanks be to God, I've had no less than five

Husbands at church door—if one may believe

14

I could be wed so often legally!

And each a man of standing, in his way.

Certainly it was told me, not long since,

That, seeing Christ had never more than once

Gone to a wedding (Cana, in Galilee[8])

He taught me by that very precedent

That I ought not be married more than once.

What's more, I was to bear in mind also

Those bitter words that Jesus, God and Man,

Spoke in reproof to the Samaritan[9]

Besides a well— "Thou hast had," said He,

"Five husbands and he whom now thou hast

Is not thy husband." He said that, of course,

But what He meant by it I cannot say.

All I ask is, why wasn't the fifth man

The lawful spouse of the Samaritan?

How many lawful husbands could she have?

All my born days, I've never heard as yet

Of any given number or limit,

However folk surmise or interpret.

All I know for sure is, God has plainly

Bidden us to increase and multiply—

A noble text, and one I understand!

And, as I'm well aware, He said my husband

Must leave father and mother, cleave to me.

But, as to number, did He specify?

He named no figure, neither two nor eight—

Why should folk talk of it as a disgrace?

…

Notes

1. **Aries, the Ram**: the first sign of the zodiac, in Chaucer's time it was supposed to govern from 12 March to 11 April.

2. **palmers**: pilgrims, so called because they carried palms to show that they had

been to Jerusalem.

3. **the holy blessed martyr**: St Thomas Becket, murdered in Canterbury Cathedral in 1170.

4. **Bath**: a city in southwest England. It is famous for hot spring.

5. **Ypres and Ghent**: both the centers of wool trade in the Middle Ages.

6. The places mentioned in these two lines used to be the famous holy lands in the late Middle Ages.

7. **For she was gap-toothed, if you take my meaning**: teeth set wide apart were a sign of a lascivious nature, and also that the owner would travel.

8. **Cana, in Galilee**: Cana of Galilee is best known as the place where, according to the Fourth Gospel, Jesus performed his tenth miracle (scholars would note that it was His first miracle in Cana): the turning of a large quantity of water into wine at a wedding feast when the wine provided by the bridegroom had run out.

9. **the Samaritan**: The Samaritans are an ethnic group of the Levant. Ethnically, they are descended from a group of Israelite inhabitants that have connections to ancient Samaria from the beginning of the Babylonian Exile up to the beginning of the Christian Era.

Questions for Study and Discussion

1. What seem to be the motives offered for the pilgrimage that is about to begin?

2. What physical disability does the Wife of Bath have?

3. How does the Wife of Bath dress herself up? What kind of impression do you have upon her appearance?

4. How many husbands has she had? What is your understanding about "not counting other company in youth"?

5. What are the Wife of Bath's teeth like? What does it mean?

6. What is your understanding of the line "For at that game she was a past mistress"? What does the "game" refer to?

Part Two   The Sixteenth Century

(1485—1603)

I. Historical Background

The Renaissance movement originated in Italy roughly in the late 14th century, spread throughout Europe in the 15th century, climaxed in the period of Michelangelo and Machiavelli in the early 16th century, and terminated in the early 17th century. The Renaissance humanists emphasized the importance of individual achievement in a wide range of fields and the significance of each individual in the society. The Renaissance movement caused a fundamental change in nearly every aspect of European intellectual life in the modern period, and its influence was strongly felt in philosophy, politics, religion, art, literature, science, architecture, and other fields of intellectual enquiry. The period of this revival marked the transition from medieval to modern times.

1. Italian Renaissance

In the late 14th century, the Italian Renaissance began the opening phase of the movement in the cities of Florence and Siena. Soon, it spread to Venice, where the manuscripts of ancient Greek culture and Roman culture attracted the earliest Renaissance humanists, such as Francesco Petrarch, and Giovanni Boccaccio. Humanist scholars searched monastic libraries and studied the writings of the ancient Greeks and Romans for new inspiration and ideology. They sought intellectual independence by breaking away from the current religious ideology dominated by the Catholic Church.

The Italian Renaissance gave birth to some extraordinary talented masters who made great contributions to the civilization of the human society. In literature, Francesco Petrarch (1304—1374), the founder of Renaissance Humanism, and the foremost writer of sonnets in Italian, and his sonnets were translated into English by Thomas Wyatt (1503—1542). Giovanni Boccaccio (1313—1375), an important Renaissance humanist and author of a number of significant works. His masterpiece was *The Decameron*, regarded as a masterpiece and a model for Italian classical prose. Baldassare Castiglione (1478—1529) wrote his most famous work, *The Book of the Courtier*, defining the ideal Renaissance gentleman. Niccolo Machiavelli's (1469—1527) best-known work was *Il Principe* (*The Prince*), considered one of the first works of political science, in which he described the means by which a prince may gain and maintain his power.

The significance of the Renaissance movement can be summed up as follows:

1. The Renaissance gave a great impetus to art, architecture, learning and literature which reached tremendous heights. It also generated great respect for antiquity and a reverence for the ancient Greek and Roman classics.

2. Politically, it strengthened the power of the monarchy. Feeling tired of feudal anarchy, the people in Europe expected the monarchy to ensure peace and order, political stability and economic prosperity.

3. In religion, it set off and intensified the Religious Reform and weakened the Catholic Church, which could not occupy the position of unquestioned authority.

4. Greater emphasis is placed on man's dignity and on human potentiality for personal growth and excellence.

5. It led to the formation of humanism, and gave a stimulus to the growth of vernacular literature. As a result, the Italian, French, German, Spanish and English languages blossomed at that time.

6. It generated many far-reaching scientific inventions and geographical discoveries. The rise of the rational spirit and of scientific investigation weakened absolute conformity and obedience, and the emphasis was laid on the importance of critical examination and evaluation of ideas and principles.

7. With the discovery of many historical manuscripts, the study of history was made more critical and scientific under the guidance of a more curious and inquisitive spirit that demanded accuracy and reliability.

8. The Renaissance brought in new conceptions of life and the world, which invigorated the strong desire and hot pursuit of personal independence and individual expression, and brought into focus the timely appreciation of worldly

pleasures in the present life rather than in the afterlife.

9. The Renaissance movement spawned a massive explosion of the dissemination of knowledge brought on by the advent of printing.

10. Most important for our study of humanities and arts, the Renaissance movement procreated in Europe a large number of great humanist thinkers and scholars, whose works are forever a main part of sources from which we can draw to form our learning.

2. Introduction of the Printing Press

Two events proved a powerful stimulus to the formation of the English Renaissance. The first is the introduction of the printing, and the second, the Religious Reformation.

William Caxton (1422—1492), was the first English person to work as a printer, and more important, the first person to introduce a printing press into England. In 1475, he printed *The Recuyell of the Historyes of Troye* (a French courtly romance written by Raoul le Fevre), his own translation from the French, and the first book printed in English. All his life, Caxton printed about 100 books.

Because of Caxton's introduction of the printing press, the English literature began to flourish with the publication of many works, including Chaucer's *Canterbury Tales* (1843) and Malory's *Le Morte d'Arthur* (1485). The printing press rendered easier and more profitable the translation of many literary works from the European continent of both ancient and modern times. Thus, Caxton's introduction of the printing press fostered a national interest in book reading, created a commercial market for academic and literary writings, and provided various reading materials for people's serious learning and leisurely enjoyment.

3. Religious Reformation

The Religious Reformation, originating from the continent and initiated by Martin Luther, spread to England. Henry VIII used to be faithful to the Roman Catholic Church, but his wish to have a male heir to continue the Tudor dynasty by divorcing his first wife Katharine and marrying Anne Boleyn did not gain the approval of Pope Clement VII. Henry defied the Pope and married Ann Boleyn. The Pope's refusal to allow the annulment of Henry's marriage to Catherine prompted the English King to break away from the Roman Catholic Church. In

1534, the England's breach with Rome was completed by the Act of Supremacy. Henry VIII seized the good opportunity to reduce the power of the Roman Catholic Church by pushing ahead the Religious Reform, and by confiscating the property of the monasteries. He declared himself the head of the new Anglican Church. From 1534 to 1536, the English Parliament enacted a number of acts. In consequence, all direct payments to the Pope in Rome were halted, and the Archbishop of Canterbury was endowed with the power to grant a wide variety of dispensations previously held only by the Papacy. The English King had the right to appoint all senior churchmen and determine the definition of beliefs—both again had been held by the Papacy.

Under the reign of the Tudors, Britain became a centralized, rationalized bureaucratic country. The establishment of the English Church, the increased power of the feudal nobility, the growing influence of the new rising bourgeoisie, and the growth of a strong, centralized monarchy under the Tudors heralded the end of the medieval period in England and the movement towards the English renaissance.

4. The Elizabethan Age

After Mary Tudor's death in 1558, Elizabeth I became Queen of England at the age of 25. She was the daughter of Henry VIII and his second wife, Anne Boleyn. Elizabeth was a very intelligent woman. In both intellect and temperament, she was well qualified for the role of a monarch. She was exceptionally well-educated, under the instruction of Roger Ascham—one of the most outstanding scholars and thinkers of the age. She could speak Latin, French and German. She showed a broad interest in subjects, ranging from art and literature, to history, philosophy and science. And she was a remarkably sagacious political strategist. As a strong, resolute monarch, Elizabeth I returned England to Protestantism, quelled a great deal of internal turmoil, and unified the nation. She provided the country with a long period of general peace and increasing prosperity. She was also a strong supporter of the arts, and this sparked a surge of various activities in learning and literature.

Elizabeth I ruled Britain for a long term until her death in 1603. During her long reign, England emerged from a weak, humble nation as a country of tremendous political and military power and unparalleled cultural achievements. She is generally credited with leading England to nearly the height of a powerful state among European nations. Both Spain and France felt the impact of England's rapidly increasing strength and audacity under Elizabeth's rule. In fact, the earlier period of the Elizabeth's reign scarcely produced any work of permanent importance. But after 50 years of religious disturbances and upheavals, time was required for the restoration of the domestic peace and confidence from which a great literature could spring. At long last, the hour grew ripe and there came the greatest outrush of creative power in the whole history of the English literature. Much of the English renaissance is considered directly attributable to Elizabeth's personal temperament and influence, and it is well appropriate that the second half of the 16th century in England is identified as the Elizabethan Age.

Some characteristics of the Elizabethan Age are summed up as follows:

Firstly, it was an age of new tolerant attitudes towards the religious affairs under the Queen's influence.

Secondly, it was an era of comparative social contentment.

Thirdly, it was a time of hopes and dreams, of glorious adventures and of great enthusiasm springing from the exotic lands with incredible riches.

Lastly, it was a period of intellectual freedom, of unbounded patriotism, of growing intelligence and comfort among all social status, and of peace and stability at home and abroad.

II. Literary Review

1. The English Renaissance

The Renaissance movement in Britain began with the introduction of Italian art and philosophy during the reign of Henry VIII. The period is also referred to as "the age of Shakespeare" or "the Elizabethan Age".

The English Renaissance produced a lot of prominent literary masters. Sir Thomas More (1478—1535) was a leading humanist scholar, famous for his book *Utopia* (1515) in which, the author depicted an ideal state, where the three great concepts Liberty, Fraternity and Equality were for the first time conveyed as the foundations of civilized society, where all is ordered for the best for humanity as a whole, and where the evils of society, such as poverty and misery, have been eliminated. Henry Howard, Earl of Surrey (1517—1547) introduced blank verse to English in translating two books of Vergil's *Aeneid*. He and his friend Sir Thomas

Wyatt (1503—1542) wrote their sonnets by imitating classical writers such as Petrarch, and they are credited as "Fathers of the English Sonnet." Edmund Spenser (1552—1599), English poet and Poet Laureate, was one of the premier craftsmen of Modern English verse in its infancy with his best known *The Faerie Queene*, an epic poem celebrating, through fantastical allegory, the Tudor Dynasty and Queen Elizabeth I. The poets and playwrights Christopher Marlowe (1564—1593), William Shakespeare (1564—1616), and Ben Jonson (1572—1637) were the three major figures of the period, with their plays representing the greatest achievements in the Renaissance drama.

Several characteristics of the English Renaissance can be listed as follows:

1. The English Renaissance generated an almost boundless creative power. Works of various kinds in prose and verse were produced, ranging in spirit from the loftiest Platonic idealism to the level of mean and vulgar realism.

2. The literary works of the period were mainly dominated by the spirit of romance.

3. The English Renaissance writings were shot through with the spirit of dramatic action, which best encouraged people to engage in fabulous and adventurous enterprises in the foreign lands.

4. The English writers originated unprecedented experiments in their literary creation. They made the bold use of any material and literary forms, sometimes regardless of false starts and grandiose failures. They made particular efforts to give prolonged poetical treatment to many subjects essentially prosaic, such as the systems of theological or scientific thought and the geography of all England.

5. The English literature continued to be largely influenced by the literature of Italy, and to a less degree by those of France and Spain.

6. The literary spirit was all-pervasive in nearly every aspect of the English society, and the English Renaissance authors were exclusively men (no women) of almost every social status, from eminent nobles, such as Thomas More, Henry Howard, Thomas Wyatt, and Philip Sidney, who lived a wealthy and comfortable life, to the company of hack writers, who starved in shabby garrets and lingered around the bustling taverns.

2. The Sixteenth Century Poetry

In the early years of the English Renaissance, there arose a flourish of lyric poetry.

Most of the lyric poems dealt with two themes: the relationship between men and women, and the treachery and hypocrisy of courtly life.

The best forerunners in this genre were Thomas Wyatt and Henry Howard. Together they introduced into English two important poetic forms: the blank verse and the sonnet. They composed their amorous sonnets modeled after the Italian Petrarch's sonnet form, which was made up of two parts: a rhyming octave (**abbaabba**), and a rhyming sestet (**cdcdcd**). Wyatt departed from the Petrarch's rime-scheme by substituting a third quatrain for the first four lines of the sestet with the different rime-arrangement: **abba abba cddc ee**. Soon after, this beautiful poetic form attracted attention from men of letters in Britain, and became the most popular among English lyric poets of the next two generations, setting a fashion which was carried to an astonishing excess during the reign of Elizabeth I.

During the Elizabethan period the sonnets were often written as part of a sequence of love poems. The sonneteers were particularly fascinated with the complexity of a sequence, in which each sonnet was both an independent poem and part of an ongoing narrative development. Among the outstanding Elizabethan sonnet sequences were Philip Sidney's (1554—1586) *Astrophel and Stella*, Samuel Daniel's (1562—1619) *Delia*, and Edmund Spenser's *Amoretti*. William Shakespeare wrote all together 154 sonnets. Shakespeare's sonnets displayed a profound meditation on the nature of love, art, procreation, sexual passion, time and death, and they are considered the greatest among the English poetry. The Shakespearean or English sonnet is made of three quatrains rhyming **abab cdcd efef** and a closing heroic couplet rhyming **gg.**

Edmund Spenser (1552—1599) forms the second great landmark in the English poetry after Chaucer. His poetic creation was greatly influenced by the classic and Italian literature. His poetry is noteworthy for four distinguishing features: wonderful beauty in art, nobility of aim, purity of spirit, and reverence for religion. *The Shepheardes Calender* (1579) was Spenser's first major poetic work. *Astrophel* (1591) was an elegy written in memory of his friend Sir Philip Sidney. In the same year *Amoretti*, Spenser's sonnet sequence commemorating his courtship of Elizabeth Boyle, was also published. In 1596, Spenser's masterpiece *The Faerie Queene* appeared with its first 6 books, and it was an unfinished long poem. The excellence of *The Faerie Queene* lies in the complexity and depth of the poet's moral vision and in his own invention—the Spenserian stanza (each stanza containing nine lines in total: eight lines in iambic pentameter followed by one line in iambic hexameter. The rhyme scheme of these lines is "**ababbcbcc**"). In style and spirit, Spenser exerted one of the most powerful influences on all succeeding English romantic poetry.

Other well-known poets are these: George Gascoigne (1530—1577), Sir Edward Dyer (1545—1607), Nicholas Breton (1545—1626), Robert Southwell (1562—1595), Thomas Nash (1567—1601), Samuel Daniel (1562—1619), Barnabe Barnes (1569—1609), Sir Walter Raleigh (1552—1618), George Chapman (1559—1631), and Michael Drayton (1563—1631).

The 16th century English poetry was notable for the following features:

1. Many of the poets tried to voice the national feeling after the defeat of the Armada, and grew silent as soon as the fervor began to wane.

2. Love was the theme of a very large part of the poetry of the period

3. The outstanding qualities of the poetry are its patriotic zeal, its enthusiastic joy in life, its theme of love, and its youthful vigor and freshness.

4. The 16th century poetry is also marked with its fluency, sweetness and melody.

5. Most of the Elizabethan lyric poetry seems artificial to the modern reader. They deal largely with goddesses and airy shepherd folk. They contain extensive allusions to classic characters and scenes, such as Venus, Olympus and many others. They are nearly all characterized by the elaboration of language.

3. The Sixteenth Century Prose

The most important and enduring contributions to English prose during the years preceding the accession of Elizabeth and perhaps of the entire century are to be found in the area of Biblical translation and devotional literature.

William Tyndale (1494—1536) was a 16th century Protestant reformer and biblical translator. He hoped to translate the New Testament into English. Finding the publication of his English version could not be possible in England, Tyndale went to Germany in 1524, and finally succeeded in getting his book printed there (1525). Much of Tyndale's work eventually found its way into the *King James Version* (or *Authorized Version*) of the Bible, which was published in 1611, and which was, to a large extent, based on his previous efforts.

Thomas More (1478—1535) was a lawyer, author, and statesman. During his lifetime he gained a reputation as a leading humanist scholar. His *History of King*

Richard III (1557) was the first important prose work in the 16th century, which heavily influenced Shakespeare's play Richard III. More's most famous work *Utopia* was a novel in which a traveler named Raphael Hythloday describes a legendary island nation *Utopia*, in which all questions of labor, government, society, and religion have been easily and perfectly settled by orderly and reasonable social arrangements.

The English prose burst into sudden glory in the late 1570s. There arose a decisive change of taste for a fluent and high artistic quality. The Elizabethan men of letters strove for grace and sophistication in their prose writings.

Richard Hooker (1553—1600) was an important prose writer during this period. His most well-known work *Of the Laws of Ecclesiastical Polity* was an epoch-making discussion of church government, written in an excellent prose style.

Philip Sidney (1554—1586) was famous as a preeminent poet and prose writer. *The Defense of Poesy* (1595) was his prominent prose criticism of the nature of poetry, written as a refutation against Stephen Gosson's *The School of Abuse*. The key point of *The Defense of Poesy* is that poetry, through the combination of the liveliness of history with the moral concern of philosophy, is more effective than either history or philosophy in rousing its readers to virtue.

Francis Bacon (1561—1626) is one of the finest prose stylists of English literature. His famous *Essays*, contain his personal reflections upon men, manners, and morals and deal with a great variety of topics, ranging from friendship to the arrangement of a house. Bacon's writings, terse, witty, pithy and packed with profound thought, are splendid examples of the English prose, which will interest and enlighten students of the English literature.

Compared with poetry, the 16th century prose was a much inferior and less practiced form of art. Though the number of its masterpieces was small, the 16th century prose was fairly attractive, for it reflected the varied interests and the complicated characteristics of the strange and wonderful age, and it foreshadowed some new forms of literature, such as criticism and fiction, which were in future to develop into genres of the first importance.

4. The Sixteenth Century Drama

4.1 The Mystery and Miracle Plays
The main body of the material for the Mystery and Miracle plays was derived from

Bible stories or from lives of the saints. Those plays were mostly staged during important Church festivals. At Christmas, for example, the beautiful story of Bethlehem (the birthplace of Jesus Christ) would be presented more vividly by placing in a corner of the church an image of a babe in a manger, with shepherds and the Magi at hand, and the choir in white garments chanting the Gloria in Excelsis (Glory in the Highest).

The early Miracle plays in Britain were classified into two kinds: the first, dealing with the birth of Christ, were performed at Christmas; the second, telling the stories about his death and triumph, were given at Easter.

Performed in the church, the Miracle plays were deeply religious in spirit. They had taken a long strong hold upon the English audience, and remained enormously popular for a long time. The English people assembled in large numbers to see the plays. Soon after, the plays spread swiftly from the churchyard to the city squares or the town common. Once outside the church, they were taken up by the guilds or trades-unions, in whose hands they lost much of their religious character. The Mystery and Miracle plays reached the height of their popularity in the 15th century before being rendered obsolete by the rise of professional theatre. Finally, they were replaced by the Elizabethan Drama in the 16th century.

4.2 The Morality Plays

In England by the end of the 15th century the Mysteries had been replaced by the Moralities.

The Morality plays, evolving from sermons, were written in part out of the desire of religious writers as didactic plays intended to infuse the audience with the principles of the Christian life. In its strict form the Morality plays are a type of theatrical allegory. The protagonist, as a representative of either the humanity or an entire social class, is challenged by personifications of various moral attributes—Love, Life, Goodness, Repentance, Greed, Death, and other abstract Virtues and Vices, who try to prompt him to choose a godly life over one of the evils. The Morality plays were most popular in Europe during the 15th and 16th centuries. As time went on, the Morality plays obtained a distinct advance over the Miracle plays by giving free scope to the imagination for new plots and incidents. Thus, the Morality plays more frequently dealt with secular topics, such as forms of knowledge, questions of good government, education, etc.

In England, the early Morality plays were a kind of dreary performance. In order to enliven the audience, the devil of the Miracle plays was introduced.

Another cheerful personage named the Vice was the predecessor of the modern clown and jester. The Vice's role was to torment the "virtues" by playing various mischievous tricks, and especially to make the Devil's life a troublesome burden by beating him with a bladder or a wooden sword at every opportunity. The Morality plays generally ended in the triumph of virtue, the devil leaping into the hell-mouth with Vice on his back. Some of the well-known Morality plays then in Britain were *Everyman*, *The Castle of Perseverance*, *Magnificence*, *The Necromancer* and *The Pride of Life*.

4.3 Shakespeare's Predecessors in the Drama

Drama was the greatest literary achievement in the 16th century England. During the period, the theatre was the focal point of the time, and the London theatre became a meeting ground of humanism and popular taste. Under royal patronage, some playwrights were able to live a comfortable life. Thus, a great deal of theatrical activity was carried on at Court, and many public theatres were built in the suburbs of London.

The best and most important playwrights in the Elizabethan Age were William Shakespeare, Ben Jonson and Christopher Marlowe, who composed their plays by means of various sources, such as the Greek tragedy, Seneca's plays, Miracle plays, Morality plays and interludes. The Elizabethan tragedies were mainly concerned with heroic themes, depicting a great persona who was destroyed unfortunately by his own passion and ambition. The comedies were usually intended to satirize the fops and gallants of the upper society.

Generally speaking, all those, who had been producing Miracles, Moralities, interludes, masques and pageants for about four centuries, could be considered Shakespeare's predecessors. But the chief immediate predecessors of Shakespeare were a small group of playwrights in the last quarter of the 16th century, who rapidly developed what is now called the Elizabethan drama. This group was called the University Wits, who were educated at the Oxford and Cambridge universities.

Among them, the forerunner was John Lyly (1554—1606), a dramatist and prose writer, who was a graduate from Magdalen College, Oxford. In his early plays, the most noteworthy were Campaspe (1584) and Endimion (1591), written in an elaborate style. But his later works adopted the realistic and vigorous manner of the Roman comedy. In Woman in the Moon (1594) he made a successful experiment with blank verse.

Thomas Lodge (1558—1625), a dramatist and writer, graduated from Trinity College, Oxford, 1577. Lodge wrote in nearly every form of literature. He wrote several euphuistic romances, the best being *Scillaes Metamorphosis* (1589). He also wrote a collection of amorous sonnets and a book of verse satires, *A Fig for Momus* (1595).

George Peele (1558—1596) was educated at Oxford. He experimented in a variety of literary forms, including the pageant, history, pastoral, comedy, and melodrama. His best-known work is The Old Wives Tale (1595), a playful piece that infuses a depiction of ordinary English life with elements of folklore and romance.

Robert Greene (1558—1592) was perhaps the first professional author in England to support himself with his pen. He was a MA graduate from Cambridge University. He began his literary career with the publication of a long romance, *Mamillia* in 1580. His romances were written in a highly wrought style, and *Pandosto* (1588) and *Menaphon* (1589) marked his highest level in playwriting.

Thomas Kyd (1558—1594) was the only one of the University Wits who was not educated in the University. His most famous play *The Spanish Tragedy* (1586) inaugurated an important Elizabethan dramatic genre—the revenge tragedy.

As the most preeminent figure of the group, the foremost Elizabethan tragedian, and also the greatest of Shakespeare's predecessors, Christopher Marlowe (1564—1593) was educated at Cambridge. His fame rested mainly on his four important plays: the three tragedies *Tamburlaine the Great* (c.1587), *Dr. Faustus* (c.1588), *The Jew of Malta* (c.1589), and a history play *Edward II* (c.1592). Marlowe's works contain heroic themes, usually centering on a great personality whose very greatness leads to his downfall. Marlowe wrote in blank verse with a rhetorical brilliance and eloquence superbly equal to the demands of high-quality drama. In his works, there is no lack of splendid imagination, poetic beauty, and dignity of the language.

William Shakespeare, as a poetic and dramatic genius, belongs not merely to England but to the whole humanity as well. Numerous people, ever since his death, have contended with each other in their wondering and zealous appreciation of his artistic achievements. A huge mass of critical literature has been produced about him, discussing problems literary, artistic, personal, of almost every aspect, and more will come out. Shakespeare and his works provide inexhaustible material for meditation upon almost every human interest and problem. After his time, there appeared some great dramatists, but none could match him in completeness and height of genius. His history plays, comedies, tragedies and romantic tragicomedies set a standard never again equaled, and he is universally regarded as one of the greatest dramatists and poets in the world.

William Shakespeare (1564—1616)

Life and Major Works

William Shakespeare was born in April 1564 and died on 23 April 1616. The exact day of his birth remains unknown, but the record reveals that he was baptized on 26 April of the year. Shakespeare is widely viewed as the greatest writer in English language and the world's prominent playwright. Few records of Shakespeare's private life have survived and considerable speculation has been made about such matters as his sexuality, religious beliefs, and whether the works attributed to him were written by others.

William Shakespeare

Born and raised in Stratford-upon-Avon, he was the third child of his parents' eight children but the eldest one to survive. His father, John Shakespeare was a successful glover and alderman, and his mother Mary Arden, was the daughter of a landowning farmer. Although no documented records about this period have been found, most researchers agree that Shakespeare was educated at the King's New School in Stratford where Latin grammar and the classics were taught. At the age of 18, Shakespeare married Anne Hathaway who was eight years superior to him. Six months after the marriage, she gave birth to their eldest daughter Susanna. Two years later (1585), twins Hamnet and Judith were born.

The period from1585 to 1592 is viewed as the "lost years" of Shakespeare for no historical traces were left. We don't know exactly when Shakespeare began to write, but based on some records, some of his plays were on the stage by 1592. He might be fairly well known for he was attacked at that time by the playwright Robert Greene. Robert Greene, possibly out of envy, declared Shakespeare to be "an upstart crow", an ambitious hack with a "tiger's heart wrapped in a player's hide."

Until 1594, Shakespeare's plays were performed only by the Lord Chamberlain's Men, a playing company in which Shakespeare worked as an actor, writer and of which he was also a part owner. The company soon became the leading company in London and later changed its name to the King's Men after being awarded by the new king, James I in 1603. In 1599, the company built their own theatre on the south bank of the Thames, which was called the Globe. As a member of the prosperous company, Shakespeare managed to earn enough money and bought the second largest house, New Place, in Stratford in 1597.

Some of his plays were published from 1594. By 1598, his name began to appear on the title pages. After becoming famous as a playwright, Shakespeare continued to act in his own plays and others. The first folio of 1623 lists him as one of "the Principal Actors in all these plays." After 1606, Shakespeare produced fewer plays. Around 1613, he retired to Stratford and died 3 years later, on 23 April 1616.

Shakespeare was buried in the chancel of the Holy Trinity Church, Stratford, two days after his death. A stone slab covering his grave is inscribed with

    "Good Friend, for Jesus' sake, forbear

    To dig the dust enclosed here;

    Blest be the man that spares these stones

    And curst be he that moves my bones."

Shakespeare wrote in all 38 plays, 154 sonnets, 2 long narrative poems and several other poems. His plays have been translated into almost all major languages in the world and are moved on to stages more often than those of other dramatists.

A generally accepted classification is to divide Shakespeare's writing career into four periods. Until the mid-1590s, Shakespeare wrote mainly comedies influenced by Roman and Italian models and history plays. His second period began from about 1595 to 1599. During this time, he wrote what are considered his greatest comedies and histories. From about 1600 to about 1608, it's Shakespeare's "tragic Period". From about 1608 to 1613, he wrote mainly tragicomedies, also called romances.

Shakespeare's first period is often called the period of apprenticeship. He wrote four comedies: *The Comedy of Errors*, *The Taming of the Shrew*, *The Two Gentlemen of Verona*, and *Love's Labour's Lost*; five history plays: three parts of *Henry VI* and *Richard III*; one tragedy: *Titus Andronicus*. Generally speaking,

Shakespeare's early plays are characterized by formal obvious plots and stylized verse.

In the second period, Shakespeare completed 6 comedies: *A Midsummer Night's Dream*, *The Merchant of Venice*, *Much Ado About Nothing*, *As You Like It*, *Twelfth Night*, and *The Merry Wives of Windsor*; four histories: *Richard II*, two parts of *Henry IV*, and *Henry V*; 2 tragedies: *Romeo and Juliet*, and *Julius Caesar*. His comedies in this period are full of romantic atmosphere. In this period, Shakespeare developed his own writing skills and styles. *Richard II* is written almost totally in verse while prose is employed in *Henry IV, parts 1 and 2,* and *Henry V* which makes the narration diverse. In order to show the complexity of humanity, the tragic scene and the comic scene are mingled, which becomes Shakespeare's typical writing device.

The third period is the tragic period in which Shakespeare created his great tragedies including *Hamlet, Othello, King Lear, Macbeth, Antony and Cleopatra, Coriolanus*, and *Timen of Athens* and several so-called dark comedies or problem plays, such as *All's Well That Ends Well, Troilus and Cressida,* and *Measure for Measure*. Most scholars believe that Shakespeare's great tragedies mark the peak of his art. Among the tragedies, *Hamlet, Othello, King Lear*, and *Macbeth* are regarded as Shakespeare's greatest tragedies. In these tragedies, the personalities of the heroes or the heroines contributed to their tragedies rather than fate or other exterior forces. Hesitation is generally considered as the fatal flaw of Hamlet, while Othello and King Lear are destroyed by their hasty judgment. Othello swallows lies made by a villain and kills his innocent wife out of jealousy. King Lear is drunk with sweet words and abandons the throne easily which brings about the murder of his daughters and the torture of himself. Macbeth and Lady Macbeth are seduced by power, kill the king and later are killed in turn. *Antony and Cleopatra, Coriolanus*, and *Timen of Athens* contain some of Shakespeare's most refined poetry. Those problem plays serve as a sharp contrast to the romantic comedies in the previous period.

In the last period, Shakespeare completed 4 principal tragicomedies: *Cymbeline, The Winter's Tale, The Tempest*, and *Pericles, Prince of Tyre,* and two final plays: *Henry VIII* and *The Two Noble Kinsmen* which are the products of collaboration with John Fletcher. These four tragicomedies begin with a grave plot but usually end with happy reunion and reconciliation.

His two long narrative poems and 154 sonnets establish his fame as a talented poet of the Renaissance. The two long narrative poems *Venus and Adonis* and *The Rape of Lucrece* were respectively published in 1593 and 1594. In *Venus and Adonis*, the bashful and innocent countryman Adonis rejects the amorous advances of Venus, the Goddess of Love. In *The Rape of Lucrece*, the virtuous Roman dame Lucrece commits suicide after being raped by the lustful Tarquin. Both poems show strong disapproval of temptation and tyranny and praise healthy love.

His *Sonnets* were published in 1609. His *Sonnets* can be divided into two groups. One is about the conflicted love for a young man of superior beauty and the other about the uncontrollable love for a mysterious "dark lady" of irresistible beauty. Critics sing highly of his sonnets as meditation on the essence of love, passion, procreation, death, and time.

Shakespeare was a less famous playwright and poet than his contemporary Ben Johnson, though he was a respected person. His fame didn't rise to the present height until the 19th century when the Romantics admired his genius and the Victorians worshiped him with reverence. In the 20th century, his works continue to be adopted, revised, performed and analyzed in various cultural contexts all over the world.

Brief Introduction and Appreciation

Hamlet is the most widely read tragedy written by Shakespeare, and one of the most powerful and influential tragedies in the English language. *Hamlet* was not set in England but in Denmark, recounting how Prince Hamlet exacts revenge on the murderer of his father, King Claudius, who, as Hamlet's uncle, after the crime, takes the throne and marries Hamlet's mother.

The story is woven around the royal family: Hamlet the protagonist, Claudius and the remarried widow Gertude, with background being Denmark's long-standing hostility with neighbouring Norway, and an invasion led by the Norwegian prince, Fortinbras.

The play opens on a night at Elsinore, the royal castle. Hamlet's friend Horatio receives report of the appearance of the ghost of the deceased king, Hamlet's father. Hamlet decides to see the ghost himself. That night the ghost emerges to Hamlet and tells him that he is the spirit of his father, poisoned and killed by Claudius. The ghost demands Hamlet to revenge him. Although Hamlet is uncertain of the reliability of the ghost, he starts to fake madness to avert suspicion.

Having noticed Hamlet's odd behaviours, the King and the Queen send two friends and former schoolmates of the Prince, Rosencrantz and Guildenstern, to find out about the cause of his strange behaviours.

Meanwhile Hamlet is courting Ophelia, daughter of Claudius' trusted chief counselor. One day Ophelia reports to her father that Hamlet rushed into her room but stared at her and said nothing. Polonius attributes Hamlet's madness to "ecstasy of love", and reports to Claudius.

Hamlet is trying to find a way to prove the authenticity of what the ghost said. He arranges for a play to be staged at court. In the play Hamlet re-enacts the murder of his father. During the play Claudius leaves in rage. Hamlet sees his reaction as a proof of his guilt. Fearing for his life, Claudius banishes Hamlet to England with Rosencrantz and Guildenstern closely watching him. Claudius gives Hamlet a letter, with the instruction that the bearer of the letter should be killed.

Gertrude summons Hamlet to her chamber for an explanation. Polonius, who is spying hidden behind an arras, makes a noise. Hamlet, thinking it is Claudius, kills Polonius with wild stabs. Too grieved for her father's death, Ophelia is mad. Laertes comes back from France, determined to look for revenge. Claudius successfully directs all Laertes' anger to Hamlet. He arranges a fencing match between the two young men, and plans to let Laertes kill Hamlet with a poison-tipped sword. Claudius also prepares a cup of poisoned wine in case the fencing does go as he expects.

Now news comes that Ophelia has committed suicide and drowned. At the funeral of Ophelia, Hamlet has a fight with Laertes but the brawl is soon stopped. When he comes back to Elsinore, Hamlet tells Horatio how he escaped from death and sent Rosencrantz and Guildenstern to their death. Now with Fortinbras' army at door, the fencing match begins. Laertes wounds Hamlet with the poisoned sword, and he is also wounded by it himself. Gertrude drinks the poisoned wine by accident and dies. Before his death, Laertes reconciles with Hamlet and tells him about Claudius' plot. Hamlet kills Claudius with his last strength. Before his death he names Fortinbras as his heir to the throne. When the latter arrives, Horatio recounts the story of Hamlet, and Fortinbras orders Hamlet's body to be borne off in honour.

The following excerpt is from the first scene of Act III. It is the most famous soliloquy made by Hamlet which is often viewed as the best part to show Hamlet's internal struggle and hesitant character.

The Merchant of Venice is believed to be written between 1596 and 1598.

The story goes like this: Bassanio, an impoverished young Venetian, asked his rich friend Antonio, a merchant, for 3,000 ducats to pay his expenditure. He planned to travel to Belmont to go after a beautiful and wealthy young heiress Portia. He announced that he had the confidence to win Portia as his wife if he could go there and meet her. Since Antonio had invested all fund in his ships and merchandise which were at sea, he decided to borrow money from the usurer Shylock, a wealthy Jew who hated Antonio very much for the latter had insulted him for being a Jew and lending money to others without interest. Shylock agreed to lend 3,000 ducats to him on the condition that if Antonio failed to return money within three months, he would cut a pound of flesh from any part of Antonio's body. Despite Bassanio's objections, Antonio accepted such a risky term. On the night when Bassanio left for Belmont, he made a conspiracy with his friend Lorenzo which resulted in Lorenzo's running off with Shylock's daughter, Jessica, who took part of her father's fortune.

At Belmont, Portia had a lot of suitors. However, according to her father's will, anyone who wanted to win Portia, must choose correctly among three caskets of gold, silver, and lead. If a suitor chose the correct casket, he would find a portrait of Portia inside and marry her; if he failed, he should swear never to reveal the casket he chose and live out his life as a bachelor.

There were two suitors before Bassanio, a Moor and the prince of Aragon, who failed to make the correct choice. Bassanio and Portia fell in love at the first sight. Portia would have Bassanio wait before he tried his luck for she was sure Bassanio would fail, too. Bassanio, however, was impatient to take the test. Without being deceived by the splendid ornaments of the gold and silver caskets, Bassanio chose the correct casket, the lead one. Portia gave Bassanio a ring to symbolize their love and declared that if Bassanio parted with the ring, it would be the end of their love.

They got married along with another couple, Gratiano, Bassanio's friend, and Nerissa, Portia's maid. Bassonio, then, heard from Antonio whose goods were reported lost at sea. The due date was over and thus, Shylock would cut a pound of Antonio's flesh in terms of the contract. Antonio hoped to see Bassanio, his good friend, once before his death. Bassanio and Gratiano left for Venice immediately with 6,000 ducats from Portia to save Antonio's life. Meanwhile, Portia and Nerissa, her maid, went Padua secretly to seek advice of Portia's cousin, Bellario, a lawyer.

The dramatic center of the play was in the court of the Duke of Venice.

Shylock accepted neither the Duke's appeal for his mercy nor Bassanio's offer to repay the doubled amount of money. The Duke wished to save Antonio but was unwilling to violate the laws of Venice. He turned to Bellario for advice who sent Portia as his representative. Portia disguised herself as a young male "doctor of the law" with the name Balthasar and Nerissa "his" lawyer's clerk. At the court, Portia demanded Shylock's mercy in a famous speech (*The quality of mercy is not strained*), but Shylock refused. Portia, then, declared that Shylock was entitled to forfeit a pound of flesh from Antonio in light of the bond. At the very moment Shylock was about to cut, Portia pointed out that the bond only allowed Shylock to take the flesh from Antonio but no blood. Therefore, if Shylock dropped any blood of Antonio in carrying out the penalty, half of his fortune and land should be given to Antonio, the remainder to the government, and his life would be at the mercy of the Duke under the Venetian law. The Duke pardoned Shylock's life and Antonio asked for the usage of only half of Shylock's property which would be left to his daughter after his death on the conditions that Shylock should convert himself to Christianity and make a will of leaving his entire fortune to Lorenzo and Jessica. The defeated Shylock accepted the terms.

Bassanio and Antonio insisted on rewarding Portia. Consequently, Portia took from Antonio a pair of gloves and the ring which herself had presented to Bassanio, who declined at first but agreed under Antonio's persuasion. Nerissa also took Gratiano's ring. Portia and Nerissa returned home shortly before Bassanio and Gratiano with Antonia as their company. The two ladies taunted their husbands before they revealed they were really the lawyer and his clerk in disguise. At the end of the play, Antonio learned his ship had returned safely. All ends happily except for Shylock.

There are two obvious plots in the play: the winning of a wife by taking a test and the demanding of a pound of human flesh by the money-lender. The plots join in the trial scene, Act IV, which is selected here for appreciation.

Sonnet is a 14-line lyric poem, usually written in rhymed iambic pentameter, which generally expresses a single theme or idea. It was a convention for contemporary English poets to dedicate sonnets to a beautiful but cold lady who had eyes like stars, lips like cherries, and cheeks like roses. The standard content contains the description of the lady's coldness in contrast to the poet's despair, the glorious beauty of the lady, and affirmation of the immortality of the poem. Shakespeare's sonnets are different in some ways though he adheres to the general tradition of Elizabethan sonnets. The persons to whom Shakespeare addresses are a young man and a dark lady who is entirely different from heroines of other sonnets. Shakespeare's sonnet 130 is viewed as the reverse of Petrarch style for he inverts the conventions, using real terms to describe his mistress. What matters more is that Shakespeare's sonnets are embodied with more profound moral and aesthetic contemplation.

Shakespeare composes his sonnets in the popular Elizabethan form which now is called Shakespearean sonnet. It is made up of three quatrains and a concluding couplet, with the rhyme scheme **abab cdcd efef gg**.

Here, two Shakespeare sonnets are chosen.

"Sonnet 18" is possibly the most famous of Shakespeare's sonnets. The first line "Shall I compare thee to a summer's day" is nearly as best known as "To be or not to be".

Englishmen are used to referring to the period from the mid May to the mid August as summer when the temperature is mild and pleasing. The poem begins with a question addressed to the beloved "Shall I compare thee to a summer's day?" The second line claims that his beloved is more beautiful than the pleasant summer. The wind in summer is too rough and the sun shines too hot or too dim. Summer's days are transient which lead to the withered autumn. All beauties fade with time going by. However, the beloved's beauty will last forever and never perish like the eternal summer because it is preserved in this eternal poem.

"Sonnet 29" praises the strong power of love, especially for the man who is in hostile environment. The poem begins with the description of the narrator's hard times, being abandoned and lonely. Thus, he cries, complains and curses his fate to no avail. Naturally, he wishes he were like some other man who has a promising future, or is bestowed with gorgeous appearance, or has many kind friends, or creates like genius, or is able to have a wide range of opportunities. The envious yearning for all those causes him to feel dissatisfied with his adverse situation. Under such a circumstance, the narrator suddenly thinks of the young man to whom the poem is addressed, and his state of mind is immediately transformed from pessimism to optimism. The poet compares such a change to a lark rising from earth to heaven. This metaphor shows vividly the poet's delightful memory with his friend which compensates wholly his misfortunes. Finally, in the couplet, the poet declares emotionally that his friend's love makes him so happy that he wouldn't even consider changing his place with a king.

In diction, the repetition of "state" in lines 2, 10, and 14 is noticeable. It has several different meanings: a condition, a state of mind, and a person's status. In rhyme scheme, it also follows the typical way with one imperfect rhyme in "possessed" and "least" in lines 6 and 8.

Selected Reading

Hamlet, Prince of Denmark
Act III SCENE I.
A room in the castle.
(Excerpt)

Enter HAMLET

HAMLET: To be, or not to be[1]: that is the question:
        Whether 'tis nobler in the mind to suffer
        The slings and arrows[2] of outrageous fortune,
        Or to take arms against a sea of troubles[3],
        And by opposing end them? To die: to sleep;
        No more[4]; and by a sleep to say we end
        The heartache and the thousand natural shocks
        That flesh is heir to[5], 'tis a consummation[6]
        Devoutly to be wish'd. To die, to sleep;
        To sleep: perchance[7] to dream: ay, there's the rub[8];
        For in that sleep of death what dreams may come
        When we have shuffled off this mortal coil[9],
        Must give us pause[10]: there's the respect[11]
        That makes calamity of so long life[12];
        For who would bear the whips and scorns of time[13],
        The oppressor's wrong, the proud man's contumely[14],
        The pangs[15] of despised love, the law's delay,
        The insolence[16] of office and the spurns
        That patient merit of the unworthy takes[17],
        When he himself might his quietus make[18]
        With a bare bodkin[19]? who would fardels[20] bear,
        To grunt[21] and sweat under a weary life,
        But that the dread of something after death,

The undiscover'd country[22] from whose bourn[23]

No traveller returns, puzzles the will

And makes us rather bear those ills we have

Than fly to others that we know not of?

Thus conscience[24] does make cowards of us all;

And thus the native hue of resolution

Is sicklied[25] o'er with the pale cast of thought,

And enterprises of great pith and moment[26]

With this regard[27] their currents turn awry,

And lose the name of action.—Soft[28] you now!

The fair Ophelia! Nymph[29], in thy orisons[30]

Be all my sins remember'd.

Notes

1. **To be, or not to be**: to live or to die; to be harmed or to harm
2. **slings and arrows**: things thrown by slings and arrows which mean attack
3. **to take arms against a sea of troubles**: to take up arms to fight against troubles which sweep upon us like sea tides
4. **No more**: only that
5. **That flesh is heir to**: that human being can't avoid
6. **consummation**: a fulfillment; an ultimate goal
7. **perchance**: perhaps
8. **rub**: obstacle
9. **shuffled off mortal coil**: shook off the confused trouble of mortal life
10. **give us pause**: make us hesitant
11. **respect**: concern
12. **calamity of so long life**: so long-lived misfortune
13. **the whips and scorns of time**: the torment of the world
14. **contumely**: disdain, contempt
15. **pangs**: sadness
16. **insolence**: contempt
17. **That patient merit of the unworthy takes**: that the worthy is taken advantage of by the unworthy
18. **might his quietus make**: might make himself free from the troubles in the world

19. **a bare bodkin**: a mere dagger
20. **fardels**: burdens
21. **grunt**: groan
22. **the undiscovered country**: the unknown place. Here, it refers to the world after death
23. **bourn**: boundary
24. **conscience**: (obsolete) consciousness
25. **sicklied**: dimmed
26. **enterprises of great pith and moment**: highly signified enterprises
27. **regard**: consideration
28. **soft**: slow
29. **Nymph**: (Roman and Greek mythology) fairy
30. **orisons**: prayers

The Merchant of Venice
Act IV Scene I.
Venice. A court of justice.

Enter the DUKE, the Magnificoes, ANTONIO, BASSANIO, GRATIANO, SALERIO, and others.

DUKE: What, is Antonio here?

ANTONIO: Ready[1], so please your grace.

DUKE: I am sorry for thee: thou art come to answer[2]
      A stony adversary, an inhuman wretch
      uncapable of pity, void and empty
      From[3] any dram[4] of mercy.

ANTONIO: I have heard
      Your grace hath ta'en great pains to qualify[5]
      His rigorous course[6]; but since he stands obdurate[7]
      And that no lawful means can carry me
      Out of his envy's reach, I do oppose
      My patience to his fury, and am arm'd
      To suffer, with a quietness of spirit,
      The very tyranny and rage of his.

DUKE: Go one, and call the Jew into the court.

SALERIO: He is ready at the door: he comes, my lord.

Enter SHYLOCK

DUKE: Make room, and let him stand before our face.

       Shylock, the world thinks, and I think so too,

       That thou but lead'st this fashion of thy malice[8]

       To the last hour of act; and then 'tis thought

       Thou'lt show thy mercy and remorse[9] more strange

       Than is thy strange apparent cruelty;

       And where thou now exact'st the penalty,

       Which is a pound of this poor merchant's flesh,

       Thou wilt not only loose[10] the forfeiture,

       But, touch'd with human gentleness and love,

       Forgive a moiety[11] of the principal;

       Glancing an eye of pity on his losses,

       That have of late so huddled on his back,

       Enow[12] to press a royal merchant[13] down

       And pluck commiseration[14] of his state

       From brassy bosoms and rough hearts of flint,

       From stubborn Turks and Tartars[15], never train'd

       To offices of tender courtesy.

       We all expect a gentle answer, Jew.

SHYLOCK: I have possess'd[16] your grace of what I purpose;

       And by our holy Sabbath[17] have I sworn

       To have the due and forfeit[18] of my bond[19]:

       If you deny it, let the danger light

       Upon your charter and your city's freedom.

       You'll ask me, why I rather choose to have

       A weight of carrion flesh than to receive

       Three thousand ducats: I'll not answer that:

       But, say, it is my humour[20]: is it answer'd?

       What if my house be troubled with a rat

       And I be pleased to give ten thousand ducats

       To have it baned[21]? What, are you answer'd yet?

       Some men there are love not a gaping pig[22];

       Some, that are mad if they behold a cat;

       And others, when the bagpipe sings i' the nose,

Cannot contain their urine: for affection[23],

Mistress of passion[24], sways it to the mood

Of what it likes or loathes. Now, for your answer:

As there is no firm reason to be render'd,

Why he cannot abide a gaping pig;

Why he, a harmless necessary cat;

Why he, a woollen bagpipe; but of force[25]

Must yield to such inevitable shame

As to offend, himself being offended;

So can I give no reason, nor I will not,

More than a lodged[26] hate and a certain[27] loathing

I bear Antonio, that I follow thus

A losing suit against him. Are you answer'd?

BASSANIO: This is no answer, thou unfeeling man,

To excuse the current[28] of thy cruelty.

SHYLOCK: I am not bound to please thee with my answers.

BASSANIO: Do all men kill the things they do not love?

SHYLOCK: Hates any man the thing he would not kill[29]?

BASSANIO: Every offence is not a hate at first.

SHYLOCK: What, wouldst thou have a serpent sting thee twice?

ANTONIO: I pray you, think you question with[30] the Jew:

You may as well go stand upon the beach

And bid the main flood[31] bate[32] his usual height;

You may as well use question with the wolf

Why he hath made the ewe bleat[33] for the lamb;

You may as well forbid the mountain pines

To wag their high tops and to make no noise,

When they are fretten[34] with the gusts of heaven;

You may as well do anything most hard,

As seek to soften that—than which what's harder?—

His Jewish heart: therefore, I do beseech you,

Make no more offers, use no farther means,

But with all brief and plain conveniency[35]

Let me have judgment and the Jew his will.

BASSANIO: For thy three thousand ducats here is six.

SHYLOCK: What judgment shall I dread, doing

    Were in six parts and every part a ducat,

    I would not draw[36] them; I would have my bond.

DUKE: How shalt thou hope for mercy, rendering none?

SHYLOCK: What judgment shall I dread, doing no wrong?

    You have among you many a purchased slave,

    Which, like your asses and your dogs and mules,

    You use in abject[37] and in slavish parts[38],

    Because you bought them: shall I say to you,

    Let them be free, marry them to your heirs?

    Why sweat they under burthens? let their beds

    Be made as soft as yours and let their palates

    Be season'd with[39] such viands[40]? You will answer

    'The slaves are ours:' so do I answer you:

    The pound of flesh, which I demand of him,

    Is dearly bought; 'tis mine and I will have it.

    If you deny me, fie upon your law!

    There is no force in the decrees of Venice.

    I stand for judgment: answer; shall I have it?

DUKE: Upon my power I may dismiss this court,

    Unless Bellario, a learned doctor,

    Whom I have sent for to determine this,

    Come here to-day.

SALERIO: My lord, here stays without

    A messenger with letters from the doctor,

    New come from Padua.

DUKE: Bring us the letter; call the messenger.

BASSANIO: Good cheer, Antonio! What, man, courage yet!

    The Jew shall have my flesh, blood, bones and all,

    Ere[41] thou shalt lose for me one drop of blood.

ANTONIO: I am a tainted wether[42] of the flock,

    Meetest[43] for death: the weakest kind of fruit

    Drops earliest to the ground; and so let me

    You cannot better be employ'd, Bassanio,

    Than to live still and write mine epitaph.

Enter NERISSA, dressed like a lawyer's clerk

DUKE: Came you from Padua, from Bellario?

NERISSA: From both, my lord. Bellario greets your grace.

Presenting a letter

BASSANIO: Why dost thou whet thy knife so earnestly?

SHYLOCK: To cut the forfeiture from that bankrupt there.

GRATIANO: Not on thy sole, but on thy soul, harsh Jew,

       Thou makest thy knife keen; but no metal can,

       No, not the hangman's axe, bear half the keenness

       Of thy sharp envy. Can no prayers pierce[44] thee?

SHYLOCK: No, none that thou hast wit enough to make.

GRATIANO: O, be thou damn'd, inexecrable[45] dog!

       And for thy life let justice be accused.

       Thou almost makest me waver in my faith

       To hold opinion with Pythagoras[46],

       That souls of animals infuse themselves

       Into the trunks[47] of men: thy currish spirit

       Govern'd a wolf, who, hang'd for human slaughter,

       Even from the gallows did his fell soul[48] fleet,

       And, whilst thou lay'st in thy unhallow'd[49] dam[50],

       Infused itself in thee; for thy desires

       Are wolvish, bloody, starved and ravenous[51].

SHYLOCK: Till thou canst rail the seal from off my bond[52],

       Thou but offend'st thy lungs to speak so loud:

       Repair thy wit, good youth, or it will fall

       To cureless ruin[53]. I stand here for law.

DUKE: This letter from Bellario doth commend[54]

       A young and learned doctor to our court.

       Where is he?

NERISSA: He attendeth here hard by[55],

       To know your answer, whether you'll admit him.

DUKE: With all my heart. Some three or four of you

       Go give him courteous conduct to this place.

       Meantime the court shall hear Bellario's letter.

Clerk: [Reads]

> Your grace shall understand that at the receipt of
> your letter I am very sick: but in the instant that
> your messenger came, in loving visitation[56] was with
> me a young doctor of Rome; his name is Balthasar. I
> acquainted him with the cause in controversy between
> the Jew and Antonio the merchant: we turned o'er
> many books together: he is furnished with my
> opinion; which, bettered with his own learning, the
> greatness whereof I cannot enough commend, comes
> with him, at my importunity, to fill up[57] your grace's
> request in my stead. I beseech you, let his lack of
> years be no impediment to let him lack a reverend
> estimation[58]; for I never knew so young a body with so
> old a head. I leave him to your gracious
> acceptance, whose trial shall better publish his
> commendation.

DUKE: You hear the learn'd Bellario, what he writes:

> And here, I take it, is the doctor come.

Enter PORTIA, dressed like a doctor of laws

> Give me your hand. Come you from old Bellario?

PORTIA: I did, my lord.

DUKE: You are welcome: take your place.

> Are you acquainted with the difference
> That holds this present question in the court?

PORTIA: I am informed thoroughly of the cause.

> Which is the merchant here, and which the Jew?

DUKE: Antonio and old Shylock, both stand forth.

PORTIA: Is your name Shylock?

SHYLOCK: Shylock is my name.

PORTIA: Of a strange nature is the suit you follow;

> Yet in such rule that the Venetian law
> Cannot impugn[59] you as you do proceed.
> You stand within his danger[60], do you not?

ANTONIO: Ay, so he says.

PORTIA: Do you confess the bond?

ANTONIO: I do.

PORTIA: Then must the Jew be merciful.

SHYLOCK: On what compulsion must I? tell me that.

PORTIA: The quality of mercy is not strain'd[61],

   It droppeth as the gentle rain from heaven

   Upon the place beneath: it is twice blest;

   It blesseth him that gives and him that takes:

   'Tis mightiest in the mightiest: it becomes

   The throned monarch better than his crown;

   His sceptre shows the force of temporal power,

   The attribute to awe and majesty,

   Wherein doth sit the dread and fear of kings;

   But mercy is above this sceptred sway;

   It is enthroned in the hearts of kings,

   It is an attribute to God himself;

   And earthly power doth then show likest God's

   When mercy seasons[62] justice. Therefore, Jew,

   Though justice be thy plea, consider this,

   That, in the course of justice, none of us

   Should see salvation: we do pray for mercy;

   And that same prayer[63] doth teach us all to render

   The deeds of mercy. I have spoke thus much

   To mitigate the justice of thy plea[64];

   Which if thou follow, this strict court of Venice

   Must needs give sentence 'gainst the merchant there.

SHYLOCK: My deeds upon my head[65]! I crave the law,

   The penalty and forfeit of my bond.

PORTIA: Is he not able to discharge the money?

BASSANIO: Yes, here I tender[66] it for him in the court;

   Yea, twice the sum: if that will not suffice,

   I will be bound to pay it ten times o'er,

   On forfeit of my hands, my head, my heart:

   If this will not suffice, it must appear

   That malice bears down truth[67]. And I beseech you,

Wrest[68] once the law to your authority:

To do a great right, do a little wrong,

And curb[69] this cruel devil of his will.

PORTIA: It must not be; there is no power in Venice

Can alter a decree established:

'Twill be recorded for a precedent,

And many an error by the same example

Will rush into the state: it cannot be.

SHYLOCK: A Daniel[70] come to judgment! yea, a Daniel!

O wise young judge, how I do honour thee!

PORTIA: I pray you, let me look upon the bond.

SHYLOCK: Here 'tis, most reverend doctor, here it is.

PORTIA: Shylock, there's thrice thy money offer'd thee.

SHYLOCK: An oath, an oath, I have an oath in heaven:

Shall I lay perjury upon my soul?

No, not for Venice.

PORTIA: Why, this bond is forfeit;

And lawfully by this the Jew may claim

A pound of flesh, to be by him cut off

Nearest the merchant's heart. Be merciful:

Take thrice thy money; bid me tear the bond.

SHYLOCK: When it is paid according to the tenor[71].

It doth appear you are a worthy judge;

You know the law, your exposition

Hath been most sound: I charge you by the law,

Whereof you are a well-deserving pillar,

Proceed to judgment: by my soul I swear

There is no power in the tongue of man

To alter me: I stay here on my bond.

ANTONIO: Most heartily I do beseech the court

To give the judgment.

PORTIA: Why then, thus it is:

You must prepare your bosom for his knife.

SHYLOCK: O noble judge! O excellent young man!

PORTIA: For the intent and purpose of the law

Hath full relation to the penalty[72],

Which here appeareth due upon the bond.

SHYLOCK: 'Tis very true: O wise and upright judge!

How much more elder[73] art thou than thy looks!

PORTIA: Therefore lay bare your bosom.

SHYLOCK: Ay, his breast:

So says the bond: doth it not, noble judge?

'Nearest his heart:' those are the very words.

PORTIA: It is so. Are there balance here to weigh

The flesh?

SHYLOCK: I have them ready.

PORTIA: Have by some surgeon, Shylock, on your charge[74],

To stop his wounds, lest he do bleed to death.

SHYLOCK: Is it so nominated in the bond?

PORTIA: It is not so express'd: but what of that[75]?

'Twere good you do so much for charity.

SHYLOCK: I cannot find it; 'tis not in the bond.

PORTIA: You, merchant, have you any thing to say?

ANTONIO: But little: I am arm'd[76] and well prepared.

Give me your hand, Bassanio: fare you well!

Grieve not that I am fallen to this for you;

For herein Fortune shows herself more kind

Than is her custom: it is still her use[77]

To let the wretched man outlive his wealth,

To view with hollow eye and wrinkled brow

An age of poverty; from which lingering penance

Of such misery doth she cut me off.

Commend me to your honourable wife:

Tell her the process of Antonio's end;

Say how I loved you, speak me fair in death[78];

And, when the tale is told, bid her be judge

Whether Bassanio had not once a love[79].

Repent but you that you shall lose your friend,

And he repents not that he pays your debt;

For if the Jew do cut but deep enough,

I'll pay it presently with all my heart[80].

BASSANIO: Antonio, I am married to a wife

Which is as dear to me as life itself;

But life itself, my wife, and all the world,

Are not with me esteem'd above thy life:

I would lose all, ay, sacrifice them all

Here to this devil, to deliver you.

PORTIA: Your wife would give you little thanks for that,

If she were by[81], to hear you make the offer.

GRATIANO: I have a wife, whom, I protest, I love:

I would she were in heaven, so she could

Entreat some power to change this currish Jew.

NERISSA: 'Tis well you offer it behind her back;

The wish would make else an unquiet house[82].

SHYLOCK: These be the Christian husbands. I have a daughter;

Would any of the stock of Barrabas[83]

Had been her husband rather than a Christian!

Aside

We trifle time[84]: I pray thee, pursue sentence.

PORTIA: A pound of that same merchant's flesh is thine:

The court awards it, and the law doth give it.

SHYLOCK: Most rightful judge!

PORTIA: And you must cut this flesh from off his breast:

The law allows it, and the court awards it.

SHYLOCK: Most learned judge! A sentence! Come, prepare!

PORTIA: Tarry a little; there is something else.

This bond doth give thee here no jot[85] of blood;

The words expressly are 'a pound of flesh:'

Take then thy bond, take thou thy pound of flesh;

But, in the cutting it, if thou dost shed

One drop of Christian blood, thy lands and goods

Are, by the laws of Venice, confiscate[86]

Unto the state of Venice.

GRATIANO: O upright judge! Mark, Jew: O learned judge!

SHYLOCK: Is that the law?

PORTIA: Thyself shalt see the act:

       For, as thou urgest justice, be assured

       Thou shalt have justice, more than thou desirest.

GRATIANO: O learned judge! Mark, Jew: a learned judge!

SHYLOCK: I take this offer, then; pay the bond thrice

       And let the Christian go.

BASSANIO: Here is the money.

PORTIA: Soft[87]!

       The Jew shall have all justice; soft! no haste:

       He shall have nothing but the penalty.

GRATIANO: O Jew! an upright judge, a learned judge!

PORTIA: Therefore prepare thee to cut off the flesh.

       Shed thou no blood, nor cut thou less nor more

       But just[88] a pound of flesh: if thou cut'st more

       Or less than a just pound, be it but so much

       As makes it light or heavy in the substance,

       Or the division of the twentieth part

       Of one poor scruple[89], nay, if the scale do turn

       But in the estimation of a hair,

       Thou diest and all thy goods are confiscate.

GRATIANO: A second Daniel, a Daniel, Jew!

       Now, infidel[90], I have you on the hip[91].

PORTIA: Why doth the Jew pause? take thy forfeiture.

SHYLOCK: Give me my principal, and let me go.

BASSANIO: I have it ready for thee; here it is.

PORTIA: He hath refused it in the open court:

       He shall have merely justice and his bond.

GRATIANO: A Daniel, still say I, a second Daniel!

       I thank thee, Jew, for teaching me that word.

SHYLOCK: Shall I not have barely my principal?

PORTIA: Thou shalt have nothing but the forfeiture,

       To be so taken at thy peril[92], Jew.

SHYLOCK: Why, then the devil give him good of it!

       I'll stay no longer question.

PORTIA: Tarry[93], Jew:

> The law hath yet another hold on you.
> It is enacted in the laws of Venice,
> If it be proved against an alien[94]
> That by direct or indirect attempts
> He seek the life of any citizen,
> The party 'gainst the which he doth contrive[95]
> Shall seize one half his goods; the other half
> Comes to the privy coffer of the state;
> And the offender's life lies in the mercy
> Of the duke only, 'gainst all other voice[96].
> In which predicament, I say, thou stand'st;
> For it appears, by manifest[97] proceeding,
> That indirectly and directly too
> Thou hast contrived against the very life
> Of the defendant; and thou hast incurr'd
> The danger formerly by me rehearsed[98].
> Down therefore and beg mercy of the duke.

GRATIANO: Beg that thou mayst have leave to hang thyself:

> And yet, thy wealth being forfeit to the state,
> Thou hast not left the value of a cord[99];
> Therefore thou must be hang'd at the state's charge.

DUKE: That thou shalt see the difference of our spirits,

> I pardon thee thy life before thou ask it:
> For half thy wealth, it is Antonio's;
> The other half comes to the general state,
> Which humbleness may drive unto a fine[100].

PORTIA: Ay, for the state, not for Antonio.

SHYLOCK: Nay, take my life and all; pardon not that:

> You take my house when you do take the prop[101]
> That doth sustain my house; you take my life
> When you do take the means whereby I live.

PORTIA: What mercy can you render him, Antonio?

GRATIANO: A halter gratis[102]; nothing else, for God's sake.

ANTONIO: So please my lord the duke and all the court

To quit[103] the fine for one half of his goods,

I am content; so he will let me have

The other half in use, to render it,

Upon his death, unto the gentleman

That lately stole his daughter:

Two things provided more, that, for this favour,

He presently become a Christian;

The other, that he do record a gift,

Here in the court, of all he dies possess'd,

Unto his son Lorenzo and his daughter.

DUKE: He shall do this, or else I do recant[104]

The pardon that I late[105] pronounced here.

PORTIA: Art thou contented, Jew? what dost thou say?

SHYLOCK: I am content.

PORTIA: Clerk, draw a deed of gift[106].

SHYLOCK: I pray you, give me leave to go from hence;

I am not well: send the deed after me,

And I will sign it.

DUKE: Get thee gone, but do it.

GRATIANO: In christening shalt thou have two god-fathers:

Had I been judge, thou shouldst have had ten more[107],

To bring thee to the gallows, not the font[108].

Exit SHYLOCK

DUKE: Sir, I entreat you home with me to dinner.

PORTIA: I humbly do desire your grace of pardon:

I must away this night toward Padua,

And it is meet[109] I presently set forth.

DUKE: I am sorry that your leisure serves you not[110].

Antonio, gratify[111] this gentleman,

For, in my mind, you are much bound to him.

Exeunt Duke and his train

BASSANIO: Most worthy gentleman, I and my friend

Have by your wisdom been this day acquitted

Of grievous penalties; in lieu whereof,

Three thousand ducats, due unto the Jew,

We freely cope your courteous pains withal[112].

ANTONIO: And stand indebted, over and above,

In love and service to you evermore.

PORTIA: He is well paid that is well satisfied;

And I, delivering[113] you, am satisfied

And therein do account myself well paid:

My mind was never yet more mercenary.

I pray you, know me when we meet again:

I wish you well, and so I take my leave.

BASSANIO: Dear sir, of force I must attempt you further[114]:

Take some remembrance of us, as a tribute,

Not as a fee: grant me two things, I pray you,

Not to deny me, and to pardon me.

PORTIA: You press me far, and therefore I will yield.

To ANTONIO

Give me your gloves, I'll wear them for your sake;

To BASSANIO

And, for your love, I'll take this ring from you:

Do not draw back your hand; I'll take no more;

And you in love shall not deny me this.

BASSANIO: This ring, good sir, alas, it is a trifle!

I will not shame myself to give you this.

PORTIA: I will have nothing else but only this;

And now methinks I have a mind to it.

BASSANIO: There's more depends on this than on the value.

The dearest ring in Venice will I give you,

And find it out by proclamation:

Only for this, I pray you, pardon me.

PORTIA: I see, sir, you are liberal in offers

You taught me first to beg; and now methinks

You teach me how a beggar should be answer'd.

BASSANIO: Good sir, this ring was given me by my wife;

And when she put it on, she made me vow

That I should neither sell nor give nor lose it.

PORTIA: That 'scuse[115] serves many men to save their gifts.

     An if your wife be not a mad-woman,

     And know how well I have deserved the ring,

     She would not hold out enemy for ever,

     For giving it to me. Well, peace be with you!

    Exeunt Portia and Nerissa

ANTONIO: My Lord Bassanio, let him have the ring:

     Let his deservings and my love withal[116]

     Be valued against your wife's commandment.

BASSANIO: Go, Gratiano, run and overtake him;

     Give him the ring, and bring him, if thou canst,

     Unto Antonio's house: away! make haste.

   Exit Gratiano

     Come, you and I will thither presently[117];

     And in the morning early will we both

     Fly toward Belmont: come, Antonio.

   Exeunt

Notes

1. **Ready**: the set answer in court
2. **answer**: to explain why you do something in court
3. **From**: of
4. **dram**: minute quantity
5. **qualify**: limit
6. **rigorous course**: harsh proceedings
7. **obdurate**: hardhearted
8. **lead'st this fashion of thy malice**: pretend to be take so cruel and wicked action
9. **remorse**: pity
10. **loose**: give up
11. **moiety**: portion
12. **Enow**: enough
13. **a royal merchant**: a merchant with king behind him. Here, it may plainly refer to a very rich businessman

14. **commiseration**: sympathy

15. **Turks and Tartars**: they stand for uneducated people.

16. **possess'd**: informed

17. **Sabbath**: a religious day for Jewish to rest.

18. **the due and forfeit:** the due forfeit

19. **bond:** contract

20. **humour:** personality

21. **baned:** driven

22. **a gaping pig:** a pig with its mouth wide open.

23. **affection:** likes and dislikes

24. **Mistress of passion:** people controlled by passion

25. **of force:** of natural power

26. **lodged:** deep-rooted

27. **certain:** sure

28. **current:** cause

29. **Hates any man the thing he would not kill?:** the correct order of the sentence is "Does any man hate the thing he would not kill?"

30. **question with**: reason with

31. **main flood:** roaring flood

32. **bate:** moderate

33. **bleat**: to utter a whine

34. **fretten**: disturbed or ruffled by high winds

35. **with all brief and plain conveniency**: as conveniently as possible

36. **draw**: take

37. **abject**: miserable

38. **parts**: services

39. **seanson'd with**: tasted of

40. **viands**: delicious food

41. **ere**: before

42. **tainted wether**: useless sick sheep

43. **Meetest**: most proper

44. **pierce**: move

45. **inexecrable**: too evil to be excused

46. **Pythagoras**: the ancient Greek philosopher who believed in the transmigration of souls.

47. **trunks**: main bodies of men

48. **fell soul**: cruel and evil soul

49. **unhallow'd**: not holy, dirty and evil

50. **dam**: mother of four-legged animals

51. **ravenous**: greedy

52. **Till thou canst rail the seal from off my bond**: till you can complain powerfully enough to remove the seal off from my contract.

53. **cureless ruin**: harm that can't be cured

54. **commend**: recommend

55. **hard by**: near by

56. **in loving visitation**: on a friendly visit

57. **fill up**: comply with

58. **reverend estimation**: thorough consideration

59. **impugn**: to express doubts about someone's honesty or ability

60. **danger**: reach

61. **strain'd**: forced

62. **seasons**: work with

63. **that same prayer**: the prayer of Lord

64. **to mitigate the justice of thy plea**: to moderate your insistence for a severe judgment

65. **My deeds upon my head**: I'll be responsible for my deeds.

66. **tender**: pay off

67. **That malice bears down truth**: that evil overpowers justice

68. **wrest**: change

69. **curb**: to control someone to prevent him from doing something harmful

70. **Daniel**: an honest and wise young judge which is mentioned in the "Apocrypha"

71. **tenor**: term

72. **Hath full relation to the penalty**: fully admitted the validity of the penalty

73. **elder**: wiser

74. **on your charge**: you pay the expense

75. **what of that**: what's the importance of that?

76. **I am arm'd**: I'm ready

77. **use**: decision

78. **speak me fair in death**: tell her my braveness and calmness in the face of

death

79. **a love**: a true friend

80. **with all my heart**: an expression to strengthen the sadness

81. **by**: present

82. **unquiet house**: a family full of quarrels

83. **Barrabas**: a robber

84. **trifle time**: waste time on trifles

85. **jot**: small quantity

86. **confiscate**: to officially take one's property away, usu., as a punishment

87. **soft**: slowly

88. **just**: exactly

89. **scruple**: a small unit weight in ancient Rome

90. **infidel**: here, it refers to the person who doesn't believe in Christianity

91. **I have you on the hip**: I have you at my mercy

92. **peril**: risk

93. **Tarry**: wait

94. **alien**: non-Christian

95. **contrive**: scheme secretly

96. **voice**: right

97. **manifest**: obvious, evident

98. **rehearsed**: mentioned

99. **cord**: rope (for Shylock to hang himself)

100. **humbleness may drive unto a fine**: if you regret and behave yourself humbly, the fine may be reduced to a smaller amount

101. **prop**: property

102. **a halter gratis**: a free rope

103. **quit**: reduce

104. **recant**: cancel

105. **late**: just now

106. **a deed of gift**: a conveyance of property

107. **thou shouldst have had ten more**: a jury made up of 12 persons

108. **font**: a container which is used in baptism

109. **meet**: proper

110. **your leisure serves you not**: you don't have spare time

111. **gratify**: reward

112. **We freely cope your courteous pains withal**: we freely offer you repayment for your proper efforts.

113. **delivering**: rescuing

114. **of force I must attempt you further**: I'm forced to try to persuade you again

115. **'scuse**: excuse

116. **withal**: furthermore

117. **presently**: soon

Sonnet 18

Shall I compare thee to a summer's day[1]?
Thou art more lovely and more temperate:
Rough winds do shake the darling buds of May,
And summer's lease[2] hath[3] all too short a date[4]:
Sometime too hot the eye of heaven[5] shines,
And often is his gold complexion dimm'd;
And every fair[6] from fair sometime declines,
By chance, or nature's changing course, untrimm'd[7];
But thy eternal summer[8] shall not fade,
Nor lose possession of that fair thou ow'st[9];
Nor shall Death brag thou wander'st in his shade[10],
When in eternal lines[11] to time thou grow'st:
So long as men can breathe, or eyes can see,
So long lives this[12], and this gives life to thee.

Notes

1. **a summer's day**: here it refers to the summer season.
2. **lease**: here it refers to the duration of summer.
3. **hath**: has
4. **a date**: a limited period
5. **the eye of heaven**: here it refers to sun
6. **fair**: beauty
7. **By chance, or nature's changing course, untrimm'd**: (beauty) is stripped of by accident or going by of time.
8. **summer**: here it is compared to youth.

9. **ow'st**: ownest. It just means own.

10. **Nor shall Death brag thou wander'st in his shade**: Death also couldn't threaten you.

11. **eternal lines**: it refers to lines of this poem or other poems.

12. **this**: this poem

Sonnet 29

When, in disgrace[1] with fortune and men's eyes,
I all alone beweep[2] my outcast state[3]
And trouble deaf heaven with my bootless[4] cries
And look upon myself and curse my fate,
Wishing me like to one more rich in hope,
Featured like him[5], like him with friends possess'd,
Desiring this man's art[6] and that man's scope[7],
With what I most enjoy contented least[8];
Yet in these thoughts myself almost despising,
Haply[9] I think on thee, and then my state[10],
Like to the lark at break of day arising
From sullen earth, sings hymns at heaven's gate;
For thy sweet love remember'd such wealth brings
That then I scorn to change my state[11] with kings.

Notes

1. **in disgrace**: out of favor

2. **beweep**: cry over

3. **my outcast state**: my condition being ignored and abandoned

4. **bootless**: useless, ineffectual

5. **Featured like him**: with the similar appearance with him who is supposed to be handsome

6. **art**: knowledge of life. It may refer to some social skills based on life experience.

7. **scope**: ability

8. **With what I most enjoy contented least**: least satisfied with what I have most.

9. **Haply**: accidentally
10. **state**: here, it refers to state of mind.
11. **state**: here, it may refer to a person's status.

Questions for Study and Discussion

1. What are the four periods in Shakespeare's writing career?
2. What does Hamlet's soliloquy ("To be, or not to be") reveal about his attitude toward revenge? What specific misgivings does he voice about seeking revenge for his father's death?
3. Examine Shylock's rhetoric. Pay special attention to the quality of his language—his use of metaphor and repetition, for instance. How do his speeches reflect his character as a whole?
4. Discuss Portia's character. How does she compare to the men around her? Is Bassanio a worthy husband for her?
5. What are the special metrical and rhyming scheme of Shakespeare's sonnets?
6. What does "this" in "Sonnet 18" refer to as in "So long lives this, and this gives life to thee"?
7. What causes "me" to reevaluate "my fate" in "Sonnet 29?"

Francis Bacon (1561—1626)

Life and Major Works

The youngest of five sons of Sir Nicholas Bacon, Lord Keeper of the Great Seal under Elizabeth I, Francis Bacon was born at York House on the Strand in London. He was raised as an English gentleman.

Bacon received an education at home in his early years because of his poor health. At the age of twelve, in 1573, he entered Trinity College, Cambridge. He lived there for three years. At Cambridge he met Queen Elizabeth, who was impressed by his precocious intellect and from then on she started calling him "the young Lord Keeper".

Francis Bacon

In 1576, he and Anthony entered *de societate magistrorum* at Gray's Inn to study law. A few months later, they joined Sir Amias Paulet, the English ambassador to Paris. Bacon returned to England at the death of his father in 1579. Sir Nicholas had laid up a considerable sum of money to purchase an estate for Francis, but the father died before doing so, and the youngest son was left with only 1/5 of the money. Bacon then got into debt. To support himself, he took up his residence in law at Gray's Inn in 1579. In 1580, he applied for a post at court through his uncle, Lord Burghley. However, His application failed and for two years he worked quietly at Gray's Inn studying law, until he was called to the Bar in 1582.

Two years later, in 1584, he entered the House of Commons. Bacon tried his very best to draw the favorable attention of the Queen, but without much success. The accession of James I, however, brought Bacon into greater favor. He became knighted in 1603. After a few years he started to experience succession of promotion in his positions until in 1618 he became Lord High Chancellor, the head of the legal system of England.

His public career ended in disgrace in 1621. Deep in debt already, Bacon was charged by a Parliamentary Committee on the administration of the law with 23 counts of corruption. He was then sentenced to a fine of £40,000, and was imprisoned in the Tower of London (though his imprisonment lasted only a few days). More seriously, parliament declared Bacon incapable of holding any future office or sitting in parliament. He barely saved his titles. Afterwards, Bacon devoted himself to writing. In March, 1626, he came to London, and died shortly after.

Bacon's works may be divided into three classes: the philosophical, the literary, and the professional works. The best of Bacon's philosophical works include *The Advancement of Learning* (1605) in English, *Novum Organum* (1620) and *De Augmentis* (1623) in Latin. Bacon's philosophy emphasized the belief that people are the servants and interpreters of nature, that truth is not derived from authority and that knowledge is the fruit of experience. Bacon is credited with the method known as implicative inference, a technique of inductive reasoning, which was a fundamental advancement of the scientific method. His literary works include mainly the essays, his chief contribution to English literature. Most of the essays were published between 1597 and 1625. These essays deal with a variety of subjects. Some of the essays are quite general, like "Of Truth" and "Of Death"; others are about individual behavior like "Of Revenge" and "Of Friendship"; some are concerning problems of statesmanship like "Of the True Greatness of Kingdom and Estates". Other literary works include *Apophthagmes New and Old* (1625), *The History of the Reign of Henry VII* (1622) and the unfinished *The New Atlantis*. In his essays, Bacon learned from Montaigne's writings, but different from the latter in temperament, outlook and style. Compared with Montaigne, Bacon emphasizes more on human nature and morality, showing the youth of his time the public life and public duty. Bacon's essays are also famous for their brevity, compactness and powerfulness. The professional works include *Maxims of the Law* (1630) and *Reading on the Statue of Uses* (1642), pleadings in law cases and speeches in Parliament.

Bacon was a representative of the Renaissance in England. He was a prominent philosopher and scientist as well as an essayist. He contributed to the foundation of modern science with his scientific way of thinking and fresh observation rather than authority as a basis for knowledge. Although he wrote much in Latin, he was capable of varied and beautiful styles in English and there is a peculiar magnificence and picturesqueness in much of his writing. Many of his sentences in *The Essays* have assumed almost the character of proverbs. His *Essays* is the first example of that genre in English literature, which has become a landmark in the development of English prose.

Brief Introduction and Appreciation

The Essays is Francis Bacon's greatest contribution to the English literature. The kaleidoscopic book intends to be read by the ambitious Elizabethan and Jacobean youth of his class and tell them how to be efficient and make their way into public life. The essays include discussions on social customs, living philosophies, academic thinking and life experience. The topics range from personal experience to statecraft. Bacon uses allusions and quotations, exemplification and reasoning. His ideas are original just as his language is compact. Parallelism and analogy are easily noted in his essays.

"Of Studies" is the one of the shortest, but probably the most popular of Bacon's 58 essays. It analyzes the major functions "Of Studies" and the different ways of pursuing studies by different people. It probes into the effects studies have upon human character. Forceful and persuasive, compact and precise, the essay best reveals Bacon's mature attitude towards learning. The essay starts with the general use and benefits "Of Studies," namely, delight, ornament and ability. Then it goes on to relate studies to experience and reveals the mutual-promoting relation between them. Bacon also points out that studies need to be treated properly and conducted in right ways. By doing it right, he reckons, our characters shall be improved in different aspects. The whole essay seems to be a manifesto of the Renaissance and a declaration of the beginning of the coming Age of Reason.

Bacon's ideas on science, reason, personal relationship and knowledge not only influenced his contemporaries, but have been cherished by many generations. His greatness in both literary form and philosophic ideas can be viewed in the selected essays.

Selected Reading

Of Studies

Studies serve for delight, for ornament, and for ability. Their chief use for delight, is in privateness and retiring[1]; for ornament, is in discourse; and for ability, is in the judgment, and disposition[2] of business. For expert men[3] can execute, and perhaps judge of particulars, one by one; but the general counsels, and the plots and marshalling of affairs[4], come best, from those that are learned. To spend too much time in studies is sloth; to use them too much for ornament, is affectation; to make judgment wholly by their rules[5], is the humour[6] of a scholar. They perfect nature, and are perfected by experience: for natural abilities are like natural plants, that need pruning[7], by study; and studies themselves, do give forth directions too much at large[8], except they be bounded in by experience[9]. Crafty men[10] contemn studies, simple men[11] admire them, and wise men use them; for they teach not their own use[12]; but that[13] is a wisdom without[14] them, and above them, won by observation. Read not to contradict and confute; nor to believe and take for granted; nor to find talk and discourse; but to weigh and consider. Some books are to be tasted, others to be swallowed, and some few to be chewed and digested; that is, some books are to be read only in parts; others to be read, but not curiously[15]; and some few to be read wholly, and with diligence and attention. Some books also may be read by deputy[16], and extracts made of them by others; but that would be only in the less important arguments, and the meaner sort of books, else[17] distilled books[18] are like common distilled waters, flashy things. Reading maketh a full man; conference a ready man[19]; and writing[20] an exact man. And therefore, if a man write little, he had need have[21] a great memory; if he confer little, he had need have a present wit[22]: and if he read little, he had need have much cunning, to seem to know that[23] he doth not. Histories make men wise; poets witty; the mathematics subtile[24]; natural philosophy[25] deep; moral[26] grave; logic and rhetoric able to contend. *Abeunt studia in mores*[27]. Nay, there is no stond[28] or impediment in the wit[29], but[30] may be wrought out[31] by fit studies; like as[32] diseases of the body, may have appropriate exercises. Bowling is good for the stone and reins[33]; shooting for the lungs and breast; gentle walking for the stomach; riding for the head; and the like. So if a man's wit be wandering, let him study the mathematics; for in demonstrations, if his wit be called away never[34] so little, he must begin again. If his wit be not apt to distinguish or find differences, let him study the schoolmen[35]; for they are *cymini sectores*[36]. If he be not apt to beat over matters[37], and to call up one thing to prove and illustrate another, let him study the lawyers' cases. So every defect of the mind, may have a special receipt[38].

Notes

1. **privateness and retiring:** the state of being alone
2. **disposition:** management
3. **expert men:** experienced men
4. **plots and marshalling of affairs:** plans and arrangements
5. **by their rules:** according to the regulations and rules listed in the books
6. **humour:** a person's characteristic disposition or temperament; a peculiarity
7. **pruning:** cultivation
8. **too much at large:** too general
9. **except they be bounded in by experience:** unless they are checked by experience
10. **crafty man:** skillful and dexterous man
11. **simple men:** ignorant person
12. **they teach not their own use:** studies themselves will not enable people to use them
13. **that:** referring to the use "Of Studies"
14. **without:** outside
15. **curiously:** attentively, carefully
16. **may be read by deputy:** may be read by someone else who gives one the

information, rather than being read by oneself.

17. **else:** or else
18. **distilled books:** excerpted or shortened books
19. **a ready man:** a person who is prompt in apprehending or reacting
20. **writing:** here means making extracts
21. **had need have:** is in need of
22. **a present wit:** a ready mind
23. **that:** what
24. **subtile:** old form of "subtle"; delicate and accurate
25. **natural philosophy:** nature science
26. **moral:** moral philosophy; ethics
27. *Abeunt studia in mores*: (Latin) studies have an influence upon the manners of those who are conversant with them.
28. **stond:** hindrance; stoppage
29. **in the wit:** in the mind
30. **but:** but what
31. **wrought out:** solved
32. **like as:** as
33. **stone and reins:** a calculus in the kidney
34. **never:** ever
35. **the schoolmen:** the scholars that belong to the medieval scholasticism
36. *cymini sectores*: (Latin) hair-splitters
37. **beat over matters:** closely examine things
38. **receipt:** recipe

Questions for Study and Discussion

1. Comment on the language style of Bacon's essays. Give examples from the three selected essays to support your idea.
2. Why is Bacon considered an important figure to the modern science?
3. Comment on Bacon's use of parallel structures in "Of Studies".
4. What lesson can we learn from "Of Studies" on the access to knowledge?

Part Three The Seventeenth Century

(1603—1700)

I. Historical Background

The death of Queen Elizabeth marked not only the end of a glorious era in history, but also the end of the Tudor dynasty. As the Queen remained single all her life, she left behind with no heir. As a result, her cousin James I, a Stuart, gained the throne at her death, and became King James I through the unification of England and Scotland. So the accession of James ushered in the era of the Stuarts.

1. King James I's Reign (1603—1625)

In his early years, James developed a great desire for knowledge and became fluent in Latin and French and competent in Italian. He had a high opinion as to his own academic ability, thinking that he was capable of outdoing almost anyone in eloquence. This character defect was to bring him into constant conflicts with the English Parliament.

James' inconsistent policy toward English Roman Catholics enraged both Catholics and Protestants alike. The Gunpowder Plot was a failed attempt by a group of provincial English Catholics to kill King James I, his family, and most of his Protestant aristocracy and of his government, by detonating gunpowder beneath the Houses of Parliament in London on November 5th, 1605. James ordered that the captured conspirators should endure the minor tortures first and then suffer the more extreme tortures before the public execution.

In the meantime, the conflict also arose between the Puritans and the Anglican Church, which was supported by the King James I. The Puritans sought to purify the Anglican Church and make reforms in the Church. They had a series of violent rejections. First, they rejected the bishops as not specifically authorized by the Bible. Second, they disapproved the practices of the Church because they believed that these practices could not serve as a safe guide to a holy life. Third, they denied humanist culture, regarding it as a temptation toward corruption and damnation. They preferred a life of thrift and hard work to that of extravagant enjoyment. They also wanted to have more freedom to develop business and industry.

James I ruled England for 22 years, and his reign is also know as Jacobean Age. After his death in 1625, James's second son, Charles I, became king of England, as the second of the Stuart kings.

2. King Charles I's Reign and English Revolution (1625—1649)

Charles I was very popular at the time of his coronation, but he soon lost his popularity with his Protestant subjects because of his marriage to the Catholic Henrietta Maria, sister of Louis XIII of France, ignoring the objections of the Parliament and public opinion. He showed great love for art, and spent a large fortune on paintings. His collection of art got him bogged down in a difficult financial situation. Charles also preferred church services to be grand with much ritual and rich color, which cost a lot of more money. Thus he became entangled in clashes with those who preferred plain and simple religious services.

Charles engaged in a long bitter struggle for supremacy with the Parliament. Like his father, he was a passionate advocate of the Divine Right of Kings, which aroused the public fear that he was attempting to seize absolute power. In 1629 he dissolved the House of Commons. In the next 11 years he ruled the country without any parliament. Many of his decisions, particularly his imposing of heavy taxes without Parliament's consent, caused widespread opposition.

The Charles' reign seethed with religious conflicts. Many people had a distrust of Charles's religious policies and felt Charles would bring the Church of England too close to Roman Catholicism. When he was fighting a war with the Scots, he was in urgent need of money. In order to collect the money, he had to summon the parliament again. But soon after, he dismissed it with rage. His attempts to reform the Scottish church sparked off the Bishops' Wars between England and Scotland (1639—1640), which weakened his government and helped precipitate his downfall. At last the break between the King and the parliament came. The English Civil War broke out in 1642. The Puritan troops led by Oliver Cromwell (1599—1658) defeated the King's supporters. Charles I was defeated and subsequently captured, tried, convicted of high treason, and beheaded on January 30, 1649.

3. Oliver Cromwell and the Commonwealth of England (1625—1649)

The English monarchy was replaced with the Commonwealth of England in 1649. But from 1649 to 1653, the Parliament had not run England effectively. Worse still, it had failed to implement reforms demanded by the army and had sought to perpetuate its power. In 1653, Oliver Cromwell, then the Parliamentary general and virtual dictator of the Commonwealth, supported by the army, dissolved the Parliament.

Oliver Cromwell was a Puritan and a highly religious person, who believed that everybody should lead a frugal life according to the Biblical doctrines. Thus Cromwell closed down many inns and theatres, and banned most of the sports. To keep the population's mind on religion, one day every month was a fast day, namely nothing should be eaten the whole day. He ordered that Puritan women should wear a long black dress that covered almost all her body up to the neck. Puritan men should wear black clothes and short hair. He banned Christmas as a holiday of celebration and enjoyment. But Cromwell himself was not strict in obeying all these rules. He enjoyed various sensuous and physical pleasures, such as music, hunting and playing bowls. By the end of his life, the English public had developed a strong antipathy to Cromwell for his severe rule.

After Cromwell's death in 1658, his son, Richard, took over leadership of the country. However, Richard Cromwell was an ineffective ruler. He was obviously not up to the task for his lack of energy, wisdom and experience to manage complicated affairs of state. Charles II, the eldest son of Charles I, was requested to return to become king of England after the restoration of the monarchy in 1660. Thus the accession of Charles II to the English throne ushered in a new era—the Restoration Period, in history.

4. The Restoration and the Glorious Revolution (1660—1702)

Soon after Charles's succession, Britain suffered three disasters. The Plague hit the country in 1665 and claimed 70,000 lives in London alone. In 1666, the Great Fire of London swept through the central parts of London, and destroyed 70,000 homes, 87 churches, and most of the buildings of the City authorities. Between 1665 and 1667 England was at war with the Dutch, ending in a Dutch victory.

Charles II was a ruler of considerable political shrewdness. His reign saw the advance of colonization and trade in India, the East Indies and America, and the great progress of England as a sea power. He founded the Royal Society in 1660. The two political parties, Whig and Tory, came into being. His pleasure-loving character set the tone of the brilliant Restoration period in art and literature. Because of his negotiations with France and his efforts at seizing absolute power, Charles often conflicted with the Parliament. Between 1681 and 1685, Charles dispensed with Parliament and ruled as an absolute monarch. Though Charles II had many children by his various mistresses, he had no legitimate offspring with his wife. Thus his younger brother James II inherited the throne.

James II had kept two things deeply ingrained in his mind before his accession to the throne: a devotion to the memory of his father Charles I, and an adherence to absolute Catholicism. James II held a strong belief that the Parliament should be controlled by an autocratic approach. Consequently, his reign proved disastrous. He suspended the hostile Parliament (1685), revived the old ecclesiastical court of high commission, and interfered with the courts and with local authorities. His attempt to propel Britain to absolute Catholicism by filling positions of authority and influence with Roman Catholics led to the 1688 Revolution, which led to his removal from the English throne.

William of Orange and his wife Mary (Protestant daughter of James II) were invited to England by both the Whig and Tory leaders. James II had few loyal followers to defend him. He fled, was captured, and was allowed to escape to France, and William and Mary took the throne. The Glorious

Revolution, also called the Bloodless Revolution, had succeeded.

William III and Mary II were crowned together at Westminster Abbey on February 13th 1689. William was the only child of Prince William II, Holland. His mother, Mary Stuart, was the daughter of Charles I. Therefore, he himself had a bloodline to the Stuarts. Soon after his coronation, he tried to kindle in his subordinates a great sense of loyalty to the country rather than to any party or any individual. With his support, the Act of Toleration was passed in 1689, which guaranteed religious toleration to the Protestant nonconformists. In the same year, the Bill of Rights was passed with his consent. It is one of the most important constitutional documents in English history.

As King of England, William III accomplished far more for the welfare of the English people than had most of the previous monarchs in the past. He eliminated the tyranny of political games and reformed the nation's political and financial institutions. His reign marked the transition from the personal government of the Stuarts to the parliamentary rule of the Hanoverians. The control of the army was transferred to the Parliament. A better system of finance was introduced and the Bank of England was established. The constitutional rights of the people were laid down on a solid basis.

On February 21st 1702, William was riding in a park when his horse stumbled on a mole hill. The king fell off of his horse and broke a collar bone. William died at Kensington Palace on March 8th, 1702.

II. Literary Review

The 17th century was a period of much turmoil—the English Revolution, the regicide of Charles I, the restoration of the monarchy, and the victory of the Parliamentary rule. Thus many serious social and religious problems had been shrouded in an atmosphere of disillusion and pessimism, during the reign of James I.

1. The Jacobean literature

The English literature of the Jacobean era (1603—1625) began with the drama, especially some of Shakespeare's greatest, and also darkest, plays. Next to Shakespeare, the poet and dramatist Ben Jonson (1572—1637) was the most commanding literary figure during the reign of James I. For 25 years he was the literary dictator of London. His versatile and dramatic works, mainly written after classic Roman and Greek models, showed his great learning, his outstanding ability, and his worldly, peculiarly English wit. His great comedy *Volpone* (1606) took a cynical view of human nature—greed in particular. The comic play shows how a group of scammers (also legacy hunters) are fooled by a top swindler, vice being punished by vice, virtue meeting its reward.

Two other dramatists who followed Ben Jonson's style were Francis Beaumont (1584—1616) and John Fletcher (1579—1625), who collaborated in their dramatic writing during the reign of James I. It is said that they wrote as many as 70 plays in all. Beaumont and Fletcher wrote a great comedy, *The Knight of the Burning Pestle* (1607), the first whole parody play in English. One of their chief merits was that of realizing how feudalism and chivalry had turned into snobbery and make-believe, and that new social classes were on the rise.

Another popular style of theatre during Jacobean times was the revenge play, popularized by John Webster (1578—1632). George Chapman (1559—1634) wrote a couple of subtle revenge tragedies, but he must be remembered chiefly on account of his famous translation of *Homer*, which was to exert a profound influence on all future English literature. Other playwrights of the revenge tragedies were John Ford (1586—1639), Thomas Middleton (1580—1627), and Cyril Tourneur (1575—1626). The revenge tragedy is a dramatic genre that flourished in the late Elizabethan and Jacobean period, of which the distinguishing features are violence, horror, pitiless intrigue and perverse passions. Drama continued to flourish until the theaters were closed by the Puritans at the onset of the English Revolution in 1642.

The King James Bible is considered one of the most massive translation projects in the history of English. In 1604, King James I commissioned the project of a new revision of the English Bible, and supervised in person the translation work of 47 scholars. It was completed in 1611. On the basis of William Tyndale's work primarily, this *Authorized Version* was widely acclaimed for its beauty and simplicity of style. It represents the culmination of the long process of the translation work of Bible into English. It became the standard Bible of the Church of England, and it is generally considered one of the greatest literary works of all time.

In poetry, the two foremost poets of the Jacobean era, Ben Jonson and John Donne, are regarded as the originators of two different poetic traditions—the Cavalier poetry and the Metaphysical poetry. Donne's poetry is noteworthy for its passionate intellect, while Jonson's is well-known for its classicism and refined guidance of passion.

The Metaphysical poets refer to a diverse group of English lyric poets of the 17th century, who shared an interest in metaphysical concerns and a common way of investigating them. The leading Metaphysical poet is John Donne (1572—1631), whose colloquial, argumentative abruptness of rhythm and tone distinguishes his works from the Elizabethan lyric tradition. Other Metaphysical poets are George Herbert (1593—1633), Andrew Marvell (1621—1678), Abraham Cowley (1618—1667), John Cleveland (1613—1658), Henry Vaughan (1622 — 1695), Richard Crashaw (1612 — 1649), and Thomas Traherne (1636—1674). Their poetry is remarkable for its ingenious use of intellectual and theological concepts in surprising conceit, strange paradoxes, and far-fetched images, and it is permeated with intellectual wit, learned imagery, and subtle argument.

The Cavalier poets refer to another school of lyric poets, most of whom are Royalists from the classes that supported King Charles I and his exiled son during the English Civil War. Among them, the predominant is Ben Jonson. Other well-known Cavalier poets are Robert Herrick (1591—1674), Richard Lovelace (1618—1658), Thomas Carew (1595—1639), John Suckling (1609—1642), Aurelian Townshend (1583—1643), William Cartwright (1611—1643) and Thomas Randolph (1605—1635). Their poetry embodies the life and culture of the English upper-classes. Focused on the courtly themes of beauty, love, and loyalty, they produced finely finished verses, expressed with wit and directness. Much of the Cavalier poetry is elegant and refined, but often frankly erotic. Their strength was the short lyric poem, and their favorite theme was carpe diem, "seize the day". The Cavaliers made one great contribution to the English lyrical tradition. Their poetry showed that it was possible for poetry to celebrate the minor pleasure and sadness of life in such a way as to impress people with a sense of ordinary day-to-day humanity, busy about its affairs, and on the whole, enjoying them very much.

2. The Caroline and Cromwellian literature

The Caroline period saw the death of many major authors and the birth of important authors of the period of the Restoration literature. Thomas Middleton died in 1627, Cyril Tourneur in 1626, John Webster in 1632, George Chapman in 1634, and John Ford in 1639. The leading literary figure Ben Jonson continued to write sporadically until his death in 1637.

The popularity of theatre fell into rapid decline. As a replacement, the masque, a courtly form of dramatic spectacle, became increasingly popular with members of the English royal court in the first half of the 17th century.

In September of 1642, the Puritans ordered all the theatres in England be closed for moral and religious reasons. The great Elizabethan dramatic impulse had thus become deeply degenerate, and the English drama was brought to a definite end.

The middle part of the 17th century, during the reign of Charles I and the subsequent Commonwealth and Protectorate, witnessed a boom of political literature in English. Political writings by sympathizers of every party or faction during the English Revolution ranged from fierce personal attacks and polemics to noble schemes aspiring to reform the nation.

Thomas Hobbes (1588—1679) was an English philosopher, and graduated from Magdalen College, Oxford, 1608. He took great interest in mathematics, physics, and the contemporary rationalism. His important works are *Leviathan* (1651), *De Corpore Politico* (1650), *De Homine* (1658), and *Behemoth* (1680). Leviathan is one of the most important works of British political philosophy, dealing mainly with the structure of society. In the book, Hobbes explicitly stated his ideal that a society should be run on the social contract and ruled by the absolute authority of a sovereign. Hobbes' political philosophy had an influence on other political theorists, such as John Locke (1632—1704, English philosopher), Baruch Spinoza (1632—1677, Dutch philosopher), and Jean-Jacques Rousseau (1712—1778, French philosopher), who, on the basis of his work, formulated their own radically different theories of the social contract.

The period also saw a flourishing of regular newspaper publications dating from the mid 17th century, with journalists such as Henry Muddiman (1629—1692), Marchamont Needham (1620—1678), and John Birkenhead (1617—1679), reporting the views and activities of the contending parties.

John Milton (1608—1674), one of the most significant writers and thinkers of all time, is often mentioned together with William Shakespeare in the history of the English literature.

He composed his most famed epic poem *Paradise Lost*, during the time from 1658 to 1664 when he became totally blind. He followed up *Paradise Lost* with two other great works *Paradise Regained*, and *Samson Agonistes,* published in 1671. In both *Paradise Lost* and *Paradise Regained*, Milton showed his master-hand in his vivid and moving characterizations of Satan, Adam, Eve, and Jesus. In the two masterpieces, Milton's language is dignified and ornate, replete with biblical and classical allusions, metaphors, puns, allegorical representations and rhetorical flourishes. Milton's works produced a far-reaching influence on the English poetry in the following centuries. His influence on later poets has been tremendous. John Dryden, William Blake, Percy Bysshe Shelley, William Wordsworth, John Keats, Alfred Tennyson, George Eliot and Thomas Hardy could not but feel his profound impact during their literary creation.

3. The Restoration literature

The English Restoration refers to a period in the history of Britain, beginning from 1660 to 1700. With the accession of Charles II, literary tastes widened. Charles II was a man who prided himself on his wit and his worldliness. He was well known as a philanderer as well. Highly witty, playful, and sexually wise poetry thus had court sanction. The lifting of Puritan restrictions and the reassembling of the court led to a relaxation of restraints, both moral and stylistic.

The English Restoration saw a sudden breakaway from the old ideals and standards in both prose and verse. As many Restoration writers had stayed abroad with Charles II and his court, they, upon their return, reacted strongly against the imaginative flights and renounced the ornate styles and forms of the previous times. They showed great admiration for Ben Jonson and his disciples. Fascinated with Jonson's lucid poetic artistry, they put a high value on good taste and moderation, and took the Greek and Latin classics as models.

Poetry was the most popular and significant form of the Restoration literature because the Restoration poems affected political events and immediately reflected the times. In the Restoration poetry, satire is the predominant poetic form of the era. The Restoration poets abandoned the conceits and irregularities of the Metaphysical poetry and managed to perfect the rimed pentameter couplet—the one great formal achievement of the time in verse.

John Dryden (1631—1700), a poet, critic and dramatist, is the most important, prolific and vigorous figure in the Restoration period. Variety, fluency, and graceful strength are the chief qualities in his verse and prose works. In satiric and didactic verse, Dryden is accepted as the chief English master, and *Absalom and Achitophel* (1681) is his greatest achievement. The other contemporary poets Edmund Waller (1606—1687), Laurence Hyde (1642—1711), George Villiers (1628—87), and Charles Sackville (1638—1706), are courtier poets, attached to the court of Charles. By contrast Matthew Prior (1664—1721) and Robert Gould (1660—1708), were outsiders who were profoundly royalist. Each of these poets wrote for the stage as well as the page. During the period of the restoration, two women poets of note emerged. These were Katherine Phillips (1632—1664) and Aphra Behn (1640—1689). Best known today for her poems on female friendship, Katherine Philips wrote some 125 poems on a variety of subjects. Aphra Behn, a successful poet, novelist, and playwright, was the first of her gender to earn a living as a writer in the English language.

During the reign of Charles II, the English prose of dissent, political theory, and economics increased significantly. The style of the Restoration prose also made a distinct advance. Dryden's prose, only less important than his verse, is mostly in the form of long critical essays, virtually the first in English. His opinions are judicious, independent, honest, and interesting. His language is clear, terse, forceful, and straightforward, and his style is easy, simple, dignified, and fluent in vocabulary, with a varied and pleasing rhythm. Thomas Sprat (1635—1713), English author, bishop of Rochester and dean of Westminster, is best remembered for his *History of the Royal Society* (1667). The Restoration was also the time when John Locke (1632—1704), wrote many of his philosophical works. Locke's empiricism was an attempt at understanding the basis of human understanding itself and thereby devising a proper manner for making sound decisions. With these scientific methods, Locke wrote his *Two Treatises on Government,* which, in future, inspired and encouraged the American thinkers during the American Revolution. John Bunyan (1628—1688), a Christian writer and preacher, wrote The Pilgrim's

Progress, the most famous published Christian allegory of personal salvation and a guide to the Christian life.

The Restoration drama exhibited the moral anarchy of the time, particularly in its comedy and "comedy of manners", a literary genre flourishing during the Restoration period. The Restoration comedy satirized the fop and the rake of the time. The plot of the comedy, often concerned with an illicit love affair or some other scandal in the setting of the Court or of fashionable London life, deliberately made fun of moral principles and institutions, especially marriage. The Restoration comedy, to a great extent, was indecent with its bawdy dialogue. Dryden wrote a lot of comedies and "tragicomedies". The other well known dramatists of the period were George Etherege (1635—1692), William Wycherley (1640—1716), John Vanbrugh (1664—1726), and William Congreve (1670—1729).

It is hard to date, for certainty, the beginning of the English novel in England. However, long fiction and fictional biographies began to appear and distinguish themselves from other forms during the Restoration period. Aphra Behn is one of the most significant authors in the rise of the novel in the Restoration period. Not only was she the first English professional female writer, but also she may be among the first professional novelists of either sex in England. Behn's most famous novel was *Oroonoko* in 1688. The novel was based on Behn's trip, in 1663, to an English sugar colony on the Suriname River, on the coast east of Venezuela.

John Donne (1572—1631)

Life and Major Works

John Donne was born into a Roman Catholic family in London at a time when anti-Catholic sentiment in England was near its height. At the age of 11, he entered the University of Oxford, where he studied for three years. He then spent another three years at the University of Cambridge. Because he refused to take the Oath of Supremacy, Donne took no degree at either university. In the following years, he studied

John Donne

law at Thavies Inn and Lincoln's Inn, but he never practiced law. Due to the fact that his Catholic faith barred him from many roads to success, Donne quietly abandoned Catholicism some time in 1590s. In 1596, Donne joined the naval expedition to Cadiz, Spain. In the next year, he joined another expedition to the Azores. Upon his return to England in 1598, he was appointed private secretary to Sir Thomas Egerton, Lord Keeper of the Great Seal. His future seemed to be secure and promising. In 1601, he became Member of Parliament for Brackley and sat in Queen Elizabeth's last Parliament. However, in the same year, Donne secretly married Lady Egerton's niece, seventeen-year-old Ann More, daughter of Sir George More. This rash union proved to be a career suicide. Donne's bad faith to his employer was neither forgotten nor forgiven. He was thrown into prison for some weeks and dismissed from his post. During the next ten years, Donne and his growing family lived in poverty. It was not until 1609 that reconciliation was effected between Donne and his father-in-law, who finally paid his daughter's dowry, which was a great help to the Donnes.

As he approached 40, Donne published two anti-Catholic polemics (*Pseudo-Martyr*, 1610; *Ignatius his Conclave*, 1611); they turned to be his public testimony of his renunciation of his Catholic faith and won him the favor of the King. In 1611 and 1612, Donne also wrote a pair of long poems, the *Anniversaries*, on the death of the daughter of Sir Robert Drury, his patron.

Although Donne had refused in 1607 to take Anglican orders, King James believed that he would be a great Anglican preacher. So the King declared that Donne could have no employment but a position in the church. In 1615, Donne gave up his Catholic faith and took orders in the Anglican Church. Later that year, he was appointed a Royal Chaplain. In 1616, he was appointed Reader in Divinity at Lincoln's Inn with a degree of Doctor of Divinity conferred by Cambridge. Soon Donne established himself as a great preacher.

The death of his wife in 1617 was a heavy blow to him, who, struck by grief, devoted whole-heartedly to his holy position. In 1618, Donne went as chaplain to Germany and he returned to London in 1620. In 1621, he was appointed Dean of Saint Paul's, where he preached to lawyers, courtiers, merchants, and tradesmen. He held this post until his death and proved to be a most excellent preacher of his time. During the last period of his life, Donne was obsessed with the idea of death, and he wrote only religious sermons and poems. He died in London on March 31, 1631.

The poetry of Donne shows a sharp break with the traditional decorative and flowery verses. The clich s of earlier love poetry, such as bleeding hearts, cheeks like roses, lips like cherries, find no way in Donne's poetry. Donne likes to distort those traditional images, ideas, and even rhythmic patterns. In the literary history, John Donne and his followers are known as the "metaphysical school" of poets.

Donne's poetry includes a wide range of secular and religious subjects. There are cynical verses about women's inconstancy (such as "Go and catch a falling star"); poems about true love (such as "The Good-Morrow"); lyrics on the mystical union of lovers' souls and bodies (such as "The Ecstasy"); hymns and holy sonnets depicting his own spiritual struggles (such as "A Hymn to God the Father"); and elegies (such as "An Anatomy of the World"). Though most of Donne's poems were widely circulated through court and literary circles in handwritten copies, they were not published in his lifetime, except for the *Anniversaries*. His collected poems were first published in 1633 and the second edition appeared in 1635. In the second edition, the poems were divided into nine groups, with *Songs and Sonnets* opening the volume, and the *Divine Poems* closing the volume.

Donne also wrote good prose. The Sermons, some 160 in all, are especially memorable. *Devotions upon Emergent Occasions* is a series of meditations, expostulations, and prayers, composed during the time of Donne's serious sickness. The work includes the celebrated "meditation X VII", which contains the following immortal lines: "no man is an island...any man's death diminishes me, because I am involved in mankind, and therefore never send to know for whom the bell tolls; it tolls for thee." The influence of this meditation is to be found in the title of one of Hemingway's famous novels *For Whom the Bell Tolls*.

From his poems and prose works, we can see the two aspects of John Donne. As a young man, he was an adventurous libertine who wrote bawdy and cynical poems to a group of mistresses. As he grew older, he became a grave and eloquent preacher. The sensual love poetry typified his youth, while the obsessive thoughts of sin and death characterized his later career.

Brief Introduction and Appreciation

If we classify Donne's love lyrics into two groups, we may find that one group takes a negative attitude towards love, while the other a positive one. "Go and Catch a Falling Star" involves a cynical tone and it belongs to the first group. It questions women's constancy and claims that you can't find a woman who is both beautiful and chaste. The poem contains 3 nine-lined stanzas and the rhyme scheme is **ababccddd**. The first stanza is an illustration of utter impossibilities. First, a falling star is a thing of great destruction, and it is impossible to catch it. Second, it is impossible to get a child on a mandrake root. Third, no one could tell where the past years are. Four, according to myths and legends, the Devil's foot is split, similar to the hoof of ox and horse. Yet no one knows the original story of the Devil's foot. Five, Mermaids are the sirens whose voices are charming but fatal. So it is impossible to hear Mermaids singing without being destroyed (with the only exception of Odysseus). Six, no man could avoid being envied in the society. Seven, no wind could help an honest man to be promoted in the society. (The last two impossibilities reflect Donne's criticism of the society). After listing all these impossibilities, the poet goes on to expound that there is something even more impossible: to find a woman fair and true. The second stanza begins with Donne's typical grandiose imagination: Suppose there is someone who is strongly drawn to see strange things and who has traveled many years, he could not find a true and fair woman. The third stanza tells the reader that, even if the traveler in the second stanza found a beautiful and faithful woman, she will turn out to be a liar in a rather short time. This is a typical love poem of cynicism.

"A Valediction: Forbidding Mourning" is a famous poem in which Donne's ideal of spiritual love is directly expressed. In this poem, Donne professes a devotion to a kind of spiritual love that transcended the physical love. The poem contains nine stanzas and each four-line stanza has a rhyme scheme of **abab** and a meter of iambic tetrameter. The poem is composed by a series of surprising metaphors and comparisons, each describing a way of looking at their separation that will help them to ward off sorrow and sadness. In the first two stanzas, the speaker, anticipating his departure, tells his lover that their farewell should be the way that virtuous men die: they die mildly without complaint. The public "tear-floods" and "sigh-tempests" are nothing but profanation to their love. Next, the speaker compares harmful "Moving of th' earth" to innocent "trepidation of the spheres." The former equals to the "sublunary lovers' love," while the latter equals to the love between the speaker and his lover. Stanza four and five offer another striking comparison between physical love and spiritual love. As for the sublunary lovers, the essence of their love is nothing but sense, so they can not bear to separate from each other. However, to the speaker and his lover, they are "Inter-assured of the mind," and care less for eyes, lips, and hands. In stanza six, the speaker declares that he and his lover share one soul, and his departure will not separate them, but expand the area of their unified soul. Even if their souls are "two" instead of "one", they are just like the feet of a drafter's compass. His lover's soul plays the role as the center foot, firm and fixed. While his is the outer foot which, under the help of the center foot, makes a perfect circle. Like many of Donne's love poems, "A Valediction: Forbidding Mourning" creates a dichotomy between the common love of the everyday world and the uncommon love of the speaker.

Selected Reading

Song

Go and catch a falling star, [1]
  Get with child a mandrake root, [2]
Tell me where all past years are, [3]
  Or who cleft[4] the Devil's foot,
Teach me to hear mermaids[5] singing,
Or to keep off envy's stinging, [6]
    And find
    What wind
Serves to advance an honest mind, [7]

If thou beest born to strange sights,
  Things invisible to see,
Ride ten thousand days and nights,
  Till age snow white hairs on thee,
Thou, when thou return'st, wilt[8] tell me
All strange wonders that befell[9] thee,
    And swear

No where

Lives a woman true, and fair.

If thou find'st one, let me know,
   Such a pilgrimage[10] were[11] sweet;
Yet do not, I would not go,
   Though at next door we might meet;
Though she were true when you met her,
And last till you write your letter, [12]
      Yet she
      Will be
False, ere I come, [13] to two, or three.[14]

Notes

1. **catch a falling star**: It is impossible for a person to catch a falling star.
2. **mandrake root**: or mandragora, forked like the lower part of the male body. It is said that an infertile woman could get pregnant by eating this. It is impossible to get a child on a mandrake root.
3. This is an unanswerable question. No one can tell where the past years are.
4. **cleft**: clove, past participle of cleave. It is said that devil's foot is split.
5. **Mermaid:** referring to the sirens in Greek mythology. It is said that only Odysseus survived their alluring song.
6. **envy**: here "envy" refers to the envious person. It is impossible to avoid being envied and libeled.
7. What wind can help an honest man to be promoted in the society?
8. **wilt**: will
9. **befell**: happen to
10. **Pilgrimage**: a journey to a sacred place. Pay attention to the irony here.
11. **were**: would be
12. **you write your letter:** referring to the correspondence after the parting of the two lovers
13. **ere I come**: before I arrive
14. **False to two or three**: to be unfaithful to a couple of lovers

A Valediction: Forbidding Mourning[1]

As virtuous men pass mildly away,
    And whisper to their souls to go,
Whilst some of their sad friends do say
    The breath goes now, and some say, No;

So let us melt, and make no noise,
    No tear-floods, nor sigh-tempests move[2],
'Twere profanation of our joys
    To tell the laity[3] our love.

Moving of th' earth[4] brings harms and fears,
    Men reckon what it did, and meant,
But trepidation of the spheres[5],
    Though greater far, is innocent[6].

Dull sublunary[7] lovers' love
    (Whose soul is sense[8]) cannot admit
Absence, because it doth remove
    Those things which elemented[9] it.

But we, by a love so much refined
    That ourselves know not what it is,
Inter-assured of the mind,
    Care less, eyes, lips, and hands to miss.

Our two souls therefore, which are one,
    Though I must go, endure not yet
A breach, but an expansion[10],
    Like gold to airy thinness beat.

If they be two, they are two so
    As stiff twin compasses[11] are two;
Thy soul, the fixed foot, makes no show
    To move, but doth[12], if th' other do.

And though it in the center sit,
    Yet when the other far doth roam,
It[13] leans and hearkens[14] after it[15],
    And grows erect, as that[16] comes home.

Such wilt thou be to me, who must
    Like th' other foot[17], obliquely run;
Thy firmness makes my circle just,
    And makes me end where I begun[18].

Notes

1. According to Izaak Walton, the biographer of John Donne, this poem was addressed to Donne's wife on the occasion of his trip to the Continent in 1612.
2. **move**: stir up
3. **laity**: layman. Here Donne compared his love to the holy religion.
4. **Moving of th' earth**: earthquake. In Donne's time, people believed that earthquake was caused by the angry God and it was disastrous.
5. **trepidation of the spheres**: shuddering of the spheres. Earthquakes are thought to threaten evil consequences, but the much greater motions of the spheres are considered harmless. Here Donne compared his departure to "trepidation of the spheres" which is great, mysterious, and totally different from common lovers' departures.
6. **innocent**: harmless
7. **sublunary**: under the moon. Earthly, changeable, and mortal
8. **Whose soul is sense**: whose essence is sense
9. **elemented**: composed
10. **expansion**: since the lovers' two souls are one, his departure will simply expand the area of their unified soul.
11. **compasses**: The compass is one of Donne's most famous metaphors, and it is the perfect image to encapsulate the values of Donne's spiritual love. Even in ancient time, compass is the symbol of faithfulness and perfection.
12. **doth**: moves

13. **It**: the foot that sits in the centre

14. **hearkens**: listen

15. **it**: the foot that draws a circle

16. **that**: the foot that draws a circle

17. **th' other foot**: the foot that draws a circle

18. **end where I begun**: draw a circle, or come back to the foot that sits in the centre.

Questions for Study and Discussion

1. Donne's love lyrics can be divided into two categories, one with a positive attitude towards love and the other with a negative attitude. Which category does the first poem belong to? Why?

2. What's the central idea of the first poem? How did the poet advance his theme?

3. How does Donne distinguish between physical and spiritual love? Which does he prefer in the second poem "A Valediction: Forbidding Mourning"?

4. One of the main characteristics of metaphysical poetry is its reliance on bizarre and unexpected imagery and symbolism. Take the second poem as an example and explain some of Donne's strangest or most surprising images and symbols.

George Herbert (1593—1633)

Life and Major Works

George Herbert was born in Montgomery, Wales, on April 3, 1593. After his father's death in 1596, Herbert, and his six brothers and three sisters, were raised by their mother alone. The lady was a patron to John Donne, who dedicated his *Holy Sonnets* to her.

Herbert was educated at Westminster School and Trinity College, Cambridge. At Cambridge he took his B.A. in 1613 and M.A. in 1616. Afterwards, Herbert was elected a major fellow of Trinity

George Herbert

College. In 1618, he was appointed Reader in Rhetoric. From 1620 to 1628, he was public orator at Cambridge. Such a post provided him with the chance to express, in Latin, the sentiments of the university on public occasions. In 1624 and 1625, Herbert was elected as representative of Montgomery in Parliament.

In 1627, Herbert's mother died and John Donne delivered her funeral sermon. In 1629, the same year he got married, Herbert's brother Edward Herbert became Lord Herbert of Cherbury.

Despite the good prospect in politics, Herbert gave up his secular ambitions. He took orders in 1630 and accepted a living in Bemerton near Salisbury, where he spent the rest of his life preaching, writing poetry and helping rebuild the church out of his own funds. In his last years, he was known as "Holy Mr. Herbert" around the countryside. On March 1, 1633, Herbert died of consumption.

Herbert's literary career could have started with his first two sonnets sent to his mother in 1610, maintaining that the love of God, compared with the love of woman, is a worthier subject for verse. His first published verses were two memorial poems in Latin on the death of the heir-apparent, Prince Henry, in 1612. In 1625, Sir Francis Bacon dedicated his translation of several psalms to Herbert. The next year, unfortunately, witnessed the death of Bacon. Grieved over the death of his friend, Herbert wrote another memorial poem in Latin. In 1633, on his own deathbed, Herbert asked to have the manuscript of his religious poems, *The Temple*, sent to his friend Nicholas Ferrar. With Ferrar's help, the book was soon published and enjoyed enormous popularity.

In his most important literary work, *The Temple*, Herbert seeks to interpret his devout meditations on the rituals and beliefs of the Church with all kinds of images. Most of the poems in *The Temple* resulted from the spiritual conflicts between God and his soul. Strong influence of Donne can be seen on Herbert: his poems contain a similar continuous argument from beginning to end; his language is almost as precise and denotative as Donne's; and his imagery, like Donne's, also works through the mind rather than the senses, and the structure of his poems is also logical.

While Herbert is closer in spirit to Donne than any other metaphysical poets, the difference between the two is also noticeable. The difference is not so much between the violence of Donne and the gentle imagery of Herbert as between the dominance of intellect over sensibility and the dominance of sensibility over intellect. Both men were highly intellectual and keenly sensitive. However, thought seems in control of feeling in Donne and in Herbert it works just the other way around. Of all the so-called metaphysical poets, Herbert is the only one whose whole source of inspiration was his religious faith. In his short life, Herbert had wide acquaintance with the great world, and he enjoyed a happy marriage. Yet it was only in the Faith, in his self-questioning and his religious meditation, that he was greatly inspired as a poet. In this sense, *The Temple* should not be regarded simply as a collection of poems, but a record of the spiritual struggles of a man of intellectual power and emotional intensity who gave much toil to perfecting his verses.

Herbert's poems are characterized by a precision of language, a metrical diversity, and an ingenious use of imagery or conceits favored by all the metaphysical poets. Herbert is a master of simple everyday words and charges them with condensed meanings. Carefully arranged in related sequences, his poems explore and celebrate God's love as he discovered them through his own experiences. As much a clergyman as a poet, Herbert surprisingly appeals to the secular audience. All kinds of readers have responded to his quiet intensity. The opinion has even been voiced that George Herbert has, since the late 20th century, displaced Donne as the leading Metaphysical poet.

Brief Introduction and Appreciation

Of all the poems in *The Temple*, "Virtue" is probably the most anthologized one. Besides its lyricalness and harmoniousness, its popularity might also be accounted for by the fact that this poem, while best demonstrating the similarity and difference between Herbert and Donne in style and subject, reflects the gentle voice of a country parson spreading the Christian message.

Herbert appreciates the beauty of nature not only for its own sake but also seeing it as a mirror of the goodness of the Creator. However, in spite of his sense of the world's beauty, Herbert's poems often reflect the transience of that beauty and question the value of such beauty. Thus, instead of presenting a world available to senses, "Virtue" exhibits an eternal world that can only be perceived by the soul.

A delicately expressed struggle between rebellion and obedience is implicated in "Virtue". The struggle lies between the desire to experience worldly pleasures and the immanent need to bow to God's will. The conflict between rebellion and obedience eventually leads to a conclusion that the experience of the natural world is less authentic than a virtuous soul seeking to receive message from God.

"Virtue" comprises four quatrains, or four-line stanzas. The carefully crafted structure can be seen in the first three quatrains which are similarly formed and interrelated. Each of the three stanzas involves a central image, namely, day (stanza 1), rose (stanza 2) and spring (stanza 3). The basic idea is these representatives of Nature's beauty will definitely die or end. Each stanza starts with the descriptions of the attractions of these images: "cool, calm, bright, bridal" for "day", "angry and brave hue" for "rose" and "sweet days [from stanza 1] and roses [from stanza 2]" for "spring". These descriptions are followed by the images that illustrate death: "day" will "fall" with "dew weep", "rose" has its "root in grave" and "spring" will have its "closes". In the fourth stanza, however, Herbert describes "Virtue" as the exception, which still "lives" like "seasoned timber" while "the whole world turn to coal".

In this poem, Herbert reflects on not only the loveliness of the mortal world but also the reality of death. By moving from the glory of daytime to the beauty of a rose to the richness of spring, the poem gradually builds momentum. Reiterating at the end of each stanza that everything "must die", Herbert leads the reader to the last quatrain, where the most cherished thing is not any tangible manifestation of nature, but the intangible "sweet and virtuous soul". When all else yields to death, the soul "chiefly lives". Through an accumulation of images, Herbert contrasts the transitory glory of the mortal world with the perpetual glory of the immortal soul, and thereby distinguishes between momentary and eternal value. Such contrasts can also be seen through the change in the refrain and rhyme scheme in the last quatrain in comparison with the first three quatrains.

Metaphysical poems are marked by the combination of the intellectual and the sensuous. In "Virtue", an example of such combination can be seen in the second line of the third stanza, when the spring is compared to a box of compressed sweets. "Sweet", the word Herbert repeats in each stanza of this poem, has often been used to describe the effect of the calm, benevolent character and the delectable sound of Herbert's poems when read aloud. But Herbert is also a poet who thought deeply and perhaps perpetually of death and resignation. The mingled finality and sweetness, harmony and destruction evoked by this poem all cohere in the word "closes", which means termination.

Herbert's beauties of thought and diction are so overloaded with far-fetched conceits and quaintness. But at the same time he shows the naked simplicity without any addition either of support or ornament. Such simplicity might be an explanation to the poem's enormous popularity not only among religious groups, but more importantly, among secular readers.

Selected Reading

Virtue[1]

Sweet day, so cool, so calm, so bright,
The bridal[2] of the earth and sky;
The dew shall weep thy fall to-night,
  For thou must die.

Sweet rose, whose hue angry and brave[3]
Bids the rash gazer wipe his eye;
Thy root is ever in its grave,
  And thou must die.

Sweet spring, full of sweet days and roses,
A box where sweets compacted[4] lie;
My music shows ye have your closes[5],
  And all must die.

Only a sweet and virtuous soul,
Like seasoned timber, never gives[6];
But though the whole world turn to coal[7],
  Then chiefly lives.

Notes

1. This poem is included in the 1633 collection *The Temple*, originally spelled as "Vertue".
2. **bridal**: marriage. Here the day is compared to the meeting of earth and sky. Notice that the word "bridal" carries more holy and ceremonial connotations

than "marriage".

3. **angry and brave:** with its red color vivid and splendid
4. **sweets compacted:** densely packed perfumes
5. **closes:** concluding cadences; here, termination
6. **gives:** yields to change
7. **the whole world turn to coal:** when all is burnt to cinder at the last judgment.

Questions for Study and Discussion

1. What is the main difference between the styles and themes of George Herbert's poetry and that of John Donne's?
2. What is the structure of "Virtue"? What metaphors or conceits does Herbert use in the poem?
3. With what thought does Herbert conclude the poem?
4. How does Herbert thematically vary the refrain and rhyme scheme in the last stanza of the poem, in contrast to the preceding three stanzas?

Andrew Marvell (1621—1678)

Life and Major Works

Andrew Marvell was born at Winstead in Holderness, Yorkshire, on March 31, 1621. When he was 3 years of age, his father was appointed lecturer at Holy Trinity Church, and the whole family moved to Hull. There Andrew attended Hull Grammar School, and in 1633 he entered Trinity College, Cambridge. In 1638, his mother died, and seven months later, his father remarried. Marvell took his B.A. degree in 1639, and he remained in Cambridge for a few more years until his father died by drowning in 1641.

Andrew Marvell

What Marvell did between 1641 and 1642 remains unknown. From 1643 to 1647, Marvell traveled widely in France, Holland, Switzerland, Spain, and Italy, learning languages and fencing. On his return, he involved himself in London literary circles and made friends among the Royalists. In 1650, Marvell became the tutor of Mary Fairfax (later Duchess of Buckingham), the twelve-year-old daughter of Sir Thomas Fairfax, the retired parliamentary general. By 1653, Marvell had been a friend to John Milton, from whom Marvell got a recommendation for the post of Assistant Latin Secretary to the Council of State. In 1657, Marvell was appointed assistant to the blind Latin Secretary for the Commonwealth, John Milton, his friend and sponsor. It is generally believed that Marvell, together with other influential figures, played an important role in saving Milton from possible execution and a long jail term at the Restoration.

Beginning from January in 1659, Marvell was elected M. P. (Member of Parliament) for his hometown Hull, and he remained one of the Hull members until his death in 1678. For the last twenty years of his life, Marvell was remarkable in political activities: from June 1662 to April 1663, he was in Holland on unknown political business (possibly espionage); from July 1663 to January 1665, he traveled with the Earl of Carlisle as private secretary on his embassy to Russia, Sweden, and Denmark; during 1674, he was a member of a fifth column promoting Dutch interest in England. During these years, he also wrote political pamphlets and satires, attacking corruption at court and in Parliament or advocating toleration for Dissenters. Marvell died in his house in Great Russell Street on 16 August, 1678, from medical treatment prescribed for a tertian ague.

Early in 1637, still a student at Trinity College, Cambridge, Marvell composed two poems (one in Greek, one in Latin) to a Cambridge volume (Musa Cantabrigiensis) congratulating Charles I on the birth of a daughter. In 1650, he published a great political poem in English: "An Horatian Ode upon Cromwell's Return from Ireland." During the period Marvell tutored young Mary Fairfax at the Yorkshire seat of the Fairfax family, he probably wrote most of his non-satiric poems, including "Upon Appleton House", "To his Coy Mistress", "The Definition of Love", "The Garden", and the Mower poems. Marvell's reputation as a poet mainly rests on these poems. In 1654, with a poem "The First Anniversary", Marvell became an unofficial laureate to Cromwell. When the latter died, the poet dedicated "Upon the Death of His Highness the Lord Protector" and took part in the funeral procession. In his last twenty years, Marvell wrote mostly political pamphlets and satires. As a result, when he died, he was known to the world chiefly as a politician and pamphleteer who wrote a few rough-and-ready satires in prose and verse. It is generally believed that Marvell's body of works would have been more considerable if he hadn't been so involved in politics.

His *Miscellaneous Poems* were published three years after his death. This volume did not contain the satires, and the reputation of it made its way slowly but steadily. Throughout the 17th and 18th centuries, Marvell's reputation was still more a statesman than a poet, and his poetry was considered to be of secondary importance to his political career. In the 19th century, Marvell's poems were more appreciated in America than in England. In the 20th century, with T.S. Eliot's *Metaphysical Lyrics*, Marvell's poetical achievements were at last recognized and the modern high estimation of his poetry began to prevail. Many critics became interested in the ambiguities of his poems and reinterpreted some of them such as the political poems "An Horatian Ode upon Cromwell's Return from Ireland" and "Upon Appleton House".

Among all his poems, "To His Coy Mistress", "The Garden", and the Mower Sequence (a group of poems including "The Mower against Gardens", "Damon the Mower", "The Mower to the Glow-Worms", and "The Mower's Song") enjoy great acclaim. "To His Coy Mistress" is one of the era's most famous expressions of the "carpe diem (seize the day)" motif. "The Garden" praises the idealized Nature and deplores the fallen state of things under human domination. The Mower Sequence depicts the conventional figure of Damon the despairing mower and the figure of Juliana the hardhearted girl: "The Mower against Gardens" praises Nature's proper mixture and attacks the sophistication of human invention; "Damon the Mower" describes the mistress's cruelty in refusing to return Damon's love and the sad consequence that Damon wounds himself; "The Mower to the Glow-Worms" continues to evoke the destructive effects of love; and "The Mower's Song" is the repetition of the paradoxical theme of a ruthless Mower being mown by the hopeless love. The Mower Sequence also touches upon the old metaphor that all flesh is grass and no one can avoid the meeting with the scythe man, or the Grim Reaper.

Marvell's poems are characterized by a light touch, a vein of mockery, and the shadow of a dark thought. He is now known for his literary accomplishments as one of the metaphysical poets.

Brief Introduction and Appreciation

"To His Coy Mistress" presents a familiar theme in literature: *carpe diem* (seize the day), a term coined by the ancient Roman poet Horace (65—8 B.C.). The title of the poem shows that the author is expressing another man's affections to a certain lady. In the 16th and 17th century, the word "coy" means not only "shy" but also "playing hard to get".

The poem is in iambic tetrameter, with eight syllables (four feet) per line. Each foot consists of an unstressed syllable followed by a stressed syllable. Every two lines are rhymed: The last syllable of line 1 rhymes with that of line 2, the last syllable of line 3 rhymes with that of line 4, and so on. This writing style of couplets influences later writers such as John Dryden and Alexander Pope.

The poem consists of 3 parts, a good example of syllogism. Part one introduces the context of the poem and gives us an extended supposition. The first two lines tell us that a young man's declaration of his love to a young lady is hesitantly and playfully declined. From line 3 to line 20, the insistent as well as imaginative young man gives his supposition: if they had enough space and time, they could spend their days in idle pursuits. However, part two reveals the cruel reality: the ruthless time urges every mortal being, and youth passes swiftly. Part three gives the conclusion: since they do not have the luxury of time, they had better "seize the day" and enjoy youth and beauty in time.

"To His Coy Mistress" is traditional in theme yet original in structure and content. It is usually classified as a metaphysical poem for the following characteristics. First, the shocking imagery: For instance, the image of "worms" enjoying the lady's "long preserved virginity," and the comparison of "love" (an abstract quality) to "a vegetable" (a common and concrete object). Second, the light and mocking tone: in part one, the speaker proposes to spend two hundred years to "adore each breast", and etc. Third, the logical argument: the supposition of idle courtship; the reality of evanescent time; the conclusion of *carpe diem*.

Selected Reading

To His Coy[1] Mistress

Had we but world[2] enough, and time,

This coyness, lady, were no crime.
We would sit down, and think which way
To walk, and pass our long love's day.
Thou[3] by the Indian Ganges'[4] side
Shouldst rubies[5] find; I by the tide
Of Humber[6] would complain. I would
Love you ten years before the Flood, [7]
And you should, if you please, refuse
Till the conversion of the Jews.[8]
My vegetable love[9] should grow
Vaster than empires, and more slow;
An hundred years should go to praise
Thine eyes, and on thy forehead gaze;
Two hundred to adore each breast,
But thirty thousand to the rest;
An age[10] at least to every part,
And the last age should show your heart.
For, lady, you deserve this state, [11]
Nor would I love at lower rate.

But at my back I always hear
Time's wing d chariot[12] hurrying near;
And yonder all before us lie
Deserts of vast eternity.
Thy beauty shall no more be found,
Nor, in thy marble vault[13], shall sound
My echoing song; then worms shall try
That long preserved virginity,
And your quaint[14] honour[15] turn to dust,
And into ashes all my lust:
The grave's a fine and private place,
But none, I think, do there embrace.

Now therefore, while the youthful hue
Sits on thy skin like morning dew,

And while thy willing soul transpires[16]
At every pore with instant fires,
Now let us sport us[17] while we may,
And now, like amorous birds of prey,
Rather at once our time devour[18]
Than languish in his slow-chapped[19] power.
Let us roll all our strength and all
Our sweetness up into one ball,
And tear our pleasures with rough strife
Thorough[20] the iron gates of life:
Thus, though we cannot make our sun
Stand still, yet we will make him run.

Notes

1. **coy**: evasive, hesitant, reluctant, playing hard to get
2. **world**: referring to space
3. **Thou**: archaic form of "you"
4. **Ganges**: River in Asia originating in the Himalayas and flowing southeast, through India, to the Bay of Bengal.
5. **rubies**: gems that may be rose red or purplish red. In folklore, it is said that rubies protect and maintain virginity. Ruby deposits occur in various parts of the world, but the most precious ones are found in Asia, including Myanmar (Burma), India, Thailand, Sri Lanka, Afghanistan, and Russia.
6. **Humber**: River in northeastern England. It flows through Hull, Andrew Marvell's hometown.
7. **the Flood**: referring to the Great Flood that Noah outlasted in his ark (Genesis 5:28—10:32).
8. **the conversion of the Jews**: Because it is rather impossible for Jews to convert to Christianity, "the conversion of the Jews" might refer to the end of the world.
9. **vegetable love**: love cultivated and nurtured like a vegetable so that it flourishes prolifically.
10. **age**: referring to a long period
11. **this state**: this lofty position; this dignity
12. **Time's wing d chariot**: In Greek mythology, the sun was personified as

the god Apollo, who rode his golden chariot from east to west each day. Thus, Marvell here associates the sun god with the passage of time.

13. **marble vault**: the young lady's tomb
14. **quaint**: fastidious
15. **honour**: purity, chastity
16. **transpires**: erupts, breaks out, emits, gives off
17. **sport us**: divert ourselves
18. **our time devour**: enjoy our time
19. **slow-chapped**: chewing or eating slowly
20. **Thorough**: Through

Questions for Study and Discussion

1. Why does the poem "To His Coy Mistress", written in the 17th Century, remain popular in the 21st Century?
2. Write an essay that analyzes the personality and character of the young man in the poem.
3. What is Marvell's tone (or attitude) in Lines 31 and 32 in the poem?
4. The theme "carpe diem" appears widely in poetry. Can you find out more poems of this theme, especially Chinese poems?
5. Identify examples of metaphor, hyperbole, personification, and other figures of speech in the poem.

John Milton (1608—1674)

Life and Major Works

John Milton was born in London in 1608. His father, John Milton Sr., was a scrivener by profession. Though he was disinherited by his Roman Catholic family (because of his conversion to Protestantism), John Milton Sr. rose to prosperity by drawing up contracts, lending money at interest, and dealing in real estate. Not only was he practical in business, but also he had talent in composing madrigals and

John Milton

psalm setting. He was Milton's first teacher in music and art.

At 12, Milton was sent to St. Paul's school, where he showed great gifts as a student of language and mastered Latin, Greek, Hebrew, and most modern European tongues. In 1625, Milton entered Christ's College, Cambridge. However, life at Cambridge was not easy for Milton: he was not content with the school curriculum; many of his fellow students disliked him and called him scornfully "The Lady Milton"; worst of all, he had a fist fight with his tutor, William Chappell, and was expelled for a term. He got B.A. in 1629 and M.A. in 1632. However, after his M.A., Milton chose not to take orders, but to leave for his father's country house at Horton in Buckinghamshire, reading widely for six years. In 1638, Milton set off on a European tour. He visited famous places like Paris, Florence, Rome, Naples, Geneva, etc., and met distinguished figures such as Hugo Grotius, Galileo Galilei, Giovanni Batista and Giovanni Diodati. In July 1639, upon hearing rumors of imminent civil war in England, Milton returned home. The civil war broke in 1640 and Milton became a revolutionary pamphleteer, writing articles on political and religious matters.

In the spring of 1642, Milton married Mary Powell, a young girl half his own age (Mary was 17 and Milton 34). In addition to the extraordinary disparity of ages, the couple had totally different family and education backgrounds: Mary was from a Royalist family, while Milton supported Parliament; Milton was splendidly well-educated, while Mary was almost completely uneducated. Within a few weeks, the bride went to visit her parents' house, and refused to come back. It was not until three years later that Mary Powell returned. In 1649, Milton was appointed Secretary for Foreign Tongues by the Cromwell regime and he worked hard, writing for the new Commonwealth and against Continental critics. Milton worked away loyally, and went totally blind in the middle of this work. The year 1652 was a difficult year for Milton: he lost his eyesight, his wife Mary, and his only son John. In 1656, Milton married Katherine Woodcock. But this happy marriage ended quickly with the death of both mother and daughter in 1658. During this brief second marriage, Milton began to work on *Paradise Lost*, and Andrew Marvell became his secretary, who proved to be a faithful assistant as well as friend. The death of Lord Protector Oliver Cromwell in 1658 foreshadowed the end of the Commonwealth and the restoration of the monarch. However, despite great danger, Milton continued publishing his political treatises in early 1659, and was eventually arrested and put into prison in autumn. For his hard and loyal service to the Commonwealth, Milton might have been easily hanged. Thanks to Andrew Marvell and other influential figures, who spoke for him, his life was spared by the newly-crowned king and he was released before Christmas, with a fine and the loss of most of his property.

In 1663, Milton married his third wife Elizabeth Minshull. In blindness, poverty, and relative isolation, Milton spent his time schooling students and completing his life's work, *Paradise Lost*, one of the greatest works ever to be written in English. It was said that he would compose lines at night in his head, and dictate them to his daughters or aides to write down in the next morning. *Paradise Lost* finally saw publication in 1667, in 10 books. In spite of the difficulties in reading; the unfamiliar meter the author adopted (blank verse was rare outside drama); and the author's reputation as a dangerous man, *Paradise Lost* met with instant success and was at once recognized as a supreme epic achievement. Even John Dryden the famous critic in Milton's time commented that "This man cuts us all out, and the ancients too."

Milton died from gout in 1674, and was buried in the church of St. Giles, Cripplegate.

Milton's writing career may be divided into three major phases: the early apprentice years (1629-39); the middle controversial years (1640-60); and the later mature years (1660-74).

At Christmas 1629, a few weeks after his 21st birthday, Milton wrote a short poem, "On the Morning of Christ's Nativity". During the six years he spent in his father's country house (1632—1638), he wrote "L'Allegro"(1632), "Il Penseroso"(1632); *Comus* (1634); and "Lycidas"(1637).

"L'Allegro" and "Il Penseroso" are companion poems, written in those dancing tetrameter couplets. And it is nearly impossible to understand and appreciate "L'Allegro" without also having read its companion piece, "Il Penseroso". The titles are almost untranslatable, and it is generally explained that "L'Allegro" is the image of a cheerful and social man, while "Il Penseroso" is the image of a melancholy and contemplative man. In composing these two poems, Milton learned from such great English poets as Edmund Spenser and William Shakespeare, for the pastoral descriptions of hobgoblins and fairies.

Comus was a masque performed at Ludlow Castle before the lord of that castle, the Earl of Bridgewater, in 1634. The play tells a dangerous journey of a young lady and her brothers. Traveling through a forest, the young lady meets an evil spirit called "Comus" who is disguised as a simple and hospitable shepherd. The evil spirit tries to persuade her to drink from a magic chalice and thus turn her into a beast. However, the lady gets the upper hand and the evil spirit is defeated. At last, the lady and her brothers arrive safely at their destination: the castle.

"Lycidas" is a pastoral elegy, dedicated to Edward King, Milton's fellow student in Cambridge. When on his way to visit his native Ireland, Edward King was drowned in 1637. Milton wrote *Lycidas*, in which Edward King was renamed "Lycidas", and Milton mourns for his death.

In his middle controversial years between 1640 and 1660, Milton set poetry aside and devoted himself to the Puritan cause, writing biting pamphlets in defense of the new Commonwealth and that of various aspects of liberty as he saw it.

From 1643 to 1645, Milton published a series of pamphlets arguing on divorce, due to his unhappy marriage with Mary Powell. In "On the Doctrine and Discipline of Divorce", Milton argued that divorce should be granted on grounds of incompatibility of temperament and personality.

In 1644, Milton published two important pamphlets: "Of Education" and "Areopagetica". "Of Education" was a response to a book written by Samuel Hartlib, a German exile in England. "Areopagetica" was a protest against a severe parliamentary ordinance to regulate printing. It is an eloquent argument calling for freedom of the press.

In 1649, after the execution of King Charles I, Milton published a pamphlet called "The Tenure of Kings and Magistrates" in which he defended the beheading of Charles I and safeguarded people's right to confer power to or withdraw power from governors. As Secretary for Foreign Languages in Cromwell's Council of State, he wrote pamphlets defending the Commonwealth and the rule of Cromwell. Even when it became obvious that a restoration was impending, Milton the staunch puritan continued publishing revolutionary pamphlets, risking his life for a cause that was lost.

After 1660, with his political dreams broken and the monarchy restored, Milton retired to private life and devoted himself whole-heartedly to the composing of his great epics. It was in his last 14 years that he produced *Paradise Lost* (1667), *Paradise Regained* (1671), and *Samson Agonistes* (1671).

Paradise Lost was an epic in 12 books, telling the story of Satan's rebellion against God and the fall of Adam and Eve. *Paradise Regained* was a short epic in only four books, and it deals with the restoration of the human race through the perfect obedience of Jesus Christ. Milton's last work, *Samson Agonistes*, was a closet tragedy (i.e., a tragedy not intended for the stage), written in the manner of the Greek tragedies. The story of Samson, one of the most colorful personalities in the Old Testament, appears in the Book of Judges (13—16). Samson, a bold and physically undefeatable Israelite falls prey to a beautiful yet deceitful Philistine woman Delilah, who turns out to be his undoing. Being a blind captive of the Philistines, Samson finally destroys the oppressors of his people as well as his own life, achieving glory more in death than in life. Milton's drama covers only the last few hours of Samson's life and it is considered the best English tragedy ever written on the Greek model.

Brief Introduction and Appreciation

Paradise Lost recounts the story of Satan's rebellion against God, and of the disobedience and fall of Adam and Eve, led astray by Satan's lies. Satan was one of the angels serving God in Heaven. He was not satisfied with his position as a subordinate and wanted to be equal to God.

The story begins with a proposition of its great theme: man's disobedience and the loss of Paradise. Milton's speaker invokes a heavenly muse and asks for help in relating his ambitious story of Adam and Eve and to justify the ways of God to men. The poem then shifts to Satan and his crew, who are found chained to a lake of fire in Hell. Satan awakens all his legions and directs his famous speech ("What though the field be lost? All is not lost..."). In a debate of whether to launch another war against God or not, a third proposal, to search the truth of a prophecy in Heaven concerning another new world, is preferred. Satan volunteers to undertake the voyage. After some difficulties, Satan passes through the gates of Hell and sees the sight of the new world he seeks.

In Heaven, God sees Satan flying towards this newly created world and foretells the success of Satan in perverting mankind. The Son volunteers to make sacrifice for humankind. Satan changes himself into the shape of a meaner angel and tries to coax Uriel, the Archangel standing guard at the sun. Uriel believes Satan's lie that he wishes to see and praise God's new creation and gives Satan the right direction. Satan enters Paradise and perches on the Tree of Life in the form of a cormorant (a large bird). Satan sees Adam and Eve, overhears their discourse of the Tree of Knowledge, and then decides to conduct his temptation. The Archangel Uriel now warns Gabriel, who is in charge of the gate of Paradise that some evil Spirit has slipped into the Garden. Gabriel promises to find the intruder before morning. Meanwhile, Adam and Eve return to their bower to rest after a long day's work. Seeing Adam and Eve asleep, Satan takes the form of a toad and tempts Eve in her dream. Gabriel finds Satan there and orders him to leave.

The next morning, God sends Raphael down to Earth to warn Adam and Eve of their enemy near at hand and the dangers they will face. At Adam's request, Raphael relates the story of Satan: how this bold angel drew his legions after him to the parts of the North, and persuaded all but Abdiel (a seraph) to rebel with him. Then Raphael continues to describe the war in Heaven: for the first two days, Michael and Gabriel served as co-leaders for Heaven's army against Satan and his legions. On the third day, God sent Messiah his Son to the battle and completely defeated the other side. Satan and his rebel angels were condemned to Hell. Now Adam asks Raphael how and wherefore this world was first created, and Raphael answers in detail. With his final admonitions, Raphael departs.

Satan returns to Paradise. Much to Satan's delight, he finds Eve working alone. Now, in the form of a serpent, he talks to Eve and praises her on her beauty and godliness. Their conversation develops, and Eve becomes eager and eager to taste the fruit from the Tree of Knowledge. At last, she follows the serpent to the root of the forbidden tree and eats. Knowing that Eve has fallen, Adam decides to share the same fate with her and so he eats from the Tree of Knowledge as well.

God knows Man's disobedience and sends the Son to give out the punishments. The Son punishes Satan and all his legions by transforming them into snakes. They are condemned never to walk upright again; and they can eat nothing but dust. The Son tells Adam and Eve of their punishment: Eve and all women must submit to their husbands and suffer the pain of childbirth; Adam and all men must lead a hard life on a depleted Earth.

God declares the banishment of Adam and Eve from Paradise. Michael is sent to carry out God's order. Hand in hand, Adam and Eve slowly leave Paradise and take their solitary way to a new world.

Despite the difficulties in reading, *Paradise Lost* is a masterpiece in English language: although blank verse (the unrhymed lines of iambic pentameter) was rare outside drama in his time, Milton employed it successfully throughout his epic; instead of using short sentences, Milton was fond of long and involved sentences, which run on many lines and achieved a grandiose effect; instead of using the common English sentence pattern of subject-verb-object order, Milton chose to use elaborate patterns drawn from Latin, which added classical savor to his epic; as a learned scholar, Milton spared no effort in citing allusions from other works, enriching his already excellent poetry.

Milton's *Paradise Lost* drew on such literary canons as Homer's *Iliad* and *Odyssey*, Virgil's *Aeneid*, and Torquato Tasso's *Jerusalem Delivered*. Milton's poetic development of the Genesis story also influenced deeply later poets, and many other works of art have been inspired by *Paradise Lost*, such as Alexander Pope's *The Rape of the Lock*, William Blake's *The Marriage of Heaven and Hell*, William Wordsworth's *Intimations of Immortality*, Lord Byron's *The Vision of Judgment*, John Keat's *Endymion*, and Yeats' *Adam's Curse*, to name only a few.

As for *Paradise Lost*, the invocation and Satan's speech in Book I are selected here. Two famous sonnets of Milton are also presented here, one to mourn for his blindness, and the other for his deceased wife.

Selected Reading

Paradise Lost

(Book I, lines 1-26: The Invocation)

Of man's first disobedience, and the fruit
Of that forbidden tree whose mortal taste
Brought death into the world, and all our woe,
With loss of Eden, till one greater Man[1]
Restore us, and regain the blissful seat,
Sing, Heavenly Muse, that on the secret top
Of Oreb[2], or of Sinai, didst inspire

That shepherd[3] who first taught the chosen seed
In the beginning how the heavens and earth
Rose out of Chaos: or, if Sion hill [4]
Delight thee more, and Siloa's[5] brook that flowed
Fast by the oracle of God, I thence[6]
Invoke thy aid to my adventrous song,
That with no middle flight intends to soar
Above th' Aonian mount[7], while it pursues
Things unattempted yet in prose or rhyme.
And chiefly thou, O Spirit[8], that dost prefer
Before all temples th' upright heart and pure,
Instruct me, for thou know'st; Thou from the first
Wast present, and, with mighty wings outspread,
Dovelike sat'st brooding[9] on the vast abyss,
And mad'st it pregnant: what in me is dark
Illumine; what is low, raise and support; [10]
That to the height of this great argument, [11]
I may assert Eternal Providence, [12]
And justify the ways of God to men.

(Book I, lines 105-191: Satan's Speech)

"...What though the field[13] be lost?
All is not lost[14]: the unconquerable will,
And study of revenge, immortal hate,
And courage never to submit or yield:
And what is else not to be overcome?
That glory[15] never shall his wrath or might
Extort from me. To bow and sue for grace
With suppliant knee, and deify his power
Who[16] from the terror of this arm so late
Doubted his empire—that were low indeed;
That were an ignominy and shame beneath[17]
This downfall; since, by fate, the strength of gods
And this empyreal substance[18] cannot fail[19];
Since, through experience of this great event,

In arms not worse, in foresight much advanced,
We may with more successful hope resolve
To wage by force or guile[20] eternal war,
Irreconcilable to our grand Foe,
Who now triumphs, and in th' excess of joy
Sole reigning holds the tyranny of Heaven."
So spake th' apostate angel, [21] though in pain,
Vaunting aloud, but racked with deep despair;
And him thus answered soon his bold compeer: [22]
"O prince, O chief of many throned powers, [23]
That led th' embattled seraphim[24] to war
Under thy conduct, and in dreadful deeds
Fearless, endangered Heaven's perpetual King,
And put to proof [25] his high supremacy,
Whether upheld by strength, or chance, or fate!
Too well I see and rue the dire event
That with sad overthrow and foul defeat
Hath lost us Heaven, and all this mighty host
In horrible destruction laid thus low,
As far as gods and heavenly essences[26]
Can perish: for the mind and spirit remains
Invincible, and vigor soon returns,
Though all our glory extinct, and happy state
Here swallowed up in endless misery.
But what if he our Conqueror, (whom I now
Of force believe almighty, since no less
Than such could have o'erpowerd such force as ours)
Have left us this our spirit and strength entire,
Strongly to suffer and support our pains,
That we may so suffice his vengeful ire[27],
Or do him mightier service as his thralls[28]
By right of war, whate'er his business be,
Here in the heart of Hell to work in fire,
Or do his errands in the gloomy deep? [29]
What can it then avail though yet we feel

Strength undiminished, or eternal being
To undergo eternal punishment?" [30]
Whereto with speedy words th' arch-fiend[31] replied:
"Fallen cherub[32], to be weak is miserable,
Doing or suffering: but of this be sure,
To do aught[33] good never will be our task,
But ever to do ill our sole delight,
As being the contrary to his high will
Whom we resist. If then his providence[34]
Out of our evil seek to bring forth good,
Our labor must be to pervert that end,
And out of good still[35] to find means of evil;
Which oft-times may succeed, so as perhaps
Shall grieve him, if I fail not, and disturb
His inmost counsels[36] from their destined aim.
But see! the angry Victor hath recalled
His ministers[37] of vengeance and pursuit
Back to the gates of Heaven; The Sulphurous hail,
Shot after us in storm, o'erblown[38] hath laid[39]
The fiery surge that from the precipice[40]
Of Heaven received us falling; and the thunder,
Winged with red lightning and impetuous rage,
Perhaps hath spent his shafts, and ceases now
To bellow through the vast and boundless deep.
Let us not slip th' occasion, whether scorn
Or satiate fury yield it from our Foe. [41]
Seest thou yon dreary plain, forlorn and wild,
The seat of desolation, void of light,
Save what the glimmering of these livid flames
Casts pale and dreadful? Thither let us tend[42]
From off the tossing of these fiery waves;
There rest, if any rest can harbor there;
And reassembling our afflicted[43] powers,
Consult how we may henceforth most offend[44]
Our Enemy, our own loss how repair,

How overcome this dire calamity,

What reinforcement we may gain from hope,

If not, what resolution from despair."

Notes

1. **one greater Man**: the Messiah. Messiah is the English transliteration of Mashiach, the Hebrew word meaning "Anointed One". The Greek form of this meaning is Xristos, from where we get the English word Christ.
2. **Oreb**: also Horeb, "the mountain of God" in Arabia near Mount Sinai, where the Lord appeared to Moses in the burning bush.
3. **That shepherd**: referring to Moses
4. **Sion hill**: the Mount Zion of David the psalmist
5. **Siloa**: a pool outside Jerusalem flowing past the Temple, with the waters of which Jesus healed a blind man.
6. **thence**: from there
7. **Aonian mount**: Helicon in Boeotia, sacred to the Moses
8. **Spirit**: referring to "Heavenly Muse" on line 6
9. **brooding**: moving
10. Illumine what is dark in me; raise and support what is low in me.
11. **argument**: subject
12. **Eternal Providence**: God
13. **field**: military campaign
14. **All is not lost**: not all is lost
15. **That glory**: the glory God wins by defeating Satan and making him subdued
16. **who**: God
17. **beneath**: worse than
18. **empyreal substance**: referring to the angels
19. **fail**: perish
20. **by force or guile**: by force or by intrigue
21. **the apostate Angel**: the disloyal Angel. referring to Satan
22. **his bold compeer**: referring to Beelzebub
23. **throned powers**: the rebellious Angels led by Satan. **throned**: of high place
24. **seraphim**: Angels. plural noun of seraph
25. **put to proof**: put to the test
26. **Heavenly essences**: angels

27. **ire**: wrath

28. **thralls**: slaves

29. **the gloomy deep**: Chaos

30. **or eternal being/To undergo eternal punishment?**: or being eternal, so as to undergo eternal punishment?

31. **the arch-fiend**: Satan

32. **cherub**: angel

33. **aught**: anything

34. **his providence**: referring to God

35. **still**: always

36. **inmost counsels**: the most secret plan

37. **His ministers**: referring to the faithful angels

38. **o'erblown**: blown over

39. **laid**: put to rest

40. **precipice**: a headlong fall

41. **whether scorn / Or satiate fury yield it from our Foe**: whether it should yield scorn or satiate fury from our Foe. **Foe**: referring to God

42. **tend**: make one's way towards

43. **afflicted**: defeated

44. **offend**: hurt

Sonnet: On His Blindness[1]

When I consider how my light is spent
    Ere half my days, in this dark world and wide[2]
    And that one talent which is death to hide, [3]
    Lodged with me useless, though my soul more bent
To serve therewith my Maker, and present
    My true account, lest he returning chide;
    "Doth God exact day-labor, light denied?" [4]
    I fondly[5] ask; but Patience to prevent
That murmur, soon replies, "God doth not need
    Either man's work or his own gifts; who best
    Bear his mild yoke, [6] they serve him best. His state
Is kingly. Thousands at his bidding speed
    And post o'er land and ocean without rest:

They also serve who only stand and wait."

Notes

1. Milton wrote another sonnet on his blindness, titled "To Mr.Cyriack Skinner upon His Blindness".
2. **in this dark world and wide**: in this dark and wide world
3. The parable of talents (Matthew 25: 14-30) loomed large in Puritan minds, and particularly in Milton's. The servants who put their master's money (talents of gold and silver) out to earn interest while he was away were called "good and faithful"; the one who simply returned what he had been given was deprived of everything and cast into outer darkness.
4. **Doth God exact day-labor, light denied**: see John 9: 4. ("We must work the works of him that sent me while it is day; the night cometh, when no man can work.")
5. **fondly**: foolishly
6. **who best/Bear his mild yoke, they serve him best**: They who best bear his mild yoke serve him best. See Matthew 11:30 ("For my yoke is easy, and my burden is light.")

Sonnet: On His Deceased Wife[1]

Methought I saw my late espoused Saint
   Brought to me like Alcestis[2] from the grave,
   Whom Jove's great son[3] to her glad husband gave,
   Rescued from death by force though pale and faint.
Mine, as whom washed from spot of childbed taint,
   Purification in the old law did save, [4]
   And such, as yet once more I trust to have
   Full sight of her in heaven without restraint,
Came vested all in white, pure as her mind.
   Her face was veiled, [5] yet to my fancied sight
   Love, sweetness, goodness, in her person shined
So clear, as in no face with more delight.
   But O, as to embrace me she inclined,
   I waked, she fled, and day brought back my night.

Notes

1. **His Deceased Wife**: referring to Milton's second wife, Katherine Woodcock
2. **Alcestis**: In Greek mythology, Alcestis was the wife of Admetus. She sacrificed her life to save her husband and was later rescued from the underworld by Hercules.
3. **Jove's great son**: referring to Hercules
4. The Mosaic law prescribing periods for the purification of women after childbirth is found in Leviticus 12.
5. When Milton married his second wife, he had already been blind.

Questions for Study and Discussion

1. While modern poetry aims to be colloquial, Milton stands on epic ceremony and aims for the exalted and grand style. Could you figure out in detail the characteristics of Milton's epic style, taking the first long sentence (line 1-16) *in Paradise Lost* as an instance?
2. *Paradise Lost* is full of biblical allusions. How many allusions could you find in the opening invocation of Book I?
3. Satan is the most well-developed character in *Paradise Lost*. Is he a sympathetic character? Take his speech in book I as an example and analyze the personality of this character.
4. What attitude does Beelzebub (Satan's "bold compeer") hold towards defeat? How does Satan reply to him?
5. Considering the poet's wretched physical condition, how do you explain the last sentence in Milton's sonnet "On His Blindness"?
6. Does Milton's sonnet "On His Deceased Wife" inspire you of a famous Chinese poem (*song ci*: Jiang Chengzi) written by Su Shi, who also grieved for his deceased wife? Compare the two poets and the two poems.

John Dryden (1631—1700)

Life and Major Works

John Dryden was born on August 9, 1631 in a country gentry's family. He attended Westminster School where he published his first poem, an elegy "Upon the Death of Lord Hastings" (1649). In 1650, he entered Trinity College, Cambridge and took a B.A. in 1654. In 1657, Dryden moved to London in the hope of some political achievement. Living in a time of political and religious turmoil, Dryden's own beliefs shift easily too. On the death of Lord Protector Cromwell, he wrote his *Heroic Stanzas* (1659). The next year, however, in the Royalist climate of the Restoration, he sensibly wrote

John Dryden

Astraea Redux (1660) to celebrate the king's return. For the coronation of Charles II, Dryden wrote "To His Sacred Majesty, a Panegyric" (1661). In 1662, Dryden was elected to the Royal Society. In 1663, Dryden married Lady Elizabeth Howard, the sister of his friend and theatrical partner Sir Robert Howard, and the daughter of the Earl of Berkshire. This marriage further established Dryden's social status.

With the theatres reopened, demand for entertainment was high, and the drama offered an attractive field to those who wanted to make a living by writing. Since 1663, Dryden had been writing for the stage and during the next 20 years, he became the most prominent dramatist in the country. His first play was the prose comedy of humor *A Wild Gallant* (1663). Another two plays, *The Rival Ladies* (1664) and *The Indian Queen* (1664) followed. The next year, *The Indian Emperor* (1665) came out as a continuation of *The Indian Queen*. The two "Indian" plays as a new genre, heroic drama, finally earned Dryden a reputation as a playwright.

In 1666, Dryden published his long poem *Annus Mirabilis* commemorating the big events of the year, including both the naval war with the Dutch and the Great Fire of London. This poem brought him the position of Poet Laureate in 1668. In the same year, he was also given the degree of M. A. by the archbishop of Canterbury. As a fellow of the Royal Society, he was furthermore made historiographer Royal in 1670, which guaranteed him of an income of 200 pounds per year.

In the year 1668, Dryden began his fruitful period of drama writing. This year he published two of his major critical essays, *An Essay of Dramatic*

Poesy (1668) and *A Defence of an Essay* (1668). In 1672, *An Essay of Heroic Plays* came out. His plays from this period include the comedy *Secret Love* (1667), the heroic drama *Tyrannic Love* (1669) and *The Conquest of Granada* (1670—1671), and the comedy *Marriage   la Mode* (1672). In 1674 Dryden published *The State of Innocence*, a musical adaptation of Milton's *Paradise Lost. Aureng-Zebe* (1676) was a tragedy in blank verse. In 1678, Dryden's masterpiece *All for Love* came out, based on the story of Anthony and Cleopatra, which is a popular subject of many playwrights, including Shakespeare.

After this golden period, Dryden's career as dramatist seemed to be less fruitful for a while. After his unsuccessful adaptation of *Troilus and Cressida* (1679) and *Spanish Friar* (1681), Dryden turned his attention to satire. His political satire *Absalom and Architophel* (1681) is one of the greatest English satires. It is written in heroic couplets, adopting biblical characters and incidents to ridicule the duke of Monmouth.

In 1682, Dryden published a long religious poem *Religio Laici* (1682), showing his keen interest in theology. Some of Dryden's best poems followed: "Threnodia Augustalis" (1685) was an ode to Charles II on his death, followed by the lyrical ode "To the Pious Memory of the Accomplished Young Lady Mrs. Anne Killigrew" (1685) and "A Song for Saint Cecilia's Day" (1687). In 1686, Dryden converted into Roman Catholicism, presumably because of the new King James II, a catholic. In 1687, Dryden published an allegorical fable, *The Hind and the Panther,* criticizing the Anglican Church. The next year, with the Glorious Revolution which put William III, the Protestant king, on the throne, Dryden lost his laureateship as well as his pension.

To make a living, Dryden returned to the theatre. He wrote *King Arthur* (1691), the libretto to Purcell's opera, *Don Sebastian* (1690), a tragicomedy, *Amphitryon* (1690), a comedy, and *Cleomenes: the Spartan Hero* (1692). His *Love Triumphant* (1694), which he claimed to be his last play in the prologue, was a failure. Then Dryden turned to translation. He translated the satires of Perseus and Juvenal (1693) and Virgil's *Aeneid* (1697). He also wrote more poems in this period. To name two of them: "An Ode, On the Death of Mr. Henry Purcell" (1696) and "Alexander's Feast" (1697). Dryden also paraphrased Ovid, Boccaccio, and Chaucer, and these narrative poems are included in the last book published before his death, *Fables Ancient and Modern* (1700).

Dryden died on April 30, 1700, of inflammation caused by gout. He was buried in the Poet's Corner in Westminster Abbey.

John Dryden is one of the greatest literary figures of the Restoration Period. In his works, we can see a panoramic England of the age. Dryden stands between the age of Shakespeare and Milton and the age of Pope and serves as a transition from one to another.

Brief Introduction and Appreciation

A much more systematic dramatic theorist than his predecessor Jonson, Dryden was called the father of English criticism by Dr. Johnson. *An Essay of Dramatic Poesy* probably best illustrates his theories on drama as a literary form.

Dryden wrote this essay as a dramatic dialogue with four characters representing four critical positions dealing with five issues concerning: 1. Ancients vs. Moderns, 2. Unities, 3. French vs. English Drama, 4. Separation of Tragedy and Comedy vs. Tragicomedy, 5. Appropriateness of Rhyme in Drama. The first speaker, Eugenius (whose name may mean "well born") prefers the moderns to the ancients. He argues that the moderns exceed the ancients as they have learned and profited from the examples set by the latter. The second speaker, Crites, however, favors the ancients. He maintains that the ancients established the unities, that dramatic rules were explicated by Aristotle first and were followed by French playwrights and that Ben Jonson, the greatest English playwright (according to Crites) followed the ancients too by adhering to the dramatic unities. The third speaker, Lisideius, argues that French drama is superior to English drama, as it follows the classical separation of comedy and tragedy. According to Lisideius, the English tragicomedy is as absurd as Bedlam (an insane asylum). The last speaker, Neander, favors the moderns, but respects the ancients. He favors English drama and more or less criticizes French drama. Neander also defends tragicomedy and maintains that tragicomedy increases the effectiveness of both tragic and comic elements by way of contrast. Neander also shows his preference for Shakespeare over Ben Jonson. Neander prefers Shakespeare for his greater scope and his faithfulness to life.

Crites objects to rhyme in plays: "since no man without premeditation speaks in rhyme, neither ought he to do it on the stage." He cites Aristotle as a support of his preference of blank verse over rhyme in drama, as blank verse lines are closer to "nature", while rhyme can never express deep thoughts naturally. Neander responds to Crites' objections by pointing out that "naturally" rhymed verse is as appropriate to dramatic as to none-dramatic poetry. The rhyme can also be "natural" if it is carefully chosen.

It is generally accepted that the fourth speaker Neander (the name probably mean "new man") is the closest to Dryden in thoughts. In the prologue of *The Rival Ladies*, Dryden states that rhyme is the best form of drama, which is much similar to Neander's ideas in the dialogue.

The excerpted part of the essay is a part of Neander's speech. In this part, he (or Dryden) compares Shakespeare and Jonson by saying that he admires Jonson but loves Shakespeare because "when he describes anything, you more than see it, you feel it too."

Compared with Jonson's dramatic theories, Dryden's essay gives a more systematic representation of his thinking on the theatre with plainer but more expressive language.

Selected Reading

An Excerpt from *An Essay of Dramatic Poesy* [1]

To begin, then, with Shakespeare. He was the man who of all modern, and perhaps ancient poets, had the largest and most comprehensive soul. All the images of Nature were still[2] present to him, and he drew them not laboriously, but luckily[3]; when he describes any thing, you more than see it, you feel it too. Those who accuse him to have wanted[4] learning, give .him the greater commendation: he was naturally learned; he needed not the spectacles of Books[5] to read Nature[6]; he looked inwards, and found her there. I cannot say he is every where alike; were he so, I should do him injury to compare him with the greatest of mankind[7]. He is many times flat, insipid[8]; his comic wit degenerating into clenches[9]; his serious swelling into bombast[10]. But he is always great, when some great occasion is presented to him: no man can say he ever had a fit subject for his wit, and did not then raise himself as high above the rest of the Poets,

Quantum lenta solent, inter viburna cupressi. [11]

The consideration of this made Mr. Hales of Eaton[12] say, That there was no subject of which any poet ever writ[13], but he would produce it much better treated of in Shakespeare; and however others are now generally preferred before him, yet the Age wherein he lived, which had contemporaries with him Fletcher[14] and Johnson[15], never equaled them to him in their esteem: And in the last kings court[16], when Ben's reputation was at highest[17], Sir John Suckling[18], and with him the greater part of the courtiers, set our Shakespeare far above him...

As for Johnson, to whose character I am now arrived, if we look upon him while he was himself, (for his last plays were but his dotages) [19], I think him the most learned and judicious writer which any theater ever had. He was a most severe judge of himself as well as others. One cannot say he wanted wit, but rather that he was frugal of it. In his works you find little to retrench or alter. Wit and language, and humour also in some measure, we had before him; but something of art was wanting to the Drama, till he came[20]. He managed his strength to more advantage than any who preceded him. You seldom find him making love in any of his scenes, or endeavouring to move the passions; his genius was too sullen and saturnine[21] to do it gracefully, especially when he knew he came after those who had performed both to such a height. Humour was his proper sphere[22], and in that he delighted most to represent mechanic people[23]. He was deeply conversant in the ancients[24], both Greek and Latin, and he borrowed boldly from them: there is scarce a poet or historian among the Roman authors of those times whom he has not translated[25] in *Sejanus* and *Catiline*[26]. But he has done his robberies so openly, that one may see he fears not to be taxed[27] by any law. He invades authors like a monarch, and what would be theft in other poets, is only victory in him. With the spoils of these writers he so represents old Rome to us, in its rites, ceremonies and customs, that if one of their poets had written either of his tragedies, we had seen less of it than in him. If there was any fault in his language, 'twas that he weaved it too closely and laboriously in his serious plays; perhaps too, he did a little to much Romanize our tongue[28], leaving the words which he translated almost as much Latin as he found them: wherein though he learnedly followed the Idiom of their language, he did not enough comply with ours. If I would compare him with Shakespeare, I must acknowledge him the more correct poet, but Shakespeare the greater wit. Shakespeare was the Homer, or father of our dramatic poets; Johnson was the Virgil, the pattern of elaborate writing; I admire him, but I love Shakespeare. To conclude of him, as he has given us the most correct Plays, so in the precepts which he has laid down in his *Discoveries*[29], we have as many and profitable rules for perfecting the stage, as any wherewith the French can furnish us.

Notes

1. The excerpt is a part of a speech by Neander, who, of the four speakers, is supposed to represent the author's viewpoints.
2. **still:** ever, always
3. **luckily:** happily
4. **wanted:** lacked
5. **the spectacles of books:** the aid from knowledge learned in books
6. **Nature:** the world of reality
7. his works are not all excellent in the same degree; otherwise he would exceed all other great writers
8. **flat, insipid:** dull
9. his talent in comedy declining and becoming puns that play upon words.
10. **his serious swelling into bombast:** his serious thoughts expanding into extravagant language.
11. *Quantum lenta solent inter viburna cupressi* (**Latin**): as the Cypresses are wont to tower above the yielding osiers (a line quoted from Virgil's *Eclogues*)
12. **Mr. Hales of Eaton:** John Hales (1584—1656), English clergyman and scholar, a fellow of Eton College.
13. **Writ:** wrote
14. **Fletcher:** John Fletcher (1579—1625), English dramatist. Dryden also comments him in the same essay.
15. **Jonson:** Ben Jonson (1572—1637), English poet actor and dramatist.
16. **the last king's court:** the court of King Charles I
17. **when Ben's reputation was at highest:** when Ben Jonson received his highest reputation.
18. **Sir John Suckling** (1609—1642)**:** English poet, one of the neoclassical or Cavalier poets.
19. if we consider his usual level of achievements, not the last plays that he wrote in his decline.
20. in earlier writers we can also find wit, language or humour, but Jonson

brought the art that the Drama lacks.

21. **sullen and saturnine:** melancholy or gloomy
22. he was good at portraying the characters' "humours" or temperaments in his drama.
23. **mechanic people:** artisans
24. he was very well acquainted with the ancient Greek and Roman writers.
25. **translated:** transferred or borrowed
26. *Sejanus* and *Catiline*: two tragedies by Ben Jonson, both based on ancient Roman history.
27. **taxed:** accused
28. **Romanize our tongue:** add Latin elements in the English language
29. *Discoveries*: referring to Ben Jonson's book of literary criticism *Timber, or Discoveries Made upon Men and Matte* (1640).

Questions for Study and Discussion

1. What is the major contribution Dryden made to English poetry?
2. What is the significant role Dryden's prose plays in the English literature?
3. What are the main issues discussed in *An Essay of Dramatic Poesy*?
4. Why does Dryden say that Shakespeare was "naturally learned"?
5. What strong and weak points does Shakespeare show in his drama according to the essay?
6. What are the merits and demerits in Jonson's drama according to the essay?
7. Why does the speaker in the essay claim that he "admires" Jonson but "loves" Shakespeare?
8. In what way are the ideas of the speaker in the essay similar to Dryden's own theories?

Part Four The Eighteenth Century

(1700—1798)

I. Historical Background

The 18th century period was a time of amazing expansion for England. Britain became a world power, an empire on which the sun never set. But it also changed internally. The world seemed quite different in many aspects in the eye of the British people. A sense of new potentialities and possibilities together with many inherent conflicts and problems transformed the daily life of the British people, and offered them fresh ways of pondering about their relations to nature and to each other.

1. Queen Anne—the Last Monarch of the House of Stuart

After the death of William III, Anne (1665—1714), the daughter of James II, became Queen of England on 8 March 1702.

As soon as she ascended the throne, Queen Anne became involved in the War of the Spanish Succession (1701—1714). The war continued until the last years of Anne's reign. In 1707, under the Act of Union, England and Scotland were "united into one kingdom by the name of Great Britain". The century-long hostility between Scotland and England came to a sudden stop. The union of the kingdoms created a peaceful island realm.

Queen Anne's reign was notable for the development of a two-party system as the new era of parliamentary rule. In the early 18th century, the Parliament was controlled by two rival political parties: the Whigs and the Tories. Generally, the Whigs were more often associated with the great noble houses, wealthy merchants, and religious dissenters, and the Nonconformist Protestant churches, while the Tories were associated with the landed gentry and the Church of England.

Queen Anne's reign was notable for the rise of John Churchill, Duke of Marlborough (1650—1722), a brilliant general, who finally succeeded in defeating the French after marching his army 600 miles across Europe.

Queen Anne's reign was also notable for an increase in the influence of ministers and a decrease in the power of the Crown.

The age of Queen Anne was one of artistic, literary, and scientific advancement. Writers such as Daniel Defoe, Alexander Pope and Jonathan Swift flourished during Anne's reign. Her name also remains associated with the world's first substantial copyright law, known as the Statute of Anne (1709), which granted exclusive rights to authors rather than printers.

As the last monarch of the House of Stuart, Queen Anne was succeeded by her second cousin, George I (1660—1727), who was a descendant of the Stuarts through his maternal grandmother, Elizabeth, daughter of James I.

2. House of Hanover

The first Hanoverian King of England, George I was Duke of Brunswick-Lunenburg. With his accession in 1714, began the long rule of the House of Hanover in Britain, which was to last for nearly two centuries until the end of Queen Victoria's reign in 1903.

George I's reign is remarkable for political stability, and social and economic development in England. George I was succeeded by his son, George Augustus, who took the throne as George II (1683—1760). George II exercised little control over policy in his early reign, leaving the government controlled by Robert Walpole Prime Minister of great Britain. His disinterest in British government contributed to the decline of the royal power.

The national anthem of the United Kingdom "God Save the King" was written during the reign of George II. It was later used in a number of Commonwealth realms. Now it remains one of the two national anthems of New Zealand (along with "God Defend New Zealand"), and the royal anthem of Australia and Canada.

George III (1738—1820) became King of Great Britain on 25 October 1760. He was the first of Hanover to be born in Britain and speak English as his first language. He ruled Britain for 59 years and both his life and his reign were longer than any previous English or British monarch.

George III's long reign was marked by a series of military conflicts involving his kingdom and much of the rest of Europe. Early in his reign, Great Britain defeated France in the Seven Years' War, becoming the dominant European power in North America and India. However, many of its American colonies were soon lost in the American Independence War. Later, the kingdom became involved in a series of wars against revolutionary and Napoleonic France. In addition, during his reign the realms of Great Britain and Ireland were joined, forming the United Kingdom.

The Hanoverian period was remarkably stable. From 1714 to 1837, there were only five monarchs, with George III remaining the longest reigning king in British History. The period was also one of political stability, and the development of constitutional monarchy. For most of the 18th century, great Whig families dominated politics, while the early 19th century saw Tory domination. It was also in this period that Britain came to acquire much of her overseas empire, mainly through various wars in the foreign lands. By the end of the Hanoverian period, the British Empire covered one third of the globe.

3. The Augustan Age

In the English literary history, the Augustan literature, or the Augustan Age, corresponds roughly with the reigns of Anne, George I, and George II, ranging from 1700 to 1760. The Augustan era is also known by two other names: the age of Neoclassicism and the Age of Reason. The term derived itself originally from a term that King George I had used in praise of himself. He regarded himself as another Augustus. Therefore, the British writers of the Augustan era took advantage of the term to honor their own efforts. They thought that with their efforts, the English social and cultural life would reach a culminating period in terms of morality and elegance, exactly the same as what was at Rome under the Emperor Caesar Augustus. The Augustan writers, headed by Alexander Pope (1688—1744) and Jonathan Swift (1667—1745), emulated in earnest the Roman writers. They adopted the Roman literary forms (notably the epistle and the satire), and aimed to create a similarly sophisticated urban literary environment. The Augustan literature was remarkable for a rapid development in novel writing, an enormous increase in satire, the transformation of drama from political satire into melodrama, and a gradual movement toward poetry of personal exploration.

4. English Enlightenment

The Enlightenment is an intellectual movement, usually associated with the 18th century in Europe, primarily in London and Paris. The Enlightenment, as a social, philosophical, political, and literary movement, sought to evaluate and understand the world by way of scientific observation and critical reasoning rather than through uncritically accepted religion, tradition, and social conventions.

In Britain, the English thinkers and writers during the 17th and 18th centuries hoped to nurture a secular view of the world and a general enthusiasm of progress and perfectibility through treating religious, social, political, and economic issues in a rational and scientific manner.

Under the influence of the philosophers who were inspired by the discoveries of the previous century and the writings of Michel de Montaigne (1533—1592), Rene Descartes (1596—1650), Francis Bacon (1561—1612), Thomas Hobbes (1588—1679) and John Locke (1632—1704), the advocates of Enlightenment movement in Britain held a strong belief that reason could be used to overcome ignorance, superstition, and tyranny and to build a perfect world. They regarded religion and hereditary aristocracy as the two greatest obstacles in the way of a better life and a better society. The English Enlightenment thinkers thought that logic and reason could be used to battle all sorts of absurd notions. "Reason", in their view, meant common sense, observation, and their own unacknowledged prejudices in favor of skepticism and freedom. They sought to discover effective principles to govern humanity, nature, and society. They launched furious attacks against dogmatism, intolerance, authority, censorship, and economic and social restraints.

The Enlightenment thinkers also believed that scientific methods could be used to study human society and to sketch the modern social sciences because rational laws could work well in the description of the social and physical behavior, and rational knowledge could be used to make better policies.

The Enlightenment thinkers put forward a set of basic principles about human society. They trusted that human beings were naturally good and could be educated to be better. If people were given freedom, social progress was

118

the inevitable outcome. The goals of an ideal society should be set to improve both material life and spiritual life.

The Enlightenment thinkers showed great interest in technological change, which would promise a great prosperity for the whole society. The Enlightenment philosophers thought they had discovered a simple formula for perpetual human happiness. They believed that individuals, once delivered from restraints, could act freely in accordance with their natures.

II. Literary Review

1. The Eighteenth Century Poetry

The 18th century English poetry was well refined, overtly political, and highly satirical, just like the Augustan poetry during the reign of Caesar Augustus (63 BC—14 AD), which was explicitly political, and distinguished by a greater degree of satire. The English poetry in the first half of the 18th century is mainly concerned with the central philosophical problem of whether the individual or the society should take priority as the subject of poetry. The English poets made the best use of all the classical forms of poetry, and they also renovated various genres of poetry to serve new functions. In their poetic practice, odes would cease to be encomium, ballads cease to be narratives, elegies cease to be sincere memorials, satires no longer be specific entertainments, parodies no longer be bravura stylistic performances, songs no longer be personal lyrics, and lyrics become a celebration of the individual rather than a lover's complaint.

Alexander Pope (1688—1744) dominated the English poetry so powerfully that few poets before or since have matched him. His first important poem, *An Essay on Criticism* (1711), sets down the guidelines for literary critics according to the prevailing classical ideals. His poetic masterpiece *The Rape of the Lock* (1712) presents a brilliant and colorful picture of the high life of his age. His translation of Homer is a Greek story told in an eighteenth-century manner. His *Essay on Man* (1734) is a poetic version of Shaftesbury's philosophy. His *Moral Essays* (1731—1735) and *The Dunciad* (1728) are didactic and satiric. Much of his poetry has a finer finish and a more subtle thrust. His poetry reflected clearly and adequately the spirit of his time, covering nearly every aspect of English life.

John Gay (1685—1732), English poet and playwright, is best known for his *The Beggar's Opera* (1728) a skillful blend of literary, political, social, and musical satire. He was not only a friend and collaborator of Pope's, but also one of the major voices of the era.

James Thomson (1700—1748), generally considered as one of the pioneers of Romanticism, is worthy to be remembered for three poems: *Rule Britannia*, *The Castle of Indolence*, and *The Seasons*. Thomson's best well-known work is his celebrated descriptive and melancholy poem *The Seasons*, written in the form of blank verse. In the poem, Thomson offered a unique image of nature in his topographical poetry but couched his descriptions in highly artificial diction. *The Seasons* heralded the romantic idealization of nature with its vivid, accurate and sensitive description. It exercised an influence on the forerunners of romanticism, such as Thomas Gray and William Cowper, and served as an inspiration to William Wordsworth and Samuel Taylor Coleridge.

Edward Young (1683—1765), English poet and dramatist, is well-known for his epic poem *Night Thoughts* (1742—1745). He wrote a series of satires, *The Universal Passion* (1725—1728) and three bombastic tragedies, *Busiris* (1719), *The Revenge* (1721), and *The Brothers* (1753). His last important work was his prose *Conjectures on Original Composition* (1759). His *Night Thoughts* is a famous Graveyard poem written in nine Nights, reflecting the poet's nocturnal meditation on the mysteries of Death and Immortality.

Thomas Gray (1716—1771) is regarded as the predominant poetic figure during the middle decades of the 18th century. His dexterous use of traditional forms and poetic diction combined with new topics and modes of expression marks him out as a forerunner of the romantic revival. His *Elegy Written in a Country Churchyard* (1751) is hailed a superior example of Graveyard poetry (also Churchyard poetry).

The Graveyard poets were a group of pre-Romantic English poets of the 18th century, who wrote primarily about human mortality. Often set in a graveyard, their poems meditated upon the predetermination of fate, the vicissitudes of life, the solitude of death and the grave, and the anguish of bereavement. The pensive, gloomy mood in their works portended the melancholy mood of the Romantic Movement. Apart from Gray and Young, other Graveyard poets include Thomas Parnell (1679—1718), Edward Young

(1683—1765), Robert Blair (1699—1746), James Thomson (1700—1748), William Shenstone (1714—1763), Elizabeth Carter (1717—1806), William Collins (1721—1759), Mark Akenside (1721—1770), Joseph Warton (1722—1800), William Mason (1724—1797), Thomas Warton (1728—1790), William Cowper (1731—1800), James Beattie (1735—1803), James Macpherson (1736—1796). Death, mortality, religion, solitude and melancholy are the recurrent themes of the Graveyard poetry. Often elegiac in tone and title, their poems make frequent use of funereal or gloomy imagery, such as night, death, stillness and gloom. The Graveyard poets were usually absorbed in their spiritual and philosophical contemplation of human mortality and man's relation to the divine. Their works demonstrate the wide range of emotional responses toward death, grief, compassion, respect, nostalgia, and other states of mind. They place a high value on personal and individual experience. Thus their subjective experience often plays a key role in their works. Furthermore, the Graveyard poetry, with its depictions of graves, churchyards, night, death, and ghosts, has been seen as laying the foundation for the Gothic literature.

In the latter part of the 18th century English literature, the most outstanding poetic figures are Oliver Goldsmith, William Cowper, Robert Burns and William Blake.

Oliver Goldsmith (1728—1774), is a prolific person, writing, translating, or compiling more than 40 volumes. The works for which he is remembered are the series of essays "The Citizen of the World", or, "Letters from a Chinese Philosopher" (1762), the poem "The Deserted Village" (1770), the novel *The Vicar of Wakefield* (1766), and the plays *The Good Natured Man* (1768) and *She Stoops to Conquer* (1771). His poetic masterpiece *The Deserted Village* contains charming, beautiful descriptions of rural life. *The Deserted Village* best conveys the predominant 18th-century spirit in so personal, poignant, and aphoristic a fashion that it remains one of the most frequently quoted poems in the English language.

William Cowper (1731—1800), is often considered as a transitional figure between the Neo-classical poetry and the Romantic poetry. As an intensely ambitious person, he attempted to contend with Pope by translating the *Iliad* and the *Odyssey*. His translations of the *Iliad* and the *Odyssey* (published in 1791) were the most significant English versions of these epic poems.

Robert Burns (1759—1796) is widely regarded as the national poet of

Scotland, and also celebrated all over the world. Like Thomson, Young, Gray and Cowper, Burns is regarded as one of the pioneers of the Romantic revival. Robert Burns is a prolific writer, composing about 400 poems in his short life. His works exerted a strong influence on Wordsworth, Coleridge, Shelley and other Romantic poets. Noteworthy for realism, strong passions, and dexterous metrical skills, his works shows his great sensitivity to nature, his natural spontaneity, his tenacious fight for freedom, his high praise of feelings and emotions of the humble people, and his great interest in folk songs and old legends.

William Blake (1757—1827) published *Songs of Innocence* (1789), *The Marriage of Heaven and Hell* (1793), and *Songs of Experience* (1794). The two lyric collections *Songs of Innocence* and *Songs of Experience* are hailed as a milestone in the history of the arts, not only for their originality and high quality but also for the successful fusion of two art media by one man. His other major works include *The Book of Thel* (1789—1791), *Vision of the Daughters of Albion* (1793), *The Marriage of Heaven and Hell* (1790—1793), *The Four Zoas* (1795—1804) and *Milton* (1804—1808). With his poetic and pictorial intelligence, he explored many important issues in politics, religion, and psychology and discussed such themes as man's relation with the Devine, humankind's fall and its subsequent redemption. He also exposed cruelty, injustice, exploitation and suppression in human society, for which the Church and the ruling class are responsible.

2. The Eighteenth Century Prose

The greatest strength of the English literature is mostly felt in prose during the period. The most talented prose writers are Swift, Addison, Steele, and Berkeley. Their works are marked by such outstanding features as maturity, variety, capacity, strength, sweetness, grace, and magnificence, which have become henceforth a rich legacy of the English literature.

Jonathan Swift (1667—1745) joined Alexander Pope, John Arbuthnot, John Gay, and others in forming the celebrated Scriblerus Club in 1713. After the publication of his two memorable works *The Drapier's Letters* (1724) and *A Modest Proposal* (1729), Swift became the national hero of Ireland, springing to her defense against the ruthless exploitation by the English oppressors. In 1704, Swift published his first major prose work *A Tale of a*

Tub, which displays many of the themes and stylistic techniques he would use in his future works. Swift's masterpiece *Gulliver's Travels* was published in 1726 which in fact, a misanthropic anatomy of the whole of human nature. It serves as a sarcastic mirror in which human beings can see their images in different aspects.

Joseph Addison (1672—1719) and Richard Steele(1672—1729) are usually mentioned together for their lifelong friendship and for their close co-operation in their literary practice in running The Tatler and The Spectator.

The partnership of the two literary figures is hailed as the most successful in the history of English literature. Though both writers differed widely in temperament, Steele being passionate and warmhearted whereas Addison reticent and serene, they shared the same political outlook and favored the middle-class culture and character. They looked at the human society humorously and humanely, and wished to turn it into a paradise of peace and happiness. They expressed their views and intentions with wit, goodwill, and fine artistry.

George Berkeley (1685 — 1753), Irish philosopher, is known for his philosophical and scientific treatises, aiming at reconciling the religious and scientific perceptions of the world through his empiricist philosophy. His chief works include *Treatise Concerning the Principles of Human Knowledge* (1710), *Three Dialogues between Hylas and Philonous*(1713), and *De Mmotin* (1721). Berkeley's philosophy of idealism has been influential in history because it laid the foundation for later secular empiricists such as David Hume (1711—1776), and his ideas have produced a great impact on the history and philosophy of science.

David Hume (1711—1776), English philosopher, economist, and historian, is considered among the most important figures in the history of the Western philosophy and the English Enlightenment. His first philosophical work is *A Treatise of Human Nature* (1739—1740). His other philosophical works include *An Enquiry Concerning Human Understanding* (1748), *An Enquiry Concerning the Principles of Morals* (1751), *Political Discourses* (1752), *The Natural History of Religion* (1755), and *Dialogues Concerning Natural Religion* (1779). In *A Treatise of Human Nature*, Hume argued that human knowledge is limited to sense-experience. The contents of sense-experience consist of impressions and ideas. Impressions are more forceful and vivacious than ideas. Thus, impressions are epistemologically superior to ideas. His exhaustive *History of England* (1754—1762), written in six volumes, was regarded as the most authoritative book on English history for sixty or seventy years until the appearance of Macaulay's work.

Adam Smith (1723—1790) is also known as the father of capitalism. His fame rests mainly on his two important treatises: *The Theory of Moral Sentiments* (1759), and *The Wealth of Nations* (1776). The main idea of his first work is that moral principles are established on the basis of social feeling or sympathy. *The Wealth of Nations*, as his most influential work, is hailed as a monumental contribution to the creation of the modern academic discipline of economics. In it, Smith gives a detailed explanation of how rational self-interest and appropriate competition can lead to common well-being. Smith's economic theories greatly influenced the writings of later economists, and David Ricardo and Carl Marx in particular.

Samuel Johnson (1709—1784) will forever stand one of the greatest and most honorable figures in the history of English literature. Johnson wrote biographies, poetry, essays, pamphlets, parliamentary reports. From 1747 to 1755, he wrote his best-known work *Dictionary of the English Language*, which gained immense popularity and produced enormous influence. In 1765, he produced his edition of *Shakespeare*. He wrote his final major work *Lives of the Most Eminent English Poets* from 1779 to 81. Johnson's style is typically neoclassical: graceful, witty, elegant, Latinate, and ponderous. All his works seem to deal with only one noble theme among many great themes of literature, which deals with man's unceasing search for happiness.

3. The Eighteenth Century Novel

The 18th century England also saw the modern novel, first emerging in the English Restoration, and soon developing into a major and serious art form. The English people take a great pride in regarding the discovery of the modern novel as England's original contribution to the world literature, because other types of literature, such as the epic, the romance, and the drama, were first created by other nations. Though at the beginning of the century, novels had a bad reputation, and were considered feminine ephemera, silly if not dangerous. The success of Richardson's novels changed the public opinion by claiming that novels entertained in order to instruct, and they were realistic and decent rather than scandalous fantasies.

Daniel Defoe (1660—1731) is universally considered the first of the great eighteenth-century English novelists. In some texts he is even referred to as one of the founders of the English novel, who helped popularize the genre in Britain. In April 1719, his masterpiece *Robinson Crusoe* came out and became an immediate success. The charm of *Robinson Crusoe* lies in its intensely realistic description. In the story, Defoe extols man's ability to endure, survive, and conquer a strange, hostile environment.

Samuel Richardson (1689—1761) is a major English 18th century novelist, best known for his three epistolary novels: *Pamela* (1740), *Clarissa* (1748) and *Sir Charles Grandison* (1753). All Richardson's novels were enormously popular in his time. His emphasis on detail, his psychological insights into women, and his dramatic technique have earned him a prominent place in English literature as one of the originators of the modern novel. He is also credited with being the first of the 18th century English "sentimental" writers.

Henry Fielding (1707—1754) is known for his rich humor and satirical prowess. Fielding's first major novel *Shamela*, published in 1741, as a parody of Richardson's work, was written to hilariously expose the virtuous heroine of "Pamela" as a scheming serving wench. Rather than a kind, humble, and chaste servant-girl, Pamela was described as a tricky and flirtatious girl, scheming to seduce her master, Squire Booby, into marrying her. Fielding continued his attack on Richardson by writing another parodic novel *Joseph Andrews* (1742), in which, the author creatively combined two classical traditions—the epic and the drama. Fielding wrote his comic masterpiece *Tom Jones* in 1749, which tells the story of Tom Jones from his infancy to his pursuit of Sophia Western, and finally to his marriage to her. The success of the book lies in its realistic account of English life in the mid-18th century.

Laurence Sterne (1713—1768) is an Irish-born English novelist. His masterpiece *Tristram Shandy* was published in nine volumes from 1759 to 1767. The story centers around domestic upsets or misunderstandings, and it is rich in characters and humor under the influence of Rabelais and Cervantes. His second novel *A Sentimental Journey Through France and Italy* (1768) is a less influential book, which has many stylistic parallels with *Tristram Shandy*. Many of the innovations suchas the endless digressions and wordplay, and the use of the narrator's psychological consciousness that Sterne introduced in his works have exercised a great influence on James Joyce, Virginia Woolf, Thomas Pynchon and David F. Wallace.

Tobias George Smollett (1721—1771) is best known for his picaresque novels. His greatest and most successful work is *Humphrey Clinker* (1771), a comical but sympathetic story of a family's adventures in Britain, written in the form of letters. His novels have abundant characters, episodes and realistic details, mainly drawn from his own rich and wide experience.

Another novelist of the period worth our attention is Oliver Goldsmith (1730-74). His works are notable for good sense, moderation, balance, order, and intellectual honesty. His finest work in his early period is *The Citizen of the World* (1762), written in letter form, in which the narrator as a foreign traveler comments upon the exotic customs of the lands through which he passed. His most enduring novel is *The Vicar of Wakefield*, published in 1766. In the novel, Goldsmith gives a detailed account of the idealized rural life, sentimental morality, and melodramatic incidents. The novel appeals to the public with its graceful style, its gentle and tolerant humor, the attractiveness of Dr. Primrose's character, the combined pathos and irony of the narrative.

4. The Eighteenth Century Drama

The 18th century England saw the flourishing of new dramas as a popular pastime, such as sentimental comedy and domestic tragedy, which were to replace the Restoration comedy.

The sentimental comedy began with the moralized comedies of Colley Cibber (1671—1757) and the sentimental dramas of Sir Richard Steele (1672—1729). With sincere intention, Cibber strove to reform and moralize the English theatre. His first play, *Love's Last Shift* (1696) is universally regarded as the first sentimental comedy in the history of the English theater. Of his 30 dramas, *She Wou'd and She Wou'd Not* (1702), *The Careless Husband* (1704), and *The Nonjuror* (1717) are the most notable.

Richard Steele wrote his first play *The Funeral* in 1701, a sentimental comedy, and later two comedies, *The Lying Lover* (1703) and *The Tender Husband* (1705). In 1722 he produced his last and most important play, *The Conscious Lovers*.

In domestic tragedy, the tragic protagonists are of ordinary or humble origins, whereas in classical and Neo-classical tragedy, the protagonists are of kingly or aristocratic rank and their downfall is an affair of state as well as a personal matter. Domestic tragedy often focused attention on ordinary merchants or citizens. Their flaws are either Christian sin or miniatures of the "tragic flaws". The consequence of the catastrophe is familial pain. The British domestic tragedy emerged more fully with the work of George Lillo.

George Lillo (1693—1739), English dramatist, is chiefly remembered as the author of *The London Merchant*; or, *The History of George Barnwell* (1731), the first domestic tragedy in English. In *The London Merchant*, an apprentice struggles with his conscience. He makes an imprudent choice and repents of his vice to attain only the hand of a worthy girl.

Richard Sheridan (1751—1816) is regarded as the most important English dramatist in the 18th century. Of all the plays Sheridan wrote and produced, the best three are *The Rivals* in 1775, *The School for Scandal* in 1777 and *The Critic* in 1779. The first two are comedies of manners that fuse the brilliant wit of the Restoration with the 18th century sensibility. Both plays hold up to ridicule the English upper class for its materialism, gossip, and hypocrisy. *The Critic* is remarkable for its depiction of a playwright unable to withstand any criticism, an unscrupulous writer of advertisements, and its thorough parody of theatrical conventions.

Alexander Pope (1688—1744)

Life and Major Works

Alexander Pope, English poet, translator, and critic, son of a linen merchant, was born in London in 1688, the year of the Glorious Revolution. His family were Roman Catholics. The religion barred him from the public schools. Under the circumstance, Pope educated himself through extensive reading in English, French, Italian, Latin, and Greek. Milton and Dryden exerted deep influences on his poems. After

Alexander Pope

extensive reading of the classics, Pope applied John Dryden's heroic couplet that stands for a perfect form of poetry to his verses.

In Pope's childhood, a tubercular infection left him deformed. He only attained a height of 4 feet 6 inches. The disease also ruined his health and subjected him to a violent headache. The undermined health distorted his view of life. He became hypersensitive, quarrelsome and irritable. In his time, Pope was famous for his witty satires and bitter quarrels with other writers. On the one hand, he attacked his literary contemporaries severely. On the other hand, he kept friendship with Joseph Addison, John Gay, Jonathan Swift and other famous writers. Pope was admitted to London's literary world by the introduction of the playwright William Wycherley in 1704. In addition, he became a member of the Scriblerus Club, a famous literary circle, in 1713.

Pope flashed into fame with the publication of *An Essay on Criticism* (1711) that expounds critical tastes and standards. In 1712 he published *The Rape of the Lock*. The satirical mock-epic poem establishes his reputation securely. It is an elegant satire about the battle between two prominent Catholic families caused by a trifle that a young man cut off a lock of hair of a beautiful maid. With their common acquaintance Pope's help, two families were reconciled in the end. Pope mocks this trivial event in an exaggerated attitude, thus sneers at the ridiculous world of his day. He satirizes the triviality and silliness of the high society with a delicate wit.

Pope came to know the commercial aspects of writing, which rendered him the first wealthy and full-time writer in England. He translated Homer's Greek works into English heroic couplets. His verse translation of *Iliad* was a great popular and financial success published from 1715 to 1720. 1726 saw the full appearance of his translation of *Odyssey*. With the money earned by the translation of *Iliad*, he became self-sufficient. But his translation was not an accurate version of the original. He recreated the work according to the British contemporary trend of thought. Bentley, a great scholar of the time, said: "It is a pretty poem, Mr. Pope, but you must not call it Homer."

In 1725 he published his edition of Shakespeare's plays, but many errors occurred because he was not familiar with the history of that period. It was heavily lampooned by some scholars such as Lewis Theobald. Pope was so ashamed into anger as to mock at him in *The Dunciad* later.

A good demonstration of satire, *The Dunciad* viciously attacked many critics and writers, Theobald in particular. Later Pope expanded it to ridicule the degenerated English society, and he gave vent to his hatred of the political and social evils.

His another great poem, *An Essay on Man* (1734) includes four letters addressed to Lord Bolingbroke. It is a series of philosophic poems about the nature of humankind, God's design for the world, happiness, etc. It intends to argue that the arrangement of nature is the best. Man should be satisfied with his position in the universe. Once men deal with reason and passion harmoniously, they'll attain virtue and happiness.

In 1717 Pope settled in a villa in Twickenham, about fifteen miles from London, where he spent the rest of his life. In 1744, Pope died of acute asthma and dropsy, and was buried in Twickenham.

Pope is a great master of heroic couplets and satires. The heroic couplet in his hands achieves the ultimate perfection. He was viewed as the outstanding classical poet in the 18th century England. He strongly advocated the classical rules, and contributed to the popularity of neoclassicism in England. However, his reputation dwindled down greatly in the next century. His poetry was regarded as outdated since the main stream of the 19th century Romanticism valued individualism and originality. But nowadays he is ranked as an important English neoclassical poet and a forceful verse satirist again.

Brief Introduction and Appreciation

Pope's outstanding work *An Essay on Criticism* (1711) appeared when he was only 23. The well-received poem cemented his reputation. Its flawless texture and profound critical insights struck the literary world, including famous writers such as Joseph Addison and Samuel Johnson.

It expresses Pope's opinions about the critics' duties and functions. It is a brilliant and comprehensive study of literary criticism, a guide to the poets' and critics' art, written in heroic couplet. Pope responds to the argument about whether poetry should be naturally or artificially written. He tends to the former writing style and advocates people to turn to the old Greek and Roman writers for guidance.

The 744-line poem contains 3 main parts. Part 1 explains common principles of good criticism, and then introduces the standards of good poetry by way of understanding the principles of good criticism. Pope reminds critics of knowing their limitation, in other words, self-awareness. In order to avoid partial and false criticism, critics should regard nature as the best judgment of art, and then study the ancient Greek and Roman rules of poetry and criticism. He admits people should produce poems according to some rules but there are exceptions. Driven by mysterious and irrational forces, gifted men may break the settled rules to compose poems.

In part 2, Pope discusses the common principles for the critics. They should consider the work as a whole unit, explore the author's purpose, and disencumber the influence of fashion and personal feeling. In addition, he criticizes that the present poems lack true taste, and lists many mistakes critics may commit, such as pride, little learning, love for parts and extremes.

The final part of the poem discusses the ideal critics' qualities and virtues: concrete, integrity, modesty, clarity, impartiality, public responsibility and so on. In conclusion, Pope sighs for the unsatisfactory actuality that the ideal critics don't exist in the degenerate contemporary world. Again, he speaks highly of ancient critics and emphasizes poets and critics to produce and comment on poetry according to classical rules of order and reason. Therefore, it is obvious he is a firm supporter and representative of Neoclassicism.

The following stanzas are taken from the second part. Here Pope thinks the fine language is unadorned and advises the critics not to focus too much on the flowery expression in case that it hinders the flow of true thoughts.

The poem is written in a plain style as the poet advocates in his own work. Besides, Pope puts forward many famous epigrams with perfect expression, which demonstrates his outstanding control of language. For example, "To err is human, to forgive divine," "A little learning is a dangerous thing," and "For fools rush in where angels fear to tread."

In short, the essay produces a great influence on his contemporary writers and makes substantial contributions to literary criticism.

Selected Reading

An Essay on Criticism

Some to Conceit[1] alone their Taste confine,
And glitt'ring Thoughts struck out[2] at ev'ry Line;
Pleas'd with a Work where nothing's just[3] or fit;
One glaring Chaos and wild Heap of Wit[4].
Poets like Painters, thus, unskill'd to trace[5]
The naked Nature[6] and the living Grace,

With Gold and Jewels cover ev'ry Part,
And hide with Ornaments their Want [7]of Art.
True Wit is Nature to Advantage[8] drest,
What oft was Thought, but ne'er so well Exprest,
Something[9], whose Truth convinc'd at Sight we find,
That gives us back the Image[10] of our Mind:
As Shades more sweetly recommend[11] the Light,
So modest Plainness sets off sprightly Wit:
For Works may have more Wit than does'em good,
As Bodies perish through Excess of Blood.
Others for Language all their Care express,
And value Books, as Women Men, for Dress:
Their Praise is still—The Stile is excellent:
The Sense, they humbly take upon Content[12].
Words are like Leaves; and where they most abound,
Much Fruit of Sense beneath is rarely found[13].
False Eloquence, like the Prismatic Glass,
Its gaudy colors spreads on ev'ry place;
The Face of Nature we no more survey,
All glares alike, without Distinction gay:
But true Expression, like th' unchanging Sun,
Clears, and improves whate'er it shines upon,
It gilds all Objects, but it alters none.
Expression is the Dress of Thought, and still
Appears more decent as more suitable[14];
A vile Conceit in pompous Words exprest,
Is like a Clown[15] in regal Purple drest;
For diff'rent Styles with diff'rent Subjects sort,
As several Garbs with Country, Town, and Court.
Some by Old Words to Fame have made Pretence;
Ancients in Phrase, mere Moderns in their Sense[16]!
Such labour'd Nothings[17], in so strange a Style,
Amaze th'unlearn'd, and make the Learned Smile.
Unlucky, as Fungoso[18] in the Play,
These Sparks[19] with awkward Vanity display

What the Fine Gentleman wore Yesterday!
And but so mimic ancient Wits at best,
As Apes our Grandsires in their Doublets drest.
In Words, as Fashions, the same Rule will hold;
Alike Fantastic, if too New, or Old[20]:
Be not the first by whom the New are try'd,
Nor yet the last to lay the Old aside.

Notes

1. **conceit:** metaphor
2. **struck out:** invented
3. **just:** proper
4. **wit:** imagination
5. **trace:** draw
6. **nature:** the objective world
7. **want:** lack
8. **advantage:** properly
9. **something:** true wit
10. **image:** the imperfect notion of something
11. **recommend:** set off
12. **content:** acquiescence
13. There are few fruit in a tree if leaves are plentiful. Similarly, the article rarelyexpresses much sense if there are too many flowery words.
14. The more suitable the expression, the more decent it appears.
15. **clown:** rudesby
16. They express the modern ideas in old language.
17. **labour'd Nothings:** pompous words
18. **Fungoso:** a foolish law student obsessed with courtly fashion in Every Man in His Humor by Ben Jonson.
19. **sparks:** dandies
20. They are both fantastic whether the words used are too new or too old.

Questions for Study and Discussion

1. Do you think the florid style is harmful to the content?
2. Why does Pope advocate plain works?
3. What are the merits of ancient Greek and Roman works?
4. How do you understand "nature" in the poem?
5. What are the features of Pope's writing?
6. What is the rhyme and rhythm of the poem?

Daniel Defoe (1659—1731)

Life and Major Works

Daniel Defoe was born in a family of Dissenters in London in 1659, the first son of James Foe, a butcher. Daniel added the "De" suggesting a genteel birth to his name in 1700 because he longed for a high family origin. His father intended him to be a minister, but he was not interested in it, and chose to be a merchant instead. He had no idea of becoming a writer at that time. Since Dissenters were barred from Oxford and Cambridge universities, Defoe attended Morton's Academy at Newington Green. When he was about eighteen, he left school, and

Daniel Defoe

started his business. In 1684 he married Mary Tuffley, who gave birth to two sons and five daughters. Due to investment mistakes, Defoe went bankrupt in 1692 and got into a large debt. The rest of his life seemed to be involved with debts and unstable fortunes. He then started writing professionally. Writing suddenly became an important part of his life.

In 1685, Defoe took part in the Duke of Monmouth's rebellion against the Catholic King James II. When the rebellion failed, Defoe was forced into semi-exile. Therefore, he was glad at William III and his wife Mary's rein. He earned fame and royal favor with his work *The True Born Englishman* (1701). The poem attacks those people who resent the new king, William III, because he is a Dutch. The work points out purified Englishmen hardly exist and those so-called "true-born" people are of mixed descents.

In 1702 Defoe anonymously published a satirical pamphlet *The Shortest Way with the Dissenters,* to protest against religious persecutions. He ironically made several savage suggestions for suppression of Dissenters. He pretended to argue that the best way to solve religious disputes was to kill Dissenters. In the following year when it was found that Defoe was the author of the pamphlet, he was sentenced to stand in the pillory and be imprisoned. Standing in the pillory, he read his mock ode *Hymn to the Pillory* to the crowd. The poem was quickly spread all over London and the public looked upon him as an obstinate fighter. He was released in 1704 on the condition that he served as a public propagandist and intelligence agent to Robert Harley, a leader of Tory government. In some sense, he was a practical and shrew man. He served the Whigs after the Tories had lost control of power, so he was despised as a man who sold his pen to the political party in charge at that time. With the support of the government, Defoe started a journal entitled *The Review* that discussed the political and social issues of England, France and other European countries. It exited for 10 years. In addition, he wrote articles on a variety of subjects including politics, religion, women, marriage, crimes and psychology for other periodicals. In a word, he makes great contribution to English journals and is considered the founder of England journals.

Besides the founder of modern journalism, Defoe is also claimed as the father of English novels. Defoe is a prolific writer who publishes over 500 books and pamphlets. His masterpiece *Robinson Crusoe* (1719) marks the formation of the modern novel, referred to as one of the first English novels because it presents the life of the common people realistically. It was published when he was almost sixty, a typical example of late-flowering. It narrates the adventures of a sailor shipwrecked alone on a deserted island, based on a true event. In the story, Robinson's many qualities are almost identical to those of the author. It is believed Defoe uses Robinson to portray himself.

The Fortunes and Misfortunes of the Famous Moll Flanders, his next important novel was published in 1722. A lowly woman is designed as the subject of literature in order to reveal how the contemporary society victimizes women. The fall and redemption of a thief and prostitute is described so vividly as to win great popularity. Virginia Woolf thinks highly of *Moll Flanders* as one of the "few English novels which we can call indisputably great."

As a businessman, Defoe had many chances to travel widely. The three-volume travel book, *Tour through the Whole Island of Great Britain* (1724—1727), recounts his true experience and introduces wonderful scenery of his motherland.

His other famous works include: *Captain Singleton* (1720), *Journal of the Plague Year* (1722), *Captain Jack* (1722), *Roxana* (1724) and *The Complete English Tradesman* (1726).

Defoe died of lethargy in Cripplegate on April 24, 1731.

Brief Introduction and Appreciation

In 1704 Scottish sailor Alexander Selkirk had a big quarrel with his captain since he thought the ship was unsuitable for sail again (it did sink soon). As a result, he was abandoned by his captain on a solitary island (now called Robinson Crusoe Island), and was rescued four years later. Defoe played his imagination and converted the true story into a widely read novel *The Life and Strange and Surprising Adventures of Robinson Crusoe*.

Under his pen, Robinson is unsatisfied with the commonplace life against the wishes of his parents so as to run away from home to seek adventure and excitement as a seaman. On a voyage, his ship is heavily attacked by a storm, and he becomes the only survivor, cast on a shore. In the desolate island, he conquers his fear and shows great courage in the face of the strict reality. He overcomes many troubles beyond our imagination, and struggles with the extraordinary circumstances persistently. At last he solves the problem of food, clothing and shelter, becoming completely self-sufficient. After a log term of isolate life, he saves a savage Friday and makes him a servant. Robinson lives there for 28 years until he helps a captain control rebellious sailors and returns to England by their ship.

Encouraged by the success of the novel, Defoe writes its sequels. In the second book, *The Farther Adventures of Robinson Crusoe* (1719), Robinson revisits the island, cultivates the residents as his subjects, looks around his plantation in Brazil, and seeks adventures in China and other places in the world. The third book, *Serious Reflections of Robinson Crusoe* (1720), consists of moral essays. Contrary to the first one, both of them disappoint most readers.

The great achievement of *Robinson Crusoe* lies in creating a hero Robinson who is typical of the rising English bourgeois. He lives in a time when capitalism is on the developing way. Since the new navigation channel was found from the 14th century, adventures became a fashion. People were curious about the outside world and aspired to the hazardous life. The character Robinson caters for the favor. His experiences of doing business, being shipwrecked in a waste island, developing the island, and at last colonizing the land present a positive image of the English bourgeois at its early stage of development. He shows boundless courage and energy in surmounting difficulties. The new type of man comes to be the hero of the public, who possesses strong enterprise in accumulating wealth.

Robinson is not only a capitalist but also a colonialist. It is obvious that Robinson shows the heart of conquering people of other origins and extending territory. He goes to sea for the slave trade. He sets up the mark of landing as soon as he resides on the waste island. He regards the land as his kingdom and refers to himself as the king of the natives. He civilizes the native Friday. The first word he teaches him is "master". All these reveal his identity as a colonist. Defoe demonstrates his colonial mind of setting up colonies overseas through the portrayal of Robinson, the prototype of colonists.

In addition, Dissenters' ethics pervade in the book. Robinson overcomes hard surroundings and enjoys fruits of labor, with his two hands. He owns vigorous power of living, and spends dozens of years independently. In the process of surviving disaster and ordeal, he shows diligence, wisdom, strong will and marvelous capacity. These qualities are consistent with the puritan values. Therefore, the book sings an ode to Dissenters. In this sense, it is a morality story.

Besides the morality story, the work also inherits the tradition of Spanish picaresque novels from Renaissance, which often portray a low-born man who achieves fortune and success by the ingenuity of his mind and the labor of his hands.

Defoe is expert in making fiction look like truth. A first-person narrative gives the story a realistic frame. He is one of the first to write stories about believable characters in fictitious and detailed conditions that resemble reality, distinguished from his predecessors. *Robinson Cruse* starts the tide of narrative fictions. Although the work lacks the structural unity and cohesiveness, Defoe lays the foundation for realistic fiction so as to be called as one of the founders of English novels. The vivid realistic story combined with the exact, plain and uncomplicated language has fascinated the world so long.

Selected Reading

Robinson Crusoe
(Crusoe visits the wreck)

A little after noon I found the sea very calm, and the tide ebbed so far out that I could come within a quarter of a mile of the ship. And here I found a fresh renewing of my grief; for I saw evidently that if we had kept on board we had been all safe, that is to say, we had all got safe on shore, and I had not been so miserable as to be left entirety destitute of all comfort and company as I now was.[1] This forced tears to my eyes again; but as there was little relief in that, I resolved, if possible, to get to the ship; so I pulled off my clothes—for the weather was hot to extremity—and took the water. But when I came to the ship my difficulty was still greater to know how to get on board; for, as she lay aground, and high out of the water, there was nothing within my reach to lay hold of. I swam round her twice, and the second time I spied a small piece of rope, which I wondered I did not see at first, hung down by the fore-chains so low, as that with great difficulty I got hold of it, and by the help of that rope I got up into the forecastle of the ship. Here I found that the ship was bulged, and had a great deal of water in her hold, but that she lay so on the side of a bank of hard sand, or, rather earth, that her stern lay lifted up upon the bank, and her head low, almost to the water. By this means all her quarter was free,[2] and all that was in that part was dry; for you may be sure my first work was to search, and to see what was spoiled and what was free. And, first, I found that all the ship's provisions were dry and untouched by the water, and being very well disposed to eat, I went to the bread room and filled my pockets with biscuit, and ate it as I went about other things, for I had no time to lose. I also found some rum in the great cabin, of which I took a large dram, and which I had, indeed, need enough of to spirit me for what was before me.

Now I wanted nothing but a boat to furnish myself with many things which I foresaw would be very necessary to me.

It was in vain to sit still and wish for what was not to be had; and this extremity roused my application. We had several spare yards, and two or three large spars of wood, and a spare topmast or two in the ship; I resolved to fall to work with these, and I flung as many of them overboard as I could manage for their weight, tying every one with a rope that they might not drive away. When this was done I went down the ship's side, and pulling them to me, I tied four of them together at both ends as well as I could, in the form of a raft, and laying two or three short pieces of plank upon them crossways, I found I could walk upon it very well, but that it was not able to bear any great weight, the pieces being too light. So I went to work, and with a carpenter's saw I cut a spare topmast into three lengths, and added them to my raft, with a great deal of labor and pains. But the hope of furnishing myself with necessaries encouraged me to go beyond what I should have been able to have done upon another occasion[3].

My raft was now strong enough to bear any reasonable weight. My next care was what to load it with, and how to preserve what I laid upon it from the surf of the sea; but I was not long considering this. I first laid all the planks or boards upon it that I could get, and having considered well what I most wanted, I got three of the seamen's chests, which I had broken open, and emptied, and lowered them down upon my raft; the first of these I filled with provisions, bread, rice, three Dutch cheeses, five pieces of dried goat's flesh (which we lived much upon), and a little remainder of European corn, which had been laid by for some fowls which we brought to sea with us, but the fowls were killed. There had been some barley and wheat together; but, to my great disappointment, I found afterwards that the rats had eaten or spoiled it all. As for liquors, I found several, cases of bottles belonging to our skipper, in which were some cordial waters[4]; and, in all, about five or six gallons of rack. These I stowed by themselves, there being no need to put them into the chest, nor any room for them. While I was doing this, I found the tide began to flow, though very calm; and I had the mortification to see my coat, shirt, and waistcoat, which I had left on the shore, upon the sand, swim away. As for my breeches, which were only linen, and open-kneed, I swam on board in them, and my stockings. However, this set me on rummaging for clothes, of which I found enough, but took no more than I wanted for present use, for I had others things which my eye was more upon, as, first, tools to work with on shore. And it was after long searching that I found out the carpenter's chest, which was, indeed, a very useful prize to me, and much more valuable than a shipload of gold would have been at that time. I got it down to my raft, whole as it was, without losing time to look into it, for I knew in general what it contained.

My next care was for some ammunition and arms. There were two very good fowling-pieces[5] in the great cabin, and two pistols. These I secured first, with some powder-horns and a small bag of shot, and two old rusty swords. I knew there were three barrels of powder in the ship, but knew not where our gunner had stowed them; but with much search I found them, two of them dry and good, the third had taken water. Those two I got to my raft with the arms. And now I thought myself pretty well freighted, and began to think how I should get to shore with them, having neither sail, oar, nor rudder; and the least capful of wind would have overset all my navigation.

I had three encouragements. 1. A smooth calm sea; 2. The tide rising, and setting in to the shore; 3. What little wind there was blew me towards the land. And thus, having found two or three broken oars belonging to the boat, and, besides the tools which were in the chest, I found two saws, an axe, and a hammer; with this cargo I put to sea[6]. For a mile or thereabouts my raft went very well, only that I found it drive a little distant from the place where I had landed before; by which I perceived that there was some indraft of the water, and consequently I hoped to find some creek or river there, which I might make use of as a port to get to land with my cargo.

(The footprint)

As this was also about half-way between my other habitation and the place where I had laid up my boat, I generally stayed and lay here in my way thither, for I used frequently to visit my boat; and I kept all things about or belonging to her in very good order. Sometimes I went out in her to divert myself, but no more hazardous voyages would I go, scarcely ever above a stone's cast or two from the shore, I was so apprehensive of being hurried out of my knowledge again by the currents or winds, or any other accident. But now I come to a new scene of my life. It happened one day, about noon, going towards my boat, I was exceedingly surprised with the print of a man's naked foot on the shore, which was very plain to be seen on the sand. I stood like one thunderstruck, or as if I had seen an apparition. I listened, I looked round me, but I could hear nothing, nor see anything; I went up to a rising ground to look farther; I went up the shore and down the shore, but it was all one; I could see no other impression but that one. I went to it again to see if there were any more, and to observe if it might not be my fancy; but there was no room for that, for there was exactly the print of a foot-toes, heel, and every part of a foot. How it came thither I knew not, nor could I in the least imagine; but after innumerable fluttering thoughts, like a man perfectly confused and out of myself, I came home to my fortification, not feeling, as we say, the ground I went on, but terrified to the last degree, looking behind me at every two or three steps, mistaking every bush and tree, and fancying every stump at a distance to be a man. Nor is it possible to describe how many various shapes my affrighted imagination represented things to me in, how many wild ideas were found every moment in my fancy, and what strange, unaccountable whimsies came into my thoughts by the way.

When I came to my castle (for so I think I called it ever after this), I fled into it like one pursued. Whether I went over by the ladder, as first contrived, or went in at the hole in the rock, which I had called a door, I cannot remember; no, nor could I remember the next morning, for never frightened hare fled to cover, or fox to earth, with more terror of mind than I to this retreat.

(Crusoe saves Friday from the cannibals)

While I was thus looking on them[7], I perceived, by my perspective, two miserable wretches dragged from the boats, where, it seems, they were laid by, and were now brought out for the slaughter. I perceived one of them immediately fall; being knocked down, I suppose, with a club or wooden sword, for that was their way; and two or three others were at work immediately, cutting him open for their cookery, while the other victim was left standing by himself, till they should be ready for him. In that very moment this poor wretch, seeing himself a little at liberty and unbound, Nature inspired him with hopes of life, and he started away from them, and ran with incredible swiftness along the sands, directly towards me; I mean towards that part of the coast where my habitation was. I was dreadfully frightened, I must acknowledge, when I perceived him run my way; and especially when, as I thought, I saw him pursued by the whole body: and now I expected that part of my dream[8] was coming to pass, and that he would certainly take shelter in my grove; but I could not depend, by any means, upon my dream, that the other savages would not pursue him thither and find him there. However, I kept my station, and my spirits began to recover when I found that there was not above three men that followed him; and still more was I encouraged, when I found that he outstripped them exceedingly in running, and gained ground on them; so that, if he could but hold out for half-an-hour, I saw easily he would fairly get away from them all.

There was between them and my castle the creek, which I mentioned often in the first part of my story, where I landed my cargoes out of the ship; and this I saw plainly he must necessarily swim over, or the poor wretch would be taken there; but when the savage escaping came thither, he made nothing of it, though the tide was then up; but plunging in, swam through in about thirty strokes, or thereabouts, landed, and ran with exceeding strength and swiftness. When the three persons came to the creek, I found that two of them could swim, but the third could not, and that, standing on the other side, he looked at the others, but went no farther, and soon after went softly back again; which, as it happened, was very well for him in the end. I observed that the two who swam were yet more than twice as strong swimming over the creek as the fellow was that fled from them. It came very warmly upon my thoughts, and indeed irresistibly, that now was the time to get me a servant, and, perhaps, a companion or assistant; and that I was plainly called by Providence[9] to save this poor creature's life. I immediately ran down the ladders with all possible expedition, fetched my two guns, for they were both at the foot of the ladders, as I observed before, and getting up again with the same haste to the top of the hill, I crossed towards the sea; and having a very short cut, and all down hill, placed myself in the way between the pursuers and the pursued, hallowing aloud to him that fled, who, looking back, was at first perhaps as much frightened at me as at them; but I beckoned with my hand to him to come back; and, in the meantime, I slowly advanced towards the two that followed; then rushing at once upon the foremost, I knocked him down with the stock of my piece. I was loath to fire, because I would not have the rest hear; though, at that distance, it would not have been easily heard, and being out of sight of the smoke, too, they would not have known what to make of it. Having knocked this fellow down, the other who pursued him stopped, as if he had been frightened, and I advanced towards him: but as I came nearer, I perceived presently he had a bow and arrow, and was fitting it to shoot at me: so I was then obliged to shoot at him first, which I did, and killed him at the first shot. The poor savage who fled, but had stopped, though he saw both his enemies fallen and killed, as he thought, yet was so frightened with the fire and noise of my piece that he stood stock still, and neither came forward nor went backward, though he seemed rather inclined still to fly than to come on. I hallooed again to him, and made signs to come forward, which he easily understood, and came a little way; then stopped again, and then a little farther, and stopped again; and I could then perceive that he stood trembling, as if he had been taken prisoner, and had just been to be killed, as his two enemies were. I beckoned to him again to come to me, and gave him all the signs of encouragement that I could think of; and he came nearer and nearer, kneeling down every ten or twelve steps, in token of acknowledgment for saving his life. I smiled at him, and looked pleasantly, and beckoned to him to come still nearer; at length he came close to me; and then he kneeled down again, kissed the ground, and laid his head upon the ground, and taking me by the foot, set my foot upon his head; this, it seems, was in token of swearing to be my slave for ever. I took him up and made much of him, and encouraged him all I could. But there was more work to do yet; for I perceived the savage whom I had knocked down was not killed, but stunned with the blow, and began to come to himself: so I pointed to him, and showed him the savage, that he was not dead; upon this he spoke some words to me, and though I could not understand them, yet I thought they were pleasant to hear; for they were the first sound of a man's voice that I had heard, my own excepted, for above twenty-five years. But there was no time for such reflections now; the savage who was knocked down recovered himself so far as to sit up upon the ground, and I perceived that my savage began to be afraid; but when I saw that, I presented my other piece at the man, as if I would shoot him: upon this my savage, for so I call him now, made a motion to me to lend him my sword, which hung naked in a belt by my side, which I did. He no sooner had it, but he runs to his enemy, and at one blow cut off his head so cleverly, no executioner in Germany could have done it sooner or better; which I thought very strange for one who, I had reason to believe, never saw a sword in his life before, except their own wooden swords: however, it seems, as I learned afterwards, they make their wooden swords so sharp, so heavy, and the wood is so hard, that they will even cut off heads with them, ay, and arms, and that at one blow, too. When he had done this, he comes laughing to me in sign of triumph, and brought me the sword again, and with abundance of gestures which I did not understand, laid it down, with the head of the savage that he had killed, just before me. But that which astonished him most was to know how I killed the other Indian so far off; so, pointing to him, he made signs to me to let him go to him; and I bade him go, as well as I could. When he came to him, he stood like one amazed, looking at him, turning him first on one side, then on the other; looked at the wound the bullet had made, which it seems was just in his breast, where it had made a hole, and no great quantity of blood had followed; but he had bled inwardly, for he was quite dead. He took up his bow and arrows, and came back; so I turned to go away, and beckoned him to follow me, making signs to him that more might come after them. Upon this he made signs to me that he should bury them with sand, that they might not be seen by the rest, if they followed; and so I made signs to him again to do so. He fell to work; and in an instant he had scraped a hole in the sand with his hands big enough to bury the first in, and then dragged him into it, and covered him; and did so by the other also; I believe he had buried them both in a quarter of an hour. Then, calling away, I carried him, not to my castle, but quite away to my cave, on the farther part of the island: so I did not let my dream come to pass in that part, that he came into my grove for shelter. Here I gave him bread and a bunch of raisins to eat, and a draught of water, which I found he was indeed in great distress for, from his running: and having refreshed him, I made signs for him to go and lie down to sleep, showing him a place where I had laid some rice-straw, and a blanket upon it, which I used to sleep upon myself sometimes; so the poor creature lay down, and went to sleep.

He was a comely, handsome fellow, perfectly well made, with straight, strong limbs, not too large; tall, and well-shaped; and, as I reckon, about twenty-six years of age. He had a very good countenance, not a fierce and surly aspect, but seemed to have something very manly in his face; and yet he had all the sweetness and softness of a European in his countenance, too, especially when he smiled. His hair was long and black, not curled like wool; his forehead very high and large; and a great vivacity and sparkling sharpness in his eyes. The color of his skin was not quite black, but very tawny; and yet not an ugly, yellow, nauseous tawny, as the Brazilians and Virginians, and other natives of America are, but of a bright kind of a dun olive-color, that had in it something very agreeable, though not very easy to describe. His face was round and plump; his nose small, not flat, like the Negroes; a very good mouth, thin lips, and his fine teeth well set, and as white as ivory.

After he had slumbered, rather than slept, about half-an-hour, he awoke again, and came out of the cave to me: for I had been milking my goats which I had in the enclosure just by: when he espied me he came running to me, laying himself down again upon the ground, with all the possible signs of an humble, thankful disposition, making a great many antic[10] gestures to show it. At last he lays his head flat upon the ground, close to my foot, and sets my other foot upon his head, as he had done before; and after this made all the signs to me of subjection, servitude, and submission imaginable, to let me know how he would serve me so long as he lived. I understood him in many things, and let him know I was very well pleased with him. In a little time I began to speak to him; and teach him to speak to me: and first, I let him know his name should be Friday, which was the day I saved his life: I called him so for the memory of the time. I likewise taught him to say Master; and then let him know that was to be my name: I likewise taught him to say Yes and No and to know the meaning of them. I gave him some milk in an earthen pot, and let him see me drink it before him, and sop my bread in it; and gave him a cake of bread to do the like, which he quickly complied with, and made signs that it was very good for him. I kept there with him all that night; but as soon as it was day I beckoned to him to come with me, and let him know I would give him some clothes; at which he seemed very glad, for he was stark naked. As we went by the place where he had buried the two men, he pointed exactly to the place, and showed me the marks that he had made to find them again, making signs to me that we should dig them up again and eat them. At this I appeared very angry, expressed my abhorrence of it, made as if I would vomit at the thoughts of it, and beckoned with my hand to him to come away, which he did immediately, with great submission. I then led him up to the top of the hill, to see if his enemies were gone; and pulling out my glass I looked, and saw plainly the place where they had been, but no appearance of them or their canoes; so that it was plain they were gone, and had left their two comrades behind them, without any search after them.

Notes

1. Sailors had to get off the ship in case that it would be broken into pieces by the furious wind.
2. **all her quarter was free:** there was no water in the after part of the ship's side.
3. **upon another occasion:** at other times
4. **cordial waters:** spirituous liquors
5. **pieces:** guns
6. **put to sea:** steer my raft in shore
7. **them:** savages
8. **dream:** Robinson once dreamed that he had saved a savage and trained him to be his servant.
9. **providence:** God
10. **antic:** strange and funny

Questions for Study and Discussion

1. What is Robinson Crusoe's attitude towards the ordeal environment?
2. What kind of man is Robinson Crusoe?
3. Why does a footprint nearly frighten Robinson Crusoe to death?
4. What is Robinson Crusoe's relationship with Friday?
5. What techniques are used by the author to achieve the lifelike effect?
6. What are the language characteristics of the novel?
7. What would you do if you were left alone in a desert island?
8. What can we learn from Robinson Crusoe?

Jonathan Swift（1667—1745）

Life and Major Works

Jonathan Swift was born in Dublin, Ireland, on November 30, 1667. His father, an attorney at King's Inn, died seven months before he was born. His mother Abigail Erick could not support the family and eventually returned to Leicester, England to live with relatives, so little Swift was brought up by his paternal uncles. From 1674 to 1682, he received education at Kilkenny Grammar School, the best school in Ireland. Then he entered Trinity College in Dublin, getting a B.A. degree in 1686.

Jonathan Swift

Since the 1688 Glorious Revolution aroused social unrest, Swift left for England and became a secretary of William Temple, an important statesman of that day as well as a distant relative of his mother. With his patron's help, Swift became acquainted with many prominent figures at Moor Park, Surrey, thus cementing his political apprenticeship. He read extensively in Temple's vast library, and received an M. A. degree from Oxford University in 1692. Although Swift worked for Temple for ten years, the position similar to a servant in the household tortured him so their relationships were a bit strained. In 1695 he interrupted his life at Moor Park to become a priest in the Church of Ireland for nearly a year, but was tempted to Temple again.

After Temple died in 1699, Swift returned to Ireland and was instituted as Vicar to Laracor and became Chaplain and secretary to the Earl of Berkeley. In 1701 Swift was awarded Doctoral Degree from Trinity College, Dublin. At the same time, he came to be known as a satiric writer by writing essays and pamphlets. While working for Temple, Swift composed his first famous work *A Tale of a Tub*, and *The Battle of the Books*. Both of them were not published until 1704, establishing Swift's reputation. *A Tale of a Tub* disputes on Roman Catholicism, Anglicanism and Calvinism in the form of three brothers' quarrel about the coats given by their father. The work is designed so exquisitely that Swift himself at his old age sighed, "Good God, what a genius I had when I

146

wrote that book." *The Battle of the Books* is also a mordant satire and mercilessly attacks pedantry, intended to defend his patron Temple's view that ancient literature is superior to that of modern.

In 1701 Swift published his first political pamphlet, *Dissensions in Athens and Rome*, favoring the Whigs. Although he was a Whig at the beginning, Swift disapproved of his party in some aspects, such as Whigs' support of Dissenters in Ireland. In 1707 Swift went to London as an emissary of Irish clergy seeking the removal of tax on the income of the Irish clergy, which was rejected by the Whig government. After a Tory government came to power in England in 1710, Swift turned to ally with the Tories, and became the editor of *The Examiner*, the official Tory publication.

Gradually, Swift became a distinguished character in London literary and political circles. He formed the Scriblerus Literary Club with Alexander Pope, Arbuthnot and others. He produced many influential pamphlets such as *The Conduct of the Allies* (1711) in which the author charged that the Whigs had prolonged the War of the Spanish Succession (1701—1714) out of self-interest. The article was so influential as to urge England to end its war with Spain.

However, the Tories fell from power after Queen Anne died in 1714. Swift had to leave London and serve as Dean of Saint Patrick's Cathedral in Dublin, a position he held from 1713 to 1742. Besides several trips to London, he spent most time in Ireland, and published some influential works on Irish problems. *A Modest Proposal* demonstrates Swift's uncommon logic wherein he suggests that the Irish sell their children to the rich English as food, and thus the Irish problem of overpopulation and poverty could be solved. Swift issued seven *Drapier Letters* (1724—1725) under the pseudonym M.B. Drapier, protesting against the scandal the royalty authorized an Englishman William Wood to make inferior copper coins in Ireland. Annoyed by the letters, English government began to investigate the real writer. However, Swift was never discovered during his lifetime since the Irish people protected the hero who devoted his life to Ireland.

Swift developed Meniere's Diseases when he was in twenties which leads to dizziness, headache, the decline of memory and the loss of hearing. But doctors of his day had little knowledge of the illness and mistook him as a mental patient. From 1742, he was taken care of by guardians because people believed he was insane. Swift died in Dublin on October 19, 1745, and was buried at St. Patrick's Cathedral in Dublin next to his beloved Stella.

Swift left behind many pamphlets on religion, human nature, politics, war, etc. His highly effective and economical language produces deep impression on readers. He expresses his opinions clearly and precisely. The plain literary words don't hinder the flow of his sharp and serious mockery. Swift is such a great master of English prose and satire that Thackeray remarked, "So great a man he seems to me, that thinking of him is like thinking of an empire falling."

Brief Introduction and Appreciation

Swift's masterpiece *Gulliver's Travels* appeared in November, 1726, and became an overnight success. The great satire narrates Gulliver, an England surgeon's adventures in fictional countries by shipwreck and other reasons.

Part I introduces Gulliver's adventure in Lilliput where the inhabitants are about six inches tall. Lilliput is the epitome of England. There exist many similarities between England and Lilliput. Officials are selected by the height that they can jump. Similar to the Tories and the Whigs in England, the Lilliput also has two parties ridiculously distinguished by the height of their heels. The country fights with his neighboring country because they dispute about whether an egg should be broken from the big end or the small one, which stands for the meaningless quarrel between Roman Catholicism and Calvinism. Swift's irony about war shows his longing for peace. Later Gulliver is forced to run for his life because he refuses to help the king evade the neighboring country, and uses his urine to extinguish the fire of the kings' palace.

Part II narrates Gulliver's experience in the giant country Brobdingnag where Gulliver is like a dwarf before men who are sixty feet high. Gulliver is captured by a giant farmer who demands him to display in public for profits until one day the queen buys him as a pet so the king is accessible to him. He narrates great achievements of England before the king. But his account cannot convince the king, who denies many regulations and systems of England in which Gulliver takes pride. He also incisively points out human beings' selfishness, coolness and brutality result in corruption, evasion, and war. Thus the corruption and evil of England are expressed through the words of the king. By a lucky accident, Gulliver returns to his native country.

In Part III, Gulliver visits Laputa, a flying island where residents are fantastic philosophers and scientists. They are immersed in impractical research, far away from common senses. Moreover, they take rude measures to their subjects. If a town rebels, the flying island will hover to deprive inhabitants of sunlight and rain, or even land on the place to grind it. It symbolizes the English atrocious rule over Ireland. Swift shows his criticism of colonialism and sympathy for the oppressed people in this way.

In Part IV, Gulliver arrives in an ideal country the Houyhnhnms. He is shocked at the fact the logical, honest and peaceful horse is the ruler, while yahoos that look like humans are animals. Yahoos are greedy, barbaric and aggressive, which hints that humans would be the same with animals if they continue degenerating. The horse reins the country in ration. Gulliver admires the place where there is no violence or oppression and wishes to stay there all along. But the Houyhnhnms find he looks like yahoos in appearance so as to drive him out. In the end, Gulliver returns to England and spends the rest of his life with horses.

Originally, *Gulliver's Travels* is designed to ridicule all false tastes in learning. But it comes to criticize the dirty society and ugly human nature. It gives a severe and full attack on the English government, society, religion, monarchism, parties, and colonialism, and expresses the author's wish of clean politics, humane and virtuous monarch. Human vices are revealed in the book, such as greed, hypocrisy, deceit, barbarity, grudge, etc. Swift bitterly mocks men in general by portraying the yahoos as savage animals with human appearance and characteristics, which demonstrates his disillusion towards his fellowmen. No wonder that the narrator would rather be accompanied by horses than people.

Besides strong irony, imagination adds to the clamor of the book as well. Swift is known for his lively imagination. He gives to these journeys an air of authenticity and realism. Facts and fiction are seamlessly combined by two ways. First, the story is based on actualities of England. Second, the detailed descriptions meet with rules of math, physics, medicines, etc. Therefore, it seems that everything is real though the author leads readers into a fantasy world. It wins children and adults' hearts for generations. Readers cannot help laughing while taking it seriously.

Selected Reading

Gulliver's Travels
(A Voyage to Lilliput)
Chapter 1

(The author gives some account of himself and family. His first inducements to travel. He is shipwrecked, and swims for his life. Gets safe on shore in the country of Lilliput; is made a prisoner, and carried up the country.)

It would not be proper, for some reasons, to trouble the reader with the particulars of our adventures in those seas; let it suffice to inform him, that in our passage from thence to the East Indies, we were driven by a violent storm to the north-west of Van Diemen's Land. By an observation, we found ourselves in the latitude of 30 degrees 2 minutes south. Twelve of our crew were dead by immoderate labor and ill food; the rest were in a very weak condition. On the 5th of November, which was the beginning of summer in those parts, the weather being very hazy, the seamen spied a rock within half a cable's length[1] of the ship; but the wind was so strong, that we were driven directly upon it, and immediately split. Six of the crew, of whom I was one, having let down the boat into the sea, made a shift[2] to get clear of the ship and the rock. We rowed, by my computation, about three leagues, till we were able to work no longer, being already spent with labor while we were in the ship. We therefore trusted ourselves to the mercy of the waves, and in about half an hour the boat was overset by a sudden flurry from the north. What became of my companions in the boat, as well as of those who escaped on the rock, or were left in the vessel, I cannot tell; but conclude they were all lost. For my own part, I swam as fortune directed me, and was pushed forward by wind and tide. I often let my legs drop, and could feel no bottom; but when I was almost gone, and able to struggle no longer, I found myself within my depth; and by this time the storm was much abated. The declivity was so small, that I walked near a mile before I got to the shore, which I conjectured was about eight o'clock in the evening. I then advanced forward near half a mile, but could not discover any sign of houses or inhabitants; at least I was in so weak a condition, that I did not observe them. I was extremely tired, and with that, and the heat of the weather, and about half a pint of brandy that I drank as I left the ship, I found myself much inclined to sleep. I lay down on the grass, which was very short and soft, where I slept sounder than ever I remembered to have done in my life, and, as I reckoned, about nine hours; for when I awaked, it was just day-light. I attempted to rise, but was not able to stir: for, as I happened to lie on my back, I found my arms and legs were strongly fastened on each side to the ground; and my hair, which was long and thick, tied down in the same manner. I likewise felt several slender ligatures across my body, from my arm-pits to my thighs. I could only look upwards; the sun began to grow hot, and the light offended my eyes. I heard a confused noise about me; but in the posture I lay, could see nothing except the sky. In a little time I felt something alive moving on my left leg, which advancing gently forward over my breast, came almost up to my chin; when, bending my eyes downwards as much as I could, I perceived it to be a human creature not six inches high, with a bow and arrow in his hands, and a quiver at his back. In the mean time, I felt at least forty more of the same kind (as I conjectured) following the first. I was in the utmost astonishment, and roared so loud, that they all ran back in a fright; and some of them, as I was afterwards told, were hurt with the falls they got by leaping from my sides upon the ground. However, they soon returned, and one of them, who ventured so far as to get a full sight of my face, lifting up his hands and eyes by way of admiration[3], cried out in a shrill but distinct voice, Hekinah Degul[4]: the others repeated the same words several times, but then I knew not what they meant. I lay all this while, as the reader may believe, in great uneasiness. At length, struggling to get loose, I had the fortune to break the strings, and wrench out the pegs that fastened my left arm to the ground; for, by lifting it up to my face, I discovered the methods they had taken to bind me, and at the same time with a violent pull, which gave me excessive pain, I a little loosened the strings that tied down my hair on the left side, so that I was just able to turn my head about two inches. But the creatures ran off a second time, before I could seize them; whereupon there was a great shout in a very shrill accent, and after it ceased I heard one of them cry aloud, Tolgo Phonac[5]; when in an instant I felt above a hundred arrows discharged on my left hand, which, pricked me like so many needles; and besides, they shot another flight into the air, as we do bombs[6] in Europe, whereof many, I suppose, fell on my body, (though I felt them not), and some on my face, which I immediately covered with my left hand. When this shower of arrows was over, I fell a groaning with grief and pain; and then striving again to get loose, they discharged another volley larger than the first, and some of them attempted with spears to stick me in the sides; but by good luck I had on a buff jerkin[7], which they could not pierce. I thought it the most prudent method to lie still, and my design was to continue so till night, when, my left hand being already loose, I could easily free myself: and as for the inhabitants, I had reason to believe I might be a match for the greatest army they could bring against me, if they were all of the same size with him that I saw. But fortune disposed otherwise of me. When the people observed I was quiet, they discharged no more arrows; but, by the noise I heard, I knew their numbers increased; and about four yards from me, over against my right ear, I heard a knocking for above an hour, like that of people at work; when turning my head that way, as well as the pegs and strings would permit me, I saw a stage erected about a foot and a half from the ground, capable of holding four of the inhabitants, with two or three ladders to mount it: from whence one of them, who seemed to be a person of quality, made me a long speech, whereof I understood not one syllable. But I should have mentioned, that before the principal person began his oration, he cried out three times, Langro Dehul San[8]: (these words and the former were afterwards repeated and explained to me); whereupon, immediately, about fifty of the inhabitants came and cut the strings that fastened the left side of my head, which gave me the liberty of turning it to the right, and of observing the person and gesture of him that was to speak.

He appeared to be of a middle age, and taller than any of the other three who attended him, whereof one was a page that held up his train, and seemed to be somewhat longer than my middle finger; the other two stood one on each side to support him. He acted every part of an orator, and I could observe many periods of threatening, and others of promises, pity, and kindness. I answered in a few words, but in the most submissive manner, lifting up my left hand, and both my eyes to the sun, as calling him for a witness; and being almost famished with hunger, having not eaten a morsel for some hours before I left the ship, I found the demands of nature so strong upon me, that I could not forbear showing my impatience (perhaps against the strict rules of decency) by putting my finger frequently to my mouth, to signify that I wanted food. The Hurgo (for so they call a great lord, as I afterwards learnt) understood me very well. He descended from the stage, and commanded that several ladders should be applied to my sides, on which above a hundred of the inhabitants mounted and walked towards my mouth, laden with baskets full of meat, which had been provided and sent thither by the king's orders, upon the first intelligence he received of me. I observed there was the flesh of several animals, but could not distinguish them by the taste. There were shoulders, legs, and loins, shaped like those of mutton, and very well dressed, but smaller than the wings of a lark. I ate them by two or three at a mouthful, and took three loaves at a time, about the bigness of musket bullets.

They supplied me as fast as they could, showing a thousand marks of wonder and astonishment at my bulk and appetite. I then made another sign, that I wanted drink. They found by my eating that a small quantity would not suffice me; and being a most ingenious people, they slung up, with great dexterity, one of their largest hogsheads, then rolled it towards my hand, and beat out the top; I drank it off at a draught, which I might well do, for it did not hold half a pint, and tasted like a small wine of Burgundy, but much more delicious. They brought me a second hogshead, which I drank in the same manner, and made signs for more; but they had none to give me. When I had performed these wonders, they shouted for joy, and danced upon my breast, repeating several times as they did at first, Hekinah Degul. They made me a sign that I should throw down the two hogsheads, but first warning the people below to stand out of the way, crying aloud, Borach Mivola[9]; and when they saw the vessels in the air, there was a universal shout of Hekinah Degul. I confess I was often tempted, while they were passing backwards and forwards on my body, to seize forty or fifty of the first that came in my reach, and dash them against the ground. But the remembrance of what I had felt, which probably might not be the worst they could do, and the promise of honour I made them, for so I interpreted my submissive behaviour, soon drove out these imaginations. Besides, I now considered myself as bound by the laws of hospitality, to a people who had treated me with so much expense and magnificence. However, in my thoughts I could not sufficiently wonder at the intrepidity of these diminutive mortals, who durst venture to mount and walk upon my body, while one of my hands was at liberty, without trembling at the very sight of so prodigious a creature as I must appear to them. After some time, when they observed that I made no more demands for meat, there appeared before me a person of high rank from his imperial majesty. His Excellency, having mounted on the small of my right leg, advanced forwards up to my face, with about a dozen of his retinue; and producing his credentials under the signet royal, which he applied close to my eyes, spoke about ten minutes without any signs of anger, but with a kind of determinate resolution, often pointing forwards, which, as I afterwards found, was towards the capital city, about half a mile distant; whither it was agreed by his majesty in council that I must be conveyed. I answered in few words, but to no purpose, and made a sign with my hand that was loose, putting it to the other (but over his Excellency's head for fear of hurting him or his train) and then to my own head and body, to signify that I desired my liberty. It appeared that he understood me well enough, for he shook his head by way of disapprobation, and held his hand in a posture to show that I must be carried as a prisoner. However, he made other signs to let me understand that I should have meat and drink enough, and very good treatment. Whereupon I once more thought of attempting to break my bonds; but again, when I felt the smart of their arrows upon my face and hands, which were all in blisters, and many of the darts still sticking in them, and observing likewise that the number of my enemies increased, I gave tokens to let them know that they might do with me what they pleased. Upon this, the Hurgo and his train withdrew, with much civility and cheerful countenances. Soon after I heard a general shout, with frequent repetitions of the words Peplom Selan[10]; and I felt great numbers of people on my left side relaxing the cords to such a degree, that I was able to turn upon my right, and to ease myself with making water; which I very plentifully did, to the great astonishment of the people; who, conjecturing by my motion what I was going to do, immediately opened to the right and left on that side, to avoid the torrent, which fell with such noise and violence from me. But before this, they had daubed my face and both my hands with a sort of ointment, very pleasant to the smell, which, in a few minutes, removed all the smart of their arrows. These circumstances, added to the refreshment I had received by their victuals and drink, which were very nourishing, disposed me to sleep. I slept about eight hours, as I was afterwards assured; and it was no wonder, for the physicians, by the emperor's order, had mingled a sleepy potion in the hogsheads of wine.

It seems, that upon the first moment I was discovered sleeping on the ground, after my landing, the emperor had early notice of it by an express[11]; and determined in council, that I should be tied in the manner I have related, (which was done in the night while I slept;) that plenty of meat and drink should be sent to me, and a machine prepared to carry me to the capital city.

This resolution perhaps may appear very bold and dangerous, and I am confident would not be imitated by any prince in Europe on the like occasion. However, in my opinion, it was extremely prudent, as well as generous: for, supposing these people had endeavoured to kill me with their spears and arrows, while I was asleep, I should certainly have awaked with the first sense of smart, which might so far have roused my rage and strength, as to have enabled me to break the strings wherewith I was tied; after which, as they were not able to make resistance, so they could expect no mercy.

These people are most excellent mathematicians, and arrived to a great perfection in mechanics, by the countenance and encouragement of the emperor, who is a renowned patron of learning. This prince has several machines fixed on wheels, for the carriage of trees and other great weights. He often builds his largest men of war, whereof some are nine feet long, in the woods where the timber grows, and has them carried on these engines three or four hundred yards to the sea. Five hundred carpenters and engineers were immediately set at work to prepare the greatest engine they had. It was a frame of wood raised three inches from the ground, about seven feet long, and four wide, moving upon twenty-two wheels. The shout I heard was upon the arrival of this engine, which, it seems, set out in four hours after my landing. It was brought parallel to me, as I lay. But the principal difficulty was to raise and place me in this vehicle. Eighty poles, each of one foot high, were erected for this purpose, and very strong cords, of the bigness of packthread, were fastened by hooks to many bandages, which the workmen had girt round my neck, my hands, my body, and my legs. Nine hundred of the strongest men were employed to draw up these cords, by many pulleys fastened on the poles; and thus, in less than three hours, I was raised and slung into the engine, and there tied fast. All this I was told; for, while the operation was performing, I lay in a profound sleep, by the force of that soporiferous medicine infused into my liquor. Fifteen hundred of the emperor's largest horses, each about four inches and a half high, were employed to draw me towards the metropolis, which, as I said, was half a mile distant.

About four hours after we began our journey, I awaked by a very ridiculous accident; for the carriage being stopped a while, to adjust something that was out of order, two or three of the young natives had the curiosity to see how I looked when I was asleep; they climbed up into the engine, and advancing very softly to my face, one of them, an officer in the guards, put the sharp end of his half-pike[12] a good way up into my left nostril, which tickled my nose like a straw, and made me sneeze violently; whereupon they stole off unperceived, and it was three weeks before I knew the cause of my waking so suddenly. We made a long march the remaining part of the day, and, rested at night with five hundred guards on each side of me, half with torches, and half with bows and arrows, ready to shoot me if I should offer to stir. The next morning at sunrise we continued our march, and arrived within two hundred yards of the city gates about noon. The emperor, and all his court, came out to meet us; but his great officers would by no means suffer his majesty to endanger his person by mounting on my body.

At the place where the carriage stopped there stood an ancient temple, esteemed to be the largest in the whole kingdom; which, having been polluted some years before by an unnatural murder, was, according to the zeal of those people, looked upon as profane, and therefore had been applied to common use, and all the ornaments and furniture carried away. In this edifice it was determined I should lodge. The great gate fronting to the north was about four feet high, and almost two feet wide, through which I could easily creep. On each side of the gate was a small window, not above six inches from the ground: into that on the left side, the king's smith conveyed four-score and eleven chains, like those that hang to a lady's watch in Europe, and almost as large, which were locked to my left leg with six-and-thirty padlocks. Over against this temple, on the other side of the great highway, at twenty feet distance, there was a turret at least five feet high. Here the emperor ascended, with many principal lords of his court, to have an opportunity of viewing me, as I was told, for I could not see them. It was reckoned that above a hundred thousand inhabitants came out of the town upon the same errand; and, in spite of my guards, I believe there could not be fewer than ten thousand at several times, who mounted my body by the help of ladders. But a proclamation was soon issued, to forbid it upon pain of death. When the workmen found it was impossible for me to break loose, they cut all the strings that bound me; whereupon I rose up, with as melancholy a disposition as ever I had in my life. But the noise and astonishment of the people, at seeing me rise and walk, are not to be expressed. The chains that held my left leg were about two yards long, and gave me not only the liberty of walking backwards and forwards in a semicircle, but, being fixed within four inches of the gate, allowed me to creep in, and lie at my full length in the temple.

Notes

1. **a cable's length:** 600 feet
2. **made a shift:** managed with difficulty
3. **admiration:** surprise
4. **Hekinah Degul:** oh, what a mouth he has!
5. **Tolgo Phonac:** come, let's kill him.
6. **bombs:** shells
7. **a buff jerkin:** a tight leather jacket
8. **Langro Dehul San:** run from the wild man!
9. **Borach Mivola:** the drunkard is going to smash his cup.
10. **Peplom Selan:** flee from the rain!
11. **express:** special messenger
12. **half-pike:** short pike carried by infantry officers

Questions for Study and Discussion

1. How are Gulliver's characteristics presented?
2. In what aspects does Lilliput resemble England?
3. Why does Swift narrate trivial things? What is the effect of the narration?
4. What is the social significance of *Gulliver's Travels*?

Thomas Gray (1716–1771)

Life and Major Works

Thomas Gray, labeled as "Graveyard poet", was born in Cornhill, London on the 26th of December 1716. His mother, Dorothy Gray, ran a millinery shop in Cornhill with her sister Mary. His father, Philip Gray, was a money-scrivener, but he was rude and selfish. In 1735, his wife managed to separate from him by taking abortion. Thomas Gray was raised and educated by this "careful, tender mother", as he called her. In 1727, he entered Eton at the expense of his mother and was under the care and education of his mother's brother, William Antrobus, one of the assistant masters at Eton.

At Eton, Thomas Gray formed friendship with Horace Walpole and Richard West, both of whom deeply influenced Thomas Gray in different ways. Horace Walpole wrote a famous Gothic novel *The Old Castle of Otranto* (1764) and created Strawberry Hill Press on which he later published

Thomas Gray

The Progress of Poetry and The Bard, an impassioned summary of English history. Being company with Horace Walpole was important to Thomas Gray's literary career. Richard West's early death indulged Gray in deep grief for years which led to his creation of some melancholy poems. In 1734, Thomas Gray was matriculated at Peterhouse, Cambridge, and Horace Walpole at King's, Cambridge, while Richard West at Christchurch, Oxford. During his first period at Cambridge, Thomas Gray leant Italian and translated some poems of Dante and Tasso. In 1738, he abandoned his degree course for some uncertain reasons. One of the possible explanations was that he accompanied Horace Walpole in some London social activities. Next year, the two friends started a three-year European tour.

Thomas Gray came back London in September, 1741. He lingered more than one year in London. During this period, Gray sent his "Ode on the Spring" to Richard West. West's death shortly afterwards was a shattering blow to Gray. The loss prompted Gray's "Sonnet on the Death of West". Possibly at that time Gray began to sketch his masterpiece "Elegy Written on a Country Churchyard" but completed eight years later, 1750. Thomas Gray returned to Cambridge in 1742. From then on, he seldom left Cambridge except for some occasional visits to London and some summer vacations to the Lake District or to Scotland. He attained his Bachelor Degree in law in 1743 but never tried to be a lawyer all his life. At his young age, he had acquired his reputation in his knowledge in English Medievalism. In 1768, he was assigned as professor of Modern History and Language at Cambridge but never gave a lecture to students. Although viewed as one of the most learned person of his time, he didn't seek fame or wealth but preferred to live a silent and uneventful studious life. In 1757, when offered the poet laureateship, he refused it. On July 30, 1771, Thomas Gray died of gout in his rooms at Pembroke college, and was buried beside his beloved mother in the small churchyard of Stoke Poges.

In contrast to other professional poets, Thomas Gray was not so prolific. He committed himself to the perfection of phrase and form. He, therefore, wrote slowly and carefully. It took him eight years to fulfill his masterpiece "Elegy Written on a Country Churchyard" until its publication in 1751. This poem soon established his fame as the leader of the sentimental poets. His other poems are also exquisite but probably not so popular. The year 1742 was extraordinarily fruitful in Gray's literary creation. He wrote "Ode on the Spring". "Ode on a Distant Prospect of Eton College" and "Hymn to Adversity" are probably regarded as the most faultless of Gray's poems. He wrote likewise some incomplete works, including a Latin Poem, "De Principiis Cogitandi", "Hymn to Ignorance" in which he contemplates his return to the university and a tragedy *Agrippina*. The year 1747 saw only "Ode on Walpole's cat". In 1748, he made an attempt on a didactic poem, "The Alliance of Education and Government", the fragments of which have many excellent lines. In 1752 he had almost completed "The Progress of Poesy", and "The Bard", which were published in 1757 as the first fruits of Walpole's Strawberry Hill Press. Gray was fond of ballad poetry and used to study Scandinavian literature. As a result, he translated two "Norse Odes" in 1761, "The Descent of Odin" and "The Fatal Sisters". He wrote in 1769 the "Installation Ode" about the appointment of Grafton as chancellor of the university.

Brief Introduction and Appreciation

Regarded as Thomas Gray's best and representative work of Sentimentalism, "Elegy Written in a Country Churchyard" is remarkable in that it laments not the death of noble or well-known men but that of common people. The poet wanders in a country churchyard at dusk, which evokes his reflection on the nature of human life. Comparing the life of great people and that of common men, he considers it true that there are no differences between them in death. He goes further to wonder what these common people can achieve if they have chances. Among these lowly people resting in the churchyard, there might have some natural poets or politicians like Milton and Cromwell but their talents were simply never discovered or cultivated. The poet admires the poor and the unknown for their simple and honest lives but jeers at the great and the noble for their contempt for the poor.

The poem was composed at the end of the Neoclassical period and at the beginning of the Romantic period, and the poem has features related to both literary periods. On one hand, it possesses the ordered, balanced diction and rational sentiments of Neoclassical poetry. Although the poetic phrasing and distorted word order make it difficult to understand the poem, they also bestow the poem with an enchantment of its own. Gray employs end rhyme every two lines in a four-line stanza instead of the prevalent couplet in the 18th century. The change of style administers to the establishment of melancholy atmosphere in the poem. On the other hand, it has some evident romantic characteristics. First, to a large extent, external nature—the landscape, together with flowers and animals—became a persistent subject of poetry in romantic period instead of human beings in neoclassical period. Gray depicts real flowers in desolate desert and jewelries under the deep ocean (stanza 14) in a context full of abstract traits of human being, such as "Ambition" and "Grandeur". Such a leap of imagination is not inferior even to Keat's. Second, Gray adds some elements of old ballads to it. From stanza 24 to stanza 29, a melancholy and wandering young man who is in pursuit of something is portrayed by a villager objectively. A small story of old ballad appears in an elegy in which the poet expresses his subjective feelings about death. Such an image is typical of the romantic poetry, as written by Wordsworth, Shelly and Keat. In a word, the poem deserves its fame—one of the best English poems in the 18th century.

Selected Reading

Elegy[1] Written in a Country Churchyard

The curfew[2] tolls the knell of parting day[3],
    The lowing[4] herd winds slowly o'er the lea[5],
The ploughman homeward plods[6] his weary way,
    And leaves the world to darkness and to me.

Now fades the glimmering landscape on the sight,
    And all the air a solemn stillness holds,
Save[7] where the beetle wheels his droning flight[8],
    And drowsy tinklings lull the distant folds[9];

Save that from yonder ivy-mantled tower[10]
    The moping owl does to the moon complain
Of such[11] as, wandering near her secret bower[12],
    Molest[13] her ancient solitary reign.

Beneath those rugged[14] elms, that yew-tree's shade,
    Where heaves the turf in many a mouldering[15] heap,
Each in his narrow cell for ever laid,
    The rude[16] Forefathers of the hamlet[17] sleep.

The breezy call of incense-breathing morn[18],
    The swallow twittering from the straw-built shed,
The cock's shrill clarion[19], or the echoing horn[20],
    No more shall rouse them from their lowly bed[21].

For them no more the blazing hearth shall burn,
    Or busy housewife ply her evening care[22]:
No children run to lisp their sire's return[23],
    Or climb his knees the envied kiss to share,

Oft[24] did the harvest to their sickle yield,
    Their furrow oft the stubborn glebe[25] has broke;
How jocund[26] did they drive their team[27] afield!
    How bow'd the woods beneath their sturdy stroke!

Let not Ambition[28] mock their useful toil,
    Their homely joys, and destiny obscure;
Nor Grandeur[29] hear with a disdainful smile
    The short and simple annals[30] of the Poor.

The boast of heraldry[31], the pomp of power,
    And all that beauty, all that wealth e'er gave,
Awaits alike th' inevitable hour[32].
    The paths of glory lead but to the grave.

Nor you, ye Proud, impute to these the fault
    If Memory o'er their tomb no trophies[33] raise,
Where through the long-drawn aisle and fretted[34] vault
    The pealing anthem swells the note of praise.

Can storied urn[35] or animated[36] bust
    Back to its mansion call the fleeting breath?
Can Honour's voice provoke[37] the silent dust,
    Or Flattery soothe the dull cold ear of Death?

Perhaps in this neglected spot is laid
    Some heart once pregnant with celestial[38] fire;
Hands, that the rod of empire[39] might have sway'd,
    Or waked to ecstasy the living lyre[40]:

But Knowledge to their eyes her ample page,
    Rich with the spoils[41] of time, did ne'er unroll;
Chill Penury[42] repress'd their noble rage,
    And froze the genial[43] current of the soul.

Full many a gem of purest ray serene
    The dark unfathom'd caves of ocean bear:
Full many a flower is born to blush unseen,
    And waste its sweetness on the desert air.

Some village-Hampden[44], that with dauntless breast
    The little tyrant of his fields withstood,
Some mute inglorious[45] Milton[46] here may rest,
    Some Cromwell[47], guiltless of his country's blood.

Th' applause of list'ning senates to command[48],
  The threats of pain and ruin to despise,
To scatter plenty o'er a smiling land,
  And read their history in a nation's eyes,

Their lot[49] forbad: nor circumscribed alone
  Their growing virtues, but their crimes confined;
Forbad to wade through slaughter to a throne,
  And shut the gates of mercy on mankind,

The struggling pangs of conscious truth to hide,
  To quench the blushes of ingenuous shame,
Or heap the shrine of Luxury and Pride
  With incense kindled at the Muse's[50] flame.

Far from the madding crowd's ignoble strife,
  Their sober wishes never learn'd to stray;
Along the cool sequester'd vale of life
  They kept the noiseless tenour[51] of their way.

Yet e'en these bones from insult to protect
  Some frail memorial still erected nigh[52],
With uncouth[53] rhymes and shapeless sculpture deck'd[54],
  Implores the passing tribute of a sigh[55].

Their name, their years, spelt by th' unletter'd[56] Muse,
  The place of fame and elegy supply:
And many a holy text around she strews,
  That teach the rustic moralist to die[57].

For who, to dumb Forgetfulness a prey,
  This pleasing anxious being e'er resign'd[58],
Left the warm precincts of the cheerful day,
  Nor[59] cast one longing lingering look behind?

On some fond breast the parting soul relies,
  Some pious[60] drops the closing eye requires;
E'en from the tomb the voice of Nature cries,
  E'en in our ashes live their wonted[61] fires.

For thee[62], who, mindful of th' unhonour'd dead,
  Dost[63] in these lines their artless tale relate;
If chance, by lonely contemplation led,
  Some kindred spirit[64] shall inquire thy fate, —

Haply[65] some hoary-headed swain[66] may say,
  "Oft have we seen him at the peep of dawn[67]
Brushing with hasty steps the dews away,
  To meet the sun upon the upland lawn;

"There at the foot of yonder[68] nodding[69] beech
  That wreathes its old fantastic roots so high.
His listless length at noontide would he stretch,
  And pore upon the brook that babbles by.

"Hard by yon[70] wood, now smiling as in scorn,
  Muttering his wayward fancies he would rove[71];
Now drooping, woeful wan, like one forlorn,
  Or crazed with care, or cross'd in hopeless love.

"One morn I miss'd him on the custom'd[72] hill,
  Along the heath, and near his favourite tree;
Another[73] came; nor yet beside the rill,
  Nor up the lawn, nor at the wood was he;

"The next with dirges[75] due in sad array
  Slow through the church-way path we saw him borne[76],
Approach and read (for thou canst[77] read) the lay[78]
  Graved[79] on the stone beneath yon aged thorn[80]."

The Epitaph[81]

Here rests his head upon the lap of Earth
    A youth to Fortune and to Fame unknown.
Fair Science[82] frowned not on his humble birth,
    And Melancholy marked him for her own.

Large was his bounty, and his soul sincere,
    Heaven did a recompense as largely send:
He gave to Misery all he had, a tear,
    He gained from Heaven ('twas[83] all he wish'd) a friend.

No farther seek his merits to disclose[84],
    Or draw his frailties[85] from their dread abode[86]
(There they alike in trembling hope repose),
    The bosom of his Father and his God.

Notes

1. **elegy**: a poem written to lament the dead
2. **curfew**: the bell to tell that night is coming
3. **tolls the knell of parting day**: to indicate the day is coming to an end
4. **lowing**: mooing
5. **o'er the lea**: over the meadow
6. **plod**: walk along slowly and difficultly
7. **save**: except
8. **wheels his droning fight**: fly in circles while humming
9. **folds**: a fence or wall surrounded sheep for protection
10. **yonder ivy-mantled tower**: the distant clock tower of the church whose outside walls are covered with ivy.
11. **of such**: of the wanderer
12. **bower**: (old use) a woman's bedroom. Here, it refers to the owl's nest.
13. **molest**: disturb
14. **rugged**: rough and irregular
15. **mouldering**: decaying slowly and gradually
16. **rude**: uneducated

17. **hamlet**: village

18. **morn**: morning

19. **shrill clarion**: sharp cock's crow

20. **horn**: here refers to the hunter's horn

21. **lowly bed**: grave

22. **ply her evening care**: work at her evening housework

23. **lisp their sire's return**: welcome their father's return with murmuring sound

24. **oft**: often

25. **stubborn glebe**: hard soil

26. **jocund**: (literary) cheerful and happy

27. **team**: here refers to livestock

28. **Ambition**: an ambitious man

29. **Grandeur**: a magnificent people

30. **annals**: the whole lives

31. **heraldry**: noble

32. **th' inevitable hour**: the death time

33. **trophies**: places or something to show the achievements of the dead

34. **fretted**: cut into complicated patterns as decoration

35. **storied urn**: a urn to contain ash of the dead body with an epitaph inscribed on it

36. **animated**: visual

37. **provoke**: evoke

38. **celestial**: related to the heaven or sky

39. **rod of empire**: scepter or regalia, badge of authority

40. **lyre**: a musical instrument with strings across a U-shaped frame, used especially in ancient Greece

41. **spoils**: things gained through time

42. **Chill Penury**: unpleasant poverty

43. **genial**: cheerful and mild

44. **Hampden**: John Hampden (1594—1643), a parliamentarian who became famous through resisting the autocratic policies of Charles I.

45. **inglorious**: unknown

46. **Milton**: John Milton (1608—1674), a great English poet and revolutionist.

47. **Cromwell**: Oliver Cromwell (1599—1658), an English military and

political leader who helped make England a republic after English bourgeois revolution from 1642 to 1649 and then ruled as Lord Protector of the Commonwealth from 1653 to 1658.

48. **command**: to deserve and receive as due

49. **lot**: destiny

50. **Muse**: a goddess presiding over art or science

51. **tenour**: ancient form of tenor which means a continuous and unwavering course.

52. **nigh**: nearby

53. **uncouth**: unrefined

54. **deck'd**: decorated

55. **implore the passing tribute of a sigh**: beg passer-bys to give a sympathetic sigh.

56. **unlettered**: untaught

57. **teach the rustic moralist to die**: teach the village moralist how to die

58. **This pleasing anxious being e'er resign'd**: ever gave up this sweet bitter life

59. **Nor**: and did not

60. **pious**: sincere

61. **wonted**: (old use) usual

62. **For thee**: as for you, here you refers to the poet himself

63. **dost**: (old use) you do

64. **kindred spirit**: people like the poet

65. **haply**: (old use) perhaps; by chance

66. **hoary-headed swain**: a villager with white hair. Swain originally means a young country man who loves a girl.

67. **at the peep of dawn**: at the very beginning of the day when light first appears

68. **yonder**: (old use) used to tell someone which place or direction you mean

69. **nodding**: drooping

70. **yon**: yonder

71. **rove**: wander

72. **custom'd hill**: the hill where the poet was used to climb

73. **Another**: another morning

74. **The next**: the next day

75. **dirges**: funeral hymns

76. **borne**: here means (he was) carried in the coffin

77. **thou canst**: (obsolete) you can

78. **lay**: a short narrative poem

79. **graved**: inscribed

80. **thorn**: hawthorn

81. **epitaph**: A brief literary piece commemorating a deceased person.

82. **Fair Science**: knowledge

83. **'twas**: it was

84. **disclose**: praise

85. **frailty**: weakness in one's character

86. **dread abode**: dark place

Questions for Study and Discussion

1. What is elegy?

2. The poem's title implies that the poem was actually written in a country churchyard, not that it is an imagination of such a scene. Why is this claim important to any interpretation of the poem's meaning?

3. How does the pastoral environment affect the narrator's emotion?

4. The purpose of this poem is to memorialize and meditate on the memory of common people. What connections still exist between the living and the dead in the churchyard?

5. An elegy is generally about someone else, but the speaker put himself into this poem, too. How does he manage to make himself an object of meditation just as those buried in the churchyard?

6. According to the poem, what is Gray's opinion of high-born persons in contrast to the low-born?

7. What's your comment on "The paths of glory lead but to the grave" in stanza 9?

8. In your opinion, what's the function of the "epitaph"?

William Blake (1757—1827)

Life and Major Works

William Blake was born on 28 November, 1757, in London, England, the third son of James Blake, a hosier and haberdasher. In his early age, Blake had shown his talent for drawing. Therefore, at the age of 10, after being taught reading and writing by his mother for several years, he was sent to Henry Pars' drawing school. During that period, he began to have a try on poetry.

At the age of 14, Blake started a seven-year apprenticeship with James Basire of Great Queen Street, the official engraver to the Society of

William Blake

Antiquaries. He learned all the necessary tools of the trade for a living that were to make him a professional engraver at the end of the term. After two years, Basire began to send him out to create sketches and drawings of statues, paintings, and monuments, including those found in Gothic churches like Westminster Abbey. The intense study of Gothic art and architecture contributed to the formation of his artistic style and ideas. In 1778, Blake attended the Royal Academy under Sir Joshua Reynolds for a time and soon left because he found Reynolds's idea about arts conflicted with his own. In 1779, he started to make a living as an engraver, receiving commissions from publishers to illustrate books and engrave pictures made by other artists.

Two years later, in 1882, Blake married Catherine Boucher, the daughter of a market gardener, who turned out to be an ideal wife to a poor and unorthodox genius. Blake taught her to draw and paint and she assisted him devoutly. Their marriage was a lifelong happiness.

In 1800, Blake moved to Felpham, on the Sussex seacoast, supported financially by William Hayley, a rich poetaster, biographer, and amateur of arts.

In 1804, Blake returned to London and decided to live in his own way although it meant a life of misunderstanding, solitary and poverty. He used to set up a one-man exhibition in his brother's shop, which proved to be a failure.

He remained obscure for some years. Only in his 60s, did he finally gather around him some young devoted admirers. In his late years, he worked on a series of water colors for Dante Alighieri's *Divine Comedy* till the day of his death. William Blake died at home on 12 August, 1827. Blake was buried in an unmarked grave in the Non-Conformist Bunhill Fields in London, where Catherine was buried four years later. In 1957, a memorial to Blake and his wife was erected in Poet's Corner of Westminster Abbey, London.

William Blake started out to write poems at the age of 12. In 1783, he published his first work *Poetical Sketch*, containing his earliest poems about joy, laughter, love and harmony.

In 1789, Blake engraved and published his first important collection of poems *Song of Innocence*. The theme of the collection is that there are still innocence and sympathy in the world, even in difficulties and sufferings. Blake, breaking thoroughly with traditions of the 18th century, experimented with new poetic forms and techniques in the volume which his contemporaries never tried. In the same year, *The Book of Thel* appeared, one of Blake's first long narrative poems with the theme similar to that of *Song of Innocence*.

Song of Experience, published in 1794, serves as a contrast to *Song of Innocence*. A world full of misery, gloom, poverty, disease and war is described instead of the bright world of the latter. A large amount of poems in these two volumes bear the same title while the content and tone are at polar opposites, such as "Holy Thursday" and "The Chimney Sweeper". Some other poems can also find their counterparts in the other volume. For example, "Lamb" is matched with the "Tiger".

Between 1790 and 1793, Blake composed and later engraved *Marriage of Heaven and Hell,* his primary prose collection which marked his spiritual independence and maturity. The work was composed in the period of radical ferment and political conflict immediately after the French Revolution. Blake explores many relationships of conflicts in the work, such as good and evil, heaven and hell, knowledge and innocence, external reality and internal world. Blake claimed, "without contraries, there is no progression."

Other works finished around this time were *The French Revolution* (1791), *America: A Prophesy* (1793), *Europe: A Prophesy* (1794), *Visions of the Daughters of Albion* (1793), *The Book of Urizen* (1794), *The Book of Ahania* (1795), and *The Book of Los* (1795).

In his late years, he completed *The Four Zoas* (1803), *Milton:a Poem* (1804—1811), *Jerusalem: The Emanation of the Giant Albion* (1804—1820) and *The Gost of Abel* (1822).

William Blake is one of the most complicated and peculiar poets in British history of literature. His genius in poetry hadn't been recognized until the end of the 19th century found that not only a great engraver but also a prominent poet was ignored. In the 20th century, William Blake was especially admired by modern poets including T. S. Eliot.

Brief Introduction and Appreciation

Among the four poems quoted here, "London", "The Tyger", and "The Chimney Sweeper" were first published in William Blake's *Songs of Experience* in 1794. At that time, Britain was suffering from political and social unrest with the upheaval of French revolution across the strait. William Blake portrays in his poems vividly the miserable life of English lower classes at that time. He, meanwhile, shows his enthusiastic support to the French Revolution. Since Blake was an engraver as well as a poet, he had a strong ability of visualization. Whatever he imagined, he could see. Therefore, one of the striking features of his poetry is imagery. He is good at showing profound connotations in simple images, such as "the mind-forg'd manacles," "blood" and "plague" in "London".

"London" was published in *Songs of Experience* in 1794. The poem was published during the upheavals of the French Revolution, and the city of London was suffering political and social unrest, due to the obvious social and working inequalities of the time. The British government had responded to the French revolution by restricting freedom of speech and sending soldiers overseas. In the poem, Blake described the dark side of London in the 18th century. The streets and the Thames were dirty, and the people lived in a desperate poverty without hope and freedom. The Churches and the Royals who ran the country were responsible for the sufferings of the people. Blake created a dark, dull and tiring atmosphere in the poem which reflected his extreme disillusionment with what he saw in London.

The poem has four stanzas, with alternate lines rhyming **abab**. The first two stanzas point out that London is restricted by rules and regulations. The third stanza shows us that Church and Monarch are restricting the people of

London. The 4th stanza tells how the youth's sinful deeds will affect the next generation.

Repetition is the most striking feature of the poem, and it serves to emphasize the prevalence of the horrors the speaker describes. For example, in the first stanza, Blake used "charter'd" to reinforce the sense of stricture the speaker feels on entering the city and "mark" to reflect the suffocating atmosphere of the city. In the second stanza Blake repeatedly uses the word "every" and "cry" to symbolize the depression that hovers over the entire society and to emphasize the idea that every person in London is suffering.

Blake also uses capitalization as a means of emphasis. He capitalizes the words referring to a particular person or thing, such as "Man", "Infant", "Church", to stand them out.

"The Tyger" was published in 1794, as a part of *Songs of Experience*. It is obviously in contrast to "The Lamb" in *Songs of Innocence*. While "the Lamb", based on Blake's pastoral youth, symbolizes good, beauty and peace by describing a child's innocent confidence in a benevolent universe, "the Tyger" suggests evil and strength, grounded on the experience of the industrialized modernity. The poem reveals a knowledge that evil exists in the world and benevolence can sometimes disappear.

"The Tyger" contains a string of unanswered questions contributing to the central idea. In the first stanza, Blake begins with an exaggerating description of a terrible tiger in the night. Shortly after seeing the tiger in the forests, Blake asks what deity could have created it. The word "immortal" is used to indicate God. In the second stanza, the poet wonders where the tiger was made. "Distant deeps" and "skies" may refer to the places where the mortal can't reach. In the third stanza, the author asks again who could make such a frightening and strong animal. In the forth stanza, Blake asks questions about what kind of tools are used by God. Then, hammer, chain, furnace and anvil are mentioned which suggest that God is an ironsmith. In the fifth stanza, the poet raised two significant questions. One is whether God is satisfied with his creation. The other is whether God is responsible for the creation of both lamb and tiger. Why and how God make such two opposite animals at the same time? No answer is offered. Blake, here, puts forward an open question for readers to think about.

To understand the poem, the most important point is to know the exact symbolic meaning of "the tyger" and "the lamb" which, however, remains the hotbed of discussion. It is generally considered that "the Lamb" stands for naivety and benevolence but in the lack of transformation. "The Tyger" may bring panic and unrest but it nurtures the strength for creation and transformation. In a word, this poem sings the praises of creation. It is considered that Blake intended to dedicate this poem to the fire-raging French Revolution.

"The Chimney Sweeper" is the title of two poems of William Blake, published in *Songs of Innocence* in 1789 and *Songs of Experience* in 1794. In the 18th century, small boys sometimes about 4 or 5 years old, were employed to climb up the narrow chimney and clean them, collecting the soot in bags. Some of them, sold by their parents to the master sweepers, were miserably treated and often suffered from lung disease and physical deformity, and died in their very young ages.

Blake wrote these two poems to arouse public's attention to the terrible state of the chimney sweepers and to protest against such harm that society did to its children. Although the two poems bear the same title, they're different in many ways. The earlier poem was written in a young chimney sweeper's viewpoint. He recounts the hard life of and then a dream had by one of his fellows, Tom. Although sold to be a chimney sweeper by his father after his mother's death, Tom was consoled by his dream in which an angel rescues all the boys from coffins and takes them to a sunny meadow. It shows Blake's optimistic view of the future. The sound of the first poem is euphonious and flowing. "Boy", "joy", "run", and "sun"—these words flow softly and smoothly which adds to the airy and light feeling of the poem. In the second poem, an adult speaker encounters a child chimney sweeper abandoned in the snow while his parents are at church. Here, the child chimney sweeper is viewed as a representative rather than a specific figure. He is called "a little black thing" and his sweeping rags "the clothes of death" which shows Blake's pessimism about chimney sweep business. In contrast to the slight hope of the future offered in the first poem, Blake, in the second one, is extremely pessimistic towards the afterlife.

Selected Reading

London

I wander thro'[1] each charter'd[2] street,
Near where the charter'd Thames does flow,
And mark in every face I meet,
Marks of weakness, marks of woe[3].

In every cry of every Man,
In every Infant's cry of fear,
In every voice, in every ban[4],
The mind-forg'd manacles[5] I hear:

How the Chimney-sweeper's cry
Every blackning[6] church appalls,
And the hapless[7] soldier's sigh
Runs in blood down palace-walls.

But most, thro' midnight streets I hear
How the youthful Harlot's[8] curse
Blasts[9] the new-born Infant's tear,
And blights[10] with plagues[11] the Marriage hearse[12].

Notes

1. **thro'**: through
2. **charter'd**: chartered, given to public, but taken privately in some way
3. **woe**: (literary) great sadness
4. **ban**: prohibition
5. **mind-forg'd manacles**: mental restraints
6. **blackning**: the wall of the church blackened by the smoke from the chimney
7. **hapless**: unfortunate and miserable
8. **Harlot**: (old use) a prostitute
9. **blast**: to make something dry up and die
10. **blight**: destroy
11. **plagues**: here refers to venereal disease

12. **the Marriage hearse**: the marriage coach was turned into a funeral coffin.

The Tyger

Tyger! Tyger! burning bright
In the forests of the night,
What immortal hand or eye
Could frame thy fearful symmetry[1]?

In what distant deeps[2] or skies
Burnt the fire of thine eyes?
On what wings dare he aspire[3]?
What the hand dare seize the fire[4]?

And what shoulder, and what art,
Could twist the sinews[5] of thy heart?
And when thy heart began to beat,
What dread[6] hand? And what dread feet?

What the hammer? What the chain?
In what furnace was thy brain?
What the anvil[7]? What dread grasp
Dare its deadly terrors clasp?

When the stars threw down their spears,
And watered heaven with their tears[8],
Did he smile[9] his work to see?
Did he who made the Lamb[10] make thee?

Tyger! Tyger! burning bright
In the forests of the night,
What immortal hand or eye,
Dare frame thy fearful symmetry?

Notes

1. **symmetry**: well-proportioned body of the tiger

2. **deep**: sea

3. **aspire**: desire strongly

4. **seize the fire**: it may allude to Prometheus's stealing of fire.

5. **sinews**: a long strong piece of tissue in one's body that connects muscle to a bone

6. **dread**: strong enough to arouse fear

7. **anvil**: a heavy iron block on which pieces of metal are shaped by using a hammer

8. **when ... tears**: the spark made by the smith's hammering the heated metal, looks like shooting stars which are usually called by children angel's tears.

9. **smile**: it probably refers to the phrase in Genesis that "God saw that it was good" after each day's creation.

10. **lamb**: Blake wrote poem "Lamb" in *Songs of Innocence* which symbolizes peace and beauty. Here, "he" in this line refers to the God who's able to create both lamb and tiger.

The Chimney Sweeper

(from *Songs of Innocence*)

When my mother died I was very young,
And my father sold me while yet my tongue
Could scarcely cry " 'weep! 'weep! 'weep! 'weep![1]"
So your chimneys I sweep, & in soot I sleep.

There's little Tom Dacre, who cried when his head,
That curl'd like a lamb's back, was shav'd: so I said
"Hush, Tom! never mind it, for when your head's bare
You know that the soot cannot spoil your white hair."

And so he was quiet, & that very night,
As Tom was a-sleeping, he had such a sight!—
That thousands of sweepers, Dick, Joe, Ned, and Jack,
Were all of them lock'd up in coffins of black.

And by came an Angel who had a bright key,
And he open'd the coffins & set them all free;

Then down a green plain leaping, laughing, they run

And wash in a river, and shine in the Sun.

Then naked & white, all their bags left behind,

They rise upon clouds, and sport in the wind;

And the Angel told Tom, if he'd be a good boy,

He'd have God for his father, & never want joy.

And so Tom awoke; and we rose in the dark,

And got with our bags & our brushes to work.

Tho'[2] the morning was cold, Tom was happy & warm;

So if all[3] do their duty, they need not fear harm.

Notes

1. **'weep**: it means "sweep". Children can't pronounce it clearly when they are crying "sweep" in the streets. Here, it also can be viewed as a pun. "weep" describes children's misery.
2. **tho'**: though
3. **all**: it refers not only to the chimney-sweepers but also angels and gods. It shows children's hope that one day, God will come to their rescue.

The Chimney Sweeper

(from *Songs of Experience*)

A little black thing[1] among the snow:

Crying " 'weep, 'weep," in notes of woe!

Where are thy father & mother? say?

They are both gone up to the church to pray.

Because I was happy upon the heath[2],

And smil'd among the winters snow:

They cloth'd me in the clothes of death[3],

And taught me to sing the notes of woe.

And because I am happy & dance & sing[4],

They think they have done me no injury:
And are gone to praise God & his Priest & King
Who make up a heaven of our misery.

Notes

1. **a little black thing**: a little boy chimney sweeper who is blackened by smoke and dust in the chimney.
2. **heath**: an open and uncultivated land covered with grass, bushes, and other small plants.
3. **the clothes of death**: clothes in dark colors
4. **I am happy & dance & sing**: it may refer to an annual dance of London sweeps and milkmaids of May Day.

Questions for Study and Discussion

1. Blake is famous for his collections of poetry *Songs of Innocence* and *Songs of Experience*. What do "innocence" and "experience" stand for here?
2. How does the poet connect the soldier's sigh with the blood running down the wall of palace in "London"?
3. What is the poet's attitude towards the city of London?
4. Why does the poet mention "the Lamb" in "The Tyger?" What relationship can be found between "the Lamb" and "the Tyger"?
5. What is the symbolic meaning of the tiger? What does the poet want to express?
6. What's the answer to the question "Did he who made the Lamb make thee?" Why does the poet ask the question?
7. What's the difference between "The Chimney Sweeper" from *Songs of Innocence* and that from *Songs of Experience*? What makes the child narrator interpret his situation so differently?
8. What relationship is between the child narrator and little Tom Dacre? What's the meaning of Tom's dream?
9. Why the child chimney sweeper uses the present tense in the last stanza of the second "The Chimney Sweeper"? What significance can be inferred from it?

Robert Burns (1759–1796)

Life and Major Works

Robert Burns was born into a peasant's home in Alloway, South Ayreshire, Scotland on 25th January, 1759. He was the eldest of his parents' seven sons. His father, William Burns, was a moderately well-educated tenant farmer who worked very hard but failed to gain enough for the family because of the barren soil. Burns grew up in poverty and hardship. At the age of 16, he had already become his father's main assistant in farm work. Robert Burns had little formal education, for poverty deprived him of the chance to keep

Robert Burns

studying in school. He dropped out after a very short schooling. From then on, Burns was chiefly educated by his father, who taught his children reading, writing, arithmetic, geography and history and even compiled a book for them. Burns' interest was aroused by his mother in the Scottish songs, ballads, legends and proverbs with which he was familiar through self-teaching. He also did a lot of reading in English literature and the Bible and acquainted himself with the major English writers, such as Shakespeare, Milton, Dryden and Pope. In 1774, Burns composed his first poem "O, Once I Lov'd A Bonnie Lass".

In 1777, William Burns moved his family to a farm at Lochlea, near Tarbolton. The family became gradually acquainted with local community. In 1781, Burns became a Freemason and fell in love with Alison Begbie to whom he wrote four songs. The love affair ended fruitlessly. In the same year, Burns went to Irving to learn flax dressing for a short time and returned home soon after the flax shop was burnt down. In 1783, his father began to fight with his landlord legally and was upheld the next January. However, two weeks later, William Burns died. Robert and his brother Gilbert failed to keep the farm and therefore, they moved to a farm at Mossegiel, near Mauchline. During the summer of 1784, he came to know Jean Armour. Despite Armour's father's disapproval, they finally got married in 1788. Totally, his wife bore him nine children but only three of them survived infancy.

In 1786, he met Mary Campbell to whom he dedicated his poems, "The Highland Lassie O, Highland Mary" and "To Mary in Heaven". He was 27 years old at that time and he decided to seek chance in Jamaica, where he planned to be a bookkeeper. In order to raise enough money for the passage, he published in July of that year his first poetry collection, *Poems, Chiefly in the Scottish Dialect* which turned out to be an immediate success. Six hundred copies at the price of 3 shillings were sold out for less than two months. Some critics in Edinburgh sang highly of his poems and advised a second edition. Burns, therefore, gave up his idea to emigrate to Jamaica. In the winter of 1786, he was invited to Edinburgh to prepare a revised edition. During his stay in Edinburgh, he encountered and made life-long friendships with Lord Glencairn and Frances Anna Dunlop who sponsored him occasionally later, and with whom he exchanged letters until his death.

In the winter of 1787, he went to Edinburgh again and encountered James Johnson, a music engraver and seller who shared with Burns the same interest in Scottish songs and resolution to preserve them. They co-worked enthusiastically for the project. As a result, the first volume of *The Scots Musical Museum* was published in the same year which included three songs of Burns. The final volume appeared in 1803. By and large, Burns contributed about 200 original and adapted songs to the whole collection of 600 songs.

In 1788, he came back to Ayrshire, married to Jean Armour and leased a farm of Elliland near Dumfries. In 1789, he was appointed as exciseman with a salary of £50 a year and finally he abandoned the farm in 1791. He was in the golden time of writing. In the November of 1790, he produced *Tam O' Shanter*. During that period, he composed more than 100 songs for George Thomson's *A Select Collection of Original Scottish Airs for the Voice*. He also collected, revised and adapted Scottish folk songs. One of these collections is *The Merry Muses of Caledonia*. Many of Burns' best-known poems are songs based on old traditional Scottish songs, such as "Auld Lang Syne", "A Red, Red Rose" and "The Battle of Sherramuir".

Arduous labor and undernourishment in his youth had reduced his health to a weak condition. His long-standing rheumatic heart condition was worsened by his bad habits of intemperance. All these factors contributed to his premature aging. In winter, 1795, he was infected bacterially after a dental extraction. On July 21, 1796 he died from bacterial endocarditis in Dumfries at the age of 37.

His first collection of his early poems, *Poems Chiefly in the Scottish Dialect* published in 1786, began to establish his fame as the "Heaven-taught Plowman". It contains "To a Mouse", "To a Mountain Daisy", "Man was Made to Mourn", and "Halloween". The majority of his works are collected in James Johnson's *The Scots Musical Museum* and George Thomson's *A Select Collection of Original Scottish Aires*, including those popular songs, "Auld Lang Syne", "Coming 'Thro' the Rye", "A Red, Red Rose", and "John Anderson, My Jo".

Robert Burns' fame as a poet lies primarily in his poems written in Scottish. The abundant Scottish literary heritage and Burns' life experience enabled him to portray sympathetically a harsh but attractive world by describing Scotch drinking habits, life manners and religion. He also tried English in composing his poems and added to his works classical English virtues of clearness and conciseness.

Robert Burns is acclaimed as the national poet of Scotland. As the most beloved figure in Scottish history and literature, his birthday, January 25, is observed annually as "Burns Night" festival with Burns Suppers served whose format has not changed yet since Burns' death in 1796. It generally includes an overview of the poet's life and works, a course of haggis which is eaten when "Address To a Haggis" is read, and an end of singing "Auld Lang Syne".

Brief Introduction and Appreciation

"My Heart's in the Highlands" shows Robert Burns' deep patriotic sentiments for Scotland. With passion, the poet describes the magnificent mountains, widespread forests, lively animals, running rivers, and deep valleys in his homeland. Wherever and whenever he goes and lives, his love for his birthplace and country will never disappear. The poem consists of four quatrains. The last quatrain is the same as the first. Both of them tell that although the narrator departs from his homeland, his heart and soul are left there, running together with deer and roe. The second and the third quatrains express further the poet's affection by saying goodbye to every concrete thing. Repetition is an indispensable ingredient of music. Undoubtedly, Robert Burns is good at employing the technique to fulfill his goal. The repetition of the first and last stanzas, the statement "My heart's in the Highlands", and the word "farewell", not only display thoroughly the narrator's love for his country but also serve as effective ways to move readers and listeners. The rhyme pattern is **aabb**.

"A Red, Red Rose" is one of Burns' most popular love songs in Scotch. The lyrics of the song are simple but effective. Readers tend to be affected by the pure and vehement love described in the song. In the first stanza, Robert Burns compared his love to a blooming flower and a sweet melody which indicate the precious beauty of his love. The second and third stanzas deal with the greatest limitation against love, "the sands o' life", i.e, time which can't wear off love. The last stanza is about the space. As long as love is real, no matter how distant the lovers are from each other, it will always be there. The song is written in four quatrains with alternating iambic tetrameter and trimeter lines. The rhyme of the poem follows the pattern **abab**.

Selected Readings

My Heart's in the Highlands[1]

My heart's in the Highlands, my heart is not here,
My heart's in the Highlands, a-chasing[2] the deer;
Chasing the wild-deer, and following the roe[3],
My heart's in the Highlands, wherever I go.

Farewell to the Highlands, farewell to the North,
The birth-place of Valour[4], the country of Worth;
Wherever I wander, wherever I rove[5],
The hills of the Highlands for ever I love.

Farewell to the mountains, high-cover'd with snow,
Farewell to the straths[6] and green valleys below;
Farewell to the forests and wild-hanging woods[7],
Farewell to the torrents and loud-pouring floods.

My heart's in the Highlands, my heart is not here,
My heart's in the Highlands, a-chasing the deer;
Chasing the wild-deer, and following the roe,

My heart's in the Highlands, wherever I go.

Notes

1. **the Highlands**: the northern area of Scotland where there are a lot of mountains
2. **a-chasing**: chasing. "a" is a kind of prefix used to mean "in a particular condition".
3. **roe**: roe deer—a small European or Asian deer living in forests
4. **Valour**: (literary) great courage
5. **rove**: travel from one place to another
6. **straths**: (Scotch) a big gully
7. **wild-hanging woods**: woods growing on cliffs in a natural way

A Red, Red Rose

O, my luve's[1] like a red, red rose
That's newly sprung in June;
O my luve's like the melodie[2]
That's sweetly played in tune[3].

As fair art thou, my bonny lass[4],
So deep in luve am I;
And I will luve thee still, my dear,
Till a' the seas gang dry[5].

Till a' the seas gang dry, my dear,
And the rocks melt wi'[6] the sun;
I will luve thee still, my dear,
While the sands[7] o' life shall run.

And fare thee weel[8], my only Luve,
And fare thee weel, a while[9]!
And I will come again, my Luve
Tho'[10] it were ten thousand mile.

Notes

1. **luve**: (Scotch) love
2. **melodie**: melody
3. **in tune**: in harmony
4. **bonnie lass**: (Scotch) a pretty young woman
5. **a' the seas gang dry**: all the seas go dry
6. **wi'**: with
7. **sands**: here refers to time for ancient people count time with the help of sandglass
8. **fare thee weel**: farewell to you
9. **a while**: for a while, for the time being
10. **Tho'**: though

Questions for Study and Discussion

1. What effective methods are employed by the poet to show his great affection towards his homeland in "My Heart's in the Highlands"?
2. How does the narrator express his love in the poem of "A Red, Red Rose"?

Part Five   The English Romanticism

(1798—1832)

I. Historical Background

Romanticism is a complex artistic, literary, and intellectual movement and a profound transition in imagination and sensibility, which originated in the second half of the 18th century in Western Europe, and gained momentum during the Industrial Revolution until about 1850. Romanticism is generally characterized by a highly imaginative and subjective approach, emotional intensity, and a dreamlike or visionary quality.

1. The English Industrial Revolution

The Industrial Revolution is a period in the late 18th and early 19th centuries when major changes in agriculture, manufacturing, and transportation produced a profound impact on the socioeconomic and cultural conditions in Britain. Several important factors contributed to this epochal change.

The vast influx of precious metals from the New World raised prices, stimulated industry, and fostered money economy in Britain. The rapid expansion of trade and the growing money economy sped up the development of new institutions of finance and credit. Capitalism appeared on a large scale, and a new type of commercial entrepreneur developed from the old class of merchant adventurers.

The *Enclosure Acts* ended arable farming in open fields and commons. Many open fields and commons were enclosed and deeded to one or more private owners, who would hold the possession and fruits of the land to the exclusion of all others. The process of enclosure was sometimes accompanied by force, resistance, and bloodshed. The rich landowners took advantage of the *Enclosure Acts* to appropriate public land for their own benefit. Thus, thousands of small farmers and tenants were forced to leave their land to make a living in industrial towns, which created a landless working class that provided the labor for the booming industries in England.

Another favorable and significant condition enabling Britain to pioneer the Industrial Revolution was that the country was abundant in three natural resources: water, iron and coal.

The increasing, wealthier population also demanded more and better goods, which stimulated the industrial output in Britain. The increase of the industrial output was made possible by the use of steam for power provided with the greatly improved engine (1769) of James Watt. Cotton textiles became the key industry in the early stage of the Industrial Revolution. John Kay's fly shuttle (1733), James Hargreaves's spinning jenny (1770), Richard Arkwright's water frame (1769), and Edmund Cartwright's power loom (1783) accelerated a massive increase in productivity. Chemical innovations and machines for making machines played an important part in various changes in the country.

Industrialization led to the rapid growth of various factories, which were mainly responsible for the rise of the modern cities, as rural workers in large numbers poured into the cities in search of employment in the factories. But in the beginning, the transition to industrialization met with strong opposition. Many unemployed workers turned their animosity towards the machines that had taken their jobs, and began destroying factories and machinery. These attackers became known as Luddites. But the British government took severe measures using the militia or army to suppress those rioters. Many of them were caught, tried and hanged, or sent in exile for life.

Because of shortage of manpower and limited opportunity for education, many children were forced to work in terrible conditions for much lower wages. In sharp contrast to the splendor of the homes of the rich owners, the poor workers lived in small and squalid houses in cramped streets. Contaminated water supply, poor toilet facilities and open filthy sewers caused the wide spread of some contagious diseases. Cholera, typhoid and smallpox were extremely common, as a result, the poor laboring people died in huge numbers. In addition, appalling working conditions contributed to frequent accidents befalling child and female workers.

The Industrial Revolution also facilitated the establishment of trade unions to promote the interests of the working people. The workers, organized by a trade union, could demand better terms by taking stride actions. The industrial capitalists had to make a choice by accepting the workers' demands or by suffering the heavy cost of the lost production. Consequently, there often arose sharp conflicts as well as compromises between the labor and the management.

2. The French Revolution

The French Revolution (1789—1799) is the politically polar opposite in France of the peaceful English Industrial Revolution. It began in 1789 with the *Declaration of the Rights of Man and Citizens*, and during a decade, the French governmental structure, previously an absolute monarchy with excessive feudal privileges for the nobility and the church, underwent radical changes based on Enlightenment principles of nationalism, citizenship, and inalienable rights. The changes were accompanied by violent turmoil, including the storming of Bastille and the executions and repression during the Reign of Terror, and a large-scale warfare involving many other European nations. Subsequent events that can be attributed to the Revolution include the Napoleonic Wars, the restoration of the monarchy, and two additional revolutions as modern France took shape.

The French Revolution triggered great terror and stubborn opposition in many British politicians who adopted a conservative philosophy. The political ideology of the conservative ruling class in Britain was represented by Edmund Burke (1729—1797), with his *Reflections on the French Revolution* published in 1790. In this pamphlet, Burke displayed his strong animosity towards the violent actions and radical changes, and the overthrow of the established privileges and the hereditary power of the monarchy and the nobility.

But the French Revolution also aroused great sympathy and enthusiasm in the English liberals and radicals, headed by Joseph Priestley (1733—1804), Thomas Paine (1737—1809), and William Godwin (1756—1836). In their writings (Priestley's *Letter to Burke*, Paine's *The Rights of Man* and Godwin's

An Enquiry Concerning the Principles of Political Justice), these liberal and radical writers hailed and supported the French cause with vigor, and argued for the rights of the people to fight against tyranny and to overthrow any government of oppression. In the meantime, Mary Wollstonecraft (1759—1797), a female British writer and philosopher, and now heralded as the first English feminist, wrote *A Vindication of the Rights of Woman* (1792) in her positive response to the French Revolution. In this classical feminist work, Wollstonecraft demanded equal rights and opportunities for women.

Frightened by the possible introduction of radical social and political changes from France into Britain, the English government suspended civil rights in 1792 and began actively prosecuting individuals for sedition. Anyone who advocated even minor political reform would be thrown in prison. In 1795, The Parliament enacted a law permitting the government to imprison without trial anyone who criticized its policies. At the same time, the English government, together with other European nations, waged wars against France till the fall of Napoleon in 1815.

II. Literary Review

1. The English Romanticism

The English Romantic period is conventionally defined as covering a period from 1798 to 1832. The English Romantic Movement, as a literary and artistic movement that reacted against the restraint and universalism of the Enlightenment, emphasized strong emotions as a source of aesthetic experience, and sang highly of such emotions as awe, horror, and trepidation as experienced in confronting the sublimity in untamed nature. It aimed at elevating folk arts and customs to a very high position. And it argued for a natural understanding of human activities as conditioned by nature in the form of language, custom and usage. The Romantics celebrated spontaneity, imagination, subjectivity, and the purity of nature. They cultivated an increasing democratic feeling, a breaking away from the interest in artificial social life and a conviction that every human being is worthy of respect. Notable English Romantic writers include William Wordsworth, Samuel Taylor Coleridge, Robert Southey, George Gordon Byron, Percy Bysshe

Shelley, John Keats and Jane Austen.

2. The English Romantic Poetry

In the Romantic poetry, the writers appreciated the beauty of nature, valued senses over intellect, and exalted emotion over reason. They were often preoccupied with the geniuses, the heroes, and the exceptional figures, with their primary concern about the passions and inner struggles of these characters. Their poetic works demonstrated their new, distinctive perspectives on life and society. In their writings, they preferred creative spirit to formal rules and traditional techniques. They stressed the importance of imagination as a gateway to transcendent experience and spiritual truth. They showed an obsessive interest in folklore, ethnic or national culture, and medieval sources. They were fascinated with the exotic, the remote, the mysterious, the weird, the occult, the supernatural, the monstrous, the diseased, the satanic, and everything that creates wonder. Most important of all, they expressed an awareness of a deeper relationship with nature.

The early generation of the Romantic poets (also called the Lake Poets), are William Wordsworth, Samuel Taylor Coleridge and Robert Southey. The Lake Poets all lived in the Lake District of England at the turn of the 19th century. These early Romantic poets started a poetic revolution by introducing a new emotionalism and introspection. Their liberating aesthetic is expressed in the *Preface to the Lyrical Ballads* (1798), which was mostly written by Wordsworth, in collaboration with Coleridge. In *Lyrical Ballads*, Wordsworth and Coleridge declared their aesthetic ideal: romantic poetry should express, in genuine language, experience derived from human emotion and imagination, and the truest experience was to be found only in nature.

William Wordsworth with Samuel Taylor Coleridge, launched the English Romantic period with their joint effort, *Lyrical Ballads*. Wordsworth's *Preface* to the second edition (1800) of *Lyrical Ballads*, in which he described poetry as "the spontaneous overflow of powerful feelings", became the manifesto of the English Romantic movement in literature. Wordsworth started his autobiographical poem and also his masterpiece, *The Prelude*, and completed it in 1805. It is a "philosophical" poem in blank verse, in which Wordsworth expressed his systematic romantic theory.

Samuel Taylor Coleridge (1772—1834) is one of the founders of the

English Romantic Movement and one of the Lake Poets, best known for his poems "The Rime of the Ancient Mariner" (1798) and "Kubla Khan" (1816), as well as his major prose work *Biographia Literaria* (1817). In 1798, he and Wordsworth collaborated on a joint volume of poetry entitled *Lyrical Ballads*, which contains his famous poem "The Rime of the Ancient Mariner". Coleridge's poetry is marked for its unique beauty and power. His use of mysterious and demonic elements in his poems influenced other poets and writers of his time. His works helped to ignite the craze for Gothic romance in Britain.

Robert Southey (1774—1843), during his life time, enjoyed great popularity and reputation and was made Poet Laureate in 1813. Perhaps his most enduring contribution to literary history is his immortal classic work *The Story of the Three Bears* (1837), a notable children's bedtime story. Today, Southey is well-known for his friendships with Coleridge and Wordsworth and his short poems, notably "The Battle of Blenheim" (1798), "The Holly Tree" (1821), and the epic *Vision of Judgment* (1821). As a prose writer, now his fame rests upon biographies of Nelson (1813), Wesley (1820), Cromwell (1821) and Bunyan (1830), several histories, ecclesiastical writings, and translations from the French and Spanish.

The second generation of the Romantic poets includes George Gordon Byron, Percy Bysshe Shelley, and John Keats. As never before in literature, the younger Romantic poets spoke of themselves, of their joys and fears, of their melancholy and triumphs, of their passions and rebellions. The younger Romantics, as unrestrained radicals, often acted against society and rejected traditional mores and religious values.

George Gordon, Lord Byron is generally seen as the epitome of a unique personality in tragic revolt against society. His stormy personal life and his poems *Childe Harold's Pilgrimage* (1812) and *Don Juan* (1819—1824) reflected the image of a generous but egotistical aristocrat, who suffered uneven pathos and who opposed society with striking irony and cynicism. In his works, Byron created his "Byronic hero", a defiant, isolated, self-reliant and melancholy young man with stormy emotions, who shuns humanity and wanders through life weighted by a sense of guilt for mysterious sins of his past. Byron's influence on European poetry, music, novel, opera, and painting has been immense.

Percy Bysshe Shelley, is universally considered to be among the finest lyric poets of the English language. His works "Ozymandias" (1818), "Ode to the West Wind" (1819), "Men of England" (1819), *The Masque of Anarchy* (1819) and "To a Skylark" (1820) are most widely read among the English poetry. His poetry expresses his two main ideas: the external tyranny of rulers, customs, or superstitions is the main enemy, and inherent human goodness will, sooner or later, eliminate evil from the world and usher in an eternal reign of transcendent love. Shelley was admired and hailed as an idol by the next two or three generations of poets, among whom were Robert Browning, Alfred Tennyson, Dante Gabriel Rossetti, and Algernon Charles Swinburne. Karl Mark also poured praise on Shelley by saying "he was essentially a revolutionary and he would always have belonged to the vanguard of socialism."

John Keats (1795—1821) is universally regarded, along with Byron and Shelley, as one of the three great Romantic poets. Most of his major poems were written between his twenty-third and twenty-fourth years. In his poetry, Keats revealed his deep love for the wild nature and simple country life. His sensuous descriptions of the beauty of nature often resonated with deep philosophic questions.

3. The English Romantic Prose and Fiction

The Romantic period is also rich in literary criticism, other nonfictional prose and fiction. The English Industrial Revolution brought about major changes in agriculture, manufacturing, and transportation, which exerted a profound impact on the socioeconomic, cultural and living conditions in Britain. With education available to more and more people, there arose an increasing demand for reading materials. Thus, newspapers, magazines and periodicals were booming in great numbers. The most famous periodicals *Edinburgh Review*, *The Quarterly Review*, *Blackwood's Magazine*, and *London Magazine*, in which leading writers were published throughout the century, were major forums of controversy, political as well as literary.

Coleridge published an influential theory of literature in his *Biographia Literaria* in 1817. The work is long and seemingly loosely structured, and although there are autobiographical elements, it is not a simple and pure autobiography. Instead, it is a meditative work with numerous essays dealing with the philosophy of Immanuel Kant, Johann Gottlieb Fichte, and Friedrich Wilhelm Joseph von Schelling.

William Godwin (1756—1836) was a libertarian anarchist and utopian proponent of a natural, rational, secular society. In his major work *An Enquiry Concerning Political Justice, and Its Influence on General Virtue and Happiness* (1793), he speaks against the rights to own private property and marriage.

William Hazlitt (1778—1830), one of the foremost literary critics of the Romantic period, is famous for his lucid and brilliant essays, in both style and content. Hazlitt wrote with deep hatred for monarchy and aristocracy, and high praise for liberty and freedom. Many of Hazlitt's essays, without abstruse intellectual inquiry and rigid moral address, are like delightful conversation poems—witty, lucid, profound, and eagerly alive to the surfaces of the work of art he is appreciating.

Charles Lamb (1774—1834), best known for his *Essays of Elia* (1823) and for the children's book *Tales from Shakespeare*. Gave a vivid account of the real human life intermixed with joy and sorrow. Through his descriptions, we can see the best pictures of many interesting men and women of his age. His influence on the English essay form cannot be overestimated.

The two major novelists of the period are Jane Austen and Walter Scott.

Jane Austen is best known for her masterpiece *Pride and Prejudice* (1813). With deep insight, full grace, and mild irony, she wrote her works which are primarily concerned with the life of the well-to-do classes of her own "provincial" region and mainly focused on practical social issues, marriage and money in particular. The theme of her works is always love and matrimony. Desirable marriage seems to be the only ambition in life of almost all her characters.

Walter Scott (1771—1832), is now the acknowledged master of the historical novel and one of the most influential authors of modern times. The wonderful series of his Waverley novels suddenly changed all the past history. The past, which had appeared as a dreary region of dead heroes, became alive and interesting again in his works. The romantic elements such as vigor, freshness, rapid action and breezy out-of-door atmosphere seem all pervasive in his stories, which attracted and fascinated numerous readers who had previously known nothing about the delights of literature.

4. The Gothic Novel

The Gothic fiction began to flourish in the later part of the 18th century in the context of the Romantic period. In fact, the Gothic is a type of imitation medievalism with its scenes invariably set in the Middle Ages. The writer's intention is not to give an accurate account of medieval life, but to arouse terror in the reader through his description of various terrifying experiences with gloomy castles, dark graveyards, subterranean dungeons, secret passageways, flickering lamps, screams, moans, bloody hands, ghosts, somber villains, distressed and sentimental heroines, and supernatural mystery.

The Gothic novel was initiated by Horace Walpole (1717—1797), a politician and writer, who published *The Castle of Otranto* (1764) as the first Gothic horror novel, in which the ingredients are a haunted castle, a villain, mysterious deaths, supernatural happenings, a moaning ancestral portrait, a damsel in distress and in violent emotions of terror, anguish, and love. The work triggered a positive response, gained a wide popularity, and imitations followed in such numbers that the Gothic stories became the commonest genre of fiction in England for the next half century. It is noteworthy in this period that the three best Gothic novelists are all women: Ann Radcliffe, Mary Shelley, and Jane Austen.

Mary Shelley (1797—1851), daughter of the literary and radical parents William Godwin and Mary Wollstonecraft, and wife of the poet Percy Bysshe Shelley, is best known for the greatest Gothic novel *Frankenstein* (1818), which is also generally thought of as the first science fiction novel. Immediately after its publication, the novel became enormously successful. The work has ever since had an influence across literature and popular culture and spawned a completely new genre of horror stories and films.

William Wordsworth (1770—1850)

Life and Major Works

William Wordsworth, the representative poet of the early romanticism, known along with Coleridge and Southey as the "Lake Poets", was born on April 7, 1770, in Cockermouth, West Cumberland, in the Lake District of northwestern

England. His father, John, was a lawyer and rent collector for Lord Lonsdale. His mother Anne died in 1778 and was followed by his father six years later. The orphan was then put under the care of his uncles who sent him to school at Hawkshead near his birthplace. Here, the fascinating nature attracted young Wordsworth so much that he came to appreciate the serenity and its sedating power on the human soul.

William Wordsworth

From 1787 to 1791, Wordsworth studied at Cambridge. In the years between 1790 and 1792, he visited France twice and these two visits gave him insights into the social iniquities and aroused his sympathy for the poor and humble folk. He became a warm supporter of the French Revolution and even joined the Gerondists, i.e., the moderate republicans.

In 1795 Wordsworth received a legacy from a friend of his, which made him financially comfortable to lead a life as a poet. He then settled down in his native Lake District with his sister Dorothy.

At the same time, Wordsworth made acquaintance with Samuel Taylor Coleridge. In 1798, they anonymously published a volume of Romantic verse called *Lyrical Ballads*. Containing poems "materially different" from those currently written, the book brought with it a fresh breath of wind of change to English poetry and marked the break with the conventional poetical tradition of the 18th century, i.e., with classicism, and the beginning of the Romantic period in English poetry.

In the winter of 1798, Wordsworth, Dorothy and Coleridge went to Germany. In the following year the brother and the sister returned to England and lived at Grasmere in the northern Lake District. In 1802, he married his childhood friend Mary Hutchinson and continued to live a quiet life in the countryside to write poetry. In 1807 he published *Poems in Two Volumes*.

In 1813, he was appointed, through the influence of the Earl of Lonsdale, Stamp Distributor (revenue collector) in the county of Westmorland with a substantial annual income.

In the same year, he moved to Rydal Mount, near Grasmere and lived there for the rest of his life. In 1839, he was honoured with the honorary degree of the Doctor of Civil Law at Oxford University. In 1842 he received a government pension after resigning from his job as a stamp distributor and in the following year he succeeded Robert Southey (1774—1843) as Poet Laureate. Wordsworth died on April 23, 1850 at the age of eighty.

Wordsworth lived a long life and wrote a great many of poems. But his major poems were written in the last decade of the 18th century and the first quarter of the 19th century.

Of all his works, the collection of *Lyrical Ballads,* to which Wordsworth contributed the majority of poems, is a monumental work in English poetical history.

In the "Preface" to the master work, which is an expansion of a brief "advertisement" in the first edition of the book, Wordsworth sets forth his principles of poetry. Unlike the classicists who focus on reason, order and the old classical traditions in poetry writing, Wordsworth maintains that "all good poetry is the spontaneous overflow of powerful feeling" and it "takes its origin from emotion reflected in tranquility" by men of deep feeling and much thought. To Wordsworth, the function of poetry lies in its power to present an unexpected splendor to familiar and common things, to incidents and situations from common life just as a prism can give a ray of commonplace sunlight the manifold miracle of colour. Wordsworth's deliberate simplicity in language and his refusal to decorate in a pompous style the common life of the poor and the wretched people in the English countryside not only reflect his own poetical principles but also produce a kind of pure and profound poetry which no other poet has ever equaled.

The Prelude, considered by many critics as one of Wordsworth's most important works, is a long poem in 14 books. It was written between 1799 and 1805, but it was not published until 1850. In this autobiographical poem, Wordsworth honestly records his own mental experiences which cover his childhood and school time, his residence at Cambridge, his first impressions of London, his experiences in France during the Revolution, and his reaction to all this.

The Excursion, was first published in 1814. The chief character here is the Wanderer, a philosophical pedlar, who, together with other characters, talks about the Church and about the graves. Then the poem further discusses the spirit in the countryside and its effect on the humbler classes of society as well as the system of national education and Christian religion.

Wordsworth's poems written after 1814 have generally been overlooked by scholars and critics as much inferior to his earlier ones. Among these poems, the most outstanding and impressive one is "The Solitary Reaper".

Wordsworth's later group of poems includes his series of "Ecclesiastical Sonnets" which, composed of total 140 pieces, traces the development of the English church from its beginnings to the poet's time and deals according to chronology with the churchmen and kings as well as with religious events and rituals. In addition, Wordsworth wrote a number of poems in eulogy of the English aristocracy and the royal family after his acceptance of poet-laureateship.

As a world famous poet, Wordsworth, is most celebrated for his poetry of nature, for which his love is really boundless. To him, nature means more than mountains and rivers, flowers and birds. It has a moral value and its philosophical significance as well.

As a great poet of nature, Wordsworth is the first to find words for the most elementary sensations of man face to face with nature. These sensations are old and universal, but once expressed in his poetry, they become charmingly new and beautiful. His deep love for nature can be found in such short lyrics as "Lines Written in Early Spring", "To the Cuckoo", "I Wandered Lonely as a Cloud", "My Heart Leaps Up", "Intimations of Immortality", and "Lines Composed a Few Miles Above Tintern Abbey".

Actually, Wordsworth is a master-hand not only in describing nature, but in searching and revealing the feelings of the common people, even children. The themes of many of his poems are drawn from rural life, and his characters belong to the lower classes in the English countryside. This derives from his intimate acquaintance with rustic life and from his belief that in rural conditions where people enjoy constant association with nature, man's elementary feelings can find a better soil than in urban life. Among a multitude of works of this kind, such poems as "The Solitary Reaper", "We Are Seven", "Michael", "The Ruined Cottage", "Simon Lee", and "The Old Cumberland Beggar" are most famous. Besides, his "Lucy" poems are also well liked. They are a series of short pathetic lyrics on the theme of harmony between humanity and nature.

Throughout Wordsworth's life, the most important contribution he has made is that he has not only started the modern poetry, the poetry of the growing inner self, but also changed the course of English poetry by using ordinary speech of the language and by advocating a return to nature.

Brief Introduction and Appreciation

Wordsworth was at his best in descriptions of mountains and rivers, flowers and birds, children and peasants, and reminiscences of his own childhood and youth. He frequently sang of birds and plants with much rapture and he also wrote lyrics to exalt nature as an important source of his inspiration. Besides, he paid close attention to common life which he thought was the subject of literary interest, so the joys and sorrows of the common people could also be his poetical themes.

For brief introduction and appreciation, here we choose the following 4 poems "She Dwelt Among the Untrodden Ways", "I Travelled Among Unknown Men", "I Wondered Lonely as a Cloud", and "The Solitary Reaper".

"She Dwelt Among the Untrodden Ways" is probably the best known of Wordsworth's five "Lucy" poems. The identity of "Lucy" is a mystery. No matter who Lucy is, the poet expresses his ardent love for her and his intense grief over her death. The first stanza of the poem shows that Lucy lives in isolation beside a river and is appreciated by very few people. But in the poet's eyes, she is delicate as a half-hidden violet, shy but beautiful, and exquisite as a single star, innocent but pure. These two comparisons in the second stanza clearly show the poet's admiration for Lucy and this causes his personal grief in the last stanza over her death. Throughout the poem prevails a mysterious tone by the poet's using of "she" and "maid" to refer to Lucy and "untrodden way" to where she has resided. But what makes the lyric most impressive here is its mournful tone in the end: Lucy lives unknown and dies unnoticed. It seems that the world is indifferent to her, and with her death its life is not affected at all. This tone is reinforced with "oh" in the last two lines of "But she is in her grave, and, oh, / The difference to me." Here "oh", simple as it is, is profound in meaning to show the poet's deep sympathy and grief. In this way, the poet's lament for the loss of Lucy reverberates.

"I Wondered Lonely as a Cloud" is one of the loveliest and most famous poems in the Wordsworth canon. According to Dorothy, Wordsworth's sister, the poet was once drunken by the sight of a patch of daffodils when walking by the lake with her, and two years later he wrote this widely read poem. In the first two lines of the poem, the speaker compares himself to a cloud, which symbolizes his integration with the natural world. Coupled with the impressive reverse personification are other images such as the dancing flowers, the lake, the breeze and the continuous stars. All this is employed to show the harmony between things in nature, and between nature and the speaker. To him, daffodils are like dancers who are dancing gaily and the stars that are shining brightly in the sky. Such unexpected beauty and consistency of nature impress the speaker so much that he not only shows his exhilaration but also turns to contemplation of the scene which he has stored in his memory. More than that, he fully realizes at the end of the poem that the scene which he has experienced has now become his spiritual wealth which will please him and comfort him when he is lonely, bored or restless and that it has even stayed with him as an inspiration. In this way, the speaker shows his reflection of the philosophical depth of his mind under then enchantment of nature.

"The Solitary Reaper" is also one of Wordsworth's most famous lyrics. In this poem, he writes specifically about real human music in a beloved rustic setting. Here a girl who is reaping alone in the field is singing by herself. Although her plaintive song is incomprehensible to the chance listener, its tone and its fluid expressive beauty leave such strong and lasting impressions on him that he listens "motionless and still", even carrying the song in his heart long after he can no longer hear it.

Structurally speaking, the poem is really simple with the first stanza setting the scene, the second offering two bird comparisons for the music, the third wondering about the content of the songs, and the fourth describing the effect of the songs on the speaker. Linguistically, it is natural and unforced. But what is more important is that the final two lines of the poem ("Its music in my heart I bore / Long after it was heard no more") return its focus to the familiar theme of memory, and the soothing effect of beautiful memories on human thoughts and feelings.

Selected Reading

She Dwelt Among the Untrodden Ways[1]

She dwelt[2] among the untrodden ways[3]
Beside the springs of Dove[4],

A Maid whom there were none to praise
And very few to love;

A violet by a mossy stone
Half hidden from the eye!
—Fair as a star, when only one
Is shining in the sky.

She lived unknown, and few could know
When Lucy ceased to be[5];
But she is in her grave, and, oh,
The difference to me[6]!

Notes

1. This verse, written in ballad form by Wordsworth while in Germany in 1799, is taken from *Lyrical Ballads* (1800). It consists of three four-line stanzas with an alternation of four and three feet iambic meter. Its rhyme scheme is **abab**.
2. **dwelt**: lived
3. **the untrodden ways**: less traveled paths; regions where people seldom go
4. **Dove**: a name of a river in England
5. **cease to be**: no longer live; die
6. **The difference to me**: her death didn't make a difference in anyone's life except for the writer. It made a huge difference in his life.

I Wandered Lonely as a Cloud[1]

I wandered lonely as a cloud
That floats on high[2] o'er vales[3] and hills,
When all at once I saw a crowd,
A host, of golden daffodils;[4]
Beside the lake, beneath the trees,
Fluttering and dancing in the breeze.

Continuous[5] as the stars that shine
And twinkle on the milky way,

They stretched in never-ending line
Along the margin of a bay[6]:
Ten thousand saw I at a glance,
Tossing their heads in sprightly[7] dance.

The waves beside them danced; but they
Out-did[8] the sparkling waves in glee[9]:
A poet could not but be gay,
In such a jocund[10] company:
I gazed—and gazed—but little thought
What wealth the show to me had brought:

For oft[11], when on my couch[12] I lie
In vacant[13] or in pensive mood[14],
They flash upon that inward eye
Which is the bliss of solitude;[15]
And then my heart with pleasure fills,
And dances with the daffodils.

Notes

1. The poem contains four six-line stanzas with each line metered in iambic tetrameter. The rhyme scheme for each stanza is **ababcc**.
2. **on high**: in the sky
3. **vales**: valleys
4. **A host, of golden daffodils**: a large number of golden daffodils
5. **Continuous**: extending without break
6. **margin of a bay**: that part of the lake extending into the land
7. **sprightly**: lively; full of spirit and vitality
8. **Out-did**: did better; excelled
9. **glee**: great merriment
10. **jocund**: cheerful; joyful; merry
11. **oft**: often
12. **couch**: bed
13. **in vacant (mood)**: unoccupied with thought
14. **in pensive mood**: in meditation; contemplating

15. **They flash upon that inward eye / Which is the bliss of solitude**: When
    alone, the poet recalls the beautiful scene, which gives him great happiness.
    Inward eye: the soul; the depth of the heart.

The Solitary Reaper[1]

Behold[2] her, single in the field,
Yon[3] solitary Highland[4] Lass[5]!
Reaping and singing by herself;
Stop here, or gently pass!
Alone she cuts and binds the grain,
And sings a melancholy strain[6];
O listen! for the Vale profound[7]
Is overflowing with the sound.

No Nightingale did ever chaunt[8]
More welcome notes[9] to weary bands[10]
Of travellers in some shady haunt[11],
Among Arabian sands[12]:
A voice so thrilling[13] ne'er was heard
In spring-time from the Cuckoo-bird,
Breaking the silence of the seas
Among the farthest Hebrides[14].

Will no one tell me what she sings?—
Perhaps the plaintive numbers[15] flow
For old, unhappy, far-off things[16],
And battles long ago:
Or is it some more humble lay[17],
Familiar matter of to-day?
Some natural[18] sorrow, loss, or pain,
That has been, and may be again?

Whate'er the theme, the Maiden sang
As if her song could have no ending;
I saw her singing at her work,

And o'er the sickle bending[19]; —
I listened, motionless and still;
And, as I mounted up the hill,
The music in my heart I bore,
Long after it was heard no more.

Notes

1. The poem contains four eight-lined stanzas of tight iambic tetrameter. Each follows a rhyme scheme of **ababccdd** with the exception of the first and last stanzas where the "a" rhyme is off (field / self and sang / work).

2. **behold**: (old English) look (at); see with attention

3. **yon**: yonder, over there

4. **Highland**: belonging to the Highlands or the northern part of Scotland

5. **lass**: (Scottish) a girl or young woman who is not married

6. **a melancholy strain**: a sad tune

7. **Vale profound**: profound Vale. **Vale**: valley; **profound**: deep

8. **chaunt**: chant; sing

9. **welcome notes**: pleasing and pleasant songs

10. **bands**: groups

11. **shady haunt**: dark and horrible places

12. **Arabian sands**: the deserts in Arabia

13. **thrilling**: causing a surge of emotion or excitement

14. **Hebrides**: a group of islands off the northwestern coast of Scotland

15. **the plaintive numbers**: the mournful verses (referring to her song)

16. **things**: events

17. **humble lay**: a simple short lyrical or narrative poem meat to be sung

18. **natural**: ordinary; belonging to the natural course of things

19. **o'er the sickle bending**: bending over the sickle

Questions for Study and Discussion

1. In "She Dwelt Among the Untrodden Ways", how does the poet describe the beauty of the maid?

2. What is the theme of "I Wandered Lonely as a Cloud"? Why does the poet compare himself to a cloud at the beginning of the poem? What does the

poet compare the daffodils to in it? Why does the poet praise them? What is "the bliss of solitude" to the poet?

3. In "I Wandered Lonely as a Cloud", how does Wordsworth achieve the seemingly effortless effect of implying the unity of his consciousness with nature? Does this technique appear in the other selected poems? Some people say this poem is one of Wordsworth's choice bits of photography. Do you agree? Why?

4. In "The Solitary Reaper", what does the poet compare the girl's song to in Stanza Two? What effect does the girl's song leave on the poet? What is the most vivid impression of the reaper which the speaker carries away with him?

5. In the poem of "The Solitary Reaper", there are two comparisons in the second stanza. Is it possible to hear the song of the nightingale in the Arabian deserts or the cry of the cuckoo-bird in the Hebrides? If not, why did Wordsworth use these comparisons?

6. How does the poem of "The Solitary Reaper" illustrate Wordsworth's view of poetry writing?

George Gordon Byron (1788—1824)

Life and Major Works

George Gordon Byron, known as Lord Byron, is one of the most important poets in the Romantic Period in England. He was born clubfooted on the 22nd of January 1788, of an impoverished noble family. His father deserted his wealthy Scottish wife after squandering away her fortune. For some years mother and son lived in loneliness and poverty in Scotland. At the age of 10, he succeeded to the baronial title and inherited a large estate of his granduncle

George Gordon Byron

William upon the latter's death. After that, Byron came back to England.

He received his education at Harrow, one of the best English public schools. In 1805, he went to Cambridge, occupied with study of history and literature. While an undergraduate, Byron showed his talent for verse writing by publishing his first collection of poems entitled *Hours of Idleness* (1807), which deals with childish recollections and early friendship. The poems were widely praised but severely attacked by a critic from *Edinburgh Review*, a conservative magazine. Two years later, he replied to the attack by publishing *English Bards and Scotch Reviewers*, a bitter satire on the journal and its supporters, including almost all literary celebrities of the day, such as Wordsworth and Southey. Compared to the roar of a young lion, this counter-attack caused great shock in the upper classes.

Byron, after graduation from Cambridge, went on the grand tour of European Continent for nearly two years between 1809 and 1811. This tour which took Byron to Portugal, Spain, Albania, Greece and Turkey turned out to be fruitful.

After his return to England, Byron took his seat in the House of Lords and made his maiden speech on February 27, 1812, showing his sympathy for the Luddites and indignation at the "Frame-breakers Bill" which would induce capital punishment to the Luddites (destroyers of machines). Later in 1816 he again raised his voice in defense of the oppressed workers in his well-known "Song for the Luddites". All this evoked hatred for him on the part of the English ruling classes.

In 1815, Byron married Miss Milbank, but their marriage turned out to be unhappy, ending with Milbank's departure one year later. Byron had already been known for his numerous love affairs, and now he was regarded by the English society as immoral. So very soon his misfortune in the family life became a pretext for the English ruling classes to turn against him. The wholesale attack was so fierce that it was impossible for Byron to stay in his native country. On April 25, 1816, he set sail for the Continent, never to return.

In the years between 1812 and 1816 before his departure from England, Byron wrote a number of long verse-tales, usually called "Oriental Tales". They are *The Giaour* (1813), *The Bride of Abydos* (1813), *The Corsair* (1814), *Lara* (1814), *Parisina* (1816) and *The Siege of Corinth* (1816). During the same period, Byron also wrote a great number of lyrical pieces, among which *Hebrew Melodies* (1815) was the most famous.

After Byron left England, Switzerland was his first stop, where he made acquaintance with Shelley and wrote *The Prisoner of Chillon*. At the end of 1816, Byron went to Italy and lived there till 1823. During this period, he kept a close touch with Shelley until the latter's tragic death in 1822. At the same time, under the influence of his intimate friend Countess Guiciolli, Byron participated actively in the revolutionary work of the Carbonari, a secret patriotic organization aiming at the liberation of Italy from Austrian domination.

Unfortunately, the Carbonari uprising in 1821 was defeated. In 1823, he went to Greece and threw himself with intense energy into the Greek struggle for its national independence from Turkey. The next year, worn out with the ardours of the campaign, Byron caught rheumatic fever and died on April 19, 1824, at Missolonghi, and he was mourned as a national hero by the Greeks.

The last and the most fruitful period of Byron's literary career coincided with the last eight years of his life during his stay in Italy and his brief expedition to Greece. The year of 1818 witnessed his completion of *Childe Harold Pilgrimage* which contains four cantos in its entirety. His poetical works of this period included more verse dramas, verse tales and more political satires and his masterpiece *Don Juan*.

The creation of "Byronic heroes" in his "Oriental Tales" is one of Byron's great contributions to the world literature. In these narrative poems, with their locale set mostly in the Near East, all have an atmosphere of the exotic, filled with great details of the brightest descriptions. The typical "Byronic heroes", with fiery passions, unbending wills and inexhaustible energy, express the poet's own ideal of freedom.

Hebrew Melodies published in 1815 is one of Byron's most famous lyrical pieces. The short poems in this book actually reflect the poet's own age, revealing his personal feelings of indignation against and his dissatisfaction with the social system, and making a comparison between the people and events of ancient biblical days and those of his day in Europe.

Generally known as the best poem among Byron's earlier group of verse tales, *The Prisoner of Chillon* deals with the story of a Swiss patriot named Fran ois Bonnivard, who dedicates himself to fighting for the freedom of his native city Geneva in the 16th century.

Childe Harold Pilgrimage (1812—1818), is a long poem chiefly about the poet's observations and reflections on his extensive travels in Europe. *Childe Harold Pilgrimage* is a great work not only for its intertwined description of the poet's great enthusiasm for freedom revealed by his passionate utterances on the national liberation movements in different countries of Europe at that time, but also for its descriptive passages about wild nature, beautiful scenery, old ruins and great architectural wonders. Its poetic style varies a great deal as the poem proceeds, ranging from the sublime to bathos, and this variety in style fits right into the occasion every time, thus resulting in a poem of great power as well as subtlety, simple yet colourful.

Don Juan, written between 1818 and 1823, is Byron's last and generally considered to be the greatest of his works. This poem, a great comic epic about adventures, is based on a traditional Spanish legend of a great lover and seducer of women, but Byron's story is completely new and is different from the original with the exception of the hero's name and his Spanish origin.

Undoubtedly, Don Juan is the central figure around whom the threads of the story are woven, but his various adventures merely provide the framework for it. The more important is that these adventures present a panoramic view of different types of society in different parts of Europe. Byron himself calls this poem an "epic satire", "a satire on abuses of the present state of society." To him, almost all Don Juan is "real life, either my own, or from people I know." So we should say in this incomplete masterpiece, Byron displays his genius not only as a romanticist but also as a realist.

Brief Introduction and Appreciation

"Sonnet on Chillon" was one of Byron's narrative poems. The story was based on the events of the historical figure of Fran ois de Bonnivard (1496—1570), a Swiss patriot who was an active fighter for the liberation of his native city of Geneva from the control of Charles III, Duke of Savoy, and who was imprisoned without trial in the Castle of Chillon off the shore of the Lake of Geneva from 1530 to 1536. This sonnet, composed in memory of Bonnivard, was written in praise of the fighters of liberty in general, and particularly of those who remained true to the ideals of freedom even when persecuted severely by their oppressors.

"When We Two Are Parted" expresses the sorrow of a lad who is betrayed by his lover. Its gist is represented by the speaker's highly subjective perceptions and feelings during and after the splitting-up. At the moment of separation the speaker senses the woman's loss of affection as it is reflected by physical touching of her cheek and falls into a state of depression. The next step in the speaker's emotional downfall is taken on the "morning" after the separation. Here the poet employs some images such as "dew in the morning" and "chill" on his brow to indicate his low spirits. However, depression is only one aspect of his conflicting emotions. Through reactions and thoughts the speaker reveals his strong disappointment at his lover's breaking of solemn promises, his shame of himself when her name with light fame is mentioned in his presence and his sympathy for her when she is publicly put to shame. With these complicated emotions, the speaker then utter ironical doubt about the worth of the relationship as a whole or of the degree of his emotional involvement by using a rhetorical question "Why wert thou so dear?" At the time when the distance between the two lovers is gained, the speaker's pains and sufferings go on, for his grief cannot be expressed openly, but only "in silence" corresponding to the "secret" character of the love affair. Then the poem ends with the speaker's imagination of a potential meeting and his emotional uncertainty expressed in the question about the first moment of the encounter, i.e. "How should I greet thee?— / With silence and tears." In conclusion, this poem, from a first-person speaker's point of view, voices the emotional aftermath of a separation. With remarkable frankness, the speaker lays open a spectrum of ambivalent feelings, brooding over the loss of love, and over his general sorrow, and specific emotions such as grief, shame, hurt pride, disappointment, disdain, regret, hope and despair.

"She Walks in Beauty", chosen from *Hebrew Melodies* (1815), was written for Mrs. Wilmot Horton, Byron's beautiful cousin by marriage, whom he met for the first time on June 11, 1814 when he attended a party. Byron was so struck by her beauty that on returning home, he wrote this poem in a single night. In this poem, the description of the beauty of a woman is prominent. In the beginning, the image of darkness is given, but it brings together two opposing forces that are at work: the night with starring skies, or rather, darkness and brightness. As the night is often thought of in terms of irrationality and the day in terms of reason, neither of them but the meeting of the two extremes is pleasing. In the lady, the perfect combination of these two opposing forces is shown not only in her aspect, or appearance, but also in her eyes. In this case, the woman's eyes are more of an internal aspect of her than a mere physical feature. Actually, by emphasizing the unique feature of this woman to contain opposites in her, Byron here agrees with the concept that not only is there a struggle between the darkness and the light, but also in the woman. In the second stanza, the opposites are shown again with the description of her nameless elegance and raven tress (or shining dark hair). So once again, it is something internal as well as external that is so attractive about this woman. In the final stanza, the poet continues to describe the woman's physical features such as soft cheeks, her winning smile and the tints in her skin, but what the poet is really convinced is that this kind of physical beauty reflects a mind at peace and a heart whose love is innocent. In other words, her physical beauty attests to her morality. The whole poem, highly rhythmic with meaningful tones, is healthy in content and impressive with the imagery that makes abstract beauty concrete. "She Walks in Beauty", with its powerful description not only of a woman's physical beauty, but also her interior strengths, tells the reader that imagery can reflect an emotion and that an innocent and well-balanced person with dignity and steadiness will win admiration and really deserve it.

Selected Reading

Sonnet on Chillon[1]

Eternal Spirit of the chainless Mind![2]
    Brightest in dungeons, Liberty! thou art:
    For there thy habitation is the heart—
The heart which love of thee alone can bind[3];

And when thy sons[4] to fetters are consign'd[5]—
    To fetters, and the damp vault's dayless gloom[6],
    Their country conquers[7] with their martyrdom[8],
And Freedom's fame finds wings on every wind[9].

Chillon! thy prison is a holy place,
    And thy sad floor an altar—for't was trod[10],
    Until his very steps[11] have left a trace
Worn, as if thy cold pavement were a sod[12],

By Bornnivard! —May none those marks efface[13]!

For they appeal from tyranny to God[14].

Notes

1. This sonnet is essentially of the Italian type, with slight modifications in the riming pattern in the octave (**abba, acca, dedede**).
   Chillon: a castle on the shore of Lake Genève, Switzerland, where François de Bonnivard, was imprisoned
2. **Eternal Spirit of the chainless Mind**: here referring to Liberty. "The chainless Mind" suggests that the body can be chained, but not the mind
3. **heart which love of thee alone can bind**: which nothing but the love of liberty can confine or restrain
4. **thy sons**: sons of liberty, those who fight for liberty
5. **to fetters are consign'd**: are consigned to fetters, referring to the loss of freedom
6. **the damp vault's dayless gloom**: here referring to the prison's deep darkness which no daylight can penetrate through
7. **conquers**: wins liberation
8. **martyrdom**: here referring to the death for the cause of liberation
9. **Freedom's fame finds wings on every wind**: The spirit of Freedom spreads everywhere.
10. **'t was trod**: 't = it, referring to the floor of the prison
11. **his very steps**: "His" here refers to Bonnivard mentioned two lines below
12. **sod**: surface layer of ground containing a mat of grass and grass roots
13. **efface**: remove completely from recognition
14. **appeal from tyranny to God**: call on God in protest against tyranny

When We Two Are Parted[1]

When we two parted
    In silence and tears,
Half broken-hearted
    To sever[2] for years,
Pale grew thy cheek and cold,
    Colder thy kiss;
Truly that hour foretold
    Sorrow to this[3].

The dew of the morning
    Sunk chill on my brow—
It felt like the warning
    Of what I feel now.
Thy vows[4] are all broken,
    And light[5] is thy fame;
I hear thy name spoken,
    And share in its shame.

They name thee before me,
    A knell[6] to mine ear;
A shudder comes o'er me—
    Why wert thou so dear?
They know not I knew thee,
    Who knew thee too well—
Long, long shall I rue[7] thee
    Too deeply to tell.

In secret we met—
    In silence I grieve,
That thy heart could forget,
    Thy spirit deceive.
If I should meet thee
    After long years,
How should I greet thee?—
    With silence and tears.

Notes

1. The metrical movement of this poem is basically a combination of iambic and anapaestic feet, with a rhyme scheme **ababcdcd**.
2. **sever**: keep apart
3. **this**: this moment
4. **vows**: solemn pledges to do something (to love the other)
5. **light**: of small account

6. **knell**: (a metaphor here) a sound of a bell run slowly to announce a death or the end of something

7. **rue**: feel remorse for; feel sorry for

She Walks in Beauty[1]

She walks in beauty, like the night
    Of cloudless climes[2] and starry[3] skies;
And all that's best of dark and bright
    Meet in her aspect[4] and her eyes:
Thus mellowed[5] to that tender light
    Which heaven to gaudy day[6] denies.

One shade[7] the more, one ray[8] the less,
    Had half impaired[9] the nameless grace[10]
Which waves[11] in every raven tress[12],
    Or softly lightens o'er her face;
Where thoughts serenely sweet express[13]
    How pure, how dear their dwelling place[14].

And on that cheek, and o'er that brow,
    So soft, so calm, yet eloquent[15],
The smiles that win,[16] the tints that glow,[17]
    But[18] tell of days in goodness spent[19],
A mind at peace with all below[20],
    A heart whose love is innocent!

Notes

1. One of the lyrics in *Hebrew Melodies* (1815), it was written to be set to adaptations of traditional Jewish tunes by the young musician Isaac Nathan. The poem contains three stanzas of iambic tetrameter with a rhyme scheme of **ababab**.

2. **climes**: climate

3. **starry**: full of stars

4. **aspect**: countenance; appearance

5. **mellowed**: became rich, sweet and soft

6. **gaudy day**: brilliant fine day. **Gaudy**: too bright in colour

7. **shade**: darkness

8. **ray**: brightness

9. **Had half impaired**: Would have half impaired

10. **nameless grace**: indescribable elegance

11. **waves**: (metaphorical use) move or swing back and forth

12. **raven tress**: shiny black hair

13. **thoughts serenely sweet express**: serene and sweet thoughts are reflected

14. **their dwelling place**: the heart

15. **eloquent**: expressive; effectively expressing

16. **The smiles that win**: the smiles that capture people's attention

17. **the tints that glow**: the glowing delicate colour

18. **But**: Simply

19. **tell of days in goodness spent**: tell of days spent in goodness. The line shows that she has been living a life of purity and moral excellence.

20. **all below**: everything in the world; the whole world. The whole line implies that she his kind towards everything below the heaven. The whole line has the implied meaning of her great kindness.

Questions for Study and Discussion

1. What is the rhyme scheme of "Sonnet on Chillon"? What do you think of the poet's attitude toward the fight for freedom? Do you think this sonnet is typical of Byron's political poems? Why or why not?

2. What is the theme of the poem of "When We Two Are Parted"? What is the tone of this poem?

3. In the poem of "When We Two Are Parted", Byron uses some images to express his mood and emotion, can you cite some examples? What kind of emotion is implied in the poem besides sorrow?

4. In "She Walks in Beauty", to make abstract beauty concrete, the poet employed a variety of figures of speech, such as simile, antithesis, and parallelism. Try to identify them and explain the effects they achieve.

5. Why is the lady compared to night in the poem of "She Walks in Beauty"? What particular aspects of the night are singled out in the comparison?

6. "She Dwelt Among The Untrodden Ways" is one of Wordsworth's famous Lucy poems and "She Walks in Beauty" by Byron is also a love poem from

Hebrew Songs. Compare the two poems and find the similarities and differences between them.

Percy Bysshe Shelley (1792—1822)

Life and Major Works

Percy Bysshe Shelley, one of the major contributors to English Romantic poetry, was born on 4 August 1792, in Horsham, Sussex, England. He was the eldest of the seven children of Elizabeth Pilfold and Timothy Shelley, a conservative and narrow-minded country squire. When he was young, Shelley began to show his inclination for independent thinking and a strong love for literature. Before he was 18, he had written two

Percy Bysshe Shelley

romances and published a collection of poems, in which he extolled freedom, exposed tyranny and expressed his sympathy for the impoverished classes.

Gentle and kind by nature, Shelley had a stout heart and could not stand any injustice. When at Eton, he was known as "Mad Shelley", for he rebelled against the English school system with its brutal treatment of pupils. At that time, he not only cultivated a passion for influential philosophers of the time such as Jean Jacques Rousseau and Thomas Paine but also fell under influence of William Godwin's writings on socialist thought.

At 18, Shelley entered Oxford University, where he read the skeptical French philosophers, and his protest against all forms of tyranny became stronger and more definite. In 1811 he wrote and put into print the famous anti-religious pamphlet entitled *On the Necessity of Atheism*. For this he was promptly expelled from the university and forbidden by his conservative father to go back home.

While living alone in London at the age of 19, Shelley made acquaintance with and married Harriet Westbrook, a 16-year old school girl. Long been interested in the Irish people's struggles against British domination, the young couple went to Dublin, the Irish capital in 1812. There he published and distributed his *Address to the Irish People* and attended many other political activities to condemn the crimes committed by the English government. All this aroused great hatred in the English government.

In 1813, Shelley wrote his first important poem *Queen Mab* after returning to England. But at that time, the English government was threatening the use of death penalty to suppress the working class movements and progressive publications, so the work was refused by his publisher.

Shelley's hasty marriage with Harriet turned out to be unsuitable and unhappy due to the lack of their mutual understanding. In 1814, they separated. Shelley then fell in love with Mary Godwin, the daughter of the radical philosopher William Godwin. Two years later, they got married and lived happily with each other. But Harriet's sudden death by drowning herself broke their peaceful life—a great scandal was made out of it by Shelley's numerous political enemies. In 1817, Shelley was deprived of his right of guardianship of the two children of his by Harriet. In the same year, he completed *The Revolt of Islam*, another long narrative poem in Spenserian stanzas. An attack on the reactionary dominion throughout Europe, this poem also idealizes the French Revolution of 1789 and proclaims the regeneration of man by love. In 1818, Shelley was compelled to leave England and spent almost all the rest of his life in Italy, where his poetical powers developed rapidly and his friendship with Byron which had begun as early as 1816 grew more firmly.

When exiled in Italy in the last years of his life, Shelley never ceased to pay attention to the happenings in England. On August 16, 1819 when about 60,000 people were gathering at a rally in St. Peter's Field near Manchester, demanding universal suffrage, parliamentary reform, and the repeal of the Corn Law, a troop of cavalry opened fire on them, killing more than a dozen and wounding several hundreds, including many women and children. At the news of the massacre, Shelley wrote his magnificent allegorical poem "The Mask of Anarchy", and several political lyrics such as "Sonnet: England in 1819" and "Song to the Men of England", protesting against the government's brutal action and calling the working people to fight against the idle class.

1819 was really a great year in Shelley's literary career. He wrote besides the above mentioned political poems his great lyrical drama *Prometheus Unbounded*, a historical tragedy on an Italian subject *The Cenci*, and his famous lyric "An Ode to the West Wind". The four-act poetic drama *Prometheus Unbound* is Shelley's greatest achievement, an exultant work in praise of humankind's potential. In *The Cenci*, the young girl Beatrice symbolizes liberty and shows by her struggle and martyrdom the necessity of violence as a means of struggle against tyranny and wickedness. After 1819, Shelley also wrote, in addition to numerous short political poems and lyrics on nature and on love, a dramatic satire *Peter Bell the Third*, a parody on Wordsworth's long poem *Peter bell,* a lyrical drama inspired by the struggle of the Greeks for their freedom entitled *Hellas*, an elegy on the death of Keats *Adonais*, and his prose work "A Defence of Poetry".

In Italy, Shelley kept close ties with the Italian people fighting for their independence and at the same time showed his great concern for the liberation movements in Spain and Greece. But his sudden death prevented him from doing more for the people he sympathized with. On July 8, 1822, a swift storm swept the Mediterranean while Shelley was sailing in a small boat off Leghorn, Italy. He was drowned. His body was burned on the beach by Byron and the ashes placed in the Protestant cemetery at Rome.

Throughout Shelley's short life, he produced numerous poems, among which *Queen Mab* (1813) is his first long poem of importance with the essence of his social philosophy in it. Written in the form of a fairy-tale dream, the poem is about the fairy Queen Mab who carries off in her celestial chariot a beautiful and pure girl Ianthe and shows her the past history, the present wretched state and the happy future of the world. Through the mouth of the fairy queen the poet presents his own ideas on philosophy, religion, morality and social problems.

The Revolt of Islam is another important long poem through which Shelley expresses his social, political and aesthetic ideas. In the preface to the poem, Shelley points out the relation between the subject of the poem and the problems raised in the French Revolution. Admitting that the revolution has not been able to make come true the ideals of the progressive peoples all over the world, the poet is far from denying its significance.

"The Mask of Anarchy", with its sub-title "Written on the Occasion of the Massacre at Manchester", begins with the traditional literary device of a medieval romance, with the poet falling asleep and a vision appearing to him. But here Shelley's treatment differs from that in those romances, for he explains the allegory by directly referring to real figures in the English government of the time. Then the poet proceeds to describe the working people's miserable conditions and in the last part he preaches the doctrine of unity among the workers. Although he disapproves of violence, Shelley writes strongly against all the forms of social oppression and exploitation.

Prometheus Unbound, a symbolic lyrical drama in 4 acts, is Shelley's masterpiece. Based on ancient Greek mythology and on Aeschylus' tragedy *Prometheus Bound*, Shelley alters the ending of the story to its opposite. Here in Shelley's work, Prometheus is also punished by Zeus (or Jupiter), the all-mighty ruler among the gods, after he steals fire from heaven and teaches men how to use it. But instead of submitting eventually to Zeus as depicted in the work of Aeschylus, Prometheus remains rebellious to the end and overthrows Zeus with great support of innumerable forces. In this way, Shelley, as the champion of freedom, changes the old myth to express his own political and philosophical views.

Shelley and Byron were close friends. However, there still exist some fundamental differences between these two great poets in their world outlook. Firstly, Byron only attacks political tyranny, but Shelley also notices the cruel relations of economic exploitation in the feudal-bourgeois world. Secondly, Byron thinks more of personal ends and believes chiefly in the might of individual heroes but not that of the common people. By contrast, Shelley works for the interests of the common people and has faith in the collective strength of the masses. It is this progressive world outlook that leads Shelley not only to speak in his works for political and social freedom, but also to advocate revolution against political tyranny and economic exploitation, even to call on later in his life the people to overthrow their oppressors and exploiters in the form of armed struggle.

Brief Introduction and Appreciation

Shelley was the first poet in Europe who sang for the working class and his political lyrics are among the best of their kind in the whole sphere of European romantic poetry. His "Song to the Men of England", was written in 1819, the year of the so-called Peterloo Massacre, when the people gathering at a mass meeting and demanding reform in St. Peter's field, near Manchester, were ruthlessly attacked by the military of the government. This poem, not only calling upon the impoverished English working class to fight against their political oppressors, but also pointing out to them the intolerable injustice of economic exploitation, was later to become a rallying song of the British Communist Party.

In the poem, the speaker addresses the impoverished working people who are exploited by the ruling class. He compares the masses to bees, insects that work their whole lives away so that the Queen (or King, in the case of England) does not have to perform any honest work herself. Obviously, he sympathizes with the working class. However, his recognition that they work only to have their products and profits seized by the ruling class urges him to call on the workers to take action instead of merely complaining about their problems. So Shelley suggests that the men who do not wish to "shake the chains ye wrought" retreat to their "cellars, holes, and cells". He also implies that they live not in homes, but dark, dank and lowly places, but the elegant halls that they have decorated are being used by the tyrants. The most forceful and powerful part, however, is the end of the poem when Shelley suggests that if the labourers fail to rebel, they are actually digging graves for themselves.

As Shelley says in his note, "Ode to the West Wind" was "conceived and chiefly written in a wood that skirts the Arno, near Florence on a day when that tempestuous wind" was "collecting the vapors which pour down the autumnal rains". Inspired by the violent tempest of hail and rain, the poet eulogizes the west wind as a powerful phenomenon of nature that is both destroyer and preserver, that enjoys boundless freedom and that has the power to spread messages far and wide.

In the first 3 stanzas, the poet describes vividly the activities of the west wind on the land, in the sky and on the sea in different seasons. With these activities, the wind destroys the old world, but it heralds a new one at the same time. Envious for the boundless freedom of the west wind, the poet expresses in the fourth stanza his wishes to be a leaf, a cloud and a wave, so that he could enjoy a share of the wind's power. However, it is only a figment of his imagination, for his increasing age and his sufferings in life have bent him down, so in the end of the poem, the poet appeals to the wind, the wind of aspiration and change, to reinvigorate him and to give force and persuasiveness to his poetry so that his words can set fire to the cold and lifeless world and become a trumpet-call and a "prophecy". Here, Shelley's belief in the poet's role as prophet, which he argues so powerfully in "A Defence of Poetry", is more plainly stated than in any other of his verse. And the celebrated final line of the poem, "If Winter comes, can Spring be far behind?" clearly shows Shelley's optimistic belief in the future of mankind.

It is evident enough that with the comprehensive description of the fearless and powerful west wind in nature, the poet is actually extolling the revolution that swept across the European countries in his day. As a progressive romanticist, Shelley doesn't regard the rise-up simply as the pessimistic destructive force. On the contrary, he realizes the great power and active elements of revolution as to get rid of the social decadency and bring forth a brand-new world.

Selected Reading

Song to the Men of England[1]

Men of England, wherefore[2] plough
For the lords who lay ye low[3]?
Wherefore weave with toil[4] and care
The rich robes your tyrants wear?

Wherefore feed, and clothe, and save,
From the cradle to the grave,[5]
Those ungrateful drones[6] who would
Drain your sweat—nay[7], drink your blood?

Wherefore, Bees of England[8], forge[9]
Many a weapon, chain, and scourge[10],
That these stingless drones may spoil[11]
The forced produce of your toil?[12]

Have ye leisure, comfort, calm,
Shelter, food, love's gentle balm?
Or what is it ye buy so dear
With your pain and with your fear?[13]

The seed ye sow, another reaps;
The wealth ye find, another keeps;
The robes ye weave, another wears;

The arms ye forge, another bears.

Sow seed—but let no tyrant reap;
Find wealth—let no impostor heap;
Weave robes—let not the idle[14] wear;
Forge arms—in your defence to bear.

Shrink to your cellars, holes, and cells;
In halls ye deck[15] another dwells.
Why shake the chains ye wrought[16]? Ye see
The steel ye tempered glance on ye.[17]

With plough and spade, and hoe and loom,
Trace your grave, and build your tomb,
And weave your winding-sheet[18], till fair[19]
England be your sepulchre[20].[21]

Notes

1. This poem was written at a time of turbulent unrest, after the return of troops from the Napoleonic Wars had precipitated a great economic depression. The Song, expressing Shelley's hope for a proletarian revolution, was originally planned as one of a series for workingmen; it has become, as the poet wished, a hymn of the British labor movement. This song contains eight quatrains, the metrical pattern of each line being iambic tetrameter and the rhyme scheme for each quatrain being uniformly **aabb**.

2. **wherefore**: why; for what reason

3. **lay ye low**: oppress you; reduce you to an economically and socially humble situation

4. **toil**: physical work

5. **From the cradle to the grave**: From birth to death

6. **Drones**: the male of the honey-bees, that do no work; referring here to the exploiting class in human society who do not work but live on the labour of the working class

7. **nay**: not only so but also

8. **Bees of England**: referring here to the working people in England

9. **forge**: create by hammering

10. **scourge**: a whip used formerly for punishment

11. **spoil**: plunder

12. **The forced produce of your toil**: the products of your labour which are produced under force

13. **Or what is it ye buy so dear / With your pain and with your fear?**: Otherwise what is the reward you obtain at the high cost of your sufferings and anxieties?

14. **the idle:** the lazy people, here referring to the exploiting classes

15. **deck:** decorate

16. **wrought:** forge

17. **The steel ye tempered glance on ye**: The sword you forged is flashed before you.

18. **winding-sheet**: the sheet of cloth used to wrap up the corpse

19. **fair**: beautiful

20. **sepulchre**: here referring to grave

21. The last two stanzas of the poem are ironically addressed to those workers who submit passively to capitalist exploitation. They serve as a warning to the working people, that if the latter should give up their struggle they would be digging graves for themselves with their own hands. Compared to the preceding stanzas, these lines appear weak and ineffectual.

Ode to the West Wind[1]

O wild West Wind[2], thou breath of Autumn's being[3],
Thou, from whose unseen presence[4] the leaves dead[5]
Are driven, like ghosts from an enchanter fleeing[6],

Yellow, and black, and pale, and hectic[7] red,
Pestilence-stricken multitudes[8]: O thou,
Who chariotest[9] to their dark wintry bed[10]

The winged seeds[11], where they lie cold and low[12],
Each like a corpse within its grave, until
Thine azure sister of the Spring[13] shall blow

Her clarion[14] o'er the dreaming earth, and fill
(Driving sweet buds like flocks to feed in air[15])
With living hues and odours plain and hill:

Wild Spirit, which art moving everywhere;
Destroyer and preserver[16], hear, oh hear!

II

Thou on whose stream[17], mid the steep sky's commotion[18],
Loose clouds like earth's decaying leaves are shed,
Shook from the tangled boughs of Heaven and Ocean, [19]

Angels of rain and lightning[20]: there are spread
On the blue surface[21] of thine aery surge[22],
Like the bright hair uplifted from the head

Of some fierce Maenad[23], even from the dim verge[24]
Of the horizon to the zenith's height[25],
The locks of the approaching storm.[26] Thou dirge

Of the dying year, [27] to which this closing night[28]
Will be the dome of a vast sepulchre[29],
Vaulted[30] with all thy congregated might

Of vapours,[31] from whose solid atmosphere[32]
Black rain, and fire, and hail will burst: oh hear!

III

Thou who didst waken from his summer dreams
The blue Mediterranean[33], where he lay,
Lulled by the coil of his crystalline streams[34],

Beside a pumice isle[35] in Baiae's bay[36],
And saw in sleep old palaces and towers
Quivering within the wave's intenser day[37],

All overgrown with azure moss and flowers
So sweet, the sense faints picturing them![38] Thou
For whose path the Atlantic's level powers[39]

Cleave[40] themselves into chasms[41], while far below
The sea-blooms and the oozy woods which wear
The sapless foliage of the ocean, know

Thy voice, and suddenly grow gray with fear,
And tremble and despoil themselves:[42] oh hear!

IV

If I were a dead leaf thou mightest bear;
If I were a swift cloud to fly with thee;
A wave to pant beneath thy power,[43] and share

The impulse of thy strength, only less free
Than thou, O uncontrollable[44]! If even
I were as in my boyhood, and could be

The comrade of thy wanderings[45] over Heaven,
As then, when to outstrip thy skiey speed[46]
Scarce[47] seemed a vision; I would ne'er have striven

As thus with thee in prayer in my sore need.[48]
Oh, lift me as a wave, a leaf, a cloud!
I fall upon the thorns of life! I bleed!

A heavy weight of hours has chained and bowed
One too like thee[49]: tameless, and swift, and proud.

V

Make me thy lyre[50], even as[51] the forest is:
What if my leaves are falling like its own![52]

The tumult of thy mighty harmonies

Will take from both a deep, autumnal tone,[53]
Sweet though in sadness. Be thou, Spirit fierce,
My spirit! Be thou me, impetuous[54] one!

Drive my dead thoughts over the universe
Like withered leaves to quicken a new birth!
And, by the incantation[55] of this verse,

Scatter, as from an unextinguished hearth
Ashes and sparks[56], my words among mankind!
Be through my lips to unawakened earth

The trumpet of a prophecy![57] O, Wind[58],
If Winter comes, can Spring be far behind?

Notes

1. An ode, in ancient literature, is an elaborate lyrical poem composed for a
   chorus to chant and to dance to; in modern use, it is a rhymed lyric
   expressing noble feelings, often addressed to a person or celebrating an
   event. This ode contains five 14-lined stanzas of iambic pentameter, each
   containing four tercets and a closing couplet. The rhyme scheme in each
   part follows a pattern known as terza rima, the three-line rhyme scheme
   first used by Dante in his well-known *The Divine Comedy*. In the three-line
   terza rima stanza, the first and third lines rhyme, and the middle line does
   not; then the end sound of that middle line is employed as the rhyme for the
   first and third lines in the next stanza. The final couplet rhymes with the
   middle line of the last three-line stanza. Thus each of the five stanzas
   follows the rime scheme of **aba**, **bcb**, **cdc**, **ded**, **ee**. This linked chain gives
   a feeling of onward motion and the verse has a breathless quality which is
   in keeping with the onward motion of the wind's movement.
2. **O wild West Wind**: Pay attention to the grammatical structure of the whole
   stanza. It consists of an apostrophe, which in fact is an invocation to the

west wind. Notice the sound effect of the alliterated "w", which suggests the sound and the great power of the west wind.

3. **Autumn's being**: Autumn's life

4. **unseen presence**: invisible existence. The word "presence" further intensifies the idea of the west wind as a living being.

5. **the leaves dead**: the dead leaves

6. **ghosts from an enchanter fleeing**: ghosts fleeing from an enchanter

7. **hectic**: the kind of fever which occurs in tuberculosis

8. **Pestilence-stricken multitudes**: here referring to "a large number of withered leaves" that are like human beings hit by epidemic diseases

9. **chariotest**: "est" is here added to the verb "chariot" to indicate the second person singular after the subject "thou" .

10. **their dark wintry bed**: In winter, the seeds of plants are buried under the earth. Here "their dark wintry bed" gives a hint of "the grave". The theme of death and rebirth recurs throughout the poem.

11. **The winged seeds**: The seeds that are blown into air

12. **lie cold and low**: The seeds are compared to the dead bodies in the grave

13. **azure sister of the Spring**: here referring to the east wind that will blow in spring

14. **clarion**: a high, shrill trumpet

15. **like flocks to feed in air**: The spring wind forces upon the buds, as lambs are driven into open pasture.

16. **Destroyer and preserver**: The west wind is considered the "Destroyer" in that it drives the last signs of life from trees and the "Preserver" in that it scatters the seeds that will come to life in the next spring.

17. **stream**: flow of the wind

18. **mid the steep sky's commotion**: in the midst of the great turbulence of the high sky

19. **Shook from the tangled boughs of Heaven and Ocean**: "shook" is the old use of "shaken". The whole line means, with a metaphor, that the fragmentary clouds ("leaves") are torn by the wind from the larger and higher clouds ("boughs") which are formed by a union of air with vapor drawn up by the sun from the ocean.

20. **Angels of rain and lightning**: The "angels" here refers to the "loose clouds", the messengers of rain and lightning.

21. **the blue surface**: the azure high sky
22. **aery surge**: sea of air. Here the sky is compared to the sea
23. **Maenad**: a frenzied woman in Greek mythology in the worship of Bacchus, the God of wine and vegetation who was fabled to die in the fall and to be resurrected in the spring; a woman behaving wildly as if drunk
24. **dim verge**: the dark horizon with clouds
25. **the zenith's height**: the highest point of the sky
26. **The locks of the approaching storm**: here referring to the "clouds"
27. **Thou dirge/Of the dying year**: referring to the west wind. **dirge**: a mourning song for the dead. Here it refers to the west wind.
28. **this closing night**: the night which is darkened by the thickening clouds. Here it may also suggest the approaching doom of the ruling class.
29. **dome of a vast sepulchre**: the round top of a huge tomb
30. **vaulted**: covered with an arched roof
31. **congregated might / Of vapours**: mighty congregation of vapours (clouds)
32. **solid atmosphere**: The clouds are so dense that the sky seems to be solid.
33. **waken from his summer dreams / The blue Mediterranean**: waken the blue Mediterranean from his summer dreams
34. **Lulled by the coil of his crystalline streams**: soothed and almost hypnotized by the soft sound of the clear stream of the Mediterranean water. **Lulled**: became quiet. **coil**: referring here to the noise of the tide
35. **pumice isle**: an isle near Naples, Italy, which is formed by deposits of lava from Vesuvius, a volcano nearby
36. **Baiae's bay**: a favourite resort of the ancient Romans on the coast of Campania, at the western end of the Bay of Naples
37. **the wave's intenser day**: The translucency of the water makes its surface more dazzling than the daylight. "Day" here refers to "daylight". The whole line here means the reflections of palaces and tower (symbols of the aristocratic rule) are trembling in the intenser daylight in the water.
38. **the sense faints picturing them**: so sweet that one feels faint in describing them
39. **the Atlantic's level powers**: the waves of the Atlantic Ocean moving on its flat surface
40. **Cleave**: Separate by cutting
41. **chasms**: deep openings; deep cracks

42. **The sea-blooms and the oozy woods which wear / The sapless foliage of the ocean, know / Thy voice, and suddenly grow gray with fear, / And tremble and despoil themselves**: The plants at the bottom of the ocean, the rivers and the lakes also fall under the influence of the west wind which announces the change of the season. **oozy**: moist, slimy, muddy. **sapless foliage**: withered leaves. **Despoil themselves**: deprive themselves of their own foliage; drop their leaves.

43. **A wave to pant beneath thy power**: If I were a wave to pant beneath thy power. **Pant**: breathe quickly

44. **uncontrollable**: Here it refers to the uncontrollable west wind.

45. **thy wanderings**: you who are wandering

46. **outstrip thy skiey speed**: surpass your speed through the sky

47. **Scarce**: Scarcely

48. **I would ne'er have striven / As thus with thee in prayer in my sore need**: I would never have competed in this way with you in prayer in my great need.

49. **One too like thee**: referring to Shelley himself

50. **lyre**: a harp (a musical instrument) used by ancient Greeks for accompaniment

51. **even as**: just as

52. **What if my leaves are falling like its own**: What does it matter even if I am dying just like the leaves of the forest itself. "Falling leaves" symbolize death.

53. **The tumult of thy mighty harmonies / Will take from both a deep, autumnal tone**: The tumult of thy mighty harmonies will take a deep autumnal tone from both my depressed feelings and the falling leaves. **tumult**: confusion and excitement. "Both" here refers to "both me and the forest".

54. **impetuous**: brave, fearless

55. **incantation**: magic spell

56. **Ashes and sparks**: Here "Ashes and sparks," like "dead leaves" and "winged seeds," symbolize the double concepts of death and rebirth.

57. **The trumpet of a prophecy**: "The trumpet" refers back to "clarion" in the first stanza, and "a prophecy" refers to the last line of the poem.

58. **wind**: Although it is pronounced [wind], it forms an "eye rhyme" with "mankind" and "behind".

Questions for Study and Discussion

1. Discuss the rhetorical devices in the poem of "Song to the Men of England" and their functions.

2. The west wind in "Ode to the West Wind" is generally considered as a symbol. What does it symbolize? What is the theme of the poem? Give instances to show the various stylistic devices adopted throughout the poem, such as symbol, image, personification, metaphor and simile.

3. What are the three dominant images in the first three stanzas of "Ode to the West Wind"? How does the effect of the wind on each of these elements in the nature bear out Shelley's characterization of the wind as Destroyer and Preserver? In this poem, the speaker's relation to the wind develops in a dramatic way during the course of the poem, particularly in Stanzas 4 and 5. What is the speaker's attitude towards himself and his relation to the wind at the end of Stanza 4 and how does this change in Stanza 5?

4. Some people hold that Shelley accepted more advanced sociopolitical theory while Byron paid more attention on individual freedom. Do you agree? Why or why not?

5. How does Shelley's treatment of nature differ from that of the earlier Romantic poets? What connections does he make between nature and art, and how does he illustrate those connections?

John Keats (1795—1821)

Life and Major Works

John Keats has been considered with Shakespeare, Milton and Wordsworth as one of the indisputably great English poets. Compared with his contemporaries Byron and Shelly, Keats has a more humble social background. He was born in London in October 1795, the eldest son of a hostler and stable keeper. His father died when he was eight; his mother remarried a few months later and died of tuberculosis when he

John Keats

was 14. Her death, as he said, damaged his nature a lot and yet stirred up his imagination. His guardian, a merchant forced him to leave school at 15 and apprenticed him to a surgeon. He served his apprenticeship for 5 years. Before long, he abandoned his profession in medicine and devoted himself to literature and art. There are many reasons for which Keats made this decision, among which two were the most important: first, he has been strongly influenced by his teacher Charles Cowden Clarke (1787—1877), early when he was studying in private school, and contracted a deep love for classical literature and art; second, Keats made acquaintance with Leigh Hunt, the famous critics, by whom he made friends with many other well-known artists who were active in the field of English literature and art, such as the prosaists William Hazlitt and Charles Lamb, the poet Shelly, the painter Benjamin Robert and Haydon, and so on. Under their influence, Keats developed a stronger passion for literature and was more attracted to arts.

In 1816, Keats published his well-known Petrarchan sonnet "On First Looking into Chapman's Homer". With inimitable poetic imagery and succinct but rich language, Keats for the first time showed his artistic talent. And the next year, with the help of Shelly, he published his first collection of poems *Poem*, which did not attract the critic's attention. After the publication of *Endymion* (his long allegation poem with more than 4000 lines, which was about the love between a Greek shepherd and the moon goddess based upon ancient Greek mythology), he was brutally criticized by some conservative magazines such as *Blackwood*, the *Quarterly Review* and so on, and was slandered as "Cockney School"—a group of democratic-minded men of letters in London headed by Hunt. In the summer of 1818, he left London and started on a walking tour through England and Scotland. During his travels, Keats became acquainted with the life of small towns and villages and witnessed the poverty and privation of the people. The two years from 1818 to 1819 is hard period for Keats not only in economy but also in health and emotion—he fell deeply in love with 18-year-old Fanny Brawne, the daughter of his employer, but he refused to think about their marriage due to his sickness. However it is also the most glorious period for his creating career. During those two years, he produced almost all his works on which his high reputation now rests, *Lamia*, "The Eve of St. Mark", *Isabella*, and *Hyperion*, and the great odes: "Ode to a Nightingale", "Ode on a Grecian Urn", "Ode on Melancholy", "Ode to Psyche", and "Ode to Autumn". On account of his continuous poor health, Keats set sail for Italy in September 1820, but by the time he reached Rome he was obviously unable to move and died of consumption in February, 1821, a few months after his arrival. He was buried there beneath the epitaph he had written for himself: "here lies one whose name was writ in water." Shelly, who hailed Keats as a genius, commemorated the poet's death and the world's loss in "Adonais". In his famous lament "Adonais", Shelly calls Keats "the most active and youngest poet."

Not widely known as a great poet during his life time but severely attacked by reactionary critics of the *Quarterly* and the *Edinburgh Review*, Keats nevertheless won great poetic fame after his death. He is a singer and an advocate of the cult of beauty, a writer of "pure poesy", a sort of "art for art's sake" dreamer who indulged himself in poetic fancy and fantasy and had little interest in social or political problems. Although Keats did not attack openly the political and social evils of the day as Byron and Shelly did, and was more interested in artistic beauty in contrast with ugly social reality, yet his uncompromising attitude toward reactionary criticism, his sympathy for the poor and the oppressed mass, and his belief in the lofty mission of the poet to work for the welfare of the people have made it clear that his love of beauty in nature and in art does not make him an escapist.

Keats is now accepted as one of the most important figures of the early 19th-century romanticism, a movement that espoused the sanctity of emotion and imagination, and privileged the beauty of the natural world. The ideas and themes of Keats's poetry are mostly quintessentially Romantic concerns: the beauty of nature, the relation between imagination and creativity, the response of the passions to beauty and suffering, and the transience of human life in time. Keats was under deep influence of Spenser, Milton and Shakespeare in his early years. Later he came to realize that these influences tended to encourage the faults to which his exuberant temperament was inclined and his temperament was not merely strongly sensual but deeply reflective. Then he created his own unique style that distinguished from Hunt and Shelly, which is his sensible understanding towards nature. No English poets wrote poems as rich in sensuous imagery as in Keats's great odes. His poetry displays the most human emotion and the purest expression of personal inner experience and made a perfect combination of his sense of outside world and his understanding of beauty, which had a profound effect upon many Victorian poets such as Tennyson and Mr. and Mrs. Browning.

Brief Introduction and Appreciation

Keats's odes have generally been considered as his most important works, particularly "Ode on a Grecian Urn", "Ode on Melancholy", and "Ode to Autumn", and we may find the same dominant thoughts and feelings running through them all: the world of nature is beautiful, the realms of art and poetry and imagination are wonderful, while the existing human society contains inescapable and irremediable misery. And it is the poet's intense hatred for the human society of his time that made him love so much the beauty in the realms of nature and of art.

"Ode to a Nightingale", one of the best-known poems by Keats, was written in May 1819, when he lived at the home of his friend Charles Brown, who wrote about the situation in which Keats composed this beautiful poem: "in the spring of 1819, a nightingale had built her net near my house. Keats felt a tranquil and continual joy in her song; and one morning he took his chair from the breakfast table to the grass plot under a plum tree, where he sat for two or three hours. When he came into the house, I perceived he had some scraps of paper in his hand, and these he was quietly thrusting behind the books. On inquiry, I found those scraps, four five in numbers, contained his poetic feeling of the song of our nightingale." At that time, Keats's little brother Tom had just died, he himself suffered from the disease of consumption. The song of the nightingale symbolized for him some stable beauty which lured him temporarily away from his misery into an exquisite desire to "leave the world unseen…"

There're 8 stanzas in this ode, expressing the poet's feelings and responses on hearing the song of the nightingale, a bird that sings at night. The poet begins in the first stanza with a feeling of dullness. He is deeply moved by the joy of the nightingale with her loud and clear beautiful songs. This happiness is too sharp that he feels his "heart aches" as if he has been numbed. He longs to flee the human world and to join the bird, but he cannot because of the crucial reality. His heart is hit by the unsatisfactory facts of the real word. So in the second stanza, he thinks of resorting to the alcohol.

He longs for a "draught of vintage" to transport him out of himself into the dim forest realm of the nightingale. Then there is the question—What did the poet want to forget about? Why did he so anxiously desire to escape from the human world? The answers were discussed in detail in the next stanza. For the poet, the real world is full of tiredness, sickness and anxiety; full of pain, misery, sadness and oppression. It was just these negative factors that hurt the poet and contributed his desire to escape. The fourth stanza begins with the cry "away!" The poet rejects the wine and prefers to travel by means of imagination on the "viewless wings of poesy". He imagines that he is already with the nightingale in the dark sky to the Queen moon in a tender night. The song put him in mind of fragrant grass, flowers and fruits "on summer eves" and further carried him away to the ancient times and far-off lands. All this made him forget his painful life on earth. He was deeply indulged in this imaginary unreal world, happy and satisfied. And even longs for the end of his life.

> for many a time
> I have been half in love with easeful Death,
> Call'd him soft names in many a mused rhyme,
> To take into the air my quiet breath;
> Now more than ever seems it rich to die,
> To cease upon the midnight with no pain,
> While thou art pouring forth thy soul abroad
> In such an ecstasy!

This seems to the poet the perfect moment to die, but once the nightingale disappears with its sweet song, the poet is left alone to face the reality again with the bitter after-taste of disillusionment and perplexity. In the seventh stanza, the poet turns to think about life. The nightingale seems to live eternally because its song is the same now as it was in ancient days, perhaps the Biblical Ruth, for example, heard the nightingale's song as she gathered grain in the fields.

> Forlorn! the very word is like a bell
> To toll me back from thee to my sole self!

The poet comes back into the reality at last and realizes that it is a negative attitude to escape from the reality by means of death and imagination.

> Adieu! the fancy cannot cheat so well
> As she is famed to do, deceiving elf.

Adieu! adieu! thy plaintive anthem fades

This moment, the sound of the nightingale "Past the near meadows, over the still stream Up the hill-side; and now 'tis buried deep in the next valley-glades." The nightingale has gone and the poet came back to the real world, with both pain and happiness. And he is wondering "Was it a vision, or a waking dream"; he is not clear "do I wake or sleep?" with which the odd ends.

Keats in this poet makes a contrast between the happy world of natural loveliness and human world of agony in order to show his resentment against the social wrongs and his desire for a world of eternal happiness. The interconnection or mixture of pain and happiness, sorrow and joy, desire and disappointment, the ideal and the actual, life and death are all through the ode. The poet tells us that there are too many evils and wrongs in the human world, while the life is to accept this unhappiness and find joys in the sorrows. Life itself is neither optimistic nor miserable but real and beautiful.

Selected Reading

Ode To A Nightingale

My heart aches, and a drowsy numbness pains
My sense, as though of hemlock[1] I had drunk,
Or emptied some dull opiate to the drains[2]
One minute past, and Lethe-wards[3], had sunk;
'Tis not through envy of thy happy lot,
But being too happy in thine happiness—
That thou, light-winged Dryad[4] of the trees,
In some melodious plot
Of beechen green and shadows numberless,
Singest of summer in full-throated ease.

O, for a draught of vintage[5]! that hath been
Cooled a long age in the deep-delved earth,
Tasting of Flora[6] and the country green,
Dance, and Provencal[7] song, and sunburnt mirth!
O for a beaker full of the warm South,
Full of the true, the blushful Hippocrene,

With beaded bubbles winking at the brim,
And purple-strained mouth;
That I might drink, and leave the world unseen,
And with thee fade away into the forest dim;

Fade far away, dissolve, and quite forget
What thou among the leaves hast never known,
The weariness, the fever, and the fret
Here, where men sit and hear each other groan;
Where palsy shakes a few, sad, last gray hairs,
Where youth grows pale, and spectre-thin[8], and dies;
Where but to think is to be full of sorrow
And leaden-eyed despairs,
Where Beauty cannot keep her lustrous eyes,
Or new Love pine at them beyond tomorrow.

Away! Away! for I will fly to thee,
Not charioted by Bacchus[9] and his pards,
But on the viewless wings of Poesy,
Though the dull brain perplexes and retards:
Already with thee! Tender is the night,
And haply the Queen Moon is on her throne,
Clustered around by all her starry fays[10];
But here there is no light,
Save what from heaven is with the breezes blown
Through verdurous[11] glooms and winding mossy ways.

I cannot see what flowers are at my feet,
Nor what soft incense[12] hangs upon the boughs,
But, in embalmed darkness[13], guess each sweet
Wherewith the seasonable month endows
The grass, the thicket, and the fruit tree wild;
White hawthorn, and the pastoral eglantine[14];
Fast-fading violets covered up in leaves;
And mid-May's eldest child,

The coming musk rose, full of dewy wine,
The murmurous haunt of flies on summer eves.

Darkling[15] I listen; and, for many a time
I have been half in love with easeful Death,
Called him soft names in many a mused[16] rhyme,
To take into the air my quiet breath;
Now more than ever seems it rich to die,
To cease upon the midnight with no pain,
While thou art pouring forth thy soul abroad
In such an ecstasy!
Still wouldst thou sing, and I have ears in vain—
To thy high requiem[17] become a sod[18].

Thou wast not born for death, immortal Bird!
No hungry generations tread thee down;
The voice I hear this passing night was heard
In ancient days by emperors and clown[19];
Perhaps the selfsame song that found a path
Through the sad heart of Ruth[20], when, sick for home,
She stood in tears amid the alien corn;
The same that oft-times hath
Charmed magic casements, opening on the foam
Of perilous seas, in faery lands forlorn[21].

Forlorn! the very word is like a bell
To toll me back from thee to my sole self!
Adieu! the fancy[22] cannot cheat so well
As she is famed to do, deceiving elf[23].
Adieu! adieu! thy plaintive anthem[24] fades
Past the near meadows, over the still stream,
Up the hillside; and now 'tis buried deep
In the next valley glades.
Was it a vision, or a waking dream?
Fled is that music—Do I wake or sleep?

Notes

1. **hemlock:** highly poisonous umbelliferous plant, a poisonous herb
2. **to the drains:** to the last drop in the cup
3. **Lethe-wards:** toward Lethe. Lethe is the river in Hades, the underworld, whose waters cause forgetfulness
4. **Dryad:** a nymph inhabiting a tree and watching over it, here it is referred to the nightingale
5. **O for a draught of vintage:** longing for a drink of wine. Oh, if only I had a drink of wine
6. **Flora:** the goddess of flower
7. **Provencal:** in southern France which is famous for its love poems
8. **spectre-thin:** thin as a ghost. **Spectre:** Keats's brother Tom, had been wasted away by tuberculosis and died the previous winter
9. **Bacchus:** the god of wine
10. **fays:** archaic fairies
11. **verdurous:** green-foliaged
12. **soft incense:** scented blossoms
13. **embalmed darkness:** scented darkness
14. **eglantine:** sweet brier or honey suckle
15. **Darkling:** in the darkness
16. **mused:** meditated
17. **requiem:** special mass for the repose of the soul of a dead person
18. **became a sod:** you shall go on singing after I die
19. **by emperor and clown:** by all persons high and low
20. **Ruth:** the name of a woman, according to "The Book of Ruth" in the Old Testament, a woman named Ruth voluntarily lived with her mother-in-law after the death of her husband
21. **faery lands forlorn:** fairy lands. In ancient time, "forlorn" means "sorrowful"
22. **fancy:** imagination. "the viewless wings of poesy"
23. **deceiving elf:** Fancy is here spoken of as deceiving elf
24. **anthem:** hymn

Questions for Study and Discussion:

1. Why does his heart ache?

2. What does the author want to do?

3. How does he fly to the nightingale?

4. What can't tread the nightingale down?

5. What is the speaker's mental and emotional state at the opening of the poem? What feeling does Keats express after he hears the nightingale's singing?

6. Dying under the conditions described in stanza 6 is made to seem very attractive. How do the last two lines of the stanza affect this attractiveness?

7. In what sense is the nightingale "immortal"? How is this immortality illustrated?

8. How does Keats feel in his imaginative world? What is the difference between a "vision" and a "waking dream"?

9. Why does the poet want to be drunk so as to leave away from the present world?

10. What word brings the poet back to his present life?

11. What does the poet expose about the human society in this poem?

Jane Austen (1775—1817)

Life and Major Works

Jane Austen, an important novelist of the Romantic Period, was born on 16 December, 1775, in the rectory at Steventon, Hampshire, where her father was a rector of the parish. She was the 2nd daughter and 7th child in a family of 8. She was brought up in an intelligent but restricted family. The father was a learned scholar who encouraged his daughter's intellectual development and literary ambition. After a few years' schooling, together with her sister Cassandra, she continued her education at

Jane Austen

home and began to write at an early age. She was educated mainly through widely reading books and materials available. The family of Jane always spent time in group-reading and in performing theatricals. In such an environment, her literary talent was being cultivated and developed. Jane acquired a

thorough knowledge of the 18th century literature, including the moral philosophy of Dr. Johnson, the poetry of William Cowper and Crabbe, novels by Richardson, Fanny Burney and Henry Fielding. Moreover, she was much influenced by both the poetry and prose of Walter Scott.

Jane Austin led a quiet, peaceful and uneventful life and never got married. The first twenty-six years of her life were spent in the rectory at Steventon. In 1801, when her father retired from his post, her family moved to Bath. After her father's death in 1805, the family suffered financial difficulties and moved to Southampton. At this time, on holiday in the West Country, Jane fell in love. When the young man died, she was deeply sad. Later in 1809, together with her mother and one of her sisters, she moved to a house in Chawton provided by her brother. Later Jane went to live with her unmarried sister at Winchester. On 18 July, 1817 this bright, attractive little woman died of Addison's disease at the age of 42 and was buried in the cathedral, with 6 novels completed and 2 fragments unfinished.

Jane's life was notable for its lack of events. Such a life could furnish materials only for that class of novel which corresponds to sentimental comedy instead of furnishing material for romance. Her sunny qualities are unconsciously reflected in all her books.

Although living in a turbulent era, Jane was able to ignore the harsh social reality. She never touched upon the class conflicts of her time, and the events which stirred the Europe at that time left no impression on her works. Also the extremes of wealth and poverty are unknown in her works. She kept her eyes steadily upon the people and events around her, and wrote about the small world in which she lived. She restricted her subject matter to a narrow range of society and incidents: quiet, prosperous, gentry class families in small towns. Nevertheless, she treated her subject matter with subtlety of observation, depth of psychological penetration and delicacy of touch. Her works show a wealth of character studies and abound in wit, humour and charm. Jane knew clearly how to sketch figures with a pure and suggestive pen so that they stand out in a strong and unforgettable relief.

Jane Austen began writing at a very young age and her *Love and Friendship* (1922) dated from this period. Her early published works by amusing parody of the melodramatic novels were popular at that time. All these are clear signs of her talent for humorous and satirical writing. At first she had experimented with various styles of writing, and when she completed her masterpiece *Pride and Prejudice* at the age of twenty-two, it was clear that she had found her appropriate form.

During her lifetime Jane Austen completed 6 novels. Four of them were published anonymously and 2 were published under her signature posthumously. Jane's novels incorporate her observations on the manners of her time and class, and they always relate to courtship, love, and marriage.

Jane, herself, compared her work to a fine engraving made upon a little piece of ivory only 2 inches square. Although the ivory surface is small, she made the drawings with such a minute description of human life that she can be regarded as a real artist. Although Jane's novels were not so well-received in her lifetime, they have enjoyed steadily growing popularity, especially in the 20th century. It is not without reason that Jane Austin is credited with having brought the English novel to its maturity so that she is ranked among the truly great British novelists.

Sense and Sensibility (1811) was the first major novel of Jane Austen. The essential theme of the novel is the necessity of finding a workable idle ground between passion and reason. The story contrasts the temperaments of the two sisters. Elinor governs her life by sense or reasonableness, while Marianne rules her life by sensibility or romance. How each of the sisters reacts to their misfortunes and the lessons they draw before coming finally to the requisite happy ending forms the core of the novel. From the experiences and lessons of Elinor and Marianne, Jane Austen shows us that a truly happy marriage exists only where sense and sensibility meet and mix in proper measure.

In 1796, when Austen was twenty-one years old, she wrote the novel *First Impressions*. The work was revised and published under the title *Pride and Prejudice* in 1813. It is generally considered as one of the author's masterpieces.

In 1811 Jane Austen began *Mansfield Park*, which was published in 1814. The novel traces the career of Fanny Price, a Cinderella-like heroine, who is brought from a poor home to Mansfield Park, the country estate of her relative, Sir Thomas Bertram. She is raised with some of the comforts of her cousins, the children of Sir Thomas, but her social rank is maintained at a lower level. Despite their strict upbringing, the Bertram children become involved in marital and extramarital tangles, which bring disasters on the family. But

Fanny's upright character guides her through her own relationships with dignity and leads to her triumph at the close of the novel.

Jane Austen began a new novel, *Emma*, and published it in 1816. The heroine, Emma Woodhouse, is difficult to love but does engage the reader's sympathy and understanding. Emma is a girl of high intelligence and vivid imagination who is also marked by egotism and a desire to dominate the lives of others. She exercises her powers of manipulation on a number of neighbors who are not able to resist her prying into their lives. Most of Emma's attempts to control her friends, however, do not have happy effects for her or for them. But influenced by John Knightley, an old friend who is her superior in intelligence and maturity, she realizes how misguided many of her actions are. The novel ends with the decision of a warmer and less headstrong Emma to marry Mr. Knightley. *Emma* is Austen's most brilliant novel. The saturation of a narrow human situation with the author's satirical wit and psychological penetration is here carried to its highest point.

Persuasion, begun in 1815 and published posthumously (together with *Northanger Abbey*) in 1818, is Jane Austen's last complete novel and is perhaps the most directly expressive of her feeling about her own life. The heroine, Anne Elliot, falls in love with Captain Wentworth but is parted from him because of her class-conscious family, and when he again enters her life, their love deepens and ends in marriage. Austen's satirical treatment of social pretensions and worldly motives is perhaps at its keenest in this novel. Not only the satirical but also the romantic are the predominant tone of *Persuasion*.

Northanger Abbey, begun in 1797, had been sold in 1803 to a publisher, who neglected it. In 1816, Jane reclaimed the novel, which was published posthumously. It is a fine satirical novel, making sport of the popular Gothic novel of terror, but it does not rank among her major works.

All of Austen's works are restricted to the village life of upper-middle class of the 19th-century England. Her favorite subjects are money and marriage, which provide the framework for her novels in which women are always taken as the major characters. She thinks that marriage should be based on true love and understanding, but money is also an important element in it.

Austen's works are comedies of manners that depict the self-contained world of provincial ladies and gentlemen who appear in domestic settings. The style of Austen is easy and effortless and the plot of her works is tight and well designed. Her ingenious dialogues, subtle irony, brilliant wit, vivid characters, clear descriptive writing style, penetrating analysis and moral firmness all account for the great popularity of her works.

Brief introduction and Appreciation

Pride and Prejudice has been consistently regarded as Jane Austen's most popular and successful novel.

The plot of this novel mainly evolves around the Bennet family. Mr. and Mrs. Bennet, living in Longbourn near London, have five grown-up and unmarried daughters. The marriage prospects of the 5 daughters are the chief concern of Mrs. Bennet in life. Mr. Bennet, a gentleman of bookish nature, is disdainful of his wife and indifferent to his daughters except Elizabeth, whom he considers the most intelligent and spirited.

At the opening of the novel, Netherfield Park, an estate near the Bonnets, is leased by Mr. Bingley, a wealthy bachelor. Then he brings with him his rich and unmarried friend Mr. Darcy. Bingley falls in love with Jane, the eldest daughter of the Bennet family and a girl of sweet and gentle disposition. Darcy is attracted by lively and witty Elizabeth, the second daughter of the Bennet family, but offends her by his supercilious behaviour. Darcy proposes to Elizabeth but is rejected. Elizabeth's prejudice against Darcy increases and further misunderstandings arise. Consequently, Darcy's pride is pitted against Elizabeth's prejudice. After many twists and turns, Darcy and Elizabeth realize their errors of judgment and become engaged, meanwhile Jane and Bingley are happily reunited.

The whole story portrays life in the genteel rural society of the day, and focus on the relationship between Elizabeth Bennet and the haughty Darcy. Their relationship begins with the initial misunderstandings and ends with their mutual enlightenment. And finally they learn that their first impressions, based on pride and prejudice, were incorrect.

Chapter 1: Chapter one introduces Mr. and Mrs. Bennet of the Longbourn estate. The news that a wealthy young gentleman named Charles Bingley has rented the manor known as Netherfield Park causes a great stir in the neighboring village of Longbourn, especially in the Bennet household. The Bennets have 5 unmarried daughters, and Mrs. Bennet, an empty-headed, snobbish and vulgar woman, is the sort who agrees with the novel's opening words: "It is a truth universally acknowledged that a single man in possession of a good fortune must be in want of a wife." She sees Bingley's arrival as an opportunity for one of the girls to obtain a wealthy spouse, and she therefore insists that Mr. Bennet must go to visit Bingley, the new neighbour, "as soon as he comes," and that he should think of his daughters and what a good marriage it would be. Mr. Bennet's preference for his daughter Elizabeth also becomes evident, when he says she "has something more of quickness than her sisters," whom he describes as "silly and ignorant like other girls." Mr. Bennet teasingly questions why his visit to Bingley could be so important.

Chapter 2: Elizabeth, as well as three of her four sisters, Jane, Kitty, Mary, and Lydia is briefly introduced in Chapter Two. While in Chapter One Mr. Bennet torments his family by pretending to have no interest in visiting Bingley as soon as he arrives, but in Chapter Two we learn that indeed "Mr. Bennet was among the earliest of those who waited on Mr. Bingley." When he reveals to Mrs. Bennet and his daughters that he has made their new neighbour's acquaintance, they are overjoyed and excited. "The rest of the evening is spent in conjecturing how soon [Bingley] will return Mr. Bennet's visit, and determining when they should ask him to dinner."

In *Pride and prejudice*, Austen provides four different marriages. They are utilitarian marriage, sex-oriented marriage, moral marriage and perfect marriage. It is analyzed that one's character reflects his/her marriage and attitudes towards love and social mores are reflected in their marriage's formation. The main subject in the novel is stated in the first sentence of the novel: "It is a truth universally acknowledged that a single man in possession of a good fortune must be in want of a wife." In this statement, Jane Austen cleverly illustrates three points: she declares that the main subject of the novel will be courtship and marriage; she has established the humorous tone of the novel by taking a simple subject to elaborate and to speak intelligently of; and she has prepared the reader for a chase in the novel of either a husband in search of a wife, or a woman in pursuit of a husband. The first line also defines Jane's book as a piece of literature that connects itself to the 18th century period, in which, the emphasis on man in social environment was important, and the use of satire and wit was a common form of the 18th century literature.

Pride and Prejudice, similar to Jane Austen's other novels, is written in gentle satire, which plays a decisive part in characterization as well as in plot development. The main object of Jane's satire in the novel is the mercenary nature and the ignorance of the people, a common criticism of the 18th century. Characters in the novel which best carries these qualities are: Mrs. Bennet, a foolish woman who talks too much and is obsessed with getting her daughters married; Lydia Bennet, the youngest daughter of the Bennet family who is devoted to a life of dancing, fashions, gossips and flirting; and Mr. Williams Collins, the silly and conceited baboon who is completely stupefied by Lady Catherine in every aspect of his life that he has forgotten his own morals and duty. The tone of the novel is light, satirical, and vivid.

Selected Reading

Pride and Prejudice
Chapter I

It is a truth universally acknowledged[1], that a single man[2] in possession of a good fortune must be in want of a wife.

However little known the feelings or views of such a man may be on his first entering a neighbourhood, this truth is so well fixed in the minds of the surrounding families[3], that he is considered as the rightful property of some one or other of their daughters[4].

"My dear Mr. Bennet," said his lady[5] to him one day, "have you heard that Netherfield Park[6] is let at last?"

Mr. Bennet replied that he had not[7].

"But it is," returned she; "for Mrs. Long[8] has just been here, and she told me all about it."

Mr. Bennet made no answer.

"Do not you want to know who has taken it?" cried his wife impatiently.

"You want to tell me, and I have no objection to hearing it."

This was invitation enough.[9]

"Why, my dear, you must know, Mrs. Long says that Netherfield is taken by a young man of large fortune from the north of England; that he came down on Monday in a chaise and four[10] to see the place, and was so much delighted with it that he agreed with Mr. Morris[11] immediately; that he is to take possession before Michaelmas[12], and some of his servants are to be in the house by the end of next week."

"What is his name?"

"Bingley."

"Is he married or single?"

"Oh! single, my dear, to be sure! A single man of large fortune; four or five thousand a year[13]. What a fine thing for our girls!"

"How so? how can it affect[14] them?"

"My dear Mr. Bennet," replied his wife, "how can you be so tiresome[15]! You must know that I am thinking of his marrying one of them."

"Is that his design[16] in settling here?"

Design! nonsensed[17], how can you talk so! But it is very likely that he *may* fall in love with one of them, and therefore you must visit him as soon as he comes."

"I see no occasion for that[18]. You and the girls may go, or you may send them by themselves, which perhaps will be still better; for, as you are as handsome as any of them, Mr. Bingley might like you the best of the party."

"My dear, you flatter me. I certainly *have* had my share of beauty, but I do not pretend to be anything extraordinary[19] now. When a woman has five grown up daughters, she ought to give over thinking of her own beauty."

"In such cases, a woman has not often much beauty to think of."

"But, my dear, you must indeed go and see Mr. Bingley when he comes into the neighbourhood."

"It is more than I engage for[20], I assure you."

"But consider your daughters. Only think what an establishment[21] it would be for one of them. Sir William and Lady Lucas[22] are determined to go, merely on that account, for in general, you know they visit no new comers. Indeed you must go, for it will be impossible for *us* to visit him, if you do not[23]."

"You are over-scrupulous, surely. I dare say Mr. Bingley will be very glad to see you; and I will send a few lines[24] by you to assure him of my hearty consent to his marrying whichever he chooses of the girls; though I must throw in a good word for my little Lizzy[25]."

"I desire you will do no such thing. Lizzy is not a bit better than the others; and I am sure she is not half so handsome as Jane[26], nor half so good humoured as Lydia[27]. But you are always giving *her* the preference[28]."

"They have none of them much to recommend them," replied he, "they are all silly and ignorant like other girls; but Lizzy has something more of quickness than her sisters."

"Mr. Bennet, how can you abuse your own children in such way? You take delight in vexing[29] me. You have no compassion on my poor nerves."

"You mistake me, my dear. I have a high respect for your nerves. They are my old friends. I have heard you mention them with consideration these twenty years at least."

"Ah! you do not know what I suffer."

"But I hope you will get over it, and live to see many young men of four thousand a year come into the neighbourhood."

"It will be no use to us if twenty such should come, since you will not visit them."

"Depend upon it[30], my dear, that when there are twenty I will visit them all."

Mr. Bennet was so odd a mixture of quick parts[31], sarcastic humour, reserve, and caprice[32], that the experience of three and twenty years had been insufficient to make his wife understand his character. Her mind was less difficult to develope[33]. She was a woman of mean understanding, little information, and uncertain temper. When she was discontented, she fancied herself nervous. The business of her life was to get her daughters married; its solace was visiting and news[34].

Chapter II

Mr. Bennet was among the earliest of those who waited on[1] Mr. Bingley. He had always intended to visit him, though to the last always assuring his wife that he should not go; and till the evening after the visit was paid, she had no knowledge of it. It was then disclosed in the following manner. Observing his second daughter employed in trimming[2] a hat, he suddenly addressed her with,

"I hope Mr. Bingley will like it, Lizzy."

"We are not in a way to know *what* Mr. Bingley likes," said her mother resentfully, "since we are not to visit."

"But you forget, mama," said Elizabeth, "that we shall meet him at the assemblies[3], and that Mrs. Long has promised to introduce him."

"I do not believe Mrs. Long will do any such thing. She has two nieces of her own. She is a selfish, hypocritical woman, and I have no opinion[4] of her."

"No more have I," said Mr. Bennet, "and I am glad to find that you do not depend on her serving you."

Mrs. Bennet deigned not to make any reply, but unable to contain herself, began scolding one of her daughters.

"Don't keep coughing so, Kitty[5], for heaven's sake! Have a little compassion on my nerves. You tear them to pieces."

"Kitty has no discretion in her coughs," said her father, "she times them ill[6]."

"I do not cough for my own amusement," replied Kitty fretfully.

"When is your next ball to be, Lizzy?"

"To-morrow fortnight[7]."

"Aye, so it is," cried her mother, "and Mrs. Long does not come back till the day before; so it will be impossible for her to introduce him, for she will not know him herself."

"Then, my dear, you may have the advantage of your friend, and introduce Mr. Bingley to her."

"Impossible, Mr. Bennet, impossible, when I am not acquainted with him myself; how can you be so teasing?"

"I honour your circumspection[8]. A fortnight's acquaintance is certainly very little. One cannot know what a man really is by the end of a fortnight. But if we do not venture, somebody else will[9]; and after all, Mrs. Long and her nieces must stand their chance; and therefore, as she will think it an act of kindness, if you decline the office[10], I will take it on myself."

The girls stared at their father. Mrs. Bennet said only, "Nonsense, nonsense!"

"What can be the meaning of that emphatic exclamation?" cried he. "Do you consider the forms of introduction, and the stress that is laid on them, as nonsense? I cannot quite agree with you there. What say you, Mary[11]? for you are a young lady of deep reflection I know, and read great books, and make extracts."

Mary wished to say something very sensible, but knew not how.

"While Mary is adjusting her ideas," he continued, "let us return to Mr. Bingley."

"I am sick of Mr. Bingley," cried his wife.

"I am sorry to hear that; but why did not you tell me so before? If I had known as much this morning[12] I certainly would not have called on him. It is very unlucky; but as I have actually paid the visit, we cannot escape the acquaintance now."

The astonishment of the ladies was just what he wished; that of Mrs. Bennet perhaps surpassing the rest; though when the first tumult of joy was over, she began to declare that it was what she had expected all the while.

"How good it was in you, my dear Mr. Bennet! But I knew I should persuade you at last. I was sure you loved our girls too well to neglect such an acquaintance. Well, how pleased I am! and it is such a good joke, too, that you should have gone this morning, and never said a word about it till now."

"Now, Kitty, you may cough as much as you choose," said Mr. Bennet; and, as he spoke, he left the room, fatigued with the raptures of his wife.

"What an excellent father you have, girls," said she, when the door was shut. "I do not know how you will ever make him amends for his kindness; or me either[13], for that matter. At our time of life, it is not so pleasant I can tell you, to be making new acquaintance every day; but for your sakes, we would do any thing. Lydia, my love, though you *are* the youngest, I dare say Mr. Bingley will dance with you at the next ball."

"Oh!" said Lydia stoutly, "I am not afraid; for though I *am* the youngest, I'm the tallest."

The rest of the evening was spent in conjecturing how soon he would return Mr. Bennet's visit, and determining when they should ask him to dinner.

Notes

Chapter I

1. **acknowledged:** accepted
2. **a single man:** a bachelor
3. **the surrounding families:** the neighbouring families
4. **he is considered as the rightful property of some one or other of their daughters:** he is considered to get married to the daughter of one of those families and thus become her "legal property". Here, "the rightful property" refers to the property held or owned by just or proper claim.
5. **his lady:** here referring to Mrs. Bennet
6. **Netherfield Park:** the name of an estate in the neighbourhood of the home of the Bennets
7. **he had not:** he had not heard

8. **Mrs. Long:** a neighbour and a friend of the Bennets

9. **This was invitation enough:** This was enough to invite or encourage Mrs. Bennet to tell.

10. **a chaise and four:** a lightweight carriage pulled or driven by four horses

11. **Mr. Morris:** the owner of the Netherfield Park

12. **Michaelmas:** a church festival celebrated on September 29 in honour of the archangel St. Michael, one of the seven archangels in Jewish and Christian legend.

13. **four or five thousand a year:** a yearly income of four or five thousand pounds

14. **affect:** have something to do with

15. **tiresome:** troublesome, tedious or annoying

16. **design:** purpose, intention

17. **nonsense:** foolish talk, idea

18. **I see no occasion for that:** I see no reason or need for that

19. **anything extraordinary:** outstanding or extraordinary person

20. **It is more than I engage for:** It is more than I promise to do

21. **what an establishment:** what a marriage. Here, "establishment" refers to arrangement of marriage

22. **Sir William and Lady Lucas:** Sir William Lucas and his wife, neighbours of the Bennets

23. **Indeed you must go, for it will be impossible for *us* to visit him, if you do not:** This is because it was the etiquette of the time for the male head of a family to pay the first visit to a newly-moved-in neighbour. It would have been a shocking breath of etiquette for a mother and her daughters to call first.

24. **a few lines:** a short letter, short note

25. **I must throw in a good word for my little Lizzy:** I must say a few words in recommendation of Elizabeth. "Lizzy" is the short form for Elizabeth, the second daughter of the Bennet family.

26. **Jane:** the eldest daughter of the Bennet family

27. **Lydia:** the youngest daughter of the Bennet family

28. **giving *her* the preference:** favouring her before others, liking her the most

29. **vexing:** angering, annoying or irritating (somebody), esp. with trivial

matters

30. **Depend upon it:** There can be no doubt about it

31. **quick parts:** wit. Here, "parts" in the plural form is used in the archaic sense of "abilities", "intelligence".

32. **caprice:** sudden change in attitude or behaviour with no obvious reason; unpredictable; impulsive

33. **Her mind was less difficult to develope:** It was easier to understand her mind. "Develope" is the old spelling of "develop", meaning unwrap and unfold. In the present context, it means discover or understand.

34. **its solace was visiting and news:** The comfort of her life consisted in paying visit to her neighbours and receiving visits from them and in listening to and talking about things that happened recently in the neighbourhood. "solace" refers to (things that gives) comfort or relief (from pain, trouble, distress, etc.)

Chapter II

1. **waited on:** called on

2. **trimming:** decorate or make neat or smooth something

3. **the assemblies:** the parties, the balls

4. **opinion:** high opinion

5. **Kitty:** the short form for Catherine, the fourth daughter of the Bennet family

6. **she times them ill:** she coughs at the wrong time

7. **To-morrow fortnight:** the day after two weeks, that is to say, fifteen days later

8. **circumspection:** caution; prudence

9. **But if we do not venture, somebody else will:** But if we do not venture to introduce Mr. Bingley to Mrs. Long, somebody else will do it.

10. **office:** help, service

11. **Mary:** the third daughter of the Bennet family

12. **If I had known as much:** If I had known this morning that you were sick of Mr. Bingley

13. **or me either:** or make me amends either

Questions for Study and Discussion

1. The novel begins with one of the most famous first sentences in all novels. Explain and comment on the sentence "It is a truth universally

acknowledged, that a single man in possession of a good fortune, must be in want of a wife". What is the view of marriage that it suggests? How can it be demonstrated during the conversation between Mr. and Mrs. Bennet in Chapter I ?

2. At the beginning of the novel, Netherfield Park was mentioned. Who lives in such places? What are their economic situations? Describe the functions of such setting.

3. Why is Mrs. Bennet so happy to hear that Netherfield Park is taken by a young man?

4. Describe Mr. Bingley's social and financial status from the utterance of Mrs. Bennet. And what is her attitude toward him?

5. Chapter I has been highly praised as an opening chapter. How do you consider such praise? Is this praise justified? Would you please give some reasons for your answers?

6. After reading Chapter I and II, how would you describe the marriage between Mr. and Mrs. Bennet from the dialogue between them? And please summarize the characters of them .

7. What methods does Jane Austin use in Chapter I and II to depict the characters of Mr. Bennet, Mrs. Bennet and their daughters?

8. After reading this novel, what can we learn about the life and custom of the 18th century?

9. Would you please cite some instances to show the author's use of humour, satire and a blend of the two?

Charles Lamb (1775—1834)

Life and Major Works

Born in London Charles Lamb was the son of John Lamb, a clerk of a lawyer. Lamb was educated at Christ's Hospital, where he formed an enduring friendship with Samuel Taylor Coleridge. After leaving school, he was employed by the South Sea House. A few months later, he was transferred to the India house, where he remained from 1792 to 1825. In 1976, his mother was killed by his elder sister Mary in a fit of insanity. Lamb undertook the charge of his sister, who remained periodically insane. Lamb himself suffered from periodic mental illness too. Owing to his family commitments, Lamb lost a marriage he was looking forward to. He actually fell in love with an actress, Fanny Kelly, but she refused him and he remained until his death a bachelor.

Lamb had already established his name as a poet around the year 1795. In 1796, a volume of poems by Coleridge was published containing four sonnets written by Lamb. In 1797 he contributed some blank verse to the second edition. In his short summer holiday with

Charles Lamb

Coleridge in the same year, he met William Wordsworth, and also stroke a lifelong friendship with him. In London, Lamb became familiar with a group of young writers who favored political reform, including Shelley, Hazlitt, and Hunt. In 1802, Lamb published *John Woodvil,* a tragedy. In 1806, his farce *Mr. H* was perfomed at Drury Lane but proved a failure. In 1807, he wrote with his sister *Tales from Shakespeare.* In 1808, he cooperated with his sister again with the story of "Odyssey" in the same style they did with Shakespeare and thus appeared *The Adventures of Ulysses.* In 1809, his collection of short stories *Mrs. Leicester's School* came out. About the same time Lamb was commissioned by Longman to edit selections from the Elizabethan dramatists. He added criticism to the selections, and the collection of dramatic essays, *Specimens of English Dramatic Poets* (1808) brought him the reputation of a subtle and penetrating critic. Between 1810 and 1820 his literary output was small. He wrote intermittently for periodicals, with the major contribution being the famous *Essays of Elia*, collected in 1823 and 1833.

In 1823 Lamb moved from London to Islington, and in 1827 to Enfield, and thence in 1833 to Edmonton, where he died and was buried on December 29, 1834. His sister survived him for 13 years.

While Lamb wrote dramatic and theatrical works, his fame rested mainly as an essayist and critic. His essays cover various subjects, but with an intimate and familiar kind of tone. Not well recognized during his lifetime, Lamb went through periods of self-doubt and dismissal. However, he has left an extensive legacy of essays, stories and poetry with his particular style, wit and touching humor.

Brief Introduction and Appreciation

The Essay of Elia is a collection of miscellaneous essays written by Lamb. The first series of the essays appeared in the *London Magazine* between 1820 and 1823, and was published in a separate volume in the latter year. The second series was published in 1833. Lamb used the pseudonym Elia to save the susceptibilities of his brother John, the subject of the first series, still a clerk in the South-Sea House at the time. The name came from an Italian clerk formerly working in that office.

The essays are largely autobiographical. They deal with mankind in general as observed through Lamb's own experience and impression. They present with exquisite humor and in an inimitable style.

The excerpted part is part of "Old China", an essay from *The Essay of Elia*. It started with the narrator's affection toward old china and his appreciation of the Chinese style of arts. Then using Bridget's voice (seemingly a mixture of that of Mary Lamb and Charles Lamb himself, the essay probes into the change brought to them with the change of their financial situations.

The essay is filled with a reminiscent atmosphere and recalled details of the past time, together with the usual exquisite humor. His detailed description of the pictures on old china also shows his understanding of the mysterious Oriental arts.

Selected Reading

Old China

I have an almost feminine partiality[1] for old china. When I go to see any great house[2], I inquire for the china closet, and next for the picture gallery. I cannot defend[3] the order of preference, but by saying, that we have all some taste or other, of too ancient a date to admit of our remembering distinctly that it was an acquired one[4]. I can call to mind the first play, and the first exhibition, that I was taken to; but I am not conscious of a time when china jars and saucers were introduced into my imagination.

I had no repugnance[5] then—why should I now have?—to those little, lawless, azure—tinctured grotesques, that under the notion of men and women, float about, uncircumscribed[6] by any element, in that world before perspective[7]—a china teacup.

I like to see my old friends—whom distance cannot diminish—figuring up in the air (so they appear to our optics), yet on *terra firma*[8] still—for so we must in courtesy interpret that speck of deeper blues—which the decorous[9] artist, to prevent absurdity, had made to spring up beneath their sandals.

I love the men with women's faces, and the women, if possible, with still more womanish expressions.

Here is a young and courtly Mandarin[10], handing tea to a lady from a salver[11]— two miles off. See how distance seems to set off respect[12]! And here the same lady, or another— for likeness is identity on teacups—is stepping into a little fairy boat, moored on the hither side[13] of this calm garden river, with a dainty mincing foot[14], which in a right angle of incidence (as angles go in our world) must infallibly land her in the midst of a flowery mead—a furlong off on the other side of the same strange stream[15]!

Farther on — if far or near can be predicated of their world—see horses, trees, pagodas, dancing the hays[16].

Here — a cow and rabbit couchant[17], and coextensive[18]—so objects show, seen through the lucid atmosphere of fine Cathay[19].

I was pointing out to my cousin last evening, over our Hyson[20] (which we are old-fashioned enough to drink unmixed[21] still of an afternoon), some of these *speciosa miracula*[22] upon a set of extraordinary old blue china (a recent purchase) which we were now for the first time using; and could not help remarking, how favourable circumstances had been to us of late years, that we could afford to please the eye sometimes with trifles of this sort—when a passing sentiment seemed to overshade the brows of my companion. I am quick at detecting these summer clouds in Bridget[23].

"I wish the good old times would come again," she said, "when we were not quite so rich. I do not mean, that I want to be poor; but there was a middle state"—so she was pleased to ramble on,—"in which I am sure we were a great deal happier. A purchase is but a purchase, now that you have money enough and to spare. Formerly it used to be a triumph. When we coveted[24] a cheap luxury (and, O! how much ado I had to get you to consent in those times!) —we were used to have a debate two or three days before, and to weigh the *for* and *against*, and think what we might spare it out of, and what saving we could hit upon, that should be an equivalent. A thing was worth buying then, when we felt the money that we paid for it.

"Do you remember the brown suit, which you made to hang upon you, till all your friends cried shame upon you, it grew so threadbare[25]—and all because of that folio Beaumont and Fletcher[26], which you dragged home late at night from Barker's in Covent Garden[27]? Do you remember how we eyed it for weeks before we could make up our minds to the purchase, and had not come to a determination till it was near ten o'clock of the Saturday night, when you get off from Islington[28], fearing you should be too late—and when the old bookseller with some grumbling opened his shop, and by the twinkling taper[29] (for he was setting bedwards) lighted out the relic from his dusty treasures—and when you lugged[30] it home, wishing it were twice as cumbersome[31]—and when you presented it to me—and when we were exploring the perfectness of it (collating[32], you called it)—and while I was repairing some of the loose leaves with paste, which your impatience would not suffer to be left till daybreak—was there no pleasure in being a poor man? or can those neat black clothes which you wear now, and are so careful to keep brushed, since we have become rich and finical[33], give you half the honest vanity with which you flaunted[34] it about in that overworn suit—your old corbeau[35]—for four or five weeks longer than you should have done, to pacify[36] your conscience for the mighty sum of fifteen—or sixteen shillings was it?—a great affair we thought it then—which you had lavished on the old folio. Now you can afford to buy any book that pleases you, but I do not see that you ever bring me home any nice old purchases now.

"You are too proud to see a play anywhere now but in the pit[37]. Do you remember where it was we used to sit, when we saw the *Battle of Hexham*, and the *Surrender of Calais*[38], and Bannister and Mrs. Bland in the *Children in the Wood*[39]—when we squeezed out our shillings apiece to sit three or four times in a season in the one-shilling gallery[40]—where you felt all the time that you ought not to have brought me—and more strongly I felt obligation to you for having brought me—and the pleasure was the better for a little shame—and when the curtain drew up, what cared we for our place in the house, or what mattered it where we were sitting, when our thoughts were with Rosalind in Arden, or with Viola at the Court of Illyria[41]. You used to say that the Gallery was the best place of all for enjoying a play socially—that the relish of such exhibitions must be in proportion to the infrequency of going—that the company we met there, not being in general readers of plays, were obliged to attend the more, and did attend, to what was going on, on the stage—because a word lost would have been a chasm, which it was impossible for them to fill up. With such reflections we consoled our pride then—and I appeal to you whether, as a woman, I met generally with less attention and accommodation[42] than I have done since in more expensive situations in the house? The getting in indeed, and the crowding up those inconvenient staircases, was bad enough, —but there was still a law of civility to woman recognized to quite as great an extent as we ever found in the other passages—and how a little difficulty overcome heightened the snug seat and the play, afterwards! Now we can only pay our money and walk in. You cannot see, you say, in the galleries now. I am sure we saw, and heard too, well enough then—but sight, and all, I think, is gone with our poverty.

Bridget is so sparing[43] of her speech on most occasions, that when she gets into a rhetorical vein, I am careful how I interrupt it. I could not help, however, smiling at the phantom[44] of wealth which her dear imagination had conjured up out of a clear income of poor—hundred pounds a year. "It is true we were happier when we were poor but we were also younger, my cousin. I am afraid we must put up with the excess, for if we were to shake the superflux into the sea[45], we should not much mend ourselves. That we had much to struggle with, as we grew up together, we have reason to be most thankful. It strengthened and knit our compact closer. We could never have been what we have been to each other, if we had always had the sufficiency which you now complain of. The resisting power—those natural dilations[46] of the youthful spirit, which circumstances cannot straiten—with us are long since passed away. Competence to age is supplementary youth, a sorry supplement indeed, but I fear the best that is to be had. We must ride where we formerly walked: live better and lie softer—and shall be wise to do so—than we had means to do in those good old days you speak of. Yet could those days return—could you and I once more walk our thirty miles a day—could Bannister and Mrs. Bland again be young, and you and I be young to see them—could the good old one-shilling gallery days return—they are dreams, my cousin, now—but could you and I at this moment, instead of this quiet argument, by our well-carpeted fireside, sitting on this luxurious sofa—be once more struggling up those inconvenient staircases, pushed about, and squeezed, and elbowed by the poorest rabble[47] of poor gallery scramblers—could I once more hear those anxious shrieks of yours—and the delicious Thank God, we are safe, which always followed when the topmost stair, conquered, let in the first light of the whole cheerful theatre down beneath us—I know not the fathom line that ever touched a descent so deep as I would be willing to bury more wealth in than Croesus[48] had, or the great Jew R[49]—is supposed to have, to purchase it. And now do just look at that merry little Chinese waiter holding an umbrella, big enough for a bed-tester, over the head of that pretty insipid half Madonnaish[50] chit[51] of a lady in that very blue summer-house."

Notes

1. **an almost feminine partiality:** a delicate feeling or preference for old china that almost resembles a woman's feelings
2. **great house:** here referring to any of the houses of aristocrats that are sometimes open to the public.
3. **defend:** justify
4. **an acquired one:** one (liking, preference) gained from experience
5. **repugnance:** inconsistency
6. **uncircumscribed:** unrestricted
7. **perspective:** the technique of representing three-dimensional objects and depth relationships on a two-dimensional surface. Here Lamb shows his understanding of the ancient Chinese art: mysterious while not following the western tradition of artistic creation.
8. *terra firma:* (Latin) solid ground
9. **decorous:** characterized by or exhibiting decorum; proper
10. **Mandarin:** a high government official or bureaucrat in old China
11. **salver:** a tray for serving food or drinks
12. **set off respect:** make respect more noticeable
13. **on the hither side:** on this side
14. **a dainty mincing foot:** an affectedly refined manner
15. This sentence is a good example of Lamb's humorous expression of his understanding of the Chinese art. **furlong:** a unit for measuring distance, equal to 1/8 mile (201 meters).
16. **dancing the hays:** a kind of country dance in England; here referring to any kind of country dance.
17. **couchant:** lying down with the head raised

18. **coextensive:** having the same limits, boundaries, or scope

19. **Cathay:** a medieval name for China popularized by Marco Polo in accounts of his travels

20. **Hyson:** a type of Chinese green tea with twisted leaves

21. **drink unmixed:** drink without adding milk or sugar to it

22. *speciosa miracula:* (Latin) shining wonders

23. **Bridget:** a named to refer to Mary Lamb in *Essays of Elia*

24. **covet:** to wish for longingly

25. **threadbare:** (of clothes) having the nap worn down so that the filling or warp threads show through

26. **Francis Beaumont (1584—1616) and John Fletcher (1579—1625):** English dramatists who wrote many plays in collaboration.

27. **Covent Garden:** a district in London, located on the easternmost parts of the City of Westminster and the southwest corner of the London Borough of Camden. The area is dominated by shopping, street performers and entertainment facilities.

28. **Islington:** the central district of the London Borough of Islington, located in the north of London. Lamb and his sister lived there.

29. **taper:** a small or very slender candle

30. **lug:** to drag or haul (an object) laboriously

31. **cumbersome:** difficult to handle because of weight or bulk

32. **collate:** to examine and compare carefully in order to note points of disagreement

33. **finical:** insisting capriciously on getting just what one wants; difficult to please

34. **flaunt:** to exhibit ostentatiously or shamelessly

35. **corbeau:** black (suit)

36. **pacify:** to ease the anger or agitation of

37. **pit:** the ground floor of a theater behind the stalls

38. ***Battle of Hexhem*, and the *Surrender of Calais*:** comedies by George Colman (1762—1836), popular dramatist and miscellaneous writer of the time.

39. ***Children in the Wood*:** a play by Thomas Morton(1764—1838), early American colonist from England, a lawyer, writer and social reformer.

40. **gallery:** The cheapest seats in a theater, generally those of the uppermost

gallery (the highest upper floor).

41. **Rosalind in Arden; Viola at the Court of Illyria:** referring respectively to the heroine in Shakespeare's comedies *As You Like It* and *Twelfth Night*.

42. **accommodation:** something that meets a need; a convenience

43. **sparing:** Given to or marked by prudence and restraint in the use of material resources. Here it's used to say how Bridget is not talkative.

44. **phantom:** something apparently seen, heard, or sensed, but having no physical reality; a ghost or an apparition. Here it means the devil-like image of wealth created by Bridget.

45. **excess and superflux:** an amount or quantity beyond what is normal or sufficient; a surplus.

46. **natural dilations:** here referring to the natural ability of the youth to deal with any circumstance.

47. **rabble:** the lowest or coarsest class of people

48. **Croesus:** Last king of Lydia (560—546) whose kingdom, which had prospered during his reign, fell to the Persians under Cyrus. Now the name is often used to refer to an extremely wealthy person.

49. **the great Jew R:** Nathan Meyer Rothschild (1777—1836), a London financier and one of the founders of the international Rothschild family banking dynasty.

50. **Madonnaish:** resembling the Virgin Mary

51. **chit:** a young pretty girl

Questions for Study and Discussion

1. Who is the narrator of the essay? Who is his companion?
2. Why does the narrator have a "feminine partiality" for old china?
3. Comment on the author's "familiar tone".
4. What's the significance of Bridget's telling of old stories?
5. What does "I" think about Bridget's feeling of the old days?
6. What are the possible symbolic meanings of "old china"?
7. Summarize Lamb's understanding of Chinese art. What are the reasonable points in his understanding? Where does he make mistakes?

William Hazlitt (1778—1830)

Life and Major Works

William Hazlitt was born in Maidstone, Kent in 1778. His father was an Irish Unitarian clergyman. As a result of supporting the American Revolution, his family was forced to leave England and live in Ireland and Boston. In 1787, his family returned to England and settled at Wem in Shropshire. At the age of 15 Hazlitt was sent to New Unitarian College at Hackney in London to be trained for the ministry. However, after a few years he lost his interest and desire to become a Unitarian minister and left the college in 1797.

William Hazlitt

While in London, through the introduction of Charles Lamb, Hazlitt became acquainted with many important literary figures, among whom were Wordsworth, Coleridge, Shelley, Lamb, Southey and Byron. At first Hazlitt attempted to be a portrait painter, but soon he found himself in lack of success and then turned to writing.

In 1805 his first book *An Essay on the Principles of Human Action* was published. The following year saw his *Free Thoughts on Public Affairs*, attacking William Pitt, the young Prime Minister and his foreign policy. A series of articles and pamphlets on political corruption and the need to reform the voting system appeared after that.

Hazlitt began writing for *The Times* in 1808. In 1810 he published *The New and Improved Grammar of the English Language*. Although he was employed by the country's leading Whig newspaper, *Morning Chronicle*, as the parliamentary reporter, his criticism aimed at all political parties. Other journals he contributed to included *The Examiner*, *Edinburgh Review*, *The Yellow Dwarf* and *The London Magazine*. Because of these essays, Hazlitt was considered as a leading expert on William Shakespeare's writings.

In 1817 Hazlitt published *Characters of Shakespeare's Plays*, and the next year *A View of the English Stage*, and *English Poets*. In 1819, another book about literature, *English Comic Writers*, came out. In the same year, his most important book on politics, *Political Essays with Sketches of Public Characters* was published. In 1820, his *Dramatic Literature of the Age of Elizabeth* renewed enthusiasm for Elizabethan drama. The 1823 book *Liber Amoris* recorded his miserable marriage and love affairs. And *The Spirit of the Age: Contemporary Portraits* was a book published in 1825 containing interesting appreciations of his contemporaries. This was followed by *The Plain Speaker* (1826) and *Life of Napoleon* (4 volumes, 1828—1830).

Hazlitt was also one of the great masters of the miscellaneous essay. Most of these essays were included in *Table Talk, or Original Essays on Men and Manners* (1821—1822) and *The Plain Speaker* (1826). In these essays his keen intellect and sensibility, and his wide scope of interest and knowledge was displayed. Some of his notable essays include "On Going a Journey", "My First Acquaintance with Poets", "On the Feeling of Immortality in Youth" and "Going to a Fight".

In his essays, Hazlitt showed his impartial outlook in both political and literary matters. His most distinctive trait is the combination of intense subjectivity with strict adherence to his subject. His quest for intellectual truthfulness, his strong sense of individuality and his vehement political sympathies and antipathies always put him on the unfashionable side.

In terms of temperament, Hazlitt was of a curiously divided nature, almost as an artist as a thinker and writer. He spent much time making a careful study of English, Scottish, and Irish thinkers like Locke, Hartley, Berkeley, and Hume, and French thinkers like Helv tius, Condillac, Condorcet, and Baron d'Holbach. His thoughts were focused on man as a social and political animal, and, even more intensely, on the philosophy of mind, which was later called psychology. In his pursuit of philosophy, he was greatly influenced by Rousseau's ideas and Edmund Burke's writing style.

Hazlitt was a quarrelsome and unpleasant person, which is exemplified by his two failed marriage and the loss of many friends as the result of his quarrels with them. He died in poverty in 1830 while his literary reputation was fading.

Brief Introduction and Appreciation

Hazlitt had always been interested in the discussion of characters in literature before he wrote the book *Characters in Shakespeare's Plays*. The book was published in 1817, dedicated to Charles Lamb, as "a mark of old friendship and lasting esteem". Written with passion, the book was rather an encomium than a commentary or a critique on Shakespeare, and it was written more to show extraordinary love than extraordinary knowledge of the productions of the great master. Hazlitt revealed his feelings when reading Shakespeare. Almost all Shakespeare's important works are discussed in this book.

In general, Hazlitt believes that Shakespeare's characters are more vivid in a way that they are individuals rather than types, although one can feel that these characters are from "the same mind", they are undoubtedly "different creations". Hazlitt's book actually gives an excellent analysis of Shakespeare's craftsmanship as a dramatist, his importance in the Elizabethan period and his arts of characterization.

The selected part is mainly concerning Lady Macbeth, probably the most attractive character in *Macbeth*. Hazlitt reveals to the readers how this "great bad woman" is molded in the description of her actions and speech, in the comparison and contrast of her and her husband, and the effect she has on the murder of the King and the fate of her husband. Interestingly enough, Hazlitt also mentions the contemporary actress who plays the role of Lady Macbeth, as a re-emphasis of the uniqueness and impressiveness of this character.

Hazlitt's style is familiar but never vulgar. As one of the great Romantic prose writers, he adopts artistic language and passionate expressions with individual and original ideas.

Selected Reading

Macbeth Characters Analysis[1]

The poet's eye in a fine frenzy rolling
Doth glance from heaven to earth, from earth to heaven;
And as imagination bodies forth
The forms of things unknown, the poet's pen
Turns them to shape, and gives to airy nothing
A local habitation and a name. [2]

Macbeth and *Lear*, *Othello* and *Hamlet*, are usually reckoned as Shakespeare's four principal tragedies. *Lear* stands first for the profound intensity of the passion; *Macbeth* for the wildness of the imagination and the rapidity of the action; *Othello* for the progressive interest and powerful alternations of feeling; *Hamlet* for the refined development of thought and sentiment. If the force of genius shown in each of these works is astonishing, their variety is not less so. They are like different creations of the same mind, not one of which has the slightest reference to the rest. This distinctness and originality is indeed the necessary consequence of truth and nature. Shakespeare's genius alone appeared to possess the resources of nature. He is "your only tragedy-maker". His plays have the force of things upon the mind. What he represents is brought home to the bosom as a part of our experience, implanted in the memory as if we had known the places, persons, and things of which he treats. *Macbeth* is like a record of a preternatural[3] and tragical event. It has the rugged severity of an old chronicle with all that the imagination of the poet can engraft[4] upon traditional belief. The castle of Macbeth, round which "the air smells wooingly", and where "the temple-haunting martlet builds", has a real subsistence in the mind; the Weird Sisters[5] meet us in person on "the blasted heath"; the "air-drawn dagger" moves slowly before our eyes; the "gracious Duncan[6]", the "blood-boultered Banquo[7]" stand before us; all that passed through the mind of Macbeth passes, without the loss of a tittle[8], through ours. All that could actually take place, and all that is only possible to be conceived, what was said and what was done, the workings of passion, the spells of magic, are brought before us with the same absolute truth and vividness.

Shakespeare excelled in the openings of his plays: that of *Macbeth* is the most striking of any. The wildness of the scenery, the sudden shifting of the situations and characters, the bustle, the expectations excited, are equally extraordinary. From the first entrance of the Witches and the description of them when they meet Macbeth,

> *What are these*
> *So wither'd and so wild in their attire,*
> *That look not like the inhabitants o' th' earth*
> *And yet are on't?* [9]

the mind is prepared for all that follows.

This tragedy is alike distinguished for the lofty imagination it displays, and for the tumultuous vehemence of the action; and the one is made the moving principle of the other. The overwhelming pressure of preternatural agency urges on the tide of human passion with redoubled force. Macbeth himself appears driven along by the violence of his fate like a vessel drifting before a storm: he reels to and fro like a drunken man; he staggers under the weight of his own purposes and the suggestions of others; he stands at bay with his situation; and from the superstitious awe and breathless suspense into which the communications of the Weird Sisters throw him, is hurried on with daring impatience to verify their predictions, and with impious and bloody hand to tear aside the veil which hides the uncertainty of the future. He is not equal to the struggle with fate and conscience. He now "bends up each corporal instrument to the terrible feat[10]"; at other times his heart misgives him, and he is cowed and abashed by his success. "The deed, no less than the attempt, confounds him." His mind is assailed by the stings of remorse, and full of "preternatural solicitings[11]". His speeches and soliloquies[12] are dark riddles on human life, baffling solution, and entangling him in their labyrinths. In thought he is absent and perplexed[13], sudden and desperate in act, from a distrust of his own resolution. His energy springs from the anxiety and agitation of his mind. His blindly rushing forward on the objects of his ambition and revenge, or his recoiling[14] from them, equally betrays the harassed state of his feelings. This part of his character is admirably set off by being brought in connection with that of Lady Macbeth, whose obdurate[15] strength of will and masculine firmness gave her the ascendency[16] over her husband's faultering[17] virtue. She at once seizes on the opportunity that offers for the accomplishment of all their wished-for greatness, and never flinches from her object till all is over. The magnitude of her resolution almost covers the magnitude of her guilt. She is a great bad woman, whom we hate, but whom we fear more than we hate. She does not excite our loathing and abhorrence like Regan and Gonerill[18]. She is only wicked to gain a great end; and is perhaps more distinguished by her commanding presence of mind and inexorable[19] self-will, which do not suffer her to be diverted from a bad purpose, when once formed, by weak and womanly regrets, than by the hardness of her heart or want of natural affections. The impression which her lofty determination of character makes on the mind of Macbeth is well described where he exclaims,

Bring forth men children only;
For thy undaunted mettle should compose
Nothing but males! [20]

Nor do the pains she is at to "screw his courage to the sticking-place", the reproach to him, not to be "lost so poorly in himself", the assurance that "a little water clears them of this deed," show anything but her greater consistency in depravity[21]. Her strong-nerved ambition furnishes ribs of steel to "the sides of his intent"; and she is herself wound up to the execution of her baneful[22] project with the same unshrinking fortitude in crime, that in other circumstances she would probably have shown patience in suffering. The deliberate sacrifice of all other considerations to the gaining "for their future days and nights sole sovereign sway and masterdom," by the murder of Duncan, is gorgeously expressed in her invocation[23] on hearing of "his fatal entrance under her battlements":

Come, you spirits
That tend on mortal thoughts, unsex me here:
And fill me, from the crown to th' toe, top-full
Of direst cruelty; make thick my blood,
Stop up the access and passage to remorse,
That no compunctious visitings of nature
Shake my fell purpose, nor keep peace between
The effect and it. Come to my woman's breasts,
And take my milk for gall, you murthering ministers,
Wherever in your sightless substances
You wait on nature's mischief. Come, thick night!
And pall thee in the dunnest smoke of hell,
That my keen knife see not the wound it makes,
Nor heav'n peep through the blanket of the dark,
To cry, "hold, hold!" [24]

When she first hears that "Duncan comes there to sleep" she is so overcome by the news, which is beyond her utmost expectations, that she answers the messenger, "Thou'rt mad to say it": and on receiving her husband's account of the predictions of the Witches, conscious of his instability of purpose, and that her presence is necessary to goad[25] him on to the consummation of his promised greatness, she exclaims:

Hie thee hither,
That I may pour my spirits in thine ear,
And chastise with the valour of my tongue
All that impedes thee from the golden round
Which fate and metaphysical aid doth seem
To have thee crowned withal. [26]

This swelling exultation[27] and keen spirit of triumph, this uncontrollable eagerness of anticipation, which seems to dilate[28] her form and take possession of all her faculties, this solid, substantial flesh-and-blood display of passion, exhibit a striking contrast to the cold, abstracted, gratuitous, servile[29] malignity of the Witches, who are equally instrumental in urging Macbeth to his fate for the mere love of mischief, and from a disinterested delight in deformity and cruelty. They are hags of mischief, obscene panders to iniquity, malicious from their impotence of enjoyment, enamoured of destruction, because they are themselves unreal, abortive, half-existences—who become sublime from their exemption from all human sympathies and contempt for all human affairs, as Lady Macbeth does by the force of passion! Her fault seems to have been an excess of that strong principle of self-interest and family aggrandisement[30], not amenable[31] to the common feelings of compassion and justice, which is so marked a feature in barbarous nations and times. A passing reflection of this kind, on the resemblance of the sleeping king to her father, alone prevents her from slaying Duncan with her own hand.

In speaking of the character of Lady Macbeth, we ought not to pass over Mrs. Siddons's[32] manner of acting that part. We can conceive of nothing grander. It was something above nature. It seemed almost as if a being of a superior order had dropped from a higher sphere to awe the world with the majesty of her appearance. Power was seated on her brow, passion emanated[33] from her breast as from a shrine[34]; she was tragedy personified. In coming on in the sleeping-scene, her eyes were open, but their sense was shut. She was like a person bewildered and unconscious of what she did. Her lips moved involuntarily—all her gestures were involuntary and mechanical. She glided on and off the stage like an apparition. To have seen her in that character was an event in every one's life, not to be forgotten.

Macbeth (generally speaking) is done upon a stronger and more systematic principle of contrast than any other of Shakespeare's plays. It moves upon the verge of an abyss[35], and is a constant struggle between life and death. The action is desperate and the reaction is dreadful. It is a huddling[36] together of fierce extremes, a war of opposite natures which of them shall destroy the other. There is nothing but what has a violent end or violent beginnings. The lights and shades are laid on with a determined hand; the transitions from triumph to despair, from the height of terror to the repose of death, are sudden and startling; every passion brings in its fellow-contrary, and the thoughts pitch and jostle against each other as in the dark. The whole play is an unruly chaos of strange and forbidden things, where the ground rocks under our feet. Shakespeare's genius here took its full swing, and trod upon the farthest bounds of nature and passion.

...

Notes

1. the selected reading was part of an essay entitled "Macbeth" in Hazlitt's collection of essays *Characters of Shakespeare's Plays*; the collection covers most of Shakespeare's tragedies, comedies, history plays, sonnets and other poems. The part selected here focuses on Lady Macbeth, the most impressive female character in the play.
2. the poem's from Shakespeare's *A Midsummer Night's Dream*, Act V, Scene I.
3. **preternatural:** out of or being beyond the normal course of nature; differing from the natural
4. **engraft:** to plant firmly; establish
5. **Weird Sisters:** a name the three witches use to call themselves before Macbeth appears in the first Act. The original lines are "The weird sisters, hand in hand, / Posters of the sea and land, / Thus do go about, about: / Thrice to thine and thrice to mine / And thrice again, to make up nine. / Peace! The charm's wound up."
6. **Duncan:** King of Scotland upon the death of Malcolm in 1034. He was a

much weaker character than Malcolm. His cousin Macbeth, chief of the northern Scots, also had a claim to the throne through his mother. Macbeth formed an alliance with his cousin the Earl of Orkney, and they defeated and killed Duncan in 1040. In Shakespeare's play he is killed out of Macbeth's conspiracy.

7. **Banquo:** a character in *Macbeth*. Banquo is at first a friend to Macbeth, and they are together when they meet the three witches. The witches tell Banquo that he will not be king himself, but that his descendants will be. Therefore, Macbeth later sees Banquo as a threat to his lust for power and has him murdered.

8. **tittle:** the tiniest bit; an iota

9. This is Banquo's comment on the three witches when he and Macbeth first see them. (Act I, Scene III)

10. originally "I am settled, and bend up each corporal agent to this terrible feat" (Act I, Scene VII). It is a line said by Macbeth showing his determination in killing Duncan.

11. **solicitings:** entreaty; persuasion

12. **soliloquy:** a dramatic or literary form of discourse in which a character reveals his or her thoughts when alone or unaware of the presence of other characters.

13. **perplexed:** filled with confusion or bewilderment; puzzled

14. **recoiling:** return, reaction

15. **obdurate:** hardened against feeling; hardhearted

16. **ascendancy:** advantage

17. **faultering:** unsteady in purpose or action, as from loss of courage or confidence; hesitant

18. **Regan and Gonerill:** characters in *Lear*, Lear's two elder daughters, condemned by readers for their remorseless actions toward their father.

19. **inexorable:** not capable of being persuaded by entreaty; relentless

20. this is the lines Macbeth says to his wife when she soberly gives the detailed plan of murdering Duncan (Act I, Scene VII).

21. **depravity:** moral corruption or degradation

22. **baneful:** causing death, destruction, or ruin; harmful

23. **invocation:** the act of conjuring up a spirit by incantation

24. Lady Macbeth's soliloquy (or prayer to evil spirits) asking for more power

to be cruel enough in Duncan's murder when she hears the news of Duncan staying at her home (Act I, Scene V).

25. **goad:** to prod or urge with or as if with a long pointed stick
26. this is the lines Lady Macbeth says to encourage her husband after reading his letter telling of the witches' prophecy.
27. **exultation:** the act or condition of rejoicing greatly
28. **dilate:** to make wider or larger; cause to expand
29. **servile:** abjectly submissive; slavish
30. **aggrandizement:** increase or extension
31. **amenable:** responsive to advice, authority, or suggestion
32. referring to Sarah Siddons (1755—1831), British actress, the best-known tragedienne of the 18th century, most famous for her portrayal of the Shakespearean character Lady Macbeth.
33. **emanate:** to come or send forth, as from a source
34. **shrine:** a site hallowed by a venerated object or its associations
35. **verge of an abyss:** the edge of an unfathomable chasm
36. **huddling:** a densely packed group or crowd, as of people or animals

Questions for Study and Discussion

1. What is the significance of the quoted poem at the beginning of the selected reading?
2. For what reason does Hazlitt praise Shakespeare as a "tragedy maker"? How does Shakespeare succeed in making the great tragedy *Macbeth?*
3. What do you think makes Lady Macbeth "a great bad woman, whom we hate, but whom we fear more than we hate"?
4. Why does Hazlitt mention the actress Mrs. Siddons?
5. How are the two characters, Macbeth and Lady Macbeth, different from each other?
6. Do you consider this essay a good piece of literary critique? Give your reasons.
7. Do you agree that Hazlitt's style is "familiar but never vulgar"? Use specific examples from this essay to support your idea.
8. Compare Hazlitt's essay with that of Charles Lamb in terms of language and theme.

Part Six   The Victorian Age (1832—1900)

I. Historical Background

The Victorian age is generally agreed to stretch through the reign of Queen Victoria (1837—1901), begining with the passage of the 1832 Reform Act by the English Parliament and ending with Queen's death in 1901.

1. Queen Victoria and the Victorian Age

Alexandrina Victoria, born on May 24, 1819, was the daughter of Edward, Duke of Kent and Princess Victoria Maria Louisa of Saxe-Coburg-Saalfeld, and the grand-daughter of King George III. In 1837, at the age of 18, Victoria succeeded William IV to the throne.

In the early years of her reign, two men became the dominant influence in Victoria's life. One was Lord Melbourne, her first Prime Minister, and the other was Prince Albert, her husband, whom she married in 1840. On their advice, she managed to rule the country in a "constitutional monarchy" by using little power but exerting much influence.

An intelligent and hardworking monarch, Victoria did her utmost to serve her people and knew how to collaborate with her prime ministers by entrusting them with full leadership. During her reign, England reached the pinnacle of its economic and political power, established a vast colonial empire, and implemented numerous political and social reforms at home.

In her old age, Victoria was enormously popular with her subjects, and she was idolized as the symbol of the British Empire. Jubilees were held in 1887 and 1897 to celebrate the 50th and 60th anniversaries of the queen's accession. She died, a venerable old lady, on January 22, 1901, having reigned for sixty-four years. She was buried at Windsor beside Prince Albert, in the

Frogmore Royal Mausoleum. Above the Mausoleum door are inscribed Victoria's own words: "Farewell best beloved, here at last I shall rest with thee, with thee in Christ I shall rise again".

The early years of the Victorian age (1830—1848) saw the opening of Britain's first railway and its first Reform Parliament. The 1832 Reform Act passed by the Parliament gave the power of voting to men of the lower middle classes. Yet the economic, political and social problems associated with industrial development and urbanization made the 1830s and 1840s a "Time of Troubles", characterized by serious unemployment, desperate poverty, and violent disturbances, along with increasing class consciousness and strife. The Chartists, an organization of workers, helped create an atmosphere open to further reforms.

The middle stage of the Victorian age (1848—1870), comparatively peaking, is a time of optimism, prosperity, and stability. The Great Exhibition in Hyde Park, London (1851) displayed all the latest achievements of modern industry and science both in Britain and elsewhere in the world. The British Empire was beginning to accelerate its expansion as the defeat of Napoleonic France left Britain without any serious international rival. Britain played the role of global policeman in the world politics. Alongside the formal control it exerted over its own colonies, Britain's dominant position in world trade effectively controlled the economies of many nominally independent countries, such as some Latin American countries, China and India.

In the last phase of the Victorian age (1870—1901), the costs of Empire became increasingly apparent, and England was confronted with growing threats to its military and economic preeminence. The flourish of various artistic styles, literary schools, and social, political and religious movements enlivened the nation's intellectual and political life. A variety of socialist movements gained momentum, some influenced by the revolutionary theories of Karl Marx and Friedrich Engels.

In summary, the Victorian age was a tremendously exciting period because of its increasingly lively intellectual and political life. It was a time of prosperity, broad imperial expansion, and great political reform. It was a time of miraculous scientific achievements and enormously shocking new ideas. It was also a time of "prudishness" and "repression" in social life and people's behavior. Without a doubt, it was an extraordinarily diverse and complex period, which has sometimes been called the Second English Renaissance. It, however, also marks the beginning of Modern Times.

2. The Chartist Movement

The Chartist movement is a spontaneous movement of workers for political and social reform from 1838 to 1848, in Britain, and marked the first appearance of the English working class on the scene of history as a force in its own right. It takes its name from the *People's Charter* published in 1838, created for the London Working Men's Association. *The People's Charter*, as a public petition, aimed at redressing omissions from the electoral *Reform Act of 1832*. It quickly became a radical democratic movement for social reforms demanded by the working class, who saw in it a cure-all for all sorts of social ills.

The People's Charter stipulated 6 major demands for reform and democracy. They were: (1) institution of a secret ballot; (2) annual election of Parliament; (3) an end to the need for a property qualification for Parliament; (4) pay for Members of Parliament; (5) equal-sized electoral districts; and (6) universal electoral suffrage for all men age 21 and over.

The People's Charter was presented 3 times to the House of Commons in 1839, 1842 and 1848. On each occasion, it was rejected by the British legislators, despite the fact that it had been signed by hundreds of thousands of law-abiding individuals.

Chartism posed a serious threat to the English authority, because the aims of the Chartists, though mild and sensible by today's standards, to the Victorian government at that time, represented a real potential for upheaval and overthrow of the well-established social system. The violent turmoil of the French Revolution was still fresh in the minds of many in powerful positions. The English ruling class reacted in fear at the possibility of the violent overthrow of their authority.

Brutally crushed by the police, the Chartist movement died out eventually.

Chartism failed for a number of reasons. Most obviously, it failed to gather support in Parliament. Equally important, it failed to gather support from the middle class people. The demands of Chartism were too radical for many of the middle classes, who felt comfortably contented with their status quo. Finally, the mid-19th century spawned a variety of social-reform groups with special aims, and the Chartist movement failed to win over many of these other groups.

Although the Chartist movement came to a dead end, the movement itself was not a failure at all, with its main aims to be achieved eventually in future. The Chartist movement shocked the public into an increasing awareness of social problems, and created a framework for future working-class organizations. Many of the demands of the Chartists were eventually answered in the electoral reform bills of 1867 and 1864.

II. Literary Review

1. The Victorian Novel

The Victorian period witnessed the novel becoming the leading form of literature in English. The Victorian novel is marked with such features as realistic themes, thickly plotted stories, characters in large numbers, and long length. The Victorian novelists tried to demonstrate both the tension and the link between the adverse social and natural conditions, and the aspirations of the hero or heroine, in a larger and more comprehensive world. Their works are often idealized portraits of difficult lives, in which hard work, perseverance, love and luck win out in the end, and virtue would be rewarded and wrong-doers suitably punished. Nevertheless, the Victorian novel still cherishes the established tradition by means of Gothic scenes and characters, picaresque elements, melodrama, the Bildungsroman (of the romantic developmental self), and the I-figure, who, claiming to be the real author, seems omniscient and omnipotent, as if a puppet-master, to handle his characters with the charming ease of the 18th century humorists, and to find himself in an overt relationship with the reader.

As the novel became the ideal form to describe contemporary life and to entertain the people of middle classes, most of the Victorian novelists were now more concerned to cater for the needs and tastes of a large middle class reading public than to please aristocratic patrons. They created a lot of legacy works with permanent appeal. The Victorian period produced a host of talented novelists such as Bulwer Lytton (1803—1873), Mrs. Elizabeth Gaskell (1810—1865), William Makepeace Thackeray (1811—1863), Charles Dickens (1812—1870), Charles Reade (1814—1884), Charlotte Bront (1816—

1855), Emily Bront (1818—1848), Anne Bront (1820—1849), and Anthony Trollope (1815—1882), George Eliot (1819—1880), Charles Kingsley (1819—1875), William Wilkie Collins (1824—1889), George Meredith (1828—1909), Samuel Butler (1835—1902), Robert Louis Stevenson (1850—1894), and George Robert Gissing (1857—1903). Among them the most distinguished are the Bront sisters, Charles Dickens, William Makepeace Thackeray, and George Eliot.

The Bront sisters are Anne Bront , Emily Bront , and Charlotte Bront . Anne Bront , the youngest of the three, wrote *Agnes Grey* (1847) and *The Tenant of Wildfell Hall* (1848). Emily Bront , the middle sister, wrote only one novel, *Wuthering Heights* (1847), which is now considered a classic work of English literature. Charlotte Bront , the eldest of the three, produced four novels in all: *Jane Eyre* (1847), *Shirley* (1849), *Villette* (1853) and *The Professor* (1857). In her novels, the female characters shocked and attracted the general reading public by breaking the traditional, 19th-century fictional stereotype of a woman as gentle, lovely and beautiful, but humble, submissive, ignorant and dependent, both at home and at a social gathering.

Charles Dickens, as the foremost English novelist of the Victorian age, dominated the English fiction of the 19th century. His keen perceptiveness, intimate knowledge and understanding of the people, rich imagination, memorable characters and well-refined prose quickly gained him enormous worldwide popularity. Apart from other genres of writings, he produced more than 20 novels. Such as *The Pickwick Papers, Oliver Twist* (1837—1838), *Nicholas Nickleby* (1838—1839), *The Old Curiosity Shop* (1840—1841), *A Christmas Carol* (1843), *Dombey and Son* (1848), *David Copperfield* (1849—1850), *Hard Time* (1854), *Little Dorrit* (1857), *A Tale of Two Cities* (1859), *Great Expectations* (1860—1861), etc. Of all the novels, *David Copperfield* is regarded by many as his masterpiece. In his works, we find two remarkable features: his excessive imagination and his extreme sensibility. He is sentimental, especially over children and outcasts; he excuses the individual in view of the faults of society; he is dramatic or melodramatic; and his sensibility keeps him always close to the public, studying its taste and playing with its smiles and tears.

William Makepeace Thackeray, in a humorous and ironic tone, created an unrivaled panorama of the life of the English middle and upper classes, crowded with memorable characters displaying realistic mixtures of vanity, virtues and vices. The publication of his greatest satirical novel *Vanity Fair* in 1847 quickly established his fame as one of the major literary figures of his time. Most of Thackeray's novels were focused on the life of the middle and upper classes. As a realistic writer, his portrayal is accurate and true to life. The characters he portrayed in his works are most impressive in English literature. His satire is neither cruel nor stinging, but mild and gentle, flavored with kindness and humor.

George Eliot (1819—1880) is the pen name used by the English novelist Mary Ann Evans, the most learned and respected novelist of the late Victorian era. Her novels, largely set in provincial England, are remarkable for their realism and psychological perspicacity. Her first long novel *Adam Bede* was published in 1859. Then followed the other works: *The Mill on the Floss* (1860), *Silas Marner* (1861), *Romola* (1863), *Felix Holt* (1866), *The Spanish Gypsy* (1868), *Middlemarch* (1871—1872) and *Daniel Deronda* (1876). *Middlemarch*, her most famous work, is a study of human nature and a portrait of several memorable characters. In her novels, Eliot strives to show in individuals the play of universal moral forces, and to work out a humanistic morality capable of satisfying the deep human needs when the older, religiously based morality could no longer be satisfying and workable.

2. The Victorian Prose

The 19th century is also regarded as a high point in British nonfiction prose. The most prominent Victorian prose writers are Thomas Macaulay, Thomas Carlyle, John Stuart Mill, John Ruskin and Matthew Arnold.

The Victorian prose writers were mainly concerned in their works with such topics as the social conflicts, the working class problem, the woman question, the problem of industrialization, the political and social reforms, and the debate between science and religion.

Thomas Macaulay (1800—1859) is one of the greatest essayists of the 19th century. Macaulay's essays cover a wide range of subjects, but they can be divided into two main categories: the literary or critical, and the historical. His writings are often one-sided and inaccurate, but always interesting and enlightening. Macaulay's masterpiece *History of England* is a monumental work, now still regarded as one of the most popular historical works in the

English language.

Thomas Carlyle (1795—1881) influenced many writers, such as Charles Dickens, Matthew Arnold and John Ruskin. His style, one of the most complicated yet effective in English literature, was a compound of biblical phrases, colloquialisms, Teutonic twists, and his own coinages, arranged in unexpected sequences. His works are remarkable for the following distinctive features. First, in most of his works, Carlyle, by his style and mannerisms and positive opinions, generally attracts our attention away from his subject. Second, Carlyle has an original and interesting theory of biography and criticism. Third, Carlyle is often severe, even harsh, in his estimates of other men. Fourth, Carlyle is sometimes persuasive, grimly humorous, as if conversing, and sometimes wildly exclamatory, as if he were shouting and waving his arms at the reader. Lastly, Carlyle often violates the rules of grammar and rhetoric, and cares little for methods in his writings, but as an original genius, he expresses his distinct ideas about the political, social, and economic troubles of the time in a distinctly vivid and picturesque way.

John Stuart Mill (1806—1873) is the most influential English thinker of the Victorian age. His ideas profoundly influenced the 19th-century British thought and political discourse. His works cover logic, epistemology, economics, social and political philosophy, ethics, metaphysics, religion, and current affairs. The overall aim of his writings is to develop a positive view of the universe and the place of humans in it, one which contributes to the progress of human knowledge, individual freedom and human well-being.

John Ruskin (1819—1900), revolutionized art criticism and wrote some of the most superb prose in the English language. His essays on art and architecture were extremely influential in the Victorian age. He wrote over 250 works which cover a vast range of subjects, dealing with science, geology, ornithology, art history, literary criticism, the environmental effects of pollution, and mythology.

Matthew Arnold (1822—1888) published a lot of books of criticism, including *On Translating Homer* (1861), *Essays in Criticism* (1865; Ser. 2, 1888), and *On the Study of Celtic Literature* (1867). His *Essays in Criticism* in 1865 and 1888 remains a significant influence on critics to this day. He considered the most important criteria used to judge the value of a poem were "high truth" and "high seriousness", which he exemplified in those of

Shakespeare and Milton. Being a great literary, social and cultural critic of the Victorian age, Arnold's books are contributions to a national discussion of literature, religion, and education, and his theories of literature and culture have laid the foundations for modern literary criticism.

3. The Victorian Poetry

When Queen Victoria ascended the throne in 1837, the English poetry seemed to have entered upon a period of lean years, in sharp contrast with the poetic prosperity of the Romantic period. After the death of Coleridge, Shelley, Keats, Byron and Scott, it seemed as if no poets in Britain could fill their places. But in 1842, after the publication of his two volumes of collected poems, Alfred Tennyson was recognized as one of the great literary leaders in English poetry. With Tennyson's appearance on the English literary scene, other poets followed him in their poetic creation. Thus began a new boom of the English poetry. Among the Victorian poets, the most notable are Alfred Tennyson, Elizabeth Barrett Browning, Robert Browning, Dante Gabriel Rossetti, and Christina Rossetti.

In the early stage, the Victorian poets were heirs to the Romantics, and their works displayed their distrust of organized religion and their interest in the occult and the mysterious. Later, feeling discontented with the Romantic matter, the Victorians challenged the forms and themes of their predecessors, the Romantics, and they managed to develop a different poetry of mood and character by moving away from the Romantic tradition. Towards the end of the century, the Victorian poets began to take an interest in French symbolism and the Victorian poetry entered a decadent fin-de-siecle phase. In subject matter, the Victorian poetry covers the issues of religious faith, social change, political power, ethical value and feminism. Their work, as intellectual, public discourse, switched from self-expressionism to dramatic impersonation. Their poetry tends to be pictorial, and often uses sound to convey meaning. As the Victorian period is the great age of whimsy and nonsense, the Victorian poets are, in general, much funnier than the Romantics in terms of the poetic temperament, style, and language.

Alfred Tennyson (1809—1892), the Poet Laureate after William Wordsworth, is regarded as the chief representative of the Victorian poetry.

Tennyson's works are melancholic in tone. He used a wide range of subject matter, ranging from medieval legends to classical myths and from domestic situations to observations of nature, as source material for his poetry. His poetry reflected the intellectual ideas and moral values of his times. Tennyson is notable for his mastery of technique, his superb use of sensuous language, and his profundity of thought. He wrote a lot of phrases which have become commonplaces of the English language, and he is the second most frequently quoted writer in *The Oxford Dictionary of Quotations*, after Shakespeare.

Robert Browning, together with Alfred Tennyson, is considered one of the two leading poets of the Victorian age. A prolific person, Robert Browning wrote a huge bulk of poetry. He is especially noted for his mastery of the dramatic monologue form, for his psychological insight, for his forceful, colloquial poetic style and for his enunciation of important Victorian themes, especially progress, imperfection, and optimism. His development of the dramatic monologue techniques is regarded as his most important contribution to poetry. His use of diction, rhythm, and symbol directly influenced many later poets, including Ezra Pound, T. S. Eliot, and Robert Frost.

Elizabeth Barrett Browning (1806—1861), English poet, political thinker, and feminist, is generally considered one of the great English poets. Highly lyric and dramatic, Elizabeth's poems have a diction and rhythm that evokes an attractive, spontaneous quality though some may seem sentimental. Many of her poems show her protest against what she considered social injustice, such as the slave trade in America, the child labor in the mines and mills of England, and the restrictions placed upon women. In her poetry, Mrs. Browning tried to chasten, refine and elevate the human society so as to build up an ideal world.

Dante Gabriel Rossetti (1828—1882), English poet, translator, painter, and designer, is a cofounder of the Pre-Raphaelite Brotherhood. The Pre-Raphaelites were a group of English painters and poets, who sought to revive what they judged to be the simple, pure, rich and natural values and techniques of medieval life and art, and their pursuit of a symbolic art led them away from the mainstream. Rossetti is regarded as the leading poet amongst them. Romantic love is the main theme in Rossetti's poetry, and his works show an impassioned, mystic imagination in strong contrast to the banal sentimentality of contemporary Victorian art. His use of richly colored poetic diction achieves a sumptuous grandeur in his expression and sentiment.

Christina Rossetti (1830—1894) is one of the most important of English woman poets, the sister of the painter-designer-poet Dante Gabriel Rossetti, and a member of the Pre-Raphaelite art movement. She is best known for her ballads and her mystic religious lyrics. Much of her poetry is religious in nature with a wistful, spiritual quality. Her favorite themes are unhappy love, death, and premature resignation. As a great female poet of the era, she touched many feminist themes in her poetry. She was antipathetic to war, slavery system in the American South, cruelty to animals, and all forms of military aggression.

Some other lesser important Victorian poets meriting our attention are: Algernon Charles Swinburne (1837—1909), Gerard Manley Hopkins (1844—1889), William Morris (1834—1896), and Arthur Hugh Clough (1819—1861).

4. The Victorian Drama

In the first half of the 19th century, mediocre melodrama and Shakespeare productions were extremely popular, reigning supreme on the English stage. After Victoria's accession, the London stage witnessed a change with a profusion of farces, musical burlesques, extravaganzas and comic operas, which held the largest audience appeal all the way through the second half of the 19th century.

As a princess, Victoria herself was a great theatergoer, fascinated by various performances in different theatres. After her accession, she still kept enormous enthusiasm for drama by frequenting the two patent theatres. Between the end of March and the middle of August of 1838, she made 28 visits to opera at Her Majesty's.

As the Victorian Britain is a time and place of great change and innovation, the 19th century English drama is also marked by its transition from the rowdy spectacle to the introduction of realistic drama. Realism began around 1850 as the Romanticism period was ending around 1870. Henrik Ibsen (1828—1906), a Norwegian playwright, is considered the "father of Realism" in theater, whose plays brought to a climax the realistic movement of the 19th century. In the UK, Thomas William Robertson is an early proponent, who produced a series of realistic or naturalistic plays. His comedy *Society* (1865) is regarded as a milestone in the Victorian drama because of its realism in sets, costume, acting and dialogue. The common goal of the realistic plays was to set forth a functional or dysfunctional situation in an objective manner to an impartial audience. The audience is meant to view the characters as a visitor observes animals in a zoo. The Victorian drama encompasses a wide range of issues and topics, and displays the variety, multiple appeals, and vitality of the 19th-century English life. And it also reflected and shaped the taste of its audience.

The Victorian age is a period of very brisk dramatic activity. The public demand called for a great number of authors to write prolifically for theatrical entertainment. Among the eminent Victorian playwrights are James Robinson Planche (1796—1880), Edward Bulwer (1803—1873), Tom Taylor (1817—1880), Dion Boucicault (1820—1890), Thomas William Robertson (1829—1871), William S. Gilbert (1836—1911), Henry Arthur Jones (1851—1929), Arthur Pinero (1855—1934) and Oscar Wilde (1854—1900), with Gilbert and Wilde as the most outstanding figures of the period. The sparkling, witty comedies of Oscar Wilde and the comic operettas of W. S. Gilbert and Sir Arthur Sullivan are the brightest achievements of the Victorian drama.

William S. Gilbert (1836—1911), is best known for his 14 comic operas written in collaboration with the composer Arthur Sullivan. Gilbert is a prolific person, his creative output including over 75 plays and librettos, numerous stories, poems, lyrics and various other comic and serious pieces. His plays and his realistic style of stage direction inspired other dramatists, including Oscar Wilde, George Bernard Shaw and Oscar Hammerstein.

Oscar Wilde (1854—1900), an Irish playwright, novelist, poet, and author of short stories, most famous for his sophisticated, brilliantly witty plays. Influenced by the aesthetic theories of Walter Pater and John Ruskin, Wilde became the center of a group called the Aesthetic Movement, which advocated "art for art's sake". Wilde's creative genius found its highest expression in his brilliant series of domestic comedies *Lady Windermere's Fan* (1892), *A Woman of No Importance* (1893), *An Ideal Husband* (1895), and his masterpiece, *The Importance of Being Earnest* (1895). Scandalous in their assault on the Victorian mores, his plays took the London stage by storm with his adroitly contrived plots, pithy epigrams, clever paradoxes, brilliant dialogue and biting satire. Wilde's works sparkle with his wit, humor and intelligence, and remain a wellspring of witticisms and reflections on aestheticism, morality, and society.

Charles Dickens (1812—1870)

Life and Major Works

Charles Dickens was born on 7 February, 1812 in Portsmouth, Hampshire, England. He was the son of Elizabeth n e Barrow (1789—1863) and John Dickens (c.1785—1851), a clerk in the Navy Pay Office. John was a congenial man, hospitable and generous. But throughout his life he experienced financial difficulties. He inspired the character Mr. Micawber in Dickens' *David Copperfield* (1849—1850).

In 1814 Dickens moved to London, and then to Chatham, where he received some education. Charles Dickens' family briefly entered the

Charles Dickens

middle class and then left after his father went to prison for debt. The young Dickens was forced into manual labor in horrible conditions in the Warren's Blacking Factory to support the family. The shock of his change in position left Charles Dickens very aware of the sufferings that the Victorian poor endured. When Dickens' father was released from prison, his mother argued that Dickens should continue working rather than return to school. Dickens never forgave his mother for her lack of concern with his emotional and physical well being. His father, however, rescued him from that fate, and between 1824 and 1827 Dickens was a day pupil at a school in London. From 1824 to 1827 Dickens studied at Wellington House Academy, London, and at Mr. Dawson's school in 1827. His brief experience at the Blacking Factory haunted him all of his life — he spoke of it only to his wife and to his closest friend, John Forster. However, the dark secret became a source of creative energy without which he probably wouldn't have composed *David Copperfield* and *Great Expectations*.

He became a free-lance reporter at *Doctor's Commons Courts* in 1829. He spent much of his spare time reading in the British Museum's library and studying acting. The next year he met and fell in love with Maria Beadnell who was the daughter of a banker. By 1832 he had become a very successful shorthand reporter of Parliamentary debates in the House of Commons, and began work as a reporter for a newspaper. His relationship with Maria Beadnell ended, probably because her parents did not consider him a good match and sent her to Paris to finish her study. It is believed that she was the model for the character Dora in *David Copperfield*. In the same year his first published story "A Dinner at Poplar Walk" appeared in the *Monthly Magazine*, and was followed, very shortly thereafter, by a number of other stories and sketches.

In 1834, still a newspaper reporter, he adopted the pseudonym "Boz" and it soon became famous. His poor father (who was the original of Mr. Micawber in *David Copperfield*, as Dickens's mother was the original for the whining Mrs. Nickleby) was once again arrested for debt, and Charles was forced to come to bail him out. Later in his life his parents and his brothers frequently turned to him for financial assistance. In 1835 he met and became engaged to Catherine Hogarth, daughter of the editor of the *Evening Chronicle*.

Dickens' first book, a collection of stories titled *Sketches by Boz* was published in 1836. He married Catherine Hogarth on 2 April, 1836, at St. Luke's in Chelsea. A year later they moved into 48 Doughty Street, London, now a museum. The couple had ten children. Also in the same year, 1836, Dickens became editor for *Bentley's Miscellany* of which *Pickwick Papers* was first serialized, and to everyone's surprise, it became an enormous popular success.

After the success of *Pickwick*, Dickens started a full-time career as a novelist, although he continued his journalistic and editorial activities as well. *Oliver Twist* was begun in 1837, and continued in monthly parts until April 1839. *Oliver Twist* was finished in 1839 and followed by *Nicholas Nickleby* (1838—1839), *The Old Curiosity Shop* (1840—1841), and *Barnaby Rudge* (1841). Dickens' series of five Christmas Books were soon to follow: *A Christmas Carol* (1843), *The Chimes* (1844), *The Cricket on the Hearth* (1845), *The Battle of Life* (1846), and *The Haunted Man* (1848). In the meantime, he produced *Dombey and Son* (1846).

Among his later works are *David Copperfield* (1849—1850) in which Dickens used his own personal experiences of work in a factory, *Bleak House* (1852—1853), *A Tale of Two Cities* (1859) which was set in the years of the French Revolution, and *Great Expectations* (1860—1861). The unfinished mystery novel *The Mystery of Edwin Drood* was published in 1870.

From the 1840s Dickens spent much of his time travelling and campaigning against many of the social evils of his time. In addition to that, he gave talks and wrote pamphlets, plays, letters and so on. From 1844 to 1845 he spent some time in Italy, Switzerland and Paris. He took lecturing tours in Britain and the United States from 1858 to 1868. From 1860 Dickens lived at Gadshill Place, near Rochester, Kent. Charles Dickens died at Gad's Hill Place on June 9.

Although Dickens's career as a novelist received much attention, he produced hundreds of essays and edited and rewrote hundreds of others submitted to the various periodicals he edited. Dickens distinguished himself as a great writer in 1834 under the pseudonym Boz.

Dickens's writing style is florid and poetic, with a strong comic touch. His satires are aimed at British aristocratic snobbery. Many of his character's names provide readers with a hint as to the roles played in the story, such as Miss Murdstone in the novel *David Copperfield*, which is clearly a combination of "murder" and stony coldness. His literary style is also a mixture of fantasy and realism.

His popularity has declined little since his death and he continues to be one of the best known and most read of English authors. At least 180 motion pictures and TV adaptations were based on Dickens's works. Many of his works were adapted for the stage during his own lifetime and as early as in 1913, a silent film of *The Pickwick Papers* was made. His characters were often so memorable that they took on a life of their own outside his books.

Brief Introduction and Appreciation

Dickens is one of those rare writers who have always appealed to a wide variety of readers. Many of Dickens's books were published in popular magazines of the time. *Oliver Twist*, which was published in 1838, is one of Charles Dickens's best-known and popular works. It was written after he had already gained fame as the author of *The Pickwick Papers*. It has been adapted as a movie and a long-running Broadway musical and has been considered a classic since it was first published. Originally, each chapter of the book was published separately in order, in a magazine called *Bentley's Miscellany*, of which Dickens was editor. Each week, readers waited eagerly for the next chapter. This was partly due to the fact that each chapter ends with a "cliff-hanger" that would hold the readers' interest until the following chapter was published.

The story is set in the 1830s in England. Oliver Twist is born in a workhouse in a provincial town. His mother has been found very sick in the street, and dies just after Oliver's birth. Oliver is raised under the care of Mrs. Mann and the beadle Mr. Bumble in the workhouse. When it becomes Oliver's task to ask for more food on behalf of all the starving children in the workhouse, he is trashed. The parish beadle offers five pounds to anyone who will take the boy away from the workhouse. Oliver narrowly escapes being apprenticed to a brutish chimney sweeper and is eventually apprenticed to a local undertaker, Mr. Sowerberry. When the undertaker's another apprentice makes insulting comments about Oliver's mother, Oliver attacks him and was severely punished by Mr. Sowerberry. Desperate, Oliver runs away at dawn and heads for London. He begs food on his way and sleeps rough in the fields.

Having walked seven days in a row, he arrives at London. Outside London, Oliver, starved and exhausted, meets Jack Dawkins, a boy of his own age. Jack offers Olive shelter in London slums with Fagin, a career criminal. Fagin has trained the boys to become pickpockets. In this way, Oliver, who innocently does not understand that he is among criminals, becomes one of Fagin's boys.

When Oliver is sent out with Jack and another boy on a pickpocket expedition Oliver is so shocked when he realizes what is going on. However, he, instead of the two other boys, is caught. Fortunately, the victim Mr. Brownlow, the wealthy gentleman whose handkerchief is stolen, feels sorry for Oliver, takes him to his home and treats him very well. Mr. Brownlow is struck by Oliver's resemblance to a portrait of a young woman that hangs in his house. While the housekeeper, Mrs. Bedwin nurses him back to life after he has fallen sick, for the first time in his life he is happy.

However, two young adults in Fagin's gang, Bill Sikes and his lover Nancy, capture Oliver and return him to Fagin. Fagin is encouraged to do this by the mysterious Mr. Monks. Oliver is taken along on a burglary expedition in the country. The thieves are discovered in the house of Mrs. Maylie. Oliver is shot and wounded by a servant of the house. After Sikes escapes, he is taken in by the women who live there, Mrs. Maylie and her beautiful adopted niece Rose. Rose and Mrs. Maylie take good care of the wounded Oliver. When he tells them his story they believe him, and he stays there with them. During his stay with Rose and Mrs. Maylie, Oliver one day sees Fagin and Monks looking at him through a window. Nancy discovers that Monks is plotting against Oliver for some reason. Mr. Monks, who is interested in Oliver's origin, manages to get the gold locket left behind by Oliver's mother. As a matter of fact, Oliver is Monks half brother. Nancy also learns that there is some kind of connection between Rose and Oliver. To save Oliver she tells Rose on Monk's plot. Rose brings Oliver to Mr. Brownlow and tells him the whole story. But after Fagin tells Sikes what Nancy has done against them, Sikes brutally murders Nancy in a rage. On his frantic flight away from the crime Sikes accidentally hangs himself. Fagin and the rest of the gang are arrested. Fagin is executed after Oliver has visited him in the cell in Newgate Prison. Jack is transported after a court scene in which he eloquently defends himself and his class.

Monks' plot against Oliver failed with the help of Mr. Brownlow. As Monks is Oliver's half-brother, he tries to seek all of the inheritance for himself. Oliver's father's will states that he will leave money to Oliver on the condition that his reputation is clean. And it turns out that Oliver's dead mother and Rose were sisters. Monks gets his share of the inheritance and goes away to America. Unfortunately, he dies in prison there, and Oliver is adopted by Mr. Brownlow.

Oliver Twist is a window on English society of the 1830s. Dickens genius is in his ability to transport us back to his own time, but also to make us see clearly the flaws of his time. Dickens uses the characters in the book to make a social commentary, attacking the hypocrisy and flaws of various institutions, especially the government of the society. The laws and criminal system, and the methods of dealing with poor people are all directly or indirectly criticized. Interestingly, not any solutions are mentioned. All he does is to point out the suffering inflicted by these systems and their deep injustice. Dickens basically believed that most people were good at heart but that their good impulses could be distorted by social ills. Charles Dickens always sought to imprint upon his readers the notion that things need to be changed, and that they can be changed, and must be changed.

Selected Reading

Oliver Twist

Chapter I

Treats of the place where Oliver Twist was born, and of the circumstances attending his birth.

Among other public buildings in a certain town, which for many reasons it will be prudent to refrain from mentioning, and to which I will assign no fictitious[1] name, there is one anciently common to most towns, great or small: to wit, a workhouse; and in this workhouse was born; on a day and date which I need not trouble myself to repeat, inasmuch[2] as it can be of no possible consequence to the reader, in this stage of the business at all events; the item of mortality whose name is prefixed to the head of this chapter.

For a long time after it was ushered into this world of sorrow and trouble, by the parish surgeon, it remained a matter of considerable doubt whether the child would survive to bear any name at all; in which case it is somewhat more than probable that these memoirs would never have appeared; or, if they had, that being comprised within a couple of pages, they would have possessed the inestimable merit of being the most concise and faithful specimen of biography, extant[3] in the literature of any age or country.

Although I am not disposed to maintain that the being born in a workhouse, is in itself the most fortunate and enviable circumstance that can possibly befall a human being, I do mean to say that in this particular instance, it was the best thing for Oliver Twist that could by possibility have occurred. The fact is, that there was considerable difficulty in inducing Oliver to take upon himself the office of respiration—a troublesome practice, but one which custom has rendered necessary to our easy existence; and for some time he lay gasping on a little flock mattress, rather unequally poised between this world and the next: the balance being decidedly in favour of the latter. Now, if, during this brief period, Oliver had been surrounded by careful grandmothers, anxious aunts, experienced nurses, and doctors of profound wisdom, he would most inevitably and indubitably have been killed in no time. There being nobody by, however, but a pauper old woman, who was rendered rather misty by an unwonted allowance of beer; and a parish surgeon who did such matters by contract; Oliver and Nature fought out the point between them. The result was, that, after a few struggles, Oliver breathed, sneezed, and proceeded to advertise to the inmates of the workhouse the fact of a new burden having been imposed upon the parish, by setting up as loud a cry as could reasonably have been expected from a male infant who had not been possessed of that very useful appendage, a voice, for a much longer space of time than three minutes and a quarter.

As Oliver gave this first proof of the free and proper action of his lungs, the patchwork coverlet which was carelessly flung over the iron bedstead, rustled; the pale face of a young woman was raised feebly from the pillow; and a faint voice imperfectly articulated the words, "Let me see the child, and die."

The surgeon had been sitting with his face turned towards the fire: giving the palms of his hands a warm and a rub alternately. As the young woman spoke, he rose, and advancing to the bed's head, said, with more kindness than might have been expected of him:

"Oh, you must not talk about dying yet."

"Lor bless her heart, no! " interposed the nurse, hastily depositing in her pocket a green glass bottle, the contents of which she had been tasting in a corner with evident satisfaction. "Lor bless her dear heart, when she has lived as long as I have, sir, and had thirteen children of her own, and all on 'em dead except two, and them in the wurkus with me, she'll know better than to take on in that way, bless her dear heart! Think what it is to be a mother, there's a dear young lamb, do. "

Apparently this consolatory perspective of a mother's prospects failed in producing its due effect. The patient shook her head, and stretched out her hand towards the child.

The surgeon deposited it in her arms. She imprinted her cold white lips passionately on its forehead; passed her hands over her face; gazed wildly round; shuddered; fell back—and died. They chafed[4] her breast, hands, and temples; but the blood had stopped for ever. They talked of hope and comfort. They had been strangers too long.

"It's all over, Mrs. Thingummy! " said the surgeon at last.

"Ah, poor dear, so it is! " said the nurse, picking up the cork of the green bottle, which had fallen out on the pillow, as she stooped to take up the child. "Poor dear! "

"You needn't mind sending up to me, if the child cries, nurse, " said the surgeon, putting on his gloves with great deliberation. "It's very likely it (r)will be troublesome. Give it a little gruel[5] if it is. " He put on his hat, and, pausing by the bed-side on his way to the door, added, "She was a good-looking girl, too; where did she come from? "

"She was brought here last night," replied the old woman, "by the overseer's order. She was found lying in the street. She had walked some distance, for her shoes were worn to pieces; but where she came from, or where she was going to, nobody knows."

The surgeon leaned over the body, and raised the left hand. "The old story, " he said, shaking his head: "no wedding ring, I see. Ah! Good night! "

The medical gentleman walked away to dinner; and the nurse, having once more applied herself to the green bottle, sat down on a low chair before the fire, and proceeded to dress the infant.

What an excellent example of the power of dress, young Oliver Twist was! Wrapped in the blanket which had hitherto[6] formed his only covering, he might have been the child of a nobleman or a beggar; it would have been hard for the haughtiest stranger to have assigned him his proper station in society. But now that he was enveloped in the old calico[7] robes which had grown yellow in the same service, he was badged and ticketed, and fell into his place at once—a parish child—the orphan of a workhouse—the humble, half-starved drudge—to be cuffed and buffeted through the world—despised by all, and pitied by none.

Oliver cried lustily. If he could have known that he was an orphan, left to the tender mercies of churchwardens and overseers, perhaps he would have cried the louder.

Chapter II

Treats of Oliver Twist's growth, education, and board.

For the next eight or ten months, Oliver was the victim of a systematic course of treachery and deception. He was brought up by hand. The hungry and destitute situation of the infant orphan was duly reported by the workhouse authorities to the parish authorities. The parish authorities inquired with dignity of the workhouse authorities, whether there was no female then domiciled in "the house" who was in a situation to impart to Oliver Twist, the consolation and nourishment of which he stood in need. The workhouse authorities replied with humility, that there was not. Upon this the parish authorities magnanimously[8] and humanely resolved, that Oliver should be "farmed," or, in other words, that he should be dispatched to a branch-workhouse some three miles off, where twenty or thirty other juvenile offenders against the poor-laws, rolled about the floor all day, without the inconvenience of too much food or too much clothing, under the parental superintendence of an elderly female, who received the culprits at and for the consideration of sevenpence-halfpenny per small head per week. Sevenpence-halfpenny's worth per week is a good round diet for a child; a great deal may be got for sevenpence-halfpenny, quite enough to overload its stomach, and make it uncomfortable. The elderly female was a woman of wisdom and experience; she knew what was good for children; and she had a very accurate perception of what was good for herself. So, she appropriated the greater part of the weekly stipend[9] to her own use, and consigned the rising parochial generation to even a shorter allowance than was originally provided for them. Thereby finding in the lowest depth a deeper still; and proving herself a very great experimental philosopher.

Everybody knows the story of another experimental philosopher who had a great theory about a horse being able to live without eating, and who demonstrated it so well, that he got his own horse down to a straw a day, and would unquestionably have rendered him a very spirited and rapacious animal on nothing at all, if he had not died, four-and-twenty hours before he was to have had his first comfortable bait of air. Unfortunately for the experimental philosophy of the female to whose protecting care Oliver Twist was delivered over, a similar result usually attended the operation of her system; for at the very moment when a child had contrived[10] to exist upon the smallest possible portion of the weakest possible food, it did perversely happen in eight and a half cases out of ten, either that it sickened from want and cold, or fell into the fire from neglect, or got half-smothered by accident; in any one of which cases, the miserable little being was usually summoned into another world, and there gathered to the fathers it had never known in this.

Occasionally, when there was some more than usually interesting inquest upon a parish child who had been overlooked in turning up a bedstead, or inadvertently scalded to death when there happened to be a washing—though the latter accident was very scarce, anything approaching to a washing being of rare occurrence in the farm—the jury would take it into their heads to ask troublesome questions, or the parishioners would rebelliously affix their signatures to a remonstrance. But these impertinences were speedily checked by the evidence of the surgeon, and the testimony of the beadle; the former of whom had always opened the body and found nothing inside (which was very probable indeed), and the latter of whom invariably swore whatever the parish wanted; which was very self-devotional. Besides, the board made periodical pilgrimages to the farm, and always sent the beadle the day before, to say they were going. The children were neat and clean to behold, when they went; and what more would the people have!

It cannot be expected that this system of farming would produce any very extraordinary or luxuriant crop. Oliver Twist's ninth birthday found him a pale thin child, somewhat diminutive in stature, and decidedly small in circumference. But nature or inheritance had implanted a good sturdy spirit in Oliver's breast. It had had plenty of room to expand, thanks to the spare diet of the establishment; and perhaps to this circumstance may be attributed his having any ninth birthday at all. Be this as it may, however, it was his ninth birthday; and he was keeping it in the coal-cellar with a select party of two other young gentlemen, who, after participating with him in a sound thrashing, had been locked up for atrociously presuming to be hungry, when Mrs. Mann, the good lady of the house, was unexpectedly startled by the apparition of Mr. Bumble, the beadle, striving to undo the wicket of the garden-gate.

"Goodness gracious! Is that you, Mr. Bumble, sir?" said Mrs. Mann, thrusting her head out of the window in well-affected ecstasies of joy. "(Susan, take Oliver and them two brats up stairs, and wash'em directly.) My heart alive! Mr. Bumble, how glad I am to see you, sure-ly!"

Now, Mr. Bumble was a fat man, and a choleric[11]; so, instead of responding to this open-hearted salutation in a kindred spirit, he gave the little wicket a tremendous shake, and then bestowed upon it a kick which could have emanated from no leg but a beadle's[12].

"Lor, only think," said Mrs. Mann, running out, for the three boys had been removed by this time, "only think of that! That I should have forgotten that the gate was bolted on the inside, on account of them dear children! Walk in, sir; walk in, pray, Mr. Bumble, do, sir."

Although this invitation was accompanied with a curtsey that might have softened the heart of a churchwarden, it by no means mollified the beadle.

"Do you think this respectful or proper conduct, Mrs. Mann," inquired Mr. Bumble, grasping his cane, "to keep the parish officers a waiting at your garden-gate, when they come here upon porochial business connected with the porochial orphans? Are you aweer, Mrs. Mann, that you are, as I may say, a porochial delegate, and a stipendiary?"

"I'm sure, Mr. Bumble, that I was only a telling one or two of the dear children as is so fond of you, that it was you a coming," replied Mrs. Mann with great humility.

Mr. Bumble had a great idea of his oratorical powers and his importance. He had displayed the one, and vindicated[13] the other. He relaxed.

"Well, well, Mrs. Mann," he replied in a calmer tone; "it may be as you say; it may be. Lead the way in, Mrs. Mann, for I come on business, and have something to say."

Mrs. Mann ushered the beadle into a small parlour with a brick floor; placed a seat for him; and officiously deposited his cocked hat and cane on the table before him. Mr. Bumble wiped from his forehead the perspiration which his walk had engendered, glanced complacently at the cocked hat, and smiled. Yes, he smiled. Beadles are but men; and Mr. Bumble smiled.

"Now don't you be offended at what I'm a going to say," observed Mrs. Mann, with captivating sweetness. "You've had a long walk, you know, or I wouldn't mention it. Now, will you take a little drop of somethink, Mr. Bumble?"

"Not a drop. Not a drop," said Mr. Bumble, waving his right hand in a dignified, but placid manner.

"I think you will," said Mrs. Mann, who had noticed the tone of the refusal, and the gesture that had accompanied it. "Just a leetle drop, with a little cold water, and a lump of sugar."

Mr. Bumble coughed.

"Now, just a leetle drop," said Mrs. Mann persuasively.

"What is it?" inquired the beadle.

"Why, it's what I'm obliged to keep a little of in the house to put into the blessed infants' Daffy, when they ain't well, Mr. Bumble," replied Mrs. Mann as she opened a corner cupboard, and took down a bottle and glass. "It's gin. I'll not deceive you, Mr. B. It's gin."

"Do you give the children Daffy, Mrs. Mann?" inquired Bumble, following with his eyes the interesting process of mixing.

"Ah, bless'em, that I do, dear as it is," replied the nurse. "I couldn't see'em suffer before my very eyes, you know, sir."

"No;" said Mr. Bumble approvingly; "no, you could not. You are a humane woman, Mrs. Mann." (Here she set down the glass.) "I shall take a early opportunity of mentioning it to the board, Mrs. Mann." (He drew it towards him.) "You feel as a mother, Mrs. Mann." (He stirred the gin-and-water.) "I—I drink your health with cheerfulness, Mrs. Mann;" and he swallowed half of it.

"And now about business," said the beadle, taking out a leathern pocket-book. "The child that was half-baptized, Oliver Twist, is nine year old to-day."

"Bless him!" interposed[14] Mrs. Mann, inflaming her left eye with the corner of her apron.

"And notwithstanding a offered reward of ten pound, which was afterwards increased to twenty pound. Notwithstanding the most superlative, and, I may say, supernat'ral exertions on the part of this parish," said Bumble, "we have never been able to discover who is his father, or what was his mother's settlement, name, or con-dition."

Mrs. Mann raised her hands in astonishment; but added, after a moment's reflection, "How comes he to have any name at all, then?"

The beadle drew himself up with great pride, and said, "I inwented it."

"You, Mr. Bumble!"

"I, Mrs. Mann. We name our fondlings in alphabetical order. The last was a S,—Swubble, I named him. This was a T,—Twist, I named (r)him. The next one as comes will be Unwin, and the next Vilkins. I have got names ready made to the end of the alphabet, and all the way through it again, when we come to Z."

"Why, you're quite a literary character, sir!" said Mrs. Mann.

"Well, well," said the beadle, evidently gratified with the compliment; "perhaps I may be. Perhaps I may be, Mrs. Mann." He finished the gin-and-water, and added, "Oliver being now too old to remain here, the board have determined to have him back into the house. I have come out myself to take him there. So let me see him at once."

"I'll fetch him directly," said Mrs. Mann, leaving the room for that purpose. Oliver, having had by this time as much of the outer coat of dirt which encrusted his face and hands, removed, as could be scrubbed off in one washing, was led into the room by his benevolent protectress.

"Make a bow to the gentleman, Oliver," said Mrs. Mann.

Oliver made a bow, which was divided between the beadle on the chair, and the cocked hat on the table.

"Will you go along with me, Oliver?" said Mr. Bumble, in a majestic voice.

Oliver was about to say that he would go along with anybody with great readiness, when, glancing upward, he caught sight of Mrs. Mann, who had got behind the beadle's chair, and was shaking her fist at him with a furious countenance. He took the hint at once, for the fist had been too often impressed upon his body not to be deeply impressed upon his recollection.

"Will (r)she go with me? " inquired poor Oliver.

"No, she can't," replied Mr. Bumble. "But she'll come and see you sometimes."

This was no very great consolation to the child. Young as he was, however, he had sense enough to make a feint of feeling great regret at going away. It was no very difficult matter for the boy to call tears into his eyes. Hunger and recent ill-usage are great assistants if you want to cry; and Oliver cried very naturally indeed. Mrs. Mann gave him a thousand embraces, and, what Oliver wanted a great deal more, a piece of bread and butter, lest he should seem too hungry when he got to the workhouse. With the slice of bread in his hand, and the little brown-cloth parish cap on his head, Oliver was then led away by Mr. Bumble from the wretched home where one kind word or look had never lighted the gloom of his infant years. And yet he burst into an agony of childish grief, as the cottage-gate closed after him. Wretched as were the little companions in misery he was leaving behind, they were the only friends he had ever known; and a sense of his loneliness in the great wide world, sank into the child's heart for the first time.

Mr. Bumble walked on with long strides; little Oliver, firmly grasping his gold-laced cuff[15], trotted beside him, inquiring at the end of every quarter of a mile whether they were" nearly there." To these interrogations Mr. Bumble returned very brief and snappish replies; for the temporary blandness which gin-and-water awakens in some bosoms had by this time evaporated; and he was once again a beadle.

Oliver had not been within the walls of the workhouse a quarter of an hour, and had scarcely completed the demolition[16] of a second slice of bread, when Mr. Bumble, who had handed him over to the care of an old woman, returned; and, telling him it was a board night, informed him that the board had said he was to appear before it forthwith[17].

Not having a very clearly defined notion of what a live board was, Oliver was rather astounded by this intelligence, and was not quite certain whether he ought to laugh or cry. He had no time to think about the matter, however; for Mr. Bumble gave him a tap on the head, with his cane, to wake him up: and another on the back to make him lively: and bidding[18] him follow, conducted him into a large whitewashed room, where eight or ten fat gentlemen were sitting round a table. At the top of the table, seated in an arm-chair rather higher than the rest, was a particularly fat gentleman with a very round, red face.

"Bow to the board," said Bumble. Oliver brushed away two or three tears that were lingering in his eyes; and seeing no board but the table, fortunately bowed to that.

"What's your name, boy?" said the gentleman in the high chair.

Oliver was frightened at the sight of so many gentlemen, which made him tremble: and the beadle gave him another tap behind, which made him cry. These two causes made him answer in a very low and hesitating voice; whereupon[19] a gentleman in a white waistcoat said he was a fool. Which was a capital way of raising his spirits, and putting him quite at his ease.

"Boy," said the gentleman in the high chair, "listen to me. You know you're an orphan, I suppose?"

"What's that, sir?" inquired poor Oliver.

"The boy (r)is a fool—I thought he was," said the gentleman in the white waistcoat.

"Hush!" said the gentleman who had spoken first. "You know you've got no father or mother, and that you were brought up by the parish, don't you?"

"Yes, sir," replied Oliver, weeping bitterly.

"What are you crying for?" inquired the gentleman in the white waistcoat. And to be sure it was very extraordinary. What (r)could the boy be crying for?

"I hope you say your prayers every night," said another gentleman in a gruff[20] voice; "and pray for the people who feed you, and take care of you—

like a Christian."

"Yes, sir," stammered the boy. The gentleman who spoke last was unconsciously right. It would have been (r)very like a Christian, and a marvellously good Christian, too, if Oliver had prayed for the people who fed and took care of (r)him. But he hadn't, because nobody had taught him.

"Well! You have come here to be educated, and taught a useful trade," said the red-faced gentleman in the high chair.

"So you'll begin to pick oakum²¹ to-morrow morning at six o'clock," added the surly²² one in the white waistcoat.

For the combination of both these blessings in the one simple process of picking oakum, Oliver bowed low by the direction of the beadle, and was then hurried away to a large ward: where, on a rough, hard bed, he sobbed himself to sleep. What a noble illustration of the tender laws of England! They let the paupers go to sleep!

Poor Oliver! He little thought, as he lay sleeping in happy unconsciousness of all around him, that the board had that very day arrived at a decision which would exercise the most material influence over all his future fortunes. But they had. And this was it:

The members of this board were very sage²³, deep, philosophical men; and when they came to turn their attention to the workhouse, they found out at once, what ordinary folks would never have discovered—the poor people liked it! It was a regular place of public entertainment for the poorer classes; a tavern where there was nothing to pay; a public breakfast, dinner, tea, and supper all the year round; a brick and mortar elysium, where it was all play and no work. "Oho!" said the board, looking very knowing; "we are the fellows to set this to rights; we'll stop it all, in no time." So, they established the rule, that all poor people should have the alternative (for they would compel nobody, not they), of being starved by a gradual process in the house, or by a quick one out of it. With this view, they contracted with the water-works to lay on an unlimited supply of water; and with a corn-factor to supply periodically small quantities of oatmeal; and issued three meals of thin gruel a day, with an onion twice a week, and half a roll on Sundays. They made a great many other wise and humane regulations, having reference to the ladies, which it is not necessary to repeat; kindly undertook to divorce poor married people, in consequence of the great expense of a suit in Doctors'

Commons; and, instead of compelling a man to support his family, as they had theretofore done, took his family away from him, and made him a bachelor! There is no saying how many applicants for relief, under these last two heads, might have started up in all classes of society, if it had not been coupled with the workhouse; but the board were long-headed men, and had provided for this difficulty. The relief was inseparable from the workhouse and the gruel; and that frightened people.

For the first six months after Oliver Twist was removed, the system was in full operation. It was rather expensive at first, in consequence of the increase in the undertaker's bill, and the necessity of taking in the clothes of all the paupers, which fluttered loosely on their wasted, shrunken forms, after a week or two's gruel. But the number of workhouse inmates got thin as well as the paupers; and the board were in ecstasies.

The room in which the boys were fed, was a large stone hall, with a copper at one end: out of which the master[24], dressed in an apron for the purpose, and assisted by one or two women, ladled the gruel at meal—times. Of this festive composition[25] each boy had one porringer, and no more—except on occasions of great public rejoicing, when he had two ounces and a quarter of bread besides. The bowls never wanted washing. The boys polished them with their spoons till they shone again; and when they had performed this operation (which never took very long, the spoons being nearly as large as the bowls), they would sit staring at the copper, with such eager eyes, as if they could have devoured the very bricks of which it was composed; employing themselves, meanwhile, in sucking their fingers most assiduously, with the view of catching up any stray splashes of gruel that might have been cast thereon. Boys have generally excellent appetites. Oliver Twist and his companions suffered the tortures of slow starvation for three months: at last they got so voracious and wild with hunger, that one boy, who was tall for his age, and hadn't been used to that sort of thing (for his father had kept a small cookshop), hinted darkly to his companions, that unless he had another basin of gruel (r)per diem[26], he was afraid he might some night happen to eat the boy who slept next him, who happened to be a weakly youth of tender age. He had a wild, hungry eye; and they implicitly believed him. A council was held; lots were cast who should walk up to the master after supper that evening, and ask for more; and it fell to Oliver Twist.

The evening arrived; the boys took their places. The master, in his cook's uniform, stationed himself at the copper; his pauper assistants ranged themselves behind him; the gruel was served out; and a long grace was said over the short commons. The gruel disappeared; the boys whispered each other, and winked at Oliver; while his next neighbours nudged him. Child as he was, he was desperate with hunger, and reckless with misery. He rose from the table; and advancing to the master, basin and spoon in hand, said: somewhat alarmed at his own temerity:

"Please, sir, I want some more."

The master was a fat, healthy man; but he turned very pale. He gazed in stupefied[27] astonishment on the small rebel for some seconds, and then clung for support to the copper. The assistants were paralysed with wonder; the boys with fear.

"What!" said the master at length, in a faint voice.

"Please, sir," replied Oliver, "I want some more."

The master aimed a blow at Oliver's head with the ladle; pinioned him in his arms; and shrieked aloud for the beadle.

The board were sitting in solemn conclave, when Mr. Bumble rushed into the room in great excitement, and addressing the gentleman in the high chair, said,

"Mr. Limbkins, I beg your pardon, sir! Oliver Twist has asked for more!"

There was a general start. Horror was depicted on every countenance.

"For (r)more!" said Mr. Limbkins. "Compose yourself[28], Bumble, and answer me distinctly. Do I understand that he asked for more, after he had eaten the supper allotted by the dietary?"

"He did, sir," replied Bumble.

"That boy will be hung," said the gentleman in the white waistcoat. "I know that boy will be hung."

Nobody controverted the prophetic gentleman's opinion. An animated discussion took place. Oliver was ordered into instant confinement; and a bill was next morning pasted on the outside of the gate, offering a reward of five pounds to anybody who would take Oliver Twist off the hands of the parish. In other words, five pounds and Oliver Twist were offered to any man or woman who wanted an apprentice to any trade, business, or calling.

"I never was more convinced of anything in my life," said the gentleman in the white waistcoat, as he knocked at the gate and read the bill next morning: "I never was more convinced of anything in my life, than I am that that boy will come to be hung."

As I purpose to show in the sequel whether the white-waistcoated gentleman was right or not, I should perhaps mar the interest of this narrative (supposing it to possess any at all), if I ventured to hint just yet, whether the life of Oliver Twist had this violent termination or no.

Notes

1. **fictitious**: not true, or not real
2. **inasmuch**: since
3. **extant**: still existing in spite of being very old
4. **chafe**: rub against
5. **gruel**: a thin porridge
6. **hitherto**: up to this time
7. **calico**: heavy cotton cloth that is usually white
8. **magnanimous**: kind, generous and forgiving, especially towards an enemy
9. **stipend**: an amount of money that is paid regularly to sb, especially a priest, as wages or money to live on
10. **contrive**: devise a (plan)
11. **choleric**: easily made angry
12. **beadle**: an officer in British churches in the past, who helped the priest in various ways, especially by keeping order
13. **vindicate**: to prove something is true
14. **interpose**: interrupt
15. **cuff**: the end of a coat or shirt sleeve at the wrist
16. **demolition**: here it means eating something quickly
17. **forthwith**: immediately
18. **bid**: to order somebody to do something
19. **whereupon**: and then
20. **gruff**: (of a voice) deep and harsh, and often sounding unfriendly
21. **oakum**: a material obtained by pulling old rope to pieces
22. **surly**: bad-tempered
23. **sage**: wise
24. **mater**: the cook

25. **festive composition**: meaning gruel. Here the figure of speech oxymoron is used.
26. *per diem*: (Latin) every day
27. **Stupefied**: shocked
28. **compose yourself**: calm yourself down

Questions for Study and Discussion

1. Are the members of the board really sage, deep and philosophical? What is the implied meaning of this description?
2. What is the implied meaning of "festive composition"?
3. What kind of person is Mr. Bumble? Analyze his personalities.
4. What is Dickens's attitude towards children as can be judged in the latter half of chapter II ?
5. Give several typical examples of the use of irony and explain how the irony is achieved.
6. Compare Oliver Twist with some other boy in fiction of about the same age who grapples with adversities, for example, Huckleberry Finn.
7. What was the punishment given to Oliver for asking some more of soup?
8. What are Dickens' writing features?

William Makepeace Thackeray (1811—1863)

Life and Major Works

William Makepeace Thackeray is important not only as a great novelist but also as a brilliant satirist. Born in Calcutta, he was the son of Richmond Thackeray, a collector in the East India Company's service. He lost his father when he was only three years old. At the age of five, William was sent to England, with a short stopover at St. Helena where the imprisoned Napoleon was pointed out to him. He was educated at schools in Southampton and Chiswick and then

William Makepeace Thackeray

at Charterhouse School, where he became a close friend of John Leech. At the University, Thackeray displayed a talent for cartoon drawing and edited a student newspaper. However, Thackeray became addicted to gambling and left Cambridge in 1830 without a degree and heavily in debt.

Then he traveled for some time on the continent, visiting places like Paris and Weimar, where he met Goethe. He entered the Middle Temple, but he had little enthusiasm for law and never practiced as a barrister. At the age of 21 he inherited some money but he lost much of it on gambling. He began his career in journalism by becoming the proprietor of a struggling weekly paper, the *National Standard*, but it ceased publication a year later. He pursued his other interests, like art, and studied in a London art school and a Paris atelier. He also lost a good part of his fortune in the collapse of two Indian banks. By the end of 1833, virtually all his inherited money had been lost. Forced to find a job to support himself, he turned first to art, which he studied in Paris, but gave it up soon. So he turned to journalism. From 1834 to 1837, he made a meager living on journalism.

In 1837, Thackeray returned to London and started his career as a hardworking journalist. Thackeray began to contribute regularly to *Fraser's Magazine*, *Morning Chronicle*, *New Monthly Magazine* and *The Times*. His writings attracted first attention in *Punch*, where he satirized English snobbery. These sketches reappeared in 1848 as *The Book of Snobs*, in which he stated that "he who meanly admires mean things is a Snob."

In 1836 he married a poor Irish girl, Isabella Shawe. They had 3 daughters. However, Tragedy struck in his personal life. His wife suffered depression after the birth of their third child in 1840. Finding he could get no work done at home, he spent more and more time away, until he noticed how grave her condition was. Feeling guilty, he took his sick wife to Ireland. They fled back home after a four-week domestic battle with her mother. In 1840 Isabella Thackeray suffered a mental breakdown, from which she never recovered, though she survived Thackeray by thirty years. The author was forced to send his children to France to his mother. The children returned to England in 1846 to live with him.

In 1848, Thackeray achieved widespread popularity with his humorous *Book of Snobs* which gave a satirical description of the different strata of the ruling classes of England and is regarded as a prelude to Thackeray's major literary career. In the same year he hit the big time with *Vanity Fair*, a satirical panorama of upper-middle-class London life and manners at the beginning of the 19th century. The novel contains many fascinating characters, particularly Becky Sharp, who, although clever and unscrupulous, is also extremely appealing. It sold in the neighborhood of 7,000 numbers a month. Thackeray finally had a name that gained notice and reviews in journals such as the *Edinburgh Review*. His reputation continues to increase in 1850 with the completion of the partly autobiographical novel *Pendennis*. In 1851 he delivered a series of lectures, *English Humorists of the Eighteenth Century*, which he repeated on a tour of the United States from 1852 to 1853. In 1852 his novel of 18th-century life, *Henry Esmond*, appeared. *The Newcomes*, in which some of the characters of Pendennis reappear, came out serially during 1853 to 1855. This was the most carefully planned of Thackeray's novels, and for it he did a considerable amount of historical research. At that time, it caused a sensation thanks to its controversial ending, wherein the hero marries a woman who early in the novel seemed a "mother" to him. In 1855 and 1856 he delivered another series of lectures in the United States entitled *The Four Georges,* published in 1860. His next novel, *The Virginians* (1857—1859), is a continuation of the Esmond story. In 1860 Thackeray became editor of the newly founded *Cornhill* Magazine, in which his last novels appeared— *Lovel the Widower* (1860), *The Adventures of Philip* (1861—1862), and the unfinished historical romance, *Denis Duval* (1864).

During these years of success, Thackeray lived a bachelor life in London, even though he had his daughters and grandmother with him. He spent much time with his friends. Toward the end of his life, Thackeray was proud that through his writing he had regained the patrimony he had lost, due to bank failures and gambling in his earlier years, and that he passed on to his daughters an inheritance sufficient for their support and a grand house in Kensington he had built during his *Cornhill* years. He also took pride in his daughter Anne's first steps in her own career as a writer. His health had been declining for some years but he died suddenly from the bursting of a blood vessel in the brain on December 24, 1863. He was buried in Kensal Green Cemetery on December 30, with an estimated two thousand mourners paying their respects.

Brief Introduction and Appreciation

The title of the novel, *Vanity Fair*, was taken from Bunyan's *Pilgrim's Progress*. *Vanity Fair* has a subtitle, *A Novel Without a Hero*. In this novel, Thackeray builds his plot around the lives of Amelia Sedley and Rebecca (Becky) Sharp. Amelia Sedley is the daughter of a wealthy London merchant while Rebecca (Becky) Sharp is an orphan. Becky Sharp is a classic example of money-grubbing instinct. But she is not alone. Everyone wishes to gain something in *Vanity Fair* and acts almost in the same manner as Becky.

The story begins when Amelia Sedley, of a wealthy family, and Rebecca Sharp, a poor orphan, leave Miss Pinkerton's academy on Chiswick Mall to live out their lives in Vanity Fair—the world of social climbing and search for wealth. Amelia does not esteem the values of Vanity Fair while Rebecca cares for nothing else. At first, Rebecca tries to enter the sacred domain of Vanity Fair by inducing Joseph Sedley, Amelia's brother, to marry her. However, George Osborne, who intends to marry Amelia and does not want a governess for a sister-in-law, foils her plan. Rebecca takes a position as governess at Queen's Crawley, and marries Rawdon Crawley, second son of Sir Pitt Crawley. Because of his marriage, Rawdon's rich aunt disinherits him.

First introduced as a friend of George Osborne, William Dobbin becomes the instrument for getting George to marry Amelia, after George's father has forbidden the marriage on account of the Sedley's loss of fortune. Because of George's marriage, old Osborne disinherits him. Both young couples endeavor to live without sufficient funds. George dies at Waterloo. Amelia would have starved but for William Dobbin's anonymous contribution to her welfare. Both Rebecca and Amelia give birth to sons.

Rebecca claims she will make Rawdon's fortune, but actually she hides much of her loot, obtained from admiring gentlemen. When she becomes the favorite of the great Lord Steyne, she accumulates both money and diamonds. Rawdon, long ignored by Becky, is jailed for failing to pay a debt. Becky is slow to answer his message asking her to have him released, so he contacts Sir Pitt and Lady Jane. Lady Jane arrives without delay to free him. At home, Rawdon finds Becky entertaining Lord Steyne. He attacks Lord Steyne—he hurls a diamond pin at his forehead, leaving Lord Steyne scarred—and goes through Becky's belongings and finds her stash of money and jewelry. Innocent Rawdon draws closer to Lady Jane, wife of Rawdon's older brother, Pitt, who has inherited from the rich aunt.

When Rawdon discovers Rebecca has been betraying him, he is convinced that money means more to her than he or their son. He refuses to see her again and takes a post in Coventry Island, where he dies of yellow fever.

Because her parents are starving and she can neither provide for them nor give little Georgy what she thinks he needs, Amelia gives up her son to his grandfather. William Dobbin comes back from the service, he finds a way for the two to accept each other, and Osborne makes a will leaving Georgy half of his fortune and providing for Amelia.

Rebecca, wandering in Europe for a couple of years, finally meets Joseph, Georgy, Amelia, and William on the Continent. Rebecca sets about to finish what she started to do at the first of the book—that is, to seduce Joseph. She does not marry him, but she takes all his money and he dies in terror of her—she has, at least, hastened his death.

At the end of the book Rebecca has the money necessary to live in Vanity Fair; she appears to be respectable. William has won Amelia. Little Rawdon, upon the death of his uncle Pitt and his cousin Pitt, becomes the heir of Queen's Crawley. Little George, through the kindness of Dobbin, has given up his distorted values obtained in Vanity Fair and became a better person.

Vanity Fair, as a work of social criticism, is noted for the author's realistic depiction, the ironic and sarcastic tone, constant comment and criticism. Thackeray uses symbolism in *Vanity Fair* and employs an omniscient narrator to tell the story.

Selected Reading

Vanity Fair
A Novel without a Hero
Chapter One
Chiswick Mall

While the present century was in its teens, and on one sunshiny morning in June, there drove up to the great iron gate of Miss Pinkerton's academy for young ladies, on Chiswick Mall, a large family coach, with two fat horses in blazing harness, driven by a fat coachman in a three-cornered hat and wig, at the rate of four miles an hour. A black servant, who reposed[1] on the box beside the fat coachman, uncurled his bandy legs as soon as the equipage drew up opposite Miss Pinkerton's shining brass plate, and as he pulled the bell at least a score of young heads were seen peering out of the narrow windows of the stately old brick house. Nay, the acute observer might have recognized the little red nose of good-natured Miss Jemima Pinkerton herself, rising over some geranium pots in the window of that lady's own drawing-room.

"It is Mrs. Sedley's coach, sister," said Miss Jemima. "Sambo, the black servant, has just rung the bell; and the coachman has a new red waistcoat."

"Have you completed all the necessary preparations incident to Miss Sedley's departure, Miss Jemima?" asked Miss Pinkerton herself, that majestic lady; the Semiramis of Hammersmith, the friend of Doctor Johnson, the correspondent of Mrs. Chapone herself.

"The girls were up at four this morning, packing her trunks, sister," replied Miss Jemima; "we have made her a bow-pot."

"Say a bouquet, sister Jemima, 'tis more genteel."

"Well, a booky as big almost as a haystack; I have put up two bottles of the gillyflower water for Mrs. Sedley, and the receipt for making it, in Amelia's box."

"And I trust, Miss Jemima, you have made a copy of Miss Sedley's account. This is it, is it? Very good—ninety-three pounds, four shillings. Be kind enough to address it to John Sedley, Esquire, and to seal this billet[2] which I have written to his lady."

In Miss Jemima's eyes an autograph letter of her sister, Miss Pinkerton, was an object of as deep veneration[3] as would have been a letter from a sovereign. Only when her pupils quitted the establishment, or when they were about to be married, and once, when poor Miss Birch died of the scarlet fever, was Miss Pinkerton known to write personally to the parents of her pupils; and it was Jemima's opinion that if anything could console Mrs. Birch for her daughter's loss, it would be that pious and eloquent composition in which Miss Pinkerton announced the event.

In the present instance Miss Pinkerton's "billet" was to the following effect:—

The Mall, Chiswick, June 15, 18

MADAM,—After her six years' residence at the Mall, I have the honour and happiness of presenting Miss Amelia Sedley to her parents, as a young lady not unworthy to occupy a fitting position in their polished and refined circle. Those virtues which characterize the young English gentlewoman, those accomplishments which become her birth and station, will not be found wanting in the amiable Miss Sedley, whose INDUSTRY and OBEDIENCE have endeared her to her instructors, and whose delightful sweetness of temper has charmed her AGED and her YOUTHFUL companions.

In music, in dancing, in orthography, in every variety of embroidery and needlework, she will be found to have realized her friends' fondest wishes. In geography there is still much to be desired; and a careful and undeviating use of the backboard, for four hours daily during the next three years, is recommended as necessary to the acquirement of that dignified DEPORTMENT AND CARRIAGE, so requisite for every young lady of FASHION.

In the principles of religion and morality, Miss Sedley will be found worthy of an establishment which has been honoured by the presence of THE GREAT LEXICOGRAPHER, and the patronage of the admirable Mrs. Chapone. In leaving the Mall, Miss Amelia carries with her the hearts of her companions, and the affectionate regards of her mistress, who has the honour to subscribe herself,

Madam, Your most obliged humble servant, BARBARA PINKERTON

P.S.—Miss Sharp accompanies Miss Sedley. It is particularly requested that Miss Sharp's stay in Russell Square may not exceed ten days. The family of distinction with whom she is engaged, desire to avail themselves of her services as soon as possible.

This letter completed, Miss Pinkerton proceeded to write her own name, and Miss Sedley's, in the fly-leaf of a Johnson's Dictionary— the interesting work which she invariably presented to her scholars, on their departure from the Mall. On the cover was inserted a copy of "Lines addressed to a young lady on quitting Miss Pinkerton's school, at the Mall; by the late revered Doctor Samuel Johnson." In fact, the Lexicographer's name was always on the lips of this majestic woman, and a visit he had paid to her was the cause of her reputation and her fortune.

Being commanded by her elder sister to get "the Dictionary" from the cupboard, Miss Jemima had extracted two copies of the book from the receptacle in question. When Miss Pinkerton had finished the inscription in the first, Jemima, with rather a dubious and timid air, handed her the second.

"For whom is this, Miss Jemima?" said Miss Pinkerton, with awful coldness.

"For Becky Sharp," answered Jemima, trembling very much, and blushing over her withered face and neck, as she turned her back on her sister. "For Becky Sharp: she's going too."

"MISS JEMIMA!" exclaimed Miss Pinkerton, in the largest capitals. "Are you in your senses? Replace the Dixonary in the closet, and never venture to take such a liberty in future."

"Well, sister, it's only two-and-ninepence, and poor Becky will be miserable if she don't get one."

"Send Miss Sedley instantly to me," said Miss Pinkerton. And so venturing not to say another word, poor Jemima trotted off, exceedingly flurried and nervous.

Miss Sedley's papa was a merchant in London, and a man of some wealth; whereas Miss Sharp was an articled pupil, for whom Miss Pinkerton had done, as she thought, quite enough, without conferring upon her at parting the high honour of the Dixonary.

Although schoolmistresses' letters are to be trusted no more nor less than churchyard epitaphs[4]; yet, as it sometimes happens that a person departs this life who is really deserving of all the praises the stone cutter carves over his bones; who IS a good Christian, a good parent, child, wife, or husband; who actually DOES leave a disconsolate family to mourn his loss; so in academies of the male and female sex it occurs every now and then that the pupil is fully worthy of the praises bestowed by the disinterested instructor. Now, Miss Amelia Sedley was a young lady of this singular species; and deserved not only all that Miss Pinkerton said in her praise, but had many charming qualities which that pompous old Minerva of a woman could not see, from the differences of rank and age between her pupil and herself.

For she could not only sing like a lark, or a Mrs. Billington, and dance like Hillisberg or Parisot; and embroider beautifully; and spell as well as a Dixonary itself; but she had such a kindly, smiling, tender, gentle, generous heart of her own, as won the love of everybody who came near her, from

Minerva herself down to the poor girl in the scullery[5], and the one-eyed tart-woman's daughter, who was permitted to vend her wares once a week to the young ladies in the Mall. She had twelve intimate and bosom friends out of the twenty-four young ladies. Even envious Miss Briggs never spoke ill of her; high and mighty Miss Saltire (Lord Dexter's granddaughter) allowed that her figure was genteel; and as for Miss Swartz, the rich woolly-haired mulatto from St. Kitt's, on the day Amelia went away, she was in such a passion of tears that they were obliged to send for Dr. Floss, and half tipsify her with salvolatile. Miss Pinkerton's attachment was, as may be supposed from the high position and eminent virtues of that lady, calm and dignified; but Miss Jemima had already whimpered several times at the idea of Amelia's departure; and, but for fear of her sister, would have gone off in downright hysterics, like the heiress (who paid double) of St. Kitt's. Such luxury of grief, however, is only allowed to parlour-boarders. Honest Jemima had all the bills, and the washing, and the mending, and the puddings, and the plate and crockery, and the servants to superintend. But why speak about her? It is probable that we shall not hear of her again from this moment to the end of time, and that when the great filigree iron gates are once closed on her, she and her awful sister will never issue therefrom into this little world of history.

But as we are to see a great deal of Amelia, there is no harm in saying, at the outset of our acquaintance, that she was a dear little creature; and a great mercy it is, both in life and in novels, which (and the latter especially) abound in villains of the most sombre sort, that we are to have for a constant companion so guileless and good-natured a person. As she is not a heroine, there is no need to describe her person; indeed I am afraid that her nose was rather short than otherwise, and her cheeks a great deal too round and red for a heroine; but her face blushed with rosy health, and her lips with the freshest of smiles, and she had a pair of eyes which sparkled with the brightest and honestest good-humour, except indeed when they filled with tears, and that was a great deal too often; for the silly thing would cry over a dead canary-bird; or over a mouse, that the cat haply had seized upon; or over the end of a novel, were it ever so stupid; and as for saying an unkind word to her, were any persons hard-hearted enough to do so—why, so much the worse for them. Even Miss Pinkerton, that austere and godlike woman, ceased scolding her after the first time, and though she no more comprehended sensibility than she did Algebra, gave all masters and teachers particular orders to treat Miss Sedley with the utmost gentleness, as harsh treatment was injurious to her.

So that when the day of departure came, between her two customs of laughing and crying, Miss Sedley was greatly puzzled how to act. She was glad to go home, and yet most woefully sad at leaving school. For three days before, little Laura Martin, the orphan, followed her about like a little dog. She had to make and receive at least fourteen presents—to make fourteen solemn promises of writing every week: "Send my letters under cover to my grandpapa, the Earl of Dexter," said Miss Saltire (who, by the way, was rather shabby). "Never mind the postage, but write every day, you dear darling," said the impetuous and woolly-headed, but generous and affectionate Miss Swartz; and the orphan little Laura Martin (who was just in round-hand), took her friend's hand and said, looking up in her face wistfully, "Amelia, when I write to you I shall call you Mamma." All which details, I have no doubt, JONES, who reads this book at his Club, will pronounce to be excessively foolish, trivial, twaddling, and ultra-sentimental. Yes; I can see Jones at this minute (rather flushed with his joint of mutton and half pint of wine), taking out his pencil and scoring under the words "foolish, twaddling," &c., and adding to them his own remark of "QUITE TRUE." Well, he is a lofty man of genius, and admires the great and heroic in life and novels; and so had better take warning and go elsewhere.

Well, then. The flowers, and the presents, and the trunks, and bonnet-boxes of Miss Sedley having been arranged by Mr. Sambo in the carriage, together with a very small and weather-beaten old cow's- skin trunk with Miss Sharp's card neatly nailed upon it, which was delivered by Sambo with a grin, and packed by the coachman with a corresponding sneer—the hour for parting came; and the grief of that moment was considerably lessened by the admirable discourse which Miss Pinkerton addressed to her pupil. Not that the parting speech caused Amelia to philosophise, or that it armed her in any way with a calmness, the result of argument; but it was intolerably dull, pompous, and tedious; and having the fear of her schoolmistress greatly before her eyes, Miss Sedley did not venture, in her presence, to give way to any ebullitions[6] of private grief. A seed-cake and a bottle of wine were produced in the drawing-room, as on the solemn occasions of the visits of parents, and these refreshments being partaken of, Miss Sedley was at liberty to depart.

"You'll go in and say good-by to Miss Pinkerton, Becky!" said Miss Jemima to a young lady of whom nobody took any notice, and who was coming downstairs with her own bandbox.

"I suppose I must," said Miss Sharp calmly, and much to the wonder of Miss Jemima; and the latter having knocked at the door, and receiving permission to come in, Miss Sharp advanced in a very unconcerned manner, and said in French, and with a perfect accent, "Mademoiselle, je viens vous faire mes adieux."

Miss Pinkerton did not understand French; she only directed those who did: but biting her lips and throwing up her venerable and Roman-nosed head (on the top of which figured a large and solemn turban), she said, "Miss Sharp, I wish you a good morning." As the Hammersmith Semiramis spoke, she waved one hand, both by way of adieu, and to give Miss Sharp an opportunity of shaking one of the fingers of the hand which was left out for that purpose.

Miss Sharp only folded her own hands with a very frigid smile and bow, and quite declined to accept the proffered honour; on which Semiramis tossed up her turban more indignantly than ever. In fact, it was a little battle between the young lady and the old one, and the latter was worsted. "Heaven bless you, my child," said she, embracing Amelia, and scowling the while over the girl's shoulder at Miss Sharp. "Come away, Becky," said Miss Jemima, pulling the young woman away in great alarm, and the drawing-room door closed upon them for ever.

Then came the struggle and parting below. Words refuse to tell it. All the servants were there in the hall—all the dear friend—all the young ladies—the dancing-master who had just arrived; and there was such a scuffling, and hugging, and kissing, and crying, with the hysterical YOOPS of Miss Swartz, the parlour-boarder, from her room, as no pen can depict, and as the tender heart would fain pass over. The embracing was over; they parted—that is, Miss Sedley parted from her friends. Miss Sharp had demurely entered the carriage some minutes before. Nobody cried for leaving HER.

Sambo of the bandy legs slammed the carriage door on his young weeping mistress. He sprang up behind the carriage. "Stop!" cried Miss Jemima, rushing to the gate with a parcel.

"It's some sandwiches, my dear," said she to Amelia. "You may be hungry, you know; and Becky, Becky Sharp, here's a book for you that my sister—that is, I—Johnson's Dixonary, you know; you mustn't leave us without that. Good-by. Drive on, coachman. God bless you!"

And the kind creature retreated into the garden, overcome with emotion.

But, lo! and just as the coach drove off, Miss Sharp put her pale face out of the window and actually flung the book back into the garden.

This almost caused Jemima to faint with terror. "Well, I never"— said she—"what an audacious"—Emotion prevented her from completing either sentence. The carriage rolled away; the great gates were closed; the bell rang for the dancing lesson. The world is before the two young ladies; and so, farewell to Chiswick Mall.

Notes

1. **repose**: a state of calm or comfortable rest
2. **billet**: a brief letter
3. **veneration**: respect or awe inspired by the dignity, wisdom, dedication, or talent of a person
4. **epitaph**: a short piece of writing on the stone over someone's grave
5. **scullery**: a small room next to the kitchen in an old house, originally used for washing dishes, etc.
6. **ebullition**: a sudden violent outburst or display

Questions for Study and Discussion

1. How many characters appear in the first chapter? How many of them caught your attention? Describe them.
2. What are their personalities respectively?
3. Why does *Vanity Fair* has a subtitle *A Novel Without a Hero*? What does it imply?
4. What kind of narrative perspective did Thackeray employ to tell the story?
5. Thackeray is a satirist. His satire is caustic and his humor subtle. Can you list some examples?
6. What is the symbolic importance of Becky Sharp tossing the gift of Samuel Johnson's Dictionary out the window of her coach as she leaves Chiswick Mall?
7. Throughout the novel, Thackeray frequently interjects his own commentary

into the narrative. What is the effect of these interruptions and how do they contribute to the novel's narrative strategy?

8. What is your impression of the differences between how Becky Sharp and Amelia Sedley are characterized by Thackeray in the early stages of the novel?

Charlotte Bront (1816—1855)

Life and Major Works

Charlotte **Bront** , English author, is the eldest of the famed **Bront** sisters. She was born on 21 April 1816, in the village of Thornton near Bradford in Yorkshire County, England. She was the third daughter born to Maria Branwell and the Anglican clergyman of Irish descent, Patrick **Bront** . Charlotte's mother died in 1821, leaving 5 daughters and a son to the care of their aunt, Elizabeth Branwell. Four of the daughters were sent to a Clergy Daughters' School at Cowan Bridge, an unfortunate step which Charlotte believed to have hastened the death of her 2

Charlotte Brontë

elder sisters and to have impaired her own health. The surviving children pursued their education at home. They read widely. In 1831, Charlotte began attending school at Roe Head. In 1832, Charlotte left school and spent the next three years teaching her sisters at home. She returned to Roe Head in 1835 as a teacher, but she felt miserable there. The school moved to Dewsbury Moor in 1837, but Charlotte left a year later.

In 1839, she spent a few months working as a governess for a family named the Sidgwicks. In 1841 Charlotte worked as a governess for the Whites. In 1842 she went with Emily to study languages at the Pensionnat Heger in Brussels. In 1843, Charlotte returned alone to the Pensionnant Heger to study and teach. After a year, she returned to Haworth.

The sisters' project to found a school at Haworth proved hopeless. In 1845, she discovered the poems of Emily, and, convinced of their quality, Charlotte proposed to publish it with poems by her and Anne in a volume entitled *Poems by Currer, Acton and Ellis Bell,* and Charlotte's pseudonym was Currer Bell. The volume appeared at their own expense in 1846, but was hardly noticed and sold only two copies. Despite this discouraging start, the sisters determined to continue in their efforts to earn money by their writing. By this time, each had finished a novel. Charlotte's first work, *The Professor* never found a publisher in her lifetime, but Emily's *Wuthering Heights* and Anne's *Agnes Grey* were accepted by Thomas Newby in 1847 and published in 1848. Charlotte began *Jane Eyre* on a visit to Manchester in 1846, where she had arranged for her father to have an operation to remove a cataract from his eye. Smith and Elder published *Jane Eyre* in 1847 and it was an immediate success, arousing much speculation about its author. Newby quickly and opportunistically brought out *The Tenant of Wildfell Hall* by Anne Bronte in 1848, and encouraged rumours that Acton, Ellis, and Currer Bell were, in fact, the same person. Charlotte and Annie visited Smith and Elder in July 1848 to make themselves known as the separate authors. But Charlotte could not enjoy the success and many invitations now extended to her, because what followed was misfortune. Her alcoholic brother, Branwell, died in September and only three months later, her sister, Emily also died. Anne fell ill in 1849, so Charlotte and her friend Ellen took her to Scarborough for one last look at the sea. Anne died there in May, leaving Charlotte alone and grieving for her lost sisters at the age of 33.

Throughout this terrible time she was writing *Shirley*, which appeared in 1849 to enthusiastic reviews. She visited George Smith in London, where she met her literary hero, Thackeray. She continued her friendship with Smith and spent some time with his family in London in 1850. The two spent a few happy days together in Scotland.

In 1851, Charlotte began *Villette*. In May and June, she again stayed with George Smith and his family. Charlotte and George took a trip to Richmond, disguising themselves as "Mr. and Miss Fraser". Upon their return, they had an intense correspondence, but after a while it declined, and so did Charlotte's health. She became obsessive with waiting for letters from Smith, but she refused repeated invitations to visit his family.

In January 1852, Charlotte resumed work on *Villette*, in which she incorporated part of her friendship with Smith along with her memories of M.

Heger. In November, she shocked Smith with the third volume, in which the hero she based on Smith is dismissed in favor of a Belgian teacher. Smith underpaid Charlotte for the novel. In December, Charlotte refused a proposal from Mr. Nicholls. In 1853, Charlotte went to London to see *Villette* through the press. George Smith was engaged in November. And Charlotte relented to Mr. Nicholls and they became engaged, too. She continued to have doubts about marriage, however, which she revealed to Mrs. Gaskell.

Charlotte was married in June, 1854, at the age of thirty-eight. She was given away at the wedding by Miss Wooler because her father refused at the last moment. Ellen Nussey attended the wedding and the couple spent their honeymoon in Ireland. Charlotte was increasingly happy and well despite Nicholls' lack of encouragement about the unfinished novel *Emma* and his desire to burn her correspondence with Ellen.

In 1855, the parsonage servant, Tabby, developed a digestive tract infection that was possibly typhoid. Charlotte, who was pregnant, may have been infected by Tabby. Tabby died 6 weeks later on February 17. Charlotte died on March 31, after 6 weeks of vomiting blood and being unable to eat. Her last letters to Ellen thanked her husband and she left everything to him in her will.

Brief Introduction and Appreciation

Charlotte Bront is a representative writer of realism combined with romanticism of that time. In her works, she paints a vivid realistic picture of the English society by exposing the cruelty, hypocrisy and other evils of the upper classes and by showing the misery and suffering of the poor. Her works are famous for the depiction of the life of the middle class working women, particularly governesses. In 1847, her novel *Jane Eyre* was published and received immediate acceptance by the reading public. In this novel, Charlotte Bront successfully creates a typical new woman who has the courage to rebel and fight for freedom and equality.

On the surface, *Jane Eyre* embodies stock situations of the Gothic novel genre, such as mystery, horror, and the classic medieval castle setting; many of the incidents in the work border on melodrama. The story of the young heroine is also in many ways conventional—the rise of a poor orphan girl against overwhelming odds, whose love and determination eventually redeem a tormented hero. If this is all there were to *Jane Eyre*, the novel would soon have been forgotten. In writing *Jane Eyre*, Charlotte **Bront** did not write a mere romantic potboiler. Her book embodies serious subjects: the relations between men and women, women's equality, the treatment of children and of women, religious faith and religious hypocrisy (and the difference between the two), the realization of selfhood, and the nature of true love. It is a work of fiction with memorable characters and vivid scenes, written in a compelling prose style. In appealing to both the head and the heart, *Jane Eyre* triumphs over its flaws and remains a classic of 19th-century English literature and one of the most popular of all English novels.

Jane Eyre tells the story of an orphan who is ill-treated first by her aunt and then at a dreadful school, Lowood, before she happily becomes a governess at Thornfield Hall, teaching the daughter of the mysterious and Byronic Mr. Rochester. Charlotte draws heavily on her own and her sisters' lives, but it is not an autobiographical novel. Her own aunt was of a benevolent nature. Her personal experience and those of her sisters, were not as fantastic as what was depicted in the book. And no Rochester fell in love with her.

It was Jane's character instead of her plain looks that attracts Rochester. Her honesty, and her practical common sense which enable her to save his life, are of great value to him. However, after he proposes marriage, she discovers that he already has a wife, Bertha, a lunatic who is kept in the attic at Thornfield. Refusing to become Rochester's mistress, Jane flees from him. She is then taken in by the Rivers family when she is penniless. They coincidentally turn out to be her cousins and reveal that she is heiress to sufficient funds to give her financial security for life. The Revd. St. John Rivers, who plans to go to India as a missionary, proposes to her. As she is about to accept him, she hears a supernatural cry from Rochester. On her return to Thornfield, she finds that the house has been burnt down by Bertha, and that Rochester himself has been blinded in an unsuccessful attempt to save his wife. Now Jane can marry him, not just because he is widowed but because his physical dependence gives her the equality she aspires to.

An important episode of the novel is that Jane Eyre finally becomes rich from the inherited money yet Rochester is completely ruined. However, even when Jane has all the advantages, she goes back to Rochester, who is poor and disabled. Jane preaches a sort of individual feminism, valuing equality and individuality over societal constraints. As a Victorian woman, and an orphan, consequently making her low class, Jane Eyre had very few choices to secure her survival. To make a living, she could have been a prostitute, she could have married for money, and she could have become a servant or a governess. Jane chose the option that allowed her to be an individual, to choose her own path. The novel inspired the feminist criticism of the 1980s through Gilbert and Gulbar's *The Madwoman in the Attic* in which unstable female characters in such literature were presented as proof of the suppression of the feminine.

The romantic and realistic moods are combined in *Jane Eyre*. The novel is realistic in that its heroine is a humble governess, its other characters are mostly ordinary people, and its scenes are largely those of everyday life. But Charlotte incorporated her story with a romantic glow which transformed it and gave it some of the warmth and excitement. This romanticized realism gives the novel its peculiar charm. The novelist exhibits both her deep sympathy for the poor and the mistreated, and her exposure and condemnation of the inhuman educational system of her age.

Her style being vigorous, supple, and straightforward, she is good at describing the simple things of nature, the changing seasons, the fire-lit room, the intense emotions of the human heart. The style of the language is typical Charlotte's novels, simple and clear, vivid and concrete.

Jane Eyre is a very famous and prolonged novel since its publication. Through *Jane Eyre*, Charlotte **Bront** proved to the world of that time that the idea of a woman to become independent and successful on her own was not an unrealizable dream. Women shall not depend on men or submit to oppression; they shall fight for real equality and freedom. Even in today's world, it also has a realistic significance. It encourages women all over the world to make efforts to become strong and independent, and to pursue their happiness bravely.

Selected Reading

Jane Eyre

Chapter I

There was no possibility of taking a walk that day. We had been wandering, indeed, in the leafless shrubbery an hour in the morning; but since dinner (Mrs.

Reed, when there was no company, dined early) the cold winter wind had brought with it clouds so sombre, and a rain so penetrating, that further out-door exercise was now out of the question.

I was glad of it: I never liked long walks, especially on chilly afternoons: dreadful to me was the coming home in the raw twilight, with nipped fingers and toes, and a heart saddened by the chidings of Bessie, the nurse, and humbled by the consciousness of my physical inferiority to Eliza, John, and Georgiana Reed.

The said Eliza, John, and Georgiana were now clustered round their mama in the drawing-room: she lay reclined on a sofa by the fireside, and with her darlings about her (for the time neither quarrelling nor crying) looked perfectly happy. Me, she had dispensed from joining the group; saying, "She regretted to be under the necessity of keeping me at a distance; but that until she heard from Bessie, and could discover by her own observation, that I was endeavouring in good earnest to acquire a more sociable and childlike disposition, a more attractive and sprightly manner—something lighter, franker, more natural, as it were—she really must exclude me from privileges intended only for contented, happy, little children."

"What does Bessie say I have done?" I asked.

"Jane, I don't like cavillers or questioners; besides, there is something truly forbidding in a child taking up her elders in that manner. Be seated somewhere; and until you can speak pleasantly, remain silent."

A breakfast-room adjoined the drawing-room, I slipped in there. It contained a bookcase: I soon possessed myself of a volume, taking care that it should be one stored with pictures. I mounted[1] into the window-seat: gathering up my feet, I sat cross-legged, like a Turk; and, having drawn the red moreen curtain nearly close, I was shrined in double retirement.

Folds of scarlet drapery shut in my view to the right hand; to the left were the clear panes of glass, protecting, but not separating me from the drear November day. At intervals, while turning over the leaves of my book, I studied the aspect of that winter afternoon. Afar, it offered a pale blank of mist and cloud; near a scene of wet lawn and storm-beat shrub, with ceaseless rain sweeping away wildly before a long and lamentable blast.

I returned to my book—Bewick's *History of British Birds*: the letterpress thereof I cared little for, generally speaking; and yet there were certain introductory pages that, child as I was, I could not pass quite as a blank. They were those which treat of the haunts of sea-fowl; of "the solitary rocks and promontories" by them only inhabited; of the coast of Norway, studded with isles from its southern extremity, the Lindeness, or Naze, to the North Cape[2]—

> "Where the Northern Ocean, in vast whirls,
> Boils round the naked, melancholy isles
> Of farthest Thule; and the Atlantic surge
> Pours in among the stormy Hebrides[3]. "

Nor could I pass unnoticed the suggestion of the bleak shores of Lapland, Siberia, Spitzbergen, Nova Zembla, Iceland, Greenland, with "the vast sweep of the Arctic Zone, and those forlorn regions of dreary space,—that reservoir of frost and snow, where firm fields of ice, the accumulation of centuries of winters, glazed in Alpine heights above heights, surround the pole, and concentre the multiplied rigours of extreme cold." Of these death-white realms I formed an idea of my own: shadowy, like all the half-comprehended notions that float dim through children's brains, but strangely impressive. The words in these introductory pages connected themselves with the succeeding vignettes, and gave significance to the rock standing up alone in a sea of billow and spray; to the broken boat stranded on a desolate coast; to the cold and ghastly moon glancing through bars of cloud at a wreck just sinking.

I cannot tell what sentiment haunted the quite solitary churchyard, with its inscribed headstone; its gate, its two trees, its low horizon, girdled by a broken wall, and its newly-risen crescent, attesting the hour of eventide.

The two ships becalmed on a torpid sea, I believed to be marine phantoms.

The fiend pinning down the thief's pack behind him, I passed over quickly: it was an object of terror.

So was the black horned thing seated aloof on a rock, surveying a distant crowd surrounding a gallows.

Each picture told a story; mysterious often to my undeveloped understanding and imperfect feelings, yet ever profoundly interesting: as interesting as the tales Bessie sometimes narrated on winter evenings, when she chanced to be[4] in good humour; and when, having brought her ironing-table to the nursery hearth, she allowed us to sit about it, and while she got up Mrs. Reed's lace frills, and crimped her nightcap borders, fed our eager attention with passages of love and adventure taken from old fairy tales and other ballads; or (as at a later period I discovered) from the pages of *Pamela*, and *Henry, Earl of Moreland*.

With Bewick on my knee, I was then happy: happy at least in my way. I feared nothing but interruption, and that came too soon. The breakfast-room door opened.

"Boh! Madam Mope!" cried the voice of John Reed; then he paused: he found the room apparently empty.

"Where the dickens[5] is she!" he continued. "Lizzy! Georgy! (calling to his sisters) Joan is not here: tell mama she is run out into the rain—bad animal!"

"It is well I drew the curtain," thought I; and I wished fervently he might not discover my hiding-place: nor would John Reed have found it out himself; he was not quick either of vision or conception; but Eliza just put her head in at the door, and said at once—

"She is in the window-seat, to be sure, Jack."

And I came out immediately, for I trembled at the idea of being dragged forth by the said Jack.

"What do you want?" I asked, with awkward diffidence.

"Say, 'What do you want, Master Reed?'" was the answer. "I want you to come here;" and seating himself in an arm-chair, he intimated by a gesture that I was to approach and stand before him.

John Reed was a schoolboy of fourteen years old; four years older than I, for I was but ten: large and stout for his age, with a dingy and unwholesome skin; thick lineaments in a spacious visage, heavy limbs and large extremities. He gorged himself habitually at table, which made him bilious, and gave him a dim and bleared eye and flabby cheeks. He ought now to have been at school; but his mama had taken him home for a month or two, "on account of his delicate health." Mr. Miles, the master, affirmed that he would do very well if he had fewer cakes and sweetmeats sent him from home; but the mother's heart turned from an opinion so harsh, and inclined rather to the more refined idea that John's sallowness was owing to over-application and, perhaps, to pining after home.

John had not much affection for his mother and sisters, and an antipathy to me. He bullied and punished me; not two or three times in the week, nor once or twice in the day, but continually: every nerve I had feared him, and every morsel of flesh in my bones shrank when he came near. There were moments when I was bewildered by the terror he inspired, because I had no appeal whatever against either his menaces or his inflictions; the servants did not like to offend their young master by taking my part against him, and Mrs. Reed was blind and deaf on the subject: she never saw him strike or heard him abuse me, though he did both now and then in her very presence, more frequently, however, behind her back.

Habitually obedient to John, I came up to his chair: he spent some three minutes in thrusting out his tongue at me as far as he could without damaging the roots: I knew he would soon strike, and while dreading the blow, I mused on the disgusting and ugly appearance of him who would presently deal it. I wonder if he read that notion in my face; for, all at once, without speaking, he struck suddenly and strongly. I tottered, and on regaining my equilibrium retired back a step or two from his chair.

"That is for your impudence in answering mama awhile since," said he, "and for your sneaking way of getting behind curtains, and for the look you had in your eyes two minutes since, you rat!"

Accustomed to John Reed's abuse, I never had an idea of replying to it; my care was how to endure the blow which would certainly follow the insult.

"What were you doing behind the curtain?" he asked.

"I was reading."

"Show the book."

I returned to the window and fetched it thence[6].

"You have no business to take our books; you are a dependent, mama says; you have no money; your father left you none; you ought to beg, and not to live here with gentlemen's children like us, and eat the same meals we do, and wear clothes at our mama's expense. Now, I'll teach you to rummage my bookshelves: for they ARE mine; all the house belongs to me, or will do in a few years. Go and stand by the door, out of the way of the mirror and the windows."

I did so, not at first aware what was his intention; but when I saw him lift and poise the book and stand in act to hurl it, I instinctively started aside with a cry of alarm: not soon enough, however; the volume was flung, it hit me, and I fell, striking my head against the door and cutting it. The cut bled, the pain

317

was sharp: my terror had passed its climax; other feelings succeeded.

"Wicked and cruel boy!" I said. "You are like a murderer—you are like a slave-driver—you are like the Roman emperors!"

I had read Goldsmith's History of Rome, and had formed my opinion of Nero, Caligula, &c. Also I had drawn parallels in silence, which I never thought thus to have declared aloud.

"What! what!" he cried. "Did she say that to me? Did you hear her, Eliza and Georgiana? Won't I tell mama? but first—"

He ran headlong at me: I felt him grasp my hair and my shoulder: he had closed with a desperate thing. I really saw in him a tyrant, a murderer. I felt a drop or two of blood from my head trickle down my neck, and was sensible of somewhat pungent suffering: these sensations for the time predominated over fear, and I received him in frantic sort. I don't very well know what I did with my hands, but he called me "Rat! Rat!" and bellowed out aloud. Aid was near him: Eliza and Georgiana had run for Mrs. Reed, who was gone upstairs: she now came upon the scene, followed by Bessie and her maid Abbot. We were parted: I heard the words—

"Dear! dear! What a fury to fly at Master John!"

"Did ever anybody see such a picture of passion!"

Then Mrs. Reed subjoined—

"Take her away to the red-room, and lock her in there." Four hands were immediately laid upon me, and I was borne upstairs.

Chapter II

I resisted all the way: a new thing for me, and a circumstance which greatly strengthened the bad opinion Bessie and Miss Abbot were disposed to entertain of me. The fact is, I was a trifle beside myself[7]; or rather OUT of myself, as the French would say: I was conscious that a moment's mutiny had already rendered me liable to strange penalties, and, like any other rebel slave, I felt resolved, in my desperation, to go all lengths.

"Hold her arms, Miss Abbot: she's like a mad cat."

"For shame! for shame!" cried the lady's-maid. "What shocking conduct, Miss Eyre, to strike a young gentleman, your benefactress's son! Your young master."

"Master! How is he my master? Am I a servant?"

"No; you are less than a servant, for you do nothing for your keep. There, sit down, and think over your wickedness."

They had got me by this time into the apartment indicated by Mrs. Reed, and had thrust me upon a stool: my impulse was to rise from it like a spring; their two pair of hands arrested me instantly.

"If you don't sit still, you must be tied down," said Bessie. "Miss Abbot, lend me your garters; she would break mine directly."

Miss Abbot turned to divest a stout leg of the necessary ligature[8]. This preparation for bonds, and the additional ignominy[9] it inferred, took a little of the excitement out of me.

"Don't take them off," I cried; "I will not stir."

In guarantee whereof, I attached myself to my seat by my hands.

"Mind you don't, " said Bessie; and when she had ascertained that I was really subsiding, she loosened her hold of me; then she and Miss Abbot stood with folded arms, looking darkly and doubtfully on my face, as incredulous of my sanity.

"She never did so before," at last said Bessie, turning to the Abigail.

"But it was always in her," was the reply. "I've told Missis often my opinion about the child, and Missis agreed with me. She's an underhand little thing: I never saw a girl of her age with so much cover."

Bessie answered not; but ere long[10], addressing me, she said—"You ought to be aware, Miss, that you are under obligations to Mrs. Reed: she keeps you: if she were to turn you off, you would have to go to the poorhouse[11]."

I had nothing to say to these words: they were not new to me: my very first recollections of existence included hints of the same kind. This reproach of my dependence had become a vague sing-song[12] in my ear: very painful and crushing, but only half intelligible.

Miss Abbot joined in—"And you ought not to think yourself on an equality with the Misses Reed and Master Reed, because Missis kindly allows you to be brought up with them. They will have a great deal of money, and you will have none: it is your place to be humble, and to try to make yourself agreeable to them."

"What we tell you is for your good," added Bessie, in no harsh voice, "you should try to be useful and pleasant, then, perhaps, you would have a home here; but if you become passionate and rude, Missis will send you away, I am sure."

"Besides," said Miss Abbot, "God will punish her: He might strike her dead in the midst of her tantrums, and then where would she go? Come, Bessie, we will leave her: I wouldn't have her heart for anything. Say your prayers, Miss Eyre, when you are by yourself; for if you don't repent, something bad might be permitted to come down the chimney and fetch you away."

They went, shutting the door, and locking it behind them.

The red-room was a square chamber, very seldom slept in, I might say never, indeed, unless when a chance influx[12] of visitors at Gateshead Hall rendered it necessary to turn to account all the accommodation it contained: yet it was one of the largest and stateliest chambers in the mansion. A bed supported on massive pillars of mahogany[14], hung with curtains of deep red damask, stood out like a tabernacle in the centre; the two large windows, with their blinds always drawn down, were half shrouded in festoons and falls of similar drapery; the carpet was red; the table at the foot of the bed was covered with a crimson cloth; the walls were a soft fawn colour with a blush of pink in it; the wardrobe, the toilet-table, the chairs were of darkly polished old mahogany. Out of these deep surrounding shades rose high, and glared white, the piled-up mattresses and pillows of the bed, spread with a snowy Marseilles counterpane. Scarcely less prominent was an ample cushioned easy-chair near the head of the bed, also white, with a footstool before it; and looking, as I thought, like a pale throne.

This room was chill, because it seldom had a fire; it was silent, because remote from the nursery and kitchen; solemn, because it was known to be so seldom entered. The house-maid alone came here on Saturdays, to wipe from the mirrors and the furniture a week's quiet dust: and Mrs. Reed herself, at far intervals, visited it to review the contents of a certain secret drawer in the wardrobe, where were stored divers parchments, her jewel-casket, and a miniature of her deceased husband; and in those last words lies the secret of the red-room—the spell which kept it so lonely in spite of its grandeur.

Mr. Reed had been dead nine years: it was in this chamber he breathed his last; here he lay in state; hence his coffin was borne by the undertaker's men; and, since that day, a sense of dreary consecration had guarded it from frequent intrusion.

My seat, to which Bessie and the bitter Miss Abbot had left me riveted, was a low ottoman near the marble chimney-piece; the bed rose before me; to my right hand there was the high, dark wardrobe, with subdued, broken reflections varying the gloss of its panels; to my left were the muffled windows; a great looking-glass between them repeated the vacant majesty of the bed and room. I was not quite sure whether they had locked the door; and when I dared move, I got up and went to see. Alas! yes: no jail was ever more secure. Returning, I had to cross before the looking-glass; my fascinated glance involuntarily explored the depth it revealed. All looked colder and darker in that visionary hollow than in reality: and the strange little figure there gazing at me, with a white face and arms specking the gloom, and glittering eyes of fear moving where all else was still, had the effect of a real spirit: I thought it like one of the tiny phantoms, half fairy, half imp, Bessie's evening stories represented as coming out of lone, ferny dells in moors, and appearing before the eyes of belated[15] travellers. I returned to my stool.

Superstition was with me at that moment; but it was not yet her hour for complete victory: my blood was still warm; the mood of the revolted slave was still bracing me with its bitter vigour; I had to stem a rapid rush of retrospective thought before I quailed to the dismal present.

All John Reed's violent tyrannies, all his sisters' proud indifference, all his mother's aversion, all the servants' partiality, turned up in my disturbed mind like a dark deposit in a turbid well. Why was I always suffering, always browbeaten, always accused, for ever condemned? Why could I never please? Why was it useless to try to win any one's favour? Eliza, who was headstrong and selfish, was respected. Georgiana, who had a spoiled temper, a very acrid spite, a captious and insolent carriage, was universally indulged. Her beauty, her pink cheeks and golden curls, seemed to give delight to all who looked at her, and to purchase indemnity for every fault. John no one thwarted, much less punished; though he twisted the necks of the pigeons, killed the little pea-chicks, set the dogs at the sheep, stripped the hothouse vines of their fruit, and broke the buds off the choicest plants in the conservatory: he called his mother "old girl," too; sometimes reviled her for her dark skin, similar to his own; bluntly disregarded her wishes; not unfrequently tore and spoiled her silk attire; and he was still "her own darling." I dared commit no fault: I strove to fulfil every duty; and I was termed naughty and tiresome, sullen and sneaking, from morning to noon, and from noon to night.

My head still ached and bled with the blow and fall I had received: no one had reproved John for wantonly striking me; and because I had turned against him to avert farther irrational violence, I was loaded with general opprobrium[16].

"Unjust!—unjust!" said my reason, forced by the agonising stimulus into precocious though transitory power: and Resolve, equally wrought up, instigated some strange expedient to achieve escape from insupportable oppression—as running away, or, if that could not be effected, never eating or drinking more, and letting myself die.

What a consternation of soul was mine that dreary afternoon! How all my brain was in tumult, and all my heart in insurrection! Yet in what darkness, what dense ignorance, was the mental battle fought! I could not answer the ceaseless inward question—WHY I thus suffered; now, at the distance of—I will not say how many years, I see it clearly.

I was a discord[17] in Gateshead Hall: I was like nobody there; I had nothing in harmony with Mrs. Reed or her children, or her chosen vassalage. If they did not love me, in fact, as little did I love them. They were not bound to regard with affection a thing that could not sympathise with one amongst them; a heterogeneous thing, opposed to them in temperament, in capacity, in propensities; a useless thing, incapable of serving their interest, or adding to their pleasure; a noxious thing, cherishing the germs of indignation at their treatment, of contempt of their judgment. I know that had I been a sanguine, brilliant, careless, exacting, handsome, romping child—though equally dependent and friendless—Mrs. Reed would have endured my presence more complacently; her children would have entertained for me more of the cordiality of fellow-feeling; the servants would have been less prone to make me the scapegoat of the nursery.

Daylight began to forsake the red-room; it was past four o'clock, and the beclouded afternoon was tending to drear twilight. I heard the rain still beating continuously on the staircase window, and the wind howling in the grove behind the hall; I grew by degrees cold as a stone, and then my courage sank. My habitual mood of humiliation, self-doubt, forlorn depression, fell damp on the embers of my decaying ire. All said I was wicked, and perhaps I might be so; what thought had I been but just conceiving of starving myself to death? That certainly was a crime: and was I fit to die? Or was the vault under the chancel of Gateshead Church an inviting bourne? In such vault I had been told did Mr. Reed lie buried; and led by this thought to recall his idea, I dwelt on it with gathering dread. I could not remember him; but I knew that he was my own uncle—my mother's brother—that he had taken me when a parentless infant to his house; and that in his last moments he had required a promise of Mrs. Reed that she would rear and maintain me as one of her own children. Mrs. Reed probably considered she had kept this promise; and so she had, I dare say, as well as her nature would permit her; but how could she really like an interloper not of her race, and unconnected with her, after her husband's death, by any tie? It must have been most irksome to find herself bound by a hard-wrung pledge to stand in the stead of a parent to a strange child she could not love, and to see an uncongenial alien permanently intruded on her own family group.

A singular notion dawned upon me. I doubted not—never doubted—that if Mr. Reed had been alive he would have treated me kindly; and now, as I sat looking at the white bed and overshadowed walls—occasionally also turning a fascinated eye towards the dimly gleaning mirror—I began to recall what I had heard of dead men, troubled in their graves by the violation of their last wishes, revisiting the earth to punish the perjured and avenge the oppressed; and I thought Mr. Reed's spirit, harassed by the wrongs of his sister's child, might quit its abode—whether in the church vault or in the unknown world of the departed—and rise before me in this chamber. I wiped my tears and hushed my sobs, fearful lest any sign of violent grief might waken a preternatural voice to comfort me, or elicit from the gloom some haloed face, bending over me with strange pity. This idea, consolatory in theory, I felt would be terrible if realised: with all my might I endeavoured to stifle it—I endeavoured to be firm. Shaking my hair from my eyes, I lifted my head and tried to look boldly round the dark room; at this moment a light gleamed on the wall. Was it, I asked myself, a ray from the moon penetrating some aperture in the blind? No; moonlight was still, and this stirred; while I gazed, it glided up to the ceiling and quivered over my head. I can now conjecture readily that this streak of light was, in all likelihood, a gleam from a lantern carried by some one across the lawn: but then, prepared as my mind was for horror, shaken as my nerves were by agitation, I thought the swift darting beam was a herald of some coming vision from another world. My heart beat thick, my head grew hot; a sound filled my ears, which I deemed the rushing of wings; something seemed near me; I was oppressed, suffocated: endurance broke down; I rushed to the door and shook the lock in desperate effort. Steps came running along the outer passage; the key turned, Bessie and Abbot entered.

"Miss Eyre, are you ill?" said Bessie.

"What a dreadful noise! it went quite through me!" exclaimed Abbot.

"Take me out! Let me go into the nursery!" was my cry.

"What for? Are you hurt? Have you seen something?" again demanded Bessie.

"Oh! I saw a light, and I thought a ghost would come." I had now got hold of Bessie's hand, and she did not snatch it from me.

"She has screamed out on purpose" declared Abbot, in some disgust.

"And what a scream! If she had been in great pain one would have excused it, but she only wanted to bring us all here: I know her naughty tricks."

"What is all this?" demanded another voice peremptorily[18]; and Mrs. Reed came along the corridor, her cap flying wide, her gown rustling stormily. "Abbot and Bessie, I believe I gave orders that Jane Eyre should be left in the red-room till I came to her myself."

"Miss Jane screamed so loud, ma'am," pleaded Bessie.

"Let her go," was the only answer. "Loose Bessie's hand, child: you cannot succeed in getting out by these means, be assured. I abhor artifice, particularly in children; it is my duty to show you that tricks will not answer: you will now stay here an hour longer, and it is only on condition of perfect submission and stillness that I shall liberate you then."

"O aunt! have pity! Forgive me! I cannot endure it—let me be punished some other way! I shall be killed if—"

"Silence! This violence is all most repulsive:" and so, no doubt, she felt it. I was a precocious actress in her eyes; she sincerely looked on me as a compound of virulent[19] passions, mean spirit, and dangerous duplicity.

Bessie and Abbot having retreated, Mrs. Reed, impatient of my now frantic anguish and wild sobs, abruptly thrust me back and locked me in, without farther parley[20]. I heard her sweeping away; and soon after she was gone, I suppose I had a species of fit: unconsciousness closed the scene.

Notes

1. **mount**: go up
2. **The North Cape**: a cape on the island of Mageroya in northern Norway
3. **the Hebrides**: a group of islands off the west coast of Scotland, consisting of the Inner Hebrides and Outer Hebrides
4. **chance to be**: happen to be
5. **where the dickens**: used when asking a question to show that you are very surprised or angry
6. **thence**: Old English: from 'that place'
7. **beside myself**: in a state of extreme excitement
8. **ligature**: something that is used for tying something very tightly, for example to stop bleeding
9. **ignominy**: public shame; humiliation
10. **ere long**: before long
11. **poorhouse**: a building where very poor people in the past could live and be fed, which was paid for with public money
12. **sing-song**: a way of speaking in which a person's voice keeps rising and falling
13. **influx**: the arrival of large numbers of people or large amounts of money, goods etc, especially suddenly
14. **mahogany**: a type of hard reddish brown wood used for making furniture, or the tree that produces this wood
15. **belated**: happening or arriving late
16. **opprobrium**: strong criticism or disapproval, especially expressed publicly
17. **discord**: Lack of agreement or harmony (as between persons, things, or ideas)
18. **peremptorily**: in a way that allows no discussion or refusal
19. **virulent**: Latin; Origin: virulentus, from virus; very dangerous and affects people very quickly
20. **parley**: a discussion between enemies or people who disagree

Questions for Study and Discussion

1. In what ways is *Jane Eyre* influenced by the tradition of the Gothic novel?
2. What do the names mean in Jane Eyre? Some names to consider include: Jane Eyre, Gateshead, Lowood, Thornfield, Reed, Rivers, Miss Temple, and Ferndean.
3. In what ways might *Jane Eyre* be considered a feminist novel?
4. What points does the novel make about the treatment and position of women in Victorian society?
5. What role does Jane's ambiguous social position play in determining the conflict of her story?
6. What are the differences between Jane and the Reed children? How is Jane treated differently from them?
7. Describe the place where Jane hides in Chapter 1. Notice the colors. What is she reading? What is its mood?
8. Jane is taken into the red room as punishment. Describe the room and what happens there. Why do you think it has such an impact on Jane?

Emily Bront (1818–49)

Life and Major Works

Emily Bront is one of the famed Bronte sisters and perhaps the greatest writer of the three Bront sisters—Charlotte, Emily and Anne. Emily Bront published only one novel, *Wuthering Heights* (1847), a story of the doomed love and revenge. The sisters also published jointly a volume of verse, *Poems by Currer, Ellis and Acton Bell*, but only 2 copies of the book were sold.

Emily was born on 30 July 1818 in Thornton, Bradford, Yorkshire, England. She was daughter of Maria Branwell and Irish clergyman Patrick

Emily Brontë

Bront . She was the younger sister of Charlotte Bront and the fifth of six children. Unfortunately, her mother died of cancer when Emily was just three years old. In 1824 she attended the newly opened Clergy Daughters' School at Cowan Bridge, near Kirkby Lonsdale. While she was there along with her sisters Maria, Elizabeth and Charlotte, they suffered a lot, such as the harsh regime, cold and poor food. When Maria and Elizabeth died there a year later of tuberculosis, she and Charlotte returned home to Haworth in June 1825 for good. Then Emily was mostly home schooled. Their father was a quiet man and often spent his spare time alone, so, the motherless children entertained themselves by reading the works of William Shakespeare, Virgil, John Milton, and the Bible. They played the piano, did needlepoint, and told each other stories. The four often "paired up". Emily **Bront** was particularly close to her sister Anne, with whom she created the imaginary world of Gondal, the setting for many of her finest narrative and lyric poems; Charlotte and Branwell started writing their imaginary world "Angria". The young **Bront** girls found a creative outlet in writing stories and poetry. Emily was becoming an independent and opinionated young woman as her poem "The Old Stoic" reveals.

In 1835 Emily enrolled at Miss Wooler's school at Roe Head, Mirfield where Charlotte was teaching, but she became so homesick and ill that she returned home soon. She was for a time governess at Law Hill Hall near Halifax, West Yorkshire. In 1842, she spent nine months in Brussels, Belgium with her sisters Charlotte and Anne. There they immersed themselves in the study of French, German and literature with the aim of starting their own school someday. When their Aunt Branwell died Emily alone returned to Haworth for her funeral and stayed on there, where she stayed for the rest of her brief life. By 1845 her sisters had given up their dream of starting their own school and the three were together at Haworth again.

In September 1845 Charlotte accidentally discovered Emily's poems. Emily was angered by the intrusion into her private writings. However, her sister convinced her to collaborate on a book of poems. That's how *Poems, by Currer, Ellis and Acton Bell* appeared in 1846. It is thought that Emily started to write *Wuthering Heights* around this time. It was written between October 1845 and June 1846 and published by T. C. Newby after some delay in December 1847. Unlike Charlotte's *Jane Eyre*, it attracted considerable critical attention: many people were shocked and horrified by sheer violence of Emily's novel. Therefore it met with more incomprehension than recognition. And it was only after Emily's death that it became widely acknowledged as a masterpiece.

While the Bront sisters were on their way to becoming famous, their brother Branwell had failed as a painter and lapsed into alcoholism and drug abuse. He died in September of 1848, and Emily caught cold at her brother's funeral. In November 1848 Emily's health was poor. Tuberculosis killed her rapidly, perhaps because she stoically refused to make any concession to her ill health, continuing to get up early every day to feed her animals even when she could barely walk. On 19 December 1848, Emily Bronte died at 2 o'clock in the afternoon.

All through her life, Emily Bront could not adapt to playing the role of a genteel Victorian lady, or deal with the intrusion of strangers into her life. She could never fit in. Unlike Charlotte, Emily never made any close friends outside of her family circle. She wrote few letters but had few but strong loyalties. As far as Emily's literary creation is concerned, she is, first of all, a poet. Her 193 poems, mostly devoted to the matter of nature with its mysterious workings and its unaccountable influence upon people's life, are works of strange sublimity and beauty. They are ample proof for the poetic genius of this young, reclusive woman. But, to the common readers, she is better known today as the author of that most fascinating novel, *Wuthering Heights*. Now she is established as one of the most original poets of the century, remembered for her lyrics such as "The night is darkening round me", "Remembrance", "The Prisoner", "No coward soul is mine", "Legends of Angria" (collection, with Anne and Charlotte Bront) and "Gondal's Queen".

Brief Introduction and Appreciation

Wuthering Heights is Emily Bront 's only novel. The name of the novel comes from the Yorkshire manor house on the moors on which the story centres. "Wuthering" is a Yorkshire word, meaning turbulent weather. The book tells the tale of passionate, yet thwarted, love between Heathcliff and Catherine Earnshaw, and how this unresolved passion eventually destroys them and many around them.

The story begins 30 years before when the Earnshaw family lived at Wuthering Heights, consisting of, the mother and father, Hindley, a boy of fourteen, and 6-year-old Catherine. In that year, Mr Earnshaw travels to Liverpool where he finds a homeless, gypsy boy of about seven whom he decides to adopt as his son. He names him "Heathcliff". Hindley, who finds himself excluded from his father's affections by this newcomer, quickly learns to hate him but Catherine grows very attached to him. Soon Heathcliff and Catherine are like twins, spending hours on the moors together and hating every moment apart.

Because Hindley and Heathcliff are at enmity with each other, the former is eventually sent to college but he returns, three years later, when Mr Earnshaw dies. With a new wife, Frances, Hindley becomes master of Wuthering Heights and treated Heathcliff as a servant instead of a member of the family.

But Heathcliff and Cathy continue to run wild and, in November, a few months after Hindley's return, they make their way to Thrushcross Grange to spy on the inhabitants. As they watch the childish behaviour of Edgar and Isabella Linton, the children of the Grange, they are spotted and try to escape. Catherine, having been caught by a dog, is brought inside and helped while Heathcliff is sent home.

Five weeks later, Catherine returns to Wuthering Heights but she has changed, looking and acting like a lady. The next day, Edgar Linton visits her family to impress her. But when Edgar makes fun of Heathcliff, Catherine argues with him. Heathcliff is locked in the attic where, in the evening, Catherine climbs over the roof to comfort him.

In the summer of the next year, Frances gives birth to a child, Hareton, but she dies within a year, which leads Hindley to a life of drunkenness and waste.

As time goes by, Catherine has gradually become close to Edgar, and at the same time, growing more distant from Heathcliff.

Later, Catherine tells Ellen that Edgar has asked her to marry him and she has accepted. She says that she does not really love Edgar but Heathcliff. Unfortunately she could never marry the latter because of his lack of status and education. She therefore plans to marry Edgar and uses that position to help raise Heathcliff's standing. Unfortunately Heathcliff overheard the first part about not being able to marry him but not the second and flees from the farmhouse. He disappears without trace. Three years later, Edgar and Catherine are married.

Six months after the Catherine's marriage, Heathcliff returns as a gentleman, having become stronger and richer during his absence. Catherine is delighted to see him although Edgar is not. Isabella, Edgar's sister, now eighteen, falls madly in love with Heathcliff, viewing him as a romantic hero. He despises her but encourages her, seeing it as a chance for revenge on Edgar. When he embraces Isabella one day at the Grange, there is an argument with Edgar which causes Catherine to lock herself in her room and fall ill.

Heathcliff has been staying at the Heights, gambling with Hindley and teaching Hareton bad habits. Hindley is gradually losing his wealth, mortgaging the farmhouse to Heathcliff to repay his debts. While Catherine is ill, Heathcliff elopes with Isabella, which causes Edgar to disown his sister. Hearing that Catherine is ill, Heathcliff arranges with Ellen to visit her in secret. In the early hours of the day after their meeting, Catherine gives birth to her daughter, Cathy, and then dies.

The day after Catherine's funeral, Isabella flees Heathcliff and escapes to the south of England where she eventually gives birth to Linton, Heathcliff's son. Hindley dies six months after his sister and Heathcliff finds himself the master of Wuthering Heights and the guardian of Hareton.

The novel is a riddle which means different things to different people. To some people, it is a story about a poor man abused, betrayed and distorted by his social betters because he is a poor nobody. But as a love story, this is one of the most moving love stories that touch the hearts of numerous people: the passion between Heathcliff and Catherine proves the most intense, the most beautiful and at the same time the most horrible passion ever to be found possible in human beings.

Wuthering Heights has a unique structure: the story is told through independent narrators. Their personality is therefore completely absent from the book. The story is told mainly by Nelly, Catherine's old nurse, to Mr. Lockwood, a temporary tenant at Grange. Mr. Lockwood also gives an account of what he sees at Wuthering Heights. While part of the story is told through Isabella's letters to Nelly, the central interest is maintained, and the sequence of its development is constantly disordered by flashbacks. This makes the story all the more enticing and genuine.

Wuthering Heights is a story of doomed love and revenge. The protagonists are characterized as figures of violent emotions and typical

Yorkshire characters. The Gothic tradition is revealed by its sophisticated observation and artistic subtlety.

Selected Reading

Wuthering Heights
Chapter 15

Another week over—and I am so many days nearer health, and spring! I have now heard all my neighbour's history, at different sittings, as the housekeeper could spare time from more important occupations. I'll continue it in her own words, only a little condensed. She is, on the whole, a very fair narrator, and I don't think I could improve her style.

In the evening, she said, the evening of my visit to the Heights, I knew, as well as if I saw him, that Mr. Heathcliff was about the place; and I shunned going out, because I still carried his letter in my pocket, and didn't want to be threatened or teased any more. I had made up my mind not to give it till my master went somewhere, as I could not guess how its receipt would affect Catherine. The consequence was, that it did not reach her before the lapse of three days. The fourth was Sunday, and I brought it into her room after the family were gone to church. There was a manservant left to keep the house with me, and we generally made a practice of locking the doors during the hours of service; but on that occasion the weather was so warm and pleasant that I set them wide open, and, to fulfill my engagement, as I knew who would be coming, I told my companion that the mistress wished very much for some oranges, and he must run over to the village and get a few, to be paid for on the morrow. He departed, and I went up-stairs.

Mrs. Linton[1] sat in a loose white dress, with a light shawl over her shoulders, in the recess of the open window, as usual. Her thick, long hair had been partly removed at the beginning of her illness, and now she wore it simply combed in its natural tresses over her temples and neck. Her appearance was altered, as I had told Heathcliff; but when she was calm, there seemed unearthly beauty in the change. The flash of her eyes had been succeeded by a dreamy and melancholy softness; they no longer gave the impression of looking at the objects around her: they appeared always to gaze beyond, and far beyond—you would have said out of this world. Then, the paleness of her face—its haggard aspect having vanished as she recovered flesh—and the peculiar expression arising from her mental state, though painfully suggestive of their causes, added to the touching interest which she awakened; and—invariably to me, I know, and to any person who saw her, I should think—refuted more tangible proofs of convalescence, and stamped her as one doomed to decay.

A book lay spread on the sill before her, and the scarcely perceptible wind fluttered its leaves at intervals. I believe Linton had laid it there: for she never endeavoured to divert herself with reading, or occupation of any kind, and he would spend many an hour in trying to entice her attention to some subject which had formerly been her amusement. She was conscious of his aim, and in her better moods endured his efforts placidly, only showing their uselessness by now and then suppressing a wearied sigh, and checking him at last with the saddest of smiles and kisses. At other times, she would turn petulantly[2] away, and hide her face in her hands, or even push him off angrily; and then he took care to let her alone, for he was certain of doing no good.

Gimmerton chapel bells were still ringing; and the full, mellow flow of the beck in the valley came soothingly on the ear. It was a sweet substitute for the yet absent murmur of the summer foliage, which drowned that music about the Grange when the trees were in leaf. At Wuthering Heights it always sounded on quiet days following a great thaw or a season of steady rain. And of Wuthering Heights Catherine was thinking as she listened: that is, if she thought or listened at all; but she had the vague, distant look I mentioned before, which expressed no recognition of material things either by ear or eye.

"There's a letter for you, Mrs. Linton," I said[3], gently inserting it in one hand that rested on her knee. "You must read it immediately, because it wants an answer. Shall I break the seal?" "Yes," she answered, without altering the direction of her eyes. I opened it—it was very short. "Now," I continued, "read it." She drew away her hand, and let it fall. I replaced it in her lap, and stood waiting till it should please her to glance down; but that movement was so long delayed that at last I resumed—"Must I read it, ma'am? It is from Mr. Heathcliff."

There was a start and a troubled gleam of recollection, and a struggle to arrange her ideas. She lifted the letter, and seemed to peruse it; and when she came to the signature she sighed: yet still I found she had not gathered its import, for, upon my desiring to hear her reply, she merely pointed to the name, and gazed at me with mournful and questioning eagerness.

"Well, he wishes to see you," said I, guessing her need of an interpreter. "He's in the garden by this time, and impatient to know what answer I shall bring."

As I spoke, I observed a large dog lying on the sunny grass beneath raise its ears as if about to bark, and then smoothing them back, announce, by a wag of the tail, that some one approached whom it did not consider a stranger. Mrs. Linton bent forward, and listened breathlessly. The minute after a step traversed[4] the hall; the open house was too tempting for Heathcliff to resist walking in: most likely he supposed that I was inclined to shirk[5] my promise, and so resolved to trust to his own audacity. With straining eagerness Catherine gazed towards the entrance of her chamber. He did not hit the right room[6] directly: she motioned me to admit him, but he found it out ere[7] I could reach the door, and in a stride or two was at her side, and had her grasped in his arms.

He neither spoke nor loosed his hold for some five minutes, during which period he bestowed more kisses than ever he gave in his life before, I daresay: but then my mistress had kissed him first, and I plainly saw that he could hardly bear, for downright agony, to look into her face! The same conviction had stricken him as me, from the instant he beheld her, that there was no prospect of ultimate recovery there—she was fated, sure to die.

"Oh, Cathy! Oh, my life! how can I bear it?" was the first sentence he uttered, in a tone that did not seek to disguise his despair. And now he stared at her so earnestly that I thought the very intensity of his gaze would bring tears into his eyes; but they burned with anguish: they did not melt[8].

"What now?" said Catherine, leaning back, and returning his look with a suddenly clouded brow: her humour was a mere vane for constantly varying caprices. "You and Edgar[9] have broken my heart, Heathcliff! And you both come to bewail the deed to me, as if you were the people to be pitied! I shall not pity you, not I. You have killed me—and thriven on[10] it, I think. How strong you are! How many years do you mean to live after I am gone?"

Heathcliff had knelt on one knee to embrace her; he attempted to rise, but she seized his hair, and kept him down.

"I wish I could hold you," she continued, bitterly, "till we were both dead!

I shouldn't care what you suffered. I care nothing for your sufferings. Why shouldn't you suffer? I do! Will you forget me? Will you be happy when I am in the earth? Will you say twenty years hence[11], 'That's the grave of Catherine Earnshaw? I loved her long ago, and was wretched to lose her; but it is past. I've loved many others since: my children are dearer to me than she was; and, at death, I shall not rejoice that I are going to her: I shall be sorry that I must leave them!' Will you say so, Heathcliff?"

"Don't torture me till I'm as mad as yourself," cried he, wrenching his head free, and grinding his teeth.

The two, to a cool spectator, made a strange and fearful picture. Well might Catherine deem that heaven would be a land of exile to her, unless with her mortal body she cast away her moral character also. Her present countenance had a wild vindictiveness in its white cheek, and a bloodless lip and scintillating eye; and she retained in her closed fingers a portion of the locks she had been grasping. As to her companion, while raising himself with one hand, he had taken her arm with the other; and so inadequate was his stock of gentleness to the requirements of her condition, that on his letting go I saw four distinct impressions left blue in the colourless skin.

"Are you possessed with a devil," he pursued, savagely, "to talk in that manner to me when you are dying? Do you reflect that all those words will be branded in my memory, and eating deeper eternally after you have left me? You know you lie to say I have killed you: and, Catherine, you know that I could as soon forget you as my existence! Is it not sufficient for your infernal selfishness, that while you are at peace I shall writhe in the torments of hell?"

"I shall not be at peace," moaned Catherine, recalled to a sense of physical weakness by the violent, unequal throbbing of her heart, which beat visibly and audibly under this excess of agitation. She said nothing further till the paroxysm was over; then she continued, more kindly—

I'm not wishing you greater torment than I have, Heathcliff. I only wish us never to be parted: and should a word of mine distress you hereafter, think I feel the same distress underground, and for my own sake, forgive me! Come here and kneel down again! You never harmed me in your life. Nay, if you nurse anger[12], that will be worse to remember than my harsh words! Won't you come here again? Do!"

Heathcliff went to the back of her chair, and leant over, but not so far as to let her see his face, which was livid[13] with emotion. She bent round to look at him; he would not permit it: turning abruptly, he walked to the fireplace, where he stood, silent, with his back towards us. Mrs. Linton's glance followed him suspiciously: every movement woke a new sentiment in her. After a pause and a prolonged gaze, she resumed; addressing me in accents of indignant disappointment:—

Oh, you see, Nelly, he would not relent[14] a moment to keep me out of the grave. THAT is how I'm loved! Well, never mind. That is not my Heathcliff. I shall love mine yet; and take him with me: he's in my soul. And, added she musingly, "the thing that irks[15] me most is this shattered prison, after all. I'm tired of being enclosed here. I'm wearying to escape into that glorious world, and to be always there: not seeing it dimly through tears, and yearning for it through the walls of an aching heart: but really with it, and in it. Nelly, you think you are better and more fortunate than I; in full health and strength: you are sorry for me—very soon that will be altered. I shall be sorry for you. I shall be incomparably beyond and above you all. I WONDER he won't be near me!" She went on to herself. "I thought he wished it. Heathcliff, dear! you should not be sullen now. Do come to me, Heathcliff."

In her eagerness she rose and supported herself on the arm of the chair. At that earnest appeal he turned to her, looking absolutely desperate. His eyes, wide and wet, at last flashed fiercely on her; his breast heaved convulsively. An instant they held asunder, and then how they met I hardly saw, but Catherine made a spring, and he caught her, and they were locked in an embrace from which I thought my mistress would never be released alive: in fact, to my eyes, she seemed directly insensible. He flung himself into the nearest seat, and on my approaching hurriedly to ascertain if she had fainted, he gnashed[16] at me, and foamed like a mad dog, and gathered her to him with greedy jealousy. I did not feel as if I were in the company of a creature of my own species: it appeared that he would not understand, though I spoke to him; so I stood off, and held my tongue, in great perplexity.

A movement of Catherine's relieved me a little presently: she put up her hand to clasp his neck, and bring her cheek to his as he held her; while he, in return, covering her with frantic caresses, said wildly—

You teach me now how cruel you've been—cruel and false. Why did you despise me? Why did you betray your own heart, Cathy? I have not one word of comfort. You deserve this. You have killed yourself. Yes, you may kiss me, and cry; and wring out[17] my kisses and tears: they'll blight you—they'll damn you. You loved me—then what RIGHT had you to leave me? What right—answer me—for the poor fancy you felt for Linton? Because misery and degradation, and death, and nothing that God or Satan could inflict would have parted us, you, of your own will, did it. I have not broken your heart—You have broken it; and in breaking it, you have broken mine. So much the worse for me that I am strong. Do I want to live? What kind of living will it be when you—oh, God! would you like to live with your soul in the grave?"

"Let me alone. Let me alone," sobbed Catherine. "If I've done wrong, I'm dying for it. It is enough! You left me too: but I won't upbraid[18] you! I forgive you. Forgive me!"

"It is hard to forgive, and to look at those eyes, and feel those wasted hands," he answered. "Kiss me again; and don't let me see your eyes! I forgive what you have done to me. I love my murderer—but yours! How can I?"

They were silent—their faces hid against each other, and washed by each other's tears. At least, I suppose the weeping was on both sides; as it seemed Heathcliff could weep on a great occasion like this.

I grew very uncomfortable, meanwhile; for the afternoon wore fast away, the man whom I had sent off returned from his errand, and I could distinguish, by the shine of the western sun up the valley, a concourse thickening outside Gimmerton chapel porch.

"Service is over," I announced. "My master will be here in half an hour."

Heathcliff groaned a curse, and strained Catherine closer: she never moved.

Ere long I perceived a group of the servants passing up the road towards the kitchen wing. Mr. Linton was not far behind; he opened the gate himself and sauntered slowly up, probably enjoying the lovely afternoon that breathed as soft as summer.

"Now he is here," I exclaimed. "For heaven's sake, hurry down! You'll not meet any one on the front stairs. Do be quick; and stay among the trees till he is fairly in."

"I must go, Cathy," said Heathcliff, seeking to extricate himself from his companion's arms. "But if I live, I'll see you again before you are asleep. I won't stray five yards from your window."

"You must not go!" she answered, holding him as firmly as her strength allowed. "You shall not, I tell you."

"For one hour," he pleaded earnestly.

"Not for one minute," she replied.

"I must—Linton will be up immediately," persisted the alarmed intruder.

He would have risen, and unfixed her fingers by the act—she clung fast, gasping: there was mad resolution in her face.

"No!" she shrieked. "Oh, don't, don't go. It is the last time! Edgar will not hurt us. Heathcliff, I shall die! I shall die!"

"Damn the fool! There he is," cried Heathcliff, sinking back into his seat. "Hush, my darling! Hush, hush, Catherine! I'll stay. If he shot me so, I'd expire[19] with a blessing on my lips."

And there they were fast again. I heard my master mounting the stairs—the cold sweat ran from my forehead: I was horrified.

"Are you going to listen to her ravings?" I said, passionately. "She does not know what she says. Will you ruin her, because she has not wit to help herself? Get up! You could be free instantly. That is the most diabolical deed that ever you did. We are all done for—master, mistress, and servant."

I wrung my hands, and cried out; and Mr. Linton hastened his step at the noise. In the midst of my agitation, I was sincerely glad to observe that Catherine's arms had fallen relaxed, and her head hung down.

"She's fainted, or dead," I thought: "so much the better. Far better that she should be dead, than lingering a burden and a misery-maker to all about her."

Edgar sprang to his unbidden guest, blanched with astonishment and rage. What he meant to do I cannot tell; however, the other stopped all demonstrations, at once, by placing the lifeless-looking form in his arms.

"Look there!" he said. "Unless you be a fiend, help her first—then you shall speak to me!"

He walked into the parlour, and sat down. Mr. Linton summoned me, and with great difficulty, and after resorting to many means, we managed to restore her to sensation; but she was all bewildered; she sighed, and moaned, and knew nobody. Edgar, in his anxiety for her, forgot her hated friend. I did not. I went, at the earliest opportunity, and besought[20] him to depart; affirming that Catherine was better, and he should hear from me in the morning how she passed the night.

"I shall not refuse to go out of doors," he answered; "but I shall stay in the garden: and, Nelly, mind you keep your word to-morrow. I shall be under those larch-trees. Mind! or I pay another visit, whether Linton be in or not."

He sent a rapid glance through the half-open door of the chamber, and, ascertaining that what I stated was apparently true, delivered the house of his luckless presence.

Notes

1. **Mrs. Linton**: Catherine
2. **petulantly**: behaving in an unreasonable impatient and angry way, like a child
3. **I said**: "I" am Catherine's maid, Nelly Dean.
4. **traverse**: move across
5. **shirk**: to avoid doing something you should do
6. **hit the right room**: find the room where Catherine is in
7. **ere**: before
8. **they did not melt**: meaning he did not shed any tears
9. **Edgar**: her husband
10. **thrive on**: to enjoy or be successful in a particular situation, especially one that other people find difficult or unpleasant
11. **hence**: from now
12. **nurse anger**: be angry all the time
13. **livid**: ashen, pallid
14. **relent**: to change your attitude and become less strict or cruel towards someone
15. **irk**: annoy
16. **gnash**: to move your teeth against each other so that they make a noise
17. **wring out**: to succeed in getting something from someone
18. **upbraid**: to criticize somebody
19. **expire**: die
20. **besought**: past tense of beseech, meaning to ask somebody for something in an anxious way because you want or need it very much

Questions for Study and Discussion

1. Discuss revenge in *Wuthering Heights*. In what ways is it connected to love?
2. What is the nature of love in the novel, that it can be so closely connected to vengeance?
3. Discuss the novel's narrative structure. Are the novel's narrators trustworthy? Why or why not? With particular reference to Nelly's story, consider what might be gained from reading between the lines of the narration. What roles do the personalities of the narrators play in the way that the story is told?
4. Why does Nelly let Heathcliff in the house to see Catherine as she is dying?
5. Analyze the character of Edgar Linton. Is he a sympathetic figure? How does he compare to Heathcliff? Is Catherine really in love with him?
6. As Heathcliff and Catherine are talking, they both make many accusations against the other. What do they accuse each other of doing? What does Heathcliff mean when he says, "I love my murderer—but yours! How can I?"

Robert Browning (1812—1889)

Life and Major Works

Robert Browning, English playwright and master of dramatic monologue poetry, is considered today one of the most influential Victorian poets.

Born in a well-off and cultivated family on May 7th, 1812, Robert Browning was the eldest child of a wealthy bank clerk of England who was also a scholar and collector of books and whose massive library collections were a great source of study for young Robert. His mother, who was an accomplished musician herself, taught Browning music and cared for him with all her tenderness and love that helped to breed an

Robert Browning

optimistic character in him. Both his parents encouraged him to study and write. At an early age of 12 Browning began writing poetry and when he was

21 years old his first publication *Pauline* (1833) appeared. The book was under the financial support of his aunt but not a single volume was sold. For most of the time, Browning was tutored at home, learning at his own pace. It was during this time that he learned many languages as well as read enormous volumes of books. In his youth, Browning traveled widely in Europe and was soon to find a deep love for Italy, which he regarded as his second home.

Browning tasted the sweetness of his first success in *Paracelsus* (1835), a blank verse drama portraying a chemist who longed for learning but who constantly faced the conflict with the people around. In 1840, he wrote the historical poem *Sordello* (1840) which brought on an onslaught attack that lasted for many years. From 1841 to 1846, he published *Bells and Pomegranates* series, including the verse drama for the theater *Strafford* (1837), the narrative poem *Pippa Passes* (1841), and one of the most noted dramatic monologue poem *My Last Duchess*.

The year 1845 saw the first encounter between Robert Browning and Elizabeth Barrett, who was then far more famous a poet than he was. The love story and courtship between them found their best expression in the letters they exchanged and through Elizabeth's love sonnets. Though Elizabeth was six years older than him and despite her father's strong objection, the two lovers secretly got married in the autumn of 1846 and later they eloped to Italy where they lived happily in tranquility. It was the postnuptial life that greatly inspired Browning and that gave birth to his highly acclaimed volume of poems *Men and Women* (1855). The collection reflects his profound interest in the Italian Renaissance and proved his exquisite skills in dealing with the poetic form dramatic monologue.

After the death of his beloved wife Elizabeth, Browning returned to London. Embraced by London's literary circle again, Browning produced *Dramatis Personae* in 1864, and later *The Ring and the Book*. It is a blank verse poem consisting of 12 volumes and 21,000 lines. In various voices it narrates the 1698 trial of Count Guido Franceschini of Rome who murdered his wife Pompilia Comparini and her parents. It remained a best-seller during his lifetime. At the age of 72, Browning died. Later he was buried in Westminster Abbey.

Brief Introduction and Appreciation

Dominating Robert Browning's poem "My Last Duchess" are themes of murder, mystery and intrigue. From the speaker's indirect allusions to the death of his wife, the reader might easily guess that the speaker committed a vengeful crime out of jealousy. The poem takes its original source from the historical events of the 16th century Duke Alfonso II in Ferrara. As the speaker of the poem, the Duke is showing a messenger around his palace. Drawing back the curtain and revealing a portrait of the late Duchess, apparently a young and lovely girl, the Duke makes comments about his former wife. He claims that she was unfaithful and that she flirted with everyone and did not appreciate his "gift of a nine-hundred-years-old name". As his monologue continues, it becomes more and more clear that it is the Duke who actually caused the Duchess's early demise: "I gave commands; /Then all smiles stopped together". Having made this disclosure, the Duke returns to the business at hand: arranging for another marriage with an aristocrat's daughter.

The style and structure play a significant role in emphasizing the effect of the poem. It takes the form of dramatic monologue: one speaker relates the whole poem to another person imagines being present with him. This format suits this poem particularly well because the speaker, taken to be the Duke of Ferrara, comes across as being a very controlling and dictatorial person. And these characteristics were clearly shown in his conversational manners. For example, he takes pleasure in directing the actions of his guest with comments such as "Will't please you rise?" (Line 47) and "Nay, we'll go/ Together down, sir" (Lines 53—54).

Besides, Browning also employs the technique of enjambment and caesura to convey some important information about the speaker and the situation. The enjambed lines indicate the speaker is exerting the control over the conversation and giving the reader such feelings as the speaker is fidgeting. For instance, when the Duke is speaking of the death of his wife, he seemed to be rather nervous and rushed through the lines. The caesuras also reveal that the duke is trying to hide something or that he is pausing to think. The rhyming pentameter pattern, which is common to ballads and songs, enhances the irony of the speaker's later comment that he does not have "skill/In speech" (Lines 35—36).

Selected Reading

My Last Duchess[1]
Ferrara

That's my last Duchess painted on the wall,
Looking as if she were alive. I call
That piece a wonder, now: Fr Pandolf[2]'s hands
Worked busily a day, and there she stands.
Will 't please you sit and look at her? I said
"Fr Pandolf" by design, for never read
Strangers like you that pictured countenance,
The depth and passion of its earnest glance,
But to myself they turned (since none puts by
The curtain I have drawn for you, but I)
And seemed as they would ask me, if they durst,
How such a glance came there; so, not the first
Are you to turn and ask thus. Sir, 't was not
Her husband's presence only, called that spot
Of joy into the Duchess' cheek: perhaps
Fr Pandolf chanced to say, "Her mantle[3] laps
Over my lady's wrist too much", or "Paint
Must never hope to reproduce the faint
Half-flush that dies along her throat"; such stuff
Was courtesy, she thought, and cause enough
For calling up that spot of joy. She had
A heart—how shall I say? —too soon made glad,
Too easily impressed; she liked whate'er
She looked on, and her looks went everywhere.
Sir, 't was all one! my favour[4] at her breast,
The dropping of the daylight in the West,
The bough of cherries some officious fool
Broke in the orchard for her, the white mule
She rode with round the terrace—all and each
Would draw from her alike the approving speech,
Or blush, at least. She thanked men,—good! but thanked
Somehow—I know not how—as if she ranked

my gift of a nine-hundred-years-old name[5]
With anybody's gift. Who'd stoop to blame
This sort of trifling? Even had you skill
In speech—(which I have not)—to make your will
Quite clear to such an one, and say, "Just this
Or that in you disgusts me; here you miss,
Or there exceed the mark[6]"—and if she let
Herself be lessoned[7] so, nor plainly set
Her wits to yours, forsooth, and made excuse,
—E'en then would be some stooping; and I choose
Never to stoop. Oh, sir, she smiled, no doubt,
Whene'er I passed her; but who passed without
Much the same smile? This grew; I have commands;
Then all smiles stopped together. There she stands
As if alive. Will't please you rise? We'll meet
The company below then. I repeat,
The Count[8] your master's known munificence
Is ample warrant that no just pretence
Of mine for dowry will be disallowed;
Though his fair daughter's self, as I avowed
At starting, is my object. Nay, we'll go
Together down, sir. Notice Neptune[9], though,
Taming a sea-horse, thought a rarity,
Which Claus of Innsbruck[10] cast in bronze for me!

Notes

1. "My Last Duchess": the poem is first published in Dramatic Lyrics, 1842 and given its present title in 1849. Based on the historical events involving Alfonso II (1533—1598), fifth duke of Ferrara, in northern Italy, from 1559 to 1597. His first wife was a 14-year-old girl named Lucrezia. Three days later she died, and then Alfonso contrived to marry a niece of the Count of Tyrol. The poem represents the Duke addressing the emissary who has come to negotiate for the marriage.
2. **Fr Pandolf**: a painter not recorded in history, a painter invented by Browning
3. **Mantle**: loose cloak without sleeves

4. **My favour**: a love-gift such as a ribbon

5. **A nine-hundred-years-old name**: Lucrezia's family had their recent origin in merchants, but the Alfonso family went back 650 years.

6. **Exceed the mark:** to overshoot the target in archery. Here it means overdoing something.

7. **Lessoned**: be instructed; be educated at school; possibly the poet intends a pun on the word "lessened"—"diminished".

8. **The Count:** presumably Ferdinand II, count of Tyrol, who led the negotiations for the marriage of Alfonso II and Barbara of Austria.

9. **Neptune**: the Roman god of the sea, whose chariot is often seen pulled by sea-horses

10. **Claus of Innsbruck**: a painter unrecorded in history, from an Italian city, renowned for its sculpture, which Browning visited in 1838.

Questions for Study and Discussion

1. Why does the Duke show his collection to his guest?
2. What kind of person is the Duke? Can you find any evidence to support your point?
3. From the Duke's monologue, what can you infer about the Duchess' personality? What has this to do with her death?
4. At the end of the poem when they are about to leave, the Duke draws his guest's attention to the sculpture of Neptune. What's point of this?
5. Why does the author employ the form of dramatic monologue in the poem? How does it help to reveal the theme?

Thomas Carlyle (1795—1881)

Life and Major Works

Thomas Carlyle stood out as one of the most prominent prose writers at the end of the 19th century.

The son of a stonemason and small farmer, Thomas Carlyle was brought up in a strict Calvinist household. At the age of 15, he went to University of Edinburgh and received his B.A. in the year 1813. From the year on until 1818 he studied for the ministry of the Church of Scotland, but later he abandoned this course and studied law for a while.

Carlyle once taught at Annan Academy and Kircaldy Grammar School. From 1824 he became a full-time writer and undertook thorough study on German literature, especially Johann Wolfgang von Goethe. Carlyle's essays on German philosophy introduced to the British public many fresh ideas. He also produced a translation of a work by Goethe, which was highly acclaimed. Carlyle's first publication was "Life of Schiller", which appeared

Thomas Carlyle

in the *London Magazine* in 1823. It was during this time that he contributed regularly to Brewter's *Edinburgh Encyclopedia*, and also to such journals as *Edinburgh Review* and *Fraser's Magazine*. His career as an essayist began with two pieces in the *Edinburgh Review* in 1827. One is the long essay "Chartism" (1839), in which he expressed sympathy for the conditions of the working class. The other is "The Negro Question" (1850) which dealt with the subject of West Indian slavery. Carlyle's cynicism with the English society was evident in the *Latter-Day Pamphlets* (1850).

In 1826 Carlyle married Jane Baillie Welsh, a pretty, well-educated, doctor's daughter. Jane's wit won herself the fame as an excellent letter writer and her circle of correspondents including many eminent Victorians. Soon after their marriage the couple moved to a remote farm in Dumfriesshire, a place in which they lived an isolated life for six years. Oppressed by financial difficulties, the Carlyle's returned to Jane's farm at Craigenputtock and concentrated on writing. During their stay in London in 1831, Carlyle became acquainted with J. S. Mill, who later introduced him to Emerson, the American philosopher and essayist. The correspondence between Carlyle and Emerson lasted decades despite their different characters. Emerson once said about his friend Carlyle: "He talks like a very unhappy man, profoundly solitary, displeased and hindered by all men and things about him."

In 1834 the Carlyle's returned to London. The same year saw the publication of his breakthrough work, *Sartor Resartus*. The work, partly autobiography and partly philosophy, was written in a passionate, sophisticated language that came to be called "Carlylese". Another major work, a three volume history of the French Revolution, came out in 1837, and a biography of Fredrick the Great was produced from 1858 to 1865. During 1837 to 1840 Carlyle wrote several series of lectures, of which the most significant one was thought to be *On Heroes, Hero-Worship and the Heroic in History*. Although Carlyle acknowledged the achievements of Cromwell and Napoleon, he recognized that a thinker and writer was the hero that his own time needed.

Jane died in 1866 and it was said that Carlyle never completely recovered from his wife's death. He retired from public life, and wrote little.

Just before Jane's death, Carlyle was appointed Rector of the University of Edinburgh. In 1874 Carlyle received Prussian Order of Merit. He died on February 5, 1881 in London and was later buried in Ecclefechan.

Carlyle opposed analytic reasoning and quasi-scientific treatment of social questions advocated by the rationalist political economists. Rather he adopted the more emotional and intuitive approaches of the 18th and 19th century German thinkers like Richter and Goethe. Carlyle's *Sartor Resartus* was a disguised spiritual autobiography, in which he faces the tendencies to intellectual skepticism and dedicates himself to a life of spiritual affirmation. The first half of the book is about the ideas of a self-made philosopher who believes everything can be explained in terms of clothes. This work established Carlyle as a social critic, however, it was received with much confusion because of its unique literary style. The title of the work means "the tailor re-tailored" and highlights the main theme of the work: that social customs and religious and political institutions are merely the "clothing" of essential realities. The book is presented as the efforts of a nameless editor, aided by a German colleague, to summarize the life and theories of the German Professor Diogenes Teufelsdröckh (devil's dung). Teufelsdröckh's philosophy stresses that just as clothes go out of fashion, so do ideas and institutions, and they also must be re-envisioned or retailored. Therefore, the significance of being able to see through these symbols, or clothes, is emphasized throughout the work. Carlyle's literary style in this volume presents as many challenges to the reader as does his format in that it heavily employs allusion, metaphor, and other techniques that have been described as "eccentricities" and "syntactical aberrations". In *The French Revolution*, Carlyle sympathized with the revolutionaries to some extent but despised anarchy and appeared to fear the rule of the people. *The French Revolution* was written in dramatic language bringing the history of the revolution alive in a way that few historians have ever done. However, the manuscript was first accidentally burned by a domestic servant of John Stuart Mill and Carlyle had to rewrite the book, which was published when he was 42.

In most of his historical works such as *The French Revolution* (1837), *On Heroes and Hero–Worship* (1840), *Oliver Cromwell's Letters and Speeches* (1845), and *Frederick II of Prussia* (1858—1865), Carlyle put great emphasis on the importance of the individual and raised serious questions about democracy, mass persuasion, and politics. This isolated him from either liberal or democratic tendencies of his age. Henry James saw him as "the same old sausage, fizzing and sputtering in its own grease". In the 20th century his reputation waned, partly due to his trust in authority and admiration of strong leaders, which was interpreted as the foreshadowing of Fascism.

Brief Introduction and Appreciation

In the work *On Heroes and Hero-Worship*, Carlyle presents the view that the vast majority of people are unsuited to rule and instead heroes are needed to provide solid leadership. He advocates that it is the great men of every epoch that created history. His heroes include different types, ranging from Odin, the supreme god of Divinity, Muhammad, Luther, Napoleon, to the heroes of literature like Dante, Shakespeare and Dr. Johnson. He believes that what man has so far accomplished in the world should be attributed to these Great Men and the features of an age were the biography of its leaders.

The following is an excerpt from the author's third lecture *The Hero as Poet, Dante; Shakespeare*. In it the author identifies Dante and Shakespeare both as Heroes. He states in the beginning: "Shakespeare is the chief of all Poets hitherto; the greatest intellect who, in our recorded world, has left record of himself in the way of Literature." Carlyle views Shakespeare as a "great soul" and compares his constructing of dramas to the building of houses: "The built house seems all so fit,—every way as it should be, as if it came there by its own law and the nature of things,—we forget the rudely disorderly quarry it was shaped from. The very perfection of the house, as if Nature herself had made it,…" The author speaks highly of Shakespeare's intellect and talents as a poet. He emphasizes the poet's great insight by alluding it to God. In the second paragraph, he proceeds to say that Shakespeare's greatness lied in his "unexampled delineating of men and things." As the author observes: "the thing he looks at reveals not this or that face of it, but its inmost heart, and generic secret: it dissolves itself as in light before him, so that he discerns the perfect structure of it."

In the lecture, Carlyle employs a variety of rhetoric devices to make his speech more forceful and convincing, and these include raising questions, making comparisons, using metaphors and parallel sentences. He uses the first-person pronoun "we" in the address and this greatly decreases the distance between himself and the audiences, thus involving them in his thoughts and making them identify with his viewpoints. Apart from this, the lecture is also characteristic of concise diction and short syntax. All these have helped to highlight the author's point of view and enforced the pervasiveness of his speech.

Selected Reading

Heroes and Hero-Worship
(Lecture III, The Hero as Poet, Dante; Shakespeare)

Of this Shakespeare of ours, perhaps the opinion one sometimes hears a little idolatrously[1] expressed is, in fact, the right one; I think the best judgment not of this country only, but of Europe at large, is slowly pointing to the conclusion, that Shakespeare is the chief of all Poets hitherto; the greatest intellect who, in our recorded world, has left record of himself in the way of Literature. On the whole, I know not such a power of vision, such a faculty of thought, if we take all the characters of it, in any other man. Such a calmness of depth; placid joyous strength; all things imaged in that great soul of his so true and clear, as in a tranquil unfathomable sea! It has been said, that in the constructing of Shakespeare's Dramas there is, apart from all other "faculties" as they are called, an understanding manifested, equal to that in Bacon's *Novum Organum*[2]. That is true; and it is not a truth that strikes every one. It would become more apparent if we tried, any of us for himself, how, out of Shakespeare's dramatic materials, we could fashion such a result! The built house seems all so fit,—every way as it should be, as if it came there by its own law and the nature of things, —we forget the rude disorderly quarry it was shaped from[3]. The very perfection of the house, as if Nature herself had made it, hides the builder's merit. Perfect, more perfect than any other man, we may call Shakespeare in this: he discerns, knows as by instinct, what condition he works under, what his materials are, what his own force and its relation to them is. It is not a transitory glance of insight that will suffice; it is deliberate illumination of the whole matter; it is a calmly seeing eye; a great intellect, in short. How a man, of some wide thing that he has witnessed, will construct a narrative, what kind of picture and delineation he will give of it,—is the best measure you could get of what intellect is in the man. Which circumstance is vital and shall stand prominent; which unessential, fit to be suppressed; where is the true beginning, the true sequence and ending? To find out this, you task the whole force of insight that is in the man. He must understand the thing; according to the depth of his understanding, will the fitness of his answer be. You will try him so. Does like join itself to like; does the spirit of method stir in that confusion, so that its embroilment[4] becomes order? Can the man say, *Fiat lux*[5], Let there be light; and out of chaos make a world? Precisely as there is light in himself, will he accomplish this.

Or indeed we may say again, it is in what I called Portrait-painting, delineating of men and things, especially of men, that Shakespeare is great. All the greatness of the man comes out decisively here. It is unexampled, I think, that calm creative perspicacity[6] of Shakespeare. The thing he looks at reveals not this or that face of it, but its inmost heart, and generic secret: it dissolves itself as in light before him, so that he discerns the perfect structure of it. Creative, we said: poetic creation, what is this too but seeing the thing sufficiently? The word that will describe the thing, follows of itself from such clear intense sight of the thing. And is not Shakespeare's morality, his valor, candor, tolerance, truthfulness; his whole victorious strength and greatness, which can triumph over such obstructions, visible there too? Great as the world. No twisted, poor convex-concave mirror[7], reflecting all objects with its own convexities and concavities; a perfectly level mirror;—that is to say withal[8], if we will understand it, a man justly related to all things and men, a good man. It is truly a lordly spectacle how this great soul takes in all kinds of men and objects, a Falstaff, an Othello, a Juliet, a Coriolanus[9]; sets them all forth to us in their round completeness; loving, just, the equal brother of all. Novum Organum, and all the intellect you will find in Bacon, is of a quite secondary order; earthy, material, poor in comparison with this. Among modern men, one finds, in strictness, almost nothing of the same rank. Goethe[10] alone, since the days of Shakespeare, reminds me of it. Of him too you say that he saw the object; you may say what he himself says of Shakespeare: "His characters are like watches with dial-plates of transparent crystal; they show you the hour like others, and the inward mechanism also is all visible."

The seeing eye! It is this that discloses the inner harmony of things; what Nature meant, what musical idea Nature has wrapped up in these often rough embodiments. Something she did mean. To the seeing eye that something were discernible. Are they base, miserable things? You can laugh over them, you can weep over them; you can in some way or other genially[11] relate yourself to them;—you can, at lowest[12], hold your peace about them, turn away your own and others' face from them, till the hour come for practically exterminating and extinguishing them! At bottom, it is the Poet's first gift, as it is all men's, that he have intellect enough. He will be a Poet if he have: a Poet in word; or failing that, perhaps still better, a Poet in act. Whether he write at all; and if so, whether in prose or in verse, will depend on accidents: who knows on what extremely trivial accidents,—perhaps on his having had a singing-master, on his being taught to sing in his boyhood! But the faculty which enables him to discern the inner heart of things, and the harmony that dwells there (for whatsoever exists has a harmony in the heart of it, or it would not hold together and exist), is not the result of habits or accidents, but the gift of Nature herself; the primary outfit for a Heroic Man in what sort so ever. To the Poet, as to every other, we say first of all, See[13]. If you cannot do that, it is of no use to keep stringing rhymes together, jingling sensibilities against each other, and name yourself a Poet; there is no hope for you. If you can, there is, in prose or verse, in action or speculation, all manner of hope.

...

If I say, therefore, that Shakespeare is the greatest of Intellects, I have said all concerning him. But there is more in Shakespeare's intellect than we have yet seen. It is what I call an unconscious intellect; there is more virtue in it than he himself is aware of. Novalis[14] beautifully remarks of him, that those Dramas of his are Products of Nature too, deep as Nature herself. I find a great truth in this saying. Shakespeare's Art is not Artifice; the noblest worth of it is not there by plan or precontrivance. It grows up from the deeps of Nature, through this noble sincere soul, who is a voice of Nature. The latest generations of men will find new meanings in Shakespeare, new elucidations of their own human being; "new harmonies with the infinite structure of the Universe; concurrences[15] with later ideas, affinities with the higher powers and senses of man." This well deserves meditating. It is Nature's highest reward to a true simple great soul, that he get thus to be a part of herself. Such a man's works, whatsoever he with utmost conscious exertion and forethought shall accomplish, grow up withal unconsciously, from the unknown deeps in him;—as the oak-tree grows from the Earth's bosom, as the mountains and waters shape themselves; with a symmetry grounded on Nature's own laws, conformable to all Truth whatsoever. How much in Shakespeare lies hid; his sorrows, his silent struggles known to himself; much that was not known at all, not speakable at all: like roots, like sap and forces working underground! Speech is great; but Silence is greater.

Notes

1. **idolatrously**: to admire or worship someone too much
2. *Novum Organum*: *The New Organon or True Directions* concerning the interpretation of Nature is a treatise on methodology written by Fancis Bacon in Latin.
3. **The built house...it was shaped from:** the author compares Shakespeare's drama to a house well built with rude, disorderly materials.
4. **embroilment:** a disorderly, difficult situation
5. *Fiat lux*: it refers to God's creation of light
6. **perspicacity:** acute ability in thinking, understanding and judging
7. **convex-concave mirror:** a mirror with the surface curved outwards
8. **withal:** dated usage. It means besides; together.
9. **a Falstaff, an Othello, a Juliet, a Coriolanus:** these are characters in Shakespeare's *Henry IV, Othello, Romeo and Juliet,* and *Coriolanus* respectively.
10. **Goethe:** the great German poet Johann Wolfgang von Goethe
11. **genially:** cheerfully; in a friendly manner
12. **at lowest:** at least
13. **To the Poet, as to every other, we say first of all, See:** The vision of insight is the most important quality for a poet, as for other people.
14. **Novalis:** the pen name of the German poet Friedrich von Hardenberg

(1772—1801).

15. **concurrences:** of actions or events happening at the same time.

Questions for Study and Discussion

1. How does the author think of Shakespeare and his works?
2. According to the author, what is the most important to a poet?
3. Why does the author regard Shakespeare's works as products of Nature?
4. How do you understand "Speech is great; but Silence is greater"?
5. What's the author's attitude towards hero?

Part Seven   The Twentieth Century

(1901—1990s)

I. Historical Background

1. The Decline of the Empire

Queen Victoria died on January 22, 1901. Her son, Edward VII succeeded her. The glorious Victorian age in British history came to an end, and the Edwardian age began.

At the beginning of the 20th century, the capitalist world began to enter the new age of imperialism. But the capitalist countries did not develop at an even pace. During the process, as an old capitalist country, Britain gradually lagged behind, while the young capitalist countries, such as Germany, Austria-Hungary, Japan and America had caught up with the old ones. In the 1890s, the United States had surpassed Britain in the industrial output value, and at the beginning of the 20th century, Britain was surpassed by Germany too. However, Britain, France, Spain and Portugal had occupied many more colonies and markets than the young capitalist countries. Besides, they tried every possible means to control and hold their colonies and markets. As a newly-emerged imperial power, Germany formed the Triple Alliance with Austria and Italy. Britain, France and Russia also formed the Triple Entente. Thus, Europe was divided into two hostile camps. The rivalry among these capitalist countries at last caused the First World War in 1914.

The war lasted 4 years until the Germans signed an armistice that came into force on November 11, 1918. Britain won the greatest victory in its history, but it had suffered immense losses, and the price was high: more than a million people dead, a gigantic war debt and a loss of many foreign markets forever. Britain became very much weakened, though a victor of the war.

In 1917, the October Revolution broke out and as a result, the U.S.S.R. emerged. The British government organized a campaign of 14 countries against the newly-born socialist state in 1910—1920, but it ended in failure. The victory of the revolution led to national liberation movements in British colonies. The Indians had been demanding Home Rule. Egypt also demanded independence. When Stanley Baldwin came into power in 1924, he made an attempt to define the relations between Britain and her dominions. The clause which was accepted by the dominions was significant. It read: "Great Britain and the dominions are autonomous communities within the British empire, equal in state, in no way subordinate to one another in any aspect of their internal or domestic affairs, though united by a common allegiance to the crown and freely associated as members of the British commonwealth of nations." The definition was given official legislative recognition in 1931. In this way, all the colonies became independent states in all but name. Until 1970s, India, Pakistan, Burma, Malaysia, Singapore, Kuwait, Oman, Sudan, Ghana, Somalia, Nigeria, Kenya, Zambia and many other British colonies demanded and gained independence. In 1997, Chinese government succeeded in taking over the administration of Hong Kong. The British Empire declined and collapsed.

In 1929, a devastating economic crisis broke out in the capitalist world. For Britain, by the early summer of 1931, a warning note was sounded when foreign depositors were withdrawing large quantities of sterling from the Bank of England. The depression continued until 1933. During the depression, more than two million workers were unemployed, and the drop in production was 16 percent from 1929 to 1932. From then on, there was a substantial recovery. But Britain's share in world trade continued to decline.

In the years of economic crisis, the international situation gravely deteriorated. Confronted with the fascist threat the British government adopted a policy of appeasement with the hope of turning Hitler's attention to the Soviet Union. In 1939, the Second World War broke out, and Britain was driven into it. The war ended on May 7, 1945, when Germany surrendered unconditionally. Great Britain won again. However, the economic losses were great, and one quarter of its national wealth was lost.

For Great Britain, the two ruinous wars and the economic crises resulted in the destruction of much property and the loss of dominant position in world politics it had held during the 19th century. Britain has been subordinate to the United States and the Soviet Union in the world politics since the Second World War and to France and Japan in the size of economy since 1960s.

The end of the Second World War witnessed a landslide General Election victory for the Labour Party, for their manifesto of greater social justice with left wing policies such as the creation of a National Health Service, an expansion of the provision of council housing and the nationalization of the major industries. Poor Britain at the time relied heavily on loans from the United States of America to rebuild its damaged infrastructure. Rationing and conscription continued. What's more, the country suffered one of the worst winters on record.

Britain could no longer maintain its large Empire. As a result of decolonization, Britain was forced to withdraw from almost all of its colonies by 1970. During the 1970s and 1980s, Britain succeeded in integrating into the European Economic Community, and modernizing its economy. But it was a difficult time for the country. Firstly, the rate of unemployment was still high as deindustrialization caused the close of much of the country's manufacturing industries. The miners' strike of 1984—1985 ended Britain's coal mining after the discovery of North Sea gas. Besides, the Irish Republican Army brought a prolonged bombing campaign on the country by taking the issue of Northern Ireland to it.

1992 saw the events of Black Wednesday, when the Conservative government was forced to withdraw the pound from currency fix, the European Exchange Rate Mechanism (ERM) after they failed to keep Sterling above its agreed lower limit when currency markets believed the policy was unsustainable. After that, there was a period of continuous economic growth in Britain. What's more, the Belfast Agreement (also known as the Good Friday Agreement) was a major political development in the Northern Ireland peace process. It marked the end of a dispute between Britain and Ireland, and after it, there was little armed violence over the issue.

2. Working-class Movements

In the late 19th century, there was a rise of workers' movement. The new trade unions used strikes as a means of struggle. A variety of labor organizations were formed. They provided insurance, social benefits and collective struggle with employers. In 1893, the independent Labor Party was founded. In 1909, the Labor Party secured the allegiance of the miners' members. Financially supported by the trade unions, it was eventually to take the place of the Liberal Party as the second major party in the state, rivaling the Conservatives. Accordingly, with the emergency of the Labor party, trade unions enjoyed increasing power and rights in their struggle with employers.

Between the year of 1911 and 1914, the British working-class movement reached a new height with a wave of strikes. Among these strikes, three great ones paralyzed much of the industry of the country. The first was a great railway strike, in which over 200,000 workers participated. A coal strike was the second one. More than 3 million miners demanded chiefly the establishment of a minimum rate of wages. The strike of the transport workers were the third one, with 80,000 participants striking mainly in the district of London.

When Britain failed to win a decisive victory as expected during the First World War, discontent mounted at home, and labor unrest continued. Strikes took place in the coalfields and shipyards. In 1919—1920, the British government organized "the campaign of fourteen states" against the new Socialist State. The campaign was enthusiastically advocated by Churchill who was then at the war office. Wide-spread opposition, including that from the laboring classes, forced the expedition sent by the British government to Archangel against the Bolsheviks to withdraw. The labor movement set up councils of action and threatened to hold a general strike when the British government encouraged Poland to invade Russia. The threat effectively dissuaded the government. During this time, the British Communist Party was founded, and it played an important role in the labor movement.

During the Depression period, the coal industry, which had languished ever since its return to private owners in 1921, remained the greatest problem. When the miners refused the wage reduction urged by the owners, the Trade Union Congress (TUC) supported the miners and threatened a general strike. But the government took no action to bring about reorganization of the coal industry and it enacted a Trade Disputes Act, declaring general strikes illegal. The act aroused general indignation and protest among labors. Till now, workers' strikes are still one of the knotty problems for British government.

For the laboring class, they have made important gains in political power and living standards through their efforts and struggle.

II. Literary Review

1. The Early Twentieth Century Novel

The English realistic writers at the end of the 19th century and at the beginning of the 20th century continued and developed the tradition of the critical realism. They turned increasingly to lower middle-class and working-class life. New ways were explored to reveal the truth of life, creating a truthful picture of contemporary England. In their works they criticized the bourgeois society, condemned the existing order of things, and advocated social reforms.

George Meredith (1828—1909) is famous for his psychological analysis with which he exposed the faults and prejudices of the upper class. His main novels include *The Ordeal of Richard Feverel*, *Beauchamp's Career* and *The Egoist*, among which *The Egoist*, carefully planned and superior in strength and brilliance, is the best one. Meredith suggested in his novels that bourgeois morality and its whole system will cause the corruption of human beings, but as a bourgeois himself, he was not able to find any remedy for the social problems.

Herbert George Wells (1866—1946) enjoyed a very high position in the early 20th century English literature. As a versatile writer, he wrote a lot of scientific and fantastic novels at the end of the 19th century. He was also one of the last representatives of English realism. In the early 20th century, he moved towards anti-capitalism and wrote many realistic novels, which mainly dealt with the suffering and struggle of the ordinary people, such as *Kipps* (1905), and *Tono-Bungay* (1909). Aware of the inevitable downfall of capitalism, Wells attempted to solve the social problems in bourgeois society by devising a number of projects. One of his projects is to substitute the existing social order with a system of "technocracy", a society ruled by engineers and scientists.

Thomas Hardy (1840—1928)is one of the representatives of English critical realism at the turn of the 19th century. All together, Hardy completed

15 novels. He classified them into three groups: Novels of Characters and Environments or Wessex novels; Romances and Fantasies; Novels of Ingenuity.

Among all his novels, Hardy reached the summit of his realism with his 2 greatest ones, *Tess of the D'Urbervilles* and *Jude the Obscure*. Both novels shocked British prudery, met with hostile response from the public, and received malicious criticism. Partly because of the criticism of *Tess of the D'Urbervilles*, and partly because of his preference for poetry to prose, Hardy ceased writing novels. He announced in 1896 that *Jude the Obscure* was his last novel.

John Galsworthy (1867—1933) is regarded as one of the most prominent realistic writers in the 20th century. In his realistic novels, he was more concerned with social than political change. He attacked and satirized the propertied class, exposed the well-to-do and diagnosed the social disease. He was able to penetrate into the subtlest windings of the human heart and draw human passions with psychological depth. Nevertheless, his criticism of the bourgeois is only limited to the sphere of ethics and aesthetics. He aimed at dethroning his own class, but failed to suggest remedies to social problems.

Joseph Conrad (1857—1924) is one of the most original novelists of the early 20th century. As a prolific writer, Conrad based all his stories and novels on his life experience, and the sea plays a dominant role in his works. He excelled in presenting his characters amid violence and danger and in capturing their elusive moods with a rich and colorful vocabulary.

Katherine Mansfield (1888—1923) is a writer of remarkable talent and a master of short stories. Most of her short stories are about the upper-middle class life in England and New Zealand, showing sympathy for the poor and wretched of the lower classes. Her writing was notable for its impressionistic style and psychological conflicts.

Edward Morgan Forster (1879—1970) is a novelist, essayist and critic. His two visits to India in 1912 and 1921 supplied subject matter for him to write his masterpiece *A Passage to India* (1924), which questions the attitude to the British Empire. It has been considered by critics to be one of the finest novels of the 20th century.

2. The Early Twentieth Century Drama

Like other writers in the early 20th century, the playwrights of the period also questioned the society and values in their plays.

Bernard Shaw (1856—1950) is the greatest English dramatist of the 20th century who followed the great tradition of realism in his dramatic writing. Shaw played an important role in the development of the new drama. He defended Ibsen against the attack of the critics, and was strongly against "art for art's sake". In his long life, Shaw wrote 51 plays. In them, the injustice and inhumanity of the bourgeois society were laid bare. Shaw's plays can be classified into three cycles: "Plays Unpleasant", "Plays Pleasant", and "Three Plays for Puritans".

As a critical realist writer, Shaw tears away the mask of capitalism and exposes the social conflicts in the bourgeois society. He used his plays to deal with contemporary problems. With their wit and realism, his plays are mainly comedies of ideas in the French dramatist tradition of Moliere. His writing marks a turning to realism and naturalism which is increasingly to dominate British drama. For his achievement in producing amusing and laughable situations in his plays, Shaw is thought to be a humorist. But his humor always has a touch of satire, which functions as a sharp social lash that he uses with superb skill to expose the vice or folly of the age.

3. Modernism in Literature

Modernism is a term for a number of tendencies in the arts, prominent in the first half of the 20th century. Modernist writers rejected the traditional (Victorian and Edwardian) frame-work of narrative, description, and rational exposition in poetry and prose. Instead, they were in favor of a stream-of-consciousness presentation of personality. They relied on the poetic image as the essential vehicle of aesthetic communication, and on myth as a characteristic structural principle. Modernist literature is a literature of discontinuity, both historically and aesthetically. It is based upon a sharp rejection of the procedures and values of the immediate past, and an abrupt break with all traditions.

Modernism had a profound impact upon the development of English poetry. Under the influence of impressionism, instead of aiming at interpreting life or moralizing experience as the Victorians did, poets began to focus on individual movements of experience. It was impressionism that heralded the imagist movements in poetry. Imagism was an Anglo-American poetic movement flourishing in the 1910s. Ezra Pound led the poetic movement, followed by a group of British and American poets. As defined by Pound, "an image is that which presents an intellectual and emotional complex in an instant of time". In 1915, the English writer Richard Aldington (1892—1962) defined the principles of the movement as: "to use the language of common speech...to employ always the exact word...To create new rhythms...To present an image, poetry should render particulars exactly and not deal in vague generalities...To produce poetry that is hard and clear...concentration is of the very essence of poetry." Namely, the imagist poetry, as a kind of free verse, emphasizes on the use of common speech, new rhythms and clear images. Literary symbolism also found its expression in English poetry, with William Butler Yeats as its leading exponent. When Modernist Movement emerged, modernist poets were influenced by both impressionist and symbolist ideas, and by the ideas of the British idealists who were against the materialism that had dominated the 19th century.

Yeats and Eliot are the two most important English poets of the period.

William Butler Yeats (1865—1939), an Irish poet and dramatist, is judged by many to be one of the greatest poets who had ever lived. Young Yeats was acquainted with traditional Irish legends and lore, and began to be interested in Romantic idealism and occult philosophy. He tried to bring his poetry more into touch with the language and preoccupations of the modern world. He also sought to simplify his style, to reject late Victorian poetic modes through making his poetry free from Romantic vagueness, and to bring it close to the rhythms of everyday speech. He aimed at writing poems "as cold and passionate as the dawn". In this way, Yeats promoted the Modernist movement in poetry. As a celebrated and accomplished symbolism poet, he used an elaborate system of symbols in his poems, such as the moon, water, rose, birds and so on. For his great achievement in writing, he was awarded the Novel Prize for literature in 1923.

Thomas Stearns Eliot (1888—1965), great poet, dramatist and critic, was the acknowledged central leader among writers in English during the first half of the 20th century. Eliot's best-known poem *The Waste Land* was a classic expression of the temper of the age. Published in 1922, it brought him immediate fame. As the result of the poet's long years of meditation and feeling, the poem became a landmark in English poetry. It ended the Romantic period and signified the emergency of Modernism. The main idea of the poem is the sterility, chaos and spiritual ruins in Europe soon after the end of the First World War. It also expresses the despair of the generation of bourgeois intellectuals. The poet employed symbols from ancient myths to describe the decay and fragmentation of the Western culture. As a leader of the modernist movement in English poetry and a great innovator of verse technique, Eliot influenced 20th century English poetry profoundly.

Modernism movement in English literature was a movement of experiments in new technique in writing. Thus, modernist poets broke with the tradition of 19th century romanticism, while modernist novelists represented a new trend drifting away from the tradition of 19th century realism. Novelists turned their interests to depicting what was happening in the minds of their characters, and put emphasis on the description of the characters' psychological activities. They argued that it is the depths and recesses of personality that a novelist should explore, and the unending stream of impression, feelings, and thoughts that fiction should reveal. Lawrence, Joyce and Woolf are the renowned representatives of modernist fiction writing.

David Herbert Lawrence (1885—1930) is a pioneer in modern psychological fiction. His first important novel *Sons and Lovers* (1913), based on his early experience, is mainly autobiographical. The influence of Freudian theory of psychoanalysis, especially that of the "Oedipus complex" is obvious in the novel. *Lady Chatterley's Lover* (1928) is Laurence's last and most controversial novel which tells about Lady Chatterley's love affair with her husband's gamekeeper. It was not until 1960, long after the author's death that the full text was published. Lawrence was a controversial figure in literary history during his lifetime and even afterwards because of his frank treatment of sex. In his writing, he was against the Western industrial civilization and advocated a need for a rearrangement in the relationship between the sexes to save the decaying civilization.

James Joyce (1882—1941), one of the most original novelists in the 20th century, is the founder of "stream of consciousness", a narrative method whereby certain writers use to describe the unspoken thoughts and feelings of their characters without resorting to objective description or conventional dialogue. Joyce adapted and developed the technique in his writing.

His *Ulysses* (1922), "a modern prose epic", when it came out, became a center of controversy. In his story, Joyce adopts the technique of "stream of consciousness" to record the characters' mental activities and to reveal their inner and mental world. Besides, he was quite free with the English language and grammar by breaking through the fetters of syntax. One extreme example appears in the last chapter of the novel, where the heroine's natural and disconnected flow of thoughts is recorded in eight unpunctual pages.

Virginia Woolf (1882—1941), a great master of the stream-of-consciousness school, is regarded as one of the main exponents of Modernism and one of the greatest innovative novelists of the 20th century. Her fist two novels were written conventionally. Then, she began to try a new creative method, making experiments with a new novel form in a series of her mature novels. She rejected realism and traditional novel technique by adopting the stream-of-consciousness or interior monologue to explore problems of human personality and personal relationships. *The Waves* (1931) is regarded as "the climax of Virginia Woolf's experiments in novel form". It describes the lives of 6 characters through their stream of consciousness, each of them telling his or her story by interior monologue.

4. Post-war Literature

In the years following World War II, a diverse literature in all directions has emerged and flourished in Britain. Some of the major writers will be mentioned for their great achievements. They are novelists Evelyn Waugh, Graham Greene, George Orwell, William Golding, and Doris Lessing, and poets Ted Hughes and Philip Larkin.

Graham Greene (1904—1991), English novelist, short-story writer, playwright and journalist, is one of the most widely read novelist of the 20th-century. As a prolific and versatile writer, he wrote a great number of books, including novels, short stories, plays, books of reportage and travel, essays, books for children, and autobiographies. His first fully mature work is *Brighton Rock*, which was published in 1938 and filmed in 1948. It tells a story of gang warfare and racketeering in the underworld of Brighton, a seaside resort of South England. Actually, Greene's novels often have religious themes at the centre. In his literary criticism, he argues that in order to recover the dramatic power in the novel, the religious element, the awareness of the drama of the struggle in the soul carrying the infinite consequences of salvation and damnation, and of the ultimate metaphysical realities of good and evil, sin and grace should be recovered first. In the fallen world Greene depicts, suffering and unhappiness are omnipresent and Catholicism is presented against a background of unvarying human evil, sin and doubt.

George Orwell (1903—1950), the pseudonym of Eric Arthur Blair, is an English journalist, political essayist and novelist. He was an uncompromising individualist and political idealist. His writing is noted by concise descriptions of social conditions and events and contempt for all types of authority. His best novels include *Animal Farm* (1945), an anti-Soviet tale, and *Nineteen Eighty-Four* (1949), which is critical of totalitarianism. The former was chosen by *Time* Magazine as one of the 100 best English-language novels (1923—2005). It is an allegory in which animals play the roles of the Bolshevik revolutionaries and overthrow and oust the human owners of the farm. It describes how a society's ideologies can be manipulated and twisted by those in positions of social and political power. The latter is an anti-Utopian novel about the life of the protagonist, Winston Smith, an intellectual worker at the Ministry of Truth in an authoritarian regime. Winston is degraded and psychologically tortured after he is arrested by the thoughtpolice under the instruction of the totalitarian government of Oceania, in the year of 1984.

William Golding (1911—1994) is a British novelist and poet. His first novel *Lord of the Flies* (1954; filmed, 1963) brought him immediate success, and he won the Nobel Prize for literature for it in 1983. The novel tells of the story of a group of English schoolboys who are marooned and become isolated on an island, dealing with an unsuccessful struggle against barbarism and war, and indicating the ambiguity and fragility of civilization. Most of Golding's novels are allegorical fiction, in which he often made broad use of allusions to classical literature, mythology, and Christian symbolism. There is no distinct thread uniting his novels, and the subject matter and technique vary greatly. However it is noticeable that the settings of his novels are often in closed communities, such as islands, villages, monasteries, groups of hunter-gatherers, ships at sea or a pharaoh's court. Besides, in many of his novels, Golding revealed the dark places of human heart, when isolated individuals or small groups are pushed into extreme situations. One of the characteristics of his work is the exploration of "the darkness of man's heart", deep spiritual and ethical questions.

Doris Lessing (1919—) is a Persian-born English novelist and short-story writer. Her breakthrough work (1962) was *The Golden Notebook*, one of her most widely read and translated works. This experimental novel was greeted upon its publication as a landmark of the Women's Movement because it is concerned with the difficulties confronted by the so-called "free women", who may threaten the old tradition of western social order for their independence and strength. Most of Lessing's works are concerned with people caught in the social and political upheavals of the 20th century. The central themes in her works cover feminism, the battles of the sexes, the individuals in search of wholeness, and the dangers of technological and scientific hubris. In 2007, Lessing won the Nobel Prize for Literature at the age of 87. She is the oldest person ever to win the literature award. The Swedish Academy described her as "that epicist of the female experience, who with skepticism, fire and visionary power has subjected a divided civilization to scrutiny".

Ted Hughes (1930—1998), one of the best poets of his generation, is British Poet Laureate from 1984 until his death. In his lengthy career, Hughes published many books of poems, including: *Lupercal* (1960), *Crow* (1971), *Cave Birds* (1979), *Moortown* (1980), *Selected Poems* 1957—1981 (1982), *Flowers and Insects* (1986), *Wolfwatching* (1990), and the final collection, *The Birthday Letters* (1998). Among them, one of the most significant works is *Crow*. It is a collection of poems based around the character Crow, which borrow extensively from many world mythologies, notably Christian mythology. The character of crow is thought to be a "mythologisation" of Hughes' own life and experiences. The tone in the collection is mainly hard and bleak, and sometimes pitch black, reflecting well his view of nature as an impersonal and chaotic entity. "Crow" has been one of his most famous subjects. It is a mixture of god, bird and man, whose existence seems to be pivotal to the knowledge of good and evil.

Philip Larkin (1922—1985), English poet, novelist and jazz critic, is commonly regarded as one of the greatest English poets of the latter half of the 20th century. His first collection of poems is The North Ship (1945). It was written with short lines and carefully worked-out rhyme schemes, showing the influence of Yeats. Larkin's second volume of poetry, *The Less Deceived* appeared in 1955, establishing his position as the preeminent poet of his generation, and a leading figure of what came to be called "The Movement" (i.e., a group of young English writers who rejected the prevailing fashion for neo-Romantic writing in the style of Yeats and Dylan Thomas). Larkin's reputation as a major poet was confirmed by *The Whitsun Weddings* (1964), and by his final collection *High Windows* (1974). As a leading figure of "the Movement", who advocated addressing everyday British life in plain, straightforward language and often in traditional forms, Larkin's language was plain; his approach was cool and restricted. In his writing, he avoided "big" words, and philosophizing. Like his admired Hardy, Larkin focused on intense personal emotion but strictly avoided sentimentality or self-pity. Larkin was offered the Poet Laureateship after the death of his friend John Betjeman in 1984, but he declined the post. He never married and led an uneventful life as a university librarian in the provincial city of Hull, where he died in 1985. Larkin was chosen as "the nation's best-loved poet" in a survey by the Poetry Book Society, in 2003 and *The Times* named Larkin as the greatest post-war writer in 2008.

Thomas Hardy (1840—1928)

Life and Major Works

Thomas Hardy, English poet and novelist, was best known for his profound reflection on human circumstance and fate in a reckless world. He was also adept at portraying vividly the landscape of the English county "Wessex". In general, most of Hardy's works were characterized by a sense of deep pessimism.

Hardy was born on Egdon Heath, in Dorset, in the southwest of England on June 2, 1840. His father was a stonemason and building contractor. Hardy's mother was interested in Latin poetry and French romances and provided largely for his learning. For most of the time, Hardy received his education at home. He lived close to the land and got familiar with the life of ordinary people. The simple rural life experiences in the countryside provided him with abundant materials for his later stories. At the age of 16, Hardy was apprenticed to an architect at his father's will. He worked in an office for the restoration of churches. However, he didn't have much interest in architecture.

When Hardy was 22 he moved to London and began to write poems about the ideal rural life. In 1867 Hardy returned home in Dorset. As his poetry was not well received, Hardy decided to turn to novel writing. He finished his first novel *The Poor Man and The Lady* in 1867, but none of the publishers would publish it, so Hardy destroyed the manuscript. Later Hardy published two novels anonymously, *Desperate Remedies* (1871), a story with sophisticated plot, and *Under the Greenwood Tree* (1872), a satirical story of rustic humor. By the year 1874 he was able to earn a living by writing and he got married to Emma Lavinia Gifford. The same year saw his first success in the book *Far From the Madding Crowd*. The novel tells about the story of a young girl Bathsheba Everdene being pursued by three men. Through a series of events, she finally finds her true love and is married to the shepherd Gabriel Oak. The book won wide public attention soon after it came out and Hardy was greatly encouraged by its success. As a result, he devoted himself entirely to writing and produced quite a few novels, which include *The Return of the Native* (1878), *The Mayor of Casterbridge* (1886), *Tess of the D'Urbervilles* (1891) and *Jude the Obscure* (1895).

Compared with the later novels, *The Return of the Native* bears a less sad tone. But it is still a tragic story. Through the narrative of what happened to the heroes Damon Wildeve and Clym Yeobright and the women around them, the author revealed that the once tranquil and stable life of the English countryside was forever lost.

The Mayor of Casterbridge is one of the best known and most critically acclaimed of Hardy's novels. It explores the relationship between man's fate and his environment. Michel Henchard, the hero, is a country labourer who sells his wife and daughter at a fair during their travel to a sailor called Newson out of the drunkenness. As time goes by, Henchard manages to accumulate wealth through doing business successfully; he even becomes mayor of the town of Casterbridge and gains people's respect. Years later his wife suddenly reappears with her daughter Elizabeth-Jane who Henchard wrongly supposes is his. His tragedy begins to set in as he meets Farfrae who advocates the modern, new farming methods. But Henchard clings to the old way of doing business. The conflict between them is symbolic. Finally Farfrae takes over Henchard's business, his property and his love Lucetta. What is worse to come is when Newson arrives to take away his step-daughter Elizabeth-Jane. Henchard loses his only comfort and dies wretchedly on the outskirts of the town. One of the greatest points in the novel is the development of Henchard's character: from initial contentedness through bitter attempts to worldly success and to the final complete desperation. The hero's fate is at disposal of several joined forces that he has little control of.

The novel *Tess of the D'Urbervilles* is a most controversial one as it came in conflict with the Victorian morality of women, thus it caused public uproar in the literary circle. His next novel, *Jude the Obscure* (1895) aroused even more debate because of the extramarital relationship and the gruesome death depicted in it. The story dramatized the conflict between one's carnal and spiritual life. In 1896, disturbed by the public controversy over the unconventional subjects of two of his greatest novels, *Tess of the D'Urbervilles* and *Jude the Obscure,* Hardy put an end to his novel writing career.

During the remainder years of his life, Hardy wrote several collections of poems. He composed the blank-verse epic *The Dynasts* between 1903 and 1908. The poem is considered to be a gigantic panorama of the Napoleonic Wars. When his friend George Meredith died in 1909, Hardy succeeded on to the presidency of the Society of Authors. In 1912, the Order of Merit was conferred on him by King George V and he also received the gold medal of the Royal Society of Literature.

Hardy's wife Emma died in 1912. Two years later Hardy married his secretary, Florence Emily Dugdale. From 1920 through 1927 Hardy worked on his autobiography, which was disguised as the work of Florence Hardy. It appeared in two volumes (1928 and 1930). Hardy's last book published in his lifetime was *Human Shows* (1925).

Hardy died in Dorchester, Dorset, on January 11, 1928. His ashes were cremated in Dorchester and buried with grand ceremonies in the Poet's Corner in Westminster Abbey. Hardy's *Winter Words* came out posthumously in 1928.

Brief Introduction and Appreciation

Among his many "Wessex" novels, *Tess of the d'Urbervilles* caused quite a controversy when it appeared in 1891 as it contradicted the social morals of women in the Victorian age. At that time, Thomas Hardy was one of England's leading figures of letters. He had already authored several well-known novels, including The Return of the Native, and numerous short stories. *Tess of the d'Urbervilles* brought him both fortune and notoriety. Despite this success, Hardy was deeply wounded by the fierce personal attacks from the reviewers of the book. As he once wrote in his notebook: "Well, if this sort of thing continues no more novel-writing for me. A man must be a fool to deliberately stand up to be shot at."

The heroine of the novel Tess Durbeyfield is a 16-year-old simple country girl. She was born in an impoverished family and is the eldest daughter of John and Joan Durbeyfield. During her visit to the d'Urbervilles at the Slopes, Tess meets Alec d'Urberville. Attracted to Tess, Alec arranges for her to be the caretaker for his blind mother's poultry, so Tess moves to the Slopes to take up the position. While living at the d'Urbervilles, Alec seduces and rapes Tess.

Later Tess returns home and gives birth to a son, Sorrow. She works as a field worker on nearby farms. Unfortunately Sorrow is ill and dies in infancy. Tess becomes devastated at her son's death and decides to go away from home. She finds a job as a milkmaid to a good-natured dairyman, Mr. Crick on Talbothays Dairy. There she falls in love with a young man named Angel Clare. He does not know Tess' past, although she has tried on several occasions to tell him. After their wedding, Tess and Angel confess their pasts to each other. Tess forgives Angel for his past indiscretions, but Angel cannot forgive Tess for having a child with another man.

Angel cannot accept the stunning fact and leaves for Brazil. Heartbroken, Tess returns to her parent's house. Her seducer Alec appears in her life again and asks Tess to marry him. Tess refuses in the strongest terms, but Alec is persistent. During Angel's absence, Tess meets with misfortunes one after another. Her father is dead and her mother is ill. The burden of her family falls on Tess' shoulders. Driven by the poverty and with a hopeless belief that Angel will ever return, Tess knows that she cannot resist Alec's money and the comforts he can provide for her family. However, fate plays a joke on her. Angel returns from Brazil to look for Tess and he wants to be with her. Struck by strong despair and in a fit of fury and madness, Tess kills Alec, the source of all her miseries.

Chapter 57 and 58 is the "Fulfillment" phase. Tess murders her seducer Alec and runs to Angel for help. The two lovers travel along the country roads to avoid detection. They plan to make for a port and leave the country as soon as possible. They spend a week in a vacant house, reunited in bliss for a short time. They are discovered, however, and the trail ends at Stonehenge, the ancient pagan monument, when the police arrest Tess and take her away.

Through Tess' life, fate plays a predominant role in what happens to her. She is doomed to suffer a tragic fate as she has been too soft and kind in a relentless world filled with pretense. Her tragedy begins with her loss of virginity. As a beautiful woman, she is too attractive to men around her. As a poor woman, she is no master of her own life. She has no choice but be the prey of men. Finally, she stands up against her fate and "ends" the source of all her misery: she kills her seducer Alec. However, does she really end the source of her tragic fate? The last words in the novel answer this question "'Justice' is done, and the President of Immortals...had ended his sport with Tess." Tess is arrested and sentenced to death by the law of the society which is controlled by the rich and powerful men. These last words reveal that the unfair social treatment of women, the unjust moral demands for them and the unbalanced social structures of the Victorian England are the true source of Tess' tragedy.

Selected Reading

Tess of the D'Urbervilles
Phase the Seventh: Fulfillment
Chapter 57

Meanwhile Angel Clare had walked automatically along the way by which he had come, and, entering his hotel, sat down over the breakfast, staring at nothingness. He went on eating and drinking unconsciously till on a sudden he demanded his bill; having paid which he took his dressing-bag in his hand, the only luggage he had brought with him, and went out.

At the moment of his departure a telegram was handed to him—a few words from his mother, stating that they were glad to know his address, and informing him that his brother Cuthbert[1] had proposed to and been accepted by Mercy Chant.

Clare crumpled up the paper, and followed the route to the station; reaching it, he found that there would be no train leaving for an hour and more. He sat down to wait, and having waited a quarter of an hour felt that he could wait there no longer. Broken in heart and numbed, he had nothing to hurry for; but he wished to get out of a town which had been the scene of such an experience, and turned to walk to the first station onward, and let the train pick him up there.

The highway that he followed was open, and at a little distance dipped into[2] a valley, across which it could be seen running from edge to edge. He had traversed[3] the greater part of this depression, and was climbing the western acclivity[4], when, pausing for breath, he unconsciously looked back. Why he did so he could not say, but something seemed to impel him to the act. The tape-like surface of the road diminished in his rear as far as he could see, and as he gazed a moving spot intruded on the white vacuity of its perspective.

It was a human figure running. Clare waited, with a dim sense that somebody was trying to overtake him.

The form descending the incline was a woman's, yet so entirely was his mind blinded to the idea of his wife's following him that even when she came nearer he did not recognize her under the totally changed attire in which he now beheld her. It was not till she was quite close that he could believe her to be Tess.

"I saw you—turn away from the station—just before I got there—and I have been following you all this way!"

She was so pale, so breathless, so quivering in every muscle, that he did not ask her a single question, but seizing her hand, and pulling it within his arm, he led her along. To avoid meeting any possible wayfarers[5] he left the high road, and took a footpath under some fir-trees. When they were deep among the moaning boughs he stopped and looked at her inquiringly.

"Angel," she said, as if waiting for this, "do you know what I have been running after you for? To tell you that I have killed him!" A pitiful white smile lit her face as she spoke.

"What!" said he, thinking from the strangeness of her manner that she was in some delirium[6].

"I have done it—I don't know how," she continued. "Still, I owed it to you, and to myself, Angel. I feared long ago, when I struck him on the mouth with my glove, that I might do it some day for the trap he set for me in my simple youth, and his wrong to you through me. He has come between us and ruined us, and now he can never do it any more. I never loved him at all, Angel, as I loved you. You know it, don't you? You believe it? You didn't come back to me, and I was obliged to go back to him. Why did you go away—why did you— when I loved you so? I can't think why you did it. But I don't blame you; only, Angel, will you forgive me my sin against you, now I have killed him? I thought as I ran along that you would be sure to forgive me now I have done that. It came to me as a shining light that I should get you back that way. I could not bear the loss of you any longer—you don't know how entirely I was unable to bear your not loving me! Say you do now, dear, dear husband; say you do, now I have killed him!"

"I do love you, Tess—O, I do—it is all come back!" he said, tightening his arms round her with fervid[7] pressure. "But how do you mean—you have killed him?"

"I mean that I have," she murmured in a reverie.

"What, bodily? Is he dead?"

"Yes. He heard me crying about you, and he bitterly taunted[8] me; and called you by a foul name; and then I did it. My heart could not bear it. He had nagged me about you before. And then I dressed myself and came away to find you."

By degrees he was inclined to believe that she had faintly attempted, at least, what she said she had done; and his horror at her impulse was mixed with amazement at the strength of her affection for himself, and at the strangeness of its quality, which had apparently extinguished her moral sense altogether. Unable to realize the gravity of her conduct she seemed at last content; and he looked at her as she lay upon his shoulder, weeping with happiness, and wondered what obscure strain in the d'Urberville blood had led to this aberration[9]—if it were an aberration. There momentarily flashed through his mind that the family tradition of the coach and murder might have arisen because the d'Urbervilles had been known to do these things. As well as his confused and excited ideas could reason, he supposed that in the moment of mad grief of which she spoke her mind had lost its balance, and plunged her into this abyss[10].

It was very terrible if true; if a temporary hallucination, sad. But, anyhow, here was this deserted wife of his, this passionately-fond woman, clinging to him without a suspicion that he would be anything to her but a protector. He saw that for him to be otherwise was not, in her mind, within the region of the possible. Tenderness was absolutely dominant in Clare at last. He kissed her endlessly with his white lips, and held her hand, and said—

"I will not desert you! I will protect you by every means in my power, dearest love, whatever you may have done or not have done!"

They then walked on under the trees, Tess turning her head every now and then to look at him. Worn and unhandsome as he had become, it was plain that she did not discern the least fault in his appearance. To her he was, as of old, all that was perfection, personally and mentally. He was still her Antinous[11], her Apollo[12] even; his sickly face was beautiful as the morning to her affectionate regard on this day no less than when she first beheld him; for was it not the face of the one man on earth who had loved her purely, and who had believed in her as pure!

With an instinct as to possibilities he did not now, as he had intended, make for the first station beyond the town, but plunged still farther under the firs, which here abounded for miles. Each clasping the other round the waist they promenaded over the dry bed of fir-needles, thrown into a vague intoxicating atmosphere at the consciousness of being together at last, with no living soul between them; ignoring that there was a corpse. Thus they proceeded for several miles till Tess, arousing herself, looked about her, and said, timidly—

"Are we going anywhere in particular?"

"I don't know, dearest. Why?"

"I don't know."

"Well, we might walk a few miles further, and when it is evening find lodgings somewhere or other—in a lonely cottage, perhaps. Can you walk well, Tessy?"

"O yes! I could walk for ever and ever with your arm round me!"

Upon the whole it seemed a good thing to do. Thereupon they quickened their pace, avoiding high roads, and following obscure paths tending more or less northward. But there was an unpractical vagueness in their movements throughout the day; neither one of them seemed to consider any question of effectual escape, disguise, or long concealment. Their every idea was temporary and unforefending[13], like the plans of two children.

At mid-day they drew near to a roadside inn, and Tess would have entered it with him to get something to eat, but he persuaded her to remain among the trees and bushes of this half-woodland, half-moorland part of the country, till he should come back. Her clothes were of recent fashion; even the ivory-handled parasol that she carried was of a shape unknown in the retired spot to which they had now wandered; and the cut of such articles would have attracted attention in the settle of a tavern. He soon returned, with food enough for half-a-dozen people and two bottles of wine—enough to last them for a day or more, should any emergency arise.

They sat down upon some dead boughs and shared their meal. Between one and two o'clock they packed up the remainder and went on again.

"I feel strong enough to walk any distance," said she.

"I think we may as well steer in a general way towards the interior of the country, where we can hide for a time, and are less likely to be looked for than anywhere near the coast," Clare remarked. "Later on, when they have forgotten us, we can make for some port."

She made no reply to this beyond that of grasping him more tightly, and straight inland they went. Though the season was an English May the weather was serenely bright, and during the afternoon it was quite warm. Through the latter miles of their walk their footpath had taken them into the depths of the New Forest, and towards evening, turning the corner of a lane, they perceived behind a brook and bridge a large board on which was painted in white letters, "This desirable Mansion to be Let Furnished"; particulars following, with directions to apply to some London agents. Passing through the gate they could see the house, an old brick building of regular design and large accommodation.

"I know it," said Clare. "It is Bramshurst Court. You can see that it is shut up, and grass is growing on the drive."

"Some of the windows are open," said Tess.

"Just to air the rooms, I suppose."

"All these rooms empty and we without a roof to our heads!"

"You are getting tired, my Tess!" he said. "We'll stop soon." And kissing her sad mouth he again led her onwards.

He was growing weary likewise, for they had wandered a dozen or fifteen miles, and it became necessary to consider what they should do for rest. They looked from afar at isolated cottages and little inns, and were inclined to approach one of the latter, when their hearts failed them, and they sheered off[14]. At length their gait[15] dragged, and they stood still.

"Could we sleep under the trees?" she asked.

He thought the season insufficiently advanced.

"I have been thinking of that empty mansion we passed," he said. "Let us go back towards it again."

They retraced their steps, but it was half an hour before they stood without the entrance-gate as earlier. He then requested her to stay where she was, whilst he went to see who was within.

She sat down among the bushes within the gate, and Clare crept towards the house. His absence lasted some considerable time, and when he returned Tess was wildly anxious, not for herself, but for him. He had found out from a boy that there was only an old woman in charge as caretaker, and she only came there on fine days, from the hamlet near, to open and shut the windows. She would come to shut them at sunset. "Now, we can get in through one of the lower windows, and rest there," said he.

Under his escort she went tardily forward to the main front, whose shuttered windows, like sightless eyeballs, excluded the possibility of watchers. The door was reached a few steps further, and one of the windows beside it was open. Clare clambered in, and pulled Tess in after him.

Except the hall the rooms were all in darkness, and they ascended the staircase. Up here also the shutters were tightly closed, the ventilation being perfunctorily done, for this day at least, by opening the hall-window in front and an upper window behind. Clare unlatched the door of a large chamber, felt his way across it, and parted the shutters to the width of two or three inches. A shaft of dazzling sunlight glanced into the room, revealing heavy, old-fashioned furniture, crimson damask hangings, and an enormous four-post bedstead, along the head of which were carved running figures, apparently Atalanta's race[16].

"Rest at last!" said he, setting down his bag and the parcel of viands[17].

They remained in great quietness till the caretaker should have come to shut the windows: as a precaution, putting themselves in total darkness by barring the shutters as before, lest the woman should open the door of their chamber for any casual reason. Between six and seven o'clock she came, but did not approach the wing they were in. They heard her close the windows, fasten them, lock the door, and go away. Then Clare again stole a chink of light from the window, and they shared another meal, till by-and-by they were enveloped in the shades of night which they had no candle to disperse.

Chapter 58

The night was strangely solemn and still. In the small hours she whispered to him the whole story of how he had walked in his sleep with her in his arms across the Froom stream, at the imminent risk of both their lives, and laid her down in the stone coffin at the ruined abbey. He had never known of that till now.

"Why didn't you tell me next day?" he said. "It might have prevented much misunderstanding and woe."

"Don't think of what's past!" said she. "I am not going to think outside of now. Why should we! Who knows what tomorrow has in store?"

But it apparently had no sorrow. The morning was wet and foggy, and Clare, rightly informed that the caretaker only opened the windows on fine days, ventured to creep out of their chamber, and explore the house, leaving Tess asleep. There was no food on the premises, but there was water, and he took advantage of the fog to emerge from the mansion, and fetch tea, bread, and butter from a shop in a little place two miles beyond, as also a small tin kettle and spirit-lamp, that they might get fire without smoke. His re-entry awoke her; and they breakfasted on what he had brought.

They were indisposed to stir abroad, and the day passed, and the night following, and the next, and next; till, almost without their being aware, five days had slipped by in absolute seclusion, not a sight or sound of a human being disturbing their peacefulness, such as it was. The changes of the weather were their only events, the birds of the New Forest their only company. By tacit consent they hardly once spoke of any incident of the past subsequent to their wedding-day. The gloomy intervening time seemed to sink into chaos, over which the present and prior times closed as if it never had been. Whenever he suggested that they should leave their shelter, and go forwards towards Southampton or London, she showed a strange unwillingness to move.

"Why should we put an end to all that's sweet and lovely!" she deprecated[18]. "What must come will come." And, looking through the shutter-chink: "All is trouble outside there; inside here content."

He peeped out also. It was quite true; within was affection, union, error forgiven: outside was the inexorable.

"And—and," she said, pressing her cheek against his, "I fear that what you think of me now may not last. I do not wish to outlive your present feeling for me. I would rather not. I would rather be dead and buried when the time comes for you to despise me, so that it may never be known to me that you despised me."

"I cannot ever despise you."

"I also hope that. But considering what my life had been I cannot see why any man should, sooner or later, be able to help despising me... How wickedly mad I was! Yet formerly I never could bear to hurt a fly or a worm, and the sight of a bird in a cage used often to make me cry."

They remained yet another day. In the night the dull sky cleared, and the result was that the old caretaker at the cottage awoke early. The brilliant sunrise made her unusually brisk; she decided to open the contiguous mansion immediately, and to air it thoroughly on such a day. Thus it occurred that, having arrived and opened the lower rooms before six o'clock, she ascended to the bedchambers, and was about to turn the handle of the one wherein they lay. At that moment she fancied she could hear the breathing of persons within. Her slippers and her antiquity had rendered her progress a noiseless one so far, and she made for instant retreat; then, deeming that her hearing might have deceived her, she turned anew to the door and softly tried the handle. The lock was out of order, but a piece of furniture had been moved forward on the inside, which prevented her opening the door more than an inch or two. A stream of morning light through the shutter-chink fell upon the faces of the pair, wrapped in profound slumber, Tess's lips being parted like a half-opened flower near his cheek. The caretaker was so struck with their innocent appearance, and with the elegance of Tess's gown hanging across a chair, her silk stockings beside it, the pretty parasol, and the other habits in which she had arrived because she had none else, that her first indignation at the effrontery of tramps and vagabonds gave way to a momentary sentimentality over this genteel elopement, as it seemed. She closed the door, and withdrew as softly as she had come, to go and consult with her neighbours on the odd discovery.

Not more than a minute had elapsed after her withdrawal when Tess woke, and then Clare. Both had a sense that something had disturbed them, though they could not say what; and the uneasy feeling which it engendered grew stronger. As soon as he was dressed he narrowly scanned the lawn through the two or three inches of shutter-chink.

"I think we will leave at once," said he. "It is a fine day. And I cannot help fancying somebody is about the house. At any rate, the woman will be sure to come today."

She passively assented, and putting the room in order they took up the few articles that belonged to them, and departed noiselessly. When they had got into the Forest she turned to take a last look at the house.

"Ah, happy house—goodbye!" she said. "My life can only be a question of a few weeks. Why should we not have stayed there?"

"Don't say it, Tess! We shall soon get out of this district altogether. We'll continue our course as we've begun it, and keep straight north. Nobody will think of looking for us there. We shall be looked for at the Wessex ports if we are sought at all. When we are in the north we will get to a port and away."

Having thus persuaded her the plan was pursued, and they kept a bee-line northward[19]. Their long repose at the manor-house lent them walking power now; and towards mid-day they found that they were approaching the steepled city of Melchester, which lay directly in their way. He decided to rest her in a clump of trees during the afternoon, and push onward under cover of darkness. At dusk Clare purchased food as usual, and their night march began, the boundary between Upper and Mid-Wessex being crossed about eight o'clock.

To walk across country without much regard to roads was not new to Tess, and she showed her old agility in the performance. The intercepting city, ancient Melchester, they were obliged to pass through in order to take advantage of the town bridge for crossing a large river that obstructed them. It was about midnight when they went along the deserted streets, lighted fitfully by the few lamps, keeping off the pavement that it might not echo their footsteps. The graceful pile of cathedral architecture rose dimly on their left hand, but it was lost upon them now. Once out of the town they followed the turnpike-road, which after a few miles plunged across an open plain.

Though the sky was dense with cloud a diffused light from some fragment of a moon had hitherto helped them a little. But the moon had now sunk, the clouds seemed to settle almost on their heads, and the night grew as dark as a cave. However, they found their way along, keeping as much on the turf as possible that their tread might not resound, which it was easy to do, there being no hedge or fence of any kind. All around was open loneliness and black solitude, over which a stiff breeze blew.

They had proceeded thus gropingly two or three miles further when on a sudden Clare became conscious of some vast erection close in his front, rising sheer from the grass. They had almost struck themselves against it.

"What monstrous place is this?" said Angel.

"It hums," said she. "Hearken!"

He listened. The wind, playing upon the edifice, produced a booming tune, like the note of some gigantic one-stringed harp. No other sound came from it, and lifting his hand and advancing a step or two, Clare felt the vertical surface of the structure. It seemed to be of solid stone, without joint or moulding. Carrying his fingers onward he found that what he had come in contact with was a colossal rectangular pillar; by stretching out his left hand he could feel a similar one adjoining. At an indefinite height overhead something made the black sky blacker, which had the semblance of a vast architrave uniting the pillars horizontally. They carefully entered beneath and between; the surfaces echoed their soft rustle; but they seemed to be still out of doors. The place was roofless. Tess drew her breath fearfully, and Angel, perplexed, said—

"What can it be?"

Feeling sideways they encountered another tower-like pillar, square and uncompromising as the first; beyond it another and another. The place was all doors and pillars, some connected above by continuous architraves[20].

"A very Temple of the Winds," he said.

The next pillar was isolated; others composed a trilithon[21]; others were prostrate, their flanks forming a causeway wide enough for a carriage and it was soon obvious that they made up a forest of monoliths grouped upon the grassy expanse of the plain. The couple advanced further into this pavilion of the night till they stood in its midst.

"It is Stonehenge[22]!" said Clare.

"The heathen[23] temple, you mean?"

"Yes. Older than the centuries; older than the d'Urbervilles! Well, what shall we do, darling? We may find shelter further on."

But Tess, really tired by this time, flung herself upon an oblong slab that lay close at hand, and was sheltered from the wind by a pillar. Owing to the action of the sun during the preceding day the stone was warm and dry, in comforting contrast to the rough and chill grass around, which had damped her skirts and shoes.

"I don't want to go any further, Angel," she said, stretching out her hand for his. "Can't we bide here?"

"I fear not. This spot is visible for miles by day, although it does not seem so now."

"One of my mother's people was a shepherd hereabouts, now I think of it. And you used to say at Talbothays[24] that I was a heathen. So now I am at home."

He knelt down beside her outstretched form, and put his lips upon hers.

"Sleepy are you, dear? I think you are lying on an altar."

"I like very much to be here," she murmured. "It is so solemn and lonely —after my great happiness—with nothing but the sky above my face. it seems as if there were no folk in the world but we two; and I wish there were not— except 'Liza-Lu[25]."

Clare though she might as well rest here till it should get a little lighter, and he flung his overcoat upon her, and sat down by her side.

"Angel, if anything happens to me, will you watch over 'Liza-Lu for my sake?" she asked, when they had listened a long time to the wind among the pillars.

"I will."

"She is so good and simple and pure. O, Angel—I wish you would marry her if you lose me, as you will do shortly. O, if you would!"

"If I lose you I lose all! And she is my sister-in-law."

"That's nothing, dearest. People marry sister-in-laws continually about Marlott[26]; and 'Liza-Lu is so gentle and sweet, and she is growing so beautiful. O, I could share you with her willingly when we are spirits! If you would train her and teach her, Angel, and bring her up for your own self! ... She had all the best of me without the bad of me; and if she were to become yours it would almost seem as if death had not divided us... Well, I have said it. I won't mention it again."

She ceased, and he fell into thought. In the far north-east sky he could see between the pillars a level streak of light. The uniform concavity of black cloud was lifting bodily like the lid of a pot, letting in at the earth's edge the coming day, against which the towering monoliths and trilithons began to be blackly defined.

"Did they sacrifice to God here?" asked she.

"No," said he.

"Who to?"

"I believe to the sun. That lofty stone set away by itself is in the direction of the sun, which will presently rise behind it."

"This reminds me, dear," she said. "You remember you never would interfere with any belief of mine before we were married? But I knew your mind all the same, and I thought as you thought—not from any reasons of my own, but because you thought so. Tell me now, Angel, do you think we shall meet again after we are dead? I want to know."

He kissed her to avoid a reply at such a time.

"Angel—I fear that means no!" said she, with a suppressed sob. "And I wanted so to see you again—so much, so much! What—not even you and I, Angel, who love each other so well?"

Like a greater than himself, to the critical question at the critical time he did not answer; and they were again silent. In a minute or two her breathing became more regular, her clasp of his hand relaxed, and she fell asleep. The band of silver paleness along the east horizon made even the distant parts of the Great Plain appear dark and near; and the whole enormous landscape bore that impress of reserve, taciturnity, and hesitation which is usual just before day. The eastward pillars and their architraves stood up blackly against the light, and the great flame-shaped Sun-stone beyond them; and the Stone of

Sacrifice midway. Presently the night wind died out, and the quivering little pools in the cup-like hollows of the stones lay still. At the same time something seemed to move on the verge of the dip eastward—a mere dot. It was the head of a man approaching them from the hollow beyond the Sun-stone. Clare wished they had gone onward, but in the circumstances decided to remain quiet. The figure came straight towards the circle of pillars in which they were.

He heard something behind him, the brush of feet. Turning, he saw over the prostrate columns another figure; then before he was aware, another was at hand on the right, under a trilithon, and another on the left. The dawn shone full on the front of the man westward, and Clare could discern from this that he was tall, and walked as if trained. They all closed in with evident purpose. Her story then was true! Springing to his feet, he looked around for a weapon, loose stone, means of escape, anything. By this time the nearest man was upon him.

"It is no use, sir," he said. "There are sixteen of us on the Plain, and the whole country is reared."

"Let her finish her sleep!" he implored in a whisper of the men as they gathered round.

When they saw where she lay, which they had not done till then, they showed no objection, and stood watching her, as still as the pillars around. He went to the stone and bent over her, holding one poor little hand; her breathing now was quick and small, like that of a lesser creature than a woman. All waited in the growing light, their faces and hands as if they were silvered, the remainder of their figures dark, the stones glistening green-gray, the Plain still a mass of shade. Soon the light was strong, and a ray shone upon her unconscious form, peering under her eyelids and waking her.

"What is it, Angel?" she said, starting up. "Have they come for me?"

"Yes, dearest," he said. "They have come."

"It is as it should be," she murmured. "Angel, I am almost glad—yes, glad! This happiness could not have lasted. It was too much. I have had enough; and now I shall not live for you to despise me!"

She stood up, shook herself, and went forward, neither of the men having moved.

"I am ready," she said quietly.

Notes

1. **Cuthbert**: one of Angel's elder brothers Cuthbert Clare
2. **dipped into**: it means "went downward into..."
3. **traverse**: to travel or pass across, over or through
4. **acclivity**: ascending slope
5. **wayfarers**: old use or in literature, travelers on foot
6. **delirium**: an excited dreamy state, especially when one is seriously ill
7. **fervid**: showing too strong feeling; impassioned
8. **taunt**: to try to make someone angry or upset by unkind remarks
9. **aberration**: the state of being abnormal
10. **abyss**: a deep bottomless hole; a state of being despair
11. **Antinous**: a remarkably beautiful and intelligent youth who was a favourite of the Emperor Hadrian. While touring Egypt in late October 130 AD, which was now ruled by Rome, Antinous drowned mysteriously in the river Nile at about the age of eighteen or twenty.
12. **Apollo**: The son of Zeus and Leto, Apollo was the god of music and also of prophecy, colonization, medicine, archery, poetry, dance, intellectual inquiry and the carer of herds and flocks. He was also a god of light, known as "Phoebus"
13. **unforefending**: not taking cautious or protecting measures
14. **sheered off**: changed direction quickly to avoid something
15. **gait**: a way of walking
16. **Atalanta's race**: In Greek myth, a maiden challenged all her suitors to a footrace. Hippomenes dropped three golden apples on the course and she stopped to pick them up, therefore Hippomenes defeated her and won her love.
17. **viands**: food
18. **deprecated**: strongly disapproved of
19. **kept a bee-line northward**: kept going quickly and directly toward the north
20. **architraves**: the molding around a rectangular opening
21. **trilithon**: large and tall stone which is divided into three parts
22. **Stonehenge**: Britain's most important prehistoric monument. The history of Stonehenge dates back to about 3050 B. C., it has been used as a temple.
23. **heathen**: a person, esp. in a distant or wild place, who does not belong to

one of the large established religions.

24. **Talbothays**: the Talbothays Dairy in the Froom Valley, where Tess worked as a milkmaid and met her lover Angel.

25. **'Liza-Lu**: Tess's younger sister

26. **Marlott**: the village where Tess was born and grew up

Questions for Study and Discussion

1. What kind of feeling did Angel have after he left Tess?
2. What made Tess kill Alec? Analyze the deep reasons.
3. Why did Tess not want to leave the deserted mansion?
4. What's the symbolic meaning of Tess' lying on the Stonehenge?
5. Why the last phase of the novel is entitled "fulfillment"?

George Bernard Shaw (1856—1950)

Life and Major Works

George Bernard Shaw was born in Dublin, Ireland in1856. As the youngest child of unhappily married and inattentive parents, Shaw spent his childhood and early youth in Ireland. In 1876 at age of 20, Shaw moved to London to embark on his literary career.

Shaw spent the first three years chiefly in libraries, doing odd jobs to make a living. Before finding his first success as a music critic on the *Star* newspaper, he wrote 5 novels, all of which he

George Bernard Shaw

had a hard time getting published. In 1884 the last of the 5 novels *The Unsocial Socialist* was published. The first novel of the series, *Immaturity* was not published till 1930, while the other 3 novels, *The Irrational Knot*, *Love Among the Artists* and *Cashel Byron's Profession* appeared in 1885— 1887, 1885—1888 and 1885—1886 respectively. All of these novels have one thing in common, that is, the portrayal of a major character who is isolated and estranged from the society and his surroundings.

In the meantime Shaw took up various causes and joined several literary and political societies. In 1884 he joined the Fabian Society, which was committed to gradual rather than revolutionary means for spreading socialist principle, and placed the hopes for the world in the intellectual and intelligent few. Shaw took a leading role in the Fabian Society, serving on the executive committee from 1885 to 1911. The Fabian influence on him was very obvious in many of his plays.

In 1895, Shaw became the drama critic of the *Saturday Review*, which heralded his progress towards a lifetime's work as a dramatist. As a critic, he was strongly against the credo of "Art for Art's Sake" held by those decadent aesthetic artists. He vehemently attacked the well-constructed but very cheap, hollow plays that filled the English theaters in the late 19th century. Shaw wrote many critical essays, including *The Quintessence of Ibsenism* (1891), *The Sanity of Art* (1895) and *The Perfect Wagnerite* (1898), to express his viewpoint that art should serve the society by reflecting the real world, revealing social conflicts and educating the common people.

Shaw's first play *Widowers' House* was produced in 1892, but it met with little success. There followed *Arms and the Man* (1894), *The Devil's Disciple* (1897), *You Never Can Tell* (1898), *Mrs. Warren's Profession* (1898), *Caesar and Cleopatra* (1901) and *John Bull's Other Island* (1904). Of these plays the most important is *John Bull's Other Island*, which is Shaw's most powerful attack on English imperialism. The vices of English imperialists are all exposed via the actions and speeches of the hero Broadbent in the play. Thanks to its ironic description and characteristic "Shavian" wit, the play brought his first popular success in London.

In 1898 Shaw married Charlotte Payne-Townshend, an Irish millionairess who was also a Fabian. In 1906 they settled in the Hertfordshire village of Ayot St. Lawrence. In 1903 came a well-known play of Shaw's, *Man and Superman* (1903), which has a subtitle *A Comedy and a Philosophy* and an appendix *The Revolutionist's Handbook*. The play is a paradoxical version of the Don Juan story in which Shaw criticized capitalism and advocated socialism. Rejecting Darwinism, he embarked on the biological theory of the mysterious Life Force in this play. He believed that the Life Force was responsible for the progress in the natural world and was the explanation of the relationship between men and women.

Major Barbara (1905) is also one of Shaw's important plays. The play is significant for its vehement attack on the hypocrisy and mammonism in the capitalist society. This was followed by a number of other plays, including *Getting Married* (1908), *Misalliance* (1910) and *Fanny's First Play* (1910), centering on the problems of family and marriage. Of the numerous plays written before WWI, *Pygmalion* (1913) is better known. It describes the transformation of a Cockney flower-seller, Eliza Doolittle, into an elegant duchess by the phonetician professor Henry Higgins. With the great success on the stage, it is one of the most popular plays of Shaw.

During the war years of WWI, Shaw wrote many short plays, which have been later collected in *Playlets of the War* (1919). After the war, his status as a playwright continued to grow and he produced more serious dramas, including *Heartbreak House* (1919), *Back to Methuselah* (1921) and *Saint Joan* (1923).

In 1929 when a worldwide economic depression broke out, Shaw began to take up the political themes in his plays to attack the hypocrisy of the western societies. He wrote *The Apple Cart* (1929), a satire on Western parliamentary system, in which he elaborated his wits and sarcasm. Three years later, Shaw produced *Too True to Be Good* (1932), a three-act political extravaganza. This play seems to foreshadow the inevitable doom of the British Empire in the loss of hope among the intellectuals of the day.

One of the interesting characteristics of Shaw's published plays is the lengthy prefaces that accompany them. In those prefaces, Shaw wrote more about his opinions on the issues touched by the plays than about the plays themselves, expressing his views as a non-romantic and a great thinker. The dramatic conflict in his plays is the conflict of thought and belief rather than that of neurosis or physical passion. Discussion is the basis of the plays, and Shaw's great talent and wit have won many audiences all over the world. By the time of his death, Shaw was not only a household name in the British Isles, but also a world-famous dramatist. In 1925, he was awarded the Nobel Prize for literature.

Shaw died at Ayot St. Lawrence, Hertfordshire, on November 2, 1950. As a brilliant playwright, he wrote over 50 plays during his long career. Thanks to his great contributions to English drama, Shaw has won recognition as a leading figure in English literature in the 20th century.

Brief Introduction and Appreciation

First performed in 1913 in Vienna and published in 1916 in London, *Pygmalion* is undoubtedly the most beloved and popularly received of all of Shaw's plays. Writing the screenplay for the film version in 1938 made Shaw win an Academy Award for best screenplay. In 1957 the play was adapted into a musical *My Fair Lady*, and several film versions have been made.

In the classical legend, Pygmalion was the king of Cyprus, who fell in love with his own sculpture. Aphrodite, the goddess of love and beauty, endowed the statue with life and transformed it into the flesh-and-blood of Galatea. Based on the famous story in Ovid's *Metamorphoses*. Shaw transformed the myth in his play, which describes the transformation of a Cockney flower girl, Eliza Doolittle, into a passable imitation of a duchess by Henry Higgins, a professor of phonetics.

At the outset of the play, we are told that the so-called "correct speech" has been regarded as the mark of social status by upper classes. Then two old gentlemen—Henry Higgins, a professor of phonetics and Colonel Pickering, a linguist of Indian dialects—meet in the rain one night at Covent Garden. Higgins bets Pickering that with his knowledge of phonetics, he will be able to transform a flower girl with a vulgar cockney accent into a cultured lady in six months. The next morning, the flower girl, Eliza Doolittle, appears at his laboratory on Wimpole Street to ask for speech lessons, so that she may speak properly enough to work in a flower shop. Pickering agrees to cover the costs of the experiment if Higgins can pass Eliza off as a duchess at an ambassador's garden party. To win the bet and to prove his own points about English speech and the class system, Higgins undertakes the challenge. For a number of months, he teaches Eliza to speak standard English and introduces her successfully to social life. Some months later at an ambassador's party, Eliza turns out to be a fair lady, beautiful, cultured and elegant. Their experiment is a resounding success. The wager is definitely won, but Higgins and Pickering are now bored with the experiment, which causes Eliza to be hurt. She comes to realize that what Higgins instructs her in speech and behavior does not make her an independent and free woman.

At the close of the play, Eliza begins to rebel against Higgins and bolts from his tyranny. When she leaves the house, she says that the professor by treating her like a cultured woman has erased the real culture that she has been born with. The play ends with a truce between two of them. Higgins finally acknowledges that Eliza has obtained freedom and independence. In the sequel, Shaw tells us that Eliza marries the docile and devoted Freddy Eynsford Hill and eventually becomes a duchess.

Pygmalion probes into important problems about social class, human nature and relations between the sexes. It is a comedy in which a gifted man fashions a woman out of lifeless raw materials into a beautiful duchess. Higgins is a representation of Pygmalion, the character from the famous story of Ovid's *Metamorphoses*. However, Shaw does not allow Higgins to fall in love with his creation Eliza. Right to the last act, Higgins still shows a contemptuous and derisive attitude towards her. In addition, by creating other characters such as Mrs. Pearce and Pickering in his play, Shaw transforms the myth to suggest that the primary Pygmalion himself is incomplete and imperfect. Poking fun at middle class morality and upper class superficiality, the play reflects the social ills of the 19th England. In transforming the Pygmalion myth in such a way, Shaw further in his play exposes the inadequacies of the myth and romance that overlook the mundane, human aspects of life.

The following excerpt from *Pygmalion* is Act IV four in which we are told what happens after the ambassador's party. In this act there are more transformations in Eliza to be witnessed: When returning to the Wimpole Street laboratory, Higgins seems rather bored and more concerned with his inability to find his slippers, though they made a great success at the ambassador's party. His insensitive and inattentive response hurts Eliza. When she flings his slippers in his face, she complains to him—"You don't care. I know you don't care. You wouldn't care if I was dead. I'm nothing to you— not so much as them slippers." It means that Eliza tries to object to being treated like an object by Higgins. Moreover, when Higgins advises her to get married, she goes on to assert herself by saying that she would never sell herself. The climactic move in this act indicates the rebirth of an independent spirit in the face of Higgins's bullying superiority. Eliza's rebel against Higgins makes him reconsider what a woman can be. As a turning point of the whole play, this act marks the beginning of Higgins's considering Eliza to be an equal rather than an inferior.

To sum up, *Pygmalion* is a satire, sharply ridiculing the hypocrisy of upper class and attacking the callosity of English society. Up to now, the play has still been a food for thought to contemporary readers. By virtue of its popularity *Pygmalion* establishes Shaw's great reputation in literature.

Selected Reading

Pygmalion[1]
ACT IV

The Wimpole Street laboratory. Midnight. Nobody in the room. The clock on the mantelpiece strikes twelve. The fire is not alight: it is a summer night.
Presently Higgins[2] and Pickering[3] are heard on the stairs.

HIGGINS: (*calling down to Pickering*) I say, Pick: lock up, will you. I shan't be going out again.

PICKERING: Right. Can Mrs. Pearce[4] go to bed? We don't want anything more, do we?

HIGGINS: Lord, no!

ELIZA[5] *opens the door and is seen on the lighted landing in all the finery in which she has just won* HIGGINS's *bet for him. She comes to the hearth, and switches on the electric lights there. She is tired: her pallor[6] contrasts strongly with her dark eyes and hair; and her expression is almost tragic. She takes off her cloak; puts her fan and gloves on the piano; and sits down on the bench, brooding and silent.* HIGGINS, *in evening dress, with overcoat and hat, comes in, carrying a smoking jacket which he has picked up downstairs. He takes off the hat and overcoat; throws them carelessly on the newspaper stand; disposes of his coat in the same way; puts on the smoking jacket; and throws himself wearily into the easy-chair at the hearth.* PICKERING, *similarly attired, comes in. He also takes off his hat and overcoat, and is about to throw them on* HIGGINS's *when he hesitates.*

PICKERING: I say: Mrs. Pearce will row if we leave these things lying about in the drawing room.

HIGGINS: Oh, chuck them over the banisters[7] into the hall. She'll find them there in the morning and put them away all right. She'll think we were drunk.

PICKERING: We are, slightly. Are there any letters?

HIGGINS: I didn't look. (PICKERING *takes the overcoats and hats and goes down stairs.* HIGGINS *begins half singing half yawning an air from La Fanciulla del Golden West*[8]. *Suddenly he stops and exclaims*) I wonder where the devil my slippers are!

ELIZA *looks at him darkly; then rises suddenly and leaves the room.*

HIGGINS *yawns again, and resumes his song.*

PICKERING *returns, with the contents of the letter-box in his hand.*

PICKERING: Only circulars[9], and this coroneted billet-doux[10] for you. (*He throws the circulars into the fender, and posts himself on the hearthrug, with his back to the grate*).

HIGGINS: (*glancing at the billet-doux*) Money-lender. (*He throws the letter after the circulars*).

ELIZA *returns with a pair of large down-at-heel slippers. She places them on the carpet before* HIGGINS, *and sits as before without a word.*

HIGGINS: (*yawning again*) Oh Lord! What an evening! What a crew! What a silly tomfoollery[11]! (*He raises his shoe to unlace it, and catches sight of the slippers. He stops unlacing and looks at them as if they had appeared there of their own accord*). Oh! they're there, are they?

PICKERING: (*stretching himself*) Well, I feel a bit tired. It's been a long day. The garden party, a dinner party, and the reception! Rather too much of a good thing. But you've won your bet, Higgins. Eliza did the trick, and something to spare, eh?

HIGGINS: (*fervently*) Thank God it's over!

ELIZA *flinches*[12] *violently; but they take no notice of her; and she recovers herself and sits stonily as before.*

PICKERING: Were you nervous at the garden party? I was. Eliza didn't seem a bit nervous.

HIGGINS: Oh, she wasn't nervous. I knew she'd be all right. No, it's the strain of putting the job through all these months that has told on me. It was interesting enough at first, while we were at the phonetics; but after that I got deadly sick of it. If I hadn't backed myself to do it I should have chucked the whole thing up two months ago. It was a silly notion: the whole thing has been a bore.

PICKERING: Oh come! the garden party was frightfully exciting. My heart began beating like anything.

HIGGINS: Yes, for the first three minutes. But when I saw we were going to win hands down, I felt like a bear in a cage, hanging about doing nothing. The dinner was worse: sitting gorging there for over an hour, with nobody but a damned fool of a fashionable woman to talk to! I tell you, Pickering, never again for me. No more artificial duchesses. The whole thing has been simple purgatory[13].

PICKERING: You've never been broken in properly to the social routine. (*Strolling over to the piano*) I rather enjoy dipping into it occasionally myself: it makes me feel young again. Anyhow, it was a great success: an immense success. I was quite frightened once or twice because Eliza was doing it so well. You see, lots of the real people can't do it at all: they're such fools that they think style comes by nature to people in their position; and so they never learn. There's always something professional about doing a thing superlatively well.

HIGGINS: Yes: that's what drives me mad: the silly people don't know their own silly business. (*Rising*) However, it's over and done with; and now I can go to bed at last without dreading tomorrow.

ELIZA*'s beauty becomes murderous.*

PICKERING: I think I shall turn in too. Still, it's been a great occasion: a triumph for you. Good-night. (*He goes*).

HIGGINS: (*following him*) Good-night. (*Over his shoulder, at the door*) Put out the lights, Eliza; and tell Mrs. Pearce not to make coffee for me in the morning: I'll take tea. (*He goes out*).

ELIZA *tries to control herself and feel indifferent as she rises and walks across to the hearth to switch off the lights. By the time she gets there she is on the point of screaming. She sits down in* HIGGINS*'s chair and holds on hard to the arms. Finally she gives way and flings herself furiously on the floor raging.*

HIGGINS:(*in despairing wrath outside*) What the devil have I done with my slippers? (*He appears at the door*).

ELIZA: (*snatching up the slippers, and hurling them at him one after the other with all her force*) There are your slippers. And there. Take your slippers; and may you never have a day's luck with them!

HIGGINS: (*astounded*) What on earth—! (*He comes to her*). What's the matter? Get up. (*He pulls her up*). Anything wrong?

ELIZA: (*breathless*) Nothing wrong—with you. I've won your bet for you, haven't I? That's enough for you. *I* don't matter, I suppose.

HIGGINS: You won my bet! You! Presumptuous[14] insect! *I* won it. What did you throw those slippers at me for?

ELIZA: Because I wanted to smash your face. I'd like to kill you, you selfish brute. Why didn't you leave me where you picked me out of—in the gutter[15]? You thank God it's all over, and that now you can throw me back again there, do you? (*She crisps her fingers, frantically*).

HIGGINS: (*looking at her in cool wonder*) The creature is nervous, after all.

ELIZA: (*gives a suffocated scream of fury, and instinctively darts her nails at his face*)!!

HIGGINS: (*catching her wrists*) Ah! would you? Claws in, you cat. How dare you show your temper to me? Sit down and be quiet. (*He throws her roughly into the easy-chair*).

ELIZA: (*crushed by superior strength and weight*) What's to become of me? What's to become of me?

HIGGINS: How the devil do I know what's to become of you? What does it matter what becomes of you?

ELIZA: You don't care. I know you don't care. You wouldn't care if I was dead. I'm nothing to you—not so much as them slippers.

HIGGINS: (*thundering*) Those slippers.

ELIZA: (*with bitter submission*) Those slippers. I didn't think it made any difference now.

    A pause. ELIZA *hopeless and crushed.* HIGGINS *a little uneasy.*

HIGGINS: (*in his loftiest manner*) Why have you begun going on like this? May I ask whether you complain of your treatment here?

ELIZA: No.

HIGGINS: Has anybody behaved badly to you? Colonel Pickering? Mrs. Pearce? Any of the servants?

ELIZA: No.

HIGGINS: I presume you don't pretend that I have treated you badly.

ELIZA: No.

HIGGINS: I am glad to hear it. (*He moderates his tone*). Perhaps you're tired after the strain of the day. Will you have a glass of champagne? (*He moves towards the door*).

ELIZA: No. (*recollecting her manners*) Thank you.

HIGGINS: (*good-humored again*) This has been coming on you for some days. I suppose it was natural for you to be anxious about the garden party. But that's all over now. (*He pats her kindly on the shoulder. She writhes*). There's nothing more to worry about.

ELIZA: No. Nothing more for you to worry about. (*She suddenly rises and gets away from him by going to the piano bench, where she sits and hides her face*). Oh God! I wish I was dead.

HIGGINS: (*staring after her in sincere surprise*) Why? In heaven's name, why? (*Reasonably, going to her*) Listen to me, Eliza. All this irritation is purely subjective.

ELIZA: I don't understand. I'm too ignorant.

HIGGINS: It's only imagination. Low spirits and nothing else. Nobody's hurting you. Nothing's wrong. You go to bed like a good girl and sleep it off. Have a little cry and say your prayers: that will make you comfortable.

ELIZA: I heard your prayers. "Thank God it's all over!"

HIGGINS: (*impatiently*) Well, don't you thank God it's all over? Now you are free and can do what you like.

ELIZA: (*pulling herself together in desperation*) What am I fit for? What have you left me fit for? Where am I to go? What am I to do? What's to become of me?

HIGGINS: (*enlightened, but not at all impressed*) Oh, that's what's worrying you, is it? (*He thrusts his hands into his pockets, and walks about in his usual manner, rattling the contents of his pockets, as if condescending[16] to a trivial subject out of pure kindness*). I shouldn't bother about it if I were you. I should imagine you won't have much difficulty in settling yourself, somewhere or other, though I hadn't quite realized that you were going away. (*She looks quickly at him: he does not look at her, but examines the dessert stand on the piano and decides that he will eat an apple*). You might marry, you know. (*He bites a large piece out of the apple, and munches[17] it noisily*). You see, Eliza, all men are not confirmed old bachelors like me and the Colonel. Most men are the marrying sort (poor devils!); and you're not bad-looking; it's quite a pleasure to look at you sometimes—not now, of course, because you're crying and looking as ugly as the very devil; but when you're all right and quite yourself, you're what I should call attractive.

That is, to the people in the marrying line, you understand. You go to bed and have a good nice rest; and then get up and look at yourself in the glass; and you won't feel so cheap.

ELIZA *again looks at him, speechless, and does not stir.*

The look is quite lost on him: he eats his apple with a dreamy expression of happiness, as it is quite a good one.

HIGGINS: (*a genial*[18] *afterthought occurring to him*) I daresay my mother could find some chap or other who would do very well.

ELIZA: We were above that at the corner of Tottenham Court Road.

HIGGINS: (*waking up*) What do you mean?

ELIZA: I sold flowers. I didn't sell myself. Now you've made a lady of me I'm not fit to sell anything else. I wish you'd left me where you found me.

HIGGINS: (*slinging the core of the apple decisively into the grate*) Tosh, Eliza. Don't you insult human relations by dragging all this cant[19] about buying and selling into it. You needn't marry the fellow if you don't like him.

ELIZA: What else am I to do?

HIGGINS: Oh, lots of things. What about your old idea of a florist's shop? Pickering could set you up in one: he has lots of money. (*Chuckling*) He'll have to pay for all those togs[20] you have been wearing today; and that, with the hire of the jewellery, will make a big hole in two hundred pounds. Why, six months ago you would have thought it the millennium to have a flower shop of your own. Come! you'll be all right. I must clear off to bed: I'm devilish sleepy. By the way, I came down for something: I forget what it was.

ELIZA: Your slippers.

HIGGINS: Oh yes, of course. You shied them at me. (*He picks them up, and is going out when she rises and speaks to him*).

ELIZA: Before you go, sir—

HIGGINS: (*dropping the slippers in his surprise at her calling him sir*) Eh?

ELIZA: Do my clothes belong to me or to Colonel Pickering?

HIGGINS: (*coming back into the room as if her question were the very climax of unreason*) What the devil use would they be to Pickering?

ELIZA: He might want them for the next girl you pick up to experiment on.

HIGGINS: (*shocked and hurt*) Is that the way you feel towards us?

ELIZA: I don't want to hear anything more about that. All I want to know is whether anything belongs to me. My own clothes were burnt.

HIGGINS: But what does it matter? Why need you start bothering about that in the middle of the night?

ELIZA: I want to know what I may take away with me. I don't want to be accused of stealing.

HIGGINS: (*now deeply wounded*) Stealing! You shouldn't have said that, Eliza. That shows a want of feeling.

ELIZA: I'm sorry. I'm only a common ignorant girl; and in my station I have to be careful. There can't be any feelings between the like of you and the like of me. Please will you tell me what belongs to me and what doesn't?

HIGGINS: (*very sulky*[21]) You may take the whole damned houseful if you like. Except the jewels. They're hired. Will that satisfy you? (*He turns on his heel and is about to go in extreme dudgeon*[22]).

ELIZA: (*drinking in his emotion like nectar*[23], *and nagging him to provoke a further supply*) Stop, please. (*She takes off her jewels*). Will you take these to your room and keep them safe? I don't want to run the risk of their being missing.

HIGGINS: (*furious*) Hand them over. (*She puts them into his hands*). If these belonged to me instead of to the jeweler, I'd ram them down your ungrateful throat. (*He perfunctorily thrusts them into his pockets, unconsciously decorating himself with the protruding ends of the chains*).

ELIZA: (*taking a ring off*) This ring isn't the jeweler's: it's the one you bought me in Brighton. I don't want it now. (HIGGINS *dashes the ring violently into the fireplace, and turns on her so threateningly that she crouches over the piano with her hands over her face, and exclaims*) Don't you hit me.

HIGGINS: Hit you! You infamous creature, how dare you accuse me of such a thing? It is you who have hit me. You have wounded me to the heart.

ELIZA: (*thrilling with hidden joy*) I'm glad. I've got a little of my own back, anyhow.

HIGGINS: (*with dignity, in his finest professional style*) You have caused me to lose my temper: a thing that has hardly ever happened to me before. I prefer to say nothing more tonight. I am going to bed.

ELIZA: (*pertly*) You'd better leave a note for Mrs. Pearce about the coffee; for she won't be told by me.

HIGGINS: (*formally*) Damn Mrs. Pearce; and damn the coffee; and damn you;

and (*wildly*) damn my own folly in having lavished[24] my hard-earned knowledge and the treasure of my regard and intimacy on a heartless guttersnipe[25]. (*He goes out with impressive decorum*[26], *and spoils it by slamming the door savagely*).

ELIZA *goes down on her knees on the hearthrug to look for the ring. When she finds it she considers for a moment what to do with it. Finally she flings it down on the dessert stand and goes upstairs in a tearing rage.*

Notes

1. **Pygmalion:** a king of Cyprus who carved and then fell in love with a statue of a woman, which Aphrodite brought to life as Galatea.

2. **Higgins:** Henry Higgins, a professor of phonetics

3. **Pickering:** Colonel Pickering, Higgins's friend, who is a linguist of Indian dialects

4. **Mrs. Pearce:** Higgins's housekeeper

5. **Eliza:** Eliza Doolittle, a cockney speaking Covent Garden flower girl

6. **pallor:** extreme or unnatural paleness

7. **banisters:** one of the vertical supports of a handrail on a staircase

8. **La Fanciulla del Golden West:** *The Girl of the Golden West*, an opera in three acts by Italian composer Giacomo Puccini (1858—1924).

9. **circulars:** a printed advertisement, directive, or notice intended for mass distribution

10. **coroneted billet-doux:** a love letter decorated with a crown

11. **tomfoolery:** foolish behavior

12. **flinches:** to recoil, as from something unpleasant or difficult

13. **purgatory:** a place or condition of suffering, expiation, or remorse

14. **presumptuous:** going beyond what is right or proper; excessively forward

15. **gutter:** a degraded and squalid class or state of human existence

16. **condescending:** to descend to the level of one considered inferior; lower oneself

17. **munches:** to eat with pleasure; to chew food audibly or with a steady working of the jaws

18. **genial:** having a pleasant or friendly disposition or manner; cordial and kindly

19. **cant:** monotonous talk filled with platitudes; hypocritically pious language

20. **togs:** coat or cloak

21. **sulky:** sullenly aloof or withdrawn; gloomy; dismal

22. **dudgeon:** a sullen, angry, or indignant humor

23. **nectar:** the drink of the gods in Greek and Roman mythology

24. **lavished:** to give or bestow in abundance

25. **guttersnipe:** a person of the lowest class

26. **decorum:** appropriateness of behavior or conduct; the conventions of polite behavior

Questions for Study and Discussion

1. What is the legend of Pygmalion in Greek mythology? In what significant ways and with what effect has Shaw transformed the myth in this play?

2. Do you agree to the point that Pygmalion is not a play about turning a flower girl into a lady, but one about turning a woman into a human being? If your answer is yes, can you give us your reasons?

3. Describe the primary ways in which Eliza Doolittle changes in the course of the play. What is the most important transformation of her?

4. According to the act, what do Higgins and Pickering talk about when they get home? Do they pay attention to Eliza's feelings?

5. When Higgins looks for his slippers, Eliza flings the slippers in his face and complains that she means no more to him than his slippers. What does she mean? Can you make out the implications of her complaints?

6. Higgins says to Eliza, "Now you are free and can do what you like." Is Eliza really free?

7. What is Higgins's attitude towards Eliza according to their conversation?

8. Why does Eliza think getting married is to sell herself?

Edward Morgan Forster (1879—1970)

Life and Major Works

Edward Morgan Forster was born on 1 January 1879 in London. His father was an architect, who died soon after his son was born. Raised by his mother, aunts, and governesses, he spent his happy childhood at Rooksnest that he later evoked in the novel *Howards End* (1910). In 1893 Forster and his mother moved to Tonbridge, and he attended the Tonbridge School in Kent County. In 1897 he went to King's College, Cambridge to study history, philosophy and literature. At the college, Forster found congenial friends and blossomed under the atmosphere of intellectual freedom. He joined the Cambridge Apostles and met many lifelong friends. Through these friends, Forster was later drawn into closer contact with the Bloomsbury Group, a literary group that revolted against the artistic, social and

Edward Morgan Forster

sexual restrictions of Victorian society. After his graduation from the college in 1901, Forster chose to travel widely. A year of travel in Italy and a cruise to Greece provided rich materials for his early novels. On his return from Greece, he started his career as a journalist to write for the new *Independent Review*, launched in 1903 by a group of Cambridge friends.

Forster's first novel, *Where Angel Fear to Tread* (1905), was published in 1905. The title of the book is taken from the proverb: "Fools rush in where angels fear to tread." As an attack on the hypocritical middle classes in England, the novel is a tragic-comedy describing the consequences of the marriage of Lilia Herriton, an impulsive young widow, to the son of an Italian dentist, Gino Carella. In 1907 *The Longest Journey* (1907) appeared. In this novel, E. M. Forster explored the "idea of England" that he would later develop in *Howards End*. The third novel *A Room with a View* (1908) was published in 1908. It is a witty observation of the English middle classes as a social comedy in which Forster stressed the importance of harmony and understanding in interpersonal relationships.

Howards End (1910) is the most outstanding one of the 4 early novels by E.M. Forster, dealing with personal relationships and conflicting values. The story centers on three groups in England: the Wilcoxes who represent the upper class with their affected genteelness, the Schlegels who stand for petit-bourgeois intellectuals with their compassionate inclination, and the Basts who are poor with the lower social status. The Schlegels sisters Margaret and Helen get acquainted with the Wilcoxes.

In 1912—1913, Forster paid his first visit to India for some months. In 1921—1922, he revisited India, working as a personal secretary for the maharajah of the native state of Dewas Senior for several months. The two trips to India were responsible for the completion of Forster's last but the greatest novel, *A Passage to India* (1924). When the novel was published in 1924, it was highly acclaimed. It is a picture of society in India under the British rule, of the clash between East and West, and of the bias and misunderstandings between the English colonizer and the Indian colonized. Standing in the canon of English literature as one of the great discussions about colonialism, the novel shows Forster as an excellent stylist and a perceptive, acute observer of human nature.

In addition to the 5 novels discussed above, Forster also wrote many short stories that were published in three collections—*The Celestial Omnibus* (1911), *The Eternal Moment* (1928) and *The Life to Come* (1972). Deeply influenced by Greek mythology, his short stories are whimsical by dealing with the supernatural themes. In 1927 Forster delivered a series of Clark Lectures at Cambridge University, which were collected and published in the same year under the title of *Aspects of the Novel* (1927). The book discusses aspects that all English novels have in common: story, people, plot, fantasy, prophecy, pattern, and rhythm. His lively, informed originality and wit have made this book a classic on the theory of fiction. Forster spent his last years in King's College and was given Queen Elizabeth's Order of Merit in 1969. At the age of 90, he died at the home in Coventry on 7 June 1970.

Forster's style is marked by his sympathy for his characters, his ability to see more than one side of an argument or story, and his fondness for simple, symbolic tales. Blending tradition with innovation, he has made great contributions to the bloom of the modernist novels. In this regard, Forster is one of the finest English novelists in the 20th century.

Brief Introduction and Appreciation

A Passage to India (1924) was the last full-length novel written by E.M. Forster, and it was immediately acclaimed as his masterpiece upon its publication. Forster took the title of the book from Walt Whitman's poem *Passage to India* (1871) in which Whitman praised the completion of the Suez Canal, the laying of the Atlantic cable and the finishing of the transcontinental railroad. Different from the poem to celebrate the related themes of scientific and technological achievement and spiritual transformation, Forster's novel examines the racial misunderstandings and cultural hypocrisies that lead to the inevitable conflicts between the Indians and the English, East and West.

The story is told in 3 parts: *Mosque*, *Caves* and *Temple*. Two Englishwomen, Mrs. Moore and Miss Adela Quested travel to India. Adela expects to become engaged to Mrs. Moore's son, Ronny, a British magistrate in the Indian city of Chandrapore. Mrs. Moore happens to meet Aziz, a young Indian Muslim doctor, at a local mosque, and they soon become friends. Aziz organizes an expedition for the visitors to the nearby Marabar Caves.

In the second part of the book, as Aziz accompanies the two ladies inside one of the caves, Mrs. Moore is unnerved by the enclosed space and by the uncanny echo. Aziz, Adela, and a guide go on to the higher caves while Mrs. Moore waits below. Adela suddenly has a hallucination of being insulted by someone in the cave, and she rushes down alone. Back in Chandrapore, however, Aziz is unexpectedly arrested, being charged with attempting to rape Adela. As the trial approaches, the racial tensions between the Indians and the English flare up considerably. Aziz's friend Fielding, who is the only Englishman to believe Aziz to be innocent, angers all of British in India by joining the Indians in Aziz's defense. Ronny sends Mrs. Moore to England earlier than planned. She dies on the voyage back to England, but not before she realizes that there is no "real India"—but rather a complex multitude of different Indias. Adela suffers from mental shocks and occasionally doubts her own testimony against Aziz. At the trial, she is asked what happened in the caves. Shockingly, she declares that she has made a mistake and withdraws her charge. Aziz is set free eventually, but he turns furiously away from the British. Ronny breaks off his engagement to Adela, and she returns to England.

In the third part of the novel, Aziz has become the chief doctor two years later. He is visited by Mr. Fielding, the former principal of the Government College. They discuss the future of India, and Aziz tells Fielding that only when the British are driven out can he and Fielding really be friends.

A Passage to India is significant for its social and historical meanings. It begins and ends by posing the question of whether it is possible for an Englishman and an Indian to be friends. Using this question as a framework of the novel, Forster explores the clashes and misunderstandings between the English colonizer and the Indian colonized. In the first part *Mosque*, Forster depicts the antagonism and hostility between the British and the Indians in a tentative way. In the second part *Caves*, the inherent antagonism culminates in Adela's accusation of Aziz and her subsequent disavowal of this accusation at the trial. The racial tension between the British and the Indians seems to be irreconcilable, because the different tendencies of their cultures pull them apart. Thereafter Aziz and Fielding's friendship falls apart. In the third part *Temple*, Forster iterates his view via Aziz that the English-Indian friendship is very difficult to maintain, at least within the context of British colonialism. Forster's final vision of the possibility of English-Indian friendship is a pessimistic one, yet it is qualified by the possibility of friendship after the liberation of India.

Forster is famous for his style of symbolism that neatly encapsulates large-scale problems and conditions. The tendency is very evident in *A Passage to India*. A good case in point is the Marabar Caves, which represent all that is alien about nature. The cave's mysterious power and alien quality unsettle the visitors. The uncanny echo, the suffocating air and the enclosed space in the caves lead to Mrs. Moore's discomfort and Adela's hallucination. People are deprived of reason and sense in the caves. What happened in the Marabar Caves symbolizes that the possibility of English-Indian friendship only turns out to be a reverie. In addition to the symbolic meaning of the caves, the mosque in Part I and temple in Part III are meaningful as well. Standing for the promise of Indian openness, mysticism and friendship, the mosque and the temple play very important roles in the book.

The following excerpt comes from Chapter 24 of the novel. It depicts a climactic scene of the trial in which Aziz is accused of attempted rape by Adela, but Adela withdraws the accusation eventually and Aziz is innocent of the charge. With humor and satire, the trial scene is extremely dramatic in the few utterances of Adela that clearly show her character and create the surprising elements for the plot progress. So the trial scene is beyond all doubts the most remarkable and wittiest part in the novel.

Selected Reading

A Passage to India

(An Excerpt from Chapter 24)

While the prosecution continued, Miss Quested[1] examined the hall—timidly at first, as though it would scorch her eyes. She observed to left and right of the punkah[2] man many a half-known face. Beneath her were gathered all the wreckage of her silly attempt to see India—the people she had met at the Bridge Party, the man and his wife who hadn't sent their carriage, the old man who would lend his car, various servants, villagers, officials, and the prisoner himself. There he sat—strong, neat little Indian with very black hair, and pliant bands. She viewed him without special emotion. Since they last met, she had elevated him into a principle of evil, but now he seemed to be what he had always been—a slight acquaintance. He was negligible, devoid of significance, dry like a bone, and though he was "guilty" no atmosphere of sin surrounded him. "I suppose he is guilty. Can I possibly have made a mistake?" she thought. For this question still occurred to her intellect, though since Mrs. Moore[3]'s departure it had ceased to trouble her conscience.

Pleader Mahmoud Ali[4] now arose, and asked with ponderous[5] and ill-judged irony whether his client could be accommodated on the platform too: even Indians felt unwell sometimes, though naturally Major Callendar[6] did not think so, being in charge of a Government Hospital. "Another example of their exquisite sense of humour," sang Miss Derek[7]. Ronny[8] looked at Mr. Das[9] to see how he would handle the difficulty, and Mr. Das became agitated, and snubbed Pleader Mahmoud Ali severely.

"Excuse me—" It was the turn of the eminent barrister[10] from Calcutta[11]. He was a fine-looking man, large and bony, with grey closely cropped hair. "We object to the presence of so many European ladies and gentlemen upon the platform," he said in an Oxford voice. "They will have the effect of intimidating our witnesses. Their place is with the rest of the public in the body of the hall. We have no objection to Miss Quested remaining on the platform, since she has been unwell; we shall extend every courtesy to her throughout, despite the scientific truths revealed to us by the District Superintendent of Police; but we do object to the others."

"Oh, cut the cackle and let's have the verdict," the Major growled.

The distinguished visitor gazed at the Magistrate respectfully.

"I agree to that," said Mr. Das, hiding his face desperately in some papers. "It was only to Miss Quested that I gave permission to sit up here. Her friends should be so excessively kind as to climb down."

"Well done, Das, quite sound," said Ronny with devastating honesty.

"Climb down, indeed, what incredible impertinence!" Mrs. Turton[12] cried.

"Do come quietly, Mary," murmured her husband.

"Hi! my patient can't be left unattended."

"Do you object to the Civil Surgeon remaining, Mr. Amritrao[13]?"

"I should object. A platform confers authority."

"Even when it's one foot high; so come along all," said the Collector, trying to laugh.

"Thank you very much, sir," said Mr. Das, greatly relieved. "Thank you, Mr. Heaslop; thank you, ladies all."

And the party, including Miss Quested, descended from its rash eminence. The news of their humiliation spread quickly, and people jeered outside. Their special chairs followed them. Mahmoud Ali (who was quite silly and useless with hatred) objected even to these; by whose authority had special chairs been introduced, why had the Nawab Bahadur[14] not been given one? etc. People began to talk all over the room, about chairs ordinary and special, strips of carpet, platforms one foot high.

But the little excursion had a good effect on Miss Quested's nerves. She felt easier now that she had seen all the people who were in the room. It was like knowing the worst. She was sure now that she should come through "all right"—that is to say, without spiritual disgrace, and she passed the good news on to Ronny and Mrs. Turton. They were too much agitated with the defeat to British prestige to be interested. From where she sat, she could see the renegade Mr. Fielding[15]. She had had a better view of him from the platform, and knew that an Indian child perched on his knee. He was watching the proceedings, watching her. When their eyes met, he turned his away, as if direct intercourse was of no interest to him.

The Magistrate was also happier. He had won the battle of the platform, and gained confidence. Intelligent and impartial, he continued to listen to the evidence, and tried to forget that later on he should have to pronounce a verdict in accordance with it. The Superintendent trundled steadily forward:

he had expected these outbursts of insolence—they are the natural gestures of an inferior race, and he betrayed no hatred of Aziz[16], merely an abysmal contempt.

The speech dealt at length with the "prisoner's dupes", as they were called—Fielding, the servant Antony, the Nawab Bahadur. This aspect of the case had always seemed dubious[17] to Miss Quested, and she had asked the police not to develop it. But they were playing for a heavy sentence, and wanted to prove that the assault was premeditated. And in order to illustrate the strategy, they produced a plan of the Marabar Hills, showing the route that the party had taken, and the "Tank of the Dagger" where they had camped.

The Magistrate displayed interest in archaeology.

An elevation of a specimen cave was produced; it was lettered "Buddhist Cave".

"Not Buddhist, I think, Jain[18]..."

"In which cave is the offence alleged, the Buddhist or the Jain?" asked Mahmoud Ali, with the air of unmasking a conspiracy.

"All the Marabar caves are Jain."

"Yes, sir; then in which Jain cave?"

"You will have an opportunity of putting such questions later."

Mr. McBryde[19] smiled faintly at their fatuity[20]. Indians invariably collapse over some such point as this. He knew that the defence had some wild hope of establishing an alibi[21], that they had tried (unsuccessfully) to identify the guide, and that Fielding and Hamidullah[22] had gone out to the Kawa Dol[23] and paced and measured all one moonlit night. "Mr. Lesley says they're Buddhist, and he ought to know if anyone does. But may I call attention to the shape?" And he described what had occurred there. Then he spoke of Miss Derek's arrival, of the scramble down the gully, of the return of the two ladies to Chandrapore, and of the document Miss Quested signed on her arrival, in which mention was made of the field glasses. And then came the culminating evidence: the discovery of the field-glasses on the prisoner. "I have nothing to add at present," he concluded, removing his spectacles. "I will now call my witnesses. The facts will speak for themselves. The prisoner is one of those individuals who have led a double life. I dare say his degeneracy gained upon him gradually. He has been very cunning at concealing, as is usual with the type, and pretending to be a respectable member of society, getting a

Government position even. He is now entirely vicious and beyond redemption, I am afraid. He behaved most cruelly, most brutally, to another of his guests, another English lady. In order to get rid of her, and leave him free for his crime, he crushed her into a cave among his servants. However, that is by the way."

But his last words brought on another storm, and suddenly a new name, Mrs. Moore, burst on the court like a whirlwind. Mahmoud Ali had been enraged, his nerves snapped; he shrieked like a maniac, and asked whether his client was charged with murder as well as rape, and who was this second English lady.

"I don't propose to call her."

"You don't because you can't, you have smuggled her out of the country; she is Mrs. Moore, she would have proved his innocence, she was on our side, she was poor Indians' friend."

"You could have called her yourself," cried the Magistrate. "Neither side called her, neither must quote her as evidence."

"She was kept from us until too late—I learn too late—this is English justice, here is your British Raj[24]. Give us back Mrs. Moore for five minutes only, and she will save my friend, she will save the name of his sons; don't rule her out, Mr. Das; take back those words as you yourself are a father; tell me where they have put her; oh, Mrs. Moore..."

"If the point is of any interest, my mother should have reached Aden," said Ronny dryly; he ought not to have intervened, but the onslaught had startled him.

"Imprisoned by you there because she knew the truth." He was almost out of his mind, and could be heard saying above the tumult: "I ruin my career, no matter; we are all to be ruined one by one."

"This is no way to defend your case," counselled the Magistrate.

"I am not defending a case, nor are you trying one. We are both of us slaves."

"Mr. Mahnioud Ali, I have already warned you, and unless you sit down I shall exercise my authority."

"Do so; this trial is a farce, I am going." And he handed his papers to Amritrao and left, calling from the door histrionically yet with intense passion, "Aziz, Aziz—farewell for ever." The tumult increased, the invocation[25] of Mrs.

Moore continued, and people who did not know what the syllables meant repeated them like a charm. They became Indianized into Esmiss Esmoor, they were taken up in the street outside. In vain the Magistrate threatened and expelled. Until the magic exhausted itself, he was powerless.

"Unexpected," remarked Mr. Turton.

Ronny furnished the explanation. Before she sailed, his mother had taken to talk about the Marabar in her sleep, especially in the afternoon when servants were on the veranda[26], and her disjointed remarks on Aziz had doubtless been sold to Mahmoud Ali for a few annas: that kind of thing never ceases in the East.

"I thought they'd try something of the sort. Ingenious." He looked into their wide-open mouths. "They get just like that over their religion," he added calmly. "Start and can't stop. I'm sorry for your old Das, he's not getting much of a show."

"Mr. Heaslop, how disgraceful dragging in your dear mother," said Miss Derek, bending forward.

"It's just a trick, and they happened to pull it off. Now one sees why they had Mahmoud Ali—just to make a scene on the chance. It is his specialty." But he disliked it more than he showed. It was revolting to hear his mother travestied into Esmiss Esmoor, a Hindu goddess.

> "Esmiss Esmoor
> Esmiss Esmoor
> Esmiss Esmoor
> Esmiss Esmoor. ..."

"Ronny—"

"Yes, old girl?"

"Isn't it all queer."

"I'm afraid it's very upsetting for you."

"Not the least. I don't mind it."

"Well, that's good."

She had spoken more naturally and healthily than usual. Bending into the middle of her friends, she said: "Don't worry about me, I'm much better than I was; I don't feel the least faint; I shall be all right, and thank you all, thank you, thank you for your kindness." She had to shout her gratitude, for the chant, Esmiss Esmoor, went on.

Suddenly it stopped. It was as if the prayer had been heard, and the relics exhibited. "I apologize for my colleague," said Mr. Amritrao, rather to everyone's surprise. "He is an intimate friend of our client, and his feelings have carried him away."

"Mr. Mahmoud Ali will have to apologize in person," the Magistrate said.

"Exactly, sir, he must. But we had just learnt that Mrs. Moore had important evidence which she desired to give. She was hurried out of the country by her son before she could give it; and this unhinged Mr. Mahmoud Ali—coming as it does upon an attempt to intimidate our only other European witness, Mr. Fielding. Mr. Mahmoud Ali would have said nothing had not Mrs. Moore been claimed as a witness by the police." He sat down.

"An extraneous element is being introduced into the case," said the Magistrate. "I must repeat that as a witness Mrs. Moore does not exist. Neither you, Mr. Amritrao, nor, Mr. McBryde, you, have any right to surmise what that lady would have said. She is not here, and consequently she can say nothing."

"Well, I withdraw my reference," said the Superintendent wearily. "I would have done so fifteen minutes ago if I had been given the chance. She is not of the least importance to me."

"I have already withdrawn it for the defence." He added with forensic[27] humour: "Perhaps you can persuade the gentlemen outside to withdraw it too," for the refrain in the street continued.

"I am afraid my powers do not extend so far," said Das, smiling.

So peace was restored, and when Adela came to give her evidence the atmosphere was quieter than it had been since the beginning of the trial. Experts were not surprised. There is no stay in your native. He blazes up[28] over a minor point, and has nothing left for the crisis. What be seeks is a grievance, and this he had found in the supposed abduction of an old lady. He would now be less aggrieved when Aziz was deported.

But the crisis was still to come.

Adela had always meant to tell the truth and nothing but the truth, and she had rehearsed this as a difficult task—difficult, because her disaster in the cave was connected, though by a thread, with another part of her life, her engagement to Ronny. She had thought of love just before she went in, and had innocently asked Aziz what marriage was like, and she supposed that her question had roused evil in him. To recount this would have been incredibly painful, it was the one point she wanted to keep obscure; she was willing to give details that would have distressed other girls, but this story of her private failure she dared not allude to, and she dreaded being examined in public in case something came out. But as soon as she rose to reply, and heard the sound of her own voice, she feared not even that. A new and unknown sensation protected her, like magnificent armour. She didn't think what had happened or even remember in the ordinary way of memory, but she returned to the Marabar Hills, and spoke from them across a sort of darkness to Mr. McBryde. The fatal day recurred, in every detail, but now she was of it and not of it at the same time, and this double relation gave it indescribable splendour. Why had she thought the expedition "dull"? Now the sun rose again, the elephant waited, the pale masses of the rock flowed round her and presented the first cave; she entered, and a match was reflected in the polished walls—all beautiful and significant, though she had been blind to it at the time. Questions were asked, and to each she found the exact reply; yes, she had noticed the "Tank of the Dagger," but not known its name; yes, Mrs. Moore had been tired after the first cave and sat in the shadow of a great rock, near the dried-up mud. Smoothly the voice in the distance proceeded, leading along the paths of truth, and the airs from the punkah behind her wafted her on...

"... the prisoner and the guide took you on to the Kawa Dol, no one else being present?"

"The most wonderfully shaped of those hills. Yes." As she spoke, she created the Kawa Dol, saw the niches up the curve of the stone, and felt the heat strike her face. And something caused her to add: "No one else was present to my knowledge. We appeared to be alone."

"Very well, there is a ledge half-way up the hill, or broken ground rather, with caves scattered near the beginning of a nullah[29]."

"I know where you mean."

"You went alone into one of those caves?"

"That is quite correct."

"And the prisoner followed you."

"Now we've got'im," from the Major.

She was silent. The court, the place of question, awaited her reply. But she could not give it until Aziz entered the place of answer.

"The prisoner followed you, didn't he?" he repeated in the monotonous tones that they both used; they were employing agreed words throughout, so that this part of the proceedings held no surprises.

"May I have half a minute before I reply to that, Mr. McBryde?"

"Certainly."

Her vision was of several caves. She saw herself in one, and she was also outside it, watching its entrance, for Aziz to pass in. She failed to locate him. It was the doubt that had often visited her, but solid and attractive, like the hills, "I am not—" Speech was more difficult than vision. "I am not quite sure."

"I beg your pardon?" said the Superintendent of Police.

"I cannot be sure ..."

"I didn't catch that answer." He looked scared, his mouth shut with a snap. "You are on that landing, or whatever we term it, and you have entered a cave. I suggest to you that the prisoner followed you."

She shook her head.

"What do you mean, please?"

"No," she said in a flat, unattractive voice. Slight noises began in various parts of the room, but no one yet understood what was occurring except Fielding. He saw that she was going to have a nervous breakdown and that his friend was saved.

"What is that, what are you saying? Speak up, please." The Magistrate bent forward.

"I'm afraid I have made a mistake."

"What nature of mistake?"

"Dr. Aziz never followed me into the cave."

The Superintendent slammed down his papers, then picked them up and said calmly: "Now, Miss Quested, let us go on. I will read you the words of the deposition which you signed two hours later in my bungalow[30]."

"Excuse me, Mr. McBryde, you cannot go on. I am speaking to the witness myself. And the public will be silent. If it continues to talk, I have the court cleared. Miss Quested, address your remarks to me, who am the Magistrate in charge of the case, and realize their extreme gravity. Remember you speak on oath, Miss Quested."

"Dr. Aziz never—"

"I stop these proceedings on medical grounds," cried the Major on a word from Turton[31], and all the English rose from their chairs at once, large white figures behind which the little magistrate was hidden. The Indians rose too, hundreds of things went on at once, so that afterwards each person gave a different account of the catastrophe.

"You withdraw the charge? Answer me," shrieked the representative of Justice.

Something that she did not understand took hold of the girl and pulled her through. Though the vision was over, and she had returned to the insipidity[32] of the world, she remembered what she had learnt. Atonement and confession—they could wait. It was in hard prosaic tones that she said, "I withdraw everything."

"Enough—sit down. Mr. McBryde, do you wish to continue in the face of this?"

The Superintendent gazed at his witness as if she was a broken machine, and said, "Are you mad?"

"Don't question her, sir; you have no longer the right."

"Give me time to consider—"

"Sahib[33], you will have to withdraw; this becomes a scandal," boomed the Nawab Bahadur suddenly from the back of the court.

"He shall not," shouted Mrs. Turton against the gathering tumult. "Call the other witnesses; we're none of us safe—" Ronny tried to check her, and she gave him an irritable blow, then screamed insults at Adela.

The Superintendent moved to the support of his friends, saying nonchalantly[34] to the Magistrate as he did so, "Right, I withdraw."

Mr. Das rose, nearly dead with the strain. He had controlled the case, just controlled it. He had shown that an Indian can preside. To those who could hear him he said, "The prisoner is released without one stain on his character; the question of costs will be decided elsewhere."

And then the flimsy framework of the court broke up, the shouts of derision and rage culminated, people screamed and cursed, kissed one another, wept passionately. Here were the English, whom their servants protected, there Aziz fainted in Hamidullah's arms. Victory on this side, defeat on that—complete for one moment was the antithesis[35]. Then life returned to its complexities, person after person struggled out of the room to their various purposes, and before long no one remained on the scene of the fantasy but the beautiful naked god. Unaware that anything unusual had occurred, he continued to pull the cord of his punkah, to gaze at the empty dais[36] and the overturned special chairs, and rhythmically to agitate the clouds of descending dust.

Notes

1. **Miss Quested:** Adela Quested, a heroine in the novel, who is a young, intelligent, but somewhat repressed Englishwoman. Adela travels to India with Mrs. Moore in order to decide whether or not to marry Mrs. Moore's son Ronny.
2. **punkah:** a large cloth fan used in India on a frame suspended from the ceiling, moved backwards and forwards by pulling on a cord.
3. **Mrs. Moore:** an elderly Englishwoman who voyages to India with Adela Quested to see her son Ronny Heaslop.
4. **Mahmoud Ali:** a lawyer friend of Dr. Aziz who is deeply pessimistic about the English.
5. **ponderous:** lacking grace or fluency; labored and dull
6. **Major Callendar:** the civil surgeon at Chandrapore, Dr. Aziz's superior.
7. **Miss Derek:** a young Englishwoman who works for a wealthy Indian family and often steals their car.
8. **Ronny:** Ronny Heaslop, Mrs. Moore's son, who is the magistrate at Chandrapore. He has become prejudiced and intolerant of Indians ever since he moved to India.
9. **Mr. Das:** Ronny's assistant, who is the judge presiding over the trial of Aziz.
10. **barrister:** a lawyer admitted to plead at the bar in the superior courts.
11. **Calcutta:** a city of eastern India on the Hooghly River in the Ganges delta. It is India's largest city and a major port and industrial center.
12. **Mrs. Turton:** Turton's wife, who embodies a stereotype of the snobby, rude, and prejudiced English colonial wife in the novel.
13. **Mr. Amritrao:** the lawyer who defends Aziz at his trial. Amritrao is a highly anti-British man.
14. **the Nawab Bahadur:** a distinguished local resident in Chandrapore. He is wealthy, generous, and faithful to the English, but he gives up his title after Aziz's trial.
15. **Mr. Fielding:** Cyril Fielding, the principal of the government college near Chandrapore. He befriends Dr. Aziz, taking the doctor's side against the

rest of the English in Chandrapore when Aziz is accused of attempting to rape Adela Quested.

16. **Aziz:** an intelligent, emotional Indian doctor in Chandrapore, who is charged with attempted rape after an expedition to the Marabar Caves.

17. **dubious:** fraught with uncertainty or doubt; undecided

18. **Jain:** intermediate sect between Brahminism and Buddhism. Jina founded this ascetic, monastic sect in the 6th century B.C.

19. **Mr. McBryde:** the superintendent of police in Chandrapore

20. **fatuity:** something that is utterly stupid or silly

21. **alibi:** a form of defense whereby a defendant attempts to prove that he or she was elsewhere when the crime in question was committed.

22. **Hamidullah:** Dr. Aziz's uncle and friend. He was a close friend of Fielding before Fielding and Aziz met.

23. **the Kawa Dol:** a Jain cave

24. **Raj:** rule, sovereignty, the fact of British rule in India

25. **invocation:** a prayer or other formula used in invoking, as at the opening of a religious service.

26. **veranda:** a porch or balcony, usually roofed and often partly enclosed, extending along the outside of a building.

27. **forensic:** appropriate for courts of law or for public discussion or argumentation.

28. **blazes up:** to flare up suddenly; to rouse to impatience or anger

29. **nullah:** a dry river bed or ravine in India

30. **bungalow:** a thatched or tiled one-story house in India surrounded by a wide verandah

31. **Turton:** the collector, the man who governs Chandrapore

32. **insipidity:** something not attractive and not interesting

33. **sahib:** used formerly as a form of respectful address for a European man in colonial India

34. **nonchalantly:** coldly and indifferently

35. **antithesis:** direct contrast; opposition

36. **dais:** a raised platform, as in a lecture hall, for speakers or honored guests.

Questions for Study and Discussion

1. What is Forster's primary critique of the English in India?

2. From the outset, what do Adela and Mrs. Moore hope to get out of their visit to India?

3. What is the Englishmen's attitude towards the Indians in the novel?

4. Why does Adela accuse Aziz?

5. What qualities enable Adela to withdraw her charge at the trial finally?

6. What do you think of Adela Quested as an Englishwoman? In what ways is she different from other English people in India?

7. According to the excerpt of the trial, how does Forster portray the relationship between the British and the Indians?

8. Whether is it possible for an Englishman and an Indian to ever be friends? Why or why not?

9. What is the symbolic meaning of the Marabar Caves?

David Herbert Lawrence (1885—1930)

Life and Major Works

David Herbert Lawrence was born on 11 September 1885 at Eastwood, Nottinghamshire in central England. His father was a coal miner who was a heavy drinker, and his mother was an ex-schoolteacher, better educated than her husband. Lawrence's childhood was dominated by poverty and friction between his parents. His ill-suited parents quarreled continually, and a passionate bond grew between Lawrence and his mother. His love for his mother had a crucial influence on his early life and work, which is

David Herbert Lawrence

reflected in his closely autobiographic novel *Sons and Lovers* (1913). Lawrence attended Nottingham High School with the help of a scholarship. Then he worked as a clerk in a surgical goods factory and then became a pupil-teacher. In 1906 he studied at Nottingham University College where he obtained a teacher's certificate two years later.

Lawrence's first published work was a series of his early poems, which appeared in the *English Review* in 1909. A year later his early short story was published by the same periodical. In 1911 his first novel *The White Peacock* (1911) came out. Focusing on human relationships, the novel explores man's alienation from the natural world. His second novel *The Trespasser* (1912) was published in the next year. Based on the tragic love affair of Lawrence's friend Helen Corke and her violin teacher, the novel elaborates the theme of the tense relations between men and women.

In 1912 Lawrence met and fell in love with Frieda von Richthofen, the German wife of professor Ernest Weekley. They eloped to Bavaria and then continued to Austria, Germany and Italy. In 1913 appeared Larwence's first important novel *Sons and Lovers* (1913), which marked the beginning of his literary reputation. As a compelling portrayal of childhood, adolescence and the clash of generations, *Sons and Lovers* ranks a milestone of modern fiction in English literature.

In 1914 Lawrence married Frieda von Richthofen, and they were always on the move. Lawrence's nomadic life supplied him with material for much of his writing and he wrote four travel books including *Twilight in Italy* (1916), *Sea and Sardinia* (1912), *Mornings in Mexico* (1927) and *Etruscan Places* (1932).

Lawrence spent the war years in England and began to form friendships in literary and intellectual circles. In 1915 *The Rainbow* (1915) was published. Covering the pre–World War I period from about 1840 to 1905, the novel explores the relationships between three generations in the Brangwen family, describing the English society from the Victorian period to the modern period. The book is remarkable for the superb, complex characterizations with resonance, clarity, maturity and finesse. However, due to Lawrence's frankness about sex, *The Rainbow* is a controversial novel seized by the police and declared obscene.

In 1916 Lawrence finished his novel *Women in Love*, but he was unable to find a publisher until 1920 in New York. As the sequel to *The Rainbow* (1915), *Women in Love* is more powerful by further exploring the personal and social traumas in the wake of industrialization and urbanization. Dealing with a complex story about the love affairs of the four characters, the novel projects the tumult of post-war England and probes into the man-woman relationship against the somber social background. *Women in Love* is often regarded as Lawrence's greatest novel.

Lawrence expressed his anxiety over the post-war England in his late works. *The Lost Girl* (1920) was started in 1913 and published in 1920. It won the James Tait Black Memorial Prize, the only official honor that Lawrence was to receive in his lifetime. *Aaron's Rod* (1922), which shows the influence of Nietzsche, followed in 1922. In the same year Lawrence began his serious travels to Ceylon, Australia, America and finally to Mexico. Based on his visit to Australia, *Kangaroo* (1923) is a novel describing the political activities in Sydney. While in Mexico, Lawrence began to work on *The Plumed Serpent* (1926), a novel fraught with the violent actions, the religious rituals and myths.

Lawrence's last novel, *Lady Chatterley's Lover* (1928) roused more furor than his any other works. It was privately printed in Florence in 1928 and was finally published in unabridged editions in United States. Due to the prosecution for its obscenity, however, the novel did not come out in England until 1960 when Penguin Books took the risk of producing a complete text. It tells of the love affair between a wealthy, married woman and a man who works on her husband's estate. Lawrence's detailed description of sexual union makes the novel controversial. He believed that without a realization of sex and the body, the mind wanders aimlessly in the wasteland of modern industrial technology. In this novel Lawrence reflected upon the dehumanizing effect of mechanism and industrialism. An important recognition in *Lady Chatterley's Lover* is the extent to which the modern relationship between men and women comes to resemble the relationship between men and machines.

As a prolific writer, Lawrence's output covers novels, short stories, poems, plays, essays, travel books, paintings, translations, literary criticism and personal letters. Other non-fiction works include *Movements in European History* (1921), *Psychoanalysis and the Unconscious* (1921), *Fantasia of the Unconscious* (1922), *Studies in Classic American Literature* (1923) and *Apocalypse* (1931).

Lawrence died in Vence, France on March 2, 1930. His wife moved to the Kiowa Ranch and built a small memorial chapel where his ashes lie there. Regarded as one of the modernists among the writers in the early 20th century England, D. H. Lawrence combined social criticism with psychological exploration in his writing. Attacking on the doorstep of technology and the class system, he believed that modern industry had deprived people of individuality, making them cogs in the industrial machine, a machine driven by greed. With a bold exploration of the relations between sexes, he wanted to revive an awareness of savage sensuality in the human consciousness to free men from their enslavement. In this sense, Lawrence is an important and controversial English writer of the 20th century.

Brief Introduction and Appreciation

Set in the Nottinghamshire coalmining village of Bestwood, *Sons and Loves* (1913) is a closely autobiographic novel. It is a brilliant evocation of life in a working class mining community.

Walter Morel, a coal miner, has married a sensitive and high-minded woman Gertrude Coppard. Disappointed at her unhappy marriage, Mrs. Morel estranges herself from her husband and turns all her love towards her four children, especially the two eldest sons William and Paul. She is resolved that her boys will not become miners, so she struggles with the poverty and meanness to keep herself and her family respectable. William goes to London to work as a clerk, and Paul also gets a job as a clerk with Mr. Jordon, a manufacturer of surgical appliance. Mrs. Morel feels very upset when her boys move away from the family. William unfortunately develops pneumonia and dies a few years later. Numbed by despair, Mrs. Morel is crushed, not even noticing the rest of her children. She is roused only when her second son Paul also falls ill. She spares no efforts to nurse Paul, and subsequently their attachment deepens. From that point on, Paul becomes the focus of her life.

Paul is befriended by the Leivers family of Willey Farm, and he falls in love with the daughter Miriam. They carry on a very intimate but purely platonic relationship for many years. They read poetry together, and Paul teaches Miriam French and algebra. Afraid of being ruled out by Miriam, Mrs. Morel tries to break up their relationship. Paul himself is tired of Miriam's romantic love and her fear of physical warmth, so he wavers in his feelings toward her and becomes involved with Clara Dawes, a married woman who is separated from her husband. Paul begins to spend more time with Clara and they begin an extremely passionate affair. However, Clara does not want to divorce her husband. Paul's affair with her peters out. Meanwhile Mrs. Morel is ill with cancer, and Paul is in misery at the thought of losing her. Unable to bear her suffering, Paul and his sister Annie put an overdose of morphine in her milk. When his mother finally dies, he is broken-hearted. The novel is concluded with an opening end, offering much room for readers to surmise what would happen to Paul since his mother's death. At the close of the book, Paul resists the urges to follow his mother and goes off alone.

D. H. Lawrence was among the novelists who first introduced themes of psychology into their works. *Sons and Lovers* was possibly the first modern portrayal of a phenomenon that later, thanks to Sigmund Freud, became easily recognizable as the Oedipus complex. Paul's close relationship with his mother has provoked many Freudian and Oedipal readings of this novel. As the title of the book indicates, *Sons and Lovers* reveals two different but intertwining relationships between Paul and Mrs. Morel. The close bond between the two goes beyond the bounds of the conventional mother-son love. For Mrs. Morel's part, she projects her dissatisfaction with her marriage onto her smothering love for her son Paul. She despises all Paul's girlfriends and spares no effort to break up their relationship. On the other hand, Paul's love for his mother often borders on romantic desire. Paul hates his father Walter and often fantasizes about Walter's death, so that he would be the householder of the family. In spite of having affairs with Miriam and Clara, Paul realizes that he cannot love either of them as much as he loves his mother. When his mother dies, Paul plunges himself into deep sorrow, and his life seems to be dismal and hopeless. The Freudian and Oedipal readings of *Sons and Lovers* provide a brand new perspective to explore the submerged meanings of the novel.

Lawrence discussed the negative effect of industrialism in *Sons and Lovers*. Exploring the ordinary working-class life from the inside, the novel tells of a story about a tightly-knitted mining community. Coming from a collier family, Lawrence gave a realistic description of the mining life in the Midlands in the novel. In the course of industrialization, the pastoral landscape has been undermined; the harmonious interpersonal relationships have been estranged; men have been dehumanized without individuality or personality. To a great extent, the abnormal relation between Paul and his mother is an epitome of the English capitalist society. By debunking the so-called mechanical civilization, Lawrence presented to us a panorama of alienation in *Sons and Lovers*. From the perspective of alienation of nature, alienation of society and alienation as seen in Paul's predicaments, Lawrence explained the various conflicts brought about by the modern civilization. In this regard, *Sons and Lovers* is a great work to elaborate that the British society is an alienated world in all aspects.

The following excerpt comes from Chapter 10 of the novel in which Paul has a discussion with his mother about class system and happiness. Mrs. Morel wants her son to ascend into the middle class, but Paul says that he feels closest to the common people. Mrs. Morel wants her son to be happy, which seems mostly to mean finding a good woman and beginning to settle down. Paul argues that he worries a normal life might bore him. In this chapter, Mrs. Morel's desire to possess Paul is particularly strong. Her desire, which is constant throughout the novel, may account for Paul's failure to develop a strong relationship with Miriam and Clara.

Selected Reading

Sons and Lovers

When he was twenty-three years old, Paul[1] sent in a landscape to the winter exhibition at Nottingham Castle. Miss Jordan had taken a good deal of interest in him, and invited him to her house, where he met other artists. He was beginning to grow ambitious.

One morning the postman came just as he was washing in the scullery[2]. Suddenly he heard a wild noise from his mother. Rushing into the kitchen, he found her standing on the hearthrug wildly waving a letter and crying "Hurrah!" as if she had gone mad. He was shocked and frightened.

"Why, mother!" he exclaimed.

She flew to him, flung her arms round him for a moment, then waved the letter, crying:

"Hurrah, my boy! I knew we should do it!"

He was afraid of her—the small, severe woman with graying hair suddenly bursting out in such frenzy[3]. The postman came running back, afraid something had happened. They saw his tipped cap over the short curtains. Mrs. Morel[4] rushed to the door.

"His picture's got first prize, Fred," she cried, "and is sold for twenty guineas[5]."

"My word, that's something like!" said the young postman, whom they had known all his life.

"And Major Moreton has bought it!" she cried.

"It looks like meanin' something, that does, Mrs. Morel," said the postman, his blue eyes bright. He was glad to have brought such a lucky letter. Mrs. Morel went indoors and sat down, trembling. Paul was afraid lest she might have misread the letter, and might be disappointed after all. He scrutinized[6] it once, twice. Yes, he became convinced it was true. Then he sat down, his heart beating with joy.

"Mother!" he exclaimed.

"Didn't I *say* we should do it!" she said, pretending she was not crying.

He took the kettle off the fire and mashed the tea.

"You didn't think, mother—" he began tentatively.

"No, my son—not so much—but I expected a good deal."

"But not so much," he said.

"No—no—but I knew we should do it."

And then she recovered her composure, apparently at least. He sat with his shirt turned back, showing his young throat almost like a girl's, and the towel in his hand, his hair sticking up wet.

"Twenty guineas, mother! That's just what you wanted to buy Arthur[7] out. Now you needn't borrow any. It'll just do."

"Indeed, I shan't take it all," she said.

"But why?"

"Because I shan't."

"Well—you have twelve pounds, I'll have nine."

They cavilled[8] about sharing the twenty guineas. She wanted to take only the five pounds she needed. He would not hear of it. So they got over the stress of emotion by quarrelling.

Morel[9] came home at night from the pit, saying:

"They tell me Paul's got first prize for his picture, and sold it to Lord Henry Bentley for fifty pound."

"Oh, what stories people do tell!" she cried.

"Ha!" he answered. "I said I wor sure it wor a lie. But they said tha'd told Fred Hodgkisson."

"As if I would tell him such stuff!"

"Ha!" assented the miner.

But he was disappointed nevertheless.

"It's true he has got the first prize," said Mrs. Morel.

The miner sat heavily in his chair.

"Has he, beguy!" he exclaimed.

He stared across the room fixedly.

"But as for fifty pounds—such nonsense!" She was silent awhile. "Major Moreton bought it for twenty guineas, that's true."

"Twenty guineas! Tha niver says!" exclaimed Morel.

"Yes, and it was worth it."

"Ay!" he said. "I don't misdoubt it. But twenty guineas for a bit of a paintin' as he knocked off[10] in an hour or two!"

He was silent with conceit of his son. Mrs. Morel sniffed, as if it were nothing.

"And when does he handle th' money?" asked the collier[11].

"That I couldn't tell you. When the picture is sent home, I suppose."

There was silence. Morel stared at the sugar-basin instead of eating his dinner. His black arm, with the hand all gnarled[12] with work lay on the table. His wife pretended not to see him rub the back of his hand across his eyes, nor the smear in the coal-dust on his black face.

"Yes, an' that other lad 'ud'a done as much if they hadna ha' killed 'im[13]," he said quietly.

The thought of William went through Mrs. Morel like a cold blade. It left her feeling she was tired, and wanted rest.

Paul was invited to dinner at Mr. Jordan[14]'s. Afterwards he said:

"Mother, I want an evening suit."

"Yes, I was afraid you would," she said. She was glad. There was a moment or two of silence. "There's that one of William's," she continued, "that I know cost four pounds ten and which he'd only worn three times."

"Should you like me to wear it, mother?" he asked.

"Yes. I think it would fit you—at least the coat. The trousers would want shortening."

He went upstairs and put on the coat and vest. Coming down, he looked strange in a flannel[15] collar and a flannel shirt-front, with an evening coat and vest. It was rather large.

"The tailor can make it right," she said, smoothing her hand over his shoulder. "It's beautiful stuff. I never could find in my heart to let your father wear the trousers, and very glad I am now."

And as she smoothed her hand over the silk collar she thought of her eldest son. But this son was living enough inside the clothes. She passed her hand down his back to feel him. He was alive and hers. The other was dead.

He went out to dinner several times in his evening suit that had been William's. Each time his mother's heart was firm with pride and joy. He was started now. The studs[16] she and the children had bought for William were in his shirtfront; he wore one of William's dress shirts. But he had an elegant figure. His face was rough, but warm-looking and rather pleasing. He did not look particularly a gentleman, but she thought he looked quite a man.

He told her everything that took place, everything that was said. It was as if she had been there. And he was dying to introduce her to these new friends who had dinner at seven-thirty in the evening.

"Go along with you[17]!" she said. "What do they want to know me for?"

"They do!" he cried indignantly. "If they want to know me—and they say they do—then they want to know you, because you are quite as clever as I am. "

"Go along with you, child!" she laughed.

But she began to spare her hands. They, too, were work-gnarled now. The skin was shiny with so much hot water, the knuckles rather swollen. But she began to be careful to keep them out of soda. She regretted what they had been—so small and exquisite. And when Annie[18] insisted on her having more stylish blouses to suit her age, she submitted. She even went so far as to allow a black velvet bow to be placed on her hair. Then she sniffed in her sarcastic manner, and was sure she looked a sight. But she looked a lady, Paul declared, as much as Mrs. Major Moreton, and far, far nicer. The family was coming on[19]. Only Morel remained unchanged, or rather, lapsed slowly.

Paul and his mother now had long discussions about life. Religion was fading into the background. He had shoveled away all the beliefs that would hamper him, had cleared the ground, and come more or less to the bedrock[20] of belief that one should feel inside oneself for right and wrong, and should have the patience to gradually realize one's God. Now life interested him more.

"You know," he said to his mother, "I don't want to belong to the well-to-do middle class. I like my common people best. I belong to the common people."

"But if anyone else said so, my son, wouldn't you be in a tear. *You* know you consider yourself equal to any gentleman."

"In myself," he answered, "not in my class or my education or my manners.

But in myself I am."

"Very well, then. Then why talk about the common people?"

"Because—the difference between people isn't in their class, but in themselves. Only from the middle classes one gets ideas, and from the common people—life itself, warmth. You feel their hates and loves."

"It's all very well, my boy. But, then, why don't you go and talk to your father's pals?"

"But they're rather different."

"Not at all. They're the common people. After all, whom do you mix with now—among the common people? Those that exchange ideas, like the middle classes. The rest don't interest you."

"But—there's the life—"

"I don't believe there's a lot more life from Miriam[21] than you could get from any educated girl—say Miss Moreton. It is *you* who are snobbish about class."

She frankly *wanted* him to climb into the middle classes, a thing not very difficult, she knew. And she wanted him in the end to marry a lady.

Now she began to combat him in his restless fretting. He still kept up his connection with Miriam, could neither break free nor go the whole length of engagement. And this indecision seemed to bleed him of his energy. Moreover, his mother suspected him of an unrecognized leaning towards Clara[22], and, since the latter was a married woman, she wished he would fall in love with one of the girls in a better station of life. But he was stupid, and would refuse to love or even to admire a girl much, just because she was his social superior.

"My boy," said his mother to him, "all your cleverness, your breaking away from old things, and taking life in your own hands, doesn't seem to bring you much happiness."

"What is happiness!" he cried. "It's nothing to me! How *am* I to be happy?"

The plump question disturbed her.

"That's for you to judge, my lad. But if you could meet some *good* woman who would *make* you happy—and you began to think of settling your life—when you have the means—so that you could work without all this fretting— it would be much better for you."

He frowned. His mother caught him on the raw[23] of his wound of Miriam. He pushed the tumbled hair off his forehead, his eyes full of pain and fire.

"You mean easy, mother," he cried. "That's a woman's whole doctrine for life—ease of soul and physical comfort. And I do despise it."

"Oh, do you!" replied his mother. "And do you call yours a divine discontent?"

"Yes. I don't care about its divinity. But damn your happiness! So long as life's full, it doesn't matter whether it's happy or not. I'm afraid your happiness would bore me."

"You never give it a chance," she said. Then suddenly all her passion of grief over him broke out. "But it does matter!" she cried. "And you *ought* to be happy, you ought to try to be happy, to live to be happy. How could I bear to think your life wouldn't be a happy one!"

"Your own's been bad enough, mater, but it hasn't left you so much worse off than the folk who've been happier. I reckon you've done well. And I am the same. Aren't I well enough off?"

"You're not, my son. Battle—battle—and suffer. It's about all you do, as far as I can see."

"But why not, my dear? I tell you it's the best—"

"It isn't. And one *ought* to be happy, one *ought*."

By this time Mrs. Morel was trembling violently. Struggles of this kind often took place between her and her son, when she seemed to fight for his very life against his own will to die. He took her in his arms. She was ill and pitiful.

"Never mind, Little," he murmured. "So long as you don't feel life's paltry[24] and a miserable business, the rest doesn't matter, happiness or unhappiness."

She pressed him to her.

"But I want you to be happy," she said pathetically.

"Eh, my dear—say rather you want me to live."

Mrs. Morel felt as if her heart would break for him. At this rate she knew he would not live. He had that poignant[25] carelessness about himself, his own suffering, his own life, which is a form of slow suicide. It almost broke her heart. With all the passion of her strong nature she hated Miriam for having in this subtle way undermined his joy. It did not matter to her that Miriam could not help it. Miriam did it, and she hated her.

She wished so much he would fall in love with a girl equal to be his mate—educated and strong. But he would not look at anybody above him in station. He seemed to like Mrs. Dawes. At any rate that feeling was wholesome. His mother prayed and prayed for him, that he might not be wasted. That was all her prayer—not for his soul or his righteousness, but that he might not be wasted. And while he slept, for hours and hours she thought and prayed for him.

He drifted away from Miriam imperceptibly, without knowing he was going. Arthur only left the army to be married. The baby was born six months after his wedding. Mrs. Morel got him a job under the firm again, at twenty-one shillings a week. She furnished for him, with the help of Beatrice[26]'s mother, a little cottage of two rooms. He was caught now. It did not matter how he kicked and struggled, he was fast. For a time he chafed[27], was irritable with his young wife, who loved him; he went almost distracted when the baby, which was delicate, cried or gave trouble. He grumbled for hours to his mother. She only said: "Well, my lad, you did it yourself, now you must make the best of it." And then the grit came out in him. He buckled[28] to work, undertook his responsibilities, acknowledged that he belonged to his wife and child, and did make a good best of it. He had never been very closely inbound into the family. Now he was gone altogether.

The months went slowly along. Paul had more or less got into connection with the Socialist, Suffragette, Unitarian people in Nottingham, owing to his acquaintance with Clara. One day a friend of his and of Clara's, in Bestwood, asked him to take a message to Mrs. Dawes. He went in the evening across Sneinton Market to Bluebell Hill. He found the house in a mean little street paved with granite cobbles and having causeways of dark blue, grooved bricks. The front door went up a step from off this rough pavement, where the feet of the passersby rasped[29] and clattered. The brown paint on the door was so old that the naked wood showed between the rents. He stood on the street below and knocked. There came a heavy footstep; a large, stout[30] woman of about sixty towered above him. He looked up at her from the pavement. She had a rather severe face.

She admitted him into the parlour, which opened on to the street. It was a small, stuffy, defunct room, of mahogany[31], and deathly enlargements of photographs of departed people done in carbon. Mrs. Radford[32] left him. She was stately, almost martial. In a moment Clara appeared. She flushed deeply, and he was covered with confusion. It seemed as if she did not like being discovered in her home circumstances.

Notes

1. **Paul:** Paul Morel, the son who is his mother's favorite and struggles throughout the novel to balance his love for her with his relationships with other women

2. **scullery:** a small room adjoining a kitchen, in which dishwashing and other kitchen chores are done

3. **frenzy:** a state of violent mental agitation or wild excitement

4. **Mrs. Morel:** Gertrude Morel, the mother in the novel who becomes unhappy with her husband Walter and devotes herself to her children

5. **guineas:** a gold coin issued in England from 1663 to 1813 and worth one pound and one shilling

6. **scrutinized:** to examine or observe with great care; inspect critically

7. **Arthur:** Arthur Morel, Paul's younger brother

8. **cavilled:** to find fault unnecessarily; raise trivial objections

9. **Morel:** Walter Morel, Gertrude's husband, who is a coal miner

10. **knocked off:** finished very quickly

11. **collier:** a coal miner

12. **gnarled:** rugged and roughened, as from old age or work

13. **an' that other lad 'ud'a done as much if they hadna ha' killed 'im:** (local dialect) and that other boy (William, their eldest son) would have done as well, if they had not killed him.

14. **Mr. Jordan:** Thomas Jordan, the owner of the factory where Paul works

15. **flannel:** a soft woven cloth of wool or a blend of wool and cotton or synthetics

16. **studs:** a small ornamental button mounted on a short post for insertion through an eyelet, as on a dress shirt

17. **go along with you:** (informal) do not believe what someone says

18. **Annie:** Paul's older sister

19. **coming on:** improving or making progress

20. **bedrock:** the basis or the foundation

21. **Miriam:** Miriam Leivers, the daughter of the family at Willey Farm. She befriends Paul and becomes his first love.

22. **Clara:** Clara Dawes, a friend of Miriam's. She is Paul's second love, and they have a passionate affair.

23. **caught him on the raw**: said something that distressed him.

24. **paltry:** lacking in importance or worth; trivial

25. **poignant:** keenly distressing to the mind or feelings

26. **Beatrice:** Beatrice Wyld, a friend of the Morel family. She eventually marries Arthur when he returns from the army.

27. **chafed:** to annoy or vex

28. **buckled:** to succumb; to give in

29. **rasped:** rough; grating

30. **stout:** bulky in figure; strong in body; sturdy

31. **mahogany:** the wood of any of various tropical American evergreen trees used in making furniture

32. **Mrs. Radford:** Clara's mother

Questions for Study and Discussion

1. Much of the novel is concerned with Paul's relationship with women, most importantly his mother, Miriam and Clara. According to their relationships, what can we tell of Paul?

2. How to understand the relationship between Paul and his mother? Why does Paul always come back to his mother in the end?

3. Walter Morel, the coal miner, always speaks in a dialect throughout the novel. Why might Lawrence have chosen to make Morel use a dialect?

4. What do you think Mrs. Morel's relationship with her husband? How about their marriage?

5. What kind of woman does Mrs. Morel want Paul to marry?

6. What is going wrong between Paul and Miriam? Is it just that Miriam cannot compete with Paul's love for his mother? What is the real reason for their breakup?

7. According to the excerpt, can you describe Mrs. Morel's character?

8. Why does Mrs. Morel feel so sad at the mention of her eldest son William?

9. The close relationship between the son and the mother has provoked many Oedipal readings of this novel. Do you agree with the interpretation of the novel from the perspective of psychoanalytical criticism? Why or why not?

10. In what significant ways and with what effect has Lawrence criticized industrialization in the novel?

Virginia Woolf (1882—1941)

Life and Major Works

Born in London to Sir Leslie Stephen (1832—1904), and Julia Prinsep Stephen (1846—1895), Virginia Woolf (1882—1941) was considered to be an exceptionally lucky person because of her father's eminence. Sir Leslie Stephen was famous as an editor, critic and biographer. Coming from a family of renowned beauties who left their mark in the Victorian society as models for Pre-Raphaelite artists and early photographers, Virginia's mother, Julia Stephen was equally well connected. Woolf was educated at home, and raised in an environment

Virginia Woolf

filled with the influences of Victorian literary society for her frequent contact with her father's friends, all "high brows" with super culture and great learning. Among the visitors to the house were Henry James, George Eliot, George Henry Lewes, Julia Margaret Cameron (an aunt of Julia Stephen), and James Russell Lowell (Virginia's godfather). The Woolfs and some of their friends formed the well-known intellectual circle, the "Bloomsbury Group", among which Woolf was to be a significant figure. In addition to these influences was the immense library at 22 Hyde Park Gate, where Virginia was taught the classics and English literature. Furthermore, in 1912 Virginia Woolf married a keenly intelligent writer Leonard Woolf, her brother's friend at Cambridge. He encouraged her to write novels. They also found together the Hogarth Press in 1917, which published her books and those by other promising young writers of the time, including Katherine Mansfield's *Prelude* (1918) and T.S. Eliot's *The Waste Land* (1923). In such a cultured world of middle-class and upper-class London intelligentsia, it was natural for Woolf to begin her career as a writer.

Woolf began her literary career as a reviewer for the *Times Literary Supplement*. In her writing, Woolf, as a feminist, showed her concern for the position of women, and often wrote articles which appealed for women's rights. Her first novel *The Voyage Out* (1915) was written in the traditional technique. It was not until the publication of her second novel *Night and Day* (1919) that she began to try to make experiments with new and creative methods. She rejected the traditional method of realism by attacking such realists as Arnold Bennett, John Galsworthy and H.G. Wells. In her experiment, the plot is secondary to philosophical introspection. She tried her best to adopt the stream-of-consciousness, or interior monologue method. Her novels became series of impression, musings and reflections. She tried to penetrate into the innermost of human nature, and to explore problems of human personality and personal relationship.

Woolf's most important works include *Mrs. Dalloway* (1925), *To the Lighthouse* (1927) and *The Waves* (1931). It was the publication of *Mrs. Dalloway* that established her reputation as an important psychological writer. The next two novels *To the Lighthouse* and *The Waves* secured her reputation as an outstanding writer of the 20th century.

The following novels are also among Woolf's mature ones: *Orlando* (1928), a fantastic saga, *The Years Out* (1938), her longest novel depicting the history of a family, and *Between the Acts* (1941), her last novel in which she issued her final statement on art. Woolf was also a famous critic. Her best critic essays were collected in two volumes, *The Common Reader* (1925) and *The Second Common Reader* (1932). In her book-length essay *A Room of One's Own* (1929), with its famous dictum, "a woman must have money and a room of her own if she is to write fiction," she showed her concern with the difficulties of women writers to write in a man's world.

As one of the foremost modernist literary figures of the 20th century, Woolf tried her best to go beyond the "tyranny of plot" in order to get close to life as it is experienced. She wrote, "Examined for a moment an ordinary mind on an ordinary day. The mind receives myriad impressions—trivial, fantastic, evanescent, or engraved with the sharpness of steel." And it is the writer's task to "convey this varying, this unknown and uncircumscribed spirit." It is the stream-of-consciousness technique that she employed in her writing to approach the true experience of life. Concentrating on moments of great subtlety and sensitivity, she tried to assemble fragments of perception with her method and poetic language.

Being diligent and sensitive, Woolf's health deteriorated because of the intensity of her creative writing. Her nervous depression from which she suffered periodically since her childhood was aggravated when she finished the manuscript of her last novel *Between the Acts*. On March 28, 1941, after having a nervous breakdown, she drowned herself in the River Ouse near her home. Her beloved husband buried her under a tree in the garden of their house in Rodmell, Sussex.

Brief Introduction and Appreciation

Mrs. Dalloway was published in 1925. As one of Virginia Woolf's best books, it established her reputation as a remarkable English novelist of the 20th century. It has generated the most critical attention and continues to be one of her best known and most widely studied novels. *Mrs. Dalloway* is a novel with little plot. There are mainly movements from one character to another, or movements from the internal thoughts of one character to the internal thoughts of another in the novel. It covers only one day from morning to night in Mrs. Dalloway's life, recording the events of a single day when Mrs. Dalloway was giving an evening party at her home in Westminster.

At the beginning, Clarissa Dalloway, an upper-class housewife, walks through her London neighborhood to buy flowers for the party. When she returns from flower shopping, an old suitor and friend, Peter Walsh, drops by her house unexpectedly. Their meeting in the present intertwines with their thoughts of the past. Peter has never gotten over Clarissa's refusal to marry him years earlier, and it still obsesses him. When Peter was lost in thoughts in Regent's Park, we learn about another main character, Septimus, a veteran and victim of World War I. He now sees nothing valuable in the England he fought for. What he experienced in the war has permanently scarred him. He suffers from serious mental problems and he is suicidal. He is going to be sent to a mental institution in the country. Mr. Richard Dalloway is a thick-headed politician and a matter-of-fact man. Clarissa believes that the void exists between people, even between husband and wife. She feels somewhat disturbed because Richard doesn't know all about her although she values the privacy she maintains in her marriage. When Clarissa sees off Miss Kliman, Elizabeth's history teacher we learn from their thoughts that the two despise each other passionately, because each believes the other to be an oppressive force over Elizabeth. Meanwhile, Septimus commits suicide just before he is taken to the asylum for fear that his doctor would destroy his soul. Peter marvels ironically at the level of London's civilization, and he goes to Clarissa's party where most of the novel's main characters are assembled and their thoughts are presented. Clarissa feels dissatisfied with the party by her role and the critical eyes of Peter. She understands and identifies with Septimus, admiring him for not compromising his soul.

Many themes expressed in the novel have been discussed and still more are to be explored. There is the snobbishness of the upper class and the servile flattery of those in the lower society as Peter sees. Besides, nearly all the characters feel isolated. One of the major themes is isolation and community. Communicativeness is possible but at the same time, limited, as evidenced by Clarissa's enduring sense of being alone and by her social skills, which bring people together at her parties. People struggle to find ways for communication as well as adequate privacy, and they feel the balance between the two is difficult to attain. Mrs. Dalloway and her contemporaries live in a time when the old establishment and its oppressive values are nearing their end. Together with those English citizens who still cherish the old tradition, they inevitably feel strongly the feeling of the failure of the Empire, in addition to the feeling of their personal failures. The feelings can be detected in the minds of Clarissa, Peter, and Septimus. Living being not easy, as is mentioned in the novel, Mrs. Dalloway "always had the feeling that it was very, very dangerous to live even one day". Attitudes towards death also find their expressions in the characters. On that day, Clarissa repeats a line from Shakespeare's *Cymbeline* over and over again as the day goes on: "Fear no more the heat o' the sun / Nor the furious winter's rages." The line is from a funeral song that celebrates death as a comfort after a difficult life. Middle-aged Clarissa has experienced the deaths of her parents and sister. She witnessed the calamity of the war. It is natural for her to grow to believe that living is dangerous, so she ultimately becomes at peace with her own mortality. Septimus, who enlisted for romantic patriotic reasons was injured in trench warfare and now suffers from shell shock. He has become numb to the horrors of the war, and even felt little madness at his friend's death. Believing his lack of feeling is a crime, he chooses to embrace death by jumping from a window. He faces death most directly. As for Peter Walsh, he is insecure in his identity and grows frantic at the idea of death.

The author presented all these themes and ideas through examining and studying the minds of the characters, and through revealing their thoughts and silent soliloquies. As a master of the stream-of-consciousness school, Woolf made a good use of the technique to draw a vivid sketch of her characters. She develops Clarissa Dalloway, and other characters by chronicling their interior thoughts with little pause or explanation. In order to craft her characters deep enough to be realistic while dealing with only one day in their lives, the author made her story travel forwards and backwards in time, and in and out of the characters' minds. With the interior perspective of the novel, the author seemed to have a mirror to reflect the image of her characters, even an image of the post First World War social structure in England. Woolf is considered to have discovered a new literary form capable of expressing the new realities of postwar England.

The following excerpt is taken form the first part of the novel. It is a faithful record of Mrs. Dalloway's interior thoughts on her way to the flower shop, which serves as a good example to illustrate the employment of stream-of-consciousness technique of the author.

Selected Reading

Mrs. Dalloway (excerpt)

She had reached the Park gates[1]. She stood for a moment, looking at the omnibuses in Piccadilly[2].

She would not say of any one in the world now that they were this or were that. She felt very young; at the same time unspeakably aged. She sliced like a knife through everything; at the same time was outside, looking on. She had a perpetual sense, as she watched the taxi cabs, of being out, out, far out to sea and alone; she always had the feeling that it was very, very dangerous to live even one day. Not that she thought herself clever, or much out of the ordinary. How she had got through life on the few twigs of knowledge Fr ulein Daniels[3] gave them she could not think. She knew nothing; no language, no history; she scarcely read a book now, except memoirs in bed; and yet to her it was absolutely absorbing; all this; the cabs passing; and she would not say of Peter[4], she would not say of herself, I am this, I am that.

Her only gift was knowing people almost by instinct, she thought, walking on. If you put her in a room with some one, up went her back like a cat's; or she purred[5]. Devonshire House, Bath House[6], the house with the china cockatoo[7], she had seen them all lit up once; and remembered Sylvia, Fred, Sally Seton—such hosts of people; and dancing all night; and the wagons plodding[8] past to market; and driving home across the Park. She remembered once throwing a shilling into the Serpentine[9]. But every one remembered; what she loved was this, here, now, in front of her; the fat lady in the cab. Did it matter then, she asked herself, walking towards Bond Street[10], did it matter that she must inevitably cease completely; all this must go on without her; did she resent it; or did it not become consoling to believe that death ended absolutely? But that somehow in the streets of London, on the ebb and flow of things, here, there, she survived, Peter survived, lived in each other, she being part, she was positive, of the trees at home; of the house there, ugly, rambling all to bits and pieces as it was[11]; part of people she had never met; being laid out like a mist between the people she knew best, who lifted her on their branches as she had seen the trees lift the mist, but it spread ever so far, her life, herself. But what was she dreaming as she looked into Hatchard's shop window[12]? What was she trying to recover? What image of white dawn in the country, as she read in the book spread open:

> Fear no more the heat o' the sun
>
> Nor the furious winter's rages. [13]

This late age of the world's experience had bred in them all, all men and women, a well of tears. Tears and sorrows; courage and endurance; a perfectly upright and stoical[14] bearing. Think, for example, of the woman she admired most, Lady Bexborough[15], opening the bazaar.

There were Jorrocks' Jaunts and Jollities; there were Soapy Sponge and Mrs. Asquith's Memoirs and Big Game Shooting in Nigeria[16], all spread open. Ever so many books there were; but none that seemed exactly right to take to Evelyn Whitbread[17] in her nursing home. Nothing that would serve to amuse her and make that indescribably dried-up little woman look, as Clarissa came in, just for a moment cordial; before they settled down for the usual interminable talk of women's ailments. How much she wanted it—that people should look pleased as she came in, Clarissa thought and turned and walked back towards Bond Street, annoyed, because it was silly to have other reasons for doing things. Much rather would she have been one of those people like Richard who did things for themselves, whereas, she thought, waiting to cross[18], half the time she did things not simply, not for themselves; but to make people think this or that; perfect idiocy[19] she knew (and now the policeman held up his hand) for no one was ever for a second taken in. Oh if she could have had her life over again! She thought, stepping on to the pavement, could have looked even differently!

She would have been, in the first place, dark like Lady Bexborough, with a skin of crumpled[20] leather and beautiful eyes. She would have been, like Lady Bexborough, slow and stately; rather large; interested in politics like a man; with a country house; very dignified, very sincere. Instead of which she had a narrow pea-stick figure[21]; a ridiculous little face, beaked like a bird's. That she held herself well was true; and had nice hands and feet; and dressed well, considering that she spent little. But often now this body she wore (she stopped to look at a Dutch picture), this body, with all its capacities, seemed nothing—nothing at all. She had the oddest sense of being herself invisible; unseen; unknown; there being no more marrying, no more having of children now, but only this astonishing and rather solemn progress with the rest of them, up Bond Street, this being Mrs. Dalloway; not even Clarissa any more; this being Mrs. Richard Dalloway.

Bond Street fascinated her; Bond Street early in the morning in the season; its flags flying; its shops; no splash; no glitter; one roll of tweed in the shop where her father had bought his suits for fifty years; a few pearls; salmon on an ice block.

"That is all," she said, looking at the fishmonger's. "That is all," she repeated, pausing for a moment at the window of a glove shop where, before the War[22], you could buy almost perfect gloves. And her old Uncle William used to say a lady is known by her shoes and her gloves. He had turned on his bed one morning in the middle of the War. He had said, "I have had enough." Gloves and shoes; she had a passion for gloves; but her own daughter, her Elizabeth, cared not a straw for either of them.

Not a straw, she thought, going on up Bond Street to a shop where they kept flowers for her when she gave a party. Elizabeth really cared for her dog most of all. The whole house this morning smelt of tar. Still, better poor Grizzle[23] than Miss Kilman[24]; better distemper and tar and all the rest of it than sitting mewed in a stuffy bedroom with a prayer book! Better anything, she was inclined to say. But it might be only a phase, as Richard said, such as all girls go through. It might be falling in love. But why with Miss Kilman? Who had been badly treated of course; one must make allowances for that, and Richard said she was very able, had a really historical mind. Anyhow they were inseparable, and Elizabeth, her own daughter, went to Communion[25]; and how she dressed, how she treated people who came to lunch she did not care a bit, it being her experience that the religious ecstasy made people callous (so did causes); dulled their feelings, for Miss Kilman would do anything for the Russians, starved herself for the Austrians, but in private inflicted positive torture, so insensitive was she, dressed in a green mackintosh coat. Year in year out she wore that coat; she perspired; she was never in the room five minutes without making you feel her superiority, your inferiority; how poor she was; how rich you were; how she lived in a slum without a cushion or a bed or a rug or whatever it might be, all her soul rusted with that grievance sticking in it, her dismissal from school during the War—poor embittered unfortunate creature! For it was not her one hated but the idea of her, which undoubtedly had gathered in to itself a great deal that was not Miss Kilman; had become one of those spectres with which one battles in the night; one of those spectres who stand astride us and suck up half our life-blood, dominators and tyrants; for no doubt with another throw of the dice[26], had the black been uppermost and not the white, she would have loved Miss Kilman! But not in this world. No.

It rasped her, though, to have stirring about in her this brutal monster! To hear twigs cracking and feel hooves planted down in the depths of that leaf-encumbered forest, the soul; never to be content quite, or quite secure, for at any moment the brute would be stirring, this hatred, which, especially since her illness, had power to make her feel scraped, hurt in her spine; gave her physical pain, and made all pleasure in beauty, in friendship, in being well, in being loved and making her home delightful rock, quiver, and bend as if indeed there were a monster grubbing at the roots, as if the whole panoply of content were nothing but self love! This hatred!

Nonsense, nonsense! She cried to herself, pushing through the swing doors of Mulberry's the florists.

She advanced, light, tall, very upright, to be greeted at once by button-faced Miss Pym, whose hands were always bright red, as if they had been stood in cold water with the flowers.

There were flowers: delphiniums, sweet peas, bunches of lilac; and carnations, masses of carnations. There were roses; there were irises. Ah yes—so she breathed in the earthy garden sweet smell as she stood talking to Miss Pym who owed her help, and thought her kind, for kind she had been years ago; very kind, but she looked older, this year, turning her head from side to side among the irises and roses and nodding tufts of lilac with her eyes half closed, snuffing in, after the street uproar, the delicious scent, the exquisite coolness. And then, opening her eyes, how fresh like frilled linen clean from a laundry laid in wicker trays the roses looked; and dark and prim the red carnations, holding their heads up; and all the sweet peas spreading in their bowls, tinged violet, snow white, pale—as if it were the evening and girls in muslin frocks came out to pick sweet peas and roses after the superb summer's day, with its almost blue-black sky, its delphiniums, its carnations, its arum lilies was over; and it was the moment between six and seven when every flower—roses, carnations, irises, lilac— glows; white, violet, red, deep orange; every flower seems to burn by itself, softly, purely in the misty beds; and how she loved the grey-white moths spinning in and out, over the cherry pie, over the evening primroses!

And as she began to go with Miss Pym from jar to jar, choosing, nonsense, nonsense, she said to herself, more and more gently, as if this beauty, this scent, this colour, and Miss Pym liking her, trusting her, were a wave which she let flow over her and surmount that hatred, that monster, surmount it all; and it lifted her up and up when—oh! A pistol shot in the street outside!

"Dear, those motor cars," said Miss Pym, going to the window to look, and coming back and smiling apologetically with her hands full of sweet peas, as if those motor cars, those tyres of motor cars, were all HER fault.

Notes

1. **Park gates:** the gates of St. James Park in London
2. **Piccadilly:** a street in London, which is a center of fashionable shops, clubs and hotels.
3. **Fr ulein Daniels:** Fr ulein is German word for "miss". Miss Daniels here refers to the German governess who taught Mrs. Dalloway in her childhood.
4. **Peter:** Peter Walsh, Mrs. Dalloway's former lover
5. **purred:** made a soft and low sound in its throat in order to show it is

pleased, as a cat does

6. **Devonshire House, Bath House:** some buildings Mrs. Dalloway remembered she had seen in the past.

7. **china cockatoo:** large crested parrot made of porcelain

8. **plodding:** walking very slowly in a boring or bored way

9. **Serpentine:** ornamental water in Hyde Park in London

10. **Bond Street:** a street in the west end of London

11. **the house there, ugly, rambling all to bits and pieces as it was:** the house here refers to the house where Mrs. Dalloway lived, ugly, big but somewhat old and dilapidated.

12. **Hatchard's shop window:** the shop window of Hatchard's. Hachard's is the name of the shop

13. **Fear no more the heat o' the sun / Nor the furious winter's rages:** the two lines are the first two ones of the dirge on Imogen in Shakespeare's Cymbeline that Mrs. Dalloway remembered.

14. **stoical:** not complaining or feeling unhappy when bad things happen

15. **Lady Bexborough:** an artistic lady whom Mrs. Dalloway knew and admired. She was asked to open the bazaar somewhere some time ago.

16. **Jorrocks' Jaunts and Jollities; there were Soapy Sponge and Mrs. Asquith's Memoirs and Big Game Shooting in Nigeria:** these are popular books in the 1920s that came into the mind of Mrs. Dalloway at the moment.

17. **Evelyn Whitbread:** Mrs. Dalloway's friend, whose husband is Huge Whitbread, a coal merchant.

18. **waiting to cross:** waiting to cross the street

19. **idiocy:** extreme stupidity of silliness or a very stupid remark or action

20. **crumpled:** having a lot of lines

21. **Instead of which she had a narrow pea-stick figure:** unlike Lady Bexborough who is large and stately, Mrs. Dalloway was slender, with a figure as thin as the pea-stick.

22. **the War:** the first World War

23. **Grizzle:** the dog at the Dalloway's

24. **Miss Kilman:** servant at the Dalloway's

25. **Communion:** referring to the Holy Communion, a solemn religious ceremony in the Christian Church where bread and wine are consecrated and

received as the body and blood of Jesus Christ.

26. **with another throw of the dice:** if her fate should be otherwise.

Questions for Study and Discussion

1. Please analyze Virginia Woolf's "stream-of-consciousness" device in the excerpt.
2. Can you imagine what kind of person Mrs. Dalloway is?
3. What did Mrs. Dalloway think of on her way to the flower shop?
4. Please analyze why Mrs. Dalloway "always had the feeling that it was very, very dangerous to live even one day"?
5. The lines "Fear no more the heat o' the sun / Nor the furious winter's rages" come from a funeral hymn in one of Shakespeare's play. What do the lines suggest? And why did Mrs. Dalloway repeat the lines at that time?
6. Will you please analyze the themes of the novel?
7. How many characters are involved in the excerpt? Who are they and what are their relationships to Mrs. Dalloway?
8. Flowers are important images in the novel. How do they suggest the feeling and emotion? What's their relationship to Mrs. Dalloway and what does the relationship reveal about her?

William Butler Yeats (1865—1939)

Life and Major Works

William Butler Yeats, a celebrated and accomplished Irish poet and dramatist, was born of Protestant parents in Dublin, Ireland on June 13, 1865. His father was a portrait painter, and his mother was the daughter of a prosperous merchant in Sligo Country, a wild and beautiful port town in the west of Ireland. Yeats learned a lot of old Irish legends, and songs by talking with the peasants and

William Butler Yeats

fishermen when he spent much of his time with his grandparents in Sligo Country. Yeats had a lifelong love for the scenery and folklore of this region, which greatly influenced his work. When he was 2 years old, the family moved to London, and he was educated at schools there. But when he was 16, the family moved back to Dublin. Then, Yeats became an art student at the School of Art in conformity with his father's profession, and he grew interested in the occult. Six years later, he left and went to London. He got acquainted with William Morris and Oscar Wild, became active in literary circles and devoted to creation of new Irish literature. His early work was not especially Irish but he sought to transform Irish folklore and legend into poetry. During this period together with Edwin J. Ellis, he began to work on an edition of William Blake. When he was 24, his book *The Wanderings of Oisin* was brought out, and in the same year, he met and fell desperately in love with Maud Gonne, a famous actress and a passionate Irish nationalist. He wrote a great many of love poems to her, and she, although she had issued many of her refusals to his proposals and married another fellow revolutionary, was to figure so successfully in his plays. His love for her also kindled his interest in the country's political struggle for independence. In 1890, Yeats joined the Order of the Golden Dawn, a secret society. He took part in the Irish nationalist movement and spoke for "the new Ireland". But after the death of the Irish nationalist leader, C.S. Parnell (1846—1891), Yeats turned his mind from politics to literature, believing that poems and plays would create a national unity capable of transforming the country.

In 1891, Yeats helped found The Rhymers' Club, an organization consisting of a group of poets and made acquaintance with fellow members Johnson and Ernest Dowson. His first verse play, *The Countess Catheleen*, with Maude Gonne originating the title role, appeared in 1892. Yeats visited Paris in 1894, and became acquainted with some modern French poetry and met the poet-critic Arthur Synons who explained him the Symbolist aesthetic, which aroused his new interest. Yeats used an elaborate system of symbols in his writing. In 1895 his *Poems* which collected the lyrics of his early years was published.

In 1896, Yeats met Lady Augusta, an aristocrat and playwright, who shared his interest in Ireland's past, especially its folklore. She became his lifelong friend and had a profound effect on his life. He visited Lady Gregory frequently at Coole in Country Galway, and he now had both theatrical and political interests. He wrote a great deal of prose in this period, but produced another volume of lyrics, *The Wind among the Reeds*, in 1899. Together with Lady Gregory, Yeats found Irish National Theater in Dublin, the predecessor of the Abby Theory. He was its manager for 7 years. His becoming president of the Irish National Dramatic Society was also out of his theoretical interest. And eventually, the Abbey Theater, the center of Irish dramatic revival, was opened in 1904 with the help of Lady Gregory. Yeats wrote 26 plays for the Abbey Theater, some in verse and others in prose. In his work for the Abbey, he persuaded John Millingtong Synge, who was among the leaders of the Irish literary revival, to return to Irish folklore for subject material, and Synge wrote some of the finest Irish plays ever produced.

In 1911 Yeats met Ezra Pound after his American tour with the Abbey troupe. The two poets influenced each other, and Pound's influence was perhaps stronger although he was 20 years junior. Besides, Yeats also studied John Donne, a metaphysical poet in the 17th century. In 1914, Yeats had his so far most important volume of poetry *Responsibilities* published while he was working on the first part of his *Autobiography*. The year of 1916 saw the Easter Rising in Dublin. Still concerned about the troubles of Ireland, he wrote "EASTER 1916" in memory of the incident. On October 21, 1917, Yeats's proposal to Georgie Hyde-Lees was accepted and they were happily married. Their daughter was born two years later, and a son in 1921. In 1922, Yeats was invited to become a member of the Irish Senate.

Many volumes of Yeats' representative poems were published during the years from 1919 to 1937, including *The Wild Swans at Coole* (1919), *Michael Robartes and the Dancer* (1921), *The Tower* (1928), *The Winding Stair* (1933) and *A Vision* (1937).

In his lifetime, Yeats completed all together 11 volumes of poetry, 26 plays, 9 books of prose, 5 autobiographical works and 4 books of philosophy and literary criticism. He was awarded the Nobel Prize for literature in 1923. His health was poor during the late years in his life, but he continued to think and write, also spent some time with the dying Lady Gregory. In 1938, he moved to the south of France. He fell ill at the beginning of 1939 and died on January 28 in Roquebrune. His body remained buried there throughout the World War II. In September, 1948 it was taken back and laid to rest in Drumcliffe Churchyard near Sligo.

Brief Introduction and Appreciation

The poem "Down by the Salley Garden" is a typical story of inexperienced youth in the realm of love. It is just like a folk song, lyrical, charming and repetitive. It was originally entitled "An Old Song Resung" written when Yeats was 24 years old and had just met Maude Gonn who became the inspiration for many of Yeats's early poems. Yeats made an attempt to reconstruct a half-forgotten old song which an old woman in the village of Ballysodare Sligon often sang to herself. The language is simple to understand, and so is the theme. The poem is about the relationship between the narrator, a boy and a woman whom the boy idealizes as having "little snow-white feet", and the narrator's failure to be able to deal with their relationship. He loves her, but she is carefree and wants to enjoy herself and "take life easy". She advises him not to be serious about love and life. But he doesn't take her advice and suffers many torments as a result.

Written only 4 years after "Down by the Salley Garden", "The lake Isle of Innisfree" is also a widely quoted poem, typical of Yeats' early lyrics. "Innisfree", meaning "heather island" in Gaelic, is an island of intense natural beauty off the coast of Ireland. It is located in County Sligo, where Yeats' mother's home was and he spent many days with his grandmother. Yeats identified it as the part of Ireland and the world closest to his heart, and here the author is referring to a place for hermitage. The poem came into the poet's mind as he walked in a London street. Yeats first wrote the poem in London in 1890, when he was feeling intensely homesick. It consists of 3 quatrains with iambic pentameter, with each stanza rhymed **abab**. The **abab** rhyme structure enforces the feeling of nature, lending a flowing and soothing rhythm to the poem. Compared with "Down by the Salley Garden", it is far more sophisticated and mature. The themes explored and the techniques used are much more complex. The central theme is exile. The poet reveals his tiredness of the noisy city life and his desire to escape the cruel reality by building a small cabin at Innisfree and living alone there. Longing for peace in a fairyland from the bottom of his heart, he wants to leave immediately, because when he "stands on a roadway" or on the city pavement, he hears the lapping of the lake waters in his heart. When portraying his ideal life, he uses strong pastoral images. The world described here is almost a paradise, there being no interference of man to spoil natural things except the narrator and the small cabin built to blend in with the surroundings. Technically, Yeats has achieved in this poem a suggestive pattern of meaning by a careful counterpointing of contrasting images like human and fairly, natural and artificial. Around the "fairyland", the poem is closely woven, easy, subtle and music. A haunting quality has been given to the poem with the clarity and control of the imagery.

"Sailing to Byzantium" was created in 1926 and published 2 years later as part of Yeats' greatest collection. It is considered as one of Yeats' most inspired works, and one of the greatest poems of the 20th century. The poem explores the dichotomies between art and ordinary life, age and youth, as well as sensuality and spirituality, expressing most effectively the poet's mysterious poetic system. The poem consists of four open-form stanzas and the eight-line stanzas, named ottava rima, metered in iambic pentameter and rhymed **abababcc**, with a couplet following two trios of alternating rhyme. The literary device alliteration is also applied in the poem. Without conventional characters or plot, the lyric is narrated by "an aging man" between two worlds. Realizing that his prime has passed, and youth and the sensual life are no longer a choice for him, the speaker determines to go on a spiritual journey and sail to the ideal world of Byzantium, a rich symbol of eternity and paradise.

In the first stanza, a world of youth and sensuality is introduced. It is a world full of life and youth with the young lying in one another's arms, birds singing in the trees and fish swimming in the waters. But the old is neglected by the young who indulge themselves in the "sensual music", and therefore, "this is no country for old men". In the second stanza, the old man, deprived of physical strength, is depicted as of little consequence. The lifelessness of old age is inevitable unless he focuses on the intellect of soul and seeks to free himself from the constraints of the human body. And only in an ideal environment can he learn to sing the songs of the soul. Consequently, the speaker resolves to make a spiritual and metaphorical voyage to Byzantium, the holy city, which is a symbol of artistic magnificence and eternity. In the third stanza, the poet interprets that at the moment that the sages died, they moved from the mortal life to the immortal one and achieved an eternity through both the life of the soul and the Byzantine painting. The speaker now addresses the sages and asks them eagerly to make him immortal like the figures in the gold mosaic in Byzantium art through breaking free from his body, the "dying animal". Once he has been taken out of the natural world, as he declares in the fourth stanza, he will free himself from the restraints of the physical body and will never find form in any natural thing, but rather be a hammered bird made of hammered gold. Placed in a golden tree the narrator has now completely transformed himself into a work of art, enduring and unable to be susceptible to the ravages of time, decay and death.

Throughout the poem, the use of symbolism is very important. Firstly, the title contains two important symbols: "sailing" depicts a metaphorical and psychological journey and "Byzantium" is a symbol of a world of artistic magnificence and permanence, creating in the readers' mind the rich culture associated with the Byzantium Empire. In the first stanza, those images of birds, fish and young lovers symbolize transience and mortality. In the second stanza, "a tattered coat upon a stick", the image of scarecrow is applied to represent the decrepitude of the old. The golden bird in the last stanza is Yeats' chosen image of which he wants to take permanent form. Owning to its physical permanence, the golden bird is the representation of the artistic existence the poet yearns for. Besides, the symbol of music and song is used throughout the poem, which unifies the sensual world and the intellectual one. The birds' song in the first stanza is sensual and fleeing; the "singing school" suggests the joy experienced in the intellectual paradise; the song of the golden bird that entertains the lords and ladies of Byzantium symbolizes the intellectual joy the poet desires to enjoy.

Selected Reading

Down by the Salley Garden

Down by the salley[1] Meanwhile gardens my love and I did meet;
She passed the Salley gardens with little snow-white feet.
She bid me take love easy, as the leaves grow on the tree;
But I, being young and foolish, with her would not agree.

In a field by the river my love and I did stand,
And on my leaning shoulder she laid her snow-white hand.
She bid me take life easy, as the grass grows on the weirs[2];
But I was young and foolish, and now am full of tears.

Notes

1. **Salley:** the Irish name for a type of willow tree, a variant of "sallow".
2. **weirs:** barriers or walls built across a river in order to control or divert the flow of water.

The Lake Isle of Innisfree[1]

I will arise and go now, and go to Innisfree
And a small cabin build there, of clay and wattles[2] made;
Nine bean-rows will I have there, a hive for the honeybee,
And live alone in the bee-loud glade[3].
And I shall have some peace there, for peace comes dropping low,
Dropping from the veils[4] of the mourning to where the cricket sings;
There midnight's all a glimmer, and noon a purple glow,
And evening full of the linnet's[5] wings.
I will arise and go now, for always night and day
I hear lake water lapping[6] with low sounds by the shore;
While I stand on the roadway, or on the pavements grey,
I hear it in the deep heart's core[7].

Notes

1. **Isle of Innisfree**: the Irish name for a type of willow tree, a variant of "sallow"
2. **wattles**: barriers or walls built across a river in order to control or divert the flow of water
3. **the bee-loud glade**: an open place where bees buzz noisily
4. **veils**: fog in the morning
5. **linnet**: a kind of small brown singing bird, common in Europe
6. **lapping**: beating of waves
7. **in the deep heart's core**: at the the bottom of my heart

Sailing to Byzantium[1]

I

That is no country[2] for old men. The young
In one another's arms, birds in the trees

—Those dying generations—at their song,
The salmon[3]-falls, the mackerel[4]-crowded seas,
Fish, flesh, or fowl[5], commend all summer long
Whatever is begotten[6], born, and dies.
Caught in that sensual music all neglect
Monuments of unageing intellect[7].

II

An aged man is but a paltry[8] thing,
A tattered[9] coat upon a stick, unless
Soul clap its hands and sing, and louder sing
For every tatter[10] in its mortal dress,
Nor is there singing school but studying
Monuments of its own magnificence;
And therefore I have sailed the seas and come
To the holy city of Byzantium.

III

O sages standing in God's holy fire
As in the gold mosaic of a wall[11],
Come from the holy fire, perne in a gyre[12],
And be the singing-masters of my soul.
Consume[13] my heart away; sick with desire
And fastened to a dying animal[14]
It knows not what it is; and gather me
Into the artifice[15] of eternity.

IV

Once out of nature I shall never take
My bodily form from any natural thing,
But such a form as Grecian goldsmiths make
Of hammered gold and gold enameling
To keep a drowsy Emperor awake[16];
Or set upon a golden bough to sing
To lords and ladies of Byzantium
Of what is past, or passing, or to come.

Notes

1. **Byzantium:** the ancient city of Byzantium, capital of Eastern Roman Empire (also Byzantine) ruled by the Turkish Sultan, and the center of Orthodox Church. The city is now known as Istanbul. In Yeats' mind, the civilization of Byzantium stood for a highest point in art, spirituality, and philosophy. Here, symbolic of the world of art and poetry, it symbolizes a world of artistic magnificence and eternity. In reality, Yeats had never visited the city himself. But he went to a closer place, Sicily and the Northern Italian Ravenna where he saw in the museums there mosaics, sages and saints. All of these things are mentioned in the third stanza of the poem. So, the poem is about an imaginative journey, not an actual one.

2. **country:** the sensual world or natural world

3. **salmon:** a kind of large fish with silver skin and pink flesh that lives in the ocean but swims up rivers to lay its eggs.

4. **mackerel:** a kind of ocean fish which has oily flesh and a strong taste.

5. **fish, flesh, or fowl:** the three represent all living things of nature on the earth, in the water and in the air. "Fowl" is archaic form of "bird".

6. **begotten:** born or brought into being

7. **unaging intellect:** a reference to the works of art

8. **paltry:** unimportant, worthless and silly

9. **tattered:** old and torn

10. **tatter:** piece of cloth that are old and torn

11. **O sages standing in God's holy fire / As in the gold mosaic of a wall:** Here, Yeats refers to a particular painting which he saw in the church of San Apollinare Nuovo at Ravenna when he visited it in 1907. The painting depicted martyrs being burned for their faith. **Mosaic:** a pattern or picture made by fitting together small pieces of colored stone, glass, paper, etc.

12. **perne in a gyre:** whirl round in a spiral motion; "perne" or "pirn", a bobbin, reel or spoon on which something is wound. It may be a thing such as those Yeats would have seen in Sligo when he was young.

13. **consume:** destroy by fire

14. **a dying animal:** a decrepit and dying body

15. **artifice:** art, the works of art, art products created by the human mind

16. **But such a form as Grecian goldsmiths make / Of hammered gold and gold enamelling / To keep a drowsy Emperor awake:** Yeats once wrote:

"I have read somewhere that in the Emperor's palace at Byzantium was a tree made of gold and silver, and artificial birds that sang." And later in 1937, he mentioned that the tree symbolized the intellectual joy of eternity.

Enamelling: glass-like substance covering used to coat metal or pottery for decoration or as protection.

Questions for Study and Discussion

1. Who is the narrator of the first poem?
2. In the first poem, what's the narrator's attitude towards love? Do you think it's right or wrong? And why?
3. In the first poem, what's the lady's attitude towards love and life? Do you agree with her? Can you figure out what kind of person she is?
4. In the first poem, why didn't the narrator take the lady's advice? What's the result?
5. What kind of world is portrayed in the second poem? Can you see the contrast between his present location and the ideal land?
6. Can you imagine what the speaker in the second poem will do at Innisfree? What is the speaker's current emotional state? How do you know?
7. How do various rhythmic and other sound effects convey the messages of the poem?
8. In the fourth poem, why does the narrator say "this is no country for old man"?
9. What are the differences between the sensual world and the intellectual world?
10. Various images and symbols are used in the third poem. What do they stand for?
11. What does the old poet yearn to be turned into? And why?

Wilfred Owen (1893—1918)

Life and Major Works

The eldest of 4 children of Tom and Susan Owen, Wilfred Owen was born on the 18th of March, 1893 in Oswestry, Shropshire, and brought up in the Anglican religion of the evangelical school. His father was a railway worker, and his mother a domineering pious evangelical who urged him to become an Anglican priest from his early days. For an evangelical, man is saved not by the good he does; but by the faith he has in the redeeming power of Christ's sacrifice. The influence of religion remains visible in his poems and in their themes: sacrifice, Biblical language and his description of Hell, though he had rejected much of his belief by 1913. In 1897, the family moved to Birkenhead, Merseyside where Owen's education

Wilfred Owen

began at the Birkenhead Institute 3 years later, and then continued at the Technical School in Shrewsbury when the family moved there in 1906. Owen was a shy, intense, and scholarly boy who read widely and constantly, showing keen interest and gift in arts. He began writing from an early age and his earliest experiments in poetry began at the age of 17. But he didn't do well academically and failed to attain entrance to the University of London for the entrance results were disappointing.

Then, from October, 1911, Owen spent a year as a lay assistant to the Revd. Herbert Wigan at Dunsden, near Reading, but returned to Shrewsbury. In 1913 he went to Bordeaux, France, where he was teaching English to children in the Berlitz School of Language when the World War I broke out in the summer of 1914. Owen visited the local hospitals and became acquainted with many of the war's wounded. The 22-year-old young man was deeply affected by those visits. Besides, he was increasingly aware of the magnitude of the war. As a result, he returned to England in September 1915, and enlisted in the war effort, becoming a solider in the British Army. He joined the Artists' Rifles, only to find no artists in the unit. In June 1916, he was commissioned as a second lieutenant in the Manchester Regiment and spent the rest of the year training in England.

The year of 1917 was of great importance to him. In January, the worst war winter, he was transferred to the hell of the trenches in France where he was to be thoroughly shocked by horrors of war and his outlook on life would change permanently. There, he saw his first action in which he and his soldiers were forced to hold a flooded dug-out in no-man's land for fifty hours under heavy bombardment. In March he got injured with concussion from a fall and evacuated to a military hospital, but returned to the front-line in April. In late April, when Owen led his men through an artillery barrage to the German trenches, he was severely shaken and disoriented by the bombardment, and barely avoided being hit by an exploding shell, but returned to his base camp confused and stammering. He was diagnosed with "neurasthenia" (shell-shock). Owen was evacuated from the front to a French hospital and subsequently returned to Britain, where on June 26th, he was checked into the Craiglockhart War Hospital for Neurasthenic Officers near Edinburgh.

We wonder what might have happened to his literary career, had Owen not arrived at Craiglockhart War Hospital, because it was there that he wrote most of his great poetry while recovering, and above all it was there that he met with Siegfried Sassoon, who was also a patient and had gained a reputation as a poet. The meeting seemed to be the real beginning of Owen's career as a mature and genuine poet, and Sassoon was to be his major influence on his work. Sassoon agreed to look over Owen's poems after an awkward introduction, and it was the poem "Anthem for Doomed Youth" that impressed Sassoon greatly. In addition to encouraging Owen to continue writing poems, he introduced him to such literary figures as Robert Graves to whom Owen showed one of his poems "Disabled" when he came to Craiglockhart to visit his friend Sassoon. Owen was struck by the fact that "Graves was very impressive by the piece", as Owen remarked in a letter to Sally Owen, his sister. Besides, Graves introduced Owen to such luminaries as Arnold Bennett and H. G. Wells after his release from hospital.

After his treatment, Sassoon went back in service, but was severely injured on head by "friend fire" and sent back to England. In August 1918, Owen returned to the front in France to replace Sassoon in spite of Sassoon's threat to wound his own legs if Owen would go. Owen seemed to know he would be killed there. On November 4, 1918 — exactly 7 days before the signing of the Armistice, he was shot to death by a German machine-gunner at the Sambre Canal, near the French village of Ors. On November 11, 1918, the day of the armistice, it was after the bells had been ringing for one hour in Shrewsbury, England, to celebrate the end of the war that the telegram informing their son's death arrived at Tom and Susan Owen's home.

Killed young and premature, Owen's most mature works were all created in the very short period of time between August 1917 and September 1918. Only five of Owen's poems had been published before his death. Siegfried Sassoon arranged for the publication of *Poems by Wilfred Owen* in 1920. Owen's best known poems include "Anthem for Doomed Youth", "Dulce Et Decorum Est", "The Parable of the Old Man and the Young", and "Strange Meeting".

Owen is well known as the leading poet of the First World War for his war poetry on the horrors of trench and gas warfare, as well his condemnation of the horrors of war. It's impossible to predict had he lived, he would have gone on to even greater glory in his writing. But he had left behind enough for us to acknowledge his immense stature as a poet in the history of literature. His poetry reflects a special historic viewpoint, the prevailing "mentality" of most of the thinking men in the trenches, and the poet's vision at a certain moment in history, encompassing both hope and despair. Characteristic of his poetry is alliteration, assonance and pararhyme. His use of pararhyme, with its heavy reliance on consonance was innovative and quiet brilliant in his works.

Brief Introduction and Appreciation

Based on an earlier poem "Earth's Wheels", "Strange Meeting" was written in the spring or early summer of 1918, the year Owen died. It stands in the forefront of his achievements, and it was called "Owen's passport to immortality" by Siegfried Sassoon. The famous quotation from the poem — "I am the enemy you killed, my friend" is engraved on the poet's memorial in the grounds of Shrewsbury Abbey.

The title of the poem was taken from Shelley's "The Revolt of Islam". In Shelley's poem, it reads "Gone forth whom no strange meeting did befall." Owen got from his brothers and sister the complete poetical works of Shelley as a 21 birthday present. "Strange Meeting" is a short elegy lamenting a soldier-poet's participation in the First World War, the most cataclysmic and most futile event in which a whole generation with hope and shining futures was slaughtered. The poem is written in the first person, and it can be assumed that the narrator and Wilfred Owen are the same person. Perhaps drawing from many trips into the underworld by characters in earlier literature works, Owen seems to escape the horrors of the battlefield and go on a private journey into hell. It's also assumed that in the poem, Owen makes a totally literal account of a night raid, one of many he and his soldiers surely made, into a German trench and down into its underground shell shelter and sleeping quarters. The entire disembodied nature of the experience fills the account with the perfect poetic ambiguity of the "probing" (bayoneting) of the sleeping Germans and the impossibility of mercy with risk to losing his own life.

Thematically, the poem is not difficult to understand. The story tells of an English soldier at the Front, dreaming that he goes to hell, and there he meets the German soldier he killed in hand-to-hand combat the day before. They now have been made allies by Death, and before they sleep for ever they can talk, agree on the horrors of war, and mourn the potential that has gone with them. A dark and solemn tone is employed in the poem to convey to us the sheer senselessness of war which is neither glorious or honorary, and Owen's hostility towards the war effort and the futility of the actions is apparently displayed.

Structurally the poem consists of 44 lines, divided into 3 irregular stanzas. It begins with the relief of a soldier as he escapes the war. The opening line "It seemed that out of battle I escaped" ushers readers into a dream-like world in which a meeting for the two heroes takes place, a strange meeting and fate for them, innocent victims of the war, and an ambiguous meeting for us.

The scene is set in lines 1–3, the first stanza: holes, caverns, tunnels in sight. We don't know whether it is trench or hell because of the deliberate ambiguity set by the poet. The implication of "Titanic Wars" makes us realize that past and present are linked, and in the future, Owen's tragic war may reoccur.

In the second stanza, the soldier meets the spirit of a dead soldier and that is when he realizes where he is. Among those "encumbered" (with uniform and kit? Ambiguous.) and suffering sleepers, the two men who have already shared one terrible, intimate moment—the moment of bayoneting now comes to recognition. "Probed" is another example of ambiguous word for its lacking of an indirect object. "Piteous" explains why the distressful hands are lifted. To bless or surrender?

In the third stanza, the spirit tells the soldier that going into war is simply a waste of one's life. The cruelty and harshness of war is described here. From lines 12-13, we see the contrast between the hell and the war—war is somewhat worse than hell since in this hell there is "no blood", "no guns thumped, or down the flues made moan", but relief and peace. With a paradox "strange friend", the narrator introduces an apparent one-sided dialogue in line 14. However, through careful examination, we can find Owen subtly merges the two figures in the monologue, the enemy and friend, the friend with the enemy, by mixing verbal tenses and pluralizing the personal pronoun. In this way, the seeming one-sided dialogue actually becomes a monologue of both as one, and as readers, we know not who is who. But perhaps the realization is not of significance since as human, they are a whole. Through the dialogue with the dead—"I am the enemy you killed, my *friend*", a moment of mutual recognition of their common inhumanity illuminates their common humanity. And therefore, in killing another you kill yourself, you kill each other.

"Strange Meeting" has been regarded as Owen's most "problematic" poem perhaps for its ambiguity, deep meaning and superb craftsmanship. Examples for ambiguity have been shown above. Besides, it's a poem with deep meanings: this Hell is in fact a place of peace and reconciliation, and there dead enemies become brothers in their loathing of war. Quite different from being of an eternity of everlasting torment at the beginning, the two soldiers are freed from all pain and horror in the Hell. The real Hell is the war which they have left behind. Naturally, here lies the harsh condemnation of war.

Technically, when we read the poem, the unusual rhyme is very impressive. It is pararhyme, or double consonance, a particular feature of the poetry of Wilfred Owen. It is a near rhyme in which the consonants in two words are the same, but the vowels are different, for example, hall—hell, grained—ground, years—yours, laughed—left and etc. To sustain the rhyme is a challenge, but it gives a sonorous effect to the poem, and it works better than obvious rhymes, which are likely to distract from the meaning. Metrically, it is written in iambic pentameters, the same as most of the great poems in English. It is a powerful meter and Owen uses powerful words for his powerful theme but causes no violence but gentleness.

In addition, in the poem, some critics have "heard" many voices, far more than the two soldiers, including Owen himself, observing, the voice of history, the voice of prophecy, the voice of peace and maybe many others. The discerning of them is also painstaking, which makes the poem more complex and fascinating.

Selected Reading

Strange Meeting[1]

It seemed that out of battle I escaped
Down some profound dull tunnel, long since scooped
Through granites which titanic wars[2] had groined[3]
Yet also there encumbered[4] sleepers groaned,
Too fast in thought or death to be bestirred.
Then, as I probed them, one sprang up, and stared
With piteous[5] recognition in fixed eyes,
Lifting distressful hands, as if to bless.
And by his smile, I knew that sullen[6] hall,—
By his dead smile I knew we stood in Hell.

With a thousand pains[7] that vision's face was grained;
Yet no blood reached there from the upper ground,
And no guns thumped, or down the flues made moan.
"Strange friend," I said, "here is no cause to mourn."
"None," said that other, "save the undone years,
The hopelessness. Whatever hope is yours,
Was my life also, I went hunting wild
After the wildest beauty in the world, [8]
Which lies not calm in eyes, or braided hair,
But mocks the steady running of the hour,
And if it grieves, grieves richlier than here.
For by my glee might many men have laughed,
And of my weeping something had been left,
Which must die now I mean the truth untold,
The pity of war, the pity war distilled.[9]
Now men will go content with what we spoiled,
Or, discontent, boil bloody, and be spilled.
They will be swift with swiftness of the tigress.
None will break ranks, though nations trek from progress.
Courage was mine, and I had mystery,
Wisdom was mine, and I had mastery:
To miss the march of this retreating world

Into vain citadels[10] that are not walled.

Then, when much blood had clogged their chariot-wheels,

I would go up and wash them from sweet wells,

Even with truths that lie too deep for taint.

I would have poured my spirit without stint[11]

But not through wounds; not on the cess[12] of war.

Foreheads of men have bled where no wounds were.

I am the enemy you killed, my friend.

I knew you in this dark: for so you frowned

Yesterday through me as you jabbed and killed.

I parried; but my hands were loath and cold.

Let us sleep now ..."

Notes

1. The poem is one of the last Wilfred Owen wrote in 1918. It's said to be unfinished because of the kind of weird ending. This poem shows his use of "pararhyme" (sight rhyme, e.g. hall—hell, wild—world, spoiled—spilled), one of his innovative experiments which have influenced later poets, such as W. H. Auden (1907—1973) and Stephen Spender (1909—1995).

2. **Titanic wars:** here referring to conflicts throughout history on a gigantic scale, not just Owen's war.

3. **groined:** formed curved edge

4. **encumbered:** prevent someone from moving or acting freely or easily

5. **pitious:** not pitying, but calling for pity

6. **sullen:** silent, gloomy

7. **a thousand pains:** the legacy of war inflicted in life not after life

8. **hunting wild after the wildest beauty in the world:** the poet's high-sounding quest for beauty and truth

9. **the pity of war, the pity war distilled:** "pity" here refers to without any emotional by-products, and stands for the useless sacrifice of human lives during war. "distilled" means the pure essence.

10. **citadels:** fortress on high ground overlooking and protecting a city

11. **without stint:** generously and in large amount

12. **cess:** a somewhat Anglo-Irish word meaning "tax, levy" or "luck"(more probably, here)—as used in the phrase "bad cess to you" (may evil befall

you).

Questions for Study and Discussion

1. What does "seemed" in the first line suggest?
2. According to the scene set in the first stanza, what does the place remind you of? What place does it turn out to be? And how do you know it?
3. What does "also" hint in the forth line?
4. Where does the "strange meeting" take place?
5. In what relation do "war" and "hell" stand to each other?
6. Who is the first speaker? And who is the second one?
7. How is the dead enemy of the first speaker humanized in the poem?
8. What does "the truth untold" in line 24 mean?
9. What might he mean when the "strange friend" mentions "the undone years" for which he has to mourn?
10. What kind of future will Europe / humankind have as predicted in the poem?
11. And what aspects of this future does the speaker lament?
12. How do you understand the poem's subject matter?

Thomas Stearns Eliot (1888—1965)

Life and Major Works

Thomas Stearns Eliot was born in a prominent Unitarian Saint Louis, Missouri family; his fifth cousin, Tom Eliot, was Chancellor of Washington University, and his grandfather, William Greenleaf Eliot, was the school's founder. Eliot's major work shows few signs of St. Louis, although there was a Prufrock furniture store in town in his youth.

Eliot graduated from Harvard University in 1909. Eliot made his life and literary career in Britain following a tour of Germany which was

Thomas Stearns Eliot

curtailed by the outbreak of World War I. After the war, in the 1920s, he would spend time with other great artists in the Montparnasse Quarter in Paris, France. He dabbled in the study of Sanskrit and eastern religions and was a student of G. I. Gurdjieff.

In 1915, Eliot published a poem through the assistance of Ezra Pound, *The Love Song of J. Alfred Prufrock*, which brought him to prominence. His style was famous at the time for its freshness and modernism.

Eliot sent a letter to Conrad Aiken late in December 1914. Less than four months later he was introduced to Vivienne Haigh-Wood, a Cambridge governess. At the end of the year, Eliot and Vivienne, both 27 years old, were married in register office.

In the 1960s, Eliot wrote: "I came to persuade myself that I was in love with [Vivienne] simply because I wanted to burn my boats and commit myself to staying in England. And she persuaded herself (also under the influence of Pound) that she would save the poet by keeping him in England. To her the marriage brought no happiness ... to me it brought the state of mind out of which came *The Waste Land*."

Eliot published the long poem, *The Waste Land*, in The Criterion in October 1922. At that time, Eliot was in a period of enormous personal difficulty—his ill-fated marriage was already foundering, and both he and Vivienne suffered from precarious health. *The Waste Land* became one of the principal examples of a new trend in English poetry and came to represent the disillusionment of the post-World War I generation. By the time The Dial republished the poem in November of 1923, Eliot had already distanced himself from the poem's vision of despair, and he wrote "My present ideas are very different" at that time.

The poem has become a familiar touchstone of modern literature despite the alleged obscurity of the poem—its slippage between satire and prophecy, its abrupt and unannounced changes of speaker, location and time, its elegiac but intimidating summoning up of a vast and dissonant range of cultures and literatures. There are famous phrases in the poem, "April is the cruellest month", "I will show you fear in a handful of dust", and "Shantih shantih shantih".

Eliot separated from his wife in 1933. His wife was confined to a mental hospital for the last 9 years of her life, where Eliot did not visit. She tried many times to waylay him, but succeeded only in November 1935 when she was able to get close enough to him after one of his public lectures and ask when he would be coming home.

Eliot's later work is often, but by no means exclusively, religious in nature, but it also attempts to preserve historical English values which Eliot thought important. He expressed his beliefs at the time by saying, "I am an Anglo-Catholic in religion, a classicist in literature and a royalist in politics." This period includes works such as *The Hollow Men*, *Ash-Wednesday*, *The Journey of the Magi*, and *Four Quartets*. Eliot considered *Four Quartets* as his masterpiece, because it draws upon his vast knowledge of mysticism and philosophy. It consists of four poems, *Burnt Norton*, *The Dry Salvages*, *East Coker*, and *Little Gidding*. Each of these is written in several hundred lines totally and broken into five sections. They have many things in common although they resist easy characterization. Each begins with a rumination on the geographical location of its title and each meditates on the nature of time in some important respect — theological, historical, physical, and on its relation to the human condition. A reflective early reading suggests an inexact systematicity among them; they approach the same ideas in varying but overlapping ways, although they do not necessarily exhaust their questions.

Burnt Norton asks what it means to consider things which are not the case but might have been. We see the shell of an abandoned house, and Eliot toys with the idea that all these "merely possible" realities which are invisible to us are present together: all the possible ways people might walk across a courtyard add up to a vast dance we can't see; children who aren't there are hiding in the bushes.

Eliot's plays, mostly in verse, include *Murder in the Cathedral* (1935), *The Family Reunion* (1939), *The Cocktail Party* (1949), *The Confidential Clerk* (1953) and *The Elder Statesman* (1958).

Murder in the Cathedral is a frankly religious work about the death of St. Thomas Becket. Eliot confessed to being influenced by the works of the 17th century preacher, Lancelot Andrewes. Later, Eliot was appointed to the committee which was formed to produce the "New English" translation of the Bible. In 1939 he published a book of poetry for children, *Old Possum's Book of Practical Cats* ("Old Possum" being a name Pound had bestowed upon him), which was to become the basis of the successful West End and Broadway musical, *Cats* that was composed by Andrew Lloyd Webber in 1981. Eliot won two Tony Awards for this.

He was awarded the Nobel Prize in literature "for his outstanding, pioneer contribution to present-day poetry" on November 4, 1948.

After his death, his body was cremated. The ashes were taken to St. Michael's Church in East Coker, the village from which Eliot's ancestors had immigrated to America, according to Eliot's wishes. A simple plaque commemorates him.

Brief Introductions and Appreciation

The dramatic monologue *The Love Song of J. Alfred Prufrock* (1915), a landmark of emerging modernism, is an artistically fresh, visually inventive work. It blends the Victorian forms and rhythms of Alfred, Lord Tennyson, and Robert Browning, and it was composed during the poet's period of casting about for a career and lifestyle with the disdain and self-doubt of Charles Baudelaire. Eliot began the poem with an epitaph in Italian from Inferno, Dante's epic journey into hell. The 131-line main text opens in a seedy part of London, a modern parallel of hell in its joylessness and perpetual torment. The action propelled by the walk of the speaker and an unidentified "you" moves over doubts and questions neatly unified by rhymed couplets, interspersed in lines 3 and 10 with the odd incidents of unrhymed endings. The skewering of the protagonist Prufrock, surreal and menacing, on a surgical table, terrorizes at the same time that it draws the viewer to a subject pinned down for study like an insect in the lab.

The theme is an overt admission of weakness: The speaker confesses an inability to commit to sexual love. Prufrock, unlike Eliot himself, has become a 20th-century clich for the prissy, conflicted bachelor obsessed with a balding head and prim wardrobe and mannerisms. Like the sinuous fog, another reference to his flaccid character, his gaze glides indoors, then outdoors, from surgery to street, social gathering, storm drains, terrace, and back into the "soft October night". The juxtaposition of trivialities with life-disturbing doubts stretches out the tedium of modern life over "a hundred visions and revisions", an internal rhyme with "decisions". Prufrock's inner turmoil threatens to "disturb the universe", unlike the outward control of selecting a tie pin or creasing his slacks. The pathetic hyperbole forms his chaotic thoughts, which swirl around the unexpressed question that dogs him.

Prufrock is not alone in courting disaster through uninvolvement. Passing acquaintances discuss the arts, take tea and coffee, but take no action. That is typical of the modern quandary. Still transfixed in line 57, Prufrock, once more, wriggles away from a decision, choking on "the butt-ends of my days and ways". Aware of the fear of intimacy, he envisions himself as "a pair of ragged claws / Scuttling across the floors of silent seas", a starkly sibilant, crablike image that echoes Macbeth's terror of scorpions in his mind. Well past his prime, Prufrock the shirker ironically envisions himself beheaded like John the Baptist, the prophet of Christ. More realistic is the companion image of the sissy gentleman stretching his arm for death, "the eternal Footman", to dress in burial shroud.

Returning to biblical allusion, Prufrock considers himself as Lazarus, a character in hell, proposed in Luke 16 as a messenger warning mortals to change their ways. Prufrock, who is Fearful of rejection, of being misunderstood, lies splayed on a screen, his nervous system illumined by a magic lantern. Prufrock, unable to claim the tragic significance of Hamlet, settles for Polonius, the fuddy-duddy court adviser who gets himself killed by lurking at the edge of the action. Dismayed by the effects of age, Prufrock imagines women on the beach tittering to each other without summoning him with their songs. In the greater scope, the overripe bachelor merely becomes a symptom. The modern world, like Prufrock, too long enthralled by fancy, has lingered in romanticism and self-indulgent skip until the realities of the modern world threaten to consume it.

Selected Reading

The Love Song of J. Alfred Prufrock[1]
S'io credesse che mia risposta fosse
A persona che mai tomasse at mondo,
Questa fiamma staria senza piu scosse.
Ma perciocche giammai di questo fondo
Non torno vivo alcun, s'i'odo if vero,
Senza tema d'infamia ti rispondo.[2]

Let us go then, you and I[3],
When the evening is spread out[4] against the sky

Like a patient etherised[5] upon a table;
Let us go, through certain half-deserted streets,
The muttering retreats[6]   5
Of restless nights in one-night cheap hotels[7]
And sawdust[8] restaurants with oyster-shells:
Streets that follow like a tedious argument
Of insidious intent
To lead you to an overwhelming question[9]...   10
Oh, do not ask, 'What is it? '
Let us go and make our visit.

In the room the women come and go
Talking of Michelangelo[10].

The yellow fog[11] that rubs its back upon the window-panes,   15
The yellow smoke that rubs its muzzle on the window-panes
Licked its tongue into the comers of the evening,
Lingered upon the pools that stand in drains,
Let fall upon its back the soot that falls from chimneys,
Slipped by the terrace, made a sudden leap,   20
And seeing that it was a soft October night,
Curled once about the house, and fell asleep.[12]

And indeed there will be time
For the yellow smoke that slides along the street,
Rubbing its back upon the window-panes;   25
There will be time, there will be time
To prepare a face to meet the faces that you meet;
There will be time to murder and create,
And time for all the works and days of hands
That lift and drop a question on your plate;[13]   30
Time for you and time for me,
And time yet for a hundred indecisions,
And for a hundred visions and revisions,[14]
Before the taking of a toast and tea.

In the room the women come and go   35
Talking of Michelangelo.

And indeed there will be time
To wonder, 'Do I dare? ' and, 'Do I dare? '
Time to turn back and descend the stair[15],
With a bald spot in the middle of my hair—   40
[They will say: 'How his hair is growing thin!']
My morning coat, my collar mounting firmly to the chin[16],
My necktie rich and modest, but asserted[17] by a simple pin—
[They will say: 'But how his arms and legs are thin! ']
Do I dare   45
Disturb the universe?
In a minute there is time
For decisions and revisions which a minute will reverse.[18]

For I have known them all already, known them all[19]—
Have known the evenings, mornings, afternoons,   50
I have measured out my life with coffee spoons;[20]
I know the voices dying with a dying fall[21]
Beneath the music from a farther room.
So how should I presume[22]?

And I have known the eyes already, known them all—   55
The eyes that fix you in a formulated[23] phrase,
And when I am formulated, sprawling on a pin[24],
When I am pinned and wriggling on the wall,
Then how should I begin
To spit out all the butt-ends of my days and ways?[25]   60
And how should I presume?

And I have known the arms already, known them all—
Arms that are braceleted and white and bare[26]
[But in the lamplight, downed with light brown hair!]

Is it perfume from a dress   65
That makes me so digress?
Arms that lie along a table, or wrap about a shawl.
And should I then presume?
And how should I begin?

Shall I say, I have gone at dusk through narrow streets   70
And watched the smoke that rises from the pipes
Of lonely men in shirt-sleeves, leaning out of windows? ...

I should have been a pair of ragged claws
Scuttling across the floors of silent seas.

And the afternoon, the evening, sleeps so peacefully!   75
Smoothed by long fingers[27],
Asleep... tired... or it malingers,
Stretched on the floor, here beside you and me.
Should I, after tea and cakes and ices[28],
Have the strength to force the moment to its crisis?   80
But though I have wept and fasted, wept and prayed,
Though I have seen my head [grown slightly bald] brought in upon a
platter[29],
I am no prophet-and here's no great matter;
I have seen the moment of my greatness flicker,
And I have seen the eternal Footman[30] hold my coat, and snicker, 85
And in short, I was afraid.[31]

And would it have been worth it[32], after all,
After the cups, the marmalade, the tea,
Among the porcelain, among some talk of you and me,
Would it have been worth while,   90
To have bitten off the matter with a smile,
To have squeezed the universe into a ball[33]
To roll it toward some overwhelming question,
To say: 'I am Lazarus[34], come from the dead,

Come back to tell you all, I shall tell you all' —   95
If one, settling a pillow by her head,
Should say: 'That is not what I meant at all.
That is not it, at all.'

And would it have been worth it, after all,
Would it have been worth while,   100
After the sunsets and the dooryards and the sprinkled streets,
After the novels, after the teacups, after the skirts that trail along the
floor —
And this, and so much more? —
It is impossible to say just what I mean!
But as if a magic lantern[35] threw the nerves in patterns on a screen: 105
Would it have been worth while
If one, settling a pillow or throwing off a shawl,
And turning toward the window, should say:
'That is not it at all,
That is not what I meant, at all.'   110

No! I am not Prince Hamlet[36], nor was meant to be;
Am an attendant lord[37], one that will do
To swell a progress[38], start a scene or two,
Advise the prince; no doubt, an easy tool,
Deferential, glad to be of use[39],   115
Politic, cautious, and meticulous;
Full of high sentence, but a bit obtuse;
At times, indeed, almost ridiculous —
Almost, at times, the Fool[40].

I grow old ... I grow old ...   120
I shall wear the bottoms of my trousers rolled.[41]

Shall I part my hair behind?[42] Do I dare to eat a peach?
I shall wear white flannel trousers, and walk upon the beach.
I have heard the mermaids singing[43], each to each.

I do not think that they will sing to me. 125

I have seen them riding seaward on the waves
Combing the white hair of the waves blown back
When the wind blows the water white and black.[44]

We have lingered in the chambers of the sea
By sea-girls wreathed with seaweed red and brown 130
Till human voices wake us, and we drown.[45]

Notes

1. **The Love Song of J. Alfred Prufrock:** the title of this poem is ironical. A love song should be full of warm emotions, but what we find in the poem is the contrary. This poem was originally entitled "Prufrock among the Women". "J. Alfred Prufrock" follows the early form of Eliot's signature "T. Stearns Eliot". The name "Prufrock" is also ironical, which is the combination of "prude" and "frock". "Prude" means "a person who is excessively attentive to propriety to slight breaches of decorum"; "frock" means "an outer garment, chiefly worn by men when formally dressed". From the name we can have the first glimpse and social status of the character.

2. **S'io credesse che mia risposta fosse ...Senza tema d'infamia ti rispondo:** these lines are taken from Dante's *Inferno*, and are spoken by the character of Count Guido da Montefelltro. Dante meets the punished Guido in the Eighth chasm of Hell. Guido explains that he is speaking freely to Dante only because he believes Dante is one of the dead who could never return to earth to report what he says. Translated from the original Italian, the lines are as follows: "If I thought that my reply would be to someone who would ever return to earth, this flame would remain without further movement; but as no one has ever returned alive from this gulf, if what I hear is true, I can answer you with no fear of infamy."

3. **you and I:** here "you" and "I" are regarded by most critics as two opposite sides or two selves that make up the whole being, that is Prufrock, rather than two individual persons—Prufrock and the lady he invites.

4. **spread out:** this metaphor occurs many times in Bergson's *Time and Free Will* (1910), the work which Eliot, while in Harvard, quoted from most frequently in his writings about Bergson.

5. **etherised:** anesthetized with ether; but also suggesting "made etherial", less real

6. **retreats:** a place of shelter which should give one peace and calm, but there is no restfulness

7. **one-night cheap hotels:** hotels which were cheap and where people would stay for one night

8. **sawdust:** cheap bars and restaurants used to spread sawdust on the floor to soak up spilled beer, etc.

9. **an overwhelming question:** in James Fenimore Cooper's *The Pioneers* (1823), a book Eliot loved as a child, a metaphorical "overwhelming question" occurs.

10. **Michelangelo:** the great Renaissance Italian artist

11. **fog:** according to Eliot, the smoke that blew across the Mississippi from the factories of St. Louis, his hometown.

12. **Licked its tongue into the corners of the evening ... Curled once about the house, and fell asleep:** these lines bring up in our mind a picture of a leisurely cat whose existence does not have any meaning or purpose at all. In this sense, the lines show that human world is totally under the spell of this meaninglessness.

13. **That lift and drop a question on your plate:** the reader is expecting something important to occur after such sentences as "There will be time... to prepare a face to meet the faces that you meet" and "There will be time to murder and create", but unexpectedly he finds something very insignificant.

14. **visions and revisions:** something seen in the mind and change of mind

15. **descend the stair:** indicates that Prufrock is too timid to follow his desire

16. **my collar mounting firmly to the chin:** the hard collar of a coat and the coat were separated and linked by a hidden clasp at that time. Prufrock was wearing a morning coat which could match the hard collar standing straight.

17. **asserted:** made fixed

18. **In a minute there is time / For decisions and revisions which a minute will reverse:** even within such a short period of time as one minute, there is still a multitude of possibilities to change one's mind. This well explains Prufrock's situations of life and his mental conditions, that is, he is always hesitating and drifting.

19. **For I have known them all already, known them all:** here "them" refers to "the evenings, mornings, afternoons", "voices", "eyes", "arms" etc. in the following lines.

20. **I have measured out my life with coffee spoons:** the implied meaning is that he has spent his life in trivial things.

21. **a dying fall:** in Shakespeare's *Twelfth Night*, the lovesick Duke Orsino orders an encore of a moody piece of music: "That strain again! It had a dying fall."

22. **presume:** to claim something that one has no right to. The sudden shift from the question "Do I dare?" to "how should I presume?" shows that his resolution to make the proposal is getting weaker.

23. **formulated:** means "to be reduced to a formular, or to be expressed in a short clear form".

24. **sprawling on a pin:** in the study and collection of insects, specimens are pinned into place and kept in cases. Prufrock feels as though he is being brutally analyzed in a similar manner.

25. **When I am pinned and wriggling on the wall ... To spit out all the butt-ends of my days and ways:** in these lines, Prufrock's inability to do anything against the society he is in is made strikingly clear by using a sharp comparison. Prufrock imagines himself as a kind of butterfly or house lizard pinned on the wall and struggling in vain to get free. This image of a life pinned on the wall is vividly presented to show Prufrock's current predicament. Mere looks from other people would melt Prufrock's courage to assert his existence and make him incapable of doing anything. "Butt-ends" means the ends of smoked cigarettes.

26. **Arms that are braceleted and white and bare:** a bracelet of bright hair about the bone in John Donne's *The Relic*, a line with a "powerful effect" Eliot remarking upon in *The Metaphysical Poets* (1921).

27. **Smoothed by long fingers:** as it is getting late, the shadows grow longer before sunset.

28. **cakes and ices:** cookies and ice cream

29. **Though I have seen my head [grown slightly bald] brought in upon a platter:** Matthew 14:3-11, Mark 6:17-29 in the Bible; the death of John the Baptist. King Herod was enamored of a dancing girl named Salome. He offered her a gift of anything she wanted in his kingdom. Salome's mother told her to request the head of John the Baptist on a silver platter. Herod complied.

30. **eternal Footman:** death

31. **And in short, I was afraid:** in this candid confession, Prufrock blurts out the reason why he is all the time delaying of taking actions. He is simply afraid. Yet afraid of what. The answer can be rather open, but essentially he is afraid because he is unsure of himself in the first place.

32. **And would it have been worth it:** the change into the past tense of the subjective mood shows that the time for Prufrock to ask the hand of the lady is over.

33. **To have squeezed the universe into a ball:** an allusion to Andrew Marvell (1621—1678). His poem *To His Coy Mistress* says: "Let us roll all our strength and all / Our sweetness up into one ball, / And tear out pleasures with rough strife / Through the iron gates of life."

34. **Lazarus:** another Biblical story. In Luke 16:19—31, a Lazarus is a beggar associated with a rich man named Dives in a parable. When they died Lazarus went to Heaven while Dives went to Hell. Dives wanted to warn his brothers about Hell and asked Abraham if Lazarus could be sent back to tell them. Abraham refused saying, "if they hear not Moses and the prophets, neither will they be persuaded, though one rose from the dead."

35. **magic lantern:** early form of slide projector

36. **Prince Hamlet:** Shakespeare's most famous character. The hero Hamlet, like Prufrock, is crippled by indecisiveness. Prufrock echoes Hamlet's famous "to be or not to be" at the end of this line.

37. **attendant lord:** Prufrock having an inferiority complex, stating that he will never be a main character with a purpose, like Hamlet, but rather an "attendant lord" (in this case Polonius), a side character who may slightly move the plot but is buffoonish, a fool (see below).

38. **progress:** a royal journey marked by pageant

39. **Deferential, glad to be of use:** I, Prufrock, am humble and happy to be useful.

40. **Fool:** besides the common meaning, a standard character in Elizabethan drama, as in a court jester who entertains the nobility and speaks in seeming nonsense which contained paradoxical wisdom. Hamlet's court jester was Yorick ("Alas poor Yorick—I knew him Horatio..."). The fool was often also another character in the play, not a court jester, who was used as comic relief. In *Hamlet* it is the gravedigger; in *The Merchant of Venice* it is Launcelot Gobbo, in *Henry IV Part I and II,* it is Falstaff, and so on.

41. **I shall wear the bottoms of my trousers rolled:** it was fashionable to have bottoms of trousers rolled up at that time.

42. **Shall I part my hair behind:** at that time such a hairstyle was considered "daringly bohemian".

43. **the mermaids singing:** Prufrock visualizes mermaids singing. The mermaids symbolize life and vitality and they are in contrast with the women in the drawing room.

44. **have seen them riding seaward on the waves...When the wind blows the water white and black:** here through these lines, Prufrock shows clearly his strong desire for a more vigorous and meaningful existence as the one those fish in Mother Nature have. In the mind of Prufrock, the vitality and healthiness of mermaid's life make his existence, and in the case, the existence of human race as a whole, all the more purposeless and meaningless.

45. **Till human voices wake us, and we drown:** Prufrock has lingered in his visions of the world of mermaids, till human voices call him back to the world of reality.

Questions for Study and Discussion

1. Why does the poet open the poem with a quoted passage from Dante's *Inferno*?

2. Do you think Prufrock has a good sense of who he is, or do you think he is deluded? Give evidence to support your answer.

3. Does Prufrock, the name of a character, suggest extra meaning?

4. "In the room the women come and go / Talking of Michelangelo". Why does the poem describe this phenomenon in the eyes of Prufrock? Try to find as many as ironies as possible in this poem and analyze them.
5. What do the images of "fog" and "smoke" in line 15-16 suggest?
6. Why does Eliot repeat the sentence "there will be time" for many times?
7. In the line "And when I am formulated, sprawling on a pin, / When I am pinned and wriggling on the wall", what does Prufrock compare himself to and why?
8. In the line "I should have been a pair of ragged claws / Scuttling across the floors of silent seas", what does Prufrock compare himself to and why?
9. Discuss religious images in "The Love Song of J. Alfred Prufrock". How do such images function in the poem? Does Eliot treat religion seriously?
10. If you rewrite this poem as a short story, covering one night in the life of Prufrock, where does he go? What does he see that makes him bring up the subjects that he does? In your story, who will you have Prufrock talking to?

Ted Hughes (1930—1998)

Life and Major Works

Ted Hughes, one of the greatest English poets in the 20th century, was born in west Yorkshire on August 17th, 1930. His father, who worked as a carpenter and shopkeeper, was one of the few survivors in his regiment to have survived the battle of Gallipoli during World War I. When Ted was 7, the whole family moved to Mexborough in south Yorkshire. There, he went on many fishing and shooting expeditions with his brother and acquired an impression of the nature as "red in

Ted Hughes

tooth and claw", with creatures killing other creatures for their own survival. This crude and cruel natural landscape of the moors in Yorkshire, coupled with the atrocities and casualties of World War I, impressed Hughes' poetic imagination and decided in large measure his thematic concerns in the future poetic creation.

467

After high school, Hughes entered the Royal Air Force and served for two years as a ground wireless mechanic. During that period of time, he spent a great deal of time reading Shakespeare. Then he began his studies in English at Cambridge but later switched to archaeology and anthropology. The latter subject enabled him to cultivate an inclination for mythology and mythic structures. At the same time, he spent much time in reading Yeats and folklore as well as Shakespeare. In 1956, Hughes married Sylvia Plath, a talented American poet whom he met at Cambridge. After marriage, they lived in the United States for some years and their marriage proved to be fruitful to both of them. During their stay in the USA, Hughes' first book of poems *Hawk in the Rain*, with its harsh rhythms and diction and its vivid grandiose imagery, won Harper Publication Contest and was published to immediate acclaim in both England and the United States in 1957.

In 1959, Hughes' second collection of poems *Lupercal* won the Somerset Maugham Award and the Hawthornden Prize. In December, the two poets returned to England and the following year saw the publication of the book, which firmly established Hughes' reputation as a major poet. In these years Hughes also wrote 2 collections of poems for children: *Meet my Folks!* (1961) and *Earth Owl and Other Moon people* (1963).

However, Hughes' growing professional success was at odds with his personal life. In 1962 Hughes separated from Plath, who killed herself in 1963. But further family tragedy was to follow for Hughes when Wevill, his second wife also committed suicide, taking their daughter with her in 1969. The next year, Hughes married Carol Orchard in 1970 and finally settled in her home county of Devon where he became a farmer and began to enjoy the domestic peace, showing great reluctance to live in the public eye even after 1985, the year when Hughes was honoured with the title of the Poet Laureate of the United Kingdom, a post he held until his death. During all these years of his poetic career, Hughes published more volumes of poems such as *Wodwo* (1967), *Crow* (1970), *Season Songs* (1974), *Gaudete* (1977), *Cave Birds* (1978), *Remains of Elmet* (1979), *Moortown* (1980) and *River* (1983) and won many of Europe's highest literary honors. Besides, he wrote many short stories, plays for radio and stage, and some very fine critical essays in which he went straight to the heart of the matter, conveying somewhat single-minded critical insights with enthusiasm and power. Hughes' creative energies remained high in the late years of his life, during which he published books of poems including *Flowers and Insects* (1986) and *Wolfwatching* (1990). On October 28, 1998, Hughes died of cancer in Devonshore, England. In the same year, his final collection, *The Birthday Letters* (Farrar, Straus & Giroux, 1998) was published, documenting his relationship with Plath.

Ted Hughes began to write poems when he was only 15 and today, he has become reputedly one of the best English poets and is often regarded along with Philip Larkin as representative of the English poetry since World War II. Hughes is a poet of nature in the raw, of primitivism, pessimism, and natural destruction. Under the influence of Blake, Yeats, D. H. Lawrence and Samuel Bechett, Hughes writes the poetry which shows a clear break with the poetic ambitions of The Movement, a group of 1950s British writers who shared a concern with straightforward prose style instead of the extreme romanticism.

His point of view towards life is determined in large measure by two aspects: one is the aftermath of the two world wars which severely affected Europe culturally, historically and psychologically and the other is an "awareness of nature" and an enchantment for the animal world. In his poetry, Hughes is preoccupied with the writing of nature, of animal life, and of the elemental forces of non-human life and the inner turbulence of modern man who is seen as cut off from the instinctual sources of his power. He focuses on the struggle for survival and the pain and suffering that come along with it. With a keen sense of the inadequacy of humanism and the breakdown of all the conventional values, Hughes lays bare the sterility and nihilism in modern man's response to life. His themes express the powerful, often violent energies of nature as well as the relationship between these energies and the divided nature of modern man.

Hughes is a poet writing in the Romantic tradition, who prefers to express an individual insight rather than present traditional values of the society. Hughes constructs a mythic rather than explicitly political framework for this world, using both lyric form and dramatic monologue to give voice to the intense struggle between the hunter and the hunted, the human and the divine. He makes use of freer poetic forms, relies less on strict metrical schemes, and is more inclined towards an arrogant tone and an exaggerated diction. His images are usually simple, vivid but grim with a stark, hard-edged quality; his rhythms are bold, strong and rapid, with heavy stresses and obtrusive alliterations, producing an effect of urgent violence and primitive strength; his language, colloquial and varied, tends to move from comic levity and violence to grotesque surrealism. It is undeniable that Hughes is a talented poet with great gifts of imagination and originality of expression.

Brief Introduction and Appreciation

Ted Hughes, regarded often as a poet of "nature in the raw, of primitivism, pessimism, and natural destruction", published a number of animal poems during his long and distinguished literary career. As a keen countryman and hunter from a young age, he viewed writing poems as a continuation of his earlier passion—"This is hunting and the poem is a new species of creature, a new specimen of the life outside your own."

In the poem of "Hawk Roosting", Hughes attempts to speak with the voice of his animal subject and we see everything through the hawk's eyes, the center upon which everything in the poem pivots. Perched high atop a tree, like a king on his throne, the hawk appears with his eyes closed to be sleeping in a vast wood but his body is still alive to instinct. He has none of man's "falsifying dream", no vision of the world, but he is the embodiment of lordly grandeur. He exults in his domain and fits perfectly into his environment. The whole world is what he sees and the creatures in it exist to assist the survival of the hawk. The high trees, the air that keeps him afloat, the sun that provides warmth and light, and the earth whose surface is open to his keen-eyed scrutiny or inspection, are made so that he may function perfectly. His feet and each single feather on him are the product of numerous years of evolution and adaptation. His life goes on because all the others die for him and he can kill them at will. He even believes himself to be God's supreme creation and is himself a Godlike arbiter of life and death: "My feet are locked upon the rough bark./ It took the whole of Creation/ To produce my foot, my each feather: / Now I hold Creation in my foot." When Hughes has his hawk say, "there is no sophistry in my body", he is emphasizing that the bird is not subject to self-doubt and that it is an absolute solipsist who will not permit things to change: "I am going to keep things like this." So compared with man who is unable to accept nature for what it is, but attempts to tame it, the hawk, with his purely functional purpose built into his blood and body, tries at no stage to hide what he is or apologize for his brutal ways, but merely delights in the essence of his being and is therefore seen as superior to the humans.

As we have seen, throughout the poem Hughes actually describes three aspects about the hawk—his manners, his relations with the nature around him and the change of the nature since his appearance—to show the hawk's great power and his command of the earth below him, and the massive egotism running through the poem may be telling in its implications for the human world. However, the unstated theme lying underneath the animal's soliloquy is that the hawk is a product of nature and his personality is determined by nature. That is to say, the hawk is proper to the nature alone.

Selected Reading

Hawk Roosting

I sit in the top of the wood, my eyes closed.
Inaction[1], no falsifying dream[2]
Between my hooked head and hooked feet:
Or in sleep rehearse perfect kills and eat.

The convenience of the high trees!
The air's buoyancy[3] and the sun's ray
Are of advantage to me;
And the earth's face[4] upward for my inspection.

My feet are locked upon[5] the rough bark.
It took the whole of Creation[6]
To produce my foot, my each feather:
Now I hold Creation in my foot

Or fly up, and revolve it all slowly—
I kill where I please because it is all mine.
There is no sophistry in my body:[7]
My manners are tearing off heads –

The allotment[8] of death.
For the one path of my flight is direct

Through the bones of the living.
No arguments assert my right:

The sun is behind me.
Nothing has changed since I began[9].
My eye has permitted no change.
I am going to keep things like this.

Notes

1. **Inaction**: absolute immobility
2. **no falsifying dream**: It implies that the hawk has no hopes of the impossible and that his only concern is the practical one of killing
3. **The air's buoyancy**: The air that lifts the hawk or keeps him afloat
4. **earth's face**: surface of the earth
5. **are locked upon**: hold firmly
6. **Creation**: the universe and everything in it; the whole world
7. **There is no sophistry in my body**: I do not need to resort to sophistry when I take action. **Sophistry**: the use of false deceptive arguments.
8. **allotment**: distribution; appointment
9. **I began**: I began to exist or appear

Questions for Study and Discussion

1. Who is the speaker? Why did the poet choose "Hawk Roosting" instead of "Roosting Hawk" as the title?
2. How do you comment on the Hawk's "manners"?
3. Is this poem merely a matter-of-fact depiction of the hawk at roosting or an analogy of a human tyranny? What's your understanding?
4. Throughout the poem, the hawk is described as a self-centered creature. Can you find some details to support your idea of the hawk's arrogance?
5. Is there any symbolism adopted in the poem? If so, can you cite some examples to support your idea?
6. Give examples to show how the poet describes the ruthless brutality of the hawk and the contrast between the hawk and the humans.
7. Does the hawk fit right into the environment? Why do you think so?

William Golding (1911—1993)

Life and Major Works

William Golding is one of the famous contemporary novelists in Britain. He was born on 19 September, 1911 in Cornwall, on the south-western tip of England. His father, Alec Golding, was a distinguished school master. The family Golding came from had produced a long line of schoolmasters. Golding was especially interested in literature from his young age. He wrote a play revised from a story in old Egypt at the age of seven. From the age of 12, Golding began to compile a book about the history of the British Chamber of Commerce, which was

William Golding

prepared to consist of 12 volumes. He became a very famous novelist in his middle age. His novels are permeated with the sense of man's sin and guilt.

He was educated at a famous boys' school, Marlborough Grammar School, where his father was the Senior Master. He was expected to be a scientist by his parents; however, he had a very different plan for his own future. According to the wishes of his parents he studied sciences at Oxford University for two years, and then he changed his major to English literature and Anglo-Saxon history. It was during his university years that he published his book—a collection of poems.

After his graduation, Golding followed his family tradition and worked as an English and philosophy teacher at Bishop Wordsworth's School in Salisbury, which was a job he did not like at all. So he quit this job 5 years later in 1940. Then he joined the Royal Navy in command of a rocket ship in the Second World War. He took part in a number of battles during the next five years and fought fiercely because he was bitterly opposed to the Nazi philosophy that advocated the German superiority over all other races.

His wartime experiences played a large part in helping him to form his view of life and also made him witness everything about the ferocity of the war. And also the influence of the war was shown in most of his works. He once explain how his first novel arose from his insights cultivated in the war:

"Anyone who moved through those years without understanding that man produces evil as a bee produces honey, must have been blind or wrong in the head." "The basic point my generation discovered about man was that there was more evil in him than could be accounted for simply by social pressure." The idea he got underlie all of his works that human beings constantly desert opportunities to make a good world, not because of the conscious intention in their mind but because of the weak qualities in their nature that overwhelm them.

When the war was over, Golding returned to his former post as a teacher at Bishop Wordsworth School in 1945, he settled down to go on teaching and furthering his literary career. Although he had written a few books at that time, he was unsuccessful except for a few minor reviews and magazine articles. However, at the same time he did produce three manuscript novels. In 1954, Golding published his first novel *Lord of the Flies* after having been turned down by 21 publishers. It tells about the story of a group of English schoolboys being evacuated by plane to a place of safety during a nuclear war in the near future. Their plane crashes and the boys are stranded on an uninhabited tropical island. Through this adventure story the reader is presented with an analysis of some of the most important philosophical and psychological issues of modern thought. This book became an immediate success in the western countries, through which Golding achieved international fame and wide critical acceptance. This novel is universally considered his masterpiece. This famous novel derives from Defoe's *Robinson Crusoe* and R. M. Ballantyne's *The Coral Island* (1057). In this book, as well as in his many other books, his purpose is to explore into the darkest place of human heart and make people realize the truth of man. At the initial stage of its publication, most people thought that it was really not a success literary work, because in their view it was so completely out of key with contemporary realism and provincialism. Nevertheless, it was recognized as a major literary work later and established him as a prominent contemporary novelist in Britain.

Successively, Golding published a science fiction, *The Inheritors* in 1955. Golding thought this novel is his best book, while other people prefer his first work, *The Lord of the Flies*. *The Inheritors* shows how the arrival of rapacious homo sapiens overruns and corrupts the man. In 1956, Golding published his third novel, *Pincher Martin*, in which he dramatized a shipwrecked sailor who desperately struggled for his life by clinging to a barren rock. His next novel, *Free Fall*, was published in 1959. This work is an elaborate account of the life-drama of Sammy Mountjoy, who runs back his evasive life which was full of wrong choices and failures. From the title, we can realize that one's fall or descent into evil is upon his free will. His another novel entitled *The Spire* came out in 1964. This story is about the building of the spire of a medieval Cathedral. But this seeming holy project of building the spire of the Cathedral turns out to be not an innocent work but a filthy one with all kinds of bad intentions. His another recent novel *Darkness Visible* was published in 1979 after a long gap. The title is taken from Milton's description about the Hell in his *Paradise Lost*. In this novel, evil is even more terribly present.

Golding is a very genuinely serious writer because he held a very strong pessimistic view towards human nature. He thinks that modern civilization, the institutions and order are fragile and temporary, and that man's irrationality and innate evil are strong and enduring. His primary aim in his work is to deal with the innate evil and original sin of man, which operates counter to the forces of reason and civilization. As to himself, he did not trust human nature, so we can say that he is the most pessimistic English writer after the World War II. He thought that human beings are inherently savage and violent, which reflects the whole mood of the postwar years. In 1983 Golding received the Nobel Prize for literature and the Nobel Foundation cited: "his novels which, with the perspicuity of realistic narrative art and the diversity and universality of myth, illuminate the human condition in the world of today."

Brief Introduction and Appreciation

The publication of *Lord of the Flies* established Golding's place in contemporary English literature. To author his masterpiece *Lord of the Flies*, Golding derived inspiration from the popular 19th-century children's adventure tale *the Coral Island* by R. M. Ballantyne. The story of *The Coral Island* revolves around a group of shipwrecked English boys who reach a tropical island and in the true Robinson Crusoe fashion create an idyllic society, namely a reasonable imitation of the pious Victorian English society. The novel intends to manifest that the English people had reached the highest point of evolution in the world, and they serve as a splendid example to all others because of their "natural" superiority. It seemed shallow and hypocritical as modern western society underwent numerous disasters and crises in two terrible world wars. Regarding morality in *The Coral Island* as unrealistic, Golding deliberately re-wrote this story and set an opposite ending for it in *Lord of the Flies*.

Lord of the Flies tells a story of a group of English schoolboys who, marooned on a desert island, are undergoing a striking transition from civilized to barbaric in their horrific exploits. The story begins with a plane crash in the midst of an atomic war, which leaves a bunch of English schoolboys, aged five to twelve, scattered throughout a tropical island somewhere in the Pacific Ocean. Since there are no adult survivors in the plane crash, the boys are excited and enjoy freedom to their hearts' content. Initially, the boys attempt to establish a democratic and civilized social system on the island, and Ralph, a representative of civilization, is elected as the leader. With aids and support from the intellectual Piggy and the highly-perceptive Simon, Ralph strives to establish rules for housing and sanitation. Ralph also makes a signal fire—the group's first priority, hoping that a passing ship will see the smoke signal and rescue them. A major challenge to Ralph's leadership is Jack, who commands a group of choirboys-turned hunters and enjoys the excitement of hunting for pigs. For the sake of hunting, Jack and his followers paint their faces and become savages. Jack draws the other boys slowly away from Ralph's influence. Simon and Piggy remain sober and are murdered by Jack and his dehumanized tribe. Hence the tribe has progressed from butchering pigs to slaying their fellow humans and turned their island paradise into a hellish slaughter house. Then Jack prepares to track down and kill Ralph. They start a fire to smoke him out of one of his hiding places, creating an island-wide forest fire. A passing cruiser sees the smoke from the fire, and a British naval officer arrives on the beach just in time to save Ralph from certain death at the hands of the schoolboys-turned savages.

In a sense, *Lord of the Flies* is a tragic parody of children's adventure tales, illustrating humankind's intrinsic evil nature. This novel reflects Golding's pessimistic outlook which seems to show that without restrictions of society, human beings would likely return to savagery, the primitive part of their nature. The primal, darker human instincts emerges with the steady falling away of civilization. Golding presents the reader with a chronology of events leading a group of young schoolboys from hope to disaster as they attempt to survive the uncivilized, unsupervised, isolated environment until rescued. Golding doesn't simply describe a whole process of the boys' dehumanization, but looks for its source—the dark side of human nature, the savagery that underlies even the most civilized human beings. He exposes the basic evil of human nature and believes that perfection of society is pointless because man's basic evil nature cannot be improved by a better society and man's anarchic nature eventually leads to the downfall of civilization.

Lord of the Flies is an allegorical novel, for throughout the book, there are symbolic characters and objects that directly represent Golding's view of the world and human nature. In Golding's own words, "The whole book is symbolic in nature except the rescue in the end where adult life appears, dignified and capable, but in reality enmeshed in the same evil as the symbolic life of the children on the island." Each of the main characters represents a certain idea or aspect of the spectrum between civilization and savagery. Ralph, the protagonist, embodies the civilizing impulse, as he strives from the start to create order among the boys and to build a stable society on the island. Jack, the antagonist, embodies the impulse toward savagery and the unchecked desire for power and domination. Meanwhile, Piggy represents the scientific and intellectual aspects of civilization. Furthermore, just as various characters embody thematic concepts in the novel, a number of objects do as well. The island is an allegorical microcosm of the human world. What happens there becomes a commentary on the contemporary world. The conch shell, which is used to summon the boys to gatherings and as an emblem of the right to speak at those gatherings, represents order, civilization, and authority. Piggy's glasses, which are used to make fire, symbolize the power of science and intellectual endeavor. The Lord of the flies, the sow's head on a stick in the jungle, meanwhile, embodies the human impulse toward savagery, violence, and barbarism that exists within each person.

Lord of the Flies is remarkable in its style. Golding is a master at controlling the length and types of sentences. When he wants the action to move slowly, he uses long, complex sentences that slow the reader's pace, making us feel as though we were having a leisurely time. When he wants to create tension, the short, choppy sentences are applied and can be read quickly to give the reader a threatening sensation. Golding's deliberate use of imagery enhances the meaning of the story by appealing to the senses. Simon's meditation is surrounded by butterflies, and the Lord of the Flies is covered by flies. While birds make witchlike cries, and coconuts are described as skulls. Golding also uses a mirroring technique. At the beginning of the story, when the boys explore the island, they are excited and jolly with what they find. Here the description is filled with light, color, and friendship. The second exploration recalls the first, but the boys have lost innocence. They are searching for the beast; there are gloom, fear, and isolation in the description.

Lord of the Flies is considered a classic in both theme and form. It is thought-provoking and the major theme is implied in the title, which is the literal translation of the Greek word "Beelzebub", a term used for the Judeo-Christian idea of Satan, meaning the Devil.

Selected Reading

Lord of the Flies

Chapter 9 A View to a Death

Over the island the build-up of clouds continued. A steady current of heated air rose all day from the mountain and was thrust to ten thousand feet; revolving masses of gas piled up the static until the air was ready to explode. By early evening the sun had gone and a brassy glare had taken the place of clear daylight. Even the air that pushed in from the sea was hot and held no refreshment. Colors drained from water and trees and pink surfaces of rock, and the white and brown clouds brooded. Nothing prospered but the flies who blackened their lord and made the spilt guts look like a heap of glistening coal. Even when the vessel broke in Simon's nose and the blood gushed out they left him alone, preferring the pig's high flavor.

With the running of the blood Simon's fit passed into the weariness of sleep. He lay in the mat of creepers[1] while the evening advanced and the cannon[2] continued to play. At last he woke and saw dimly the dark earth close by his cheek. Still he did not move but lay there, his face sideways on the earth, his eyes looking dully before him. Then he turned over, drew his feet under him and laid hold of the creepers to pull himself up. When the creepers shook the flies exploded from the guts with a vicious note and clamped back on again. Simon got to his feet. The light was unearthly. The Lord of the Flies[3] hung on his stick like a black ball.

Simon spoke aloud to the clearing.

"What else is there to do?"

Nothing replied. Simon turned away from the open space and crawled through the creepers till he was in the dusk of the forest. He walked drearily between the trunks, his face empty of expression, and the blood was dry round his mouth and chin. Only sometimes as he lifted the ropes of creeper aside and chose his direction from the trend of the land, he mouthed words that did not reach the air.

Presently the creepers festooned the trees less frequently and there was a scatter of pearly light from the sky down through the trees. This was the backbone of the island, the slightly higher land that lay beneath the mountain where the forest was no longer deep jungle. Here there were wide spaces interspersed with thickets and huge trees and the trend of the ground led him up as the forest opened. He pushed on, staggering sometimes with his weariness but never stopping. The usual brightness was gone from his eyes and he walked with a sort of glum determination like an old man.

A buffet of wind made him stagger and he saw that he was out in the open, on rock, under a brassy sky. He found his legs were weak and his tongue gave him pain all the time. When the wind reached the mountain-top he could see something happen, a flicker of blue stuff against brown clouds. He pushed himself forward and the wind came again, stronger now, cuffing the forest heads till they ducked and roared. Simon saw a humped thing[4] suddenly sit up on the top and look down at him. He hid his face, and toiled on.

The flies had found the figure too. The life-like movement would scare them off for a moment so that they made a dark cloud round the head. Then as the blue material of the parachute collapsed the corpulent[5] figure would bow forward, sighing, and the flies settle once more.

Simon felt his knees smack the rock. He crawled forward and soon he understood. The tangle of lines showed him the mechanics of this parody; he examined the white nasal bones, the teeth, the colors of corruption. He saw how pitilessly the layers of rubber and canvas held together the poor body that should be rotting away. Then the wind blew again and the figure lifted, bowed, and breathed foully at him. Simon knelt on all fours and was sick till his stomach was empty. Then he took the lines in his hands; he freed them from the rocks and the figure from the wind's indignity.

At last he turned away and looked down at the beaches. The fire[6] by the platform appeared to be out, or at least making no smoke. Further along the beach, beyond the little river and near a great slab of rock, a thin trickle of smoke was climbing into the sky. Simon, forgetful of the flies, shaded his eyes with both hands and peered at the smoke. Even at that distance it was possible to see that most of the boys—perhaps all of the boys—were there. So they had shifted camp then, away from the beast[7]. As Simon thought this, he turned to the poor broken thing that sat stinking by his side. The beast was harmless and horrible; and the news must reach the others as soon as possible. He started down the mountain and his legs gave beneath him. Even with great care the best he could do was a stagger.

"Bathing," said Ralph, "that's the only thing to do." Piggy was inspecting the looming-sky through his glass. "I don't like them clouds. Remember how it rained just after we landed?"

"Going to rain again."

Ralph dived into the pool. A couple of littluns[8] were playing at the edge, trying to extract comfort from a wetness warmer than blood. Piggy took off his glasses, stepped primly into the water and then put them on again. Ralph came to the surface and squirted a jet of water at him.

"Mind my specs[9]," said Piggy. "If I get water on the glass I got to get out and clean 'em."

Ralph squirted again and missed. He laughed at Piggy, expecting him to retire meekly as usual and in pained silence. Instead, Piggy beat the water with his hands.

"Stop it!" he shouted. "D'you hear?"

Furiously he drove the water into Ralph's face.

"All right, all right," said Ralph. "Keep your hair on.[10]"

Piggy stopped beating the water.

"I got a pain in my head. I wish the air was cooler."

"I wish the rain would come."

"I wish we could go home."

Piggy lay back against the sloping sand side of the pool. His stomach protruded and the water dried on it. Ralph squinted up at the sky. One could guess at the movement of the sun by the progress of a light patch among the clouds. He knelt in the water and looked round.

"Where's everybody?"

Piggy sat up.

"P'raps they're lying in the shelter."

"Where's Samneric[11]?"

"And Bill?"

Piggy pointed beyond the platform.

"That's where they've gone. Jack's party."

"Let them go," said Ralph, uneasily, "I don't care."

"Just for some meat—"

"And for hunting," said Ralph, wisely, "and for pretending to be a tribe, and putting on war-paint[12]."

Piggy stirred the sand under water and did not look at Ralph.

"P'raps we ought to go too."

Ralph looked at him quickly and Piggy blushed.

"I mean—to make sure nothing happens."

Ralph squirted water again.

Long before Ralph and Piggy came up with Jack's lot, they could hear the party. There was a stretch of grass in a place where the palms left a wide band of turf between the forest and the shore. Just one step down from the edge of the turf was the white, blown sand of above high water, warm, dry, trodden. Below that again was a rock that stretched away toward the lagoon[13]. Beyond was a short stretch of sand and then the edge of the water. A fire burned on the rock and fat dripped from the roasting pig meat into the invisible flames. All the boys of the island, except Piggy, Ralph, Simon, and the two tending the pig, were grouped on the turf. They were laughing, singing, lying, squatting, or standing on the grass, holding food in their hands. But to judge by the greasy faces, the meat eating was almost done; and some held coconut shells in their hands and were drinking from them. Before the party had started a great log had been dragged into the center of the lawn and Jack, painted and garlanded[14], sat there like an idol. There were piles of meat on green leaves near him, and fruit, and coconut shells full of drink.

Piggy and Ralph came to the edge of the grassy platform; and the boys, as they noticed them, fell silent one by one till only the boy next to Jack was talking. Then the silence intruded even there and Jack turned where he sat. For a time he looked at them and the crackle of the fire was the loudest noise over the droning of the reef. Ralph looked away; and Sam, thinking that Ralph had turned to him accusingly, put down his gnawed bone with a nervous giggle. Ralph took an uncertain step, pointed to a palm tree, and whispered something inaudible to Piggy; and they both giggled like Sam. Lifting his feet high out of the sand, Ralph started to stroll past. Piggy tried to whistle.

At this moment the boys who were cooking at the fire suddenly hauled off a great chunk of meat and ran with it toward the grass. They bumped Piggy, who was burnt, and yelled and danced. Immediately, Ralph and the crowd of boys were united and relieved by a storm of laughter. Piggy once more was the center of social derision so that everyone felt cheerful and normal.

Jack stood up and waved his spear.

"Take them some meat."

The boys with the spit gave Ralph and Piggy each a succulent chunk. They took the gift, dribbling. So they stood and ate beneath a sky of thunderous brass that rang with the storm-coming.

Jack waved his spear again.

"Has everybody eaten as much as they want?"

There was still food left, sizzling on the wooden spits, heaped on the green platters. Betrayed by his stomach, Piggy threw a picked bone down on the beach and stooped for more.

Jack spoke again, impatiently.

"Has everybody eaten as much as they want?"

His tone conveyed a warning, given out of the pride of ownership, and the boys ate faster while there was still time. Seeing there was no immediate likelihood of a pause, Jack rose from the log that was his throne and sauntered to the edge of the grass. He looked down from behind his paint at Ralph and Piggy. They moved a little farther off over the sand and Ralph watched the fire as he ate. He noticed, without understanding, how the flames were visible now against the dull light. Evening was come, not with calm beauty but with the threat of violence[15].

Jack spoke.

"Give me a drink."

Henry brought him a shell and he drank, watching Piggy and Ralph over the jagged rim. Power lay in the brown swell of his forearms: authority sat on his shoulder and chattered in his ear like an ape.

"All sit down."

The boys ranged themselves in rows on the grass before him but Ralph and Piggy stayed a foot lower, standing on the soft sand. Jack ignored them for the moment, turned his mask down to the seated boys and pointed at them with the spear.

"Who's going to join my tribe?"

Ralph made a sudden movement that became a stumble. Some of the boys turned toward him.

"I gave you food," said Jack, "and my hunters will protect you from the beast. Who will join my tribe?"

"I'm chief," said Ralph, "because you chose me. And we were going to keep the fire going. Now you run after food—"

"You ran yourself!" shouted Jack. "Look at that bone in your hands!"

Ralph went crimson.

"I said you were hunters. That was your job."

Jack ignored him again.

"Who'll join my tribe and have fun?"

"I'm chief," said Ralph tremulously. "And what about the fire? And I've got the conch[16]—"

"You haven't got it with you," said Jack, sneering. "You left it behind. See, clever? And the conch doesn't count at this end of the island—"

All at once the thunder struck. Instead of the dull boom there was a point of impact in the explosion.

"The conch counts here too," said Ralph, "and all over the island."

"What are you going to do about it then?"

Ralph examined the ranks of boys. There was no help in them and he looked away, confused and sweating. Piggy whispered.

"The fire—rescue."

"Who'll join my tribe?"

"I will."

"Me."

"I will."

"I'll blow the conch," said Ralph breathlessly, "and call an assembly."

"We shan't hear it."

Piggy touched Ralph's wrist.

"Come away. There's going to be trouble. And we've had our meat."

There was a blink of bright light beyond the forest and the thunder exploded again so that a littlun started to whine. Big drops of rain fell among them making individual sounds when they struck.

"Going to be a storm," said Ralph, "and you'll have rain like when we dropped here. Who's clever now? Where are your shelters? What are you going to do about that?"

The hunters were looking uneasily at the sky, flinching from the stroke of the drops. A wave of restlessness set the boys swaying and moving aimlessly. The flickering light became brighter and the blows of the thunder were only just bearable. The littluns began to run about, screaming.

Jack leapt on to the sand.

"Do our dance[17]! Come on! Dance!"

He ran stumbling through the thick sand to the open space of rock beyond the fire. Between the flashes of lightning the air was dark and terrible; and the boys followed him, clamorously. Roger became the pig, grunting and charging at Jack, who side-stepped. The hunters took their spears, the cooks took spits, and the rest clubs of firewood. A circling movement developed and a chant. While Roger mimed the terror of the pig, the littluns ran and jumped on the outside of the circle. Piggy and Ralph, under the threat of the sky, found themselves eager to take a place in this demented but partly secure society. They were glad to touch the brown backs of the fence that hemmed in the terror and made it governable.

"Kill the beast! Cut his throat! Spill his blood!"

The movement became regular while the chant lost its first superficial excitement and began to beat like a steady pulse. Roger ceased to be a pig and became a hunter, so that the center of the ring yawned emptily. Some of the littluns started a ring on their own; and the complementary circles went round and round as though repetition would achieve safety of itself. There was the throb and stamp of a single organism.

The dark sky was shattered by a blue-white scar. An instant later the noise was on them like the blow of a gigantic whip. The chant rose a tone in agony.

"Kill the beast! Cut his throat! Spill his blood!"

Now out of the terror rose another desire, thick, urgent, blind.

"Kill the beast! Cut his throat! Spill his blood!"

Again the blue-white scar jagged above them and the sulphurous explosion beat down. The littluns screamed and blundered about, fleeing from the edge of the forest, and one of them broke the ring of biguns[18] in his terror.

"Him! Him!"

The circle became a horseshoe. A thing was crawling out of the forest. It came darkly, uncertainly. The shrill screaming that rose before the beast was like a pain. The beast stumbled into the horseshoe.

"Kill the beast! Cut his throat! Spill his blood!"

The blue-white scar was constant, the noise unendurable. Simon was crying out something about a dead man on a hill.

"Kill the beast! Cut his throat! Spill his blood! Do him in[19]!"

The sticks fell and the mouth of the new circle crunched and screamed. The beast was on its knees in the center, its arms folded over its face. It was crying out against the abominable noise something about a body on the hill. The beast struggled forward, broke the ring and fell over the steep edge of the rock to the sand by the water. At once the crowd surged after it, poured down the rock, leapt on to the beast, screamed, struck, bit, tore. There were no words, and no movements but the tearing of teeth and claws.

Then the clouds opened and let down the rain like a waterfall. The water bounded from the mountain-top, tore leaves and branches from the trees, poured like a cold shower over the struggling heap on the sand. Presently the heap broke up and figures staggered away. Only the beast lay still, a few yards from the sea. Even in the rain they could see how small a beast it was; and already its blood was staining the sand.

Now a great wind blew the rain sideways, cascading the water from the forest trees. On the mountain-top the parachute filled and moved; the figure slid, rose to its feet, spun, swayed down through a vastness of wet air and trod with ungainly feet the tops of the high trees; falling, still falling, it sank toward the beach and the boys rushed screaming into the darkness. The parachute took the figure forward, furrowing the lagoon, and bumped it over the reef and out to sea.

Toward midnight the rain ceased and the clouds drifted away, so that the sky was scattered once more with the incredible lamps of stars. Then the breeze died too and there was no noise save the drip and trickle of water that ran out of clefts and spilled down, leaf by leaf, to the brown earth of the island. The air was cool, moist, and clear; and presently even the sound of the water was still. The beast lay huddled on the pale beach and the stains spread, inch by inch.

The edge of the lagoon became a streak of phosphorescence which advanced minutely, as the great wave of the tide flowed. The clear water mirrored the clear sky and the angular bright constellations. The line of phosphorescence bulged about the sand grains and little pebbles; it held them each in a dimple of tension, then suddenly accepted them with an inaudible syllable and moved on.

Along the shoreward edge of the shallows the advancing clearness was full of strange, moonbeam-bodied creatures with fiery eyes. Here and there a larger pebble clung to its own air and was covered with a coat of pearls. The tide swelled in over the rain-pitted sand and smoothed everything with a layer of silver. Now it touched the first of the stains that seeped from the broken body and the creatures made a moving patch of light as they gathered at the edge. The water rose farther and dressed Simon's coarse hair with brightness. The line of his cheek silvered and the turn of his shoulder became sculptured marble. The strange attendant creatures, with their fiery eyes and trailing vapors, busied themselves round his head. The body lifted a fraction of an inch from the sand and a bubble of air escaped from the mouth with a wet plop. Then it turned gently in the water.

Somewhere over the darkened curve of the world the sun and moon were pulling, and the film of water on the earth planet was held, bulging slightly on one side while the solid core turned. The great wave of the tide moved farther along the island and the water lifted. Softly, surrounded by a fringe of inquisitive bright creatures, itself a silver shape beneath the steadfast constellations, Simon's dead body moved out toward the open sea.

Notes

1. **creeper:** the vine-like plants that grow by creeping and encompass the island.
2. **the cannon:** the sound of thunder, foreshadowing the coming storm
3. **the Lord of the Flies:** the sow's head on a stick presented by Jack and his hunters as a gift for the imaginary beast. It is now rotting and covered by

crowds of flies.

4. **a humped thing:** the sham beast on the mountain-top—a dead parachute man

5. **corpulent:** excessively fat

6. **the fire:** the signal fire kept by the boys with the hope that a passing ship will see the smoke and come to rescue.

7. **the beast:** an imaginary object on the island which frightens the boys. Actually the beast is something internal: it exists in the man himself.

8. **littluns:** little ones, refers to the younger boys around the age of six

9. **specs:** spectacles

10. **keep your hair on:** (idiom) keep calm and not to over-react or lose your temper.

11. **Samneric:** Sam and Eric are twin brothers who do everything together and because of this become like one person with the address Samneric.

12. **war-paint:** Jack and his hunters paint their faces for the sake of hunting pigs.

13. **the lagoon:** the place where Ralph finds the conch and encounters Piggy at the opening of the story.

14. **painted and garlanded:** Jack thrones himself as the tribe leader, with paint on his face and a garland round his neck.

15. **the threat of violence:** the foreboding of a violent storm

16. **the conch:** the object used to call an assembly and to preserve order during the assembly. It is the symbol of order and authority, for who holds it has the right to speak and all boys on the island have the same right.

17. **dance:** a ritual around the fire that savages perform when engaged in desperate, destructive hunting. Here the choirboys-turned hunters act out the reenactment of the hunting by dancing, chanting and killing, and the human depravity to savagery reaches its climax. The charm is even irresistible to Ralph and Piggy.

18. **biguns:** big ones, refers to the bigger boys between the ages of ten and twelve.

19. **do him in:** (slang) kill him

Questions for Study and Discussion

1. There are descriptions of the coming storm on the tropical island. How does

the storm function in the events of this chapter?

2. Simon insists on climbing the mountain to find out what the beast is. Against the boys' derision he says, and against the warning of the Lord of the flies he repeats, "What else is there to do?" What does Simon imply when he speaks it aloud to the clearing in paragraph 4?

3. Study the Golding's description of Simon in paragraph 6: "The usual brightness was gone from his eyes and he walked with a sort of glum determination like an old man." What a man do you think Simon is, and what causes the unusualness of Simon?

4. What does Simon find on the mountain-top? Why is he eager to inform the news to the other boys? What is the significance of Simon's discovery?

5. What role does Piggy play? Why is he always the center of derision? What might he and his glasses represent?

6. How does Golding make use of certain symbols to convey his philosophy of human nature? Find out three most significant symbols in this chapter and explain what each symbolizes.

7. Describe the ritual around the fire. What are the hunters preoccupied with? Why do they repeat the chant, "Kill the beast! Cut his throat! Spill his blood!"? How is the dehumanization of the boys coming to a climax?

8. What devices does Golding use to create tension as the event reaches its climax?

9. Does Ralph and Piggy take part in killing Simon? Do you think Ralph and Piggy are responsible for Simon's death? Explain your reason.

10. What Biblical parallel is there to Simon's death? In view of the fate of the saintly Simon, can visionary insight into the human condition save the boys?

Doris Lessing (1919—)

Life and Major Works

Doris Lessing was born Doris May Tayler to Captain Alfred Tayler and Emily Maude Tayler on October 22, 1919. Although she was born in Persia (now Iran), both of her parents were British. Her father, who had lost a leg during his service in World War I, was a clerk in the Imperial Bank of Persia. Her mother had been a nurse at the Royal Free Hospital. In 1925, the family moved to the British Colony of Southern Rhodesia (now Zimbabwe), wishing to get rich through maize farming. Captain Tayler purchased one thousand acres of bush for that purpose. Doris's mother adapted to the rough life in the settlement, and tried energetically to reproduce what she thought was a civilized, Edwardian life among savages. But the family business turned out to be a failure, and the promised wealth never came as the Taylers had expected.

Doris Lessing

Doris' childhood was described by herself as a mixture of pleasure and pain. In the natural world, she enjoyed the fun of exploration with her brother Harry. But at home and in school, she was faced with the rigid or even cruel education from her mother and the nuns. Doris was educated at the Dominican Covent High School but left school at 14, and thereafter was self-educated. She left home at 15 and worked as a nursemaid, and started to read and write. In fact, Lessing made herself into a self-educated intellectual. Her miserable childhood became her literary inspiration and loads of books ordered from London became her source of imagination and a retreat into other worlds.

In 1937, Doris Lessing moved to Salisbury, where she worked as a telephone operator for one year. She met Frank Wisdom there and soon married him. They had two children. The marriage, however, did not last long. They had a divorce in 1943, but Doris remained in Salisbury and was drawn to the Left Book Club, a group of Communists. There she met her second husband, Gottfried Lessing. Soon after their marriage they had a son. But the year of 1949 saw the end of their marriage.

After their divorce, Doris took the son of Gottfried and herself to London, and soon established her name as a writer. She joined the British Communist Party, but left it in 1956. Between 1956 and 1995, Doris Lessing was prohibited from entering South Africa because of her criticism of the country.

In 2001 she was awarded the Prince of Asturias Prize in Literature, one of Spain's most important distinctions, for her brilliant literary works in defense of freedom and Third World causes. She also received the David Cohen

British Literature Prize. She was on the shortlist for the first Man Booker International Prize in 2005. In 2007 she was awarded the Nobel Prize for Literature. She was described by the Swedish Academy as "that epicist of the female experience, who with scepticism, fire and visionary power has subjected a divided civilisation to scrutiny". Lessing is the 11th woman to win the Nobel Prize in its 106-year history, and also the oldest person ever to win the literature award.

Being a famous writer, Lessing declined a damehood, but accepted a Companion of Honour at the end of 1999 for "conspicuous national service". She has also been made a Companion of Literature by the Royal Society of Literature.

Lessing's fiction is commonly divided into three phases: the Communist theme (1944—1956), when she was writing radically on social issues; the psychological theme (1956—1969); and after that the Sufi theme, which was explored in a science fiction setting in the *Canopus* series. Lessing's switch to science fiction was not welcomed by many critics. To this Lessing replied: "What they didn't realize was that in science fiction is some of the best social fiction of our time." Unlike some authors primarily known for their mainstream work, she has never hesitated to admit that she writes science fiction. She was Writer Guest of Honour at the 1987 World Science Fiction Convention (Worldcon). When asked about which of her books she considered most important, Lessing chose the *Canopus in Argos* science fiction series (1979—1983).

Doris Lessing's first book as a novelist was *The Grass is Singing* (1950), which examines the relationship between a white farmer's wife and her black servant. The semi-autobiographical *Children of Violence* series, usually called the Martha Quest series for its main character, is largely set in Africa. The series comprises *Martha Quest* (1952), *A Proper Marriage* (1954), *A Ripple from the Storm* (1958), *Landlocked* (1965) and *The Four-Gated City* (1969). The masterpiece is the final volume of the series, *The Four-Gated City*, a period fresco apparently enveloping all of England.

The Golden Notebook (1962) is Doris Lessing's real breakthrough. It has been considered a pioneering work by the feminist movement and it belongs to the handful of books that informed the 20th-century view of the male-female relationship.

Briefing for a Descent into Hell (1971) was considered by the author herself as "inner-space fiction": an attempt in the spirit of Romanticism to expand human knowledge to encompass regions beyond the control of reason and the ego.

In the novel series *Canopus in Argos: Archives* (vol. 1–5, 1979—1984) Lessing expanded the science fiction genre. The series studies the post-atomic war development of the human species. Lessing depicts the opposition of opinions about colonialism, nuclear war and ecological disaster between female and male.

Lessing returned to realistic narrative in *The Good Terrorist* (1985). In this novel she provided a satirical picture of the need of the contemporary left for total control and the female protagonist's misdirected sacrifice.

The autobiographical *Under My Skin* (1994) and *Walking in the Shade* (1997) marked a new peak in her literary career. Lessing recalls not only her own life but the entire epoch: England in the last days of the empire.

A common theme in science fiction: the global catastrophe, forcing mankind to return to a more primitive life, has had special appeal for Doris Lessing. It has appeared in some of her books of recent years: the fantasy novel *Mara and Dann* (1999) and its sequel *The Story of General Dann and Mara's Daughter, Griot and the Snow Dog* (2005).

Lessing's most recent novel is *Alfred and Emily*. She has announced it is her final book.

Brief Introduction and Appreciation

Lessing grew up on a farm in Africa where she spent her childhood exploring the wild life on the veld. The veld is a huge grassy land with few bushes and trees. She was allowed to roam the veld and carry with her a rifle to shoot game for the family's food. With this unusual experience for a female at her time, she claimed that her real education came from the observation of nature on the veld. The veld actually became the setting of her many stories, among which is "A Sunrise on the Veld".

"A Sunrise on the Veld" tells the story of a boy who experiences the transfer from the wonder of life to the awareness of the ending of life—death. It is a story that explores feelings of fear, anger and grief that most human beings feel when they must face the reality of suffering and death.

At the beginning of the story, the boy gets up early in the morning and feels proud for his ability of controlling himself and the environment around. The boy has trained himself to wake up exactly at half past four without using the alarm clock. He considers the desire to stay longer in bed a weakness he should overcome. When he does, he feels he has full control over his limbs, muscles, thought and even brain. Dressed yet bare footed, the boy crept through the house in the cold of the early morning. He went out with his dogs and a gun. He began to run on the grassy land. During his enjoyment of the moment, he was being bothered by small cries of a creature in pain. The boy then went to find out the source of the cries and saw a buck dying, covered in black ants. He realized there was nothing he could do for the poor animal. The feeling of having everything under his control disappeared—he had no control over this situation. After the buck has been eaten clean and become a skeleton, the boy went over to look at it closely. He imagined what it looked like when it was alive. He imagined how the buck had run happily in the grass early in the morning, like he was doing. The boy discovered that the buck's leg had been broken. He began to realize that death happens to all creatures. He also realized that even though he could control the situation to some extent, a lot of things in this world no one can control.

The most impressive thing about the story is probably Lessing's talent of depicting the personality of a character. She describes the boy's intense feelings by using various rhetorical devices.

To begin with, she pictures the feel of an early morning on the grasslands with her creative use of the language. Repetition is often considered something to be avoided in writing; however in this story, Lessing constructively uses repetition to emphasize the coldness of the morning air. In addition, the frequent use of metaphors and similes helps the story to appeal to the reader's senses. For example, she describes the simile as "springing out like a fish", which reminds the reader of the sting of chilly water. Personification is another device she adopts when she describes the wait for the sun to "paint the world afresh", like an artist. Furthermore, Lessing uses contrast to reinforce ideas. For instance, she contrasts the cold morning air with the stuffiness of the parents' room.

With her vivid description and careful observation, Lessing best portraits a young boy in his process of becoming mature.

Selected Reading

A Sunrise on the Veld[1]

Every night that winter he said aloud into the dark of the pillow: Half-past four! Half-past four! till his brain had gripped[2] the words and held them fast. Then he fell asleep at once, as if a shutter had fallen; and lay with his face turned to the clock so that he could see it first thing when he woke.

It was half-past four to the minute, every morning. Triumphantly pressing down the alarm-knob of the clock, which the dark half of his mind had outwitted, remaining vigilant[3] all night and counting the hours as he lay relaxed in sleep, he huddled down for a last warm moment under the clothes, playing with the idea of lying abed for this once only. But he played with it for the fun of knowing that it was a weakness he could defeat without effort; just as he set the alarm each night for the delight of the moment when he woke and stretched his limbs, feeling the muscles tighten, and thought: Even my brain— even that! I can control every part of myself.

Luxury of warm rested body, with the arms and legs and fingers waiting like soldiers for a word of command! Joy of knowing that the precious hours were given to sleep voluntarily!—for he had once stayed awake three nights running, to prove that he could, and then worked all day, refusing even to admit that he was tired; and now sleep seemed to him a servant to be commanded and refused.

The boy stretched his frame full-length, touching the wall at his head with his hands, and the bedfoot with his toes; then he sprung out, like a fish leaping from water. And it was cold, cold.

He always dressed rapidly, so as to try and conserve his night-warmth till the sun rose two hours later; but by the time he had on his clothes his hands were numbed and he could scarcely hold his shoes. These he could not put on for fear of waking his parents, who never came to know how early he rose.

As soon as he stepped over the lintel, the flesh of his soles contracted on the chilled earth, and his legs began to ache with cold. It was night: the stars were glittering, the trees standing black and still. He looked for signs of day, for the greying[4] of the edge of a stone, or a lightening in the sky where the sun would rise, but there was nothing yet. Alert as an animal he crept past the dangerous window, standing poised with his hand on the sill for one proudly fastidious moment, looking in at the stuffy blackness of the room where his parents lay.

Feeling for the grass-edge of the path with his toes, he reached inside another window further along the wall, where his gun had been set in readiness the night before. The steel was icy, and numbed fingers slipped along it, so that he had to hold it in the crook of his arm for safety. Then he tiptoed to the room where the dogs slept, and was fearful that they might have been tempted to go before him; but they were waiting, their haunches[5] crouched in reluctance at the cold, but ears and swinging tails greeting the gun ecstatically. His warning undertone kept them secret and silent till the house was a hundred yards back: then they bolted off into the bush, yelping excitedly. The boy imagined his parents turning in their beds and muttering: Those dogs again! before they were dragged back in sleep; and he smiled scornfully. He always looked back over his shoulder at the house before he passed a wall of trees that shut it from sight. It looked so low and small, crouching there under a tall and brilliant sky. Then he turned his back on it.

He would have to hurry. Before the light grew strong he must be miles away; and already a tint of green stood in the hollow of a leaf, and the air smelled of morning and the stars were dimming.

He slung the shoes over his shoulder, veld skoen[6] that were crinkled and hard with the dews of a hundred mornings. They would be necessary when the ground became too hot to bear. Now he felt the chilled dust push up between his toes, and he let the muscles of his feet spread and settle into the shapes of the earth; and he thought: I could walk a hundred miles on feel like these! I could walk all day, and never tire!

He was walking swiftly through the dark tunnel of foliage[7] that in day-time was a road. The dogs were invisibly ranging the lower travelways of the bush, and he heard them panting. Sometimes he felt a cold muzzle on his leg before they were off again, scouting for a trail to follow. They were not trained, but free-running companions of the hunt, who often tired of the long stalk before the final shots, and went off on their own pleasure. Soon he could see them, small and wild-looking in a wild strange light, now that the bush stood trembling on the verge of colour[8], waiting for the sun to paint earth and grass afresh.

The grass stood to his shoulders; and the trees were showering a faint silvery rain. He was soaked; his whole body was clenched in a steady shiver.

Once he bent to the road that was newly scored with animal trails, and regretfully straightened, reminding himself that the pleasure of tracking must wait till another day.

He began to run along the edge of a field, noting jerkily how it was filmed over with fresh spiderweb, so that the long reaches of great black clods seemed netted in glistening grey. He was using the steady lope he had learned by watching the natives, the run that is a dropping of the weight of the body from one foot tot the next in a slow balancing movement that never tires, nor shortens the breath; and he felt the blood pulsing down his legs and along his arms, and the exultation and pride of body mounted in him till he was shutting his teeth hard against a violent desire to shout his triumph.

Soon he had left the cultivated part of the farm. Behind him the bush was low and black. In front was a long vlei[9], acres of long pale grass that sent back a hollowing gleam of light to a satiny sky. Near him thick swathes of grass were bent with the weight of water, and diamond drops sparkled on each frond.

The first bird woke at his feet and at once a flock of them sprang into the air calling shrilly that day had come; and suddenly, behind him, the bush woke into song, and he could hear the guinea fowl calling far ahead of him. That meant they would now be sailing down from their trees into thick grass, and it was for them he had come: he was too late. But he did not mind. He forgot he had come to shoot. He set his legs wide, and balanced from foot to foot, and swung his gun up and down in both hands horizontally, in a kind of improvised exercise, and let his head sink back till it was pillowed in his neck muscles and watched how above him small rosy clouds floated in a lake of gold.

Suddenly it all rose in him: it was unbearable, and he leapt up into the air, shouting and yelling wild, unrecognisable noises. Then he began to run, not carefully, as he had before, but madly, like a wild thing. He was clean crazy, yelling mad with the joy of living and a superfluity[10] of youth. He rushed down the vlei under a tumult of crimson and gold, while all the birds of the world sang around him. He ran in great, leaping strides, and shouted as he ran, feeling his body rise into the crisp rushing air and fall back surely on to sure feet; and thought briefly, not believing that such a thing could happen to him, that he could break his ankle any moment, in this thick tangled grass. He cleared bushes like a duiker, leapt over rocks; and finally came to a dead stop at a place where the ground fell abruptly away below him to the river. It had been a two-mile-long dash through waist-high growth, and he was breathing hoarsely and could no longer sing. But he poised on a rock and looked down at stretches of water that gleamed through stooping trees, and thought suddenly, I am fifteen! Fifteen! The words came new to him; so that he kept repeating them wonderingly, with swelling excitement; and he felt the years of his life with his hands, as if he were counting marbles, each one hard and separate and compact, each one a wonderful shining thing. That was what he was: fifteen years of this rich soil, and this slow-moving water, and air that smelt like a challenge whether it was warm and sultry at noon, or as brisk as cold water, like it was now.

There was nothing he couldn't do, nothing! A vision came to him, as he stood there, like when a child hears the word "eternity" and tries to understand it, and time takes possession of the mind. He felt his life ahead of him as a great and wonderful thing, something that was his; and he said aloud, with the blood rushing to his head: all the great men of the world have been as I am now, and there is nothing I can't become, nothing I can't do; there is no country in the world I cannot make part of myself, if I choose. I contain the world. I can make of it what I want. If I choose, I can change everything that is going to happen: it depends on me, and what I decide now.

The urgency and the truth and the courage of what his voice was saying exulted him so that he began to sing again, at the top of his voice, and the sound went echoing down the river gorge. He stopped for the echo, and sang again: stopped and shouted. That was what he was!—he sang, if he chose; and the world had to answer him.

And for minutes he stood there, shouting and singing and waiting for the lovely eddying sound of the echo; so that his own new strong thoughts came back and washing round his head, as if someone were answering him and encouraging him; till the gorge was full of soft voices clashing back and forth from rock to rock over the river. And then it seemed as if there was a new voice. He listened, puzzled, for it was not his own. Soon he was leaning forward, all his nerves alert, quite still: somewhere close to him there was a noise that was no joyful bird, nor tinkle of falling water, nor ponderous movement of cattle.

There it was again. In the deep morning hush that held his future and his past, was a sound of pain, and repeated over and over: it was a kind of shortened scream, as if someone, something, had no breath to scream. He came to himself, looked about him, and called for the dogs. They did not appear; they had gone off on their own business, and he was alone. Now he was clean sober, all the madness gone. His heart beating fast, because of that frightened screaming, he stepped carefully off the rock and went towards a belt of trees. He was moving cautiously, for not so long ago he had seen a leopard in just this spot.

At the edge of the trees he stopped and peered, holding his gun ready; he advanced, looking steadily about him, his eyes narrowed. Then all at once, in the middle of a step, he faltered, and his face was puzzled. He shook his head impatiently, as if he doubted his own sight.

There, between two trees, against a background of gaunt black rocks, was a figure from a dream, a strange beast that was horned and drunken-legged, but like something he had never even imagined. It seemed to be ragged. It looked like a small buck that had black ragged tufts of fur standing up irregularly all over it, with patches of raw flesh beneath ... but the patches of rawness were disappearing under moving black and came again elsewhere; and all the time the creature screamed, in small gasping screams, and leaped drunkenly from side to side, as if it were blind.

Then the boy understood: it was a buck. He ran closer, and again stood still, stopped by a new fear. Around him the grass was whispering and alive. He looked wildly about, and then down. The ground was black with ants, great energetic ants that took no notice of him, but hurried and scurried towards the fighting shape, like glistening black water flowing through the grass.

And, as he drew in his breath and pity and terror seized him, the beast fell and the screaming stopped. Now he could hear nothing but one bird singing, and the sound of the rustling, whispering ants.

He peered over at the writhing blackness that jerked convulsively with the jerking nerves. It grew quieter. There were small twitches from the mass that still looked vaguely like the shape of a small animal.

It came into his mind that he should shoot it and end its pain; and he raised the gun. Then he lowered it again. The buck could no longer feel; its fighting was a mechanical protest of the nerves. But it was not that which made him put down the gun. It was a swelling feeling of rage and misery and protest that expressed itself in the thought: if I had not come it would have died like this:

so why should I interfere? All over the bush things like this happen; they happen all the time; this is how life goes on, by living things dying in anguish. He gripped the gun between his knees and felt in his own limbs the myriad[11] swarming pain of the twitching animal that could no longer feel, and set his teeth, and said over and over under his breath: I can't stop it. I can't stop it. There is nothing I can do.

He was glad that he did not have to make a decision to kill it even when he was feeling with his whole body: this is what happens, this is how things work.

It was right—that was what he was feeling. It was right and nothing could alter it.

The knowledge of fatality, of what has to be, had gripped him and for the first time in his life; and he was left unable to make any movement of brain or body, except to say: "Yes, yes. That is what living is." It had entered his flesh and his bones and grown in to the furthest corners of his brain and would never leave him. And at that moment he could not have performed the smallest action of mercy, knowing as he did, having lived on it all his life, the vast, unalterable, cruel veld, where at any moment one night stumble over a skull or crush the skeleton of some small creature.

Suffering, sick, and angry, but also grimly satisfied with his new stoicism, he stood there leaning on his rifle, and watched the seething black mound grown smaller. At his feet, now, were ants trickling back with pink fragments in their mouths, and there was a fresh acid smell in his nostrils. He sternly controlled the uselessly convulsing muscles of his empty stomach, and reminded himself: the ants must eat too! At the same time he found that the tears were streaming down his face, and his clothes were soaked with the sweat of that other creature's pain.

The shape had grown small. Now it looked like nothing recognisable. He did not know how long it was before he saw the blackness thin, and bits of white showed through, shining in the sun—yes, there was the sun, just up, glowing over the rocks. Why, the whole thing could not have taken longer than a few minutes.

He began to swear, as if the shortness of the time was in itself unbearable, using the words he had heard his father say. He strode forward, crushing ants with each step, and brushing them off his clothes, till he stood above the skeleton, which lay sprawled under a small bush. It was clean-picked.[12] It might have been lying there years, save that on the white bone were pink fragments of gristle. About the bones ants were ebbing away, their pincers full of meat.

The boy looked at them, big black ugly insects. A few were standing and gazing up at him with small glittering eyes.

"Go away!" he said to the ants, very coldly. "I am not for you—not just yet, at any rate. Go away." And he fancied that the ants turned and went away.

He bent over the bones and touched the sockets in the skull: that was where the eyes were, he thought incredulously, remembering the liquid dark eyes of a buck. And then he bent the slim foreleg bone, swinging it horizontally in his palm.

That morning, perhaps an hour ago, this small creature had been stepping proudly and free through the bush, feeling the chill on its hide even as he himself had done, exhilarated by it. Proudly stepping the earth, tossing its horns, frisking a pretty white tail, it had sniffed the cold morning air. Walking like kings and conquerors it had moved through this fee-held bush, where each blade of grass grew for it alone, and where the river ran pure sparkling water for its slaking.

And then—what had happened? Such a swift surefooted[13] thing could surely not be trapped by a swarm of ants?

The boy bent curiously to the skeleton. Then he saw that the back leg that lay uppermost and strained out in the tension of death, was snapped midway in the thigh, so that broken bones jutted over each other uselessly. So that was it! Limping into the ant-masses it could not escape, once it had sensed the danger. Yes, but how had the leg been broken? Had it fallen, perhaps? Impossible, a buck was too light and graceful. Had some jealous rival horned it?

What could possibly have happened? Perhaps some Africans had thrown stones at it, as they do, trying to kill it for meat, and had broken its leg. Yes, that must be it.

Even as he imagined the crowd of running, shouting natives, and the flying stones, and the leaping buck, another picture came into his mind. He saw himself, on any one of these bright ringing mornings, drunk with excitement, taking a snap shot at some half-seen buck. He saw himself with the gun lowered, wondering whether he had missed or not; and thinking at last that it was late, and he wanted his breakfast, and it was not worth while to track miles after an animal that would very likely get away from him in any case.

For a moment he would not face it. He was a small boy again, kicking sulkily[14] at the skeleton, hanging his head, refusing to accept the responsibility.

Then he straightened up, and looked down at the bones with an odd expression of dismay, all the anger gone out of him. His mind went quite empty; all around him he could see trickles of ants disappearing into the grass. The whispering noise was faint and dry, like the rustling of a cast snakeskin.

At last he picked up his gun and walked homewards. He was telling himself half defiantly that he wanted his breakfast. He was telling himself that it was getting very hot, much too hot to be out roaming the bush.

Really, he was tired. He walked heavily, not looking where he put his feet. When he came without sight of his home he stopped, knitting his brows. There was something he had to think out. The death of that small animal was a thing that concerned him, and was by no means finished with it. It lay at the back of his mind uncomfortably.

Soon, the very next morning, he would get clear of everybody and go to the bush and think about it.

Notes

1. **veld:** The term veld, or veldt, refers primarily (but not exclusively) to the wide open rural spaces of South Africa or southern Africa and in particular to certain flatter areas or districts covered in grass or low scrub. The word comes from the Afrikaans (ultimately from Dutch), literally meaning "field".
2. **grip:** hold the attention of ; intellectually hold
3. **vigilant:** on the alert; watchful
4. **greying:** showing the color of grey
5. **haunch:** The hip, buttock, and upper thigh in human beings and animals
6. **skoen:** Afrikaans word for shoe
7. **foliage:** a cluster of plant leaves, especially tree leaves
8. **on the verge of colour:** about to change in colour
9. **vlei:** Afrikaans word for valley
10. **superfluity:** the quality or condition of being beyond what is required or sufficient
11. **myriad:** innumerable

12. **clean-picked:** all eaten up

13. **surefooted:** not liable to error in judgment or action

14. **sulkily:** in a gloomy way

Questions for Study and Discussion

1. What type of *imagery* does Lessing use in order to describe the African landscape?

2. What significance does the fact that he is white have in the story?

3. What is the significance of the title of the story?

4. Do you find any significant symbols in the story? What are they?

5. What is the possible allegorical meaning of the story?

6. What do you think is the theme of the story?

7. What are the boy's thoughts about his life and his future?

8. What similarity does the boy see between himself and the dead buck?

References

[1] Abrams, M.H., ed. *A Glossary of Literary Terms*. 7th edition. Beijing: Foreign Language Teaching and Research Press, 2004.

[2] Abrams, M.H., ed. *English Literature*. New York: W.W. Norton & Company, 1993.

[3] Abrams, M.H., ed. *The Norton Anthology of English Literature*. New York: Norton, 1986

[4] Acheson, J. *Samuel Beckett's Later Fiction and Drama*. New York: St. Martin's Press, 1987.

[5] Alcorn, J. *The Nature Novel from Hardy to Lawrence*. London and Basingstoke: Macmillan Press, 1977.

[6] Allen, W. *The English Novel, a Short Critical History*. New York: E. P. Dutton & Co., INC., 1955.

[7] Alexander, M. *A History of English Literature*. London: Macmillan Education, 2000.

[8] Austen, J. *Pride and Prejudice*. London: Redwood Burn Limited Trowbridge and Esher, 1978.

[9] Axthelm, P.M. *The Modern Confessional Novel. London*: Yale University Press, 1967.

[10] Barnard, Robert. *A Short History of English Literature*. 2nd edition. Oxford: Oxford University Press, 1994.

[11] Beckett, Samuel. *Waiting for Godot*. London: Faber & Faber, 1965.

[12] Bell, Arthur et al. *English Literature: 1900 to the Present*. 2nd edition. New York: Barron's Educational Series, Inc., 1994.

[13] Bergonzi, Bernard. *The Situation of the Novel*. London and Basingstoke: Macmillan Press, 1970.

[14] Bloom, Harold. *Samuel Beckett's Waiting for Godot*. New York: Chelsea House Publishers, 1985.

[15] Bloom, Harold. *Samuel Beckett's Molly, Malone Dies, The Unnamable.* New York: Chelsea House publishers, 1988.

[16] Boitani, Piero., ed. *The Cambridge Chaucer Companion.* Shanghai: Shanghai Foreign Language Education Press, 2000.

[17] Booz, Elisabeth B. *A Brief Introduction to Modern English Literature, 1914-1980.* Shanghai: Shanghai Foreign Language Education Press. 1984.

[18] Boyd, S.J. *The Novels of William Golding.* Bnghton: Haveston, 1988.

[19] Bradbury, Malcolm. *The Modern English Novel.* London: Penguin Books, 1993.

[20] Brooks, Cleanth and Robert Penn Warren, *Understanding Poetry.* 4th edition. Beijing: Foreign Language Teaching and Research Press, 2004.

[21] Brooks, Cleanth and Robert Penn Warren, *Understanding Fiction.* 3rd edition. Beijing: Foreign Language Teaching and Research Press, 2004.

[22] Brown, Julia Prewitt. *A Reader's Guide to the Nineteenth Century English Novel.* New York: Macmillan Publishing Company, 1985.

[23] Buckley, William K. *Lady Chatterley's Lover, Loss and Hope.* New York: Twayne Publishers, 1993.

[24] C. Baldwin, Edward. *The Character Books of the 17th Century in Elation to the Development of the Novel.* Western Reserve University, 1900.

[25] Carey, J. *William Golding: The Man and His Books.* New York: Farra, Straus & Giroux, 1987.

[26] Chaucer, Geoffrey. *The Canterbury Tales.* Oxford: Oxford University Press. 1995.

[27] Chen Jia. *A History of English Literature.* Beijing: Commercial Press, 1986

[28] Chen Jia. *Selected Readings in English Literature.* Beijing: Commercial Press, 1986

[29] Claudia and Johnson. *Jane Austen.* Chicago: The University of Chicago Press, 1984.

[30] Collie, J. and S. Slater. *Literature in the Language Classroom.* London: CUP., 1987.

[31] Cooper, John Xiros. *The Cambridge Introduction to T. S. Eliot.* London: Cambridge University Press. 2006.

[32] Coote, Stephen. *The Penguin Short History of English Literature.* New

York: Penguin Books Ltd ., 1993

[33] Corns, Thomas N. *The Cambridge Companion to English Poetry Donne to Marvell.* Shanghai: Shanghai Foreign Language Education Press, 2001.

[34] Curran, Stuart. *The Cambridge Companion to British Romanticism.* Shanghai: Shanghai Foreign Language Education Press, 2001.

[35] Danielson, Dennis., ed. *The Cambridge Companion to Milton.* Shanghai: Shanghai Foreign Language Education Press, 2000.

[36] David, Monaghan. *Jane Austen: Structure and Social Vision.* London: Macmillan, 1980.

[37] Donne, John (Craik, R.J.ed. lit.; Craik, T.W., ed. lit). *John Donne: Selected Poetry and Prose.* London: Methuen, 1986.

[38] Drabble, Margaret, ed. *The Oxford Companion to English Literature.* New York: Oxford University Press, 1985.

[39] Eagleton, Terry. *Literary Theory: An Introduction.* Oxford: Blackwell Publishers Ltd , 1983.

[40] Eliot, Thomas Stearns. *Prufrock and Other Observations.* London: The Egoist, Ltd, 1917.

[41] Evans, Ifor. *A Short History of English Literature.* Middlesex: Penguin Books. 1976

[42] Gaskell, Philip. *Landmarks in English Literature.* Wuhan: Wuhan University Press, 2006.

[43] Fleischmann, W.B., ed. *Encyclopedia of World Literature in the 20th Century.* New York: Frederick Ungan Publishing Co., INC., 1969.

[44] Gittings, Robert. *John Keats.* London: Penguin Books, 1971.

[45] Grierson, Herbert, J.C. ed. *Metaphysical Lyrics and Poems of the Seventeenth Century: Donne to Butler.* Oxford: Oxford University Press, 1987.

[46] Gross, John., ed. *The New Oxford Book of English Prose.* Oxford: Oxford University Press, 1998.

[47] Guerin, Wilfred L., ed. *A Handbook of Critical Approaches to Literature.* Beijing: Foreign Language Teaching and Research Press, 2004.

[48] Guo Qunying. *British Literature.* Vol. 1. Beijing: Foreign Teaching and Research Press, 2001.

[49] Harris, Lanzen. *Nineteenth-Century Criticism.* Detroit: Gale Research Company, 1986.

[50] He Oixin. *A History of English Drama.* Nanjing: Yilin Press, 1999.

[51] Holman, C. Hugh and William Harmon. *A Handbook to Literature*. 7th edition. New York: Macmillan, 1995.

[52] Hou Weirui. *A Comprehensive History of English Literature*. Shanghai: Shanghai Foreign Language Education Press, 1999.

[53] Hyder, Edward Rollins. *The Keats Circle*. Harvard University Press, 1955.

[54] James, Edward Austen-Leigh. *Memoir of Jane Austen*, ed., R. W. Chapman. Oxford: Clarendon Press, 1926.

[55] Keymer, Thomas and Jon Mee, *The Cambridge Companion to English Literature, 1740-1830*. Cambridge: Cambridge University Press, 2004.

[56] Lascelles, Marry. *Jane Austen and Her Art*. Oxford: Clarendon Press, 1939.

[57] Litz，A. Walton，Jane Austen: *A Study of Her Artistic Development*. London: Chatto & Windus, 1965.

[58] Long, William J. *English Literature*. London: Ginn and Company, 1909.

[59] Luo, Jingguo. *A New Anthology of English Literature*. 2 vols., Beijing: Beijing University Press, 1966

[60] Marvell, Andrew. (Wilcher, Robert, ed. lit.). *Andrew Marvell: Selected Poetry and Prose*. London: Methuen, 1986.

[61] Milton, John. *Paradise Lost*. Edinburgh: R. & R. Clark, Limited. 1996.

[62] Milton, John. (Davies, Tony, ed. lit.). *John Milton: Selected Longer Poems and Prose*. London: Routledge, 1992.

[63] Moody, David. *The Cambridge Companion to T.S. Eliot*. Cambridge University Press. 1995.

[64] Morton, A.L. *A People's History of England*. London: Lawrence & Wishart Ltd. 1979.

[65] Potter, Lois. *A Preface to Milton*. Beijing: Peking University Press, 2005.

[66] Purkis, John. *A Preface to Wordsworth*. Beijing: Peking University Press, 2005.

[67] Richardson, Joanna. *The Everlasting Spell —A Study of Keats and Friends*, London: Ebeneser Baylis and Son Limited, 1963.

[68] Richetti, John., ed. *The Columbia History of British Novel*, Beijing: Foreign Language Teaching and Research Press, Columbia University Press, 2005.

[69] Roe, Sue and Susan Sellers. *The Cambridge Companion to Virginia Woolf*.

Shanghai: Shanghai Foreign Language Education Press, 2001.

[70] Rogers, Pat. *An Outline of English Literature.* Oxford: Oxford University Press, 1998.

[71] Selden, Raman. *A Reader's Guide to Contemporary Literature Theory.* 2nd Edition. Kentucky: The University Press of Kentucky, 1989.

[72] Sharrock, Roger. *Keats: Selected Poems and Letters.* London: Oxford University Press, 1971.

[73] Southam, B.C. *A Student's Guide to the Selected Poems of T.S. Eliot.* London: Faber & Faber, 1990.

[74] Thornley, G.C. *An Outline of English Literature.* New York: Longman Scientific & Technical Pub., 1984.

[75] Uhlmann, Anthony. *Beckett and Poststructuralism.* Cambridge: Cambridge University Press, 1999.

[76] Walsh, William. *Introduction to Keats.* London: Methucm & Co. Ltd, 1981.

[77] Wang Zuoliang. *A History of English Literature.* Beijing: Commercial Press, 1996

[78] Ward, Aileen. *John Keats—The Making of a Poet.* New York: The Viking Press, 1967.

[79] Watts, Cedric. *A Preface to Keats.* London: Longman, 1985.

[80] Williams, Merryn. *A Preface to Hardy.* Beijing: Peking University Press, 2005.

[81] Williamson, George. *A Reade's Guide to T.S. Eliot: A Poem-by-Poem Analysis.* New York: Syracuse University Press, 1998.

[82] Whitley, J.S. *Golding: Lord of the Flies.* London: Arnold, 1979.

[83] Zhang Dingquan and Wu Gang. *A New Concise History of English Literature.* Shanghai: Shanghai Foreign Language Education Press, 2002.

[84] 常耀信.英国文学简史.王塔译.天津：南开大学出版社，2006.

[85] 查尔斯·米尔斯·盖雷.英美文学和艺术中的古典神话.上海：上海人民出版社，2005.

[86] 陈嘉.英国文学作品选读.北京：商务印书馆，1983.

[87] 戴继国.英国诗歌教程.北京：对外经济贸易出版社，2005.

[88] 戴维·罗伯兹.英国史：1688 年至今.鲁光桓译.广州：中山大学出版社，1990.

[89] 邓绪新. *An Introduction to Literature of English.* 武汉：武汉大学出版

社，2002.

[90]丁廷森.英国文学选读.重庆：重庆大学出版社，2005.

[91]董翔晓，鲁效阳，谢天振，包幼华.英国文学名家.哈尔滨：黑龙江人民出版社，1984.

[92]方重.乔叟文集.上海：上海译文出版社，1979.

[93]何树，苏友芬主编.英国文学导读与应试指南.上海：上海世界图书出版公司，2005.

[94]何其莘.英国戏剧史.南京：译林出版社，1999.

[95]何其莘，张剑，侯毅凌编.英国文学选集.北京：外语教学与研究出版，2004.

[96]亨利·詹姆斯.小说的艺术.朱雯，朱乃长等译.上海：上海译出版社，2001.

[97]侯维瑞主编.英国文学通史.上海：上海外语教育出版社，1999.

[98]侯维瑞.现代英国小说史.上海：上海外语教育出版社，2001.

[99]侯维瑞，李维屏.英国小说史.南京：译林出版社，2005.

[100]胡家峦.英国名诗详注.北京：外语教学与研究出版社，2001.

[101]胡全生等.20世纪英美文学选读——后现代主义卷.上海：上海交通大学出版社，2003.

[102]胡全生.20世纪英美文学选读 现代主义卷.上海：上海交通大学出版社，2003.

[103]蹇昌槐.西方小说与文化帝国.武汉：武汉大学出版社，2004.

[104]李赋宁.英国文学论述文集.北京：外语教学与研究出版社，1997.

[105]李美华.英国生态文学.上海：学林出版社，2008.

[106]李维屏.英国小说人物史.上海：上海外语教育出版社，2008.

[107]李维屏.英国小说艺术史.上海：上海外语教育出版社，2003.

[108]李维屏.英美现代主义文学概观.上海：上海外语教育出版社，1998.

[109]利维斯.F.R.伟大的传统.袁伟译.北京：生活·读书·新知 三联店，2002.

[110]李正栓.英国文学学习指南.北京：清华大学出版社，2006.

[111]李正栓，郭群英主编.新编英国文学教程.石家庄：河北教育出版社，2006.

[112]刘炳善.英国文学简史.郑州：河南人民出版社，2006.

[123]刘炳善，罗益民.英国文学选读.郑州：河南人民出版社，2006.

[114]刘世沐等.英美文学欣赏.北京：北京出版社，1982.

[115]刘守兰.英美名诗解读.上海：上海外语教育出版社，2003.

[116]刘文荣.19世纪英国小说史.北京：中国社会科学出版社，2002.

[117]刘晓鹏，田野，廖国强，孟宏党主编.应用英语教程.汕头：汕头大学出版社，2002.

[118]刘意青主编.英国18世纪文学史.北京：外语教学与研究出版社，2005.

[119]刘英，张建萍.英国短篇小说导读.天津：南开大学出版社，2006.

[120]罗经国.新编英国文学选读.（第二版）.北京：北京大学出版社，2005.

[121]罗选民主编.英美文学赏析教程·散文与诗歌.北京：清华大学出版社，2002.

[122]钱青.英国19世纪文学史.北京：外语教学与研究出版社，2005.

[123]瞿世镜.当代英国小说.北京：外语教学与研究出版社，1998.

[124]孙汉云.英国文学教程.南京：河海大学出版社，2005.

[125]孙建主编.英国文学辞典·作家与作品.上海：复旦大学出版社，2005.

[126]孙建，汪洪章等.英国文学选读.上海：复旦大学出版社，2008.

[127]陶洁主编.美国文学选读.北京：高等教育出版社，2002.

[128]田野，蒋璐，高传香，邓云华.新编英美概况.汕头：汕头大学出版社，2002.

[129]田野，王跃，王莎烈主编.英语知识365天.吉林：吉林大学出版社，1996.

[130]王军.英美女性作家与作品赏析.北京：新华出版社，2007.

[131]王蕾，陆燕敏主编.英国文学选读.天津：天津大学出版社，2007.

[132]王守仁，英国文学选读.（第二版）.北京：高等教育出版社，2005.

[133]王守仁，方杰著.英国文学简史.上海：上海外语教育出版社，2006.

[134]王佐良.英国诗史.南京：译林出版社，1997.

[135]王佐良.英国文学史.北京：商务印书馆，1996.

[136]王佐良，何其莘著.英国文艺复兴时期文学史.北京：外语教学与研究出版社，1996.

[137]王佐良，李赋宁等.英国文学名篇选注.北京：商务印书馆，1983.

[138]王佐良，周珏良主编.英国二十世纪文学史.北京：外语教学与研究出版社，1994.

[139]吴伟仁.英国文学史及选读.北京：外语教学与研究出版社，1996.

[140]杨明生.英国文学名家.哈尔滨：黑龙江人民出版社，1984.

[141]杨晓峰.英美文学精华.开封：河南大学出版社，2006.

[142]杨岂深，孙铢.英国文学选读.上海：上海译文出版社，2005.

[143]杨周翰.十七世纪英国文学.北京：北京大学出版社，1996.

[144]殷企平，高奋等.英国小说批评史.上海：上海外语教育出版社，2001.

[145]约翰·但恩.英国玄学诗鼻祖约翰·但恩诗集.傅浩译，北京：北京十月文艺出版社，2006.

[146]张伯香.英国文学教程.武汉：武汉大学出版社，2005.

[147]张瑾,赵嘉颖主编.英国文学习题集.哈尔滨:哈尔滨工业大学出版社,2005.

[148]张锦涛.英语国家现代文学选读.北京:外语教学与研究出版社,2001.

[149]詹姆斯·诺尔森文约翰·海恩斯摄影.贝克特肖像.王绍祥译.上海:上海人民出版社,2006.

[150]郑克鲁.外国文学史.北京:高等教育出版社,2006.

[151]朱坤领主编.英语文学赏析.重庆:重庆大学出版社,2008.

[152]http://andromeda.rutgers.edu/

[153]http://www.bartleby.com/198/

[154]http://www.bibliomania.com/

[155]http://www.biography.com/

[156]http://www.bookrags.com/

[157]http://www.britannia.com/

[158]http://www.classicreader.com/author/

[150]http://www.cliffsnotes.com/

[160]http://dictionary.reference.com/

[161]http://en.allexperts.com/

[162]http://encarta.msn.com/

[163]http://www.encyclopedia.com/

[164]http://en.wikipedia.org/

[165]http://www.gradesaver.com/

[166]http://www.historylearningsite.co.uk/

[167]http://www.iep.utm.edu/

[168]http://www.infoplease.com/

[169]http://library.thinkquest.org/

[170]http://www.literatureclassics.com/

[171]http://www.luminarium.org/

[172]http://www.mapability.com/travel/p2i/book.html

[173]http://www.novelguide.com/

[174]http://www.online-literature.com/

[175]http://www.poets.org/

[176]http://www.poetseers.org/

[177]http://www.sparknotes.com/

[178]http://www.spartacus.schoolnet.co.uk/

[179]http://www.thefreedictionary.com/

[180]http://www.victorianweb.org/authors/index.html/

后 记

习近平在文化传承发展座谈会上强调：担负起新的文化使命努力建设中华民族现代文明。"在新的起点上继续推动文化繁荣、建设文化强国、建设中华民族现代文明，是我们在新时代新的文化使命。要坚定文化自信、担当使命、奋发有为，共同努力创造属于我们这个时代的新文化，建设中华民族现代文明。"（《人民日报》（2023 年 06 月 03 日 01 版 ））

教材是教学之本，它规范着某一门课程的基本内容，保证教学内容的规范化和科学化，以实现教学目的。因此，教材建设是实现教学计划和达到教学目的的基本建设工程。根据杭州电子科技大学和浙江省教育厅有关"精品课程"立项建设的要求，我们组织编写了《精编英国文学教程》，作为校级与省级"精品课程"《英美文学导论》建设的重要组成部分。具体分工如下：

陈庆生，陈许(主编)：Historical Background and Literary Review of Part One,
　　　　　　Part Two, Part Three, Part Four, Part Five and Part Six

田 野（副主编 ）：John Keats，Jane Austen，Thomas Stearns Eliot，William
　　　　　　Golding

田 颖（副主编 ）： George Bernard Shaw，E.M. Forster，D.H. Lawrence

蓝云春：Historical Background and Literary Review of Part Seven,Virginia
　　　　Woolf，William Butler Yeats，Wilfred Owen

周小娉：Geoffrey Chaucer，John Donne，Andrew Marvell，John Milton

王银瓶：William Shakespeare，Francis Bacon，Thomas Gray，William Blake，
　　　　Robert Burns

黄 巍：George Herbert，John Dryden，Charles Lamb，William Hazlitt，Doris
　　　　Lessing

秦 宏：Alexander Pope，Daniel Defoe，Jonathan Swift

郑 玮：William Wordsworth，George Gordon Byron，Percy Bysshe Shelley，
　　　　Ted Hughes

方 璞：Charles Dickens，William Makepeace Thackeray，Charlotte Bronte，
　　　　Emily Bronte

杨鲁平：Robert Browning，Thomas Carlyle，Thomas Hardy

　　在本书的编写过程中，我们吸收了许多专家学者的研究成果，参阅了大量的书籍和资料，在此，我们谨向有关著作者和出版单位表示衷心感谢！

陈庆生　陈　许
2023 年 8 月于杭州电子科技大学

图书在版编目（CIP）数据

精编英国文学教程 / 陈庆生，陈许主编. —杭州：浙江
大学出版社,2009.10(2023.8 重印)
ISBN 978-7-308-07130-7

Ⅰ.精… Ⅱ.①陈…②陈… Ⅲ.文学史－英国－高等学
校－教材 Ⅳ.I561.09

中国版本图书馆 CIP 数据核字（2009）第 188481 号

精编英国文学教程

陈庆生　陈　许　主编

责任编辑	葛　娟
封面设计	刘依群
出版发行	浙江大学出版社
	（杭州市天目山路 148 号　邮政编码 310007）
	（网址:http://www.zjupress.com）
排　　版	杭州青翔图文设计有限公司
印　　刷	广东虎彩云印刷有限公司绍兴分公司
开　　本	710mm×1000mm　1/16
印　　张	32.75
字　　数	675 千
版 印 次	2009 年 11 月第 1 版　2023 年 8 月第 6 次印刷
书　　号	ISBN 978-7-308-07130-7
定　　价	69.00 元